Rick Steves'
GERMANY
& AUSTRIA
2006

W9-BNU-328

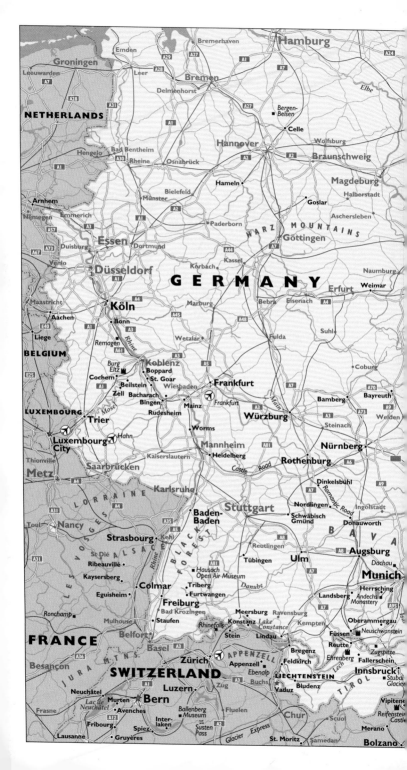

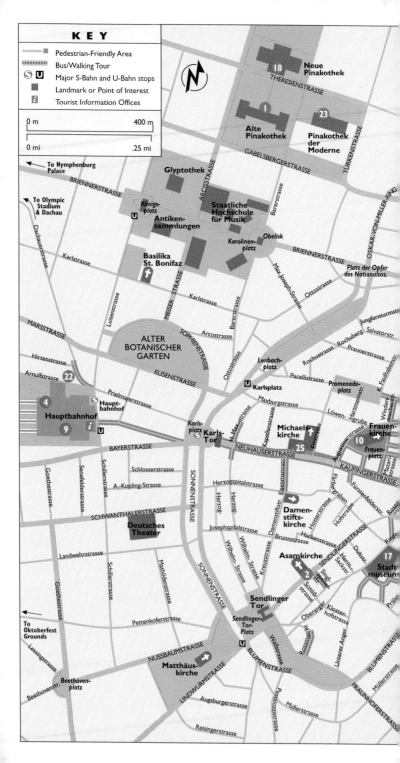

KEY

Pedestrian-Friendly Area

Bus/Walking Tour

Ⓢ Ⓤ Major S-Bahn and U-Bahn stops

Landmark or Point of Interest

ⓘ Tourist Information Offices

0 m		400 m

0 mi		.25 mi

Neue Pinakothek 18

THERESIENSTRASSE

Alte Pinakothek 1

Pinakothek der Moderne 23

GABELSBERGERSTRASSE

To Nymphenburg Palace →

BRIENNERSTRASSE

Glyptothek

ARCISSTRASSE

To Olympic Stadium & Dachau →

Königs-platz Ⓤ

Antiken-sammlungen

Staatliche Hochschule für Musik

Barerstrasse

Dachauerstrasse

Karlstrasse

Basilika St. Bonifaz ✝

Karolinen-platz

Obelisk

BRIENNERSTRASSE

OSKAR-VON-MILLER-RING

Max-Joseph-strasse

Ottostrasse

Platz der Opfer des Nationalsoz.

MARSSTRASSE

Luisenstrasse

MEISER STRASSE

Karlstrasse

Barerstrasse

SOPHIENSTRASSE

Arcostrasse

Jungfernturmstr.

Hirtenstrasse

ALTER BOTANISCHER GARTEN

Ottostrasse

Lenbach-platz

Rochusberg Salvatorstr.

Rochusstrasse Rochberg

Prannerstrasse

Arnulfstrasse

22

ELISENSTRASSE

Pacellistrasse

Promenade-platz

K.-Faulhaberstr.

Prielmayerstrasse

Ⓢ **Haupt-bahnhof**

Ⓤ **Karlsplatz**

Maxburgstrasse

Löwen-grube

Windenmacherstr.

4

Hauptbahnhof

ⓘ

Karls-platz

Karls-Tor Ⓢ

H.-Max-strasse

Kapellenstrasse

Michaels-kirche

Frauen-kirche ✝

9

Ⓤ

BAYERSTRASSE

NEUHAUSERSTRASSE

25

Färbergraben

Augustiner-strasse

10 **Frauen-platz**

KAUFINGERSTRASSE

Mazari-strasse

Schillerstrasse

Schlosserstrasse

SONNENSTRASSE

Herzogspitalstrasse

A.-Kopling-Strasse

Herzog-

Herzog-

Damenstift-str.

Eisenmannstr.

Färbergraben

Fürstenfelderstr.

Rosen-

SCHWANTHALERSTRASSE

Sendelfeldstrasse

Josephspitalstrasse

Damen-stifts-kirche

Hotterstrasse

Roses

Goethestr.

Deutsches Theater

Damenstiftstr.

Brunnstrasse

Hackenstrasse

SENDLINGERSTRASSE

Hofer-strasse

Dultst.

Landwehrstrasse

Mathildenstrasse

Wilhelm-Strasse

Kreuzstrasse

Asamkirche

2

Singlspieler str.

Herm.-Sack-str.

17 **Stadt-museum**

Schillerstrasse

Wilhelm- Strasse

Schmid-strasse

Pral-

Goethestrasse

Sendlinger Tor

Oberanger

Klosterhofstrasse

Rosstmarkt

Unterer Anger

To Oktoberfest Grounds →

Pettenkoferstrasse

Sendlinger-Tor-Platz

Ⓤ

BLUMENSTRASSE

Wallstrasse

Pestalozzistrasse

Müllerstrasse

BLUMENSTRASSE

Lessingstrasse

NUSSBAUMSTRASSE

Matthäus-kirche ✝

LINDWURMSTRASSE

Pestalozzistrasse

FRAUNHOFERSTRASSE

Beethoven-platz

Beethovenstr.

Augsburgerstrasse

Müllerstrasse

Reisingerstrasse

MUNICH

1. Alte Pinakothek
2. Asam Church
3. Bavarian National Museum
4. Bike Rental (2)
5. To Chinese Tower
6. Cuvilliés Theater
7. Deutsches Museum
8. English Garden
9. EurAide Office
10. Frauenkirche
11. Fünf Höfe Shops
12. Haus der Kunst
13. Hofbräuhaus
14. Kunsthalle Art Center
15. Marienplatz
16. Müllersches Pool
17. Munich City Museum
18. Neue Pinakothek
19. New Town Hall (Glockenspiel)
20. Odeonsplatz
21. Old Town Hall
22. Panorama Bus Tours Office
23. Pinakothek der Moderne
24. Residenz (Royal Palace)
25. St. Michael's Church
26. St. Peter's Church
27. Viktualien Markt

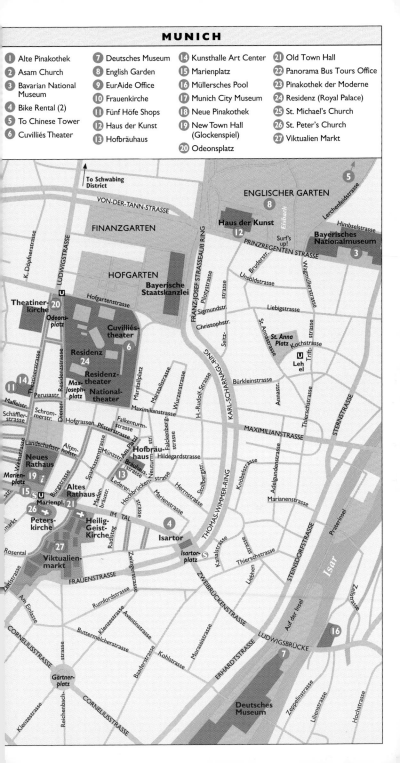

BERLIN

Erasmusstr.

Zwinglistrasse

TURMSTRASSE

KAISERIN AUGUSTE ALLEE

ALT MOABIT

Otto-Dix Str.

Lesser Ury Weg

Hallerstr.

HELMHOLTZSTRASSE

LEVETZOWSTRASSE

Jagowstrasse

Eberfelder Strasse

Essener Strasse

Bundesratufer

LESSINGSTRASSE

Holsteiner Ufer

KIRCHSTRASSE

Thomasiusstrasse

Calvinstr.

Spenerstrasse

PAULSTRASSE

Werftstr.

Lüneburger Strasse

Agricolastrasse

Wullenweberstr.

Flensburger

Bellevue

Haus der Kulturen der Welt

Salzufer

FRANKLINSTRASSE

Spree

Spree

MARCHSTR.

To Charlottenburg

Einsteinufer

BACHSTRASSE

KLOPSTOCKSTR.

ALTONAERSTRASSE

Händelallee

Schloss Bellevue

SPREEWEG JOHN FOSTER DULLES ALLEE

Flea Market

Siegessäule

Bremer Weg

STRASSE DES 17 JUNI

Tiergarten

Tiergartenufer

Fasanenallee

Grosser Weg

TIERGARTEN

Herzallee

Fasanenstrasse

Neuer See

GROSSE STERNALLEE

HARDENBERGSTRASSE

Gartenufer

Rauchstrasse

Corneliusstrasse

HOFJÄGERALLEE

Köbisstrasse

Hiroshimastr.

Hildebrandstr.

Bahnhof Zoo

Jebenstr.

ZOOLOGISCHER GARTEN

36

BUDAPESTER STRASSE

Keithstrasse

Lützowufer

Reichpietschufer

13

Carmerstr.

Savignyplatz

KANTSTRASSE

8

18

Europa Center

9

Wichmannstrasse

KURFÜRSTENSTRASSE

LÜZOWSTRASSE

Knesebeckstr.

Grolmanstr.

Uhlandstr.

Rankestrasse

Marburger Str.

Bayreuther Strasse

TAUENTZIENSTRASSE

EINEMSTRASSE

Derfflingerstr.

Genthiner Str.

Kückstrasse

KURFÜRSTENDAMM

19

Fasanenstr.

Meinekestr.

Augsburger Str.

Eiselbener Str.

Passauer Str.

17

Wittenbergplatz

KLEISTRASSE

Kalckreuthstr.

Motzstrasse

Nollendorfpl.

BÜLOWSTRASSE

POTSDAMERSTRASSE

LIETZENBURGER STRASSE

Schaperstrasse

Fuggerstrasse

MARTIN LUTHER STRASSE

Eisenacher Strasse

Nollendorfstr.

Massenstr.

Zietenstr.

Frober-

Steinmetzstrasse

Pfalzburger Strasse

Fasanenstrasse

BUNDESALLEE

NÜRNBERGER STRASSE

Bamberger Strasse

Anhalter Strasse

Welserstrasse

Winterfeldtstrasse

Luitpoldstr.

Geldtschstrasse

UHLANDSTRASSE

Pariserstrasse

NACHODSTRASSE

Motzstrasse

Münchener Str.

Heilbronner Str.

HOHENSTAUFENSTRASSE

Kyffhäuserstrasse

Goltzstrasse

HOHENZOLLERNDAMM

Landhausstrasse

Barbarossastrasse

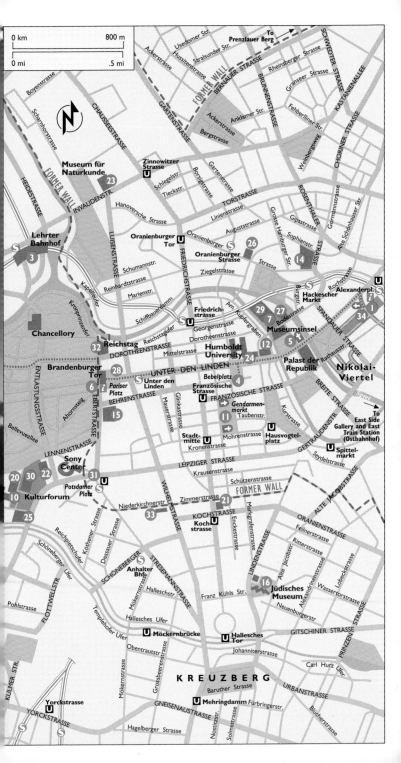

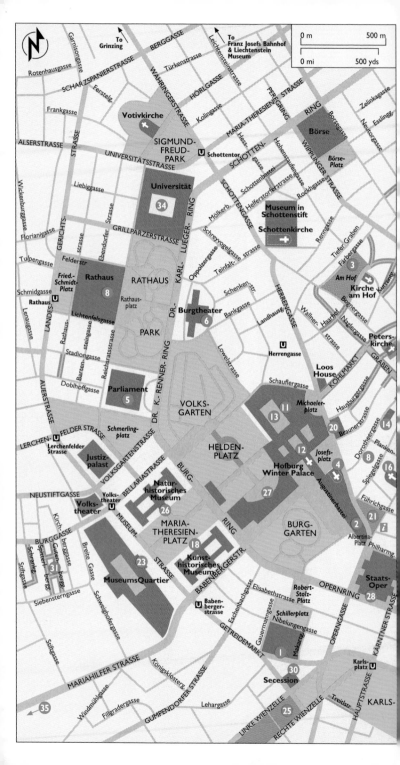

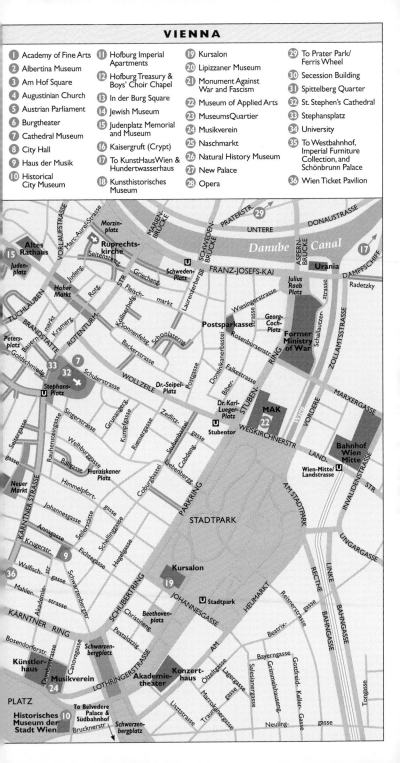

VIENNA

1. Academy of Fine Arts
2. Albertina Museum
3. Am Hof Square
4. Augustinian Church
5. Austrian Parliament
6. Burgtheater
7. Cathedral Museum
8. City Hall
9. Haus der Musik
10. Historical City Museum
11. Hofburg Imperial Apartments
12. Hofburg Treasury & Boys' Choir Chapel
13. In der Burg Square
14. Jewish Museum
15. Judenplatz Memorial and Museum
16. Kaisergruft (Crypt)
17. To KunstHausWien & Hundertwasserhaus
18. Kunsthistorisches Museum
19. Kursalon
20. Lipizzaner Museum
21. Monument Against War and Fascism
22. Museum of Applied Arts
23. MuseumsQuartier
24. Musikverein
25. Naschmarkt
26. Natural History Museum
27. New Palace
28. Opera
29. To Prater Park/ Ferris Wheel
30. Secession Building
31. Spittelberg Quarter
32. St. Stephen's Cathedral
33. Stephansplatz
34. University
35. To Westbahnhof, Imperial Furniture Collection, and Schönbrunn Palace
36. Wien Ticket Pavilion

Rick Steves'

GERMANY
& AUSTRIA
2006

AVALON
TRAVEL

CONTENTS

Top Destinations in Germany & Austria

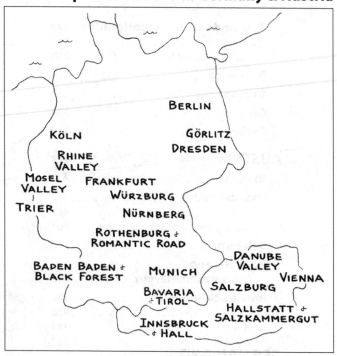

INTRODUCTION

In many ways, Germany and Austria are Teutonic twins, offering alpine scenery, dramatic castles, cobbled quaintness, and tasty wurst and strudel. But Germany is more of a mover and shaker, rattling Europe in the last century and leading the way for the new united Europe in the 21st century. Meanwhile, Austria is content to bask in its good living and opulent past. Taken together, the two countries are intriguing and rewarding for travelers to explore.

This book breaks Germany and Austria into their top big-city, small-town, and rural destinations. It then gives you all the information and opinions necessary to wring the maximum value out of your limited time and money in each of these destinations. If you plan a month or less in this region, this lean and mean little book is all you need.

Experiencing this region's culture, people, and natural wonders economically and hassle-free has been my goal for three decades of traveling, tour guiding, and travel writing. With this new edition, I pass on to you the lessons I've learned, updated for your trip in 2006.

Rick Steves' Germany & Austria is your friendly Franconian, your German in a jam, a tour guide in your pocket. The book includes a balance of cities and villages, mountaintop hikes and forgotten Roman ruins, sleepy river cruises and sky-high gondola rides. It covers the predictable biggies while mixing in a healthy dose of Back Door intimacy.

Along with visiting Rhine castles, Mozart's house, chunks of the Berlin Wall, and the Vienna Opera, you'll ride a thrilling Austrian mountain luge, soak in a Black Forest mineral spa, share a beer with Bavarian monks, and ramble through traffic-free alpine towns. I've been selective, including only the most exciting sights. For example, there are dozens of quaint villages in Austria's Lake

District. I take you to only the most charming: Hallstatt. And of the passel of castles in the Mosel Valley, I guide you to the best: Burg Eltz.

The best is, of course, only my opinion. But after spending half my adult life researching Europe, I've developed a sixth sense for what stokes the traveler's wanderlust. Just thinking about the places featured in this book makes me want to slap dance and yodel.

This Information Is Accurate and Up-to-Date

This book is updated every year. Most publishers of guidebooks that cover a region from top to bottom can afford an update only every two or three years (and even then, it's often by e-mail or fax). Since this book is selective, covering only the top destinations in Germany and Austria, I can update it in person each summer. The telephone numbers, hours, and prices of the places listed in this book are accurate as of mid-2005. Even with annual updates, things change. Still, if you're traveling with the current edition of this book, I guarantee you're using the most up-to-date information available in print. For the latest, visit www.ricksteves.com/update. Also at my Web site, you'll find a valuable list of reports and experiences—good and bad—from fellow travelers who have used this book (www.ricksteves.com/feedback).

Use this year's edition. People who try to save a few bucks by traveling with an old book are not smart. They learn the seriousness of their mistake...in Europe. Your trip costs about $10 per waking hour. Your time is valuable. This guidebook saves lots of time.

About This Book

This book is organized by destination. Each destination is covered as a mini-vacation on its own, filled with exciting sights and homey, affordable places to stay. In the following chapters, you'll find:

Planning Your Time, a suggested schedule with thoughts on how best to use your limited time.

Orientation, including tourist information, city transportation, and an easy-to-read map designed to make the text clear and your arrival smooth.

Self-Guided Walks, taking you through interesting neighborhoods, with a personal tour guide in hand.

Sights, a succinct overview of Germany's and Austria's most important sights, arranged by neighborhood, with ratings: ▲▲▲—Don't miss; ▲▲—Try hard to see; ▲—Worthwhile if you can make it; No rating—Worth knowing about.

Sleeping and **Eating,** with addresses, phone numbers, and Web sites of my favorite good-value hotels and restaurants.

Transportation Connections, including train information and route tips for drivers, with recommended roadside attractions along the way.

The **appendix** is a traveler's tool kit, with a climate chart, telephone tips, rail routes, and German survival phrases.

Browse through this book, choose your favorite destinations, and link them together. Then have a great trip! You'll travel like a temporary local, getting the absolute most out of every mile, minute, and euro. As you travel the route I know and love, I'm happy you'll be meeting some of my favorite Europeans.

PLANNING

Trip Costs

Five components make up your trip cost: airfare, surface transportation, room and board, sightseeing/entertainment, and shopping/miscellany.

Airfare: Don't try to sort through the mess. Get and use a good travel agent. A basic round-trip flight from the U.S. to Frankfurt should cost $500 to $1,000 (even cheaper in winter), depending on where you fly from and when. Always consider saving time and money in Europe by flying "open jaw" (flying into one city and out of another).

Surface Transportation: For a three-week whirlwind trip of all my recommended destinations, allow $650 per person for public transportation (train pass and buses) or $750 per person (based on 2 people sharing) for a three-week car rental, parking, gas, and insurance. Car rental is cheapest when reserved from the U.S. Train passes are normally sold only outside of Europe. You may save money by simply buying tickets as you go (see "Transportation," page 16).

Room and Board: You can travel comfortably in this region on an average of $80 a day per person for room and board (less in small towns). An $80-a-day budget allows $10 for lunch, $15 for dinner, and $55 for lodging (based on 2 people splitting the cost of a $110 double room that includes breakfast). That's doable. Students and tightwads do it on $40 a day ($20 per hostel bed, $20 for meals and snacks).

Sightseeing and Entertainment: In big cities, figure $9 to $12 per major sight (Munich's Deutsches Museum-$9, Vienna's Kunsthistorisches Museum-$12), $3 to $5 for minor ones, and $25 to $50 for bus tours and splurge experiences (such as concert tickets, alpine lifts, and conducting the beer-hall band). An overall average of $25 a day works for most. Don't skimp here. After all, this category is the driving force behind your trip—you came to sightsee, enjoy, and experience Germany and Austria.

Germany and Austria: Best Three-Week Trip by Car

Day	Plan	Sleep in
1	Fly into Frankfurt, to the Rhine	Bacharach
2	Rhine Valley	Bacharach
3	To Baden-Baden via the Mosel Valley	Baden-Baden
4	Relax and soak in Baden-Baden	Baden-Baden
5	Drive through the Black Forest	Staufen
6	To the Tirol	Reutte
7	Bavaria and castles	Reutte
8	To Hallstatt via Innsbruck and Hall	Hallstatt
9	Hallstatt and Salzkammergut Lake District	Hallstatt
10	To Vienna via Schönbrunn Palace	Vienna
11	Vienna	Vienna
12	To Salzburg via Melk and Mauthausen	Salzburg
13	Salzburg	Salzburg
14	To Munich	Munich
15	Munich	Munich
16	To Rothenburg via the Romantic Road	Rothenburg
17	Rothenburg	Rothenburg
18	To Nürnberg	Nürnberg
19	To Dresden	Dresden
20	To Berlin	Berlin
21	Berlin	Berlin
22	Fly home	

Shopping and Miscellany: Figure $1 per postcard and $2 per coffee, beer, and ice-cream cone. Shopping can vary in cost from nearly nothing to a small fortune. Good budget travelers find that this category has little to do with assembling a trip full of lifelong and wonderful memories.

When to Go

The "tourist season" runs roughly from May through September.

Summer has its advantages: best weather, snow-free alpine trails, very long days (light until after 21:00), and the busiest schedule of tourist fun.

In spring and fall—May, June, September, and early October—travelers enjoy fewer crowds, milder weather, and the ability to grab a room almost whenever and wherever they like. Also, in fall, fun harvest and wine festivals pop up all over.

Note: This itinerary is designed to be done by car, but could be done by train with some modifications: Take the train from Baden-Baden to Rothenburg, spend the night, take the train to Munich, visit Bavaria and the castles (possibly as a day trip from Munich), see all of the Austrian sights (Salzburg, Hallstatt, Mauthausen, Melk) on the way to Vienna, and take a night train from Vienna to Berlin (skipping Dresden and Nürnberg).

Winter travelers find concert seasons in full swing, with absolutely no tourist crowds, but some accommodations and sights are either closed or run on a limited schedule. Confirm your sightseeing plans locally, especially when traveling off-season. The weather can be cold and dreary, and nighttime will draw the shades on your sightseeing before dinnertime. You may find the climate chart in the appendix helpful.

Sightseeing Priorities
Depending on the length of your trip, and taking geographic proximity into account, here are my recommended priorities.

3 days:	Munich, Salzburg
5 days, add:	Rhine Valley, Rothenburg
7 days, add:	Bavaria and Tirol
10 days, add:	Berlin

World Cup 2006

On July 9, 2006, the world's two best football (a.k.a. soccer) teams meet in Berlin's 76,000-seat Olympic Stadium for the World Cup Final, capping two years of competition between nations around the world. Germany hosts this year's Cup, with the semi-final matches held throughout June in 12 cities, including Berlin, Munich, Frankfurt, Köln, and Nürnberg. (For a full list of game dates and cities, see page 590 in the appendix.)

Even if you're not a sports fan, if you're traveling in Germany during May, June, or July of 2006, you'll feel the buzz. In train stations, you may see boisterous groups of Brits, Dutch, or Italians arriving for a match, dressed in team colors and singing team songs. On game nights, regular life grinds to a halt as locals crowd the bars to watch on TV. After a victory, impromptu parades fill the streets, with fans in cars honking horns and waving team flags. You'll experience firsthand just how big soccer is in Germany, Europe, and the rest of the world...except the U.S.

What's all the excitement about? The World Cup takes place every four years (opposite the Summer Olympic Games). Just as they do for the Olympics, countries assemble all of their best players into a single, star-studded national team. For two years, these national teams compete in qualifying matches to earn the right to go to the World Cup. The qualification process is long and difficult, particularly for the players: They must leave the professional club teams they play for most of the year (often in other countries—for example, David Beckham, the world's best-known player, is English but plays for Real Madrid), fly halfway around the globe for crucial national team matches, then fly back to play in a club match a day later. Eventually, however, some 150

14 days, add:	Vienna, Hallstatt, Danube Valley
16 days, add:	Baden-Baden, Black Forest
More time:	Choose among Würzburg, Mosel Valley, Trier, Frankfurt, Köln, Nürnberg, Dresden, Görlitz, and Innsbruck/Hall.

(The itinerary and map on page 17 include nearly everything on this list.)

Travel Smart

Your trip to Germany and Austria is like a complex play—easier to follow and really appreciate on a second viewing. While no one does the same trip twice to gain that advantage, reading this book in its entirety before your trip accomplishes much the same thing.

Reread entire chapters as you travel, and visit local tourist information offices. Upon arrival in a new town, lay the countries are whittled down to the final 32 who will compete in the World Cup. Perennial powerhouses Italy, France, England, Argentina and Brazil will all be there, along with upstarts like Iran, Saudi Arabia, and Togo (the host country automatically qualifies). The U.S., no longer an upstart but not yet a powerhouse, will try to better their remarkable run to the quarterfinals of the 2002 World Cup, a run that was ended by—who else?—Germany.

The first match is June 9 in Munich. For the next month, there's at least one game played every day somewhere in Germany. Tickets range from €35 for a nose-bleed seat in the preliminaries to €600 for the best seats in the finals.

Most stadiums are located outside the city center, so you needn't worry too much about game-day crowds or security. But host cities (and their hotels) will be more crowded than usual. Hopefully, you won't have to deal with any "hooligans"—the pan-European word for fans that get too rowdy and violent. What you will see everywhere is the World Cup logo of three smiley faces forming "006," the slogan "A Time to Make Friends," the acronym "FIFA" (the sport's governing body), and the ubiquitous official mascots—a lion muppet named Goleo VI and a talking soccer ball named Pille. Germans, who are crazy for soccer even during the regular season (6 million Deutsch play in some kind of organized league, and 10 million attend pro games), will get even crazier as they welcome the whole world.

It all culminates in the Final on July 9 in Berlin: The two best teams battling it out to become World Cup Champion, the hopes, dreams, and national pride of two countries on the line, with one out of three members of the human race following the action... very few of whom live in the United States.

groundwork for a smooth departure. Buy a phone card and use it for reservations and confirmations. Enjoy the hospitality of the Germanic people. Ask questions. Most locals are eager to point you in their idea of the right direction. Wear your money belt, pack along a pocket-size notebook to organize your thoughts, and practice the virtue of simplicity. Those who expect to travel smart, do.

Design an itinerary that enables you to hit the festivals and museums on the right days. The World Cup will clog hotels around game days in 2006 (see the sidebar). As you read through this book, note the days when sights are closed. Saturday morning feels like any bustling weekday morning, but at lunchtime, many shops close down through Sunday. Sundays have pros and cons, as they do for travelers in the U.S. (special events, limited hours, shops and banks closed, limited public transportation, no rush hours). Popular places are even more popular on weekends. Many sights are closed on Monday.

Plan ahead for laundry, Internet stops, and picnics. To maximize rootedness, minimize one-night stands. Mix intense and relaxed periods. Every trip (and every traveler) needs at least a few slack days. Pace yourself. Assume you will return.

RESOURCES

Tourist Information Offices

In the U.S.

The German and Austrian national tourist offices in the U.S. offer a wealth of information. Before your trip, get the free general-information packet and request any specifics you want (such as regional and city maps and festival schedules).

German National Tourist Office: Maps, Rhine schedules, castles, biking, genealogical information, and city and regional information. Visit www.cometogermany.com and contact the nearest office:

In New York: 122 E. 42nd St. #2000, New York, NY 10168, tel. 800/651-7010 or 212/661-7200, fax 212/661-7174, gntonyc@d-z-t.com.

In Illinois: P.O. Box 59594, Chicago, IL 60659, tel. 773/539-6303, fax 773/539-6378, gntoch@aol.com.

In California: 501 Santa Monica Blvd. #607, Santa Monica, CA 90401, tel. 310/394-2580, fax 310/260-2923, info@gntolax.com.

Austrian Tourist Office: P.O. Box 1142, New York, NY 10108-1142, tel. 212/944-6880, fax 212/730-4568, www.austria.info, travel@austria.info. Ask for their "Austria Kit" with map. Fine hikes and city information.

In Germany and Austria

The tourist information office is your best first stop in any new town or city. Try to arrive, or at least telephone, before it closes. In this book, I'll refer to a tourist information office as a **TI**. Throughout Germany and Austria, you'll find TIs are usually well-organized and have English-speaking staff.

As national budgets tighten, many TIs have been privatized. This means they become sales agents for big tours and hotels, and their "information" becomes unavoidably colored. While TIs are eager to book you a room, you should use their room-finding service only as a last resort. TIs can as easily book you a bad room as a good one—they are not allowed to promote one place over another. Go direct, using the listings in this book.

Rick Steves' Guidebooks, Public Television Show, and Radio Show

Rick Steves' Europe Through the Back Door gives you budget-travel skills, such as minimizing jet lag, packing light, planning your itinerary, traveling by car or train, finding rooms, changing money, avoiding rip-offs, buying a mobile phone, hurdling the language barrier, staying healthy, taking great photographs, using a bidet, and much more. The book also includes chapters on 38 of my favorite "Back Doors," two of which are in Germany and Austria.

Country Guides: These annually updated books offer you the latest on the top sights and destinations, with tips on how to make your trip efficient and fun. Here are the titles:

Rick Steves' Best of Europe	*Rick Steves' Great Britain*
Rick Steves' Best of	*Rick Steves' Ireland*
Eastern Europe	*Rick Steves' Italy*
Rick Steves' England	*Rick Steves' Portugal*
(new in 2006)	*Rick Steves' Scandinavia*
Rick Steves' France	*Rick Steves' Spain*
Rick Steves' Germany	*Rick Steves' Switzerland*
& Austria	

City and Regional Guides: Updated every year, these focus on Europe's most compelling destinations. Along with specifics on sights, restaurants, hotels, and nightlife, you'll get self-guided, illustrated tours of the outstanding museums and most characteristic neighborhoods.

Rick Steves' Amsterdam,	*Rick Steves' Prague*
Bruges & Brussels	*& the Czech Republic*
Rick Steves' Florence	*Rick Steves' Provence*
& Tuscany	*& the French Riviera*
Rick Steves' London	*Rick Steves' Rome*
Rick Steves' Paris	*Rick Steves' Venice*

Rick Steves' Phrase Books: In Germany and Austria, a phrase book is as fun as it is necessary. This practical and budget-oriented series covers German, French, Italian, Spanish, Portuguese, and French/Italian/German. You'll be able to make hotel reservations over the phone, chat with your cabbie, and bargain at street markets.

And More Books: *Rick Steves' Europe 101: History and Art for the Traveler* (with Gene Openshaw) gives you the story of Europe's people, history, and art. Written for smart people who were sleeping in their history and art classes before they knew they were going to Europe, *101* helps Europe's sights come alive.

Rick Steves' Easy Access Europe, geared for travelers with limited mobility, covers London, Paris, Bruges, Amsterdam, and the Rhine Valley.

Rick Steves' Postcards from Europe, my autobiographical book, packs 25 years of travel anecdotes and insights into the ultimate 2,000-mile European adventure.

My latest book, *Rick Steves' European Christmas,* covers the joys, history, and quirky traditions of the holiday season in seven European countries, including both Germany and Austria.

Public Television Show: My series, *Rick Steves' Europe,* keeps churning out shows (60 at last count), including several featuring the sights in this book.

Radio Show: My new weekly radio show, which combines call-in questions (à la *Car Talk*) and interviews with travel experts, airs on public radio stations. For a schedule of upcoming topics and an archive of past programs (just click on a topic of your choice to listen), see www.ricksteves.com/radio.

Other Guidebooks

Especially if you'll be traveling beyond my recommended destinations, you may want some supplemental information. When you consider the improvements they'll make in your $3,000 vacation, $30 for extra maps and books is money well spent. Especially for several people traveling by car, the weight and expense are negligible. One good tip can save the price of an extra guidebook.

Lonely Planet's guides to Germany and Austria are thorough, well-researched, and packed with good maps and hotel recommendations for low- to moderate-budget travelers (but they're not updated annually—check the copyright date). The similar Rough Guides are written by insightful British researchers (also not updated annually).

Students and vagabonds like the highly opinionated Let's Go series (updated annually by Harvard students, has thorough hostel listings). Let's Go is best for backpackers who have railpasses and are interested in the youth and nightlife scene.

The popular, skinny, green Michelin Guides are excellent, especially if you're driving. Michelin Guides are known for their city and sightseeing maps, dry but concise and helpful information on all major sights, and good cultural and historical background. English editions are sold locally at gas stations and tourist shops.

More Recommended Reading and Movies

For information on Germany and Austria past and present, consider these books and films:

Non-Fiction Books: *Germany and the Germans* (by John Ardagh), *A Tramp Abroad* (by Mark Twain), *The Story of the Trapp Family Singers* (Maria von Trapp), *Inside the Third Reich* (Albert Speer), *Germany: A New History* (H. Schulze), *Culture Shock! Germany* (Richard Lord), and *Of German Ways* (Lavern Rippley).

Fiction Books: *Stones from the River* and *Floating in My Mother's Palm* (both by Ursula Hegi), *The Reader* (Bernard Schlink), *1632* (Eric Flint), *Summer at Gaglow* (Esther Freud), *Airs Above the*

Begin Your Trip at www.ricksteves.com

At www.ricksteves.com you'll find a wealth of **free information** on destinations covered in this book, including fresh European travel and tour news every month and helpful "Graffiti Wall" tips from thousands of fellow travelers.

While you're there, the **online Travel Store** is a great place to save money on travel bags and accessories designed by Rick Steves to help you travel smarter and lighter, plus a wide selection of guidebooks, planning maps, and DVDs.

Traveling through Europe by rail is a breeze, but choosing the right railpass for your trip—amidst hundreds of options—can drive you nutty. At www.ricksteves.com, you'll find **Rick Steves' Annual Guide to European Railpasses**—your best way to convert chaos into pure travel energy. Buy your railpass from Rick, and you'll get a bunch of free extras to boot.

Travel agents will tell you about mainstream tours of Europe, but they won't tell you about **Rick Steves' tours.** Rick Steves' Europe Through the Back Door travel company offers more than two dozen itineraries and 300 departures reaching the best destinations in this book...and beyond. You'll enjoy the services of a great guide, a fun bunch of travel partners (with small groups of around 25), and plenty of room to spread out in a big, comfy bus. You'll find trips to fit every vacation size, from week-long city getaways to longer cross-country adventures. For details, visit www.ricksteves.com or call 425/771-8303 ext. 217.

Ground (Mary Stewart), *The Tin Drum* (Günter Grass), *All Quiet on the Western Front* (Erich Maria Remarque), *Berlin Noir* (Philip Kerr), *Saints and Villains* (Denise Giardina), *The Silent Angel* (Heinrich Böll), *Buddenbrooks* and *The Magic Mountain* (both by Thomas Mann), and *Narcissus and Goldmund* (Herman Hesse).

Films: *The Third Man* (1949); *The Sound of Music* (1965); *Before Sunrise* (1995); *Amadeus* (1984); *Immortal Beloved* (1994); *Schindler's List* (1993); *The White Rose* (1982); *Swing Kids* (1993); *Das Boot* (1981); *The Tin Drum* (1979); *Cabaret* (1972); *Marriage of Maria Braun* (1979); *Triumph of the Will* (1935); *Run, Lola, Run* (1998); *Mephisto* (1981); *Wings of Desire* (1987); *Far Away, So Close!* (1993); *Nowhere in Africa* (2001); *Goodbye, Lenin* (2003); and *Downfall* (2004).

Maps

The black-and-white maps in this book, drawn by Dave Hoerlein, are concise and simple. Dave, who is well traveled in Germany and Austria, has designed the maps to help you locate recommended places and get to the tourist offices, where you can pick up a more in-depth map (usually free) of the city or region. Better maps are sold at newsstands—take a look before you buy to be sure the map has the level of detail you want.

European bookstores, especially in touristy areas, have good selections of maps. For drivers, I'd recommend a 1:200,000- or 1:300,000-scale map for each country. Train travelers usually manage fine with the freebies they get with the train pass and from the local tourist offices.

PRACTICALITIES

Red Tape: Currently, Americans need only a passport, but no visa or shots, to travel in Germany and Austria. Even as borders fade, when you change countries, you must still change telephone cards, postage stamps, and *Unterhosen*.

Time: In Europe—and throughout this book—you'll be using the 24-hour clock. After 12:00 noon, keep going: 13:00, 14:00, and so on. For anything over 12, subtract 12 and add p.m. (14:00 is 2:00 p.m.).

Germany and Austria are six/nine hours ahead of the East/West Coasts of the U.S.

Discounts: While discounts for sightseeing and transportation are not listed in this book, youths (under 18) and students (only with International Student Identity Card; www.isic.org) often get discounts—but only by asking.

Watt's Up? If you're bringing electrical gear, you'll need a two-prong adapter plug and a converter. Travel appliances often have convenient, built-in converters; look for a voltage switch marked 120V (U.S.) and 240V (Europe).

News: Americans keep in touch in Europe with the *International Herald Tribune* (published almost daily via satellite). Every Tuesday, the European editions of *Time* and *Newsweek* hit the stands with articles of particular interest to travelers in Europe. Sports addicts can get their fix from *USA Today*. Good Web sites include www.europeantimes.com and http://news.bbc.co.uk.

MONEY

Banking

Bring plastic (ATM, debit, or credit cards) along with several hundred dollars in hard cash as an emergency backup. Traveler's checks are a waste of time and money.

Before you go, verify with your bank that your card will work, inquire about fees (can be up to $5 per transaction), and alert them that you'll be making withdrawals in Europe; otherwise, the bank may not approve transactions if it perceives unusual spending

---

Exchange Rates

Germany, Austria, and this book all use the euro currency.

1 euro (€) = about $1.20

Like dollars, one euro (€) is broken down into 100 cents. You'll find coins ranging from one cent to two euros, and bills from five euros to 500 euros. To convert prices in euros to dollars, add 20 percent: €20 is about $24, €45 is about $55, and so on. So, that €65 German cuckoo clock is about $80, and the €90 taxi ride through Vienna is...uh-oh.

---

patterns. Bring an extra card in case one gets demagnetized or gobbled up by a machine.

The best and easiest way to get cash in euros is to use the omnipresent bank machines (always open, low fees, and quick processing). You'll need a PIN code—numbers only, no letters—to use with your Visa or MasterCard. The German word for "cash machine" is *Bankomat*.

In case you need a bank in Germany, they're generally open Monday through Friday 8:00 to 12:00 and 14:00 to 16:00; in Austria, Monday through Friday 8:00 to 15:00 and until 17:30 on Thursday.

Just like at home, credit or debit cards work easily at larger hotels, restaurants, and shops. Visa and MasterCard are more commonly accepted than American Express. Smaller businesses prefer payment in local currency. Smart travelers function with hard cash and plastic.

Keep your credit and debit cards and most of your money hidden away in a money belt (a cloth pouch worn around your waist and tucked under your clothes). Thieves target tourists. A money belt provides peace of mind and allows you to carry lots of cash safely. Don't be petty about getting money. Withdraw a week's worth of money, stuff it in your money belt, and travel!

Tips on Tipping

Tipping in Europe isn't as automatic and generous as it is in the U.S.—but for special service, tips are appreciated, if not expected. As in the U.S., the proper amount depends on your resources, tipping philosophy, and the circumstance, but some general guidelines apply.

Restaurants: Tipping is an issue only at restaurants that have waiters and waitresses. If you order your food at a counter, don't tip.

At German and Austrian restaurants that have a wait staff,

service is included, although it's common to round up the bill after a good meal (usually 5–10 percent; so, for an €18.50 meal, pay €20). Rather than leaving coins on the table, Germans usually pay with paper, saying how much they'd like the bill to be (for example, for an €8.10 meal, give a €20 bill and say *"Neun Euro"*—"Nine euros"—to get €11 change).

Taxis: To tip the cabbie, round up. For a typical ride, round up to the next euro on the fare (to pay a €13 fare, give €14); for a long ride, to the nearest €10 (for a €75 fare, give €80). If the cabbie hauls your bags and zips you to the airport to help you catch your flight, you might want to toss in a little more. But if you feel like you're being driven in circles or otherwise ripped off, skip the tip.

Hotels: I don't tip at hotels, but if you do, give the porter a euro for carrying bags and leave a couple of euros in your room at the end of your stay for the maid if the room was kept clean.

Special Services: Tour guides at public sites sometimes hold out their hands for tips after they give their spiel; if I've already paid for the tour, I don't tip extra, though some tourists do give a euro or two, particularly for a job well done. In general, if someone in the service industry does a super job for you, a tip of a couple of euros is appropriate...but not required.

When in doubt, ask. If you're not sure whether (or how much) to tip for a service, ask your hotelier or the tourist information office; they'll fill you in on how it's done on their turf.

VAT Refunds for Shoppers

Wrapped into the purchase price of your souvenirs is a Value Added Tax (VAT) of 16 percent in Germany and 16 to 20 percent in Austria. If you make a purchase of more than a certain amount (€30 in Germany, €75 in Austria) at a store that participates in the VAT refund scheme, you're entitled to get most of that tax back. Personally, I've never felt that VAT refunds are worth the hassle, but if you do, here's the scoop.

If you're lucky, the merchant will subtract the tax when you make your purchase (this is more likely to occur if the store ships the goods to your home). Otherwise, you'll need to do all this:

Get the paperwork: Have the merchant completely fill out the necessary refund document, called a "cheque." You'll have to present your passport at the store.

Get your stamp at the border or airport: Process your *cheque*(s) at your last stop in the EU with the customs agent who deals with VAT refunds. It's best to keep your purchases in your carry-on for viewing, but if they're too large or dangerous (such as knives) to carry on, then track down the proper customs agent to inspect them before you check your bag. You're not supposed to use your

Damage Control for Lost or Stolen Cards

If you lose your credit, debit, or ATM card, you can stop people from using your card by reporting the loss immediately to the respective global customer-assistance centers. Call these 24-hour U.S. numbers collect: Visa (tel. 410/581-9994), MasterCard (tel. 636/722-7111), and American Express (tel. 336/393-1111).

Have, at a minimum, the following information ready: the name of the financial institution that issued you the card, along with the type of card (classic, platinum, or whatever). Ideally, plan ahead and pack photocopies of your cards—front and back—to expedite their replacement. Providing the following information will allow for a quicker cancellation of your missing card: full card number, whether you are the primary or secondary cardholder, the cardholder's name exactly as printed on the card, billing address, home phone number, circumstances of the loss or theft, and identification verification (your birth date, your mother's maiden name, or your Social Security number—memorize this, don't carry a copy). If you are the secondary cardholder, you'll also need to provide the primary cardholder's identification verification details. You can generally receive a temporary card within two or three business days in Europe.

If you promptly report your card lost or stolen, you typically won't be responsible for any unauthorized transactions on your account, although many banks charge a liability fee of $50.

purchased goods before you leave. If you show up at customs wearing your new lederhosen or dirndl, officials might look the other way—or deny you a refund.

Collect your refund: You'll need to return your stamped documents to the retailer or its represen-tative. Many merchants work with services such as Global Refund or Premier Tax Free, with offices at major airports, ports, or border cross-ings. These services, which extract a 4 percent fee, can refund your money immediately in your currency of choice or credit your card (within 2 billing cycles). If you have to deal directly with the retailer, mail the store your stamped documents and then wait. It could take months.

Customs Regulations

You can take home $800 in souvenirs per person duty-free. The next $1,000 is taxed at a flat 3 percent. After that, you pay the individual item's duty rate. You can also bring in duty-free a liter of alcohol (slightly more than a standard-size bottle of wine), a carton of cigarettes, and up to 100 cigars. As for food, anything in cans or sealed jars is acceptable. Skip dried meat, cheeses, and fresh fruits and veggies. To check customs rules and duty rates, visit www.customs.gov.

TRANSPORTATION

By Car or Train?

The train is best for single travelers, those who'll be spending more time in big cities, and those who don't want to drive in Europe. While a car gives you the ultimate in mobility and freedom, enables you to search for hotels more easily, and carries your bags for you, the train zips you effortlessly from city to city, usually dropping you in the center and near the tourist office. Cars are great in the countryside but a worthless headache in cities such as Munich, Berlin, Frankfurt, and Vienna.

Trains

Trains are generally slick, speedy, and punctual, with synchronized connections. They cover cities well, but some frustrating schedules make a few out-of-the-way recommendations (such as the concentration camp at Mauthausen) not worth the time and trouble for the less determined.

Schedules: For timetables, visit http://bahn.hafas.de/bin/query.exe/en (German Rail, but also good for much of Europe, including Austria) or www.oebb.at (Austrian Rail). At most train stations, attendants will print out a step-by-step itinerary for you, free of charge. You can also produce an itinerary yourself using the track-side machines marked *Fahrkarten*. The touch-screen display gives you an English option; choose "Timetable Information," indicate your point of departure and destination, and then hit "Print" for a personalized schedule, including transfers and track numbers. Don't try to buy tickets from these machines—they only accept European bankcards. Major German stations also have handy Service Points offering general help to travelers. Each country has train information numbers you can dial from anywhere in the country: for Germany—tel. 11861 (€0.50/min); for Austria—tel. 051-717 (to get an operator, dial 2, then 1). Ask for an English speaker.

Railpasses: Eurail's new Germany and Austria-specific pass will probably be the best-value railpass if you are traveling

Major Train Lines

exclusively in these two countries. If you're traveling in neighboring countries as well, consider the Eurail Selectpass, which gives you up to 15 travel days (within a 2-month period) in three, four, or five adjacent countries—you could choose Germany, Austria, and bordering Western European countries. If you're planning a whirlwind tour of Europe, another possibility is the 18-country Eurailpass. These passes are available in a Saverpass version, which gives a 15 percent discount on railpasses for two or more companions traveling together. Each country also has its own individual train passes that offer good value for trips limited to one country. But patch-working second-class country passes together is complicated and unlikely to save you money. To sort through the options, explore my online Railpass Guide at www.ricksteves.com/rail. You

Railpasses

Prices listed are for 2005. My free *Rick Steves' Guide to European Railpasses* has the latest prices and details (and easy online ordering) at www.ricksteves.com/rail.

GERMAN FLEXIPASS

	1st Cl. Indiv.	1st Cl. Twin	2nd Cl. Indiv.	2nd Cl. Twin	2nd Cl. Youth
4 days in a month	$260	$195	$180	$135	$142
Extra rail days (max 6)	34	25.50	24	18	13

Covers KD Line boats on the Rhine and Mosel, 60% off Romantic Road and Castle bus ride. Twin prices are per person for 2 traveling together. Youth passes are for travelers under 26 only. Kids 6-11: half of full fare. Kids 5 and under: free. Five and ten-day versions available at some main train stations in Germany.

AUSTRIAN FLEXIPASS

	1st Class	2nd Class
Any 3 days out of 15 days	$164	$112
Add-on days (max 5)	22	16

Kids 6-11 half of adult fare, under 4: free.

SWITZERLAND–AUSTRIA FLEXI PASS

	1st Class Indiv.	1st Class Saver	2nd Class Youth
4 days in 2 months	$309	$269	$209
Extra rail days (max 6)	36	30	27

Saver prices are per person for 2 or more people traveling together. Youth passes are for travelers under 26 only. Kids 4-11: half of adult fare or Saver price, under 4: free.

GERMANY–BENELUX FLEXIPASS

	1st Cl. Indiv.	1st Cl. Saver	2nd Cl. Indiv.	2nd Cl. Saver	2nd Cl. Youth
5 days in 2 months	$328	$246	$246	$200	$199
6 days in 2 months	$362	$272	$272	$218	$217
8 days in 2 months	$430	$324	$324	$258	$258
10 days in 2 months	$498	$374	$374	$298	$299

Saver prices are per person for 2 or more traveling together. Youth passes are for travelers under 26 only. Kids 4-11 pay half of first class or Saver fare, under 4: free.

Germany and Austria by train

These schematic maps indicate the cost in dollars for a one-way second-class train trip between the cities shown. First class costs 50 percent more. Add up the approximate ticket costs for your trip to see if a railpass will save you money.

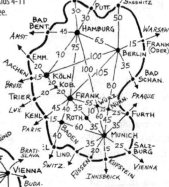

Germany

EURAIL SELECTPASSES

This pass covers travel in three, four, or five adjacent countries. Visit www.ricksteves.com/rail for additional country choices.

1st Class Individual	3 Countries	4 Countries	5 Countries
5 days in 2 months	$370	$414	$456
6 days in 2 months	410	454	496
8 days in 2 months	488	532	574
10 days in 2 months	564	608	650
15 days in 2 months			826

1st Class Saver	3 Countries	4 Countries	5 Countries
5 days in 2 months	$316	$352	$388
6 days in 2 months	348	386	422
8 days in 2 months	414	452	488
10 days in 2 months	480	516	552
15 days in 2 months			702

2nd Class Youth	3 Countries	4 Countries	5 Countries
5 days in 2 months	$241	$269	$296
6 days in 2 months	267	295	322
8 days in 2 months	317	345	372
10 days in 2 months	367	395	422
15 days in 2 months			537

Saverpass prices are per person for 2 or more people traveling together at all times. Youthpasses: Under age 26 only. Kids 4-11 pay half of adult fare; under 4: free.

Selectpass diagram key:

A **Selectpass** can be designed to connect a "chain" of any three, four, or five countries in this diagram linked by direct lines. (Examples that qualify: Norway-Sweden-Germany; Spain-France-Italy; Austria-Italy-Greece.) "Benelux" is considered one country.

SELECTPASS DRIVE

Any 3 days of rail travel + 2 days of Hertz or Avis car rental in 2 months within 3 adjoining countries.

Car Category	First Class	Extra Car Day
Economy	$310	$49
Compact	320	65
Intermediate	340	75
Small Automatic	350	95

Extra rail day $40 (max 7). Price shown is per person for 2 traveling together. Third and fourth persons sharing car get a 3-day out of 2-month railpass for approx. $256 (kids 4-11: $128). A fourth or fifth country adds about $35 to these prices. For more info, call your travel agent or Rail Europe at 800/438-7245.

can purchase any of these railpasses from your travel agent or
Rick Steves' Europe Through
the Back Door.

Eurailers (including Select
and single-country passholders) should know what extras
are covered by their pass; for
example, travel on any German
buses marked "Deutshe Bahn"
or "DB" (run by the train company); travel on city S-Bahn systems;
covered or discounted boats on the Rhine, Mosel, and Danube
Rivers; and a 60 percent discount on the Romantic Road bus tour.
Flexipass holders should note that discounted trips don't use up a
flexi-day, but fully covered ("free") trips do. The "used" flexipass
day can also cover your train travel on that day (but if you're not
planning to travel more that day, it makes sense to pay for, say, a
short boat ride rather than use up a day of your pass for it).

Note that if you take a night train between Germany and
Italy, your railpass must also include Austria (which these trains
pass through). This means you can no longer simply buy a separate
ticket covering the Austrian segment; rather, you must buy a ticket
for the entire route.

Tickets: Ticket fares are shown on the map on page 18 or
at http://bahn.hafas.de/bin/query.exe/en. If you decide to buy
train tickets as you go, look into local specials. Germany offers
several different point-to-point discounts (which can all be combined): If two to five people travel together on one ticket, the first
person pays the regular price, and the rest pay half of that price.
Kids under 14 travel free when named on one of their parent's
or grandparent's ticket. Off-peak specials in Germany include a
wild *Schönes Wochenende* ticket for €32; it gives groups of up to five
people unlimited second-class travel on non-express trains all day
Saturday or Sunday. *Länder-Tickets* are a similar deal (€26 for up
to 5 people after 9:00 on weekdays on local trains within a single
region, such as Bavaria). Those staying longer in Germany can get
additional discounts for a full year by purchasing one of several
BahnCards (starting at €25; see www.bahn.de).

While Eurailers over 26 automatically travel in first class,
people of any age buying individual tickets or single-country passes
should remember that traveling in second class provides the same
transportation for 33 percent less.

Train plus Bike: Hundreds of local train stations rent bikes
for about $5 a day, and sometimes have easy "pick up here and drop
off there" plans. For more on mixing train and bike travel, ask at
stations for information booklets.

Car Rental and Leasing

It's cheaper to arrange your car rental in advance in the U.S. than in Europe. You'll want a weekly rate with unlimited mileage. Comparison-shop through your agent. DER, a German company, often has the best rates (U.S. tel. 800-782-2424, www.dertravel .com).

Expect to pay about $750 per person (based on 2 people sharing the car) for a small economy car for three weeks with unlimited mileage, including gas, parking, and insurance. I normally rent a small, inexpensive model like a Ford Fiesta. For a bigger, roomier, more powerful but inexpensive car, move up to a Ford Focus or VW Polo. If you drop your car off early or keep it longer, you'll be credited or charged at a fair, prorated price.

For peace of mind, I spring for the Collision Damage Waiver insurance (CDW, about $15–25 per day), which limits my financial responsibility in case of an accident. Unfortunately, CDW now has a high deductible hovering around $1,200. When you pick up your car, many car-rental companies will try to sell you "super CDW" at an additional cost of $7 to $15 per day to lower the deductible to zero.

Some credit cards offer CDW-type coverage for no charge to their customers. Quiz your credit-card company on the worst-case scenario. You have to choose either the coverage offered by your car-rental company or by your credit-card company. This means that if you go with the credit-card coverage, you'll have to decline the CDW offered by the car-rental company. In this situation, some car-rental companies put a hold on your credit card for the amount of the full deductible (which can equal the value of the car). This is bad news if your credit limit is low—particularly if you plan on using that card for other purchases during your trip.

Another alternative is buying CDW insurance from Travel Guard for $9 a day (U.S. tel. 800-826-4919, www.travelguard .com). It's valid throughout Europe, but some car-rental companies refuse to honor it, especially in Italy and the Republic of Ireland. Oddly, residents of some states (including Washington) are not allowed to buy this coverage.

In sum, buying CDW—and the supplemental insurance to buy down the deductible, if you choose—is the easiest but priciest option. Using the coverage that comes with your credit card is cheaper, but can involve more hassle. If you're taking a short trip, an easy solution is to buy Travel Guard's very affordable CDW. For longer trips, look into leasing.

Leasing: For trips of two and a half weeks or more, leasing (which automatically includes CDW insurance with no deductible) is the best way to go. By technically buying and then selling back the car, you save lots of money on tax and insurance. Leasing

Driving: Distance and Time

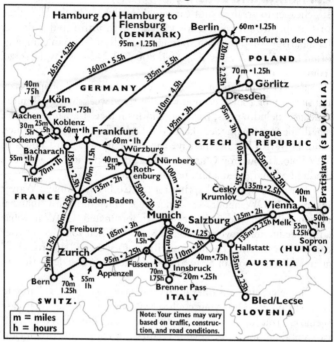

provides you a new car with unlimited mileage and a 24-hour emergency assistance program. You can lease for as little as 17 days to as long as six months. Car leases must be arranged from the U.S. A reliable company offering 17-day lease packages for about $750–800 is Europe by Car (U.S. tel. 800-223-1516, www .europebycar.com).

Driving

If you plan to drive Germany or Austria, get an International Driving Permit before your trip (at your local AAA office or online at www.aaa.com/vacation/idpf.html—send $10 plus 2 passport-type photos). Also bring along your U.S. driver's license.

Every long drive between my recommended destinations is via the autobahn (super freeway), and nearly every scenic backcountry drive is paved and comfortable.

Austria charges drivers who use their roads. In Austria, you'll need a *Vignette* sticker for your rental car (buy at the border crossing, big gas stations near borders, or a rental-car agency)—€8 for 10 days or €22 for two months. (Dipping into the country on regular roads—such as around Reutte in Tirol—requires no special payment.)

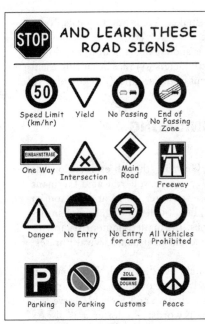

STOP AND LEARN THESE ROAD SIGNS

Speed Limit (km/hr) — Yield — No Passing — End of No Passing Zone

One Way — Intersection — Main Road — Freeway

Danger — No Entry — No Entry for cars — All Vehicles Prohibited

Parking — No Parking — Customs — Peace

Learn the universal road signs (explained in charts in most road atlases and at service stations; see above). Seat belts are required, and two beers under those belts are enough to land you in jail.

Use good local maps and study them before each drive. Learn which exits you need to look out for, which major cities you'll travel toward, where the ruined castles lurk, and so on.

To get to the center of a city, follow signs for *Zentrum* or *Stadtmitte.* Ring roads go around a city. For parking, you can pick up the "cardboard clock" (*Parkscheibe,* available free at gas stations, police stations, and *Tabak* shops) and display your arrival time on the dashboard so parking attendants can see you've been there less than the posted maximum stay (blue lines indicate 90-min zones on Austrian streets).

In Europe, the shortest distance between any two points is the autobahn. Signs directing you to the autobahn are green in Austria, blue in Germany. To understand the complex but superefficient autobahn (no speed limit, toll-free), look for the *Autobahn Service* booklet at any autobahn rest stop (free, lists all stops, services, road symbols, and more). Learn the signs: *Dreieck* (literally, "three corners") means a "Y" in the road; *Autobahnkreuz* is an intersection. Exits are spaced about every 20 miles and often have a gas station (*bleifrei* means "unleaded"), a restaurant, a minimarket, and sometimes a tourist information desk. Exits and intersections refer to the next major or the nearest small town. Study the map and anticipate which town names to look out for. Know what you're looking for—miss it, and you're long autobahn-gone. When navigating, you'll see *nord, süd, ost,* or *west.*

Autobahns generally have no speed limit, but you will commonly see a recommended speed posted. While no one gets a ticket for ignoring this recommendation, exceeding this speed means your car insurance no longer covers you in the event of an accident. Don't cruise in the passing lane; stay right. In fast-driving Germany, the backed-up line caused by an insensitive slow driver is called an *Autoschlange,* or "car snake." What's the difference between a car snake and a real snake? According to locals, "on a real snake, the ass is in the back."

Get used to metric. A liter is about a quart, four to a gallon; a kilometer is 0.6 mile. Convert kilometers to miles by cutting them in half and adding back 10 percent of the original (120 km: 60 + 12 = 72 miles).

COMMUNICATING

Language Barrier

Germans and Austrians speak German (though each region has its own distinct dialect). Most young or well-educated Germans and Austrians—especially those in larger towns and the tourist trade—speak at least some English. Still, you'll get more smiles by using the German pleasantries. In smaller, nontouristy towns, the language barrier is higher. See the "German Survival Phrases" near the end of this book.

German—like English, Dutch, Swedish, and Norwegian—is a Germanic language, making it easier on most American ears than Romance languages (such as Italian and French). These tips will help you pronounce German words: The letter *w* is always pronounced as "v" (e.g., the word for "wonderful" is *wunderbar*, pronounced VOON-der-bar). In these vowel combination—*ie* and *ei*—you pronounce only the second letter, so *ie* sounds like the letter E (as in *hier* and *Bier,* the German words for "here" and "beer"), while *ei* sounds like the letter I (as in *nein* and *Stein,* the German words for "no" and "stone"). The vowel combination of *eu* is pronounced "oy" (as in *treu* and *Deutsch,* the German words for "true" and "German"). To pronounce a vowel with an umlaut *(ä, ö, ü)*, purse your lips when you say it. The letter *Eszett (ß)* represents *ss.* Written German always capitalizes all nouns.

Give it your best shot. The locals will appreciate your efforts.

Telephones

Smart travelers learn the phone system and use it daily to reserve or reconfirm rooms, get tourist information, reserve restaurants, confirm tour times, or phone home.

Types of Phones

You'll encounter various kinds of phones in Germany and Austria.

Public pay phones, which used to be coin-operated, now almost always take insertable phone cards. A few coin-operated phones still exist; if you use coins to make your calls, have a bunch handy. You can also use an international phone card to make calls from pay phones that take coins or insertable cards. For details on the different phone cards, see below.

Hotel room phones are fairly cheap for local calls, but pricey for international calls, unless you use an international phone card (see below).

American mobile phones work in Europe if they're GSM-enabled, tri-band (or quad-band), and on a calling plan that includes international calls. With a T-Mobile phone, you can roam using your home number, and pay $1 to $2 per minute for making or receiving calls.

Some travelers buy a **European mobile phone** in Europe. For about $125, you can get a phone that will work in most countries once you pick up the necessary chip (about $30) per country. Or you can buy a cheaper, "locked" phone that only works in the country where you purchased it (about $100, includes $20 worth of calls). If you're interested, stop by any European shop that sells mobile phones; you'll see prominent store-window displays. You aren't required to (and shouldn't) buy a monthly contract—buy prepaid calling time instead (as you use it up, buy additional minutes at newsstands or mobile-phone shops). If you're on a budget, skip mobile phones and use phone cards instead.

Paying for Calls

You can spend a fortune making phone calls in Europe...but why would you? Here's the skinny on different ways to pay, including the best deals.

German and Austrian **phone cards** come in two types: phone cards that you insert into a pay phone (best for local calls or quick international calls), and phone cards that come with a dial-up code and can be used from virtually any phone (best for international calls; note that these are not a good value when used from German public pay phones—see below).

Insertable phone cards are a convenient way to pay for calls from public pay phones. Buy these cards at TIs, tobacco shops, post offices, and train stations. The price of the call (local or international) is automatically deducted while you talk. They are sold in several denominations starting at about €5. Calling the U.S. with one of these phone cards is reasonable (about 2–3 min per euro), but more expensive than using an international phone card. Each European country has its own insertable phone card—so your German card won't work in an Austrian phone.

International phone cards can be used from virtually any phone. These are not inserted into the phone. Instead, you dial the toll-free number listed on the card, reaching an automated operator. When prompted, you dial a code number, also written on the card. A voice tells you how much is left in your account. Then dial your number. Usually you can select English, but if the prompts are in German, experiment: Dial your code, followed by the pound sign (#), then the number, then pound again, and so on, until it works. Since you don't insert the card in the phone, you can use these to make inexpensive calls from most phones, including the one in your hotel room, avoiding pricey hotel rates. Remember that you don't need the actual card to use a card account, so it's sharable. You can write down the access and code numbers in your notebook and share it with friends.

Calls to the U.S. are very cheap (about 20–25 min per euro). You can use the cards to make local and domestic long-distance calls as well. Buy cards at small newsstand kiosks and hole-in-the-wall long-distance phone shops. Because there are so many brand names, simply ask for an international telephone card and tell the vendor where you'll be making most calls ("to America"), and he'll select the brand with the best deal. Some international calling cards work in multiple countries—if traveling to both Germany and Austria, try to buy a card that will work in both places. Because cards are occasionally duds, avoid the high denominations.

These international phone cards are such a good deal that the irritated German phone company is making them less cost-effective. In Germany, the cards are only cheap if you use them from a fixed line, like a hotel-room phone. From a pay phone, you'll get far fewer minutes for your money (for example, 10 min instead of 100 on a €5 card). No such pay-phone problem exists in Austria (at least, not yet).

Dialing direct from your hotel room without using an international calling card is usually quite expensive for international calls. (I always ask first how much I'll be charged.) Keep in mind that you might have to pay for local and occasionally even toll-free calls.

Receiving calls in your hotel room is often the cheapest way to keep in touch with the folks back home—especially if your family has an inexpensive way to call you (either a good deal on their long-distance plan, a prepaid calling card with good rates to Europe, or access to an Internet phone service such as Skype—www.skype.com). Give them a list of your hotels' phone numbers before you go. As you travel, send your family an e-mail or make a quick payphone call to set up a time for them to call you, and then wait for the ring.

U.S. calling cards (such as the ones offered by AT&T, MCI, or Sprint) are the worst option. You'll nearly always save a lot of money by paying with a phone card.

How to Dial

Calling from the U.S. to Germany or Austria, or vice versa, is simple—once you break the code. The European calling chart on page 586 will walk you through it. Remember that German and Austrian time is six/nine hours ahead of the East/West Coasts of the U.S.

Dialing Domestic Calls: Germany and Austria, like much of the U.S., use an area-code dialing system. If you're dialing within an area code, you just dial the local number to be connected; but if you're calling outside your area code, you have to dial both the area code (which starts with a 0) and the local number. For example, Munich's area code is 089 and the number of one of my recommended Munich hotels is 515-530. To call the hotel within Munich, you'd dial 515-530. To call it from Frankfurt, you'd dial 089/515-530.

Don't be surprised if local phone numbers in Germany and Austria have different numbers of digits within the same city or even the same hotel (for example, a hotel can have a 6-digit phone number and an 8-digit fax number).

Dialing International Calls: For a listing of country codes, see the appendix. When making an international call to Germany or Austria, first dial the international access code of the country you're in (011 from the U.S. or Canada, 00 if you're calling from Europe), then—depending on the country you're calling—dial either Germany's country code (49) or Austria's country code (43), then the area code (*without* its initial 0) and the local number. For example, to call the Munich hotel from home, you'd dial 011 (the international access code for the U.S. and Canada), 49 (Germany's country code), 89 (Munich's area code without the initial 0), and 515-530.

To call my office from anywhere in Europe, I dial 00 (Europe's international access code), 1 (U.S. country code), 425 (Edmonds' area code), and 771-8303.

E-mail and Mail

E-mail: Internet cafés are available at just about every destination in this book, giving you reasonably inexpensive and easy Internet access. Your hotelier can direct you to the nearest place. Many hotels have Internet terminals in their lobbies for guests, and some offer Wi-Fi wireless connections for travelers with laptops.

Mail: While you can arrange for mail delivery to your hotel (allow 10 days for a letter to arrive), phoning and e-mailing are so easy that I've dispensed with mail stops altogether.

SLEEPING

In the interest of smart use of your time, I favor hotels and restaurants handy to your sightseeing activities. Rather than list hotels scattered throughout a city, I describe two or three favorite neighborhoods and recommend the best accommodations values in each, from $10 bunks to plush $200+ doubles.

While accommodations in Germany and Austria are fairly expensive, they are normally very comfortable and come with breakfast. Plan on spending $80 to $120 per hotel double in big cities, and $40 to $80 in towns and in private homes.

A triple is much cheaper than a double and a single. While hotel singles are most expensive, private accommodations *(Zimmer)* have a flat per-person rate. Hostels and dorms always charge per person. Especially in private homes, where the boss changes the sheets, people staying several nights are most desirable. One-night stays are sometimes charged extra.

In recommending hotels, I favor small, family-run places that are central, inexpensive, quiet, clean, safe, friendly, English-speaking, and not listed in other guidebooks. I also like local character and simple facilities that don't cater to American "needs." Obviously, a place meeting every criterion is rare, and all of my recommendations fall short of perfection—sometimes miserably. But I've listed the best values for each price category, given the above criteria. The very best values are family-run places with showers down the hall and no elevator.

Any room without a bathroom has access to a bathroom in the corridor (free unless otherwise noted). All rooms have a sink. For environmental reasons, towels are often replaced in hotels only when you leave them on the floor. In cheaper places, they aren't replaced at all, so hang them up to dry and reuse.

Unless I note otherwise, the cost of a room includes a breakfast (sometimes continental, but usually buffet). The price is usually posted in the room. Before accepting, confirm your understanding of the complete price. I appreciate feedback on your hotel experiences.

Making Reservations

It's possible to travel at any time of year without reservations, but given the high stakes, erratic accommodations values, and the quality of the gems I've found for this book, I'd highly recommend calling for rooms at least several days in advance as you travel (and book well in advance for festivals, such as Munich's Oktoberfest, and around World Cup game dates in 2006—see sidebar on page 6).

If tourist crowds are minimal, you might make a habit of calling between 9:00 and 10:00 on the day you plan to arrive, when the hotel knows who'll be checking out and just which rooms will be available. I've taken great pains to list telephone numbers with long-distance instructions (see "Telephones," page 24; also see the appendix). Use the telephone and the convenient telephone cards. Most hotels listed are accustomed to English-only speakers. Most hotel receptionists will trust you and hold a room until 16:00 without a deposit, though some will ask for a credit-card number. Honor (or cancel by phone) your reservations. Long distance is cheap and easy from public phone booths. *Trusting people to show up is a hugely stressful issue and a financial risk for B&B owners. Don't*

Sleep Code

To help you easily sort through the accommodations listed, I've divided the rooms into three categories based on the price for a standard double room with bath.

$$$ Higher Priced
$$ Moderately Priced
$ Lower Priced

To give maximum information with a minimum of space, I use the following code to describe accommodations listed in this book. Prices are listed per room, not per person. When a range of prices is listed for a room, the price fluctuates with room size or season. You can assume a hotel takes credit cards unless you see "cash only" in the listing. Hotel clerks speak at least some English unless otherwise noted.

S = Single room (or price for one person in a double).
D = Double or Twin. Double beds are usually big enough for non-romantic couples.
T = Triple (often a double bed with a single bed moved in).
Q = Quad (an extra child's bed is usually cheaper).
b = Private bathroom with toilet and shower or tub.
s = Private shower or tub only (the toilet is down the hall).

According to this code, a couple staying at a "Db-€90" hotel would pay a total of 90 euros (about $110) for a double room with a private bathroom. The hotel accepts credit cards or cash in payment.

---

let these people down—I promised you'd call and cancel if for some reason you can't show up. Don't needlessly confirm rooms through the tourist offices; they'll take a commission.

If you know exactly which dates you need and really want a particular place, reserve a room long before you leave home. To reserve from home, call, e-mail, or fax the hotel. E-mail is free, phone and fax costs are reasonable, and simple English is usually fine. To fax, use the form in the appendix (also at www.ricksteves .com/reservation). A two-night stay in August would be "2 nights, 16/8/06 to 18/8/06." (Europeans write the date day/month/year, and European hotel jargon uses your day of departure.) Hotels often require one night's deposit to hold a room. Usually a credit-card number and expiration date will be accepted as the deposit. Faxing your card number (rather than e-mailing it) keeps it private, safer, and out of cyberspace. If you do reserve with a credit card, you can pay with your card or cash when you arrive;

if you don't show up, you'll be billed for the night.

Hotels in larger cities sometimes have strict cancellation policies (you might lose, say, a deposit if you cancel within 2 weeks of your reserved stay, or you might be billed for the entire visit if you leave early); ask about cancellation policies before you book.

On the road, reconfirm your reservations a day or two in advance for safety (or you may be bumped—really). Also, don't just assume you can extend. Take the time to consider in advance how long you'll stay.

Camping and Hosteling

Campers can manage with Let's Go listings (see "Other Guidebooks," page 10) and help from the local TI (ask for a regional camping listing). Your hometown travel bookstore should also have guidebooks on camping in Europe. You'll find campgrounds just about everywhere you need them. Look for *Campingplatz* signs. You'll meet lots of Europeans—camping is a popular, middle-class-family way to go. Campgrounds are cheap ($6–10 per person), friendly, safe, more central and convenient than rustic, and rarely full.

Hostelers can take advantage of the wonderful network of hostels. Follow signs marked *Jugendherberge* (with triangles) or with the logo showing a tree next to a house. Generally, travelers without a membership card ($28 per year, sold at hostels in most U.S. cities or online at www.hiusa.org, U.S. tel. 202/783-6161) are admitted for an extra $5.

Hostels are open to members of all ages (except in Bavaria, where a maximum age of 26 is strictly enforced at official hostels, though not at independent hostels). They usually cost $10 to $20 per night (cheaper for those under 27, plus $4 sheet rental if you don't have your own) and serve good, cheap meals and/or provide kitchen facilities. If you plan to stay in hostels, bring your own sheet. While many hostels have a few doubles or family rooms available upon request for a little extra money, plan on gender-segregated dorms with 4 to 20 beds per room. Hostels can be idyllic and peaceful, but school groups can raise the rafters. School groups are most common on summer weekends and on school-year weekdays. I like small hostels best. While many hostels may say over the telephone that they're full, most hold a few beds for people who drop in, or they can direct you to budget accommodations nearby.

EATING

Germanic cuisine is heavy, hearty, and—by European standards—inexpensive. Though it's tasty, it can get monotonous if you fall into the schnitzel or wurst-and-potatoes rut. Be adventurous.

Each region has its specialties, which, though not cheap, are often good values.

There are many kinds of restaurants. Hotels often serve fine food. A *Gaststätte* is a simple, less-expensive restaurant. For smaller portions, order from the *kleine Hunger* (small hunger) section of the menu.

Ethnic restaurants provide a welcome break from Germanic fare. Foreign cuisine is either the legacy of a crumbled empire (Hungarian and Bohemian, from which Austria gets its goulash and dumplings) or a new arrival to feed the many hungry-but-poor guest workers. Italian, Turkish, and Greek food are good values.

The cheapest meals are found in department-store cafeterias, *Schnell-Imbiss* (fast-food) stands, university cafeterias *(Mensas)*, and hostels. For a quick, cheap bite, have a deli make you a *Wurstsemmel*—a meat sandwich.

Most restaurants tack a menu onto their door for browsers and have an English menu inside. Only a rude waiter will rush you. Good service is relaxed (slow to an American). In Germany and Austria, you might be charged for bread you've eaten from the basket on the table; have the waiter take it away if you don't want it. To wish others "Happy eating!" offer a cheery *"Guten Appetit!"* When you want the bill, say, *"Zahlen (TSAH-lenn), bitte."* For tips on tipping, see page 13.

For most visitors, the rich pastries, wine, and beer provide the fondest memories of Germanic cuisine. The wine (85 percent white) is particularly good from the Mosel, Rhine, and Danube river valleys and eastern Austria. Order wine by the *Viertel* (quarter liter, or 8 oz.) or *Achtel* (eighth liter, or 4 oz.). You can say, *"Ein Viertel Weisswein* (white wine), *bitte* (please)." Order it *süss* (sweet), *halb trocken* (medium), or *trocken* (dry). *Rotwein* is red wine and *Sekt* is German champagne. Menus list drink size by the tenth of a liter, or deciliter (dl). Ask for a *Weinschorle* and you'll get a spritzer—white wine pepped up with a little sparkling water.

The Germans enjoy a tremendous variety of great beer. The average German, who drinks 40 gallons of beer a year, knows that *dunkles* is dark, *helles* is light, *Flaschenbier* is bottled, and *vom Fass* is on tap. *Pils* is barley-based, *Weizen* is wheat-based, and *Malzbier* is the malt beer that children learn with. *Radler* is half beer and half lemon-lime soda. When you order beer, ask for *eine Halbe* for a half-liter (not always available) or *eine*

Send Me an E-mail, Drop Me a Line

If you enjoy a successful trip with the help of this book and would like to share your discoveries, please fill out the survey at www.ricksteves.com/feedback. I personally read and value all feedback.

Mass for a whole liter (about a quart). Tap water—which many waiters aren't eager to bring you—is *Leitungswasser.* They would rather you buy *Mineralwasser* (*mit/ohne Gas*, with/without carbonation). Popular soft drinks include *Apfelschorle* (half apple juice, half sparkling water) and *Spezi* (Coke and orange soda).

TRAVELING AS A TEMPORARY LOCAL

We travel all the way to Europe to enjoy differences—to become temporary locals. You'll experience frustrations. Certain truths that we find "God-given" or "self-evident," such as cold beer, ice in drinks, bottomless cups of coffee, and bigger being better, are suddenly not so true. One of the benefits of travel is the eye-opening realization that there are logical, civil, and even better alternatives. A willingness to go local ensures that you'll enjoy a full dose of European hospitality.

If there is a negative aspect to the image Europeans have of Americans, it is that we are big, aggressive, impolite, rich, loud, and a bit naive. Americans tend to be noisy in public places, such as restaurants and trains. Our raised voices can demolish Europe's reserved and elegant ambience. Talk softly. While Europeans look bemusedly at some of our Yankee excesses—and worriedly at others—they nearly always afford us individual travelers all the warmth we deserve.

Judging from all the happy postcards I receive from travelers who have used this book, it's safe to assume you'll enjoy a great, affordable vacation—with the finesse of an independent, experienced traveler. Thanks, and happy travels—*gute Reise!*

BACK DOOR TRAVEL PHILOSOPHY

From *Rick Steves' Europe Through the Back Door*

Travel is intensified living—maximum thrills per minute and one of the last great sources of legal adventure. Travel is freedom. It's recess, and we need it.

Experiencing the real Europe requires catching it by surprise, going casual..."Through the Back Door."

Affording travel is a matter of priorities. (Make do with the old car.) You can travel—simply, safely, and comfortably—anywhere in Europe for $100 a day plus transportation costs (even less in Germany and Austria). In many ways, spending more money only builds a thicker wall between you and what you came to see. Europe is a cultural carnival, and, time after time, you'll find that its best acts are free and the best seats are the cheap ones.

A tight budget forces you to travel close to the ground, meeting and communicating with the people, not relying on service with a purchased smile. Never sacrifice sleep, nutrition, safety, or cleanliness in the name of budget. Simply enjoy the local-style alternatives to expensive hotels and restaurants.

Extroverts have more fun. If your trip is low on magic moments, kick yourself and make things happen. If you don't enjoy a place, maybe you don't know enough about it. Seek the truth. Recognize tourist traps. Give a culture the benefit of your open mind. See things as different but not better or worse. Any culture has much to share.

Of course, travel, like the world, is a series of hills and valleys. Be fanatically positive and militantly optimistic. If something's not to your liking, change your liking. Travel is addictive. It can make you a happier American as well as a citizen of the world. Our Earth is home to six billion equally important people. It's humbling to travel and find that people don't envy Americans. They like us, but, with all due respect, they wouldn't trade passports.

Globe-trotting destroys ethnocentricity. It helps you understand and appreciate different cultures. Regrettably, there are forces in our society that want you dumbed down for their convenience. Don't let it happen. Thoughtful travel engages you with the world—more important than ever these days. Travel changes people. It broadens perspectives and teaches new ways to measure quality of life. Many travelers toss aside their hometown blinders. Their prized souvenirs are the strands of different cultures they decide to knit into their own character. The world is a cultural yarn shop. And Back Door travelers are weaving the ultimate tapestry. Come on, join in!

GERMANY

GERMANY

(Deutschland)

Deutschland is energetic, efficient, and organized—it's Europe's muscleman, both economically and wherever people line up (Germans have a reputation for pushing ahead). Its bustling cities hold 85 percent of its people, and average earnings are among the highest in the world. Ninety-seven percent of the workers get one-month paid vacations, and, during the other 11 months, they create a Gross Domestic Product (GDP) that's about one-quarter of the United States'. Germany has risen from the ashes of World War II to become the world's fifth-largest industrial power. Germany also shines culturally, beating out all but two countries in production of books, Nobel laureates, and professors.

Though its East-West division lasted about 40 years, historically Germany has been divided between north and south. Northern Germany was barbarian, is predominantly Protestant, and tackles life aggressively, while southern Germany was Roman, is largely Catholic, and enjoys a more relaxed tempo of life. The romantic American image of Germany is beer-and-pretzel Bavaria (probably because that was "our" sector after the war). This historic North-South division is less pronounced these days as Germany becomes a more mobile society. The big tasks facing Germany today include its continual efforts to revive the former East Germany and to strengthen the country's economy while maintaining its generous social services.

Germany's tourist route today—Rhine, Romantic Road, Bavaria—was yesterday's trade route, connecting its most thriving medieval cities. Germany as a nation is just 130 years old. In 1850, there were 35 independent countries in what is now Germany. In medieval times there were 350, each with its own weights, measures, coinage, king, and lottery.

Many visitors can't help but associate Germany with its dark Nazi past. While a small neo-Nazi skinhead element still survives in the back alleys of German society, for the most part the nation has evolved into a surprisingly progressive, almost touchy-feely place. A genuine sense of shame and responsibility for World War II and the Holocaust pervades much of German society, and

Germany

the last few generations of German kids have been raised to fully understand their nation's destructive role in the 20th century. If you visit a concentration camp memorial, you'll likely see several field-trip groups of German teens, and other reminders of the Nazi chapter are everywhere: Imagine sitting down after dinner and watching *Schindler's List* or *Band of Brothers* on national TV...featuring your grandparents as the bad guys. As Germany leads the way in forming a healthy European Union—with peace, unity, tolerance, and human rights as its central motivations—it seems that most Germans are trying to make up for the ugliness their ancestors subjected Europe to not so long ago.

Germany Almanac

Official Name: Bundesrepublik Deutschland, or simply Deutschland.

Population: Germany's 82 million people (4 times the population of Texas) are largely of Teutonic DNA (90 percent), plus a small but significant minority (2.5 percent) of Turkish-descended citizens. A third of Germans are Catholic, a third Protestant, and a third unaffiliated or Muslim.

Latitude and Longitude: 51°N and 9°E. The latitude is similar to Alberta, Canada.

Area: At 138,000 square miles, Germany is smaller than Montana and about half the size of Texas. Its land is bordered by nine countries.

Geography: The terrain gradually rises—from flat land in the north to the rugged Alps in the south, culminating in the 9,700-foot Zugspitze mountain. The climate is temperate.

Biggest Cities: The capital city of Berlin has 3.4 million people, followed by Hamburg's 1.7 million and Munich's more than 1.3 million.

Economy: With a GDP of $2.4 trillion—similar to America's Midwest states combined—Germany is Europe's largest economy. Still, the GDP per capita is $29,000, or about 25 percent less than America's. Their high-tech industries pump out iron and steel (ThyssenKrupp), cars (BMW, DaimlerChrysler, Volkswagen), chemicals and drugs (Bayer), and global electronics (Siemens, T-Mobile/Deutsche Telekom). There are 1,280 breweries, but much of the production is consumed locally. Germany trades almost equally with a half-dozen neighboring countries, and the United States.

All over Germany, you'll likely see written on doorways a mysterious message: "20 + C + M + B + 06." This is marked in chalk on Epiphany (January 6), the Christian holiday celebrating the arrival of the Magi to adore the newborn Baby Jesus. In addition to being the initials of the three wise men (Caspar, Melchior, and Balthazar), the letters also stand for the Latin phrase *Christus mansionem benedicat*—"May Christ bless the house." The little crosses separating the letters remind all who enter that the house has been blessed in this year (20-06).

Germans eat lunch and dinner about when we do. Order house specials whenever possible. Pork, fish, and venison are good, and don't miss the bratwurst and sauerkraut. Potatoes are the standard vegetable, but *Spargel* (giant white asparagus) is a must in-season. The bread and pretzels in the basket on your table often cost extra. When I need a break from pork, I order the *Salatteller* (big, varied

Since the 1990 reunification, Germany's economy has been burdened by the cost (about $70 billion a year) of integrating the former East Germany into the modern West. Germany's expensive social security system gets even costlier as the population ages. Thanks to powerful trade unions, workers get good benefits, but unemployment seems permanently fixed at 10 percent. Recently, the deficit has even exceeded the 3-percent-of-GDP level required to be a euro currency member.

Government: Germany's September 2005 elections were extremely close, with no single party, left or right, sweeping to victory. Conservative Chancellor Angela Merkel now heads a coalition government that leans slightly to the right. A small but powerful minority party, the Greens, presses the pro-environment agenda. Germany's chancellor, similar to the prime minister in other countries, is not elected directly by the people but is the head of the lead party in parliament. The less-powerful president (Horst Köhler) is also elected by parliament. The legislative branch includes the *Bundestag* (613 seats, elected by both direct and proportional representation) and the *Bundesrat* (69 votes by local officials of Germany's 16 states).

Flag: *Deutschland*'s flag is composed of three horizontal bands of (starting from the top) black, red, and gold.

The Average Deutsch: The average German is 42 years old—six years older than the average American—has 1.39 kids, and will live to be almost 79. He or she lives in a household with two other people, watches 2.5 hours of TV a day, spends 20 minutes reading the daily newspaper, and says the word *der* more often than any other word. The average German drinks a pint of beer every 32 hours, which is slightly less than the average Irish or Czech.

dinner-size salad). Great beers and white wines abound. Go with whatever beer is on tap.

Gummi bears are local gumdrops with a cult following (beware of imitations—you must see the word *Gummi*), and Nutella is a chocolate-hazelnut spread that may change your life.

When it comes to drink, the Germans enjoy an embarrassment of riches. In addition to being famous for their excellent brew and rowdy beer halls, Germany is also known for its fine wine— from the sweet, white "Rhine wines" to some good reds. For more on German consumption, see page 31 in this book's Introduction.

MUNICH

(München)

Munich, Germany's most livable and "yuppie" city, is also one of its most historic, artistic, and entertaining. It's big and growing, with a population of more than 1.3 million. Until 1871, it was the capital of an independent Bavaria. Its imperial palaces, jewels, and grand boulevards constantly remind visitors that this was once a political and cultural powerhouse. And its recently bombed-out feeling reminds us that 75 years ago it provided a springboard for Nazism, and 60 years ago it lost a war.

Orient yourself in Munich's old center with its colorful pedestrian mall. Immerse yourself in Munich's art and history—crown jewels, Baroque theater, Wittelsbach palaces, great paintings, and beautiful parks. Munich evenings are best spent in frothy beer halls, with their oompah, bunny-hopping, and belching Bavarian atmosphere. Pry big pretzels from buxom, no-nonsense beer maids.

Planning Your Time

Munich is worth two days, including a half-day side-trip to Dachau. If necessary, its essence can be captured in a day (walk the center, tour a palace and a museum, and enjoy a beer-filled evening). Those in a hurry and without a car can see "Mad" King Ludwig's castles (covered in the Bavaria and Tirol chapter) as a day trip from Munich by tour. Even Salzburg (2 hrs one-way by train) is within day-tripping distance.

World Cup Warning: The big news in 2006 is the World Cup, which will clog cities throughout Germany in June and July (see page 6). Six big games will be played in Munich's new stadium: on June 9, 14, 18, 21, and 24, and a semifinal match on July 5. On and around these dates, hotels will be jam-packed.

ORIENTATION

(area code: 089)
The tourist's Munich is circled by a ring road (site of the old town wall) marked by four old gates: Karlstor, also known as Stachus (near the main train station, known as the Hauptbahnhof), Sendlinger Tor, Isartor (near the river), and Odeonsplatz (no surviving gate, near the palace). Marienplatz marks the city's center. A great pedestrian-only zone (Kaufingerstrasse and Neuhauserstrasse) cuts this circle in half, running nearly from Karlstor and the train station through Marienplatz to Isartor. Orient yourself along this east–west axis. Ninety percent of the sights and hotels I recommend are within a 20-minute walk of Marienplatz and each other.

Despite its large population, Munich feels small. This big-city elegance is possible because of a law that no building can be taller than the church spires. Despite ongoing debate about changing this policy, there are still no skyscrapers in downtown Munich.

Tourist Information

Official TIs: Munich has two helpful TIs (www.muenchen-tourist .de). One is in front of the **main train station** (with your back to the tracks, walk through the central hall, step outside, and turn right; Mon–Sat 9:00–20:00, Sun 10:00–18:00, less off-season, tel. 089/233-0300). The other TI is on Munich's main square, **Marienplatz,** below the glockenspiel (Mon–Fri 10:00–20:00, Sat 10:00–16:00, closed Sun).

At either TI, pick up brochures and a city map (€0.30, often free in hotel lobbies) and confirm your sightseeing plans. Consider the *Monats-programm* (€1.55, German-language list of sights and events calendar) and the free, twice-monthly magazine *In München* (in German, lists all movies and entertainment in town). The TI can book you a room (you'll pay a down payment of about 15 percent, then pay the rest at the hotel), but you'll get a better value with my recommended hotels—contact them directly. If you're interested in a Panorama/Gray Line tour of the city or to nearby castles (described on page 46), don't buy your ticket at the TI; instead, buy discounted tickets for these same tours at EurAide (see below).

The **München Welcome Card,** sold by the TI and EurAide, covers transportation plus small discounts on minor sights (€6.50/1 day, €16/3 days). For most visitors, the transportation-only tickets are a better deal (see "Getting Around Munich," page 44).

If the line at the TI is bad, go to EurAide.

EurAide: The industrious, eager-to-help EurAide office in the main train station is a godsend for Eurailers and budget travelers (June–Sept daily 7:45–12:45 & 14:00–18:00; Oct–May Mon–Fri 8:00–12:00 & 13:00–16:00, closed Sat–Sun; room 3 at track 11, tel. 089/593-889, fax 089/550-3965, www.euraide.com, see www.euraide.com/ricksteves for Rhine cruise schedules, euraide@compuserve.com). EurAide sells a €0.50 city map and offers a free, information-packed newsletter, *The Inside Track* (described on page 44; it's always available in a rack at their door). They also book rooms for a €3 fee.

EurAide helps 600 visitors per day in the summer; do your homework, have a list of questions ready, and keep in mind that they're busiest in the morning. Alan Wissenberg and his EurAide staff know your train-travel and accommodations questions and have answers in clear American English. (Chances are that your questions are already answered by their *Inside Track* newsletter— scan it first.) The German rail company pays them to help you design your train travels, and they make reservations and sell tickets, *couchettes,* and sleepers for the train at the same price as at the station ticket windows. EurAide also sells a Prague Excursion train pass, convenient for Prague-bound Eurailers—good for train travel from any Czech border station to Prague and back to any border station within seven days (1st class-€50, 2nd class-€40, youth 2nd class-€35; also sold through their U.S. office: tel. 941/480-1555, fax 941/480-1522).

EurAide also sells tickets for Panorama/Gray Line city tours (see page 46), as well as for tours to Neuschwanstein and Linderhof castles (see page 48). If you show EurAide this book in 2006, you'll get a 15 percent discount on these tickets.

Arrival in Munich

By Train: Munich's main train station (Hauptbahnhof) is a sight in itself—one of those places that can turn an accountant into a fun-loving vagabond. For a quick rest stop, the Burger King's toilets (upstairs, free) are as pleasant and accessible as its hamburgers. More toilets are downstairs near track 26 (clean, but €1.10). Check out the bright and modern complex of **restaurants** and shops opposite track 14. For a quick train picnic, I shop at **Yorma's,** by track 26. The **k presse + buch** shop (across from track 23) is great for English-language books, newspapers, and magazines, including *Munich Found* (informative English-speaking residents' monthly, €3). You'll also find two **tourist information** offices (the city TI and EurAide—see "Tourist Information" above) and **lockers** (€2, tracks 18, 26, and 31). **Car-rental agencies** are up the steps opposite track 21 (Mon–Fri 7:00–21:00, Sat–Sun 8:00–17:00). A **pharmacy** is out the front door to the right, next to the TI (Mon–Fri 8:00–18:30, Sat 8:00–14:00, closed Sun, tel. 089/594-119). A quiet, non-smoking **waiting room** *(Warteraum)* is open to anybody (across from track 23 and up the escalator), but the nearby, plush **DB Lounge** is only for those with a first-class ticket (railpasses don't get you in).

Subway lines, trams, and buses connect the station to the rest of the city (though many of my recommended hotels are within walking distance of the station). If you get lost in the underground maze of subway corridors while you're simply trying to get to the station, follow the signs for *DB* (DeutscheBahn) to surface successfully.

By Plane: There are two good ways—by subway or airport bus—to connect the airport and downtown Munich. You can take an easy 40-minute ride on the S-1 or S-8 **subway,** which runs every 20 minutes between the airport and Marienplatz (€9 or free with a validated and dated railpass). Or hop on the Lufthansa **airport bus,** which links the airport with the main train station (€10, 3/hr, 45 min, buy tickets on bus; at the station, buses line up near taxi stands facing Arnulfstrasse—to get there from the station, exit near track 26). Airport info: tel. 089/97500, www.munich-airport.de.

Helpful Hints

Museum Hours: A few sights—including the Alte Pinakothek, Munich City Museum, and Dachau Concentration Camp— are closed on Monday. The art galleries are generally open late one night a week.

Useful Phone Numbers: Pharmacy (at train station next to TI)—tel. 089/594-119; EurAide train info—tel. 089/593-889; American Express travel agency—tel. 089/2909-0145 (no train tickets, Mon–Fri 9:00–18:00, Sat 9:30–12:30, closed Sun, Promenade Platz 6); Taxi—tel. 089/21610.

Internet Access: There's plenty of online access in Munich; easy-Internetcafé dominates the scene, with great rates and an ideal location near the train station (daily 24 hrs, 500 terminals and a convenient phone center with cheap international rates, opposite station's main entrance at Bahnhofplatz 1). Down by Isartor, Munich Walk has 100 terminals and good prices (daily 24 hrs, Im Tal 31, tel. 089/2070-2737, www.munichwalktours .de).

Laundry: A handy self-service *Waschcenter* is a 10-minute walk from the train station (€6.50/15 lbs, €11/25 lbs, drop-off service for €8–16 depending on load size, daily 7:00–23:00, English instructions, Paul-Heyse-Strasse 21, near intersection with Landwehrstrasse, tel. 089/531-311).

Bikes and Pedestrians: Signs painted on the sidewalk or blue-and-white street signs show which side of the sidewalk is designated for pedestrians and which is for cyclists. The strip of pathway closest to the street is usually reserved for bikes.

Pedestrians wandering into the bike path may hear the cheery ding-ding of a cyclist's bell just before being knocked unconscious by a local biker.

Private Driver: Johann Fayoumi is reliable and speaks English (€50/hr, mobile 0174-183-8473, johannfayoumi@compuserve.de).

Car Rental: Allround Car Rental has reasonable rates (around €40/24 hrs including insurance, Boschetsrieder Strasse 12, U-3: Obersendling, tel. 089/723-8383, www.allroundrent.de). Several car-rental agencies are located upstairs at the train station, opposite track 21 (Mon–Fri 7:00–21:00, Sat–Sun 9:00–17:00).

The Inside Track **Train Travelers' Newsletter:** Anyone traveling by train should pick up the wonk-ish yet brilliant quarterly newsletter published by Alan at EurAide (free, readily available in a rack by the EurAide door—see EurAide listing under "Tourist Information," above). You'll find all the tedious but important details on getting to Neuschwanstein, Dachau, Nymphenburg, and Prague; the ins and outs of supplements and reservations necessary for railpass-holders; a daily schedule of various tours in Munich; and (of course) plenty of tips on how to take advantage of EurAide's services.

What's With Monaco? People walking around with guidebooks to Monaco aren't lost. "Monaco" means "Munich" in *Italiano*.

Getting Around Munich

Much of Munich is walkable. To reach sights away from the city center, use the fine tram, bus, and subway systems. Taxis are honest and professional, but expensive and generally unnecessary (except perhaps to avoid the time-consuming trip by tram and foot to Nymphenburg Palace).

By Public Transit: Subways are called U-Bahns or S-Bahns (actually an underground-while-in-the-city commuter railway). Subway lines are numbered (for example, S-3 or U-5). Eurailpasses are good on the S-Bahn, but if you use a flexipass, it'll cost you a travel day.

The entire system (bus/tram/subway) works on the same tickets, sold at TIs and in the subway at booths and easy-to-use ticket machines (which take coins and €5 and €10 bills). There's a wide array of ticket types. A **regular ticket** costs €2.20 and is good for two hours of changes in one direction. For the shortest rides (1 or 2 stops), buy the €1.10 *Kurzstrecke* ("short stretch") ticket. The €4.50 **all-day pass** is a great deal for a single traveler. But for more than one person, the €8 "**partner**" all-day pass is an even better deal—it covers all public transportation for up to five adults and a dog (2 kids count as 1 adult, so 2 adults, 6 kids, and a dog can travel with

Central Munich

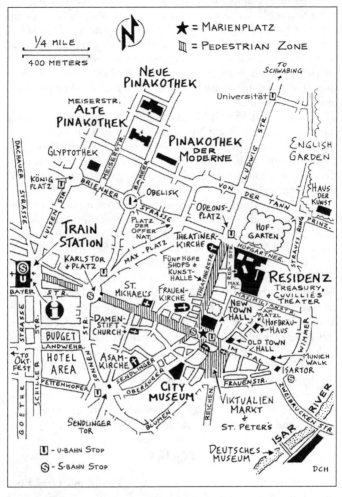

this ticket). The **XXL ticket** includes the extended transportation network, which covers the trip to Dachau Concentration Camp (€6/1 person, €10.50/partner ticket). For longer stays, consider a **three-day ticket** (€11/1 person, €18.50/partner ticket for the gang). All-day and multi-day passes are valid until 6:00 the following morning.

Partner tickets—while seemingly impossibly cheap—are for real. Read it again and do the arithmetic. Even two people traveling together save money. And for groups, it's a real steal. The only catch is you've got to stay together.

You must stamp your ticket with the date and time prior to using it (for all-day or multi-day passes, you only have to stamp it the first time you use it). For the subway, punch your ticket in the blue machine *before* going down to the platform. For buses and trams, stamp your ticket once on board. Plainclothes ticket-checkers enforce this honor system, rewarding freeloaders with stiff €40 fines. For more information, call tel. 089/4142-4344 or see www.mvv-muenchen.de.

Important: All S-Bahn lines connect the Hauptbahnhof (main station) with Marienplatz (main square). If you want to use the S-Bahn and you're either at the station or Marienplatz, follow signs to the S-Bahn (U is not for you), and concern yourself only with the direction (Hauptbahnhof/Pasing or Marienplatz). "Direction" in German is *Richtung*.

By Bike: Munich, level and compact with plenty of bike paths, feels good on two wheels. You can rent bikes quickly and easily at the train station from **Radius Tours** (May–mid-Oct daily 10:00–18:00, closed mid-Oct–April, city bikes–€3/hr, €14/day, €17/24 hrs, €25/48 hrs, mountain bikes 25 percent more; in front of track 32, tel. 089/596-113, www.radiusmunich.com). Closer to the river and Isartor, **Munich Walk** also rents bikes (open daily 24 hours, €3/hr, €15/24 hrs, Im Tal 31, tel. 089/2070-2736, www.munichwalktours.de). Both outfits have maps and good advice, and both offer bike tours (mentioned below). Also see "Bikes and Pedestrians" warning above.

For a longer trip, consider this great day on a bike: English Garden to Olympic Park, then along the canal to Nymphenburg Palace, around the palace grounds, and back to the center (in 30 min) via Arnulfstrasse, which has a bike path the entire way. Or consider the Isar River bike ride described on page 73.

TOURS

Munich has three major tour companies. **Panorama/Gray Line** specializes in bus tours of the city and to the Bavarian castles of "Mad" King Ludwig (Neuschwanstein and Linderhof; their office is next to the train station, near track 26, Arnulfstrasse 8, 3 doors left of Eden-Hotel Wolff, tel. 089/5490-7560, www.autobusoberbayern.de; you'll get a 15 percent discount on Panorama/Gray Line tours if you buy tickets at EurAide—see "Tourist Information," above). The two other major companies compete directly with each other, offering walking tours, bike tours, and day trips to Dachau Concentration Camp and Neuschwanstein Castle; in my experience, they're comparable: **Radius Tours** (office in the main train station, in front of track 32, tel. 089/5502-9374, www.radiusmunich.com, info@radiusmunich.com) and the newer **Munich Walk** (near

Isartor at Im Tal 31, tel. 089/2070-2736, www.munichwalktours
.de). Munich Walk offers €1 off any of their services to readers of
this book in 2006.

Of Munich

Walking Tours—Radius Tours runs two city walking tours
daily April through October (fewer tours off-season): "Munich
Highlights" (at 10:00) and "Hitler and the Third Reich" (at 15:00).
Their guides are reliably good. Each tour costs €10, lasts 2.5 hours,
and departs from the Radius office (in front of track 32 at the train
station). There's no need to register—just show up.

Munich Walk offers similar walks: a "City Walk" (€10, May–
mid-Oct daily at 10:45 and 14:45) and "Hitler's Munich" tour (€10,
April–Oct daily at 10:00, fewer tours off-season). Their "Beer &
Brewery" tour is more mature than your typical hard-partying pub
crawl. You visit Munich's oldest brewery to learn, eat, and drink in
the city that made beer famous (€17, May–mid Sept daily at 18:15,
fewer tours off-season). All Munich Walk tours depart from under
the glockenspiel on Marienplatz; no reservations are necessary.

"New Munich" advertises free walking tours. This youthful
outfit (which started with the same guerilla business plan in Berlin)
has an irreverent, boisterous approach to walking tours—it's basically an hour of entertainment sprinkled with some historical
"facts." The first basic tour is free (although you'll be hit up for tips,
as that's how their guides are paid). They sell the other standard
Munich tours. Their nightly pub crawl offers a fun way to make
drunken friends from around the world. For details, see their free
magazine (all over town) or www.newmunich.com.

Local Guides—I've had great days with three good local guides,
each charging the same prices (€100/2 hrs, €120/3 hrs): Georg
Reichlmayr (tel. 08131/86800, mobile 0170-341-6384, www
.muenchen-stadtfuehrung.de, info@muenchen-stadtfuehrung
.de), Monika Hank (tel. 089/311-4819, monika.hank@web.de),
and Renate Suerbaum (tel. 089/283-374, renate@suerbaum.de).
They helped me with much of the historical information in this
chapter, and Georg was my sidekick on the Munich episode of my
public television series.

Bike Tours—Mike's Bike Tours, popular with the college crowd,
are four-hour frat parties on wheels. The tours are slow-paced and
the guides are better comedians than historians, but you do ride
through the English Garden (€24, tips encouraged, bikes provided,
1-hr break in Chinese Tower beer garden, at least 1 tour daily
March–Oct—at 11:30, can be up to 3 tours daily in summer, no need
to reserve, meet under tower of Old Town Hall on Marienplatz;
for schedule, call tel. 089/651-4275 or mobile 0172-852-0660, visit
www.mikesbiketours.com, or pick up brochure at TI). **Radius**

Tours, described above, offers similar bike tours. **Munich Walk** is unique in offering private guided bike tours to small groups at any time (€22 per person for groups of at least 4). Team up with a small gang, then call 089/2070-2736 and set a date.

Quickie Orientation City Bus Tour—Panorama/Gray Line Tours offers many itineraries, including one-hour orientation bus tours (departs from Hertie department store, Elisenstrasse 3, directly in front of train station). This tour is actually well worthwhile—sitting upstairs on the topless double-decker bus, you'll see lots of things the typical visitor wandering around the center never sees. It complements the information in this book beautifully. The live guide narrates in German and English. Just show up and pay the driver, or save a euro by picking up your ticket in advance at EurAide (€11, daily in season on the half-hour 10:00–17:00; Panorama/Gray Line office is near track 26 across the street at Arnulfstrasse 8, tel. 089/5502-8995, www.autobusoberbayern.de). Note that hop-on, hop-off bus tours are not allowed in Munich.

From Munich

"Mad" King Ludwig's Castles—Two spectacular Bavarian castles, Neuschwanstein and Linderhof, make a logical day trip from Munich. For more on these destinations, see the Bavaria and Tirol chapter.

    Panorama/Gray Line Tours offers rushed all-day bus tours of the two castles that also include 30 minutes in Oberammergau (€43, 15 percent discount with this book in 2006 if you buy your ticket at EurAide in the train station, castle admissions-€15 extra, daily April–Oct, Nov–March most days but not Mon). In summer, it's wise to purchase tickets a day ahead. Tours meet at 8:10 and depart at 8:30 from the Hertie department store (across from the station). While **Munich Walk** advertises a similar tour, they're simply selling tickets for the Panorama/Gray Line trip.

    Radius Tours runs all-day tours to Neuschwanstein Castle by train (€32, €25 with railpass, castle admission-€9 extra, departs May–Oct daily at 9:30 from in front of track 32 at train station, you're home by 19:00, book ahead; off-season tours run Mon, Wed, and Sat at 10:30; tel. 089/5502-9374, www.radiusmunich .com, info@radiusmunich.com). This "tour" is basically an escort on public transportation (not really necessary, but it allows you to avoid the ticket line at the castle).

Dachau Concentration Camp—**Radius Tours** offers English-language-only tours of the camp year-round (€19 includes the €6 cost of public transportation, €2 discount with this book in 2006, April–Oct Tue–Sun at 9:15 and 12:30, Nov–March Tue–Sun at 12:00, no Mon tours, depart from Radius office in Munich station—in front of track 32, it's smart to confirm times, but you can just show up, allow 5 hrs round-trip). **Munich Walk** does a similar tour (€19 includes €6 transport costs, Tue-Sun at 10:20 and 13:15, no tours Mon). While several other companies do Dachau tours, only Radius and Munich Walk are allowed to actually guide inside the camp.

SIGHTS AND ACTIVITIES

Central Munich

▲▲**City Views**—Downtown Munich's three best city viewpoints (all described below) are from the tops of: St. Peter's Church (stairs only), Frauenkirche (stairs plus elevator), and New Town Hall (elevator).

▲▲**Marienplatz and the Pedestrian Zone**—Riding the escalator out of the subway into sunlit Marienplatz (literally, "Mary's

Square") gives you a fine first look at the glory of Munich: great buildings bombed flat and rebuilt, outdoor cafés, and people bustling and lingering like the birds and breeze with which they share this square. Notice the ornate facades of the gray, pointy Old Town Hall and the neo-Gothic New Town Hall, with its beloved glockenspiel.

The **New Town Hall** (Neues Rathaus), built from 1867 until 1906, dominates the square. Munich was a very royal city. Notice the politics of the statuary. The 40 statues—though sculpted only in 1900— decorate New Town Hall not with civic leaders, but with royals and blue-blooded nobility. Because this building survived the bombs and had a central location, it served as the U.S. military headquarters in 1945.

The New Town Hall is famous for its **glockenspiel**—only 100 years old— which "jousts" daily at 11:00 and 12:00 all year (also at 17:00 May–Oct). The *Spiel* recreates a royal wedding from the 16th century: The duke and his bride watch the action as the Bavarians (in white and blue) forever beat their enemies. Below, the coopers—famous for being the first to dance in the streets after a deadly plague lifted—do their popular jig.

The New Town Hall tower offers **views** of the city (€2, elevator from

Munich at a Glance

In the Center

▲▲▲Deutsches Museum Germany's version of our Smithsonian Institution, with 10 miles of exhibits on science and technology. **Hours:** Daily 9:00–17:00.

▲▲Marienplatz Munich's main square, at the heart of a lively pedestrian zone, watched over by New Town Hall (and its glockenspiel show). **Hours:** Always open; glockenspiel jousts daily at 11:00 and 12:00, plus 17:00 May–Oct.

▲▲Hofbräuhaus World-famous beer hall, worth a visit even if you're not chugging. **Hours:** Daily 9:00–24:00.

▲▲Alte Pinakothek Bavaria's best painting gallery, with a wonderful collection of European masters from the 14th–19th centuries. **Hours:** Tue–Sun 10:00–17:00, Tue until 20:00, closed Mon.

▲▲Residenz Museum The elegant family palace of the Wittelsbachs, awash with Bavarian opulence. **Hours:** Daily April–mid-Oct 9:00–18:00, mid-Oct–March 10:00–16:00.

▲▲Residenz Treasury Shows off a thousand years of Wittelsbach family crowns and royal knickknacks. **Hours:** Daily April–mid-Oct 9:00–18:00, mid-Oct–March 10:00–16:00.

▲Munich City Museum The history of the city in five floors. **Hours:** Tue–Sun 10:00–18:00, closed Mon.

▲Neue Pinakothek The Alte's hip twin sister, with paintings from 1800–1920. **Hours:** Wed 10:00–20:00, Thu–Mon 10:00–17:00, closed Tue.

▲Pinakothek der Moderne Modern art museum near the Alte and Neue Pinakotheks—with a building as interesting as the art. **Hours:** Tue–Sun 10:00–17:00, Thu–Fri until 20:00, closed Mon.

▲English Garden The largest city park on the Continent, packed with locals, tourists, surfers, and nude sunbathers. **Hours:** Always open.

St. Michael's Church Renaissance church housing Baroque decor and a crypt of 40 Wittelsbachs. **Hours:** Church—daily 9:00–19:00; crypt—Mon–Fri 9:30–16:30, Sat 9:30–14:30, closed Sun, less off-season.

Frauenkirche Huge, distinctive twin-domed church looming over the city center. **Hours:** Open long hours daily.

St. Peter's Church Munich's oldest church, packed with important relics. **Hours:** Open long hours daily.

Viktualien Markt Munich's "small-town" open-air market, perfect for a quick snack or meal. **Hours:** Mon–Sat, food stalls open until late, closed Sun.

Haus der Kunst Once Hitler's former temple of Nazi art, now hosting various modern-art exhibitions. **Hours:** Daily 10:00–20:00, Thu until 22:00.

Bavarian National Museum Collection of artifacts celebrating the culture of Germany's biggest state. **Hours:** Tue–Sun 10:00–17:00, Thu until 20:00, closed Mon.

Away from the Center
▲▲Nymphenburg Palace The Wittelsbachs' impressive summer palace, three miles from downtown, featuring a hunting lodge, coach museum, fine royal porcelain collection, and vast park. **Hours:** Daily April–mid-Oct 9:00–18:00, mid-Oct–March 10:00–16:00.

▲▲Dachau Concentration Camp Notorious Nazi camp on the outskirts of Munich, now a powerful museum. **Hours:** Tue–Sun 9:00–17:00, closed Mon.

▲Andechs Monastery Baroque church, hearty food, and Bavaria's best brew, in the countryside near Munich. **Hours:** Beer garden open daily 10:00–23:00, last meal order 20:00, church open until 18:00.

▲Olympic Park The stadium and sports complex from Munich's 1972 Olympic stadium, now a lush park with a view tower and swimming pool. **Hours:** Grounds always open; tower daily 9:00–24:00, pool daily 7:00–23:00.

BMW Museum The BMW headquarters, temporarily closed to the public except for a small exhibit and factory tours. **Hours:** Museum daily 10:00–20:00, tours by appointment only—call several weeks in advance.

under glockenspiel, Mon–Fri 9:00–19:00, Sat–Sun 10:00–19:00).

Marienplatz is marked by a statue of the **Virgin Mary,** moved here in 1638 from its original location in the Frauenkirche out of thanks that the Swedes didn't sack the town during their occupation. It was also a rallying point for the struggle against the Protestants. The cherubs are fighting against the four great biblical enemies of civilization: war, hunger, disease, and the wrong faith. The serpent represents the "wrong faith," a.k.a. Martin Luther.

The **Old Town Hall** (Altes Rathaus; at the right side of square as you face New Town Hall) was completely destroyed by WWII bombs and later rebuilt. Ludwig IV, an early Wittelsbach who was Holy Roman Emperor (back in the 14th century), stands in the center of the facade. He donated this great square to the people. On the bell tower, find the city seal with its monk and towers. Munich flourished because, in its early days, all salt trade had to stop here on Marienplatz.

Back at Marienplatz, the **pedestrian mall** (Kaufingerstrasse and Neuhauserstrasse) leads you through a great shopping area, past carnivals of street entertainers and good old-fashioned slicers and dicers, the towering twin-domed Frauenkirche (built in 1470, rebuilt after WWII), and several fountains, to Karlstor and the train station. As one of Europe's first pedestrian zones, the mall enraged shopkeepers when it was built in 1972 for the Olympics. Today, it is "Munich's living room." Nearly 9,000 shoppers pass through it each hour. The shopkeepers are happy...and merchants nearby are begging for their streets to become traffic-free. Imagine this street in hometown U.S.A.

Three Churches near Marienplatz—In the pedestrian zone around Marienplatz are three noteworthy churches: St. Michael's, the Frauenkirche, and St. Peter's. Each was heavily bombed in World War II, and each displays photos of that destruction near its entrance. To locate these churches: As you face New Town Hall, St. Michael's is a few blocks down the pedestrian street to your left; the Frauenkirche is the big twin-domed church at 10 o'clock; and St. Peter's is over your right shoulder.

St. Michael's Church, while one of the first great Renaissance buildings north of the Alps, has a brilliantly Baroque interior. The crypt contains 40 stark royal tombs, including the resting place of King Ludwig II, the "mad" king still loved by Romantics (church entry free, daily 9:00–19:00; crypt-€2, Mon–Fri 9:30–16:30, Sat 9:30–14:30, closed Sun, less off-season; frequent concerts—check the schedule outside).

The twin onion domes of the 500-year-old **Frauenkirche** (Church of Our Lady) are the symbol of the city. While much of the church was destroyed in World War II, the towers survived and the rest has been gloriously restored. It was built in Gothic style, but money problems meant the domes weren't added until Renaissance times. Late Gothic buildings in Munich were generally built of brick—easy to make locally and cheaper and faster to use than stone. This church was constructed in a remarkable 20 years. It's located on

the grave of Ludwig IV (who died in 1348). His big, black, ornate tomb (now in the back) was originally in front at the high altar. Standing in the back of the nave, notice how your eyes go right to the altar... Christ...and (until recently) Ludwig. Those Wittelsbachs—always trying to be associated with God. In fact, this alliance was instilled in people through the prayers they were forced to recite: "Virgin Mary, mother of our duke, please protect us."

You can ascend the tower for the city's highest public viewpoint, at 280 feet (€3, 86 steps to elevator, April–Oct Mon–Sat 10:00–17:00, closed Sun and Nov–March).

St. Peter's Church, the oldest in town, overlooks Marienplatz. It's built on the hill where Munich's original monastic inhabitants probably settled. Outside, notice the old tombstones plastered onto the wall—a reminder that in the Napoleonic age, the cemeteries surrounding most city churches were (for hygienic and practical space reasons) dug up and moved. Inside, check out the photos of the bomb damage (near the entrance). Then look at the marvelously restored altar and ceiling frescoes—possible with the help of Nazi catalog photos (see "Munich Bombed," above).

Munich has more relics than any city outside of Rome. For more than a hundred years, it was the pope's bastion against the rising tide of Protestantism in northern Europe during the Reformation. Favors done in the defense of Catholicism earned the Wittelsbachs neat relic treats. For instance, check out the tomb of Mundita (2nd side chapel on left as you enter). She's a second-century martyr whose remains were given to Munich by Rome as thanks and a vivid reminder that those who die for the cause of the Roman Church go directly to heaven without waiting for Judgment Day.

It's a long climb to the top of the spire (306 steps, no elevator)—much of it with two-way traffic on a one-lane staircase—but the

Munich Bombed

As World War II drew to a close, it was clear that Munich would be destroyed. Hitler did not allow the evacuation of much of the town's portable art treasures and heritage. A mass emptying of churches and civil buildings would have caused hysteria and been a statement of no confidence in his leadership. While museums were closed (and could be systematically emptied over the war years), public buildings were not. Rather than save the treasures, the Nazis photographed everything. What the bombs didn't get was destroyed by 10 years of rain and freezing winters. The first priority after the war was to get roofs over the ruined buildings. Only now, nearly 60 years after the last bombs fell, are the restorations—based on those Nazi photographs—finally being wrapped up.

Shortly after World War II, German cities established commissions to debate how they'd rebuild their cities: restoring the old towns or bulldozing and going modern. While Frankfurt voted to bulldoze (hence its Manhattan-like feel today), Munich voted—by a close margin—to rebuild its old town. Buildings cannot exceed the height of the church spires. Today, Munich has no real shopping malls. Instead, its downtown is vital, filled with people who come to shop.

view is dynamite (€1.50, Mon–Sat 9:00–19:00, Sun 10:00–19:00, off-season until 18:00, last entry 30 min before closing). Try to be two flights from the top when the bells ring at the top of the hour, and then, when your friends back home ask you about your trip, you'll say, "What?"

Viktualien Markt—Early in the morning, you can still feel small-town Munich here, long a favorite with locals for fresh produce and good service (closed Sun). The most expensive real estate in town could never really support such a market, but the town charges only a percentage of the gross income, enabling these old-time shops to carry on (and keeping fast-food chains out).

The huge maypole is a tradition. Fifteenth-century town market squares posted a maypole decorated with various symbols to explain which crafts and merchants were doing business in the market. Munich's maypole shows the city's six great brews and the crafts and festivities associated with brewing. (You can't have a kegger without coopers—find the merry barrel-makers.)

Munich's breweries each take turns here—notice the beer counter. A sign *(Heute im Ausschank),* which changes every day or two, announces which of the six Munich beers is being served. Here, unlike at other beer gardens, you can order half a liter (for shoppers who want to have a quick sip and then keep on going).

The Viktualien Markt is ideal for a light meal (see page 86). Or, for a more expensive selection, try the...

Alois Dallmayr Delicatessen—When the king called out for dinner, he called Alois Dallmayr. As you enter, read the black plaque with the royal seal by the door: *Königlich Bayerischer Hof-Lieferant* ("Deliverer for the King of Bavaria and his Court"). This place became famous for its exotic and luxurious food items: tropical fruits, seafood, chocolates, fine wines, and coffee. Catering to royal and aristocratic tastes (and budgets), it's still the choice of Munich's old rich. Today, it's most famous for its coffee, dispensed from fine hand-painted Nymphenburg porcelain jugs (Mon–Fri 9:30–19:00, Sat 9:00–18:00, closed Sun, Dienerstrasse 14, behind New Town Hall).

▲▲Hofbräuhaus—Whether or not you slide your lederhosen on its polished benches, it's a great experience just to see the world's most famous beer hall in all its rowdy glory (daily 9:00–24:00, live oompah music during lunch and dinner, Platzl 6, 5-min walk northeast of Marienplatz). As you wander, look for the following: Various *Stammtisch* signs (meaning "reserved") hang above tables where different clubs meet regularly; don't sit here unless you're specifically invited. Racks of locked steins, made of pottery and metal, are for regulars. You'll see locals stuffed into lederhosen and dirndls; giant gingerbread cookies that sport romantic messages; and postcards of the new German (and apparently beer-drinking) pope. The men's room has two dozen urinals around a vomitorium. The bouncer at the door nabs 20 to 50 people (mostly Italians, he says) trying to steal mugs as souvenirs. The staircase to the left of the entrance displays historic old Hofbräuhaus photos and prints. For more details, see page 85.

▲Munich City Museum (Münchner Stadtmuseum)—Five floors of exhibits tell the story of Munich. The ground floor traces the development of National Socialism. The first floor focuses on life in Munich through the centuries (including WWII), illustrated with paintings, photos, and models. The second floor hosts more city history and "monk culture" exhibits. The third floor features historic carnivals and puppets, and the fourth floor displays musical instruments from around the world (€4, free on Sun, Tue–Sun 10:00–18:00, closed Mon, few English descriptions, no crowds, bored and playful guards, 3 blocks off Marienplatz at St.-Jakobs-Platz 1, tel. 089/2332-2370, www.stadtmuseum-online.de). The museum's Stadt Café is handy for a good meal (see page 89).

Across the street from the entrance, Munich's new **Jewish Museum** is being built (due to be completed in 2007, www .juedisches-museum-muenchen.de). This, along with a new school and community center, is part of a revitalization of Munich's Jewish quarter.

Rococo Churches—Near the Munich City Museum, the private church of the Asam brothers **(Asamkirche)** is a gooey, drippy, Baroque-concentrate masterpiece by Bavaria's top two rococonuts. A few blocks away, the small **Damenstift Church** has a sculptural rendition of the Last Supper so real that you feel you're not alone (at intersection of Altheimer Ecke and Damenstiftstrasse, a block south of the pedestrian street).

Munich's Cluster of Art Museums (Pinakotheks)

This cluster of blockbuster museums (Alte, Neue, and Moderne Pinakotheks) displays art spanning from the 14th century to modern times. The three museums sit around a grassy square just northeast of Königsplatz. They're a 10-minute walk from the nearest U-Bahn stops, but handy tram #27 whisks you right there from Karlsplatz (near the train station). For more information on any of these, see www.pinakothek.de.

▲▲**Alte Pinakothek**—Bavaria's best painting gallery (literally, the "Old Art Gallery," pronounced "ALL-tuh pee-nah-koh-TAYK") shows off a world-class collection of European masterpieces from the 14th to 19th centuries, starring the two tumultuous centuries (1450-1650) when Europe went from medieval to modern. See paintings from the Italian Renaissance (Raphael, Leonardo, Botticelli, Titian) and the German Renaissance it inspired (Albrecht Dürer). The Reformation of Martin Luther eventually split Europe into two subcultures—Protestants and Catholics— with their two distinct art styles (exemplified by Rembrandt and Rubens, respectively).

Cost, Hours, Location: €5, Tue–Sun 10:00–17:00, Tue until 20:00, closed Mon, last entry 30 min before closing, free and excellent audioguide, €1.50 English booklet, obligatory lockers, no flash photos, U-2 or U-8: Königsplatz, Barer Strasse 27, tel. 089/2380-5216.

☉ Self-Guided Tour: All the paintings we'll see are on the upper floor, which is laid out like a barbell. Start at one fat end and work your way through the "handle" to the other end. Along the way you'll find the following paintings, roughly in this order.

German Renaissance—Room II: Albrecht Dürer's larger-than-life *Four Apostles* (*Johannes und Petrus* and *Paulus und Marcus*) are saints of a radical new religion—Martin Luther's Protestantism. Just as Luther challenged Church authority, Dürer—a friend of Luther's—strips these saints of any rich clothes, halos, or trappings

Alte Pinakothek

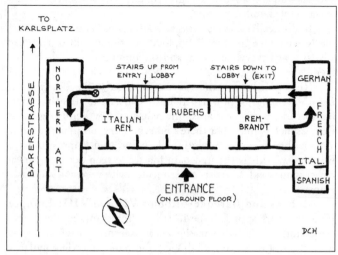

of power and gives them down-to-earth human features: receding hairlines, wrinkles, and suspicious eyes. The inscription warns German rulers to follow the Bible rather than Catholic Church leaders. The figure of Mark—a Bible in one hand and a sword in the other—is a fitting symbol of the dangerous times.

Dürer's *Self-Portrait in Fur Coat (Selbstbildnis im Pelzrock)* looks like Jesus Christ but is actually 28-year-old Dürer himself, gazing out, with his right hand solemnly giving a blessing. This is the ultimate image of humanism: the artist as an instrument of God's continued creation. Get close and enjoy the intricately braided hair, the skin texture, and the fur collar. To the left of the head is Dürer's famous monogram—"A.D." in the form of a pyramid.

Italian Renaissance—Room IV: With the Italian Renaissance—the "rebirth" of interest in the art and learning of ancient Greece and Rome—artists captured the realism, three-dimensionality, and symmetry found in classical statues. Leonardo da Vinci's *Virgin and Child (Maria mit dem Kind)* need no halos—they radiate purity. Mary is a solid pyramid of maternal love, flanked by Renaissance-arch windows that look out on the hazy distance. Baby Jesus reaches out to play innocently with a carnation, the blood-colored symbol of his eventual death.

Raphael's *Holy Family at the Canigiani House (Die hl. Familie aus dem Hause Canigiani)* takes Leonardo's pyramid form and runs with it. Father Joseph forms the peak, with his staff as the strong central axis. Mary and Jesus (on the right) form a pyramid-within-the-pyramid, as do Elizabeth and baby John the Baptist on the left. They all exchange meaningful contact, safe within the bounds of the stable family structure.

In Botticelli's *Lamentation over Christ (Die Beweinung Christi)*, the Renaissance "pyramid" implodes, as the weight of the dead Christ drags everyone down, and the tomb grins darkly behind them.

Room V: In Titian's *Christ Crowned with Thorns (Die Dornenkronung)*, a powerfully built Christ sits silently enduring torture by prison guards. The painting is by Venice's greatest Renaissance painter, but there's no symmetry, no pyramid form, and the brushwork is intentionally messy and Impressionistic. By the way, this is the first painting we've seen done on canvas rather than wood, as artists experimented with vegetable-oil-based paints.

Rubens and Baroque—Rooms VII and VIII: Europe's religious wars split Europe in two—Protestants in the northern countries, Catholics in the south. (Germany itself was split, with Bavaria remaining Catholic.) The Baroque style popular in Catholic countries features large canvases, bright colors, lots of flesh, rippling motion, wild emotions, grand themes...and pudgy winged babies, the sure sign of Baroque.

Rubens and Isabella Brant shows the Baroque painter Peter Paul Rubens of Flanders with his first wife, both of them the very picture of health, wealth and success. They lean together unconsciously, as people in love will do, with their hands clasped in mutual affection. When his first wife died, 53-year-old Rubens found a replacement—16-year-old *Hélène Fourment*, shown in her wedding dress. You may recognize Hélène's face in other Rubens paintings.

The Rape of the Daughters of Leucippus (Der Raub der Tochter des Leukippos) has many of Rubens' most typical elements—fleshy, emotional, rippling motion, bright colors, and a classical subject. The legendary twins Castor and Pollux crash a wedding and steal the brides as their own. The chaos of flailing limbs and rearing horses is all held together in a subtle X-shaped composition. Like the weaving counterpoint in a Baroque fugue, Rubens balances opposites.

In Rubens' 300-square-foot *Great Last Judgment (Das Grosse Jüngste Gericht)*, Christ raises the righteous up to heaven (left side) and damns the sinners to hell (on the right). This swirling cycle of nudes was considered risqué and kept under wraps by the very monks who'd commissioned it.

Notice that Rubens' canvases were—to a great extent—cranked out by his students and assistants from small "cartoons" the master himself made (displayed in the next room).

Room IX: Rembrandt van Rijn of Holland's *Six Paintings from the Life of Christ* are a down-to-earth look at supernatural events. The *Adoration* of baby Jesus takes place in a 17th-century Dutch barn with ordinary folk as models. The canvases are dark brown, lit by strong light. The *Adoration*'s light source is the baby Jesus himself—literally the "light of the world." In the *Deposition (Kreuzabnahme),* the light bounces off Christ's pale body onto his mother Mary, showing how his death also hurts her. The drama is underplayed, with subdued emotions. Looking on is a man dressed in blue—a self-portrait of Rembrandt.

Room XI: Albrecht Altdorfer's *The Battle of Issus (Schlacht bei Issus)* shows a world at war. The masses of soldiers are swept along in the currents and tides of a battle completely beyond their control, their confused motion reflected in the swirling sky. We see the battle from a great height, giving us a Godlike perspective. Though the painting depicts Alexander the Great's victory over the Persians (find the Persian king Darius turning and fleeing), it could as easily have been Germany in the 1520s. Christians were fighting Muslims, peasants battled masters, and Catholics and Protestants were squaring off for a century of conflict. The armies melt into a huge landscape, leaving the impression that the battle goes on forever.

▲**Neue Pinakothek**—The Alte Pinakothek's hip sister is a twin building across the square, showing off paintings from 1800 to 1920: Romanticism, realism, Impressionism, *Jugendstil,* Monet, Renoir, van Gogh, Goya, and Klimt (€5, Wed 10:00–20:00, Thu–Mon 10:00–17:00, closed Tue, €1.50 English booklet, classy Café Greco in basement spills into park and offers fine salads, U-2 or U-8: Theresienstrasse, Barer Strasse 29 but enter on Theresienstrasse, tel. 089/2380-5195).

▲**Pinakothek der Moderne**—This new museum picks up where the other two leave off, covering the 20th century. Four permanent displays (graphics, design, architecture, and paintings) are layered within the striking minimalist architecture. You'll find works by Picasso, Dalí, Miró, Magritte, Beckmann, Max Ernst, and abstract artists. The big, white, high-ceilinged building itself is worth a look. Even if you don't pay to visit the exhibits, step into the free entrance hall to see the sky-high atrium and the colorful blob-column descending the staircase (€9, free on Sun, Tue–Sun 10:00–17:00, Thu–Fri until 20:00, closed Mon, U-4 or U-5: Odeonsplatz, Barer Strasse 40, tel. 089/2380-5360). This far-out collection offers no audioguide and little information in English.

In and near the English Garden

▲**English Garden (Englischer Garten)**—Munich's "Central Park," the largest on the Continent, was laid out in 1789 by an American. Over 100,000 locals commune with nature here on a sunny summer day. The park stretches three miles from the center, past the university to the trendy and bohemian Schwabing quarter. For the best quick visit, follow the river from the surfers (under the bridge just past Haus der Kunst) downstream into the garden. Just beyond the hilltop temple (walk up for a postcard view of the city), you'll find the big Chinese-pagoda beer garden and other places to enjoy a drink or a meal (see page 87). A rewarding

respite from the city, the park is especially fun on a bike under the summer sun (bike rental at train station or near Isartor—see page 46; unfortunately, there are no bike-rental agencies in or near the park). Caution: While local law requires sun-worshippers to wear clothes on the tram, this park is sprinkled with buck-naked sun-bathers—quite a shock to prudish Americans (who end up riding their bikes into the river and trees).

Haus der Kunst—Built by Hitler as a temple of Nazi art, this bold and fascist building is now an impressive shell for various temporary art exhibits. Ironically, the art displayed in Hitler's "house of art" is the kind that annoyed the Führer most—modern (€7 per exhibit, combo-ticket for €10 if there are 2 exhibits, daily 10:00–20:00, Thu until 22:00, at south end of English Garden, tram #17 or bus #100 to Nationalmuseum/Haus der Kunst, Prinzregentenstrasse 1, tel. 089/211-270, www.hausderkunst.de).

Just beyond the Haus der Kunst, where Prinzregentenstrasse crosses the Eisbach canal, you can watch adventure-seekers actually surfing in the rapids created as the small river tumbles underground.

Bavarian National Museum (Bayerisches Nationalmuseum)—This tired but interesting collection features Riemenschneider carvings, manger scenes, traditional living rooms, and old Bavarian houses (€3, Tue–Sun 10:00–17:00, Thu until 20:00, closed Mon, tram #17 or bus #100 to Nationalmuseum/Haus der Kunst, Prinzregentenstrasse 3, tel. 089/211-2401, www.bayerisches-nationalmuseum.de).

The Deutsches Museum

Germany's answer to our Smithsonian Institution, the ▲▲▲ Deutsches Museum traces the evolution of science and technology.

Green Munich

Although the capital of a very conservative part of Germany, Munich has long been a liberal stronghold. For 15 years, the city council has been controlled by a Social Democrat/Green Party coalition. The city policies are pedestrian-friendly—you'll find most of the town center closed to normal traffic, with plenty of bike lanes and green spaces. Talking softly and hearing birds rather than motors, it's easy to forget you're in the center of a big city. On summer Mondays, the peace and quiet makes way for "blade Monday"—when streets in the center are closed to cars and as many as 30,000 in-line skaters swarm around town in a giant rolling party.

With 10 miles of exhibits from astronomy to zymurgy, even those on roller skates will need to be selective. Enjoy wandering through well-described rooms of historic airplanes (Hitler's flying bomb from 1944), spaceships, mining, the harnessing of wind and water power, hydraulics, musical instruments, printing, chemistry, computers, clocks, and astronomy...it's the Louvre of science and technology. The museum is designed to be hands-on; if you see a button, push it.

Cost, Hours, Location: €7.50, daily 9:00–17:00 (worthwhile €4 English guidebook, self-service cafeteria). To get to the museum, take the S-Bahn to Isartor, then walk 300 yards over the river, following signs (tel. 089/21791, www.deutsches-museum.de).

 Self-Guided Tour: First head to the **mines**, which trace the history of mining since prehistoric times (mines closed during daily German-language tours at 9:45 and 13:45). As you follow the spiral stairs down to the mines, notice the 19th-century miners' chapel on the left. (Also notice the handy WC on the right.) While descriptions are only in German, the reconstructions of coal, potash, and salt mines are still impressive. It's a fun, haunted house–type experience, with creepy life-like miners tucked away in dark corners. Enjoy the photo ops, like the chairlift that used to transport miners. (Hop in!) Apart from the fun and games, the museum has made great efforts to include realistic, accurate details to show what rigorous, dangerous work mining has always been. When you emerge from the mines, skip the mineral oil and natural gas section (Erdöl und Erdgas) and follow the signs for *Ausgang* (exit).

The fascinating, compact exhibit on **marine navigation** (on the ground floor) has small and often large models of sail, steam, and diesel vessels, from early canoes to grand sailing ships. Take the staircase down into the galley, below the main floor, to check out how life on passenger ships has changed—and don't miss the bisected U1 submarine. This first German submarine, dating from 1906, has been in the museum since 1921.

Flying high above the masts of the marine navigation exhibit is the section on **aeronautics** (1st floor). Displays cover the most basic airborne flights (flying insects and seed pods), Otto Lilienthal's 1891 successful efforts to imitate bird flight, and the development of hot-air balloons and gas-powered zeppelins. Many of the planes here are original, including the Wright brothers' Type A (1909), fighters and cargo ships from the two world wars, and the first functioning helicopter, made in 1936. Climb into the planes whenever permitted, and try out the flight simulator.

The **astronautics** exhibit is located on the second floor. Back in the 1920s, Germany was working on rocket-propelled cars and sleds. Germany's research provided the U.S. and Soviet space teams with much of their technical know-how. Here, you can peer at models of the A4 (one of the first remote-controlled rockets/weapons, from WWII), motors from the American Saturn rockets, and various space capsules, including Spacelab. The main focus is the walk on the moon, the Apollo missions, and the dogs-in-space program (monkeys, too)... but if you've ever been curious about space underwear, you'll find your answer here. Skip the nearby Altamira Caves exhibit, a replica of the 15,000-year-old drawings found in a cave in northern Spain; they're so dark you can barely see anything.

The third floor traces the **history of measurement,** including time (from a 16th-century sundial and an 18th-century clock to a scary Black Forest wall clock complete with grim reaper), weights, geodesy (surveying and mapping), and computing (from 18th-century calculators to antiquated computers from the 1940s and 1950s).

On your way to the state-of-the-art planetarium (worth a visit if open, requires extra ticket, lecture in German), poke your head out into the **sundial garden** located above the third floor. Even if you're not interested in sundials, this is a great place for a view of the surrounding landscape. On a clear day, you can see the Alps.

Most sections of the museum are well-described in English. The much-vaunted high-voltage demonstrations (3/day, 15 min, all in German) show the noisy creation of a five-foot bolt of lightning.

Imax Theater: Adjacent to the Deutsches Museum, big-screen movies play hourly in regular format and 3-D (€8.50, daily 11:00–22:00, 12 different movies/day, call on weekends for reservations, Museumsinsel 1, tel. 089/2112-5180).

Deutsches Museum Annex: The museum celebrated its 100th anniversary in 2003 by opening an annex across town called the **Verkehrszentrum** (Transportation Center), showing off all aspects of transport, from old big-wheeled bikes to Benz's first car (a three-wheeler from the 1880s) to sleek ICE super-trains. This branch museum is in a recently renovated early 20th-century conference hall near the Oktoberfest grounds, a.k.a. Theresienwiese (€2.50, daily 9:00–17:00, Thu until 20:00, Theresienhöhe 14a, U-4 or U-5: Theresienwiese, tel. 089/2179-529).

The Residenz

For a long hike through corridors of gilded imperial Bavarian grandeur, tour the Wittelsbach's family palace (largely rebuilt after World War II). The Wittelsbachs, who ruled Bavaria for more than 700 years, modeled the front of their enormous palace on the Medici family's Pitti Palace in Florence. The sprawling place evolved from the 14th through the 19th centuries—as you'll see on the charts near the entrance. Whatever happened to the Wittelsbachs, the longest continuously ruling family in European history? They're still around—but since they're no longer royalty, most of them have real jobs now.

Cost, Hours, Location: €6 each to visit the Residenz Museum (palace apartments) and the Treasury; the €9 combo-ticket covers both. The Halls of the Nibelungen are free. All parts of the palace are open daily April–mid-Oct 9:00–18:00, mid-Oct–March 10:00–16:00, last entry 30 min before closing. The complex is located three blocks north of Marienplatz. Tel. 089/290-671, www.schloesser.bayern.de.

Orientation: While impressive, the Residenz can be confusing for visitors. Enter the complex from the main entrance on Max-Joseph-Platz (at the corner of the palace nearest Marienplatz) or from the entrance on Residenzstrasse. Just inside the main entrance are the Halls of the Nibelungen (free) and the ticket booth for the Residenz Museum and the Treasury (which are located in separate wings, but share the same ticket booth).

Halls of the Nibelungen—The mythological scenes in these fascinating halls were the basis of Wagner's *Der Ring des Nibelungen*. Wagner and "Mad" King Ludwig were friends and spent time hanging out here (c. 1864). These very images could well have inspired Wagner to write his *Ring* and Ludwig to build his "fairy-tale castle," Neuschwanstein. Even if you're not touring the rest of the Residenz, note that these rooms are free to enter.

▲▲**Residenz Museum (Residenzmuzeum)**—This "museum" actually includes the most spectacular halls and private apartments of the Wittelsbachs' palace complex. It's the best place to get a glimpse of the opulent lifestyle of Bavaria's late, great royal family.

Ø Self-Guided Tour: Since it's so big, different sections of the Residenz Museum are open in the mornings and in the afternoons (after 13:30 in summer, 12:30 in winter). Follow the

Rundgang signs and the self-guided tour below, which is designed to coincide with the afternoon route (a little more interesting than the morning). Due to ongoing renovations, either tour route can change without notice. To help you find the highlights, I have numbered the rooms as they appear on the official map (free at entry), though be warned the rooms themselves aren't all numbered. Your ticket includes an English audioguide; for even more information, consider the €10 English guidebook.

Shell Grotto (Room 6, actually outside, ground floor): This artificial grotto was an exercise in man controlling nature—a celebration of humanism. Renaissance humanism was a big deal when

this was built in the 1550s. Imagine the ambience here during that time, with Mercury—the pre-Christian god of trade and business—overseeing the action, and red wine spurting from the mermaid's breasts and dripping from Medusa's head in the courtyard. The strange structure is made from Bavarian freshwater shells. This palace was demolished by WWII bombs. After the war, people had no money to contribute to the reconstruction—but they could gather shells. All the shells you see here were donated by small-town Bavarians as the grotto was rebuilt according to Nazi photos (see "Munich Bombed" sidebar, page 54). Next to the shells, the door marked *OO* leads to public toilets.

Antiquarium (Room 7, ground floor): In the mid-16th century, Europe's royal families (such as the Wittelsbachs) collected and displayed busts of emperors—implying a connection between

themselves and the ancient Roman rulers. Given the huge demand for these classical statues in the courts of Europe, many of the "ancient busts" are fakes cranked out by crooked Romans. Still, a third of the statuary you see here is original. This was, and still is, a festival banquet hall. Two hundred dignitaries can dine here, surrounded by alle-

gories of the goodness of just rule on the ceiling. Notice the small paintings around the room—these survived the bombs because they were painted in arches. Of great historic interest, these paintings show 120 Bavarian villages as they looked in 1550. Even today, when a Bavarian historian wants a record of how his village once looked, he comes here. Notice the town of Dachau in 1550 (above the door on the right as you leave).

Gallery of the Wittelsbach Family (Room 4, ground floor): This room is from the 1740s (about 200 years younger than the Antiquarium). All official guests had to pass through here to meet the duke. The family tree in the center is labeled "genealogy of an imperial family." A big Wittelsbach/Hapsburg rivalry was worked out through 500 years of marriages and wars—when weddings failed to sort out a problem, they had a war. Opposite the tree are portraits of Charlemagne and Ludwig IV, each a Holy Roman Emperor and each wearing the same crown (now in Vienna). Ludwig IV was the first Wittelsbach HRE—an honor used for centuries to substantiate the family's claim to power. You are surrounded by a scrapbook covering 738 years of the Wittelsbach family.

Allied bombs took their toll on this hall. Above, the central ceiling painting is restored, but since there were no photos of the other two ceiling paintings, those spots remain empty. On the walls, notice how each painting was hastily cut out of its frame. Museums were closed in 1939 and would gradually be evacuated in anticipation of bombings. But public buildings like this palace could not prepare for the worst. Only in 1944, when bombs were imminent, was the hasty order given to slice each portrait out of its frame and hide them all away.

Nymphenburg Porcelain (Room 5, at the end of the family gallery, ground floor): In the 18th century, a royal family's status was bolstered by an in-house porcelain works (like Meissen for the Wettins in Dresden). The Wittelsbach family had their own Nymphenburg porcelain made for the palace. Notice how the mirrors give the effect of infinite pedestals with porcelain vases. If this inspires you to own some Nymphenburg porcelain, it's for sale at the Nymphenburg boutique in the Fünf Höfe (see "Shopping," page 77).

Reliquary (Room 95, upper floor, often closed in the morning): Meet St. John the Baptist and his mother, Elizabeth (#47 and #48—skulls on jeweled pillows). The case in the center contains skeletons of three babies from the slaughter of the innocents in Bethlehem (when Herod, in an attempt to kill the baby Jesus, ordered all sons of a certain age killed).

Chapel (ground-floor Room 89, but also viewable from upper-floor room 96, likely closed in the morning): Dedicated to Mary, this late-Renaissance/early-Baroque gem was the site of "Mad" King Ludwig's funeral after his mysterious murder—or suicide—in 1886. (He's buried in St. Michael's Church; see page 52.) While Ludwig was not popular in the political world, he was beloved by his people, and the funeral drew huge crowds.

"Mad" King Ludwig's grandfather (Ludwig I) was married here in 1810. After the wedding ceremony, carriages rolled his guests to a rollicking reception, which turned out to be such a hit that it became an annual tradition—Oktoberfest.

Private Chapel of Maximilian I (Room 98, upper floor, probably closed in the morning): Maximilian I, the dominant Bavarian figure in the Thirty Years' War, built one of the most precious rooms in the palace. The miniature pipe organ (from around 1600) still works. The room is sumptuous, from the gold leaf and the fancy hinges to the stucco marble. (Stucco marble is fake marble—a mix of stucco, applied and polished. Designers liked it because it was less expensive than real marble and the color could be controlled.) Note the post-Renaissance perspective tricks decorating the walls; they were popular in the 17th century.

Precious Rooms (Rooms 55–62, upper floor): The Wittelsbachs were always trying to keep up with the Hapsburgs, and this long string of ceremonial rooms was all for show. The decor and furniture are rococo. The family art collection, now in the Alte Pinakothek, once decorated these walls. The bedroom (Room 60) was the official sleeping room, where the duke would get up and go to bed publicly, à la Louis XIV.

Red Room (Room 62, upper floor): The ultimate room is at the end of the corridor—the coral red room from 1740. (Coral red was *the* most royal of colors in Germany.) Imagine visiting the duke and having him take you here to ogle at miniature copies of the most famous paintings of the day, painted with one-haired brushes. Notice the fun effect of the mirrors around you—the corner mirrors make things go forever and ever.

▲▲**Treasury (Schatzkammer)**—The Treasury, next door to the Residenz, shows off a thousand years of Wittelsbach crowns and knickknacks. Vienna's jewels are better, but this is Bavaria's best, with fine 13th- and 14th-century crowns and delicately carved ivory and glass (for cost and hours, see above).

❺ Self-Guided Tour: A long clockwise circle through the eight rooms takes you chronologically through a thousand years of royal treasure. (It's a one-way system—getting lost is not an option.) Your ticket includes an English audioguide, but I've explained the highlights below.

The oldest jewels in the first room are 200 years older than Munich itself. Many of these came from various prince-bishop collections when they were secularized (and their realms came under the rule of the Bavarian king from Munich) in the Napoleonic Era (c. 1800). The tiny mobile altar allowed a Carolingian king (from Charlemagne's family of kings) to pack light in 890—and still have a little Mass while on the road.

In Room 3, study the reliquary with St. George killing the

dragon—sparkling with more than 2,000 precious stones (#58). Get up close—you can almost hear the dragon hissing. It was made to contain the relics of St. George, who never existed (Pope John Paul II declared him nothing more than a legend). If you could lift the miniscule visor, you'd see that the carved ivory face of St. George is actually the Wittelsbach duke (the dragon represents the "evil" forces of Protestantism).

In the next room (#4), notice the vividly carved ivory crucifixes from 1630 (#157 and #158, on the right). These incredibly realistic sculptures were done by local artist Georg Petel, a friend of Peter Paul Rubens (whose painting of Christ on the cross—which you'll see across town in the Alte Pinakothek—is Petel's obvious inspiration). Look at the flesh of Jesus' wrist pulling around the nails.

Continue into the next room (#5). The freestanding glass case (#245) holds the never-used royal crowns of Bavaria. Napoleon ended the Holy Roman Empire and let the Wittelsbach family rule as kings of Bavaria. As a sign of friendship, this royal coronation gear was made in Paris by the same shop that made Napoleon's crown. But before the actual coronation, Bavaria joined in an all-Europe get-rid-of-Napoleon alliance, and suddenly these were too French to be used.

Cuvilliés Theater—Attached to the Residenz is the Cuvilliés Theater, dazzling enough to send you back to the days of divine monarchs. Unfortunately, it's closed for renovation until 2008.

Near the Residenz

To get to the Hofgarten, face the Residenz entrance, then go left around the Residenz one long block to the palace's original entryway (flanked by the second set of lions—rub their noses for good luck) and enter the complex. After the first arch, bear left across the courtyard and cut through the entry to the Egyptian collection to the park.

Hofgarten—The elegant people's state garden (Hofgarten) is a delight on a sunny afternoon. The "Renaissance" temple centerpiece has great acoustics (and usually a musician performing for tips from lazy listeners). The lane leads to a building housing the government of Bavaria and the Bavarian war memorial, which honors the fallen *heroes* of World War I, but only the *fallen* of World War II. The venerable old **Café Tambosi**—with a Viennese elegance inside and a relaxing garden setting outside—is a good antidote to all the beer halls (daily 8:00–24:00, Odeonsplatz 18, tel. 089/298-322).

Odeonsplatz—This square near the Hofgarten is a part of the grand, imperial Munich vision. The church on Odeonsplatz (Theatinerkirche) contains nearly all the Wittelsbach tombs. The loggia in the Hofgarten (honoring Bavarian generals) is modeled in the Florence Renaissance style. A Roman-type triumphal arch hovers in the distance to the north (at the end of Ludwigstrasse). And to the west, a grand axis (Briennerstrasse) heads towards the Greek-inspired museum quarter.

Briennerstrasse: From Odeonsplatz, look (or wander) down Briennerstrasse to get a taste of the ambitious city planning of the Wittelsbachs. At Karolinenplatz, the black obelisk commemorates the 30,000 Bavarians who marched with Napoleon to Moscow and never returned. Beyond that is the grand Königsplatz, or "King's Square," with its stern neoclassicism, evocative of ancient Greece.

On the way to this imperial splendor, Briennerstrasse goes through a square called Platz der Opfer des Nationalsozialismus, literally, "Square of the Victims of Nazism." Nearby you'll find two former Nazi administration buildings; one is now the music academy, though it's still very much fascist in its architecture. A plaque on the street explains the history.

Nymphenburg Palace Complex

Nymphenburg Palace and the surrounding one-square-mile park are good for a royal stroll or bike ride. Here you'll find a pair of palaces, the Royal Stables Museum, and playful extras such as a bathhouse, pagoda, and artificial ruins.

Cost, Hours, Information: €10 for everything, less for each of the six individual parts. All sights are open daily April–mid-Oct 9:00–18:00, mid-Oct–March 10:00–16:00. The park is open daily 6:00–dusk. Tel. 089/179-080, www.schloesser.bayern.de.

Getting There: The palace is three miles northwest of central Munich. Getting there from the center is easy, if a bit time-consuming: Take tram #17 from Karlstor (20 min to palace) or the train station (15 min to palace) to the Schloss Nymphenburg stop. From the bridge by the tram stop, you'll see the palace, but you'll have to walk another 10 minutes to get there. A pleasant bike path follows Arnulfstrasse from the train station all the way to the palace (a 30-min pedal).

▲▲**Nymphenburg Palace**—In 1662, after 10 years of trying, the Bavarian ruler Ferdinand Maria and his wife, Henriette Adelaide of Savoy, finally had a son, Max Emanuel. In gratitude for a male heir, Ferdinand gave this land to his Italian wife, who proceeded to build an Italian-style Baroque palace. Their son expanded the palace to today's size. For 200 years, this was the Wittelsbach family's summer escape from Munich. (They still refer to themselves as princes and live in one wing of the palace.) If "Wow!" is your first impression, that's intentional.

Your visit is limited to 16 main rooms on one floor: the Great Hall (where you start), the King's Wing (to the right), and the Queen's Wing (on the left). The €2.50 audioguide is informative

Greater Munich

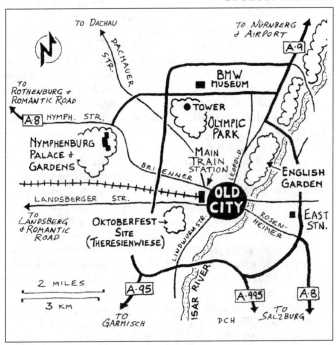

and easy to use (better than the €6 English guidebook). For most visitors, the following self-guided tour is all you'll need.

◐ Self-Guided Tour: The **Great Hall** in the middle was the dining hall. One of the grandest rococo rooms in Bavaria, it was decorated by Zimmermann (of Wieskirche fame) and Cuvilliés around 1760. The painting on the ceiling shows Olympian gods keeping the peace (the ruler's duty).

The **King's Wing** (right of entrance) has walls filled with Wittelsbach portraits and stories. In the second room straight ahead, notice the painting showing the huge palace grounds, with Munich (and the twin onion domes of the Frauenkirche) three miles in the distance. Imagine the logistics when the royal family—with their entourage of 200—decided to move out to the summer palace. The Wittelsbachs were high rollers because, from 1624 until 1806, a Wittelsbach was one of seven electors of the Holy Roman Emperor. In 1806, Napoleon ended that institution and made the Wittelsbachs kings. (Note: For simplicity, I've referred to the Wittelsbachs as kings and queens, even though before 1806, these rulers were technically electors.)

In the **Queen's Wing** (left of entrance), enter the first room, then head to the right to find the very red room. You'll see the founding couple, Henriette Adelaide and Ferdinand Maria (after the Counter-Reformation, Bavarian men were named Maria—but his high heels and leggings were another story altogether). The inlaid table was a wedding present. The real pay-off, this palace, didn't come until Henriette (who was 14 when married) got pregnant. The green room is the ceremonial bedroom. The painting to the right of the bed shows Max Emanuel as a kid in a double portrait with his older sister. Both are dressed in the latest French fashions.

King Ludwig I's Gallery of Beauties, near the end of the long hall in the Queen's Wing, is decorated with portraits of 36 beautiful women—all of them painted by Joseph Stieler from 1827 to 1850. King Ludwig I was a consummate girl-watcher who prided himself on the ability to appreciate beauty regardless of social rank. He would pick the prettiest women from the general public and invite them to the palace for a portrait. The women range in status from royal princesses to a humble cobbler's daughter...but Ludwig seemed to prefer brunettes. The portraits reflect the modest Biedermeier style, as opposed to the more flamboyant Romanticism of the same period. If only these creaking floors could talk. Something about the place feels highly sexed, in a Prince Charles kind of way.

The next rooms are decorated in the neoclassical style of the Napoleonic Era. At the rope, see the room where Ludwig II was born (August 25, 1845). Royal births were carefully witnessed. The mirror allowed for a better view. While Ludwig's death was shrouded in mystery (see page 97), his birth was well-documented.

Amalienburg Palace—Three hundred yards from the palace, hiding in the park (ahead and to the left as you go through to back of palace), you'll find one of the finest rococo buildings in all of Europe. In 1734, Elector Karl Albrecht had this hunting lodge built for his wife, Maria Amalia—another rococo jewel designed by Cuvilliés and decorated by Zimmermann. Above the pink-and-white grand entryway, notice Diana, goddess of the chase, flanked by busts of satyrs. Look for the perch atop the roof where the queen would do her shooting. Behind a wall in the garden, dogs would scare non-flying pheasants. When they jumped up in the air above the wall, the sporting queen—as if shooting skeet—would pick them off.

Tourists enter this tiny getaway through the back door. The first room has doghouses under gun cupboards. Next, in the fine yellow-and-silver bedroom, see Vulcan forging arrows for amorous cupids at the foot of the bed. The bed is flanked by portraits of Karl Albrecht and Maria Amalia—decked out in hunting attire. She liked her dogs. The door under the portrait leads to stairs to the rooftop pheasant-shooting perch.

The mini–Hall of Mirrors is a blue-and-silver commotion of rococo nymphs designed by Cuvilliés in the mid-1700s. Cuvilliés, short and hunchbacked, showed a unique talent for art and was sent to Paris to study. In the next room, paintings show court festivities, formal hunting parties, and no-contest kills (where the animal is put at an impossible disadvantage—like shooting fish in a barrel). Finally, the kitchen is decorated with Chinese picnics on blue Dutch tiles.

Royal Stables Museum (Marstallmuseum)—This huge garage is lined with gilded Cinderella coaches. The highlight is just inside the entrance: the 1742 Karl Albrecht coronation coach. Because Karl Albrecht was an emperor, this coach has eight horses. Kings only get six.

Wandering through the collection, you can trace the evolution of 300 years of coaches—getting lighter and with better suspension as they were harnessed to faster horses. The carousel for the royal kids made development of dexterity fun—lop off noses and heads and toss balls through the snake. The glass case is filled with accessories.

In the room after the carousel, find the painting on the right of "Mad" King Ludwig on his sleigh at night. In his later years, Ludwig was a Howard Hughes-type recluse who stayed away from the public eye and only went out at night. (At his nearby Linderhof Palace, he actually had a hydraulic-powered dining table that would rise from the kitchen below, completely set for the meal—so he wouldn't be seen by his servants.) In the next room, you'll find

Ludwig's actual sleighs. Next to them is the coach designed for his wedding, but it was never used. Ludwig's over-the-top coaches were Baroque. But this was 1870. The coaches, like the king, were in the wrong century. Notice the photos (c. 1865, in the glass case) of Ludwig with the Romantic composer Richard Wagner. Ludwig cried on the day Wagner was married. Hmmm.

Across the passage from the museum entrance, the second hall is filled with coaches for everyday use. Upstairs is a collection of **Nymphenburg porcelain** (described by an English loaner booklet at the entrance). Historically, royal families such as the Wittelsbachs liked to have their own porcelain plants to make fit-for-a-king plates, vases, and so on. The Nymphenburg palace porcelain works is still in operation. Ludwig ordered the masterpieces of his royal collection (now at the Alte Pinakothek) to be copied in porcelain for safekeeping into the distant future. Take a close look—these are exquisite.

The Olympic Park and Nearby

▲Olympic Park (Olympiapark München)—Munich's great 1972 Olympic stadium and sports complex is now a lush park. You can get a good look at the center's striking "cobweb" style of architecture while enjoying the park's picnic potential. In addition, there are several activities on offer at the park, including a tower with a commanding but so-high-it's-boring view from 820 feet (Olympiaturm, €4, daily 9:00–24:00, last trip 23:00, tel. 089/3067-2750) and an excellent swimming pool (Olympia-Schwimmhalle, €3, daily 7:00–23:00, last entry 22:00, tel. 089/3067-2290). With the construction of Munich's new soccer stadium for the 2006 World Cup, the Olympic Park has been left in the past. It will now melt into the neighborhood as just a fine park and swimming pool. So, in an effort to zip up its image, the park is offering roof-climbing tours with a dizzying zip-cord finale (the TI has details). To reach the park, take U-3 to Olympia-Zentrum direct from Marienplatz (www.olympiapark-muenchen.de).

BMW Museum—The museum at the BMW headquarters is closed for remodeling until 2007. In the meantime, the temporary exhibit here may appeal to hardcore BMW aficionados (€2, daily 10:00–20:00, U-3: Olympia-Zentrum, tel. 089/3822-5652), but the Deutsches Museum's annex has a much better old-car exhibit (see page 62). True BMW fans should call several weeks in advance for factory tours (free, 2.5 hrs, by appointment, books up fast July–Aug, same tel. as above).

Near Munich

▲▲▲"Mad" King Ludwig's Castles—The spectacular Neuschwanstein and Linderhof castles make a great day trip. For all the details, see the Bavaria and Tirol chapter. Your easiest option is to take a tour (see page 46). Without a tour, only Neuschwanstein is easy (2 hrs by train to Füssen, then 10-min bus ride to Neuschwanstein). If you want to visit the castles on your own by train, consider getting the Bayern ticket, which covers up to five people from Munich to the castles and back for only €30 (explained in *The Inside Track* newsletter and sold at EurAide—see page 44).

▲▲Nürnberg—In 2006, a new express train gets you to Nürnberg in just 60 minutes (hourly departures), making this very historic city a viable day trip from Munich. For information, see the Nürnberg chapter.

▲Berchtesgaden—This resort, near Hitler's Eagle's Nest getaway, is easier as a day trip from Salzburg (just 12 miles away); see page 523.

Near Munich

G E R M A N Y

TO ROTHENBURG
┤─┤ RAIL
--- ROMANTIC ROAD BUS

B A V A R I A

AIRPORT

AUGSBURG

DACHAU

MUNICH

DCH

BUCHLOE

LANDSBERG

HERRSCHING

HERRENCHIEMSEE

SALZ-BURG

KEMPTEN

ANDECHS

AMMER-SEE

CHIEMSEE

ROSENHEIM

PRIEN

WIES-KIRCHE

MURNAU

HALLEIN

FÜSSEN

OBERAMMERGAU

KUFSTEIN

BERCHTES-GADEN

KÖNIG-SEE

NEUSCHWANSTEIN

LINDERHOF

REUTTE

GARMISCH

KITZBÜHEL

LERMOOS

MITTEN-WALD

50 MILES

ZUG-SPITZE

HALL

80 KM

INNSBRUCK

T I R O L

A U S T R I A

▲**Isar River Bike Ride**—Munich's river, lined by a gorgeous park, leads bikers into the pristine countryside in just a few minutes. From downtown (easy access from the English Garden or Deutsches Museum), follow the riverside bike path south (upstream) along the east (left) bank. You can't get lost. Just stay on the lovely bike path. It crosses the river after a while, passing tempting little beer gardens and lots of Bavarians having their brand of fun—including gangs enjoying Munich's famous river party rafts. Go as far as you like, then to get home, retrace your route. The closest bike rental is at Munich Walk, near Isartor (see page 46).

▲**Andechs Monastery**—The monastery crouches quietly with a big smile between two lakes just south of Munich. For a fine Baroque church in a rural Bavarian setting at a monastery that serves hearty food and perhaps the best beer in Germany, consider a short side-trip here. The cafeteria terrace offers first-class views and second-class prices (beer garden open daily 10:00–23:00, last meal order 20:00, church until 18:00, tel. 08152/3760). Reaching Andechs from Munich without a car is frustrating (take the S-5 train to Herrsching, then catch a shuttle bus, taxi, or hike 3 miles). Don't miss the stroll up to the church, where you can sit peacefully and ponder the striking contrasts a trip through Germany offers.

▲▲**Dachau Concentration Camp Memorial (KZ-Gedenkstätte Dachau)**—Dachau was the first Nazi concentration camp (1933). Today, it's the most accessible camp for travelers and an effective voice from our recent but grisly past, pleading "Never again." A visit here is a valuable experience and, when approached thoughtfully, well worth the trouble. After this most powerful sightseeing experience, many people gain more respect for history and the dangers of mixing fear, blind patriotism, and an evil government. You'll likely see lots of students here, as all German schoolchildren are required to visit a concentration camp. It's interesting to think that a couple of generations ago, people greeted each other with a robust *"Sieg Heil!"* Today, almost no Germans know the lyrics of their national anthem, and German flags are a rarity.

In the 1930s, the camp was outside the town, surrounded by a mile-wide restricted area. A huge training center stood next to the camp. While a relatively few 32,000 inmates died in Dachau between 1933 and 1945 (in comparison, over a million were killed at Auschwitz in Poland), the camp is notorious because the people who ran the entire concentration-camp system were trained here. Given the strict top-down Nazi man-agement style, it's safe to assume that most of the demonic innovations for Hitler's mass killing originated at Dachau. This was a work camp, where inmates were used for slave labor. It was also a departure point for shipments of people destined for gas chambers in the east, mostly in Poland—where most of the mass murder took place (conveniently distant, far out of view of the German public).

Few realize that Dachau actually housed people longer *after* the war than during the war. After liberation, the fences were taken down, but numerous survivors who had nowhere else to go stayed. The camp served as a prison for camp officials convicted in the Dachau trials. And later, the camp was used for refugees from Eastern Europe. Until the 1960s, it was like a small town, with a cinema, shops, and so on.

Cost, Hours, Tours: The memorial camp is free. Open Tue–Sun 9:00–17:00, last entry 30 min before closing, closed Mon, www.memorial-site-dachau.org. For maximum understanding, rent the €2.50 audioguide, consider the English guided walk (daily in summer at 13:30, 2 hrs, donation requested, call 08131/669-970 or ask at door to confirm), or take a tour from Munich (see page 48).

Dachau

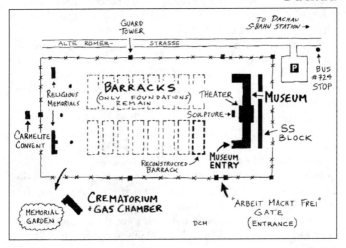

A visit to the Dachau memorial consists of the museum, the bunker behind the museum, the restored barracks, and a pensive walk across the huge but now-empty camp to the shrines and crematorium at the far end. Upon arrival, pick up the mini-guide (€0.50), consider the excellent €2 booklet, and note when the next documentary film in English will be shown (20 min, normally shown at 11:30, 14:00, and 15:30, verify times on board as you enter museum).

 Self-Guided Tour: You enter, like the inmates did, through the infamous iron gate with the taunting slogan *Arbeit macht frei* ("Work makes you free"). The museum—which tries valiantly to personalize the plight of the inmates—is thoughtfully described in English. Computer tap-screens let you watch early newsreels. The theater shows a powerful documentary movie (see above for times).

The bunker behind the theater was for "special prisoners," such as failed Hitler assassins and politicians who challenged Nazism. It contains an exhibit on the notorious SS (you have direct access to the bunker after the movie lets out, otherwise walk around museum past the *Arbeit macht frei* sign.)

The big square between the museum and the reconstructed barracks was used for roll call. Twice a day, the entire camp population assembled here. They'd stand at attention until all were accounted for. If someone was missing (more likely dead than escaped), everyone would have to stand—often through the night—until the person was located.

Beyond the two reconstructed barracks (one is open to the public—where you can rent an audioguide), a long walk takes you past the foundations of the other barracks to four places of meditation and worship (Jewish, Catholic, Protestant, and Russian Orthodox). Beyond that is a Carmelite Convent.

To the left of the shrines, a memorial garden surrounds the camp crematorium. Look at the smokestack. You're standing on ground nourished by the ashes of those who died at Dachau.

While the Dachau gas chamber is like those at all other concentration camps, this one was never used.

Getting There: Dachau is a 45-minute trip from downtown Munich. Take S-2 (direction: Petershausen) to Dachau, then from the station, catch bus #724 or #726 (Dachau-Ost) to KZ-Gedenkstätte (the camp). The XXL ticket covers the entire trip, both ways (€6/1 person, €10.50/partner ticket). Drivers follow Dachauerstrasse from downtown Munich to Dachau-Ost. Then follow the *KZ-Gedenkstätte* signs.

The town of Dachau is more pleasant than its unfortunate image (TI tel. 08131/75286). With 40,000 residents, located midway between Munich and its airport, it's now a high-priced and in-demand place to live.

EXPERIENCES

Oktoberfest

When King Ludwig I had his marriage reception in 1810, it was such a success that they made it an annual bash. These days, the Oktoberfest lasts more than two weeks (Sept 16–Oct 3 in 2006), starting on the third Saturday in September and usually ending on the first Sunday in October (but never before Oct 3—the day Germany celebrates its recent reunification).

Oktoberfest kicks things off with an opening parade of more than 6,000 participants. Every night, it fills eight huge beer tents with about 6,000 people each. A million gallons of beer later, they roast the last ox.

It's best to reserve a room early, but if you arrive in the morning (except Fri or Sat) and haven't called ahead, the TI can normally help. The Theresienwiese fairground (south of the main train station), known as the "Wies'n," erupts in a frenzy of rides, dancing, and strangers strolling arm-in-arm down rows of picnic tables while the beer god stirs tons of beer, pretzels, and wurst in a bubbling cauldron of fun. The

three-loops roller coaster must be the wildest on earth (best before the beer-drinking). During the fair, the city functions even better than normal. It's a good time to sightsee, even if beer-hall rowdiness isn't your cup of tea. For details, see www.oktoberfest.de.

SHOPPING

You'll find beer steins to take home at shops on the pedestrian zone by St. Michael's Church and at the gift shops that surround the Hofbräuhaus. Müncheners take their shoes very seriously; the pedestrian zone abounds with shoe stores featuring everything from expensive Italian models to Birkenstocks (substantially cheaper here than in the U.S.).

Here are a few areas and stores in particular to consider:

On Marienplatz: Beck's has been a local institution since 1861, when it began meeting the needs of the royal family, including "Mad" King Ludwig. This shop has long been to fabrics what Alois Dallmayr is to fine food (see page 55). Today, it's an upscale department store, with stationery, cosmetics, and its own clothing label and designer duds. If you're facing the glockenspiel on New Town Hall, look to your right—you can't miss it on the corner. Also on Marienplatz is the **Hugendubel** bookstore, with an extensive selection of English-language books (Mon–Sat 9:30–20:00, closed Sun, coffee shop on top floor).

Weinstrasse/Theatinerstrasse: Shoppers will want to stroll from Marienplatz down the pedestrianized Weinstrasse, which becomes Theatinerstrasse). As you walk down Weinstrasse (it runs alongside the left of New Town Hall—as you face it), look for **Fünf Höfe** on your left—named for its five courtyards and filled with Germany's top shops (open until 20:00, includes the Nymphenburg porcelain store, www.fuenfhoefe.de). Soon after is the **Kunsthalle,** a big bank-sponsored art center with excellent temporary exhibits and impressive events (daily 10:00–20:00, Theatinerstrasse 8, tel. 089/224-412, www.hypo-kunsthalle.de). Note how its Swiss architects (who also designed Munich's grand new soccer stadium for the 2006 World Cup) play with light and color. Even if you're not a shopper, wander through the Kunsthalle to appreciate the architecture.

Maximilian Strasse: For the most exclusive shops, stroll this street. Ludwig I made the grand but very impersonal Ludwigstrasse. As a reaction to this unpopular street by this unpopular king, his son Maximilian built a street designed for the people and for shopping. It leads from the National Theater over the Isar River to the Bavarian Parliament (which you can see from the theater end).

SLEEPING

Unless you hit Munich during a fair, convention, or big holiday, you can sleep reasonably here. Lots of student hotels around the station house anyone who's young at heart for €20 and it's easy to find a fine double with breakfast in a good basic hotel for €80. I've listed accommodations in two neighborhoods: within a few blocks of the central train station (Hauptbahnhof) and in the old center. Many of these places have complicated, slippery pricing schemes. I've listed the normal non-convention, non-festival prices. There are major conventions about 30 nights a year—prices increase from 20 percent to as much as 300 percent during Oktoberfest (Sept 17–Oct 3 in 2006; reserve well in advance). And 2006 brings the World Cup to Germany, so hotel prices will be sky-high from about June 8 through July 9 (especially when Munich hosts matches on June 9, 14, 18, 21, and 24, and July 5). Prices can also go up slightly for smaller conventions. On the other hand, during slow times, you may be able to do better than the rates listed here—always ask.

Near the Train Station

Budget hotels cluster in the area immediately south of the station. It feels seedy after dark (erotic cinemas and men with moustaches in the shadows), but it's dangerous only for those in search of trouble. Neighborhoods in the old center (see page 82) might feel more comfortable to many readers.

$$$ King's Hotel First Class, a fancy 90-room business-class hotel, is an elegant splurge that becomes a good deal on weekends. You'll get a lobby with chandeliers and carved wooden ceilings, rooms with canopy beds, and a well-polished staff (Db-€170; cheaper Fri–Sun: Db-€110; save €15 per person by skipping breakfast, air-con, 500 yards north of station at Dachauer

---

Sleep Code

(€1 = about $1.20, country code: 49, area code: 089)
S = Single, **D** = Double/Twin, **T** = Triple, **Q** = Quad, **b** = bathroom, **s** = shower only. Unless otherwise noted, credit cards are accepted, a buffet breakfast is included, and English is spoken.

To help you sort easily through these listings, I've divided the rooms into three categories based on the price for a standard double room with bath:

$$$ **Higher Priced**—Most rooms €95 or more.
$$ **Moderately Priced**—Most rooms between €70–95.
$ **Lower Priced**—Most rooms €70 or less.

Munich's Train Station Area

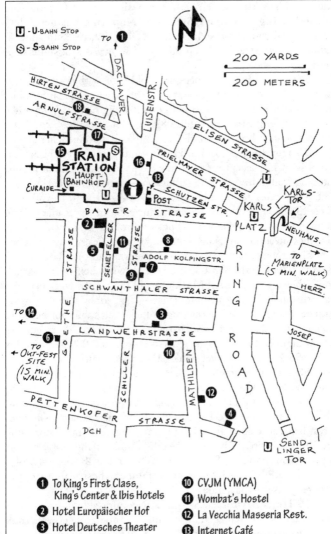

- **1** To King's First Class, King's Center & Ibis Hotels
- **2** Hotel Europäischer Hof
- **3** Hotel Deutsches Theater
- **4** Hotel Bristol
- **5** Hotel Mark
- **6** Hotel Schweiz
- **7** Hotel Monaco
- **8** Alpen Hotel
- **9** Hotel Royal
- **10** CVJM (YMCA)
- **11** Wombat's Hostel
- **12** La Vecchia Masseria Rest.
- **13** Internet Café
- **14** To Launderette
- **15** Bike Rental
- **16** City Tour Bus Stop
- **17** Romantic Road Bus Stop
- **18** Panorama Tour Office

Strasse 13, tel. 089/551-870, fax 089/5518-7300, www.kingshotels
.de, 1stclass@kingshotels.de). Their sister hotel (around the
corner), **King's Center Hotel,** also rents fine business-class
canopy-bed rooms but is less plush (Db-€120; Fri-Sun special:
Db-€75; Marsstrasse 15, tel. 089/515-530, www.kingshotels.de,
center@kingshotels.de).

$$$ Alpen Hotel, a once-grand old hotel with gorgeous pub-
lic spaces close to the train station, rents 57 simple, comfortable,
slightly overpriced rooms (small Db-€105, big Db-€115, Tb-€145,
Adolf-Kolping-Strasse 14, tel. 089/559-330, fax 089/559-33100,
www.alpenhotel-muenchen.de, info@alpenhotel-muenchen.de).

$$ Hotel Europäischer Hof is a huge, impersonal business
hotel with 158 decent rooms. They have four categories of rooms,
ranging from fairly cheap to outrageous (official rates are sky-high,
but actual rates are usually closer to S-€40, Sb-€80, D-€50, Db-
€92, 10 percent discount on prevailing rate for my readers if you
reserve ahead and mention this book or if you pay cash; no discounts
during conventions, major events, and Oktoberfest weekends; non-
smoking rooms, family rooms, free Internet access, Bayerstrasse
31, tel. 089/551-510, fax 089/5515-1222, www.heh.de, info@heh
.de). They also run **Hotel Mark,** around the corner, with a similar
institutional-slumbermill ambience—large lobby, dim hallways,
and 95 plain, cheaper rooms (high official rates, but normal rates
usually around S-€35, D-€50, basic Db-€88, ask for 10 percent discount described above, Senefelderstrasse 12, tel. 089/559-820, fax
089/5598-2323, www.hotel-mark.de, mark@heh.de).

$$ Hotel Deutsches Theater is a brass-and-marble-filled
place with 28 tight, modern, three-star rooms. The back rooms
face the courtyard of a neighboring theater; when there's a show,
there can be some street noise. Hardworking manager Johannes
promises these special cash-only rates for readers of this book
in 2006 (Sb-€65, Db-€85, Tb-€95, more during fairs, pricier
suites, non-smoking floor, Landwehrstrasse 18, tel. 089/545-
8525, fax 089/5458-5261, www.hoteldeutschestheater.de, info
@hoteldeutschestheater.de).

$$ Hotel Bristol has 57 similarly comfortable business-class
rooms and is also managed by Johannes. While a longer walk from
the station, this is pleasantly located just across the street from
Sendlinger Tor (Sb-€61, Db-€81, Tb-€91, these rates promised
in 2006 with this book and cash payment, more during fairs,
non-smoking rooms, elevator, hearty buffet breakfast on terrace, 1 U-Bahn stop from station, U-1 or U-2: Sendlinger Tor,
Pettenkoferstrasse 2, tel. 089/548-2220, fax 089/5482-2299, www
.bristol-muc.com, hotel@bristol-muc.com).

$$ Hotel Monaco is a delightful and welcoming little zone
hiding on the fifth floor of a giant, nondescript building two

blocks from the station. Emerging from the elevator, you're warmly greeted by Frau Sevdas into her flowery, cherub-filled oasis. It's homey rather than slick, with 20 clean and fresh rooms, all with fake blond-hardwood floors (Sb-€50–70, Db-€66–80, €5 cheaper if you pay in cash, Schillerstrasse 9, entrance on Adolf-Kolping-Strasse, tel. 089/545-9940, fax 089/550-3709, www.hotel-monaco .de, info@hotel-monaco.de).

$$ Hotel Schweiz is built like a bomb shelter. Solid and efficient, with a warm welcome, 57 new-feeling rooms, and a tasty breakfast, this is a good value (Sb-€58, Db-€75, Tb-€90, non-smoking rooms, free Internet access in lobby, from the station walk 2 blocks down Goethestrasse to #26, tel. 089/543-6960, fax 089/5436-9696, www.hotel-schweiz.de, info@hotel-schweiz.de).

$$ Hotel Ibis is a big, plain, efficient chain hotel offering 200 simple but comfortable little industrial-strength staterooms for a good price to businesspeople on a tight per diem (Sb-€69, Db-€81, often €10 cheaper Fri–Sun, breakfast-€9, non-smoking rooms, air-con, Dachauer Strasse 21, tel. 089/551-930, fax 089/5519-3102, www.ibishotel.com, h1450@accor.com).

$$ Hotel Royal is perhaps the best value in its price range (if you don't mind the strip joints flanking the entry). While a bit institutional, it's clean, fresh, efficient, and plenty comfortable. Most importantly, it's energetically run by Pasha and Changiz. Each of its 40 rooms are mod, fresh, and bright (Sb-€45–55, Db-€65–75, Tb-€75–95, book direct and claim your 10 percent discount off their prevailing price with this book in 2006, ask for a room on the quiet side, free Internet and Wi-Fi, Schillerstrasse 11a, tel. 089/591-021, fax 089/550-3657, www.hotel-royal.de, info@hotel -royal.de).

$ CVJM (YMCA), open to all ages, rents 85 beds in modern rooms (S-€32–37, D-€54, T-€75, €25/bed in a shared triple, those over 26 pay about 10 percent more, cheaper for 3 nights or more and in winter, €10/night more during Oktoberfest, free showers, Landwehrstrasse 13, tel. 089/552-1410, fax 089/550-4282, www .cvjm-muenchen.org, hotel@cvjm-muenchen.org).

$ Wombat's Hostel, casual and welcoming anyone young at heart, seems to be the best option near the station for budget backpackers. They have cheap doubles and six- to eight-bed dorms with lockers, a bar open until 2:00 in the morning, a relaxing and peaceful winter garden, all the normal services, and a creative management. All bedrooms are fresh and modern, with good bathrooms (dorm bed-€22, Db-€62, breakfast-€4, cheaper off-season, open 24 hours, a block from the station at Senefelderstrasse 1, tel. 089/5998-9180, www.wombats-hostels.com, office@wombats -munich.de).

In the Old Center

$$$ **Mercure München Altstadt Hotel** is a huge, impersonal, basic business-class hotel with all the modern comforts on a boring street very close to the Marienplatz action. If you want an American-style hotel room buried deep in Munich for a good price, this place has 70 of them (Db-€103 for most days, breakfast-€13, non-smoking floors, air-con, a block south of the pedestrian zone at Hotterstrasse 4, tel. 089/232-590, fax 089/2325-9127, www .mercure.com, h3709@accor.com).

$$$ **Hotel Blauer Bock,** formerly a dormitory for Benedictine monks, has been on the same corner across from the Munich City Museum since 1841. It's a little pricey and feels spartan, but offers clean, decent rooms and has a straightforward pricing system (the same prices every day of the year). Breakfast is served in its very mod and sleek restaurant next door, though most of the decor feels like the monks still run the place (S-€41–49, Sb-€60–65, D-€66–71, Db-€93–102, Sebastianplatz 9, tel. 089/231-780, fax 089/2317-8200, www.hotelblauerbock.de, info@hotelblauerbock.de).

$$ **Hotel am Viktualienmarkt,** located just a block off of the market, was recently renovated by Elke Glöckle and her daughter Stephanie. Light-colored wood gives the rooms a fresh, clean feeling. The prices are very good for this central location (Sb-€39–45, Db-€80–95, Tb-€95–110, Qb-€110–125, lower prices are for weekends, Utzschneiderstrasse 14, tel. 089/231-1090, fax 089/2311-0955, www.hotel-am-viktualienmarkt.de, reservierung@hotel-am -viktualienmarkt.de).

$$ **Pension Lindner** is clean, quiet, and modern, with 10 pastel-bouquet rooms, mediocre plumbing, and—at times—indifferent service (S-€39, D-€55, Ds-€65, Db-€75, these special prices promised with this book through 2006, more during conventions and Oktoberfest, reception and breakfast in café below, elevator, Dultstrasse 1, tel. 089/263-413, fax 089/268-760, www.pension -lindner.com, info@pension-lindner.com, Marion Sinzinger).

$$ **Hotel Atlanta** is conveniently located 50 yards from the Sendlinger Tor U-Bahn stop and a 10-minute walk from Marienplatz. Its 20 rooms are split between two buildings connected by a peaceful patio. To minimize street noise, ask for a room in the older back building (S-€40, Ss-€55, Sb-€70, Ds-€70, Db-€80–90, Sendlingerstrasse 58, tel. 089/263-605, fax 089/260-9027, www.hotel-atlanta.de, info@hotel-atlanta.de).

$$ **Hotel Münchner Kindl** is jolly, with 16 decent rooms above a friendly neighborhood bar (S-€52, Ss-€66, Sb-€77, D-€72, Ds-€82, Db-€92, Tb-€107, Qb-€120, these prices through 2006 with this book, same rates during festivals and fairs; cheaper June–Aug: D-€60, Ds-€70, Db-€80; non-smoking rooms, night noises travel up central courtyard, Damenstiftstrasse 16, tel.

Central Munich Hotels and Restaurants

★ = MARIENPLATZ

1. Hotel am Viktualienmarkt
2. Pension Lindner
3. Hotel Münchner Kindl
4. Hotel Atlanta
5. Hotel Blauer Bock
6. Mercure München Altstadt Hotel
7. Hofbräuhaus
8. Weisses Bräuhaus
9. To Augustiner Beer Garden
10. Jodlerwirt Pub
11. Rest. Nürnberger Bratwurst Glöckl am Dom & Andechser am Dom
12. Restaurant Altes Hackerhaus
13. Restaurant Spatenhaus
14. To Chinesischer Turm Biergarten & Seehaus
15. Suppenküche Cafeteria
16. Glockenspiel Café & Hugendubel Books
17. Alois Dallmayr Deli
18. Buxs Self-Service Vegetarian Restaurant
19. Forum Speisecafé
20. Prinz Myshkin Vegetarian Restaurant
21. Riva Bar Pizzeria
22. Café Tambosi
23. Stadt Café

089/264-349, fax 089/264-526, www.hotel-muenchner-kindl.de, reservierung@hotel-muenchner-kindl.de, Renate Dittert).

Away from the Center

$$$ **Hotel Uhland** is a stately mansion renting 31 delightful rooms in a safe-feeling residential neighborhood near the Theresien-wiese Oktoberfest grounds. It's been in the same wonderful Hauzenberger family for 50 years and is a worthwhile splurge (Sb-€68–75, small Db-€80, big Db-€95, Tb-€115, save about €10 a night by booking online, great family rooms and deals, non-smoking floor, free loaner bikes, free parking; from station, take bus #58 to Georg-Hirth-Platz, or walk 15 minutes: go up Goethestrasse and turn right on Pettenkoferstrasse, cross Georg-Hirth-Platz to Uhlandstrasse and find #1; tel. 089/543-350, fax 089/5433-5250, www.hotel-uhland.de, info@hotel-uhland.de).

$ Munich's venerable **International Youth Camp Kapuz-inerhölzl** (a.k.a. "The Tent") offers 400 spots on the wooden floor of a huge circus tent and never fills up. You'll get a mattress (€8.50) or bed (€11), blankets, showers, lockers, washing machines, bike rental, Internet access, and breakfast. It can be a fun but noisy experience—kind of a cross between a slumber party and Woodstock. There's a cool table-tennis-and-Frisbee atmosphere throughout the day and no curfew at night (June–Aug only, catch tram #17 from train station for 17 minutes to Botanischer Garten, direction Amalienburgstrasse, and follow the crowd down Franz-Schrank-Strasse, tel. 089/141-4300, www.the-tent.com, see-you@the-tent.de).

EATING

Munich cuisine is best seasoned with beer. You have two basic choices: beer halls such as the Hofbräuhaus, where you'll find music and tourists; or the mellower beer gardens, where you'll find the Germans. I'm here for the beer-garden fun. But when the wurst and kraut get to be too much for you, Munich has more Michelin-star restaurants than any other German city, plus a galaxy of good, more affordable alternatives.

In beer halls, beer gardens, or at the Viktualien Markt, try the most typical meal in town: *Weisswurst* (white-colored veal sausage) with *süss Senf* (sweet mustard), a salty *Brezel* (pretzel), and *Weissbier*. Also unique and memorable is a *Stecherlfisch*—fish on a stick (great with a pretzel and a big beer).

Beer Halls and Beer Gardens

These are my favorite places to sip or chug some Munich brew. For tips on enjoying this quintessential Munich experience, see the "Munich's Beer Scene" sidebar.

Munich's Beer Scene

In Munich's beer halls *(Bräuhäuser)* and beer gardens *(Biergarten)*, meals are inexpensive, white radishes are salted and cut in delicate spirals, and surly beer maids pull mustard packets from their cleavage.

Beer gardens go back to the days when monks brewed their beer and were allowed to sell it directly to the thirsty public. They stored their beer in cellars under courtyards kept cool by the shade of bushy chestnut trees. Eventually, tables were set up, and these convivial eateries evolved. The tradition (complete with chestnut trees) survives, and any real beer garden will keep a few tables (identified by not having a tablecloth) available for customers who buy only beer and bring in their own food.

Huge liter beers (called *ein Mass* in German, or *ein* pitcher in English) cost about €6. You can order your beer *helles* (light but not "lite"—which is what you'll get if you say *"ein* beer"), *dunkles* (dark), or *Radler* (half lemon-lime soda, half beer). Beer gardens have a deposit system for their big glass steins: You pay €1 extra, and when you're finished, you can take the mug to the return man for your refund, or leave it on the table and lose your money. (Men's rooms come with vomitoriums.)

Many beer halls have a cafeteria system. Eating outside is made more pleasant by the *Föhn* (warm winds that come over the Alps from Italy), which gives this part of Germany 30 more days of sunshine than the North—and sometimes even an Italian ambience. (Many natives attribute the city's huge increase in outdoor dining to global warming.)

Beer halls take care of their regular customers. You'll notice many *Stammtische* (tables reserved for regulars and small groups, such as the "Happy Saturday Club"). They have a long tradition of being launch pads for grassroots action. The Hofbräuhaus was the first place Hitler talked to a big crowd.

The **Hofbräuhaus** is the world's most famous beer hall. Although it's grotesquely touristy, it's a Munich must. Even if you don't eat here, check it out; it's fun to see 200 Japanese people drinking beer in a German beer hall...across from a Hard Rock Café. Germans go for the entertainment—to sing "Country Roads," see how Texas girls party, and watch tourists try to chug beer (daily 9:00–24:00, music during lunch and dinner, Platzl 6, 5-min walk from Marienplatz, tel. 089/290-1360, www.hofbraeuhaus.de). You can drop by anytime for their €20 buffet, order a light meal (my favorite: €6.10 for *ein paar Schweins-wurst mit Kraut*—pork sausages with sauerkraut), or just order a drink. They only sell beer by the one-liter mug (€6.20). And they sell lots—10,000 of these liters every day. The Hofbräuhaus is the only beer hall in town offering

regular live oompah music. This music-every-night atmosphere is thick, and the fat, shiny-leather bands even get church mice to stand up and conduct three-quarter time with breadsticks. They also host a gimmicky folk evening in the upstairs *Festsaal* (2nd floor) nightly from 19:00 to 22:30. Walk up the stairs to the left of the entrance just to see the historic old Hofbräuhaus photos and prints. For more on this Munich institution, see page 55.

Weisses Bräuhaus is much less rowdy than the Hofbräuhaus, but still very touristy. It's famous as the birthplace of Weissbier (fizzy, unfiltered wheat beer). The menu features a full selection of very traditional Bavarian specialties. While the food menu is in English, the drink menu—with a huge and confusing variety of beers—is only in German. The food is very good here, and you'll pay a few extra euros for the history (€5–14 main dishes, daily 9:00–24:00, Im Tal 7, between Marienplatz and Isartor, 2 blocks from Hofbräuhaus, tel. 089/290-1380). Hitler met with fellow fascists here in 1920, when his Nazi party had yet to ferment.

The **Viktualien Markt Beer Garden** taps you into about the best budget eating in town (closed Sun, see page 54). Countless stalls surround the beer garden and sell wurst, sandwiches, produce, and so on. This B.Y.O.F. tradition goes back to the days when monks served beer but not food. To picnic, choose a table without a tablecloth. This is a good spot to grab a typical Munich *Weisswurst* and some beer. The self-service **Suppenküche** (soup kitchen) is fine for a small, cozy, sit-down lunch (€4 soup meals, go straight into market 50 yards from the intersection of Frauenstrasse and Reichenbachstrasse, green shop with black-and-white awning).

Augustiner Beer Garden is a sprawling haven for well-established local beer-lovers on a balmy evening. For a true under-the-leaves beer garden packed with Müncheners—many of whom claim that Augustiner is the best beer in town—this is very good (daily 10:00–24:00, food until 22:00, across from train tracks, 3 loooong blocks from station, away from the center at Arnulfstrasse 52, tram #17, taxis always waiting at the gate).

Tiny **Jodlerwirt** is a smart-alecky, yodeling kind of pub. The food is great, and the ambience is as Bavarian as you'll find. Avoid the basic ground-floor bar and climb the stairs into the action. Good food and lots of belly laughs...completely incomprehensible to the average tourist (Mon–Sat 19:00–3:00 in the morning, food until 23:00, closed Sun, accordion act nightly from 20:30, Altenhofstrasse 4, between Hofbräuhaus and Marienplatz, tel. 089/221-249).

Nürnberger Bratwurst Glöckl am Dom, popular with tourists, offers a classier, fiercely Bavarian evening. Dine outside under the trees; or in the dark, medieval, cozy interior—patrolled by wenches and spiked with antlers. I come here to enjoy the explosively tasty little *Nürnberger* sausages (€7–15 dinners, daily 9:30–24:00, Frauenplatz 9, at the rear of the twin-domed Frauenkirche, tel. 089/291-9450).

The trendier **Andechser am Dom,** on the same breezy square, serves Andechs beer and great food to appreciative regulars. Müncheners favor the dark beer (ask for *dunkles*), but I love the light *(helles)*. The €10.50 *Gourmetteller* is a great sampler of their specialties (€5–15 main dishes, daily 10:00–24:00, Weinstrasse 7, reserve during peak times, tel. 089/298-481).

Altes Hackerhaus is liked by locals—especially the workers from the newspaper—for its traditional *Bayerischer* (Bavarian) fare with a fancier feel. It offers a small courtyard and a fun forest of characteristic nooks festooned with old-time paintings and posters (€10–20 meals, €5–10 wurst dishes, daily 9:00–24:00, Sendlinger Strasse 14, tel. 089/260-5026).

Spatenhaus is the opera-goers' beer garden, serving more elegant food in a woodsy, traditional setting since 1896. Or eat outside, on the square facing the opera and palace. It's pricey, but you won't find better-quality beer-garden cuisine (€20 meals, daily 9:30–24:00, on Max-Joseph-Platz opposite opera, Residenzstrasse 12, tel. 089/290-7060).

In the English Garden: For outdoor ambience and a cheap meal, spend an evening at the English Garden's **Chinesischer Turm** (Chinese pagoda) **Biergarten.** You're welcome to B.Y.O. food and grab a table, or buy from the picnic stall *(Brotzeit)* right there. Don't bother to phone ahead—they have 6,000 seats. This is a fine opportunity to try a *Steckerlfisch,* sold for €9 at a separate kiosk (daily, long hours in good weather, usually live music, tel. 089/3838-7327, www.chinaturm.de). **Seehaus im Englischen Garten** is famous among Müncheners for its idyllic lakeside setting and excellent Mediterranean and traditional cooking. It's dressy and a bit snobbish, and understandably filled with locals who fit the same description. Choose from classy indoor or lakeside seating (€20 meals, daily 10:00–24:00, a fine 15-min hike into the English Garden—located on all the city maps—or tram

#44 or taxi to the doorstep, Kleinhesselohe 3, tel. 089/3816-130).
Seehaus Beer Garden, adjacent to the fancy Seehaus restaurant,
is a less expensive, more casual beer garden with all the normal
wurst, kraut, pretzels, and fine beer at typical prices. What makes
this spot special: You're buried in the English Garden, enjoying
the fine lakeside setting (daily, long hours from 11:00 when the
weather's fine).

Non-Beer Hall Restaurants
Man does not live by beer alone. Well, maybe some do. But for the
rest of us, I recommend the following alternatives to the beer-hall
scene.

On or near Marienplatz
With a Bird's-Eye Marienplatz View: **Glockenspiel Café** is
good for a coffee or a meal with a view down on the Marienplatz
action. There are several dining zones. Locals like the sunroof, but
regardless of the weather, I grab a seat overlooking Marienplatz
(Mon–Sat 10:00–24:00, Sun 10:00–19:00, ride elevator from
Rosenstrasse entrance, opposite glockenspiel at Marienplatz 28,
tel. 089/264-256). For a quicker and less crowded option, go to the
Starbucks-style café on the top floor of **Hugendubel** bookstore
(described under "Shopping" on page 77).

An Elegant Picnic or Café: The crown in **Alois Dallmayr**'s
emblem indicates that the royal family assembled its picnics at this
historic and expensive delicatessen. Explore this dieter's purgatory
and put together a royal picnic to munch in the nearby Hofgarten.
A classy but pricey café serves light meals on the ground floor
(Mon–Fri 9:30–19:00, Sat 9:00–18:00, closed Sun, Dienerstrasse
14, behind New Town Hall). For more information, see page 55.

A Budget Picnic: To save money, browse at Dallmayr's but
buy in the basement **supermarkets** of the Kaufhof stores across
Marienplatz or at Karlsplatz (Mon–Sat 9:30–20:00, closed Sun).

Trendy Eateries South of Marienplatz
The area south of Marienplatz is becoming a kind of Soho, with
lots of fun shops, wine bars, and bistros handy for a healthy and
quick lunch. All of these recommended restaurants are located on
the map on page 83, except for the last one (La Vecchia Masseria),
on the map on page 79.

Buxs Self-Service Vegetarian Restaurant is a cafeteria where
you'll find exactly what you want—as long as it's vegetarian. Fill a
plate with your choice of organic soups, salads, and hot dishes,
then pay by weight (about €10 for a meal, Mon–Fri 11:00–18:45,
Sat 11:00–15:00, closed Sun, non-smoking, at bottom end of
Viktualien Markt at Frauenstrasse 9, tel. 089/291-9550).

Forum Speisecafé—young, stylish, and without a hint of tourism—features international cuisine. It's famous for its creative breakfasts (served all day long) and for its imaginative weekly specials posted outside on the chalkboard (€6 lunches available 11:30–14:30, €10 dinners, open daily 8:00–24:00, later on Fri–Sat, smoky interior or breezy outdoor seating, corner of Corneliusstrasse and Müllerstrasse, tel. 089/268-818).

Stadt Café is a lively, smoky diner/café serving great daily specials (€5-7) and an inventive menu of Italian, German, salads, and vegetarian dishes. This high-energy, no-frills restaurant and its cobbled courtyard is packed with enthusiastic local eaters, newspaper-readers, and coffee-sippers (daily 11:00–24:00, in Munich City Museum, St.-Jakobs-Platz 1, tel. 089/266-949).

Prinz Myshkin is everybody's favorite upscale vegetarian eatery in the old center. You'll find a clever, appetizing selection of €10–13 plates. The decor is mod and the clientele is entirely local (daily 11:30–23:00, non-smoking section doesn't quite work, Hackenstrasse 2, tel. 089/265-596).

Riva Bar Pizzeria is a long, skinny bar with an open oven popping out great pizzas to a crowd of young Müncheners. It's very popular for its fresh, homemade-quality pizzas, pastas, and salads. There's a crowded dining area in back and a few pleasant tables outside on the busy sidewalk (€7–10 pizzas, Mon–Sat 8:00–24:00, Sun 11:00–24:00, 50 yards toward Marienplatz from Isartor at Im Tal 44, tel. 089/220-240).

La Vecchia Masseria is a world apart. As soon as you step inside, you know this is a winner—a favorite among Munich's residents for simple Italian food served inside with a cozy Tuscan farmhouse decor or outside in a beautiful courtyard. Energetic and charismatic Giovanni greets his guests at the door, and the staff makes sure you're never wanting for pizza, pasta, or *vino*. The food is so phenomenal, I'd order high on the menu or try the €22 tasting *menu* (daily 11:30–24:00, reservations smart, cash only, near train station, Mathildenstrasse 3, tel. 089/550-9090, fax 089/550-9091).

TRANSPORTATION CONNECTIONS

Munich is a super transportation hub (one reason it was the target of so many WWII bombs). Train info: tel. 11861 (€0.50/min). For quick help at the main train station, stop by the train service counter in front of track 18. For better English and more patience, drop by EurAide at track 11 (see page 41).

From Munich by Train to: Füssen (hrly, 2 hrs; for a Neuschwanstein Castle day trip, depart at 6:50 and arrive at 9:00 with transfer in Buchloe; or go direct at 8:51 and arrive at 10:57—confirm times at station), **Berlin** (hrly, 7 hrs), **Nürnberg** (hrly,

1 hr), **Würzburg** (hrly, 2 hrs), **Rothenburg** (hrly, 3–4 hrs, 2 transfers), **Frankfurt** and **Frankfurt Airport** (hrly, 4 hrs), **Salzburg** (hrly, 2 hrs), **Reutte,** Austria (every 2 hrs, 3-hr trip, transfer in Garmisch or Kempten), **Vienna** (3/day direct, 5 hrs; otherwise about hrly, 5 hrs, transfer in Salzburg), **Venice** (2/day, 8 hrs), **Paris** (3/day, 9 hrs), **Prague** (3/day, 6–9 hrs—see "EurAide," page 41, for a Prague Excursion pass to supplement your railpass), and just about every other point in Western Europe. Night trains run daily to Berlin, Vienna, Venice, Florence, Rome, Paris, Amsterdam, Budapest, Milan (via Switzerland), Copenhagen, and Prague (at least 7 hours to each city). To use a railpass for a night train to Italy, your pass must include all countries on the train route (i.e., Austria or Switzerland). Otherwise, you must buy a ticket covering the entire trip.

Romantic Road Bus: My long love affair with the Romantic Road bus tour (once the delightful way to connect "Mad" King Ludwig's castles, Munich, Dinkelsbühl, Rothenburg, and the Rhine) is officially dead. In 20 years, the service has gone from an efficient, friendly, and free-with-a-train-pass bus tour to none of the above. It's still famous, but it was recently purchased by a Spanish company and promises only to stray farther from its original intent. I'd stick with the trains for your Bavarian explorations. If you're still interested in the tour, see page 173.

BAVARIA AND TIROL

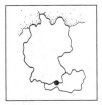

Two hours south of Munich, between Germany's Bavaria and Austria's Tirol, is a timeless land of fairy-tale castles, painted buildings shared by cows and farmers, and locals who still yodel when they're happy.

In Germany's Bavaria, stop by the Wieskirche, a textbook example of Bavarian rococo bursting with curly curlicues, and browse through Oberammergau, Germany's woodcarving capital and home of the famous Passion Play. Tour "Mad" King Ludwig II's ornate Neuschwanstein Castle, Europe's most spectacular.

In Austria's Tirol, hike to the ruined Ehrenberg castle, scream down a ski slope on an oversized skateboard, and then catch your breath for an evening of yodeling and slap dancing.

In this chapter, I'll cover Bavaria first, then Tirol. Austria's Tirol is easier and cheaper than touristy Bavaria. My favorite home base for exploring Bavaria's castles is actually in Austria, in the town of Reutte. Füssen, in Germany, is a handier home base for train travelers.

Planning Your Time

While Germans and Austrians vacation here for a week or two at a time, the typical speedy American traveler will find two days' worth of sightseeing. With a car and more time, you could enjoy three or four days, but the basic visit ranges anywhere from a long day trip from Munich to a three-night, two-day visit. If the weather's good and you're not going to Switzerland, be sure to ride a lift to an alpine peak.

By Car: Here's a good one-day circular drive from Reutte: 7:30–Breakfast, 8:00–Depart hotel, 8:30–Arrive at Neuschwanstein

Highlights of Bavaria and Tirol

to pick up tickets (which you reserved by phone a few days ear-lier—see page 95) for the two castles—Neuschwanstein and Hohenshwangau, 9:00–Tour Hohenschwangau, 11:00–Tour Neuschwanstein, 13:00–Drive to the Wieskirche (20-min stop) and on to Linderhof Castle, 14:30–Tour Linderhof, 16:30–Drive along scenic Plansee lake back into Austria, 17:30–Back at hotel, 19:00–Dinner at hotel and perhaps a folk evening. In peak season, you might arrive later at Linderhof to avoid the crowds. Off-season (Oct–March), start your day an hour later, since Neuschwanstein and Hohenschwangau don't open until 10:00.

The next morning, you could stroll through Reutte, hike to the Ehrenberg ruins, and ride the luge on your way to Innsbruck, Munich, Switzerland, Venice, or wherever.

By Public Transportation: Train travelers can use Füssen as a base and bus or bike the three miles to Neuschwanstein. Reutte is connected by bus with Füssen (except Sat–Sun; taxi €30 one-way). If you're based in Reutte, you can bike to the Ehrenberg ruins (just outside Reutte) and to Neuschwanstein Castle/Tegelberg luge (90 min). A one-way taxi from Reutte to Neuschwanstein costs about €35. Or, if you stay at the recommended Gutshof zum Schluxen hotel, you can hike through the woods to Neuschwanstein (1 hr).

Getting Around Bavaria and Tirol

By Car: This region is ideal by car. All the sights are within an easy 60-mile loop from Reutte or Füssen. Even if you're doing the rest of your trip by train, consider renting a car in Füssen for the day here (as cheap as €50/day; see "Car Rental," page 95).

By Public Transportation: It can be frustrating. Local bus service in the region is spotty for sightseeing. If you're rushed and without wheels, Reutte, the Wieskirche, Linderhof, and the luge rides are probably not worth the trouble (but the Tegelberg luge near Neuschwanstein is within walking distance of the castle).

Füssen, with hourly train connections to and from Munich (hrly, 2-hr trip, some with transfer in Buchloe), is three miles from Neuschwanstein Castle, easily reachable by bus or bike (see "Getting to the Castles from Füssen or Reutte," page 100). **Reutte** is a 30-minute bus ride from Füssen (Mon–Fri 6/day, none Sat–Sun, €3.40; taxis from Reutte to the castles are €35 one-way; to Füssen, €30).

Buses also run from Füssen to **Oberammergau** (4–5/day, less off-season, 1.5 hr, some with transfer in Echelsbacher Brücke; bus often marked *Garmisch*, confirm with driver that bus will stop in Oberammergau). From Munich, visiting Oberammergau directly by train is easier (hrly, 1.75 hrs, change in Murnau) than going to Füssen to catch the bus.

Füssen to **Linderhof** by public transportation will burn most of a valuable sightseeing day; you'll spend more time on the bus (or waiting for it) than you will at the castle. Skip Linderhof—or rent a car for the day. If you must go, take an early bus to Oberammergau, which has direct bus connections to Linderhof (4/day in summer, less off-season, 30 min).

Confirm all bus schedules in Füssen by checking the big board at the bus stop across from the train station, buying a bus timetable (€0.30) at the TI or train station, or calling 08362/939-0505. For longer-distance bus trips (such as to Garmisch or Linderhof), you'll save money if you buy a *Tagesticket* (day pass).

By Tour: If you're interested only in Bavarian castles, consider an all-day organized bus tour of the Bavarian biggies as a side-trip from Munich (see page 72 in the Munich chapter).

By Bike: This is great biking country. Shops in or near train stations rent bikes for €8 to €15 per day. The ride from Reutte to Neuschwanstein and the Tegelberg luge (90 min) is great for those with the time and energy.

By Thumb: Hitchhiking, always risky, is a slow-but-possible way to connect the public-transportation gaps.

Füssen

Füssen has been a strategic stop since ancient times. Its main street sits on the Via Claudia Augusta, which crossed the Alps (over Brenner Pass) in Roman times. The town was the southern terminus of a medieval trade route now known among modern tourists as the "Romantic Road." Dramatically situated under a renovated castle on the lively Lech River, Füssen just celebrated its 700th birthday.

Unfortunately, Füssen is overrun by tourists in the summer. Traffic can be exasperating. Apart from Füssen's cobbled and arcaded town center, there's little real sightseeing here. The striking-from-a-distance **Castle** (Hohes Schloss) houses a boring picture gallery. The mediocre **City Museum** in the monastery below the castle exhibits lifestyles of 200 years ago and the story of the monastery, and offers displays on the development of the violin, for which Füssen is famous (€2.50, €3 includes castle gallery; April–Oct Tue–Sun 10:00–17:00, closed Mon; Nov–March Tue–Sun 13:00–16:00, closed Mon; English descriptions, tel. 08362/903-146).

Füssen's **Model Railroad Museum** (Modelleisenbahn-Museum ZeitscHieneN) is small and overpriced but interesting, featuring model trains of all types—including, probably, the one you rode to town. The collection, gathered over a lifetime by brothers Ulf and Falk Haase, was donated by their mom to the town under the condition that this museum would be built (€4.50, Mon–Fri 10:00–18:00, Sat 10:00–14:00, closed Sun, Kemptener Strasse 7, tel. 08362/929-678). In 2006, the museum may be incorporated into the City Museum or perhaps closed down altogether. Check with the TI for details.

Halfway between Füssen and the border (as you drive, or a woodsy walk from the town) is the **Lechfall,** a thunderous waterfall (with a handy WC).

ORIENTATION

(area code: 08362)
Füssen's train station is a few blocks from the TI, the town center (a cobbled shopping mall), and all my hotel listings (see "Sleeping," page 105). If necessary, the **TI** can help you find a room (June–mid-Sept Mon–Fri 8:30–18:30, Sat 10:00–13:00, Sun 10:00–14:00, less off-season, 3 blocks down Bahnhofstrasse from station, tel. 08362/93850, fax 08362/938-520, www.stadt-fuessen.de). After hours, the little self-service info pavilion (7:00–24:30) near the front of the TI features an automated room-finding service.

Arrival in Füssen: Exit left as you leave the train station (lockers available, €1–2) and walk a few straight blocks to the center of town and the TI. To get to Neuschwanstein or Reutte, catch a bus from in front of the station.

Helpful Hints

Internet Access: Try Videoland (€2/30 min, €3/hr, Mon–Sat 11:00–22:00, Sun 14:00–20:00, Luitpoldstrasse 11, tel. 08362/38300).

Bike Rental: Friendly Christian runs Preisschranke next to the train station (€8/24 hrs; May–Sept Mon–Sat 9:00–19:00, closed Sun; Oct–April Mon–Fri 10:00–18:00, Sat 10:00–15:00, closed Sun; mobile 0178-374-0219 or 0176-2205-3080). Rad Zacherl has a bigger selection, but a less convenient location (€8/24 hrs, mountain bikes-€15/24 hrs, passport number for deposit; May–Sept Mon–Fri 9:00–18:00, Sat 9:00–13:00, closed Sun; Oct–April Mon–Fri 9:00–12:00 & 14:00–18:00, Sat 9:00–13:00, closed Sun; three-quarters of a mile out of town at Kemptener Strasse 26, tel. 08362/3292). For a strenuous but enjoyable 20-mile loop trip, see page 101.

Car Rental: Peter Schlichtling is more central and cheaper (€50/24 hrs, includes insurance, Kemptener Strasse 26, tel. 08362/922-122, www.schlichtling.de) than Hertz (Füssenerstrasse 112, tel. 08362/986-580).

SIGHTS AND ACTIVITIES

Neuschwanstein and Hohenschwangau Castles

The most popular tourist destination in Bavaria is the "King's Castles" *(Königsschlösser)*. With fairy-tale turrets in a fairy-tale alpine setting built by a fairy-tale king, they are understandably popular. The well-organized visitor can have a great four-hour visit. Others will just stand in line and possibly not even see the castles. The key: Phone ahead for a reservation (details below) or arrive by 8:00 to wait in line for tickets (you'll have time to see both castles,

Füssen

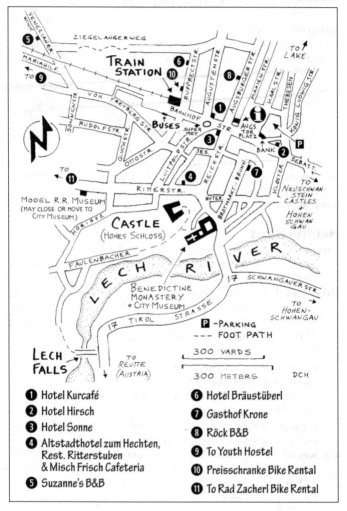

1 Hotel Kurcafé
2 Hotel Hirsch
3 Hotel Sonne
4 Altstadthotel zum Hechten, Rest. Ritterstuben & Misch Frisch Cafeteria
5 Suzanne's B&B
6 Hotel Bräustüberl
7 Gasthof Krone
8 Röck B&B
9 To Youth Hostel
10 Preisschranke Bike Rental
11 To Rad Zacherl Bike Rental

consider fun options nearby—mountain lift, luge course, Füssen town—and get out by early afternoon). Off-season (Oct–June), you have a little more flexibility, but it's still a good idea to get an early start (try to arrive by 9:00).

▲▲▲**Neuschwanstein Castle**—Imagine "Mad" King Ludwig as a boy, climbing the hills above his dad's castle, Hohenschwangau (see below), dreaming up the ultimate fairy-tale castle. He had the power to make his dream concrete and stucco. Neuschwanstein (noy-SHVAHN-shtine) was designed by a painter first...then an architect. It looks medieval, but it's only about as old as the

"Mad" King Ludwig

Ludwig II (a.k.a. "Mad" King Ludwig), a tragic figure, ruled Bavaria for 23 years until his death in 1886 at the age of 41. Politically, his reality was to "rule" either as a pawn of Prussia or a pawn of Austria. Rather than deal with politics in Bavaria's capital, Munich, Ludwig frittered away most of his time at his family's hunting palace, Hohenschwangau. He spent much of his adult life constructing his fanciful Neuschwanstein Castle—like a kid builds a tree house—on a neighboring hill upon the scant ruins of a medieval castle. Although Ludwig spent 17 years building Neuschwanstein, he lived in it only 172 days.

Ludwig was a true Romantic living in a Romantic age. His best friends were artists, poets, and composers such as Richard Wagner. His palaces are wallpapered with misty medieval themes—especially those from Wagnerian operas. Eventually he was declared mentally unfit to rule Bavaria and taken away from Neuschwanstein. Two days after this eviction, Ludwig was found dead in a lake. To this day, people debate whether the king was murdered or committed suicide.

Eiffel Tower. It feels like something you'd see at a home show for 19th-century royalty. Built from 1869 to 1886, it's the epitome of the Romanticism popular in 19th-century Europe. Construction stopped with Ludwig's death (only a third of the interior was finished), and within six weeks, tourists were paying to go through it.

Today, guides herd groups of 60 through the castle, giving an interesting—if rushed—30-minute tour. You'll go up and down more than 300 steps, through lavish Wagnerian dream rooms, a royal state-of-the-19th-century-art kitchen, the king's gilded-lily bedroom, and his extravagant throne room. You'll visit 15 rooms with their original furnishings and fanciful wall paintings. After the tour, you'll see a room lined with fascinating drawings (described in English) of the castle plans, construction, and drawings from 1883 of Falkenstein—a whimsical, over-the-top, never-built castle that makes Neuschwanstein look stubby. Falkenstein occupied Ludwig's fantasies the year he died. Following the tour, a 20-minute slide show (alternating German and English) plays continuously. If English is on, pop in. If not, it's not worth waiting for.

Mary's Bridge (Marienbrücke)—Before or after the Neuschwanstein tour, climb up to Mary's Bridge to marvel at Ludwig's castle, just as Ludwig did. This bridge was quite an engineering accomplishment 100 years ago. From the bridge, the frisky can hike even higher to the *Beware—Danger of Death* signs and an

Neuschwanstein and Hohenschwangau

even more glorious castle view. (Access to the bridge is closed in bad winter weather, but many travelers walk around the barriers to get there—at their own risk, of course.) For the most interesting descent from Neuschwanstein (15 min longer and extremely slippery when wet), follow signs to the Pöllat Gorge.

▲▲**Hohenschwangau Castle**—Standing quietly below Neuschwanstein, the big, yellow Hohenschwangau (hoh-en-SHVAHN-gow) Castle was Ludwig's boyhood home. Originally built in the 12th century, it was ruined by Napoleon. Ludwig's father, Maximilian, rebuilt it, and you'll see it as it looked in 1836. It's more lived-in and historic, and excellent 30-minute tours actually give a better glimpse of Ludwig's life than the more-visited and famous Neuschwanstein Castle tour.

Cost and Hours: Each castle costs €9, a *Königsticket* for both castles costs €17, and children under 18 are admitted free (castles open April–Sept daily from 9:00 with last tour departing at 18:00, Oct–March daily from 10:00 with last tour at 16:00).

Getting Tickets for the Castles: Every tour bus in Bavaria converges on Neuschwanstein, and tourists flush in each morning from Munich. A handy reservation system (described below) sorts out the chaos for smart travelers. Tickets come with admission times. To tour both castles, you must do Hohenschwangau first (logical, since this gives a better introduction to Ludwig's short life). You'll get two tour times: Hohenschwangau and then, two hours later, Neuschwanstein. If you miss your appointed tour time, you can't get in.

If you arrive late and without a reservation, you'll spend two hours in the ticket line and may find all tours for the day booked. A **ticket center** for both Neuschwanstein and Hohenschwangau is located at street level between the two castles (daily April–Sept 8:00–17:00, Oct–March 9:00–15:00, last tickets sold for Neuschwanstein 1 hour before closing, for Hohenschwangau 30 min before closing). First tours start around 9:00 (or 10:00 Oct–March). Arrive by 8:00 in summer, and you'll likely be touring by 9:00. Warning: During the summer, tickets for English tours can run out by 16:00.

It's best to **reserve ahead** in peak season (July–Sept, especially Aug). You can make reservations a minimum of 24 hours in advance by contacting the ticket office by phone (tel. 08362/930-830), e-mail (info@ticket-center-hohenschwangau.de), or booking online (www.ticket-center-hohenschwangau.de). Tickets reserved in advance cost €1.60 extra (per person, per castle), and ticket holders must be at the ticket office well before the appointed entry time (30 min before for Hohenschwangau, 60 min before for Neuschwanstein—this allows you sufficient time to make your way up to the castle). Remember that many of the businesses are owned by the old royal family, so they encourage you to space the two tours longer than necessary in hopes that you'll spend a little more money. Insist on the tightest schedule—with no lunch break—if you don't want too much down time.

Services: The helpful TI, bus stop, ATM, and telephones cluster around the main intersection (TI hours are sporadic, but generally open daily May–Sept 13:00–19:00, Oct–April 10:00–16:00, tel. 08362/819-765, www.schwangau.de). The "village" at the foot of Europe's Disney castle feeds off the droves of hungry, shop-happy tourists. The Bräustüberl cafeteria serves the cheapest grub (often with live folk music). The Alpsee lake is ideal for a picnic, but there are no grocery shops in the area. Your best bet is getting food to go from one of the many bratwurst stands (between the ticket center and TI) for a lazy lunch at the lakeside park or in one of the old-fashioned rowboats (rented by the hour in summer).

Getting to the Castles: From the ticket booth, Hohenschwangau is an easy 10-minute climb. Neuschwanstein is a steep 30-minute hike. To minimize hiking to Neuschwanstein, you can take a shuttle bus (from in front of Hotel Lisl, just above ticket office and to the left) or horse-drawn carriage (from in front of Hotel Müller, just above ticket office and to the right), but neither gets you to the castle doorstep. The frequent shuttle buses drop you off at Mary's Bridge, leaving you a steep 10-minute downhill walk from the castle—be sure to see the view from Mary's Bridge before hiking down (€1.80 up, €2.60 round-trip not worth it since you have to hike up to bus stop for return trip). Carriages (€5 up, €2.50 down) are slower than walking and they stop below Neuschwanstein, leaving you a five-minute uphill hike. Note: If it's less than an hour until your Neuschwanstein tour time, you'll need to hike, and even at a brisk pace, it still takes 30 minutes. For a lazy, varied, and economical plan, ride the bus to Mary's Bridge for the view, hike down to the castle, and then catch the carriage from there back down.

Getting to the Castles from Füssen or Reutte: If arriving by **car,** note that road signs in the region refer to the sight as *Königsschlösser,* not Neuschwanstein. There's plenty of parking (all lots-€4). Get there early, and you'll park where you like. Lot E—past the ticket center and next to the lake—is my favorite.

From **Füssen,** those without cars can catch the roughly hourly **bus** (€1.55 one-way, €3.10 round-trip, 10 min, note times carefully on the meager schedule, catch bus at train station), take a **taxi** (€9 one-way), or ride a rental **bike** (2 miles).

From **Reutte,** take the bus to Füssen (Mon–Fri 6/day, none Sat–Sun, €3.40, 30 min), then hop a city bus to the castle.

For a romantic twist, hike or mountain-bike from the trailhead at the recommended hotel **Gutshof zum Schluxen** in Pinswang (see page 119). When the dirt road forks at the top of the hill, go right (downhill), cross the Austria–Germany border (marked by a sign and deserted hut), and follow the narrow paved road to the castles. It's a 60- to 90-minute hike or a great circular bike trip (allow 30 min; cyclists can return to Schluxen from the castles on a different 30-min bike route via Füssen).

Near Neuschwanstein Castle

▲**Tegelberg Gondola**—Just north of Neuschwanstein is a fun play zone around the mighty Tegelberg gondola. Hang gliders circle like vultures. Their pilots jump from the top of the Tegelberg gondola. For €15, you can ride the lift to the 5,500-foot summit and back down (daily May–Oct 9:00–17:00, Dec–April 9:00–16:30, closed Nov, frequency depends on demand, last lift goes up 10 min before closing time, in bad weather call first to confirm, tel. 08362/98360). On a clear day you get great views of the Alps and Bavaria and the vicarious thrill of watching hang gliders and paragliders leap into airborne ecstasy. Weather permitting, scores of adventurous Germans line up and leap from the launch ramp at the top of the lift. With one leaving every two or three minutes, it's great spectating. Thrill-seekers with exceptional social skills may talk themselves into a tandem ride with a paraglider. From the top of Tegelberg, it's a steep 2.5-hour hike down to Ludwig's castle. Avoid the treacherous trail directly below the gondola. At the base of the gondola, you'll find a playground, a cheery eatery, and a very good luge ride (below).

▲**Tegelberg Luge**—Next to the Tegelberg Gondola is a luge course. A luge is like a bobsled on wheels (for more details, see "Luge Lesson" on page 115). This stainless-steel track is heated, so it's often dry and open when drizzly weather shuts down the concrete luges. It's not as scenic as Austria's Bichlbach or Biberwier (see page 115), but it's handy (€2.50/ride, 6-ride sharable card-€10, July–Sept daily 10:00–18:00, otherwise same hours as gondola, in winter sometimes opens later due to wet track, in bad weather call first to confirm, tel. 08362/98360). A funky cable system pulls riders (in their sleds) to the top without a ski lift.

Ludwig² **Musical**—The newest song-and-dance incarnation of the king's life seems to be big success. Even those who rolled their eyes at its ill-fated predecessor (*Ludwig II: Longing for Paradise,* which went bankrupt a couple years ago) say this show is filled with catchy tunes performed by a great cast. The theater, the Festspielhaus Neuschwanstein, is situated on the beautiful Forggensee lake, an easy cab ride from Füssen. Consider dinner before the show at the adjoining restaurant (€25–110, tickets available at most hotels, Tue–Sun at 19:30, Sat–Sun also at 14:30, no shows on Mon, tel. 08362/507-7333, www.ludwig2musical.de).

Bike Ride around Forggensee—On a beautiful day, nothing beats a bike ride around the bright-turquoise Forggensee lake. This 20-mile ride is almost exclusively on bike paths, with just a few stretches on country roads. Locals swear going clockwise is less work, but either way has a couple of strenuous uphill parts. Still, the amazing views of the surrounding Alps will distract you from your churning legs—so this is still a great way to spend the afternoon. Pack a picnic lunch and figure about three hours round-trip. From Füssen, follow *Ludwig² Musical* signs; once you reach the theater, follow *Forggensee Rundweg* signs.

More Sights in Bavaria

These are listed in driving order from Füssen.

▲▲**Wies Church (Wieskirche)**—Germany's greatest rococo-style church, this "Church in the Meadow" is newly restored and looking as brilliant as the day it floated down from heaven. Overripe with decoration but bright and bursting with beauty, this church is a divine droplet, a curly curlicue, the final flowering of the Baroque movement (donation requested, summer daily 8:00–19:00, winter daily 8:00–17:00, parking-€1, tel. 08862/932-930, www.wieskirche.de).

This pilgrimage church is built around the much-venerated statue of a scourged (or whipped) Christ, which supposedly wept in 1738. The carving—too graphic to be accepted by that generation's church—was the focus of worship in a peasant's barn. Miraculously, it shed tears—empathizing with all those who suffer. Pilgrims came from all around. A tiny and humble chapel was built to house the statue in 1739. (You can see it where the lane to the church leaves the parking lot.) Bigger and bigger crowds came. Two of Bavaria's top rococo architects, the Zimmermann brothers, were commissioned to build the Wieskirche that stands here today.

Follow the theological sweep from the altar to the ceiling: Jesus whipped, chained, and then killed (notice the pelican above the altar—recalling a pre-Christian story of a bird that opened its breast to feed its young with its own blood); the painting of a baby Jesus posed as if on the cross; the sacrificial lamb; and finally, high on the ceiling, the resurrected Christ before the Last Judgment. This is the most positive depiction of the Last Judgment around. Jesus, rather than sitting on the throne to judge, rides high on a rainbow—a symbol of forgiveness—giving any sinner the feeling that there is still time to repent, with plenty of mercy on hand. In the back, above  the pipe organ, notice the empty throne—waiting for Judgment Day—and the closed door to paradise.

Above the entrances to both side aisles are murky glass cases with 18th-century handkerchiefs. People wept, came here, were healed, and no longer needed their hankies. Walk up either aisle flanking the high altar to see votives—requests and thanks to God (for happy, healthy babies, and so on). Notice how the kneelers are positioned so that worshippers can meditate on scenes of biblical miracles painted high on the ceiling and visible through the ornate tunnel frames. A priest here once told me that faith, architecture, light, and music all combine to create the harmony of the Wieskirche.

Two paintings flank the door at the rear of the church. One shows the ceremonial parade in 1749 when the white-clad monks of Steingaden carried the carved statue of Christ from the tiny church to its new big one. The second painting, from 1757, is a votive from one of the Zimmermann brothers, the artists and architects who built this church. He is giving thanks for the successful construction of the new church.

The Wieskirche is 30 minutes north of Neuschwanstein. The Romantic Road bus tour stops here for 15 minutes. You can take a bus from Füssen to the Wieskirche, but you'll spend more time waiting for the bus back than you will seeing the church. By car, head north from Füssen, turn right at Steingaden, and follow the signs. Take a commune-with-nature-and-smell-the-farm detour back through the meadow to the parking lot.

If you can't visit Wieskirche, visit one of the other churches that came out of the same heavenly spray can: Oberammergau's church, Munich's Asamkirche, Würzburg's Hofkirche Chapel (at the Residenz), the splendid Ettal Monastery (free and near Oberammergau), and, on a lesser scale, Füssen's cathedral.

If you're driving from Wieskirche to Oberammergau, you'll cross the Echelsbacher Bridge, which arches 230 feet over the Pöllat Gorge. Thoughtful drivers let their passengers walk across (for the views) and meet them at the other side. Any kayakers? Notice the painting of the traditional village woodcarver (who used to walk from town to town with his art on his back) on the first big house on the Oberammergau side, a shop called Almdorf Ammertal. It has a huge selection of overpriced carvings and commission-hungry tour guides.

▲**Oberammergau**—The Shirley Temple of Bavarian villages, exploited to the hilt by the tourist trade, Oberammergau wears way too much makeup. If you're passing through anyway, it's worth a wander among the half-timbered *Lüftlmalerei* houses frescoed (in a style popular throughout the town in the 18th century) with Bible scenes and famous fairy-tale characters. Browse through woodcarvers' shops—small art galleries filled with very expensive whittled works. The beautifully frescoed Pilate's House on Ludwig-Thomas-Strasse is a living workshop full of woodcarvers and painters in action (free; May–Oct, Dec, and Feb Mon–Sat 13:00–18:00, closed Sun; closed Nov, Jan, and March–April). Or see folk art at the town's Heimatmuseum (Tue–Sun 14:00–18:00, closed Mon; **TI** generally open June–Oct Mon–Fri 8:30–18:00, Sat–Sun 10:00–12:00; Nov–May Mon–Fri 8:30–18:00, Sat 9:00–12:00, closed Sun; tel. 08822/92310, www.oberammergau.de).

Oberammergau Church: Visit the church, a poor cousin of

the one at Wies. This church looks richer than it is. Put your hand on the "marble" columns. If they warm up, they're fakes—"stucco marble." Wander through the graveyard. Ponder the deaths that two wars dealt Germany. Behind the church are the photos of three Schneller brothers, all killed within two years in World War II.

Passion Play: Still making good on a deal the townspeople struck with God when they were spared devastation by the Black Plague several centuries ago, once each decade Oberammergau presents its Passion Play. For 100 summer days in a row, the town performs an all-day dramatic story of Christ's crucifixion (in 2000, 5,000 people attended per day). Until the next performance, in 2010, you'll have to settle for reading the book, seeing Nicodemus tool around town in his VW, or browsing through the theater's exhibition hall (€3.50, German tours daily 10:00–17:00, tel. 08822/945-8833). English speakers get little respect here, with only two theater tours a day scheduled (often at 11:00 and 14:00). They may do others if you pay the €25 or gather 20 needy English speakers.

Sleeping in Oberammergau: **$$ Hotel Bayerischer Löwe** is central, with a good restaurant and 18 comfortable rooms (Db-€56, cash only, Dedlerstrasse 2, tel. 08822/1365, fax 08822/882, www.bayerischerloewe.com, gasthof.loewe@freenet.de, Reinhofer family). **$$ Gasthof zur Rose** is a big, central, family-run place with 21 rooms (Sb-€35, Db-€58, Tb-€75, Qb-€84, kids under 14 cheaper—ask, Dedlerstrasse 9, tel. 08822/4706, fax 08822/6753, gasthof-rose@t-online.de). **$ Frau Magold's** three bright and spacious rooms are twice as nice as the cheap hotel rooms, for much less money (Db-€40–44, cash only, immediately behind Gasthof Zur Rose at Kleppergasse 1, tel. & fax 08822/4340, no English spoken). The **$ youth hostel** on the river is a short walk from the center (€17 beds, includes taxes, breakfast, and sheets, tel. 08822/4114, fax 08822/1695, jhoberammergau@djh-bayern.de).

Getting to Oberammergau: From Füssen to Oberammergau, four to five buses run daily (fewer in winter, 1.5 hrs). Trains run from Munich to Oberammergau (hrly, 1.75 hrs, change in Murnau). Drivers entering the town from the north should cross the bridge, take the second right, and park in the free lot a block beyond the TI. Leaving town, head out past the church and turn toward Ettal on Road 23. You're 20 miles from Reutte via the scenic Plansee. If heading to Munich, Road 23 takes you to the autobahn, which gets you there in less than an hour.

▲▲**Linderhof Castle**—This homiest of "Mad" King Ludwig's castles is small and comfortably exquisite—good enough for a minor god. Set in the woods 15 minutes from Oberammergau and surrounded by fountains and sculpted, Italian-style gardens, it's the only palace I've toured that actually had me feeling envious.

Don't miss the grotto, which is located outside and uphill from the palace; 15-minute tours are included with the palace ticket (€7, daily April–Sept 9:00–18:00, Oct–March 10:00–16:00, last tour 30 min before closing; English tours every 30 min or when 15 gather—sparse off-season, so you may have to wait; parking-€2.50, fountains often erupt on the hour, tel. 08822/92030). Plan for lots of walking and a two-hour stop to fully enjoy this royal park. Pay at the entrance and get an admission time. Visit outlying sights in the garden to pass any wait time. The outside of the palace is undergoing a long-term renovation, with lots of scaffolding. But the interior, freshly refurbished, is glorious. Without a car, getting to (and home from) Linderhof is a royal headache—skip it (but diehards can find details under "Getting Around Bavaria and Tirol," page 93).

▲▲**Zugspitze**—The tallest point in Germany is a border crossing. Lifts from Austria and Germany travel to the 9,700-foot summit of the Zugspitze. You can straddle the border between two great nations while enjoying an incredible view. Restaurants, shops, and telescopes await you at the summit.

On the German side, the 75-minute trip from Garmisch costs €44 round-trip; family discounts are available (buy a combo-ticket for cogwheel train to Eibsee and cable-car ride to summit, drivers can park for free at cable-car station at Eibsee, daily 8:15–14:15 to go up, last cable car down around 17:00, tel. 08821/7970, www.zugspitze.de). Allow plenty of time for afternoon descents: If bad weather hits in the late afternoon, cable cars can be delayed at the summit, causing tourists to miss their train from Eibsee back to Garmisch. Hikers enjoy the easy six-mile walk around the lovely Eibsee (German side, 5 min downhill from cable-car).

On the Austrian side, from the less-crowded Talstation Obermoos above the village of Erwald, the tram zips you to the top in 10 minutes (€32 round-trip, cash only, goes every 20 min, late May–Oct daily 8:40–16:40, tel. in Austria 05673/2309, www.zugspitze.com).

The German ascent from Garmisch is easier for those without a car, but buses connect the Erwald train station and the Austrian lift nearly every hour.

SLEEPING

Prices listed are for one-night stays. Most hotels give about 5 to 10 percent off for two-night stays—always request this discount. Competition is fierce, and off-season prices are soft. High season is mid-June through September. Rooms are generally about 12 percent less in shoulder season and much cheaper in off-season.

Sleep Code

(**€1 = about $1.20, country code: 49, area code: 08362**)
S = Single, **D** = Double/Twin, **T** = Triple, **Q** = Quad, **b** = bathroom,
s = shower only. Unless otherwise noted, credit cards are accepted, English is spoken, and breakfast is included.

To help you sort easily through these listings, I've divided the rooms into three categories, based on the price for a standard double room with bath:

$$$ **Higher Priced**—Most rooms €100 or more.
$$ **Moderately Priced**—Most rooms between €60–100.
$ **Lower Priced**—Most rooms €60 or less.

In Füssen

Though I prefer sleeping in Reutte (see page 116), convenient Füssen is just three miles from Ludwig's castles and offers a cobbled, riverside retreat. It's very touristy, but it has plenty of rooms. All recommended accommodations are within a few blocks of the train station and the town center. Parking is easy at the station. To locate these hotels, see the map on page 96.

$$$ **Hotel Kurcafé** is deluxe, with 30 spacious rooms and all of the amenities. The standard rooms are comfortable, and the newer, bigger rooms have elegant touches and fun decor—like canopy drapes and cherubic frescoes over the bed (Sb-€85, standard Db-€109, bigger Db-€116–141 depending on size, Tb-€127, Qb-€141, 4-person suite-€161, €10 more for weekends and holidays, ask about package deals, cheaper off-season, non-smoking rooms, elevator, parking-€5/day, carries some U.S. newspapers, on tiny traffic circle a block in front of station at Bahnhofstrasse 4, tel. 08362/930-180, fax 08362/930-1850, www.kurcafe.com, info@kurcafe.com, Schöll family).

$$$ **Hotel Hirsch** is a big, romantic, old tour-class hotel with 53 rooms on the main street in the center of town. Their standard rooms are fine, and their theme rooms are a fun splurge (Sb-€56–82, standard Db-€87–133, theme Db-€118–162, prices depend on room size and demand, cheaper Nov–March and during slow times, only the expensive theme rooms are non-smoking, family rooms, elevator, free parking, Kaiser-Maximilian Platz 7, tel. 08362/93980, fax 08362/939-877, www.hotelhirsch.de, info@hotelhirsch.de).

$$$ **Hotel Sonne,** in the heart of town, rents 32 mod, institutional, yet comfy rooms (Sb-€85, Db-€105, Tb-€129, cheaper Oct–mid-June, non-smoking rooms, elevator, kitty-corner from TI at Reichenstrasse 37, tel. 08362/9080, fax 08362/908-100,

www.hotel-sonne.de, info@hotel-sonne.de).

$$ Altstadthotel zum Hechten offers all the modern comforts in a friendly, traditional shell right under Füssen Castle in the old-town pedestrian zone (35 rooms, S-€32, Sb-€45, D-€60, Db-€78–80, Tb-€100, Qb-€116, free parking, cheaper off-season and for longer stays, non-smoking rooms, fun miniature bowling alley in basement, nearby church bells ring hourly at night; from TI, walk down pedestrian street, take 2nd right to Ritterstrasse 6, tel. 08362/91600, fax 08362/916-099, www.hotel-hechten.com, hotel.hechten@t-online.de, Pfeiffer and Tramp families).

$$ Suzanne's B&B is run by a plain-spoken, no-nonsense American woman who strikes some travelers as brusque. Suzanne runs a tight ship, offering lots of local travel advice, backyard-fresh eggs, local cheese, a children's yard, laundry (€25/load), and bright, woody, spacious rooms (Db-€80, Tb-€115, Qb-€145, suite from €120 can hold up to 10—ask for details; attic special: €70 for 2, €100 for 3, €120 for 4; cash only, non-smoking, Internet access €5/hr, exit station right and backtrack 2 blocks along tracks, cross tracks at Venetianerwinkel to #3, tel. 08362/38485, fax 08362/921-396, www.suzannes.de, svorbrugg@t-online.de). Her kid-friendly loft has very low ceilings (you'll crouch), a private bathroom (you'll crouch), and up to six beds.

$$ Hotel Bräustüberl has 16 decent rooms at fair rates attached to a gruff, musty, old beer hall–type place. Don't expect much service (S-€25, Sb-€45, D-€52, Db-€64–78, cash only, Rupprechtstrasse 5, a block from station, tel. 08362/7843, fax 08362/923-951, brauereigasthof-fuessen@t-online.de).

$ Gasthof Krone, a rare bit of pre-glitz Füssen in the pedestrian zone, has dumpy halls and stairs and big, time-warp rooms at good prices (S-€28, D/Ds-€52, extra bed-€26, extra bed for kids under 12-€20, €3 more per person for 1-night stays, reception in restaurant, closed Nov–June, from TI head down pedestrian street, take first left to Schrannengasse 17, tel. 08362/7824, fax 08362/37505, www.krone-fuessen.de, info@krone-fuessen.de).

$ Wilhelm and Elisabeth Röck, a sweet old couple, rent out two rooms in their home a block from the TI (D-€51, Db-€55, Tb-€75, cash only, non-smoking, Augsburgerstrasse 7, tel. 08362/6353, just enough English spoken).

$ Füssen Youth Hostel, a fine, German-run place, welcomes travelers under 27 (€18 dorm beds in 2- to 6-bed rooms, D-€42, €3 more for non-members, includes breakfast and sheets, non-smoking, laundry-€3.20/load, dinner for a few euros, office open 7:00–12:00 & 17:00–23:00, until 22:00 off-season, from station backtrack 10 min along tracks, Mariahilferstrasse 5, tel. 08362/7754, fax 08362/2770, jhfuessen@djh-bayern.de).

In Hohenschwangau, near Neuschwanstein Castle

Inexpensive farmhouse *Zimmer* (B&Bs) abound in the Bavarian countryside around Neuschwanstein, offering drivers a decent value. Look for *Zimmer Frei* signs ("room free," or vacancy). The going rate is about €50 to €65 for a double, including breakfast.

$$ Alpenhotel Meier is a small, family-run hotel with 15 rooms in a bucolic setting within walking distance of the castles, just beyond the lower parking lot (Sb-€46, Db-€77, plus €1.35 "tourist tax" per person, 5 percent discount with cash and this book in 2006, cheaper for longer stays, non-smoking rooms, all rooms have porches or balconies, family rooms, sauna, easy parking, just before tennis courts at Schwangauer Strasse 37, tel. 08362/81152, fax 08362/987-028, www.alpenhotel-allgaeu.de, info@alpenhotel -allgaeu.de, Frau Meier).

$$ Romantic Pension Albrecht, in the shadow of the castle, offers seven rooms in a historic home. Just a three-minute walk from the ticket booth, you enjoy proximity to the castle without all the hustle and bustle. This charming house is a little tired—but at 102 years old, you would be, too. Many of the rooms have balconies, and friendly Frau Strauss—who welcomes her guests as her mother did before her—is happy to share her garden with you (S-€29–35, Sb-€39, Db-€67, more for 1-night stays, cash only, free parking, Pfleger Rothut Weg 2, tel. & fax 08362/81102, www .albrecht-neuschwanstein.de, info@albrecht-neuschwanstein.de).

$ Beim "Landhannes" is a hundred-year-old working dairy farm run by Johann and Traudl Mayr. They rent six creaky, well-antlered rooms and keep flowers on the balconies, big bells in the halls, and cows in the yard (Sb-€30, Db-€60, 20 percent discount for 3 or more nights, cash only, poorly signed in the village of Horn on the Füssen side of Schwangau, look for the farm 100 yards in front of Hotel Kleiner König, Am Lechrain 22, tel. 08362/8349, fax 08362/819-646, www.landhannes.de, mayr@landhannes.de).

$ Sonnenhof is a big, woody, old house with four spacious, traditionally decorated rooms (all with balconies) and a cheery garden. It's a 15-minute walk through the fields to the castles (S-€30, D-€45, Db-€55, cash only; at Pension Schwansee on the Füssen–Neuschwanstein road, follow the small lane 100 yards to Sonnenweg 11; tel. 08362/8420, Frau Görlich).

EATING

In Füssen

Füssen's old town and main pedestrian drag are lined with a variety of eateries. The first three listings cluster on Ritterstrasse, just under the castle, off the top of the main street.

Ritterstuben offers delicious, reasonably priced fish, salads, veggie plates, and a fun kids' menu (€6–12 meals, Tue–Sun 11:30–14:30 & 17:30–23:00, closed Mon, Ritterstrasse 4, tel. 08362/7759). Demure, English-speaking Gabi serves while her husband cooks.

Zum Hechten Restaurant serves hearty, traditional Bavarian fare and specializes in pike *(Hecht)* pulled from the Lech River (€8–12 meals, Thu–Tue 11:00–14:00 & 17:00–20:30, closed Wed, tel. 0836/91600, Ritterstrasse 6).

Misch Frisch is a clever and modern self-service eatery that sells its hot meals and salad bar by weight and offers English newspapers (about €3 for a filling salad, €5 meals, Mon–Fri 11:00–18:00, Sat 10:30–15:00, closed Sun, Ritterstrasse 6).

Hotel Kurcafé's fine restaurant, right on Füssen's main traffic circle, has good weekly specials, plus a tempting bakery (daily 11:30–14:30 & 17:30–22:00, choose between a traditional dining room and a pastel "winter garden," €11 Bavarian BBQ on Fri nights, live Bavarian zither music most Fri–Sat during dinner, tel. 08362/930-180).

TRANSPORTATION CONNECTIONS

From Füssen to: Neuschwanstein (hrly buses, 10 min, €1.55 one-way, €3.10 round-trip; taxis cost €9 one-way), **Reutte** (by bus: Mon–Fri 6/day, none Sat–Sun, 30 min, €3.40 one-way; taxis cost €30 one-way), **Munich** (hrly trains, 2 hrs, some change in Buchloe). Train info: tel. 11861 (€0.50/min).

Romantic Road Buses: I don't recommend the bus (which has declined in value and service over the years), but here's the scoop if you want to take it. The northbound Romantic Road bus departs Füssen at 9:50; the southbound bus arrives Füssen at 19:05 (bus stops at train station). A railpass gets you a 60 percent discount on the Romantic Road bus (without using up a day of a flexipass). For more information, see page 173 in the Rothenburg chapter.

Reutte

Reutte (ROY-teh, with a rolled *r*), a relaxed Austrian town of 5,700, is located 20 minutes across the border from Füssen. It's far from the international tourist crowd, but popular with Germans and Austrians for its climate. Doctors recommend its "grade 1" air. Reutte's one claim to fame with Americans: As Nazi Germany was falling in 1945, Hitler's top rocket scientist, Werner von Braun, joined the Americans (rather than the Russians) in Reutte. You could say the American space program began here.

Reutte isn't featured in any other American guidebook. While its generous sidewalks are filled with smart boutiques and lazy coffeehouses, its charms are subtle. It was never rich or important. Its castle is ruined, its buildings have painted-on "carvings," its churches are full, its men yodel for each other on birthdays, and

lately, its energy is spent soaking its Austrian and German guests in *Gemütlichkeit*. Most guests stay for a week, so the town's attractions are more time-consuming than thrilling. If the weather's good, hike to the mysterious Ehrenberg ruins, ride the luge, or rent a bike. For a slap-dancing bang, enjoy a Tirolean folk evening. For accommodations, see page 116.

ORIENTATION

(€1 = about $1.20, country code: 43, area code: 05672)

Tourist Information: Reutte's TI is a block in front of the train station (Mon–Fri 8:00–12:00 & 14:00–17:00, Sat 8:30–12:00, closed Sun, tel. 05672/62336 or, from Germany, 00-43-5672/62336, www.reutte.com). Go over your sightseeing plans, ask about a folk evening, pick up city and biking maps and the *Sommerprogramm* events schedule (in German only), and ask about discounts with the hotel guest cards. Their informational booklet has a good self-guided town walk.

Helpful Hints

Laundry: There isn't an actual launderette in town, but the recommended Hotel Maximilian lets even non-guests use their self-service machines (see page 118). Or stay at the recommended Gutshof zum Schluxen or the local campground, which both have washing machines and dryers.

Bike Rental: Try Intersport (€15/day, Mon–Fri 8:30–18:00, Sat 8:30–17:00, closed Sun, Lindenstrasse 25, tel. 05672/62352) or Hotel Maximilian.

SIGHTS AND ACTIVITIES

Ehrenberg Castle Ensemble (Festungsensemble Ehrenberg)

Just a mile outside of Reutte are the brooding ruins of four castles that once made up the largest fort in Tirol (built for defense against the Bavarians). Today, these castles are gradually being

Reutte

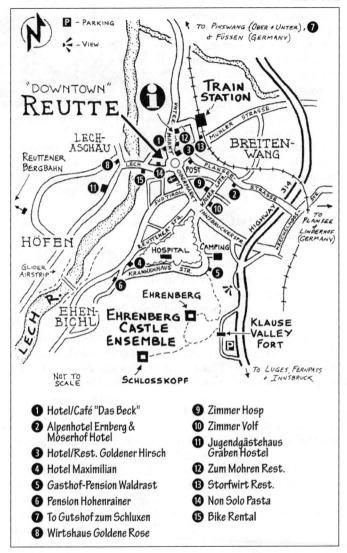

● Hotel/Café "Das Beck"
● Alpenhotel Ernberg & Moserhof Hotel
● Hotel/Rest. Goldener Hirsch
● Hotel Maximilian
● Gasthof-Pension Waldrast
● Pension Hohenrainer
● To Gutshof zum Schluxen
● Wirtshaus Goldene Rose
● Zimmer Hosp
● Zimmer Volf
● Jugendgästehaus Graben Hostel
● Zum Mohren Rest.
● Storfwirt Rest.
● Non Solo Pasta
● Bike Rental

turned into a European Castle Museum, showing off 500 years of military architecture in one swoop (due to be completed in 2007; www.ehrenberg.at). The European Union is helping fund the project because it promotes the heritage of a multinational region—Tirol—rather than a country (the EU's vision includes a zone of regions rather than nations).

Three of the castles cluster together; the fourth (Fort Claudia) is across the valley, though all four used to be connected by walls. The first three—the easiest and most interesting to visit—are described below, from lowest to highest. New signs throughout the castle complex will help you find

your way and explain some background on the region's history, geology, geography, culture, flora, and fauna.

Getting to the Castle Ensemble: The Klause, Ehrenberg, and Schlosskopf castles are on the road to Lermoos and Innsbruck. These are a pleasant walk or a short bike ride from Reutte; bikers can use the *Radwanderweg* along the Lech River (the TI has a good map).

▲**Klause Valley Fort**—At the parking lot at the base of the ruin-topped hill, you'll find the recently modernized remains of a Gothic fortification. It was located on the medieval salt road (which used to be the ancient Roman road, Via Claudia Augusta). Beginning in the 14th century, this fort controlled traffic and levied tolls on all who passed through this strategic valley. Today it houses a new 60-minute multimedia **Sound and Vision Show** about the castles (€10, in English at 18:15 on Tue and Thu, tel. 05672/62007). You'll sit inside the shell of the old castle while the 2,000-year history of this valley's fortresses is projected on the old stone walls and modern screens around you. By early 2006, this will also be the home to an extensive museum about the "castle ensemble." If you're hungry, drop by the nearby café/guest house, Gasthof Klause (closed Mon), which offers a German-language flier and a wall painting of the intact castle.

▲▲**Ehrenberg Ruins**—Ehrenberg, a 13th-century rock pile, provides a great contrast to King Ludwig's "modern" castles and a super opportunity to let your imagination off its leash. Hike up 20 minutes from the parking lot for a great view from your own private

ruins. Facing the hill from the parking lot, find the gravelly road at the *Klause* sign. Follow the road to the saddle between the two hills. From the saddle, notice how the castle stands high on the horizon. This is Ehrenberg (which means "Mountain of Honor"), the first of the four ensemble castles, built in 1296. Thirteenth-century castles were designed to stand boastfully tall. With the advent of gunpowder, castles dug in. Notice the **ramparts** around you. They are from the 18th century. Approaching Ehrenberg castle, look for the small door to the left. It's the night entrance (tight and awkward, therefore safer against a surprise invasion). While hiking up the hill, you go through two doors. Castles allowed step-by-step retreat, giving defenders time to regroup and fight back against invading forces.

Before making the final and steepest ascent, follow the path around to the right to a big, grassy courtyard with commanding views and a fat, newly restored **turret.** This stored gunpowder and held a big cannon that enjoyed a clear view of the valley below. In medieval times, all the trees approaching the castle were cleared to keep an unobstructed view.

Look out over the valley. The pointy spire marks **Breitenwang,** which was a stop on the ancient Via Claudia Augusta. In A.D. 46, there was a Roman camp there. In 1489, after the Reutte bridge crossed the Lech River, Reutte (marked by the onion-domed church) was made a market town and eclipsed Breitenwang in importance. Any gliders circling? They launch from just over the river in Höfen (see "Flying and Gliding," page 114).

For centuries, this castle was the seat of government—ruling an area called the "judgment of Ehrenberg" (roughly the same as today's "district of Reutte"). When the emperor came by, he stayed here. In 1604, the ruler moved downtown into more comfortable quarters, and the castle was no longer a palace.

Now climb the steep hill to the top of the castle. Take the high ground. There was no water supply here—just kegs of wine, beer, and a cistern to collect rain.

Ehrenberg repelled 16,000 Swedish soldiers in the defense of Catholicism in 1632. Ehrenberg saw three or four other battles, but its end was not glorious. In the 1780s, a local businessman bought the castle in order to sell off its parts. Later, when vagabonds moved in, the roof was removed to make squatting miserable. With the roof gone, deterioration quickened, leaving this evocative shell and a whiff of history.

▲**Schlosskopf**—If you have energy left after conquering Ehrenberg, hike up to the mighty Schlosskopf (literally "Castle Head"). When the Bavarians captured Ehrenberg in 1703, the Tiroleans climbed up to the bluff above it to rain cannonballs down on their former fortress. In 1740, a mighty new castle—designed to defend against modern artillery—was built on this same sky-high strategic location. By the end of the 20th century, the castle was completely overgrown with trees—you couldn't see it from Reutte. But today the trees are shaved away, and the castle has been excavated. In 2005, the Castle Ensemble project reconstructed the original equipment used to build this fortress (such as wooden cranes)—and then began using those same means to restore parts of it. By

2007, Schlosskopf will be partially rebuilt, and the 18th-century construction equipment will retire and become part of the exhibit.

In Reutte

Folk Museum (Heimatsmuseum)—Reutte's Heimatmuseum, offering a quick look at the local folk culture and the story of the castles, is more cute than impressive. Ask to borrow the packet of information in English (€2, May–Oct Tue–Sun 10:00–17:00, closed Mon and Nov–April, in the bright-green building on Untermarkt, around corner from Hotel Goldener Hirsch, tel. 05672/72304).

▲▲Tirolean Folk Evening—Ask the TI or your hotel if there's a Tirolean folk evening scheduled. During the summer (July–mid-Sept), Reutte and nearby towns sometimes put on an evening of yodeling, slap dancing, and Tirolean frolic worth the €8 to €10 and short drive. Off-season, you'll have to do your own yodeling. There are also weekly folk concerts featuring the local brass band in Reutte's park (free, July–Aug only, ask at TI). For listings of these and other local events, pick up a copy of the German-only *Sommerprogramm* schedule at the TI.

▲Flying and Gliding—For a major thrill on a sunny day, drop by the tiny airport in Höfen across the river, and fly. A small single-prop plane can buzz the Zugspitze and Ludwig's castles and give you a bird's-eye peek at Reutte's Ehrenberg ruins (2 people for 30 min-€110, 1 hr-€220, tel. 05672/62827, phone rarely answered and then not in English, so your best bet is to show up at the Höfen airport on good-weather afternoons). Or, for something more angelic, how about *Segelfliegen*? For €36, you get 30 minutes in a glider for two (you and the pilot). Just watching the towrope launch the graceful glider like a giant, slow-motion rubber-band gun is exhilarating (May–mid-Sept 12:00–19:00, in good but breezy weather only, find someone in the know at the "Thermic Ranch," tel. 05672/71550 or 05672/64010, or mobile 0676-711-0100).

Reuttener Bergbahn—This mountain lift swoops you high above the tree line to a starting point for several hikes and an alpine flower park, with special paths leading you past countless varieties of local flora. Unique to this lift is a barefoot hiking trail *(Barfusswanderweg)*, designed to be walked without shoes—no joke (€9 one-way, €13 round-trip, flowers best in late July, lift usually mid-May–Oct daily 9:00–11:50 & 13:00–16:30, tel. 05672/62420, www.reuttener-seilbahnen.at).

Near Reutte

▲▲Luge Courses (Sommerrodelbahn)—Near Lermoos, on the road from Reutte to Innsbruck, you'll find two exciting luge courses. Both luges charge the same price (€6 per run, 5- and

Luge Lesson

Taking a wild ride on a luge (pronounced "loozh") is a quintessential alpine experience. It's also called *Sommerrodelbahn* or "summer toboggan." To try one of Europe's great cheap thrills (€2–6), take the lift up to the top of a mountain, grab a wheeled, sled-like go-cart, and scream back down the mountainside on a banked course. Then take the lift back up to the top and start all over again.

Luge courses are highly weather-dependent, and can close at the slightest hint of rain. If the weather's questionable, call ahead to confirm that your preferred luge is open. Stainless steel courses are more likely to stay open in drizzly weather than concrete ones.

Operating the sled is simple: Push the stick forward to go faster, pull back to apply brakes. Even a novice can go very, very fast. Most are cautious on their first run, speed demons on their second...and bruised and bloody on their third. A woman once showed me her journal illustrated with her husband's dried five-inch-long luge scab. He disobeyed the only essential rule of luging: Keep both hands on your stick. To avoid getting into a bumper-to-bumper traffic jam, let the person in front of you get way ahead before you start. You'll emerge from the course with a windblown hairdo and a smile-creased face.

10-trip discount cards) and shut down at the least hint of rain (call ahead to make sure they're open; you're more likely to get luge info in English if you call the TIs, listed below). If you're without a car, these are not worth the trouble (consider the luge near Neuschwanstein instead—see "Tegelberg Luge," page 101).

The short and steep luge: Bichlbach, the first course (330-foot drop over a 2,600-foot course), is four miles beyond Reutte's castle ruins. Look for a chairlift on the right, and exit on the tiny road at the *Almkopfbahn Rosthof* sign (June–Sept daily 10:00–17:00, sometimes opens in spring and fall—especially weekends—depending on weather, closed in winter, call first, tel. 05674/5350, or contact the local TI at tel. 05674/5354).

The longest luge: The Biberwier *Sommerrodelbahn* is a better luge and, at 4,250 feet, the longest in Austria (15 min farther from Reutte than Bichlbach, just past Lermoos in Biberwier—the first exit after a long tunnel). The only drawbacks are its short season and hours (late-May–June Sat–Sun 9:00–16:30 only, closed Mon–Fri; July–Sept daily 9:00–16:30; call first, tel. 05673/2323 or 05673/2111, TI tel. 05673/2922).

▲**Fallerschein**—Easy for drivers and a special treat for those who may have been Kit Carson in a previous life, this extremely remote log-cabin village is a 4,000-foot-high, flower-speckled world of serene slopes and cowbells. Thunderstorms roll down the valley like it's God's bowling alley, but the pint-size church on the high ground, blissfully simple in a land of Baroque, seems to promise that this huddle of houses will survive, and the river and breeze will just keep flowing. The couples sitting on benches are mostly Austrian vacationers who've rented cabins here. Many of them, appreciating the remoteness of Fallerschein, are having affairs.

Getting to Fallerschein: The village, at the end of the 1.25-mile Berwang Road, is near Namlos and about 45 minutes southwest of Reutte. You'll find a parking lot at the end of the road, leaving you with a two-mile walk down a drivable but technically closed one-lane road.

SLEEPING

In and near Reutte
(€1 = about $1.20, country code: 43, area code: 05672)
Reutte is a mellow Füssen with fewer crowds and easygoing locals with a contagious love of life. Come here for a good dose of Austrian ambience and lower prices. Those with a car should make their home base here; those without should consider it. (To call Reutte from Germany, dial 00-43-5672, then the local number.) You'll drive across the border without stopping. Reutte is popular with Austrians and Germans, who come here year after year for one- or two-week vacations. The hotels are big, elegant, and full of comfy, carved furnishings and creative ways to spend lots of time in one spot. They take great pride in their restaurants, and the owners send their children away to hotel-management schools. All include a great breakfast, but few accept credit cards. Most hotels give about a 5 percent discount for stays of two nights or longer.

The Reutte TI has a list of 50 private homes that rent out generally good rooms *(Zimmer)* with facilities down the hall, pleasant communal living rooms, and breakfast. Most charge €15 per person per night and speak little or no English. Reservations are nearly impossible for one- or two-night stays, but short stops are welcome if you just drop in and fill available gaps. Most *Zimmer* charge around €1.50 extra for heat in winter (worth it). I've listed a few favorites below, but the TI can always find you a room when you arrive.

Reutte is surrounded by several distinct "villages" that basically feel like suburbs—many of them, such as Breitenwang
(described below), within easy walking distance of the Reutte
town center. While there are some good hotels in central Reutte
itself, these nearby communities are also worth considering. If you
want to hike through the woods to Neuschwanstein Castle, stay at
Gutshof zum Schluxen (listed on page 119). To locate the recommended accommodations, see the map on page 111.

In Central Reutte
$$ Hotel "Das Beck" offers 16 clean, sunny, modern rooms (many
with balconies) right in the heart of town. It's a great value, and
guests are personally taken care of by Hans, Inge, and Pipi. Enjoy
their homemade marmalade at breakfast in the open kitchen/cof-
fee bar or on the sunny patio. Their small café offers tasty snacks
and specializes in Austrian and Italian wines (Sb-€42, Db-€64–
68, Tb-€83, Qb-€98, non-smoking rooms, free parking, they'll
pick you up from the station, Untermarkt 11, tel. 05672/62522,
fax 05672/625-2295, www.welcome.to/hotel-das-beck, hotel-das
-beck@eunet.at).

$$ Hotel Goldener Hirsch, located in the center of Reutte
just two blocks from the station, is a grand old hotel renovated
with Tirolean *Jugendstil* flair. It boasts 56 rooms and one lonely
set of antlers (Sb-€58, Db-€84, Tb-€117, Qb-€126–142, 2-night
discounts, family rooms, elevator, restaurant—see "Eating," below,
tel. 05672/62508, fax 05672/625-087, www.goldener-hirsch.at,
info@goldener-hirsch.at; Monika, Helmut, and daughters Vanessa
and Nina).

In Breitenwang
Right next door to Reutte is the older and quieter village of
Breitenwang (with good *Zimmer* and a fine bakery). It's a 20-
minute walk from the Reutte train station (at post office round-
about, follow Planseestrasse past onion dome to pointy straight
dome, near the two hotels; the *Zimmer* are mostly along unmarked
Kaiser Lothar Strasse, the first right past this church).

$$ Alpenhotel Ernberg is run with great care by friendly
Hermann, who combines Old World elegance with modern
touches. Nestle in for some serious coziness among the carved-
wood eating nooks and tiled stoves (Sb-€39, Db-€78, less for
longer stays, restaurant, Planseestrasse 50, tel. 05672/71912, fax
05672/191-240, www.ernberg.at, info@ernberg.at).

$$ Moserhof Hotel has 30 new-feeling rooms plus an elegant dining room (Sb-€54, Db-€84, these special rates promised
with this book in 2006—ask for the Rick Steves discount when
you reserve, extra bed-€35, most rooms have balconies, elevator,

Internet in lobby-€3/hr, restaurant, free parking, Planseestrasse 44, tel. 05672/62020, fax 05672/620-2040, www.hotel-moserhof .at, info@hotel-moserhof.at, Hosp family).

$ *Breitenwang Zimmer:* The following *Zimmer* are reasonably priced, comfortable, and quiet, have few stairs, and are within two blocks of the Breitenwang church steeple. **Walter and Emilie Hosp** rent three rooms in a modern house (D-€40, D-€36 for 2 nights or more, extra person-€15, cash only, Kaiser Lothar Strasse 29, tel. 05672/65377). **Irene and Rudolf Volf** rent three rooms closer to Reutte's main drag (D-€40, D-€30 for 2 nights or more, cash only, Kaiser Lothar Strasse 2, tel. 05672/65066).

In Ehenbichl, near the Ehrenberg Ruins

The next three listings are a bit farther from central Reutte, a couple miles upriver in the village of Ehenbichl (under the Ehrenberg ruins). From central Reutte, go south on Obermarkt and turn right on Reuttenerstrasse, following signs to Ehenbichl.

$$ **Hotel Maximilian** is a great value. It includes free bicycles, table tennis, a children's playroom, and the friendly service of the Koch family. Daughter Gabi speaks flawless English. The Kochs host many special events, and their hotel has lots of wonderful extras such as a sauna, a masseuse, and a beauty salon (Sb-€35–45, Db-€70–84, family deals, free and fast Internet in lobby, laundry service-€7/load even for non-guests, good restaurant, tel. 05672/62585, fax 05672/625-8554, www.maxihotel.com, maxhotel@netway.at). They rent cars to guests only (1 VW Golf, 1 VW van, book in advance) and bikes to anyone (€6/half-day, €10/day).

$ **Gasthof-Pension Waldrast,** separating a forest and a meadow, is run by the farming Huter family and their huge, friendly dog, Bari. The place feels hauntingly quiet and has no restaurant, but it does offer 10 nice rooms with sitting areas and castle-view balconies (Sb-€35, Db-€58, Tb-€69, Qb-€92; discounts with this book in 2006: 5 percent for 2 nights, 10 percent for 3 nights or more; cash only, non-smoking, less than 1 mile from Reutte, just off main drag toward Innsbruck, past campground and under castle ruins on Ehrenbergstrasse, tel. & fax 05672/62443, www.waldrasttirol.com, info@waldrasttirol.com).

$ **Pension Hohenrainer** is a big, no-frills alternative to Hotel Maximilian—a quiet, good value with 12 modern rooms and some castle-view balconies (Sb-€23–28, Db-€41–50, cheaper for longer stays, family rooms, free Internet in lobby, restaurant across the street, follow signs up the road behind Hotel Maximilian into village of Ehenbichl, tel. 05672/62544 or 05672/63262, fax 05672/62052, www.hohenrainer.at, hohenrainer@aon.at).

In Other Villages near Reutte

$$ **Wirtshaus Goldene Rose** is officially in the village of Lechaschau but only about a 15-minute walk from the center of Reutte. This no-nonsense, sprawling, traditional hotel—complete with antlers and portraits of the *Kaiser*—makes a good home base for those spending several days in the area who want amenities like easy parking, a restaurant, and a sauna (Sb-€40, Db-€70, from downtown Reutte cross bridge and take the first right, Dorfstrasse 2, tel. 05672/62411, fax 05672/624-117, www.hotel-goldene-rose.at, info@hotel-goldene-rose.at, Klotz family).

$ The homey **Jugendgästehaus Graben** hostel has two to six beds per room and includes breakfast and sheets. Frau Reyman and her son Rudy keep the place traditional, clean, and friendly, and serve a great €6.50 dinner for guests only. This is a super value. If you've never hosteled and are curious (and have a car or don't mind a bus ride), try it. They accept non-members of any age (dorm bed-€20, Db-€45, cash only, non-smoking rooms, Internet access, laundry service, no curfew, less than 2 miles from Reutte, bus connection to Neuschwanstein via Reutte; from downtown Reutte cross bridge and follow main road left along river, or take the bus—1 bus/hr until 19:30, ask for Graben stop, no buses Sun; Graben 1, tel. 05672/626-440, fax 05672/626-444, www.hoefen.at, info@jgh-hoefen.at).

In Pinswang

The village of Pinswang is closer to Füssen (and Ludwig's castles), but still in Austria.

$$ **Gutshof zum Schluxen,** run by helpful Hermann, gets the "Remote Old Hotel in an Idyllic Setting" award. This family-friendly working farm offers modern rustic elegance draped in goose down and pastels, and a chance to pet a rabbit and feed the deer. "Mad" King Ludwig himself is said to have slept here. Its picturesque meadow setting will turn you into a dandelion picker, and its proximity to Neuschwanstein will turn you into a hiker; the castle is just an hour's hike away—see page 100 (Sb-€41, Db-€82, extra person-€22, 10 percent discount for 4 nights or more, Internet in lobby, self-service laundry, free pickup from Reutte and Füssen, good restaurant, fun bar, mountain-bike rental, between Reutte and Füssen in village of Pinswang, tel. 05677/8903, fax 05677/890-323, www.schluxen.com, welcome@schluxen.com).

EATING

In Reutte

The hotels here take great pride in serving local cuisine at reasonable prices to their guests and the public. Rather than go to a cheap restaurant, try a hotel. Most offer €8 to €14 dinners from 18:00 to 21:00 and are closed one night a week. Reutte itself has plenty of inviting eateries, including traditional, ethnic, fast food, grocery stores, and delis.

Restaurant Goldener Hirsch, located in the hotel of the same name, offers local specialties in a traditional setting. If you need a break from Tirolean food, try the tasty vegetable plate, or *Gemüseplatte* (€8–12 entrées, closed Mon, Mühlerstasse 1, tel. 05672/62508).

Storfwirt is *the* place for a quick lunch or light dinner. You can get the usual sausages here, as well as baked potatoes, salads, and pizza. Check for daily lunch or dinner specials (€3–7 meals, Mon–Fri 8:00–24:00, Sat 17:00–24:00, closed Sun, Schrettergasse 15, tel. 05672/625-3920).

Non Solo Pasta, just off the traffic circle, is a local favorite for Italian food (€7–10 entrées, Tue–Fri 11:30–14:00 & 18:00–23:00, Sat–Sun 18:00–23:00, closed Mon, Lindenstrasse 1, tel. 05672/72714).

Zum Mohren, in the heart of Reutte, is known for its grill and game specialties. Check the menu for regionally inspired dishes featuring fresh asparagus, mushrooms, or whatever's in season (€8–14 entrées, Mon–Sat 11:00–24:00, closed Sun, Untermarkt 26, tel. 05672/62345, www.mohren.at).

TRANSPORTATION CONNECTIONS

From Reutte by Train to: Garmisch (every 2 hrs, 1 hr), **Innsbruck** (every 2 hrs, 2.5 hrs, change in Garmisch), **Munich** (hrly, 2.5–3 hrs, change in Garmisch, Pfronten-Steinach, or Kempten).

By Bus to: Füssen (Mon–Fri 6/day, none Sat–Sun, 30 min, €3.40, buses depart from in front of the train station, pay driver). Taxis cost €30 one-way.

By Car into Reutte from Germany: Skip the north *(Nord)* exit and take the south *(Süd)* exit into town. While Austria requires a toll sticker for driving on its highways (€8/10 days, buy at the border, gas stations, car-rental agencies, or Tabak shops), those just dipping into Tirol from Bavaria do not need one.

BADEN-BADEN AND THE BLACK FOREST

Combine Edenism and hedonism as you explore this most romantic of German forests and dip into its mineral spas. The Black Forest, or Schwarzwald in German, is a range of hills stretching 100 miles north–south along the French border from Karlsruhe to Switzerland. Its highest peak is the 4,900-foot Feldberg. Because of its thick forests, people called it black.

Until the last century, the Schwarzwald was cut off from the German mainstream. The poor farmland drove medieval locals to become foresters, glass blowers, and clock-makers. Strong traditions continue to be woven through the thick dialects and thatched roofs. On any Sunday, you will find Germans in traditional costumes coloring the Black Forest on *Volksmärsche* (group hikes—open to anyone; for a listing, visit www.volksmarch.com).

Popular with German holiday-goers and those looking for some serious R&R, the Black Forest offers clean air, cuckoo clocks, cherry cakes, cheery villages, and countless hiking possibilities.

The area's two biggest tourist traps are the tiny Titisee (a lake not quite as big as its tourist parking lot) and Triberg, a small town filled with cuckoo-clock shops. In spite of the crowds, the drives are scenic, the hiking is *wunderbar,* and the attractions listed below are well worth a visit. The two major (and very different) towns are Baden-Baden in the north and Freiburg in the south. Freiburg may be the Black Forest's capital, but Baden-Baden is Germany's grandest 19th-century spa resort. Stroll through its elegant streets and casino. Soak in its famous baths.

The Black Forest

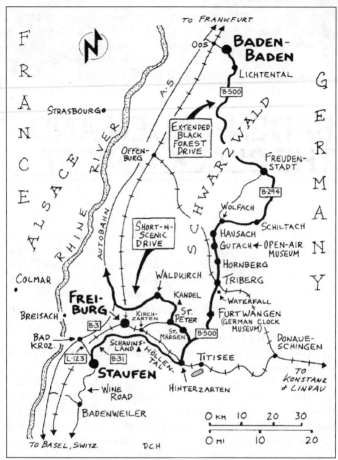

Planning Your Time

Save a day and two nights for Baden-Baden. Tour Freiburg, but sleep in charming and overlooked Staufen. By train, Freiburg and Baden-Baden are easy, as is a short foray into the forest from either. With more time, do the small-town forest medley between the two.

If you're driving, do the whole cuckoo thing—a night in Staufen, a busy day touring north, and two nights and a relaxing day in Baden-Baden. Try this blitz itinerary by car: 11:00–Arrive in Staufen (stroll town, change money, buy picnic), 12:30–Scenic drive to Furtwangen with a scenic picnic along the way, 14:30–Tour clock museum, 15:30–Drive to Gutach Waterfall just south of Triberg, 16:30–Tour Black Forest Open-Air Museum (closed during winter), 18:00–Drive to Baden-Baden, 20:00–Arrive in Baden-Baden. With an overnight in Staufen, you could spend the morning in Freiburg and arrive in Baden-Baden for some spa time (last entry 20:00).

Baden-Baden

Of all the high-class resort towns I've seen, Baden-Baden is the easiest to enjoy in jeans with a picnic. The town makes a great first stop in Germany, especially for honeymooners (1.5-hour direct train ride from Frankfurt's airport).

Baden-Baden was the playground of Europe's high-rolling elite 150 years ago. Royalty and aristocracy would come from all corners to take the *Kur*—a soak in the curative (or at least they feel that way) mineral waters—and enjoy the world's top casino.

Today, the lush town of Baden-Baden (pop. 55,000) attracts a middle-class crowd consisting of tourists in search of a lower pulse, and Germans enjoying the fruits of their generous health-care system.

ORIENTATION

(area code: 07221)

Baden-Baden is made for strolling with a poodle. The train station is in a suburb called Baden-Oos, three miles from the center but easily connected with the center by bus. Except for the station and a couple of hotels on the opposite side of town, everything that matters is clustered within a 10-minute walk between the baths and the casino.

Tourist Information

Baden-Baden's TI is in the ornate Trinkhalle building. Pick up the free monthly events program, *Baden-Baden Aktuell,* with a fine-print map. If you don't like squinting, buy the larger *zu Fuss* map (€0.50). The TI has enough recommended walks and organized excursions to keep the most energetic vacationer happy. If you're headed into the countryside, consider the good €1 Outline Map and the €5 Black Forest guidebook (Mon–Sat 10:00–17:00, Sun 14:00–17:00, WC-€0.50, tel. 07221/275-200, www.baden-baden .com, info@baden-baden.com). The TI shares space with a café (see page 134) and an agency that sells tickets to performances in town (theater, opera, orchestra, and musicals; Tue–Sat 10:00–18:00, Sun 14:00–17:00, closed Mon). Another TI is on the B-500 autobahn exit at Schwartzwaldstrasse 52 (Mon–Sat 9:00–18:00, Sun 9:00–13:00).

Baden-Baden

① To Gasthof Adler & Hostel
② Deutscher Kaiser Guesthouse
③ To Gasthof Cäcilienberg

Arrival in Baden-Baden

By Train: Walk out of the train station (€1.50–3 lockers at platform 1) and catch bus #201 (€2) in front of the kiosks on your right. Get off in about 15 minutes at the Leopoldplatz stop, usually also announced as *Stadtmitte* ("center of town"). Allow €15 for a taxi from the train station to the center.

By Plane: If you arrive at Baden-Baden's airport, catch bus #205 to Leopoldplatz in the city center (€2.50, hourly, runs 6:00–19:00). Bus #205 continues to the Merkur mountain funicular; if you plan on visiting Merkur in the next day, consider buying the €4

24-hour bus pass from the bus driver at the airport—it also covers your trip into town (see "Getting Around Baden-Baden," below for pass details; see "Mini–Black Forest Walks," below, for Merkur details).

Helpful Hints

Horse Races: Book well in advance if you'll be visiting Baden-Baden during its horse races (May 20–28 and Aug 25–Sept 3 in 2006).

Internet Access: Internet and Callshop is open late, has 10 easy-to-use terminals, and sells cheap phone cards (€2/hr, daily 10:00–22:00, Langestrasse 54, at north end of town, tel. 07221/398-400). Weblounge near Augustaplatz has 10 computers (€2.40/hr, daily 10:00–24:00, Eichstrasse 3, on south side of downtown, tel. 07221/397-868).

Laundry: Try SB-Waschcenter (€7 per load, Mon–Sat 7:30–21:00, closed Sun, uphill then down the alley at Scheibenstrasse 14, tel. 07221/24819).

Bike Rental: You can rent cheap bikes at Kurhaus Garage under the casino (€1/2 hrs, €2.50/6 hrs, €5/10 hrs, leave €20 and driver's license as deposit, half-price with *Kurkarte* discount card you'll get from your hotel—described on page 131, rental daily 8:00–18:00, return until 20:00, enter garage through casino and find main payment window near where cars exit, or easier, take the stairs on Kaiserallee behind concert hall, tel. 07221/277-203).

Train Info: The DB Reisebüro on Goetheplatz can help you with train tickets and schedules, saving a trip back out to the station (Mon–Fri 9:00–18:00, Sat 10:00–14:00, closed Sun).

Getting Around Baden-Baden

Within town, only one bus matters. Bus #201 runs straight through Baden-Baden, connecting its Oos train station, town center, and the southeast end of town (every 10 min until 19:00, then about every 20 min until 1:00 in the morning; buy tickets from driver: €2 per person, €4 24-hour pass for 1 adult, €5.20 24-hour pass for 2 adults or a family with 2 kids under age 15). Tickets are valid for 90 minutes, but only in one direction. With bus #201, you don't need to mess with downtown parking.

SIGHTS AND ACTIVITIES

▲▲**Casino and Kurhaus**—The impressive building called the *Kurhaus* is wrapped around a grand casino. Built in the 1850s in wannabe-French style, it was declared "the most beautiful casino" by Marlene Dietrich. Inspired by the Palace of Versailles, it's filled with rooms honoring French royalty who never set foot in the place. But many other French did. Gambling was illegal in 19th-century France...just over the border. The casino is licensed on the condition that it pay about 90 percent of its earnings in taxes to fund state-sponsored social programs and public works. It earns $35  million a year and is the toast of Baden-Baden—or at least its bread and butter. The staff of 300 is paid by tips from happy gamblers.

You can visit the casino on a tour (when it's closed to gamblers, see below), or you can drop by after 14:00 to gamble or just observe. (This is no problem—a third of the visitors only observe.) The place is most interesting in action; you can people-watch under chandeliers. The scene is more subdued than at an American casino; anyone showing emotion is a tourist. Lean against a gilded statue and listen to the graceful reshuffling of personal fortunes. Do some imaginary gambling or buy a few chips at the window near the entrance (an ATM is nearby). The casino is open for gambling daily from 14:00 to 2:00 in the morning (Fri–Sat to 3:00, €3 entry, €1.50 entry with *Kurkarte* discount card from your hotel—see page 131, €5 minimum bet, €10,000 maximum bet, no blue jeans or tennis shoes, tie and coat required and can be rented for €11 with an €11 deposit, passport absolutely required, under 21 not admitted, liveliest after dinner and later, pick up English history and game rules as you enter, tel. 07221/30240, www.casino-baden-baden.de). Lower rollers and budget travelers can try their luck at the casino's €0.50 slot machines *(Automatenspiel)* downstairs (€1 entry fee or included in €3 casino admission, same hours, no dress code).

Casino Tour: The casino gives 30-minute German-language tours every morning from 9:30 to 12:00 (€4, 2/hr, from 10:00 in off-season, last departure at 11:30, call a few days ahead to request an English tour, tel. 07221/30240, otherwise organize English speakers in the group and lobby for information; or just pick up the paltry English brochure). Even peasants in T-shirts, shorts, and sandals are welcome on tours.

Town Orientation: From the steps of the casino, stand between big white columns #2 and #3 and survey the surroundings (left to right): Find the ruined castle near the top of the hill, the rock-climbing cliffs next, the new castle (top of town) next to the salmon spire of the Catholic church (the famous baths are just behind that), the Merkur peak (marked by tower, 2,000 feet above sea level), and the bandstand in the Kurhaus garden. The Baden-Baden orchestra plays here most days (free, usually at 16:00).

Central Baden-Baden

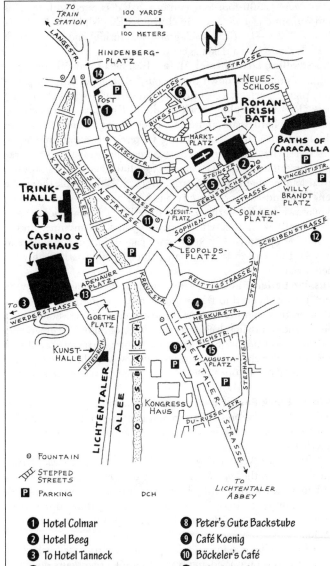

1. Hotel Colmar
2. Hotel Beeg
3. To Hotel Tanneck
4. Hotel Deutscher Kaiser im Centrum
5. Hotel am Markt & Hotel/Rest. Rathausglöckel
6. La Provence Restaurant
7. Weinstube im Baldreit
8. Peter's Gute Backstube
9. Café Koenig
10. Böckeler's Café
11. LaScala Ice Cream
12. Launderette
13. Bike Rental (Kurhaus Garage)
14. Internet & Callshop
15. Weblounge Internet Café

Trinkhalle: Beyond the colonnade on your left is the old *Trinkhalle*—a 300-foot-long entrance hall decorated with nymphs and romantic legends (explained by a €9 English book *Trinkhalle Baden-Baden—Its Tales and Legends*, sold inside) and the home of the TI, a café, and a ticket agency.

▲▲Strolling Lichtentaler Allee—Bestow a royal title on yourself and promenade down the famous Lichtentaler Allee, a pleasant, picnic-perfect, 1.5-mile-long lane. You'll stroll through a park along the babbling, brick-lined Oos River, past old mansions and under hardy oaks and exotic trees (street lit until 22:00), to the historic Lichtentaler Abbey (a Cistercian convent founded in 1245). At the elitist tennis courts, cross the bridge into the free art-nouveau rose garden (*Gönneranlage*, 100 labeled kinds of roses, great lounge chairs, best in early summer). Either walk the whole length round-trip, or take city bus #201 one-way (runs between downtown and Klosterplatz, near the Abbey). Many bridges cross the river, making it easy to shortcut to bus #201 anytime. Biking is another option (see "Bike Rental," page 125), but you'll have to stay on the road in the bike lane, since the footpath is only for pedestrians.

Russian Baden-Baden—Many Russians, including Dostoyevsky and Tolstoy, flocked to Baden-Baden after the czars banned gambling in their motherland. Many lost their fortunes, borrowed a pistol, and did themselves in on the "Alley of Sighs" (Seufzerallee, past the baths just off Sophienstrasse/Vincentistrasse). You'll find a Russian church—and cemetery—just south of the center (€0.70, Feb–Nov daily 10:00–18:00, closed Dec–Jan, near *Gönneranlage* rose garden across river from Lichtentaler Allee).

▲Mini–Black Forest Walks—Baden-Baden is at the northern end of the Black Forest. If you're not going south but want a taste of Germany's favorite woods, consider one of several hikes from town.

The best hike starts from the old town past the *Neues Schloss* (new castle) to the *Altes Schloss* (ruined old castle), which crowns a hill above town, past cliffs tinseled with rock climbers and on to Ebersteinburg, a village with a ruined castle (allow 90 min one-way; only on Sun can you catch bus #215 back into town at 13:36 or 16:36).

For another good hike, take the bus #217 to Rote Lache (bus generally runs only Wed and Sun), then hike two hours downhill via Scherrhof to the Geroldsauer Waterfall. Walk along the waterfall and stream into nearby Geroldsau to catch bus #204 back to Baden-Baden.

For less work and more views, consider riding the cogwheel Merkur Bergbahn to the 2,000-foot summit of Merkur (€4 round-trip, March–Dec daily 10:00–22:00, closed Jan–Feb, take bus

#204 or #205 from Leopoldsplatz to the end of the line and catch the funicular, tel. 07221/277-631). You can also hike down the side of the mountain you rode up, following the trails to Lichtentaler Abbey and then along Lichtentaler Allee into town.

To confirm bus schedules for any of these hikes, ask at the TI or visit www.karlsruhe.de/kvv.

The Baths

Baden-Baden's two much-loved but very different baths stand side by side in a park at the top of the old town. The Roman-Irish Bath is traditional, stately, indoors, not very social, and extremely relaxing...just you, the past, and your body. The perky, fun, and modern Baths of Caracalla are half the price, indoor and outdoor, and more social. Caracalla is better in the sunshine. Roman-Irish is fine anytime. Most visitors do both. Some hotels sell discounted tickets (10–15 percent off) to one or both of the baths; ask at your hotel.

At either bath, your admission ticket works like a subway token—you need it to get out. If you overstay your allotted time, you pay extra. You can relax while your valuables are stowed in very secure lockers. Both baths share a huge underground Bäder-Garage, which is free (for 2 hours) only if you validate your parking ticket before leaving either bath.

▲▲▲**Roman-Irish Bath (Friedrichsbad)**—The highlight of most visits to Baden-Baden is a sober two-hour ritual called the Roman-Irish Bath. Friedrichsbad pampered the rich and famous in its elegant surroundings when it opened 120 years ago. Today, this steamy world of marble, brass columns, tropical tiles, herons, lily pads, and graceful nudity welcomes gawky tourists as well as locals. For €29, you get up to three hours and the works (€21 without the 8-min massage).

Read this carefully before stepping out naked: In your changing cabin, load all your possessions onto the fancy hanger (hang it in locker across the way, slip card into lock, strap key around wrist). As you enter (in the "crème" room), check your weight on the digital kilo scale. Do this again as you leave. You will have lost a kilo...all in sweat. The complex routine is written (in English) on the walls with recommended time—simply follow the room numbers from 1 to 15.

Take a shower; grab a towel and put on plastic slippers before hitting the warm-air bath for 15 minutes and the hot-air bath for five minutes; shower again; if you paid extra, take the soap-brush massage—rough, slippery, and finished with a spank; play Gumby in the shower; lounge under sunbeams in one of several thermal steam baths; glide like a swan under a divine dome in a royal pool (one of three "mixed" pools); don't skip the cold plunge; dry in warmed towels; and lie cocooned, clean, and thinking prenatal thoughts on a bed for 30 minutes in the mellow, yellow, silent room. You don't appreciate how clean you are after this experience until you put your dirty socks back on. (Bring clean ones.)

All you need is money. You'll get a key, locker, and towel. Hair dryers are available (Mon–Sat 9:00–22:00, Sun 12:00–20:00, last admission 3 hours before closing if you're getting a massage, 2 hours before otherwise; men and women together Tue, Wed, Fri–Sun, women separate Mon and Thu; Römerplatz 1, tel. 07221/275-920, www.carasana.de—click on "Friedrichsbad").

About the dress code: It's always nude. Men and women use parallel and nearly identical facilities. During "mixed" times, men and women share only three pools in the center. On Mondays and Thursdays, two of the shared pools are reserved for women only, but the biggest pool is still used by both men and women.

Afterward, before going downstairs, browse through the Roman artifacts in the Renaissance Hall, sip just a little of the terrible but "magic" hot water *(Thermalwasser)* from the elegant fountain, and stroll down the broad royal stairway, feeling, as they say, five years younger—or at least 2.2 pounds lighter.

▲▲**Baths of Caracalla (Caracalla Therme)**—For a more modern experience, spend a few hours at the Baths of Caracalla (daily 8:00–22:00, last entry at 20:30, tel. 07221/275-940, www.carasana .de), a huge palace of water, steam, and relaxed people (professional daycare available).

Bring a towel (or pay €5 plus a €10 deposit to rent one) and swimsuit (shorts are OK for men). Buy a card (€12/2 hrs, €14/3 hrs, €16/4 hrs, 10 2-hour entries for repeat visits or a group cost €105) and put it in the locker to get a key. Change clothes, strap the key around your wrist, and go play. Your key gets you into another poolside locker if you want money for a tan or a drink. The baths are an indoor/outdoor wonderland of steamy pools, waterfalls, neck showers, Jacuzzis, hot springs, cold pools, lounge chairs, exercise instructors (extra fee), saunas, a cafeteria, and a bar. After taking a few laps around the fake river, you can join some kinky Germans for water spankings (you may have to wait a few minutes to grab a vacant waterfall). Then join the gang in the central cauldron. The steamy "inhalation" room seems like purgatory's waiting room, with misty minimal visibility, filled with strange, silently aging bodies.

The spiral staircase leads to a naked world of saunas, tanning lights, cold plunges, and sunbathing. There are three eucalyptus-scented saunas of varying temperatures: 80, 90, and 95 degrees. Follow the instructions on the wall. Towels are required, not for modesty but to separate your body from the wood bench. The highlight is the Arctic bucket in the shower room. Pull the chain. Only rarely will you feel so good. And you can do this over and over. As you leave, take a look at the Roman bath that Emperor Caracalla soaked in to conquer his rheumatism nearly 2,000 years ago (free, in the underground Bäder-Garage between the two spas).

SLEEPING

The TI can nearly always find you a room—but don't use the TI for places listed here, or you'll pay more. Go direct! The only tight times are during the horse races (May 20–28 and Aug 25–Sept 3 in 2006). If you arrive at Baden-Baden's Oos station, you can stay near the station (see page 133). But I'd hop on bus #201, which goes to the center of town (and most of the recommended hotels), and then follows the river (and Lichtentaler Allee) to the Abbey (and more hotels). Hotel am Markt, clearly the best value, is worth calling in advance.

All hotels and pensions are required to extract an additional €3.10 per person, per night "spa tax." This comes with a "guest card" *(Kurkarte)*, offering small discounts on tourist admissions around town (including casino entry and bike rental).

In the Center
For locations, see map on page 127.

$$$ Hotel Colmar, run with a personal touch by the Özcan family, offers 26 pastel-elegant rooms, some with balconies (Sb-€75–82, Db-€95, 2-room apartment Db-€110, extra bed-€30, prices guaranteed through 2006 with this book, non-smoking rooms, elevator, parking-€9/day, Lange Strasse 34, tel. 07221/93890, fax 07221/938-950, www.hotel-colmar.de, info@hotel-colmar.de).

$$$ Hotel Beeg rents 15 attractive and comfortable rooms, run from a delectable pastry shop/café on the ground floor. While it's wonderfully located on a little square in a pedestrian zone and

---

Sleep Code

(€1 = about $1.20, country code: 49, area code: 07221)
S = Single, **D** = Double/Twin, **T** = Triple, **Q** = Quad, **b** = bathroom, **s** = shower only. Unless otherwise noted, credit cards are accepted, English is spoken, and breakfast is included.

To help you sort easily through these listings, I've divided the rooms into three categories based on the price for a standard double room with bath:

  $$$ Higher Priced—Most rooms €90 or more.
   $$ Moderately Priced—Most rooms between €70–90.
    $ Lower Priced—Most rooms €70 or less.

it faces the warm baths, the staff can be a bit chilly (Sb-€80, Db-€100, balcony-€10 extra, apartment Tb-€150, elevator, reception in café, on Römerplatz at Gernsbacher Strasse 44, tel. 07221/36760, fax 07221/367-610, hccbeeg@t-online.de, Herr Beeg).

$$$ Hotel Tanneck is a funky, rambling, late-19th-century place where Persian rugs clash with flowery wallpaper. Perched on a hill behind the casino, it was once a sanitarium for the rich and aimless. Its 17 spacious rooms are now presided over by common-sense den mother Heidi (S-€31, Sb-€70–75, Ds-€80, Db-€85–100, Tb-€112–118, Qb-€138, Quint/b-€159, baby crib-€8, ground-floor rooms, family rooms, several balconies—my favorites face the south, laundry €6–8 per load, 7-min walk from casino or bus #208 stops right in front, Werderstrasse 14, tel. 07221/23035, fax 07221/38327, www.hotel-tanneck.com, info@hotel-tanneck.com).

$$$ Hotel Deutscher Kaiser im Centrum, not to be con-fused with the Deutscher Kaiser hotel below, has 28 simple, clean rooms, a friendly reception staff, and a cheerful breakfast room. It's centrally located on a quiet street, just minutes from the hubbub of town (Sb-€77–82, Db-€92–98, less Nov–March, non-smoking, Merkurstrasse 9, tel. 07221/2700, fax 07221/270-270, www .deutscher-kaiser-baden-baden.de, info@deutscher-kaiser-baden -baden.de).

$$ Hotel am Markt is a warm, 25-room, family-run hotel with all the comforts a commoner could want in a peaceful, cen-tral, nearly traffic-free location, two cobbled blocks from the baths (S-€30–32, Sb-€42–47, D-€60–62, Db-€74–80, Tb-€90, extra bed-€15, Marktplatz 18, tel. 07221/27040, fax 07221/270-444, www.hotel-am-markt-baden.de, info@hotel-am-markt-baden .de, Herr und Frau Bogner-Schindler and Frau Jung). For roman-tics, the church bells blast charmingly through each room every quarter hour from 6:15 until 22:00; for others, they're a nuisance. Otherwise, quiet rules. The ambience and the clientele make killing time on their small terrace a joy. To reach the hotel from Leopoldsplatz, locate McDonald's where Langestrasse hits the square. Walk three minutes up Langestrasse (4 sets of stairs, past stone giant) to the red-spired church on Marktplatz. By car, follow signs for *Therme* until you reach Sophienstrasse, then look for little green hotel signs leading you up the hill.

$$ Hotel Rathausglöckel, around the corner and below the Hotel am Markt at Steinstrasse 7, is a 16th-century guest house with nine cozy rooms and steep stairs (Sb-€60, Db-€60–80, 3rd person-€20, 2-room apartment with kitchen-€80–150, church bells every 15 min 6:15–22:00, parking-€6/day, tel. 07221/90610, fax 07221/906-161, www.rathausgloeckel.de, info@rathausgloeckel.de, kind Michael Rothe). To reach the hotel on foot, follow the directions for Hotel am Markt, above, but turn right at the top of the stairs.

Away from the Center

The following two listings are southeast of the center, across the Oosbach River from Lichtentaler Allee (for either hotel, take bus #201 from station, passing through center, to stop noted below).

$ Deutscher Kaiser, with spacious old rooms, is a big, traditional guesthouse run by Frau Peter, who alternates between being kind or brusque. Herr Peter cooks fine local-style meals (€7–15) in the hotel restaurant. It's right on the bus #201 line (Eckerlestrasse stop, 20 min from train station) or a 25-minute stroll from the city center down polite Lichtentaler Allee—cross the river at the green Restaurant Deutscher Kaiser sign, then turn right (S-€33, Sb-€46–49, D-€46–49, Db-€59–67, discounts on their Web site, non-smoking rooms, Internet access in lobby, free and easy parking, Hauptstrasse 35, tel. 07221/72152, fax 07221/72154, www .hoteldk.de, info@hoteldk.de). Drivers: From the autobahn, skip the town center by following Congress signs into Michaelstunnel. Take the tunnel's first exit, then another right at the end of the exit (direction Lichental). Outside, the hotel is about a half-mile down on the left. From the Black Forest, follow Zentrum signs. Just 10 yards after the Aral gas station, turn left down the small road to Hauptstrasse. For location, see map on page 127.

$ Gasthof Cäcilienberg is farther out, but still on the bus line at the end of Lichtentaler Allee (Brahmsplatz stop). It's a good fallback if the other recommended hotels are full (9 rooms, S-€35, Sb-€41, D-€45, Db-€52, cash only, closed Nov, sits above a restaurant, Geroldsauer Strasse 2, tel. 07221/72297, fax 07221/70459, a little English spoken).

Near the Station

Baden-Baden's train station is in Baden-Oos, three miles from the center (connected by bus #201).

$$ Gasthof Adler, near the train station, is clean, simple, friendly, and on a very busy intersection; ask for *ruhige Seite,* the quiet side (S-€33, Ss-€36, Sb-€45, D-€59, Ds-€64, Db-€69–79, non-smoking rooms, Kermit-green bathrooms; veer right from station, walk 3 blocks passing post office to stoplight, hotel is on left corner, Ooser Hauptstrasse 1, tel. 07221/61858 fax 07221/17145, troger.adler@t-online.de, Herr and Frau Troger speak a little English). Bus #201 stops across the street.

$ Werner Dietz Hostel, between the station and the center, has the cheapest beds in town (€18 per bed in 4- to 6-bed dorms, €3 less for 2 nights or more, €3 more if you're over 26, non-members pay €3.10 extra, S/D rooms €5 extra per person, includes sheets and breakfast, cash only, 23:30 curfew; bus #201 from station or downtown to Grosse Dollenstrasse—announced as *Jugendherberge,* about 7 stops from station, 5 from downtown; it's a steep, well-marked, 10-min climb from there, Hardbergstrasse 34; tel. 07221/52223, fax 07221/60012, jh-baden-baden@t-online .de). They give discount coupons (€2) for both city baths and serve inexpensive meals. Drivers: After the freeway to Baden-Baden ends, turn left at the first light and follow the signs. Wind your way uphill to the big, modern hostel next to the public swimming pool. For the hostel's location, see the map on page 124.

EATING

Hotel Rathausglöckel's restaurant, personal and homey, has long had a good reputation and great food. In the 16th century, prisoners were granted a last meal here before being executed. Eat here if it's the last thing you do (€8–15 entrées, Thu–Sun 11:30–14:00 & 18:00–21:30, Wed 18:00–21:30, closed Mon–Tue, reservations smart in winter, Steinstrasse 7, tel. 07221/90610, Michael).

La Provence—with a romantic setting, an eclectic menu, and good food—is popular, especially on weekends (€10–20 entrées, Mon–Fri 17:00–23:00, Sat–Sun 12:00–23:00, reservations smart, from Marktplatz hike up to Schloss Strasse 20, tel. 07221/216-515).

At **Weinstube im Baldreit,** whether you'll be having a meal or just a glass of wine, choose between their terrace courtyard and their cozy cellar (€8–14 meals, Tue–Sun from 17:00, closed Mon; from Langestrasse walk up Büttenstrasse, turn left just before the steep staircase, Küferstrasse 3; tel. 07221/23136, fax 07221/82662).

Peter's Gute Backstube ("am Leo"), a fun self-service place offering salads, pasta, fish, omelettes, and pastries, is where commoners pile their plates high. The lively staff dons lederhosen for Oktoberfest, Hawaiian shirts in sunny weather, and striped shirts for the horse races (€5 entrées, Mon–Fri 6:30–19:00, Sat 6:30–18:00, Sun 8:00–19:00, free coffee and tea refills, on Leopoldsplatz at Sophienstrasse 4, tel. 07221/392-817).

Café Koenig is *the* place to spend too much for an elegant, 19th-century cup of coffee (daily 9:00–18:30, fine shady patio, look for sign with squiggly script, just before Augustaplatz at Lichtentaler Strasse 12, tel. 07221/23573).

In der Trinkhalle, another swanky coffee joint, has comfy leather sofas, international newspapers and magazines, and a casino-view terrace (daily 10:00–24:00, next to TI in Trinkhalle building at Kaiserallee 3, tel. 07221/302-905).

For a slice of Black Forest cake, try Café Koenig (see above) or **Böckeler's Café** (Mon–Sat 8:00–18:00, Sun 9:30–18:00, Langestrasse 40-42, tel. 07221/949-594).

For good gelato or fancy ice-cream desserts and prime people watching, stop by **LaScala,** just off Leopoldplatz (daily 9:30–22:30, Lange Strasse 1, next to McDonald's).

TRANSPORTATION CONNECTIONS

From Baden-Baden by Train to: Freiburg (hrly, 45 min, sometimes with a change in Offenburg), **Triberg** (hrly, 60 min), **Heidelberg** (hrly, 60 min, catch Castle Road bus to Rothenburg), **Munich** (hrly, 4 hrs, some direct but most with 1–2 changes), **Frankfurt** (2/hr, 1.5 hrs, most with a change in Mannheim or Karlsruhe), **Frankfurt Airport** (every 2 hrs direct, 1.5 hrs, or hrly with a change in Karlsruhe, 1.5 hrs), **Koblenz** (hrly, 2.5 hrs with a change), **Mainz am Rhine** (hrly, 2 hrs, some direct but most with 1 change), **Strasbourg** (9/day, 90 min, sometimes with a change in Appenweier), **Bern** (hrly, 3.5 hrs, change in Basel). Train info: tel. 11861 (€0.50/min).

Freiburg

Freiburg im Breisgau is worth a quick look, if for nothing else than to appreciate its thriving center and very human scale. Bikers and hikers seem to outnumber cars, and trams run everywhere. This "sunniest town in Germany," with 30,000 students, feels like the university town that it is. Freiburg (FRY-burg), bombed nearly flat in 1944, skillfully put itself back together. It feels cozy, almost Austrian; in fact, it was Hapsburg territory for 500 years. This "capital" of the Schwarzwald, exuding an "I could live here" appeal, is surrounded by lush forests and filled with environmentally aware people so dedicated to solar power that they host an annual Intersolar trade fair (June 22–24 in 2006).

Marvel at the number of pedestrian-only streets. Freiburg's trademark is its system of *Bächle*, tiny streams running down each street. These go back to the Middle Ages (serving as fire protection, cattle refreshment, and a constantly flushing disposal system). Local lore says that if you fall into a *Bächle*, you are destined to marry a Freiburger. A sunny day turns any kid-at-heart into a puddle-stomper. Enjoy the ice cream and street-singing ambience of the cathedral square, which has a great produce and craft market (Mon–Sat 7:30–13:00, biggest Wed and Sat, closed Sun). To get a glimpse of the historic Altstadt (old town), be sure to stroll down the street named Gerberau and marvel at 15th-century houses and medieval city gates (Martinstor and Schwabentor).

ORIENTATION

(area code: 0761)

Tourist Information

Freiburg's busy but helpful TI sells three unnecessary city guide-books: The €4 guide has tons of practical information, the €5 city guide with photos has the most information on sights, and the €7 book is geared toward backpacker types, with lots of bar and nightlife suggestions. Persistently ask for the free city map (or €0.50 will buy you a better map—without the hassle).

The TI also offers a room-booking service (€3 per booking for Freiburg and Black Forest area), German-English **walking tours** (€7, 2 hrs, April–Oct daily at 10:30, none off-season), and lots of information on the Black Forest region (including a €5 book; TI open June–Sept Mon–Fri 9:30–20:00, Sat 9:30–17:00, Sun 10:00–12:00; Oct–May Mon–Fri 9:30–18:00, Sat 9:30–14:30, Sun 10:00–12:00; hotel availability board in front, free WC around corner, tel. 0761/388-1880, www.freiburg.de).

Arrival in Freiburg

Walk out of the bustling train station (€1.50–3 lockers, WC-€0.80, bus station next door to the right), cross the street, and head straight up Eisenbahnstrasse, the tree-lined boulevard (passing the post office). Within three blocks, you'll take an underpass under a busy road; as you emerge, the TI is immediately on your left and the town center is dead ahead.

Helpful Hints

Internet Access: Get online at Uni Kopie + Druck (€3.50/hr, Mon–Fri 8:30–19:00, Sat 9:30–16:00, closed Sun, Niemens-strasse 11). Or do your laundry while surfing the Net at Wash Tours (€6 per load, Mon–Fri 9:00–19:00, Sat until 18:00, closed Sun, Salzstrasse 22, tel. 0761/288-866). Both places are close to Martinstor.

Bike Rental: Try Mobile near the station and pick up a free route map (€5/3 hrs, €9.50/6 hrs, €12.50/24 hrs, €50 cash and pass-port for deposit, helmet and lock extra, daily 5:00–24:00; from bus station, cross tram bridge over train tracks to round building on left and walk downstairs; on Wentzingerstrasse, tel. 0761/292-7998, info@mobile-freiburg.com).

SIGHTS

▲**Cathedral (Münster)**—This impressive church, completed in 1513, took more than three centuries to build, ranging in style from late Romanesque to lighter, brighter Gothic. It was virtually the only building in town to survive WWII bombs. The lacy tower *(Münsterturm)*, considered by many the most beautiful around, is as tall as the church is long...and not worth the 329-step ascent (€1.50, Mon–Sat 9:30–17:00, Sun 13:00–17:00). From this lofty perch, watchmen used to scan the town for fires. While you could count the 123 representations of Mary throughout the church, most gawk at the "mooning" gargoyle and wait for rain.

Browse the market in the square. The ornate Historisches Kaufhaus, across from the church, was a trading center in the 16th century.

Augustiner Museum—This offers a good look at Black Forest art and culture through the ages. While there are no descriptions in English, just taking a look at the collection is interesting. Highlights are downstairs: a close-up look at some of the Münster's original medieval stained glass and statuary (€2, €4 family card, Tue–Sun 10:00–17:00, closed Mon, 2 blocks south of cathedral in big yellow building on Augustinerplatz, tel. 0761/201-2531). The historic building that houses the museum is undergoing extensive renovations until 2010, but will remain open.

Schlossberg (Castle Hill)—Schlossberg towers over the east end of Freiburg's old town. It was named Castle Hill because a 17th-century fort once stood here, built by the French to control the citizens of Freiburg during a period of French occupation. Schlossberg today is popular for its views over the city. Though the old fort is long gone, a new modern lookout tower (100 feet high) stands where the French Fort d'Aigle (eagle tower) once stood.

To get to the top of Schlossberg, you can hike or take an elevator from Schwabentor, the half-timbered tower at the east end of the old town. From the tower, look for the footbridge on Oberlinden street. Cross the bridge and hike up 10 minutes (to the left), or continue straight through the tunnel to the elevator *(Aufzug)*. At the top of the elevator and trail, you'll come to the restaurant Greiffenegg Schlössle (see "Eating," below). From there, walk another seven minutes up to the viewpoint. To continue 20 more minutes to the Fort d'Aigle lookout tower from the viewpoint, walk the level path to the left (with your back to the benches), then veer right uphill at the big white cross (look for small silver signs pointing through forest).

Schauinsland—Freiburg's own mountain, while little more than an oversized hill, is nine miles southeast of the center. This viewpoint, which won't wow Americans from Colorado, offers the handiest panorama view of the Schwarzwald for those without wheels. A gondola system, one of Germany's oldest, was designed for Freiburgers relying on public transportation (€10.70 round-trip, May–Oct daily 9:00–17:00, May–June until 18:00 Sat–Sun, Nov–April daily 9:30–17:00, catch tram #4 from town center or from tram bridge over the tracks at train station to the end, then take bus #21 seven stops to Talstation stop for gondola, tel. 0761/292-930, www.bergwelt-schauinsland.de). At the 4,000-foot summit, you'll find a view restaurant, pleasant circular walks, and the Schniederli Hof, a 1592 farmhouse museum. A tower on a nearby peak offers an even more commanding Black Forest view.

Nightlife—Night owls flock around the Martinstor in the area affectionately called Freiburg's "Bermuda Triangle." Take the street to your right just before going through the gate and get sucked in. Look at the Burger King ahead of you; mischievous Puck does a little dance and plays the pan pipes. He's a fitting mascot for a district known for its fun, colorful bars.

SLEEPING

(€1 = about $1.20, country code: 49, area code: 0761)
Though I prefer nights in sleepy Staufen (see page 141), many will enjoy a night in lively Freiburg. Prices include breakfast, and English is spoken. Hotel Alleehaus offers the most value for your money.

In the Town Center

Hotels in central Freiburg are convenient but overpriced.

$$$ Hotel Barbara, near the train station, has 21 fine and bright rooms (Sb-€69–79, Db-€92–109, extra bed-€20, prices €10 higher during fairs, nearby parking garage-€9/day, on quiet street 2 min from station, head toward TI but turn left at post office to Poststrasse 4, tel. 0761/296-250, fax 0761/26688, www.hotel-barbara.de, mail@hotel-barbara.de, friendly Erika and Armin Wahl).

$$$ City Hotel is business-class sterile with 42 clean, modern rooms. It's just off the main shopping street, a five-minute walk from the TI (Sb-€74–79, Db-€98–112, 3rd person-€25, elevator, parking-€8/day, Weberstrasse 3, tel. 0761/388-070, fax 0761/388-0765, www.cityhotelfreiburg.de, city.hotel.freiburg@t-online.de).

$$$ Markgräfler Hof is overpriced, but the rooms are clean with modern comforts, and the location is good. This place works if you can't get in anywhere else (Sb-€82–98, Db-€100–135, Gerberau 22, tel. 0761/32540, fax 0761/296-4949, www.markgraeflerhof.de, info@markgraeflerhof.de).

Outside the Town Center

These listings are a much better value, a 15-minute walk or easy bus or tram ride from the station but still handy to the center.

$$ Hotel Alleehaus is tops. Located on the edge of the center on a quiet, leafy street in a big house that feels like home, its 19 rooms are thoughtfully decorated, comfy, and warmly run by Bernd, Claudia, and their team (S-€46, Sb-€62–72, small Db-€80, larger Db-€92, suite Db-€98, Tb-€125, Qb-€145, reception closed 19:30–6:00, call by 18:00 if arriving later than 19:30, good buffet breakfast, non-smoking rooms, parking-€6/day, Marienstrasse 7, tram #4 from station to Holzmarkt, near intersection with Wallstrasse, tel. 0761/387-600, fax 0761/387-6099, www.hotel -alleehaus.de, wohlfuehlen@hotel-alleehaus.de).

$$ Hotel am Stadtgarten is on the opposite side of town (10-min walk from TI) with 37 comfortable rooms—some new and all heavy on beige (Sb-€57–70, Db-€72–85, higher prices are for May–Oct, Tb-€109, Qb-€133, Quint/b-€157, usually free parking nearby or pay €6/day, bike rental-€9/day, coupons for local restaurants and discounts for walking tours; take tram #5 or #6 from station 3 stops to Siegesdenkmal, walk 1 block in direction tram is going, then turn right at Bernhardstrasse, the hotel is at intersection with Karlstrasse; tel. 0761/282-9002, fax 0761/282-9022, www.hotelamstadtgarten.de, info@hotelamstadtgarten.de).

$ Black Forest Hostel has 105 of the cheapest beds in town. Run by friendly Tania, with a young, bohemian attitude, it's bare-bones simple (€12–20 per person in 3- to 20-bed rooms, S-€27, D-€44, cash only, non-smoking, lockers, Internet access in lobby, self-service kitchen, laundry facilities, 24-hour reception, no curfew, Kartäuserstrasse 33, 20-min walk from station or tram #1 direction Littenweiler, get off at Oberlinden stop, tel. 0761/881-7870, fax 0761/881-7895, www.blackforest-hostel.de, backpacker@blackforest-hostel.de).

$ Freiburg Youth Hostel is a big, modern option on the east edge of town (€20 per bed including sheets and breakfast, €3 less for 2 nights or more, "seniors" over 26 pay €3 extra, non-members pay €3.10 extra, 2:00 curfew, Kartäuserstrasse 151, tram #1 direction Littenweiler to Römerhof stop, then 10-min walk, tel. 0761/67656, fax 0761/60367, www.jugendherberge-freiburg.de, info@jugendherberge-freiburg.de).

EATING

Freiburg has plenty of dining options. I've listed a few good places in the town center, and a couple atop the scenic Schlossberg.

In the Town Center

Kleiner Meyerhof, around the corner from the TI, offers regional specialties, and reasonable prices (€7–17 entrées, daily 10:00–24:00, kitchen closes at 22:00, Rathausgasse 27, tel. 0761/26941).

Hausbrauerei Feierling brews its own beer and serves fine meals. On warm summer evenings, their *Biergarten* across the street offers cool, leafy shade and a lively atmosphere (€5–12 entrées, daily 11:00–24:00, Gerberau 46, tel. 0761/243-480).

Vegetarians enjoy **Caruso's** large portions and fair prices (€4–9 entrées, Mon–Sat 10:00–24:00, closed Sun, Kaiser Joseph Strasse 258, near Martinstor, tel. 0761/31000).

Tacheles appeals to student-sized appetites (big) and budgets (small). Who knew that schnitzel could be prepared in literally a dozen different ways? Here at the self-proclaimed *"Schnitzel Paradies,"* they serve up big schnitzels (€1 extra for *Pute*—turkey—instead of the traditional pork), a salad, and your choice of a side dish (french fries, *Spätzle*, and so on) for a mere €5.50 for lunch or €6.90 for dinner (after 18:00). The pub downstairs, a favorite hangout, can be crowded and smoky; instead, opt for the quiet courtyard seating upstairs (Mon–Sat 11:00–24:00, Sun 15:00–24:00, also vegetarian and fish options, nightly drink specials, live *Fussball* broadcasts Sat–Sun nights, Grünwalderstrasse 17, tel. 0761/319-6669).

Freiburg's Schlossberg

To get to these scenic restaurants, see Schlossberg under "Sights," page 137.

Greiffenegg Schlössle offers rooftop views over Freiburg, but the meals are expensive and worth it only if you can get a table on the terrace in good weather (daily 11:00–24:00, meals start at €20, reservations smart, Schlossbergring 3, tel. 0761/32728).

Biergarten Kastaniengarten is self-service, offering budget travelers a few peek-a-boo views just above the Greiffenegg Schlössle (€6–8 entrées, daily 11:00–24:00, tel. 0761/32728). Cheaper yet, consider a picnic at the Schlossberg viewpoint.

Join the cerebral grad-student crowd at **UC/Uni-Cafe** for cheap eats and a cappuccino outside on the square, or pop inside to watch a *Fussball* match on the flat-screen TV while drinking a beer (€3–6 salads and sandwiches, Mon–Sat 8:00–23:00, Sun 10:00–23:00, Niemens Strasse 7).

TRANSPORTATION CONNECTIONS

The full name of the town—and the station—is Freiburg im Breisgau (Brsg).

From Freiburg by Train to: Staufen (hrly, 30 min, 3/day are direct, others require change to train or bus in Bad Krozingen; only 7/day Sun, with none before 11:00; don't schedule yourself too tightly because cancellations can occur on milk-run trains; after 20:00 no trains to Staufen but you can take a train to Bad Krozingen station and take a shared taxi from there to Staufen for €10—call taxi 30 min before you need it, tel. 07633/5386), **Baden-Baden** (hrly, 45 min or 1.5 hrs with 1 change), **Munich** (hrly, 4.5 hrs, transfer in Mannheim), **Mainz am Rhine** (hrly, 1.5 hrs), **Basel** (hrly, 45 min), **Bern** (hrly, 2 hrs, transfer in Basel), **Frankfurt** (hrly, 2.5 hrs, 6/day are direct, others require change in Mannheim). Train info: tel. 11861 (€0.50/min).

Staufen

Staufen im Breisgau makes a peaceful and delightful home base for your exploration of Freiburg and the southern trunk of the Black Forest. Hemmed in by vineyards, it's small and off the beaten path, with a quiet pedestrian zone of colorful old buildings bounded by a happy creek that actually babbles. There's nothing to do here but enjoy the marketplace atmosphere, hike through the vineyards to the ruined castle overlooking the town, and savor a good dinner with local wine.

ORIENTATION

(area code: 07633)

Tourist Information

The TI, on the main square in the Rathaus, has a good (German-only) map of the wine road and can help you find a room (Mon 9:00–12:30 & 14:00–18:00, Tue–Thu until 17:30, Fri until 17:00, Sat 9:30–12:00, closed Sun, tel. 07633/80536, www.staufen .de, touristikinfo@staufen.de).

Arrival in Staufen

Everything I list is within a 10-min-ute walk of the station (no lockers, but try Gasthaus Bahnhof—see "Sleeping," below). To get to town, exit the station with your back to the pond and angle right up Bahnhofstrasse. Turn right at the post office on Hauptstrasse for the town center, hotels, and TI.

SIGHTS

In Staufen

Winery—Weingut Wiesler offers *Weinproben*—a wine-tasting of three different local wines and an opportunity to buy a bottle if you like it (€3, Mon–Fri 15:00–18:30, Sat 9:00–13:30, closed Sun, behind Gasthaus Bahnhof, 2nd house on left, at base of castle hill, Krozinger Strasse 26, tel. 07633/6905, Frau Wiesler).

Near Staufen

Wine Road (Badische Weinstrasse)—The wine road of this part of Germany staggers from Staufen through the tiny towns of Grunern, Dottingen, Sulzburg, and Britzingen, before collapsing in Badenweiler. If you're in the mood for some tasting, look for Winzergenossenshaft signs, which invite visitors in to taste and buy wines, and often to tour a winery.

▲**Badenweiler**—If ever a town were a park, Badenweiler is it. This idyllic, finicky-clean spa town is known only to the wealthy Germans who soak here (**TI** open Mon–Fri 9:00–13:00 & 14:00–17:30, May–Oct also Sat–Sun 9:00–12:00, tel. 07632/799-300, www.badenweiler.de). Its bath, Casseopeia Therme, is next to the ruins of a Roman mineral bath in a park of imported and exotic trees (including a California redwood). This prizewinning piece of architecture perfectly mixes trees and peace with an elegant indoor/outdoor swimming pool (daily 9:00–22:00, tel. 07632/799-200). The locker procedure, combined with the language barrier, makes getting to the pool more memorable than you'd expect (€9.90, €6.90 after 18:00, €2 towel rental with €10 deposit). Badenweiler is a 20-minute drive south of Staufen (take the train, which runs almost hourly until 20:00, to Mullheim, and bus #111 from there; covered by Regio Pass; see "Black Forest," below, for details).

SLEEPING

(€1 = about $1.20, country code: 49, area code: 07633)
The TI has a list of private *Zimmer*. Prices listed are for one night, but most *Zimmer* don't like one-nighters. Except for the last listing, breakfast is included.

$$ Gasthaus Krone, on the main pedestrian drag, has nine rooms that gild the lily but offer a good value in this price range (Sb-€60, Db-€75, Tb-€90, balconies, parking, Hauptstrasse 30, tel. 07633/5840, fax 07633/82903, www.die-krone.de, info@die-krone.de; Kurt Lahn, who looks a bit like Dan Rather, speaks a little English). Its restaurant appreciates vegetables and offers wonderful splurge meals (closed Fri–Sat).

$$ Hotel Hirschen, with a storybook location in the old pedestrian center, is family-run, with 15 plush and thoughtfully appointed rooms, balconies, and a big roof deck (Sb-€50–55, Db-€70–75, Tb-€95, elevator, free and easy parking, Hauptstrasse 19 on main pedestrian street, cozy restaurant open Wed–Sun, tel. 07633/5297, fax 07633/5295, www.hirschen-staufen.de, info @breisgaucity.com, for reservations on short notice it's best to fax, Dieter and Isabelle). They have a huge luxury penthouse for four (€130–140).

$ Hotel Sonne, at the edge of the pedestrian center, offers eight newly renovated rooms with Italian flair. Friendly Vittorio is also particularly proud of his restaurant—which offers a nice break from traditional *Deutsche Küche,* serving tasty pizzas and Italian fare (Sb-€45, Db-€60, Tb-€84; continue straight past Hotel Krone, turn right at T intersection, and take 2nd left on Mühlegasse to reach Albert-Hugard Strasse 1; tel. 07633/95300, fax 07633/953-014).

$ Bahnhof Hotel is the cheapest, simplest place in town, with a dynamite castle view from the upstairs terrace, a self-service kitchen, a *kleine* washing machine for guests, and €8 dinners served on its tree-shaded patio or in its antler-filled restaurant (S-€21, D-€41, no breakfast, across from train station, tel. 07633/6190, no English spoken). Seven comfortable and cheery rooms right out of grandma's house share two bathrooms. At night, master of ceremonies Lotte makes it the squeeze-box of Staufen. People come from all around to party with Lotte, so it can be noisy at night. If you want to eat red meat in a wine barrel under a tree, this is the place. For stays of three nights or longer, ask her about the rooms next door (Sb-€30, Db-€40).

Black Forest

▲▲Short and Scenic Black Forest Joyride (by Car or Train and Bus)—This pleasant loop from Freiburg takes you through the most representative chunk of the area, avoiding the touristy, overcrowded Titisee.

By Car: Leave Freiburg on Schwarzwaldstrasse (signs to Donaueschingen), which becomes scenic road B31 down the dark Höllental (Hell's Valley) toward Titisee. Turn left at Hinterzarten onto road B500, follow signs to St. Märgen and then to St. Peter—one of the healthy, go-take-a-walk-in-the-clean-air places that doctors actually prescribe for people from all over Germany. There's a fine four-mile walk between St. Märgen and St. Peter, with regular buses to bring you back.

To continue your drive from St. Peter, you can wind through

idyllic Black Forest scenery up to Mt. Kandel. At the summit is the Berghotel Kandel. You can park here and take a short walk to the 4,000-foot peak for a great view. Then the road winds steeply through a dense forest to Waldkirch, where a fast road takes you to the Freiburg Nord autobahn entrance. With a good car and no stops, you'll get from Staufen/Freiburg to Baden-Baden via this route in three hours.

By Train and Bus: Trains run nearly hourly from Freiburg to Kirchzarten Bahnhof, where bus #7216 goes to St. Peter and St. Märgen. Get off at St. Peter, hike four miles to St. Märgen, and bus/train back to Freiburg (€3.20 one-way, or consider the Regio Pass: €9.20/1 adult or €13/up to 5 adults for 24 hours on all regional transportation, including within Freiburg and Badenweiler). The regional bus information office has all the details on getting around the area (turn right out of Freiburg train station and walk 100 yards, tel. 0761/368-0388 during business hours; after hours, call 01805/779-966 for €0.12/min or Freiburg TI, tel. 0761/388-1880).

Town of St. Peter: The **TI,** just next to the Benedictine Abbey (private), can recommend a walk (Mon–Fri 9:00–12:00 & 14:00–17:00, Sat in July–Aug 10:00–12:00, closed Sun year-round and Sat Sept–June, Klosterhoff 11, tel. 07660/910-224). Sleep at the traditional old **Gasthof Hirschen** on the main square (Sb-€41, Db-€72–82, St. Peter/Hochschwarzwald, Bertoldsplatz 1, tel. 07660/204, fax 07660/1557, www.gasthof-hirschen.de, info @gasthof-hirschen.de), or consider **Pension Kandelblick** (D-€36–38, cash only, Seelgutweg 5, tel. 07660/349).

▲▲**Extended Black Forest Drive**—Of course, you could spend much more time in the land of cuckoo clocks and healthy hikes. For a more thorough visit, still connecting with Baden-Baden, try this drive: As described above, drive from Staufen or Freiburg down Höllental. After a short stop in St. Peter, wind up in Furtwangen with the impressive Deutsches Uhrenmuseum (German Clock Museum, €4, daily April–Oct 9:00–18:00, Nov–March 10:00–17:00, tel. 07723/920-117). More than a chorus of cuckoo clocks, this museum traces (in English) the development of clocks from the Dark Ages to the Space Age. It has an upbeat combo of mechanical musical instruments as well.

Triberg—Deep in the Black Forest, Triberg is famous for its Gutach Waterfall (which falls 500 feet in several bounces, €1.50 to see it) and, more important, the Black Forest Museum, which gives a fine look at the costumes, carvings, and traditions of the local culture (€4, daily 10:00–17:00, tel. 07722/4434, www.schwarzwaldmuseum .de). Touristy as Triberg is, it offers an easy way for travelers without cars to enjoy the Black Forest (TI tel. 07722/953-231, closed Sun, www.triberg.de).

▲**Black Forest Open-Air Museum (Schwarzwälder Freilichtermuseum)**—This offers the best look at this region's traditional folk life. (Note: It's different from the similarly-named museum in Triberg.) Built

around one grand old farmhouse, the museum is a collection of several old farms filled with exhibits on the local dress and lifestyles (€5, daily March–Nov 9:00–18:00, last entry at 17:00, closed in winter, English descriptions and €6 guidebook, north of Triberg, through Hornberg to Hausach/Gutach on road B33, tel. 07831/93560, www.vogtsbauernhof.org). The surrounding shops and restaurants are awfully touristy. Try your *Schwarzwald Kirschtorte* (Black Forest cherry cake) elsewhere.

Continue north through Freudenstadt, the capital of the northern Black Forest, and onto the Schwarzwald-Hochstrasse, which takes you along a ridge through 30 miles of pine forests before dumping you right on Baden-Baden's back porch.

ROTHENBURG AND THE ROMANTIC ROAD

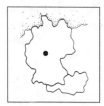

From Munich or Füssen to Frankfurt, the Romantic Road takes you through Bavaria's medieval heartland, a route strewn with picturesque villages, farmhouses, onion-domed churches, Baroque palaces, and walled cities.

Linger in Rothenburg (ROE-ten-burg), Germany's best-preserved walled town. Countless travelers have searched for the elusive "untouristy Rothenburg." There are many contenders (such as Michelstadt, Miltenberg, Bamberg, Bad Windsheim, and Dinkelsbühl), but none holds a candle to the king of medieval German cuteness. Even with crowds, overpriced souvenirs, Japanese-speaking night watchmen, and, yes, even *Schneebällen,* Rothenburg is best. Save time and mileage and be satisfied with the winner.

Planning Your Time

The best one-day drive through the heartland of Germany is the Romantic Road. The road is clearly marked for drivers, and well-described in the free brochure available at any TI. Those without wheels can take the train. Apart from Würzburg, with its Prince Bishop's Residenz (see Würzburg chapter), the only stop worth more than a few minutes is Rothenburg. Twenty-four hours is ideal for this town. With two nights and a day, you'll be able to see the essentials and actually relax a little. Spend the night, as the town is less touristy after hours, with cheap places to eat and sleep.

Rothenburg

In the Middle Ages, when Frankfurt and Munich were just wide spots on the road, Rothenburg ob der Tauber was Germany's second-largest free imperial city, with a whopping population of 6,000. Today, it's her finest medieval walled town, enjoying tremendous tourist popularity without losing its charm. Get medievaled in Rothenburg.

During Rothenburg's heyday, from 1150 to 1400, it was the crossing point of two major trade routes: Tashkent–Paris and Hamburg–Venice. Today, the great trade is tourism; two-thirds of the townspeople are employed to serve you. Too often, Rothenburg brings out the shopper in visitors before they've had a chance to see the historic town. True, this is a great place to do your German shopping, but appreciate the town's great history and sights first. While 2.5 million people visit each year, a mere 500,000 spend the night. Rothenburg is most enjoyable early and late, when the tour groups are gone. Rothenburg is very busy through the summer and in the Christmas Market month of December. Spring and fall are great, but it's pretty bleak from January through March—when most locals are hibernating or on vacation.

Rothenburg in a day is easy, with five essential experiences: the Medieval Crime and Punishment Museum, Tilman

Riemenschneider's wood carving in St. Jakob's Church, the Old Town Historic Walk, a walk along the wall, and the entertaining Night Watchman's Tour. With more time, there are several mediocre but entertaining museums, hikes and bike rides in the nearby countryside, and lots of cafés and shops. Make a point to spend at least one night. The town is yours after dark, when the groups vacate and the town's floodlit cobbles wring some romance out of any travel partner.

ORIENTATION

(area code: 09861)
To orient yourself in Rothenburg, think of the town map as a human head. Its nose—the castle garden—sticks out to the left, and the neck is the skinny lower part, with the hostel and some of the best hotels in the Adam's apple. The town is a joy on foot. No sight or hotel is more than a 15-minute walk from the train station or each other.

Most of the buildings you'll see were built by 1400. The city was born around its long-gone castle—built in 1142, destroyed in 1356—which was located on the present-day site of the castle garden. You can see the shadow of the first town wall, which defines the oldest part of Rothenburg, in its contemporary street plan. A few gates from this wall still survive. The richest and biggest houses were in this central part. The commoners built higgledy-piggledy (read: picturesque) houses farther from the center, near the present walls.

Tourist Information

The TI is on Market Square (April–Oct Mon–Fri 9:00–12:00 & 13:00–18:00, Sat–Sun 10:00–15:00, Nov–March shorter hours and closed Sun, tel. 09861/404800, www.rothenburg.de). If there's a long line, just raid the rack where they keep all the free pamphlets. The map and guide comes with a virtual walking guide to the town. The *Information* monthly guide lists all the events and entertainment. Ask about the daily English walking tour at 14:00 (€6, April–Oct; see "Tours," below). Visitors who arrive late can check the handy map with all hotels—highlighting which ones still have rooms available, with a free direct phone connection to them; it's just outside the door. The best town map is available free with this book at the Friese shop, two doors west from the TI (toward St. Jakob's Church; see "Shopping," page 161).

Arrival in Rothenburg

By Train: It's a 10-minute walk from the station to Rothenburg's Market Square (following the brown *Altstadt* signs, exit left from station, turn right on Ansbacher Strasse, and head straight into the Middle Ages). Day-trippers can leave luggage in station lockers (€2, on platform) or at the Friese shop on Market Square. Arrange train and *couchette*/sleeper reservations at the travel agency in the station (no charge for quick questions, Mon–Fri 9:00–18:00, Sat 9:00–13:00, closed Sun, tel. 09861/7711). The nearest WCs are at the snack bar next door to the station. Taxis wait at the station (€5 to any hotel).

By Car: While much of the town is closed to traffic, anyone with a hotel reservation can drive in and through pedestrian zones to get to their hotel. But driving in town can be a nightmare, with many narrow, one-way streets. If you're packing light, just park outside the walls and walk five minutes to the center. Parking lots line the town walls, and are generally free (the P1 parking lot, on the south end of town near Spitaltor, and P5 parking lot just outside Klingentor, on the north end of town, are each handy, depending on where you're staying). Only those with a hotel reservation can park within the walls after hours (but not during festivals).

Rothenburg

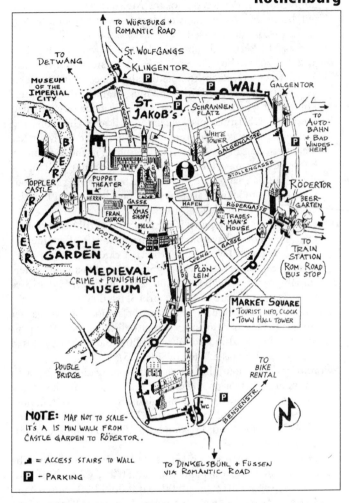

The easiest way to enter and leave Rothenburg is generally via Spittalgasse (and the Spitaltor, south end).

Helpful Hints

Festivals: Rothenburgers dress up in medieval costumes, and beer gardens spill out into the street to celebrate Mayor Nusch's Meistertrunk victory (June 2–5 in 2006, see story under "Meistertrunk Show" on page 153, more info at www .meistertrunk.de) and 700 years of history in the Imperial City Festival (Sept 1–3 in 2006, with fireworks). Really stretching it in 2006, this tourist-hungry town celebrates the 125th anniversary of the creation of the Meistertrunk myth. There will be big crowds and daily outdoor festivities from July 15 to July 23—consider yourself warned.

Christmas Market: Rothenburg is dead in November, January, and February, but December is its busiest month—the entire town cranks up the medieval cuteness with concerts and costumes, shops with schnapps, stalls filling squares, hot spiced wine, giddy nutcrackers, and mobs of earmuffed Germans. Christmas markets are big all over Germany, and Rothenburg's is considered one of the best. The festival takes place each year in the four weeks leading up to the last Sunday before Christmas (Dec 1–23 in 2006). Virtually all sights listed in this chapter are open longer hours during these four weeks. Try to avoid Saturdays and Sundays, when big-city day-trippers really clog the grog.

Internet Access: Rothenburg is in many ways still pretty medieval. Few hotels have phones in the rooms or offer Internet access. **Inter@Play,** the only Internet café in town, is more of a cheesy game room with eight good and fast coin-op terminals (€3/hr, daily 8:00–24:00, 2 blocks down Hafengasse from Market Square at Milchmarkt 3, tel. 09861/935-599).

Laundry: A handy launderette is near the station, off Ansbacher Strasse (€5.50/load, includes soap, English instructions, opens at 8:00, last load in Mon–Fri at 18:00, Sat at 14:00, closed Sun, Johannitergasse 9, tel. 09861/2775).

Swimming: Rothenburg has a fine modern recreation center with an indoor/outdoor pool *(Hallenbad)* and sauna. It's just a few minutes' walk down the Dinkelsbühl Road (adults-€3, kids-€1.70, swimsuit and towel rental-€2 each, Mon 14:00–21:00, Tue–Thu 9:00–21:00, Fri–Sun 9:00–18:00, Nordlingerstrasse 20, tel. 09861/4565).

Bike Rental: You can rent bikes at **Rad & Tat,** and follow the suggested route on page 160 (€2.50/hr, €7.50/half-day, €10/day, Mon–Fri 9:00–18:00, Sat 9:00–13:00, closed Sun, Bensenstrasse 17, outside of town near corner of Bensenstrasse and Erlbacherstrasse, passport number required, tel. 09861/87984, Daniel Lorenz).

Travel Agency: The only agency helpful for train travelers is at the train station (for hours, see above).

TOURS

▲▲**Night Watchman's Tour**—This tour is flat-out the most entertaining hour of medieval wonder anywhere in Germany. The Night Watchman (a.k.a. Hans Georg Baumgartner) jokes like a medieval

Jerry Seinfeld as he lights his lamp and takes tourists on his one-hour rounds, telling slice-of-gritty-life tales of medieval Rothenburg (€6, free for kids, mid-March–Dec nightly at 20:00, in English, meet at Market Square, www .nightwatchman.de). This is the best evening activity in town.

Old Town Historic Walk—The TI on Market Square offers 90-minute guided walking tours in English (€6, April–Oct daily at 14:00 from Market Square). While the Night Watchman's Tour is fun, take this tour for the serious history of Rothenburg, and to make sense of the town's architecture. The tours are completely different, and it would be a shame not to take advantage of this fine tour because you took the other.

Private Guides—A local historian can really bring the ramparts alive. Gisela Vogl (€53/90 min, €70/2 hr, tel. 09861/4957, werner.vogl@t-online.de) and Anita Weinzierl (tel. 09868/7993, anitaweinzierl@aol.com) are both good. Martin Kamphans, a potter, also works as a guide (tel. 09861/7941, kamphans@t-online.de).

Horse-and-Buggy Rides—These farm boys, who are generally about as charming as their horses, give a relaxing 30-minute clip-clop through the old town, starting from Market Square or Schrannenplatz. Good luck negotiating a fair price (private buggy for €30–50, or wait for one to fill up for €5 per person).

SELF-GUIDED WALK

Welcome to Rothenburg

This one-hour walk weaves Rothenburg's top sights together.

• *Start the walk on Market Square.*

Market Square Spin Tour: Stand at the bottom of Market Square (10 feet below the wooden post on the corner) and—ignoring the little white arrow—spin 360 degrees clockwise, starting with the Town Hall tower. Now do it again, this time more slowly, following these notes:

Town Hall and Tower: Rothenburg's tallest spire is the **Town Hall tower.** At 200 feet, it stands atop the old Town Hall, a white, Gothic, 13th-century building. Notice the tourists enjoying the best view in town from the black top of the tower (€1 and a rigorous but interesting climb, 214 steps, narrow and steep near the top—watch your head, April–Oct daily 9:30–12:30 & 13:30–17:00, closed Nov–March, enter on Market Square through middle

Rothenburg Town Walk

1. Market Square Spin Tour
2. Town Hall & Tower
3. Councillors' Tavern & TI
4. Print Shop
5. Baumeister's Haus Rest.
6. St. George's Fountain
7. Historical Town Hall Vaults
8. Green Market & Friese Shop
9. St. Jakob's Church
10. Museum of the Imperial City
11. Convent Garden
12. Castle Garden
13. Herrngasse
14. Eisenhut Hotel/Restaurant
15. Käthe Wohlfahrt Christmas Villages Shop & Museum
16. Doll & Toy Museum
17. Internet Café

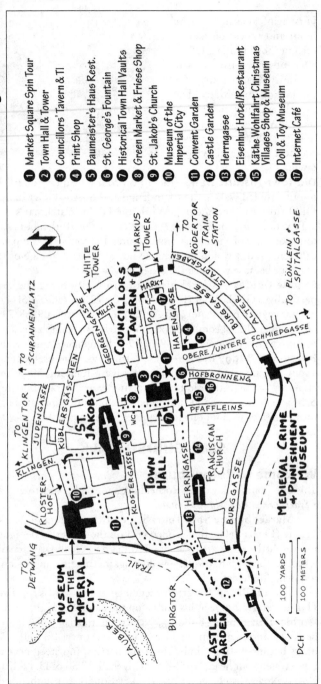

arch of new Town Hall). After a fire burned down part of the original building, a **new Town Hall** was built alongside what survived of the old one (fronting the square). This half of the rebuilt complex is in the Renaissance style from 1570.

Meistertrunk Show: At the top of Market Square stands the proud **Councillors' Tavern** (clock tower from 1466). In its day, the city council—the rich guys who ran the town government—drank here. Today, it's the TI and the focus of most tourists' attention when the little doors on either side of the clock flip open and the wooden figures (from 1910) do their thing. Be on Market Square at 11:00, 12:00, 13:00, 14:00, 15:00, 20:00, 21:00, or 22:00 for the ritual gathering of the tourists to see the less-than-breathtaking reenactment of the Meistertrunk story.

In 1631, the Catholic army took the Protestant town, and was about to do its rape, pillage, and plunder thing. As was the etiquette, the mayor had to give the conquering general a welcoming drink. The general enjoyed a huge tankard of local wine. Feeling really good, he told the mayor (according to the story): "Hey, if you can drink this entire three-liter tankard of wine in one gulp, I'll spare your town." The mayor amazed everyone by drinking the entire thing, and Rothenburg was saved.

While this is a nice story, it was dreamed up in the late 1800s for a theatrical play designed (effectively) to promote a romantic image of the town. In actuality, if Rothenburg was spared, it happened because it bribed its way out of a jam. It was occupied and ransacked several times in the Thirty Years' War, and it never recovered—which is why it's such a well-preserved time capsule today. Hint: For the best show, don't watch the clock; watch the open-mouthed tourists gasp as the old windows flip open. At the late shows, the square flickers with camera flashes.

Bottom of Market Square: On the bottom end of the square, the cream-colored building has a fine **print shop** (upstairs—see "Shopping," page 161). Adjoining that is the **Baumeister's Haus,** a touristy restaurant with a fine courtyard (see "Eating," page 169), featuring a famous Renaissance facade with statues of the seven virtues and the seven vices—the former supporting the latter. The statues are copies; the originals are in the Museum of the Imperial City (listed below). The green house below that is the former house of the 15th-century Mayor Toppler (it's now the recommended Greifen Gasthof).

Keep circling to the big 17th-century **St. George's fountain.** The long metal gutters slid, routing the water into the villagers' buckets. Rothenburg had an ingenious water system. Built on a rock, it had one real source above the town which was plumbed to serve a series of fountains; water flowed from high to low through Rothenburg. Its many fountains had practical functions beyond providing drinking water (some were stocked with fish on market days and during times of siege). Water was used for fighting fires, and because of its plentiful water supply—and its policy of requiring relatively wide lanes as fire breaks—the town never burned entirely, as so many neighboring villages did.

Two fine buildings behind the fountain show the old-time lofts with warehouse doors and pulleys on top for hoisting. All over town, lofts were filled with grain and corn. A year's supply was required by the city so they could survive any siege. The building behind the fountain is an art gallery (free, usually daily 11:00–17:00) showing off the work of local professional artists. To the right is an old-time pharmacy mixing old and new in typical Rothenburg style.

The broad street running under the Town Hall tower is **Herrngasse** (also see end of tour, below). The town originated with its castle (built in 1142 but now long gone; only the castle garden remains). Herrngasse connected the castle to Market Square. The last leg of this circular walking tour will take you from the castle garden up Herrngasse to where you now stand. For now, walk a few steps down Herrngasse to the arch under the Town Hall tower (between the new and old town halls). On the left wall are the town's measuring rods—a reminder that medieval Germany was made of 300 independent little countries, each with its own weights and measures. Merchants and shoppers knew that these were the local standards: the rod (4.3 yards), the *Schuh* (or shoe, roughly a foot), and the *Ell* (from elbow to fingertip—4 inches longer than mine...try it). Notice the protruding cornerstone. These are all over town—originally to protect buildings from reckless horse carts (and vice versa).

• *Under the arch, you'll find the...*

Historical Town Hall Vaults: This grade-schoolish little museum, worth ▲, gives a waxy but interesting look at Rothenburg during the Catholics-vs.-Protestants Thirty Years' War. With helpful English descriptions, it offers a look at "the fateful year 1631," a replica of the mythical Meistertrunk tankard, and a dungeon complete with three dank cells and some torture lore (€2, April–Oct daily 9:30–17:30, less off-season, tel. 09861/94280).

• *Leaving the museum, turn left, and walk through the courtyard to a square called...*

Green Market: Once a produce market, it's now a parking lot that fills with Christmas shops during December. Notice the clay tiled roofs. These "beaver tail" tiles became standard after thatched roofs were outlawed to prevent fires. Today, all of the town's roofs are made of these. The little fences keep the snow from falling, and catch tiles that blow off during storms. The public WC is on your left, the recommended **Friese shop** (see "Shopping," page 161) is on your right, and straight ahead is St. Jakob's Church.

Outside the church, you'll see 14th-century statues (mostly original) showing Jesus praying at Gethsemane, a common feature of Gothic churches. The artist is anonymous, because in the Gothic age (pre-Albrecht Dürer) artists were just nameless craftspeople working only for the glory of God. Five yards to the left (on the wall), notice the nub of a sandstone statue—a rare original, looking pretty bad after 500 years of weather and, more recently, pollution. Original statues are now in the city museum. Better-preserved statues you see on the church are copies.

• *If it's your wedding day, take the first entrance. Otherwise, use the second (downhill) door to enter...*

St. Jakob's Church: Built in the 14th century, this ▲▲ church has been Lutheran since 1544. The interior was "purified" by Romantics in the 19th century—cleaned of everything Baroque or not original, and refitted in the neo-Gothic style. (For example, the baptismal font and the pulpit above the second pew *look* Gothic, but are actually neo-Gothic.) The stained-glass windows behind the altar (most colorful in the morning light) are originals from the 1330s.

Take a close look at the 12 apostles' altar in front (from 1546, left permanently in its open festival-day position). Below Christ are statues of six saints. St. James (Jakob in German, pronounced "YAH-kohp") is the one with the shell. He's the saint of pilgrims, and this church was a stop on the medieval pilgrimage route to Santiago (St. James in Spanish) de Compostela in Spain. Study the painted panels—ever see Peter with spectacles? Around the back of the altarpiece (upper left) is a painting of Rothenburg's Market Square in the 15th century—looking much like it does today, with the exception of the full-Gothic Town Hall (as it was before the big fire of 1501). Notice Christ's face on the veil of Veronica (center of back side). It follows you as you walk from side to side—it must have given the faithful the religious heebie-jeebies four centuries ago.

The altar on the left side is also worth a look. It's a century older than the main altar. Notice the unusual Trinity: the Father and Son are literally bridged by a dove representing the Holy Spirit. Stepping back, you can see that Jesus is standing on a skull—clearly "overcoming death."

Before leaving the front of the church, notice the old medallions above the carved choir stalls. They feature the coats of arms of Rothenburg's leading families and portraits of city and church leaders.

Stairs in the back of the church, behind the pipe organ, lead up to the artistic highlight of Rothenburg, and perhaps the most wonderful wood carving in all of Germany: the glorious 500-year-old, 35-foot-high *Altar of the Holy Blood*. Tilman Riemenschneider, the Michelangelo of German woodcarvers, carved this from 1499 to 1504 to hold a precious rock-crystal capsule, set in a cross that contains a scrap of tablecloth miraculously stained in the shape of a cross by a drop of communion wine. It's a realistic commotion, showing that Riemenschneider—while a High Gothic artist—was ahead of his time. Below, in the scene of the Last Supper, Jesus gives Judas a piece of bread, marking him as the traitor, while John lays his head on Christ's lap. Everything is portrayed exactly as described in the Bible. On the left: Jesus enters Jericho with the shy tax collector Zacchaeus looking on from his tree. Notice the fun attention to detail—down to the nails on the horseshoe. On the right: Jesus prays in the Garden of Gethsemane. Notice how Judas, with his big bag of cash, could be removed from the scene—illustrated by photos on the wall nearby—as was the tradition for the four days leading up to Easter (€1.50, April–Oct Mon–Sat 9:00–17:30, Sun 10:30–17:30, Nov–March daily 10:00–12:00 & 14:00–16:00, free helpful English info sheet).

• *Leave the church and, from its outside steps, walk around the corner to the right and under the chapel (built over the road). Go two blocks down* **Klingengasse** *and stop at* **Klosterhof Street**. *(I've marked your spot with a small circular plaque in the middle of the road.) Looking down Klingengasse, you see the...*

Klingentor: This cliff tower was Rothenburg's water reservoir. From 1595 until 1910, a copper tank high in the tower provided clean spring water (pumped up by river-power) to the privileged. To the right of Klingentor is a good stretch of wall rampart to walk. To the left, the wall is low and simple, lacking a rampart because it guards only a cliff. Now find the shell decorating a building on the street corner next to you. That's the symbol of St. James (pilgrims commemorated their visit to Santiago de Compostela with a shell), indicating that this building is associated with the church. Walk under the shell, down Klosterhof (passing the colorful Altfränkische Weinstube; see "Eating," page 169) to the Museum of the Imperial City, housed in the former Dominican convent. Cloistered nuns used the Lazy Susan embedded in the wall (to the right of museum door) to give food to the poor without being seen.

Museum of the Imperial City (Reichsstadt Museum): You'll get a scholarly sweep through Rothenburg's history here, at this ▲▲ sight. Highlights include *The Rothenburg Passion*, a 12-panel series of paintings from 1492 showing scenes leading up to Christ's crucifixion (in the *Konventsaal*); an exhibit of Jewish culture through the ages in Rothenburg *(Judaika);* a 14th-century convent kitchen *(Klosterküche)* with a working model of the lazy Susan and a massive chimney; romantic paintings of the town *(Gemäldegalerie);* the fine Baumann collection of weapons and armor; and sandstone statues from the church and Baumeister Haus (the 7 vices and 7 virtues). Follow the *Rundgang Tour* signs (€3, €6 combo-ticket that includes Medieval Crime and Punishment Museum saves a whopping €0.50, daily April–Oct 9:30–17:30, Nov–March 13:00–16:00, English info sheet and descriptions, tel. 09861/939-043, www .reichsstadtmuseum.rothenburg.de).

• *Leaving the museum for the Castle Garden (listed below), go around to the right and into the...*

Convent Garden: This spot is a peaceful place to work on your tan...or mix a poisoned potion (free, same hours as museum). Enjoy the herb garden. Monks and nuns, who were responsible for concocting herbal cures in the olden days, often tended herb gardens. Smell (but don't pick) the *Pfefferminze, Juniper* (gin), *Chamomilla* (disinfectant), and *Origanum.* Don't smell the plants in the poison corner (potency indicated by the number of crosses... like spiciness stars in a Chinese restaurant).

• *Exit opposite from where you entered, angling left through the nuns' garden (site of the now-gone Dominican church), eventually leaving via an arch at the far end.*

See the back end of an original barn (behind a mansion fronting Herrngasse). Mansions were like small villages in themselves, with a series of buildings and spaces. The typical design included a house, a courtyard, a stable, a garden, and, finally, a barn. Go downhill to the town wall (view through bars, look to far right). This part of the wall takes advantage of the natural fortification provided by the cliff, and is therefore much smaller than the ramparts. Angle left along the wall to the big street (Herrngasse), then right under the tower *(Burgtor).* Notice the tiny "eye of the needle" door cut into the big door. If trying to get into town after curfew, you could bribe the guard to let you through this door (which was small enough to keep out any fully armed attackers).

Step through the gate and outside the wall. Look around and imagine being locked out in the year 1400. This was a wooden drawbridge (see the chain slits above). Notice the "pitch nose" mask—designed to pour boiling Nutella on anyone attacking. High above is the town coat of arms: a red castle *(roten Burg).*

Castle Garden: The garden before you was once that red castle (destroyed in the 14th century). Today, it's a picnic-friendly park. The chapel (50 yards into the park on the left) is the only bit of the original castle to survive. It's now a memorial to local Jews killed in a 1298 slaughter. A few steps beyond that is a grapevine trellis that provides a fine picnic spot. At the far end, you'll find a viewpoint (well past the tourists, and considered the best place to kiss by romantic local teenagers). But the views of the lush Tauber River Valley below are just as good from the top end of the park. Facing the town, on the left, a path leads down to the village of Detwang (you can see the church spire below)—a town even older than Rothenburg (for a walk to Detwang, see "A Walk in the Countryside," below). To the right is a fine view of the fortified Rothenburg and the "Tauber Riviera" below. Return to the tower, cross carefully under the pitch nose, and hike back up Herrngasse to your starting point.

Herrngasse: Many towns have a Herrngasse, where the richest patricians and merchants (the *Herren*) lived. Predictably, it's your best chance to see the town's finest old mansions. Strolling back to Market Square, you'll pass the old-time puppet theater (German only, on left), the Franciscan church (from 1285, oldest in town, on right), and the hippie Sawasdee shop (where the Night Watchman spends his days dreaming of his next trip to Thailand while his girlfriend sells the things they've imported, Herrngasse 23). To see the traditional house-courtyard-stables-garden-barn layout, pop into either #14 (now an apartment block) or—if that's closed—the shop next door, at #11. The Eisenhut Hotel, Rothenburg's fanciest, is worth a peek inside (see "Eating," below). The Käthe Wohlfahrt Christmas Villages shops (at Herrngasse 1 and across the street, see "Shopping," page 161) is your last, and perhaps greatest, temptation before reaching your starting and ending point: Market Square.

SIGHTS AND ACTIVITIES

Museums within a Block of Market Square

▲▲**Medieval Crime and Punishment Museum**—This museum is the best of its kind, full of fascinating old legal bits and *Kriminal* pieces, instruments of punishment and torture—even a special cage complete with a metal gag for nags. As a bonus, you get exhibits on marriage traditions and witches. Follow the yellow arrows. Exhibits are tenderly described in English (€3.50, €6 combo-ticket includes €3 Museum of the Imperial City, daily April–Oct 9:30–18:00, Nov and Jan–March 14:00–16:00, Dec 10:00–16:00, last entry 45 min before closing, fun cards and posters, Burggasse 3-5, tel. 09861/5359, www.kriminalmuseum.rothenburg.de).

▲**Doll and Toy Museum**—Two floors of historic *Kinder* cuteness is a hit with many. Pick up the free English binder (just past the entry curtain) for an extensive description of the exhibits (€4, family ticket-€10, daily March–Dec 9:30–18:00, Jan–Feb 11:00–17:00, just off Market Square, downhill from the fountain at Hofbronnengasse 13, tel. 09861/7330).

▲**German Christmas Museum**—Herr Wohlfahrt's passion is collecting and sharing historic Christmas decorations. This excellent museum, upstairs in the giant Käthe Wohlfahrt Christmas Villages shop, features a unique and thoughtfully described collection of Christmas-tree stands, mini-trees sent in boxes to WWI soldiers at the front, early Advent calendars, old-time Christmas cards, 450 clever ways to crack a nut, and a look at tree decorations through the ages—including the Nazi era and when you were a kid (€4, April–Dec daily 10:00–17:30, Jan–March only Sat–Sun 10:00–18:00, hours often change off-season, Herrngasse 1, 09861/409-365). The Wohlfahrts have agreed that with this 2006 book—if you promise to learn something—you can visit the museum at the student rate of €2.50.

More Sights and Activities in Rothenburg

▲▲**Walk the Wall**—Just over a mile and a half around, providing great views and a good orientation, this walk can be done by those under six feet tall and without a camera in less than an hour. The hike requires no special sense of balance. This covered walk is a great option in the rain. Photographers go through lots of film, especially before breakfast or at sunset, when the lighting is best and the crowds are fewest. The best fortifications are in the Spitaltor (south end). Walk from there counterclockwise to the "forehead" (note on the Rothenburg map how the town outline looks like a head). Climb the Rödertor en route. The names you see along the way are people who donated money to rebuild the wall after World War II and those who've recently donated €1,000 per meter for the maintenance of Rothenburg's heritage. You can enter or exit the ramparts at nearly every tower.

▲**Rödertor**—The wall tower nearest the train station is the only one you can climb. It's worth the 135 steps for the view and a fascinating rundown on the bombing of Rothenburg in the last weeks of World War II, when the east part of the city was destroyed (€1, unreliable hours, usually open daily but closed for lunch April–Oct, closed Nov–March, photos of WWII damage with English translations). If you climb this, you can skip the Town Hall tower.

▲▲**The Allergic-to-Tourists Wall and Moat Walk**—For a quiet and scenic break from the tourist crowds and a chance to appreciate the marvelous fortifications of Rothenburg, consider this hike: From the Castle Garden, walk outside the wall to Klingentor. At Klingentor, climb up to the ramparts and walk on the wall past Rödertor to Galgentor. Then descend, leave the old town, and hike through the park (once the moat) down to Spitaltor. Explore the fortifications here before hiking a block up Spitalgasse, turning left to pass the youth hostel, popping back outside the wall, and heading along the upper scenic reaches of the "Tauber Riviera" back to the Castle Garden.

Sightseeing Lowlights—St. Wolfgang's Church is a fortified Gothic church built into the medieval wall at Klingentor. Its dungeon-like passages and shepherd's-dance exhibit are pretty lame (€1.50, April–Sept Wed–Mon 11:00–13:00 & 14:00–17:00, Oct until 16:00, closed Tue and Nov–March). The 700-year-old **Tradesman's House** (Rothenburger Handwerkerhaus) shows the everyday life of a Rothenburger in the town's heyday (€2.20, April–Oct daily 9:00–18:00; Nov–Dec Mon–Fri 14:00–16:00, Sat–Sun 10:00–16:00; closed Jan–March, Alter Stadtgraben 26, near Markus Tower, tel. 09861/94280).

Near Rothenburg

▲**A Walk in the Countryside**—Just below the *Burggarten* (castle garden) in the Tauber Valley is the cute, skinny, 600-year-old castle/summer home of the medieval Mayor Toppler. The **Toppler Castle** (Topplerschlösschen)—the size and shape of a fortified treehouse—is in a farmer's garden and is open when-ever he's around and willing to let you in (€1.50, roughly Fri–Sun 13:00–16:00, closed Mon–Thu and Nov, 1 mile from town center at Taubertalweg 100, tel. 09861/7358). People say the mayor had this valley-floor escape to get people to relax about leaving the fortified town...or to hide a mistress.

Walk on past the covered bridge and huge trout to the peaceful village of **Detwang**. One of the oldest villages in Franconia, Detwang dates from 968. Like Rothenburg, it has a Riemenschneider altarpiece in its church. For a scenic return, loop back to Rothenburg through the valley along the river. Just past the double-arcaded bridge, follow the footpath back to town.

Franconian Bike Ride—To get a fun, breezy look at the country-side around Rothenburg, rent a bike from Rad & Tat (see "Helpful Hints," page 149). For a pleasant half-day pedal, bike along Topplerweg to Spittaltor and down into the Tauber Riviera, over the double-arcaded bridge, and along the small riverside road to Detwang, passing the cute Topplerschlösschen (described above). From Detwang, follow Liebliches Taubertal bike path signs as far up the Tauber River (direction: Bettwar) as you like.

Franconian Open-Air Museum (Fränkisches Freiland-museum)—A 20-minute drive from Rothenburg in the undiscov-ered "Rothenburgy" town of Bad Windsheim is an open-air folk museum that, compared with others in Europe, is a bit humble. But it tries very hard and gives you the best look around at tradi-tional rural Franconia (€5, daily March–Sept 9:00–18:00, Oct–Dec 10:00–16:00, closed Jan–Feb, last entry 1 hour before closing, tel. 09841/66800, www.freilandmuseum.de).

SHOPPING

Be warned...Rothenburg is one of Germany's best shopping towns. Do it here and be done with it. Lovely prints, carvings, wine-glasses, Christmas-tree ornaments, and beer steins are popular.

Christmas Stuff: The Käthe Wohlfahrt Christmas trinkets phenomenon is spreading across the half-timbered reaches of Europe. In Rothenburg, tourists flock to two **Käthe Wohlfahrt Christmas Villages** (on either side of Herrngasse, just off Market Square). This Christmas wonderland is filled with enough twinkling lights to require a special electrical hookup. You're greeted by instant Christmas mood music (best appreciated on a hot day in July) and American and Japanese tourists hungrily filling little woven shopping baskets with €5 to €8 goodies to hang on their trees. Let the spinning flocked tree whisk you in, but pause at the wall of Steiffs, jerking uncontrollably and mesmerizing little kids. (OK, I admit it, my Christmas tree sports a few KW ornaments.) Note: Prices are padded with tour-guide incentives (Mon–Sat 9:00–18:00, summer Sun 10:00–18:00, tel. 09861/4090, www .wohlfahrt.de). Their **Christmas Museum** upstairs is described above (page 159).

Traditional German Stuff: The **Friese shop** offers a charming contrast (just off Market Square, west of TI, on corner across from public WC). Cuckoo with friendliness, trinkets, and souvenirs, it gives shoppers with this book tremendous service: a 10 percent discount, 16 percent tax deducted if you have it mailed, and a free map (normally €1.50). Anneliese, who runs the place with her sons Frankie and Berni and grandson Rene (who played American football), charges only her cost for shipping and money exchange, and lets tired travelers leave their bags in her back room for free. For fewer crowds and better service, visit after 14:00 (Mon–Sat 8:00–17:00, Sun 9:30–17:00, tel. 09861/7166, fax 09861/936-619, friese-kabalo@gmx.de).

Passage 12, with a huge knickknack shop with a vast selection of steins, knives, and noisy clocks, is just a block below Market Square at Obere Schmiedgasse 12 (April–Dec Mon–Sat 9:00–19:00, Sun 10:00–19:00; Jan–March Mon–Sat 10:00–18:00, closed Sun, free WC and bag storage, tel. 09861/8196). Owner Martina promises a 10 percent discount on her prices (including sale prices) with this book in 2006.

Romantic Prints: The Ernst Geissendörfer print shop sells fine prints, etchings, and paintings. Show this book for 10 percent off marked prices on all cash purchases (or minimum €50 credit-card purchases) and a free shot of German brandy to sip while you browse (late Dec–April, Mon–Sat 10:00–18:00, Sun 10:00–17:00, closed Sun and May–late Dec, enter through bear shop on corner where Market Square hits Schmiedgasse, go up 1 floor, tel. 09861/2005).

Wine Stuff: For characteristic wineglasses, wine-making gear, and the real thing from the town's oldest wine-makers, drop by the **Weinladen am Plönlein** (daily 8:30–18:00, Plönlein 27—see "Wine-Drinking in the Old Center," page 171, for info on wine-tasting).

Shoppers who mail their goodies home can get handy €2.50 boxes at the **post office** (Mon–Fri 9:00–17:30, Sat 9:00–12:00, closed Sun, Rodergasse 11).

Those who prefer to eat their souvenirs shop the *Bäckereien* (bakeries). Their succulent pastries, pies, and cakes are pleasantly distracting...but skip the bad-tasting Rothenburger *Schneebällen*.

SLEEPING

Rothenburg is crowded with visitors, but most are day-trippers. Except for the rare Saturday night and festivals (see "Festivals," page 149), finding a room is easy throughout the year. If you want to splurge, you'll snare the best value by paying extra for the biggest and best rooms at the hotels I recommend.

Many hotels and guesthouses will pick up tired heavy-packers at the station. You may be greeted at the station by *Zimmer* skimmers who have rooms to rent. If you have reservations, resist them and honor your reservation. But if you haven't booked ahead, try talking yourself into one of these more desperate bed-and-breakfast rooms for a youth-hostel price. Be warned: These people are notorious for taking you to distant hotels and then charging

---

Sleep Code

(€1 = about $1.20, country code: 49, area code: 09861)
S = Single, **D** = Double/Twin, **T** = Triple, **Q** = Quad, **b** = bathroom, **s** = shower only. Unless otherwise noted, credit cards are accepted, English is spoken, and breakfast is included.

To help you sort easily through these listings, I've divided the rooms into three categories, based on the price for a standard double room with bath:

$$$ **Higher Priced**—Most rooms €65 or more.
  $$ **Moderately Priced**—Most rooms between €40–65.
    $ **Lower Priced**—Most rooms €40 or less.

Rothenburg Hotels

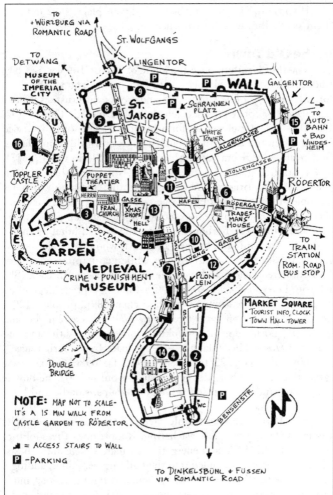

1. Gasthof Greifen
2. Hotel Gerberhaus
3. Hotel Kloster-Stüble
4. Gasthof zur Goldenen Rose
5. Hotel Altfränkische Weinstube am Klosterhof
6. Pension Elke
7. Hotel Café Uhl
8. Gästehaus Flemming
9. Gästehaus Viktoria
10. Gästehaus Raidel
11. Gasthof Marktplatz
12. Pension Pöschel
13. Frau Liebler Rooms
14. Rossmühle Youth Hostel
15. Hotel Hornburg
16. Pension Fuchsmühle

you for the ride back if you decline a room.

If you're driving and unable to find your place, stop and give them a call. They will likely rescue you.

In the Old Town

$$$ Gasthof Greifen, once the home of Mayor Toppler, is a big, traditional, 600-year-old place with large rooms and all the comforts. It's run by a fine family staff and creaks with rustic splendor (small Sb–€38, Sb–€48, small Db–€60, big Db–€82, Tb–€97–102, Qb–€117–122, 10 percent off for 3-night stay, self- or full-service laundry, free and easy parking, half a block downhill from Market Square at Obere Schmiedgasse 5, tel. 09861/2281, fax 09861/86374, www.gasthof-greifen.rothenburg.de, info@gasthof-greifen .rothenburg.de, Brigitte and Klingler family). The family also has a couple of loaner bikes free for guests, and runs a good restaurant, serving basic meals in the back garden or dining room.

$$$ Hotel Gerberhaus, a classy and stylish hotel in an old building, is warmly run by Inge and Kurt, who mix modern comforts into 20 bright and airy rooms while maintaining a sense of half-timbered elegance. Enjoy the pleasant garden in back (Sb–€48–56, Db–€56–79, Tb–€94–99, Qb–€104–114, prices depend on room size, 2-room apartment with kitchen-€89/2 people, €120/4 people, 10 percent off and a free *Schneeball* if you stay 2 nights and pay cash, most rooms non-smoking, some rooms with canopied 4-poster *Himmel* beds, laundry-€5 per load, free Internet access in lobby, Spitalgasse 25, tel. 09861/94900, fax 09861/86555, www .gerberhaus.rothenburg.de, gerberhaus@t-online.de). The downstairs café and beer garden serve good soups, salads, and light lunches.

$$$ Hotel Kloster-Stüble, deep in the old town near the castle garden, is my classiest listing. Rudolf does the cooking, while Erika—his fun and energetic first mate—welcomes guests. The hotel recently expanded into the building next door, adding a sleek-in-medieval-stones breakfast room and eight gorgeous, modern rooms within the historic shell (Sb–€55–60, fine and traditional Db–€75–90, bigger and more mod Db–€106, Tb–€110–115, family rooms-€116–155, apartment with balcony or suites-€116 for 2 or up to €215 for 6, family deals, kids under age 5 free, Heringsbronnengasse 5, tel. 09861/6774, fax 09861/6474, www .klosterstueble.de, hotel@klosterstueble.de).

$$ Gasthof zur Goldenen Rose is a classic, family-run place—simple, traditional, comfortable, and a great value—where scurrying Karin serves breakfast and stately Henni keeps everything in good order. The hotel has one shower per floor, but the rooms are clean, and you're surrounded by cobbles, flowers, and red-tiled roofs (S-€21, D-€36, Ds-€46, Db-€50, some triples;

spacious family apartment-€107 for 4 people, €128 for 5 people, €148/6 people; kid-friendly, streetside rooms can be noisy, closed Jan–Feb, Spitalgasse 28, tel. 09861/4638, fax 09861/86417, www .thegoldenrose.de, info@thegoldenrose.de). The Favetta family also serves good, reasonably priced meals (restaurant closed Wed). Keep your key to get in after hours (side gate in alley).

$$ Hotel Altfränkische Weinstube am Klosterhof is the place for well-heeled bohemians. Mario, Hanne, and their lovely daughter Viktoria rent six cozy rooms above their dark and smoky pub in a 600-year-old building. It's an upscale, *Lord of the Rings* atmosphere, with TVs, modern showers, open-beam ceilings, and *Himmel* beds—canopied four-poster "heaven" beds (Sb-€45, Db-€55, bigger Db-€65, Db suite-€75, Tb-€75, prefer cash, kid-friendly, off Klingengasse at Klosterhof 7, tel. 09861/6404, fax 09861/6410, www.romanticroad.com/altfraenkische-weinstube). Their pub is a candlelit classic, serving hot food to Hobbits until 22:30, and closing at 1:00 in the morning. Drop by on Wednesday evening (19:30–24:00) for the English Conversation Club (see "Meet the Locals," page 171).

$$ Pension Elke, run by the spry Erich Endress and his son Klaus, rents 10 bright, airy, and comfy rooms above the family grocery store (S-€25, Sb-€35, D-€38–46, Db-€58–62, prices depend on size, extra bed-€15, 10 percent discount with this book through 2006 when you stay at least 2 nights, cash only; reception in grocery store until 19:00, otherwise go around corner onto Alter Stadtgraben to first door on left and ring bell at top of stairs; near Markus Tower at Rodergasse 6, tel. 09861/2331, fax 09861/935-355, www.pension-elke-rothenburg.de, info@pension-elke-rothenburg .de).

$$ Hotel Café Uhl offers 12 fine rooms over a bakery (Sb-€30–35, Db-€50–68, prices depend on size, third person-€18, fourth person-€13, 10 percent discount with this book and cash through 2006, non-smoking rooms, parking-€4/day, reception in café, closed Jan, Plönlein 8, tel. 09861/4895, fax 09861/92820, www.hotel-uhl.de, info@hotel-uhl.de, Paul and Robert the baker).

$$ Gästehaus Flemming has seven tastefully modern, fresh, and comfortable rooms and a peaceful garden behind St. Jakob's Church (Sb-€45, Db-€57, Tb-€79, cash only, Klingengasse 21, tel. 09861/92380, fax 09861/976-384, www.gaestehaus-flemming.de, gaestehaus-flemming@t-online.de, Regina).

$$ Gästehaus Viktoria is a cheery little place right next to the town wall. Its three rooms overflow with furniture, ribbons, and silk flowers, and lovely gardens surround the house (Db-€48–55, Tb-€65, cash only, a block from Klingentor at Klingenschutt 4, tel. 09861/87682, Hanne).

$$ Gästehaus Raidel, a creaky 500-year-old house filled with beds and furniture all handmade by friendly Norry Raidel himself, rents 14 large rooms. The creaky ambience makes me want to sing the *Addams Family* theme song—but the place has a rare, time-passed, family charm (S-€19, Sb-€29, D-€39, Db-€49, Tb-€70, cash only, Wenggasse 3, tel. 09861/3115, fax 09861/935-255, best to reserve through Web site at www.romanticroad.com/raidel,  Gaestehaus-Raidel@t-online.de). Norry plays in a Dixieland Band, and invented a fascinating hybrid saxophone/trombone called the Norryphone.

$$ Gasthof Marktplatz, right on Market Square, rents nine tidy rooms with 1970s-era wallpaper and unenthusiastic staff (S-€21, D-€38, Ds-€43, Db-€48, T-€50, Ts-€57, Tb-€62, cash only, Grüner Markt 10, tel. & fax 09861/1662, www.gasthof-marktplatz .de, Herr Rosner). The maddening Town Hall bells ring through-out the night.

$$ Pension Pöschel is friendly, with six bearskin-cozy rooms in a concrete but pleasant building and an inviting garden out back (S-€20, D-€35, Db-€45, T-€45, Tb-€55, small kids free, cash only, Wenggasse 22, tel. 09861/3430, pension.poeschel@t-online.de, Bettina).

$ Frau Liebler rents two large, modern, ground-floor rooms with kitchenettes. They're great for those looking for real pri-vacy—you'll have your own room fronting a quiet cobbled lane just below Market Square (Db-€40, no breakfast, 10 percent discount for 2 or more nights with this 2006 book, laundry-€5, cash only, behind Christmas shop at Pfaffleinsgasschen 10, tel. 09861/709-215, fax 09861/709-216).

$ Rossmühle Youth Hostel—This fine hostel, run for 25 years by Eduard Schmitz, rents 184 beds in two buildings. While it's mostly four to six bed dorms, they also have 15 doubles. The droopy-eyed building (the old town horse mill, used when the town was under siege and the river-powered mill was inacces-sible) houses groups and the office. The adjacent hostel is mostly for families and individuals (dorm beds-€19, bunk-bed Db-€43, includes breakfast and sheets, dinner-€5.40, self-serve laundry-€4, entrance on Rossmühlgasse, tel. 09861/94160, fax 09861/941-620, www.rothenburg.jugendherberge.de, book through www.djh-ris .de, jhrothenburg@djh-bayern.de). Here in Bavaria, hosteling is traditionally limited to those under 27, except for families traveling with children under 18.

Outside the Wall

The first place is a hundred yards outside the wall on the train-station side of town (less than a 10-min walk from the center) and offers some of the nicest rooms I recommend here. The second is a rustic adventure below the town in what feels like a wilderness.

$$$ Hotel Hornburg, a grand 100-year-old mansion with groomed grounds and 10 spacious, tastefully decorated rooms, is a two-minute walk outside the wall and a super value (Sb-€52–67, Db-€69–98, Tb-€90–115, ground-floor rooms, non-smoking rooms, family-friendly, avoid if you're allergic to dogs, parking-€3/day; if walking, exit station and go straight on Ludwig-Siebert Strasse, turn left on Mann Strasse until you're 100 yards from town wall; if driving, exit station but go left on Vorm Würzburger Tor; Hornburgweg 28, tel. 09861/8480, fax 09861/5570, www.hotel -hornburg.de, hotelhornburg@t-online.de, friendly Gabriele and Martin).

$$ Pension Fuchsmühle is a B&B in a renovated old mill on the river below the castle end of Rothenburg. The place is a work-in-progress, with kids and a linoleum-floor feel, but if you want a rustic, countryside experience, it's great. Alex and Heidi Molitor rent six rooms and take good care of their guests (Sb-€40, Db-€60, Tb-€80, Qb-€100, 6-bed apartment-€140, extra bed-€15, €5 less after 3 nights, non-smoking, healthy farm-fresh breakfasts, piano, free tours of mill, free pickup at station, across the street from Toppler's little castle at Taubertalweg 103, tel. 09861/92633, www.fuchsmuehle.de, fuchsmuehle@t-online.de). It's a steep but pleasant 15-minute hike from the Fuchsmühle to Market Square. The Molitors provide flashlights for your return after dark.

EATING

Many restaurants stop serving meals as early as 14:00 and 20:00. Places listed are within a five-minute walk of Market Square. While all survive on tourism, many still feel like local hangouts. Your choices are typical Franconian or ethnic. A good local dish to try is Maultaschen, the Swabian ravioli; it smuggles meat in a big piece of pasta, a custom that dates back to the days when some Catholics would use this culinary trick to eat meat when it wasn't allowed.

Traditional Franconian Restaurants

Eisenhut Restaurant, in Hotel Eisenhut, is a fine place for a dress-up splurge with a surprisingly reasonable price. You'll enjoy elegantly presented, traditional dishes with formal service. Sit in their royal dining room or on their garden terrace (€11 salads, €14 daily specials, €15–20 dinner plates, €25 small

Rothenburg Restaurants

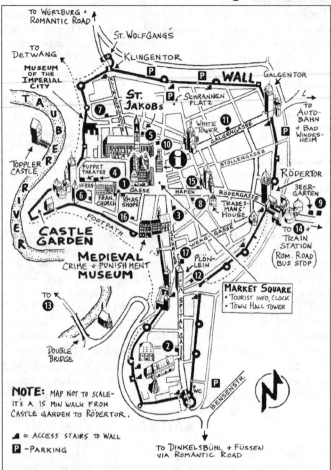

NOTE: MAP NOT TO SCALE - IT'S A 15 MIN WALK FROM CASTLE GARDEN TO RÖDERTOR.

⊿ = ACCESS STAIRS TO WALL
🅿 = PARKING

❶	Eisenhut Restaurant	❾	Gasthof Rödertor & Beer Garden
❷	Zur Goldenen Rose	❿	Lotus China
❸	Baumeister Haus & Gasthof Goldener Greifen	⓫	Pizzeria Roma
❹	Bürgerkeller	⓬	Doner Kebaps
❺	Reichs-Küchenmeister	⓭	To Unter den Linden Beer Garden
❻	Hotel Restaurant Klosterstüble	⓮	To Black Out & Club 23 Discos
❼	Altfränkische Weinstube am Klosterhof	⓯	Eis Café D' Isep (Ice Cream)
❽	Altstadt-Café Alter Keller	⓰	Trinkstube zur Hölle ("Hell")
		⓱	Restaurant Glocke

menu, €40 big *menu,* Herrngasse 3, tel. 09861/7050).

Zur Goldenen Rose, a hard-working eatery in a small hotel, is where Reno cooks up traditional German fare at great prices as Henni stokes your appetite (Tue 11:30–14:00, Thu–Mon 11:30–14:00 & 17:30–20:30, closed Wed, leafy garden terrace out back open in sunny weather, Spitalgasse 28, tel. 09861/4638).

Baumeister Haus, extremely picturesque and touristy, is a thriving place tucked deep behind a streetside pastry counter and antlered dining room. It fills an inviting courtyard with people who don't understand a German menu; the space is gorgeous, but the clientele ruins my appetite (€8–15 entrées, daily 8:00–23:00, a few doors below Market Square, Obere Schmiedgasse 3, tel. 09861/94700).

Gasthof Goldener Greifen is what you wish Baumeister Haus would be: Hardworking locals in a historic building just off the main square, who serve quality Franconian food to in-the-know locals at a good price...and with a smile. The wood is ancient and polished from generations of happy use, but the ambience isn't over-the-top—and that's just fine with me (€7–13 entrées, super-cheap kids' menus, lots of daily specials, closed Sun eve, Obere Schmiedgasse 5, tel. 09861/2281, family Klingler).

Bürgerkeller is a good place for a quiet and low-energy evening of cellar dining under medieval murals and pointy pikes. With not a burger in sight, Herr Harry Terian and his family pride themselves in quality local cuisine, offering a small but inviting menu and reasonable prices. Harry likes oldies, and you're welcome to look over his impressive playlist and request your favorite music (€6–12 entrées, Thu–Tue 11:30–14:00 & 18:00–21:00, closed Wed, a few sidewalk tables, near bottom of Herrngasse at #24, tel. 09861/2126).

Reichs-Küchenmeister is a typical big-hotel restaurant, but on a balmy evening, its pleasant, tree-shaded terrace overlooking St. Jakob's Church is hard to beat. Their *Vesperbrett* plate is a fine selection of cold cuts (€8–16 entrées, daily 11:00–22:00, Kirchplatz 8, tel. 09861/9700).

Hotel Restaurant Klosterstüble, deep in the old town near the castle garden, is a classy place for delicious and beautifully presented traditional cuisine. Rudy's food is better than his English, but head waitress Erika makes sure communication goes smoothly. The shady terrace is nice on a warm summer evening. I prefer their traditional section to the stony, sleek, non-smoking room (€10 entrées, daily 11:00–14:00 & 18:00–21:00, Heringsbronnengasse 5, tel. 09861/6774).

Altfränkische Weinstube am Klosterhof seems designed for Hobbits to celebrate their anniversaries. At this very dark and smoky pub, classically candlelit in a 600-year-old building,

Mario whips up gourmet pub grub (€6–12 entrées, hot food served 18:00–22:30, closes at 1:00 in the morning, off Klingengasse at Klosterhof 7, tel. 09861/6404). If you'd like dinner company, drop by on Wednesday evening, when the English Conversation Club has a big table reserved from 19:00 on (see "Meet the Locals," page 171). You'll eat well and with new friends—both travelers and locals.

Altstadt-Café Alter Keller is just right for a light meal near the center—but without the tourists. Eat indoors under walls festooned with old pots and jugs, or outdoors on a quiet little square. Herr Hufnagel, a baker and pastry chef, whips up a tempting array of cakes, pies, and giant meringue cookies, while gracious Christine makes sure you understand your options (€3–7 dishes, Sat–Thu 11:00–20:00, Sun until 18:00, closed Fri, Alter Keller 8, tel. 09861/2268).

Gasthof Rödertor, just outside the wall through the Rödertor gate, is a lively place where Rothenburgers go for a hearty meal at a good price. Their passion is potatoes: an entire *Kartoffeln Stube* menu is dedicated to spud plates (€6–11 entrées, daily 11:30–14:00 & 17:30–22:30, tel. 09861/2022). They also run a popular beer garden (see below).

Ethnic-Food Breaks from Pork and Potatoes

Lotus China is a peaceful world apart, serving good Chinese food (€8–10 entrées, €6 2-course lunch specials, daily 11:30–14:30 & 17:30–23:00, 2 blocks behind TI near church, Eckele 2, tel. 09861/86886).

Pizzeria Roma is smoky because it's the locals' favorite for €6.50 pizza and pastas with good Italian wine. Thirty-six years ago, the Magrini family moved here from Tuscany. They've been cooking pasta for Rothenburg ever since (Thu–Tue 11:30–24:00, closed Wed and mid-Aug–mid-Sept, Galgengasse 19, tel. 09861/4540, Ricardo).

Doner Kebaps, run by Osman Gul, serves cheap and tasty food to go. His tiny place offers what must be the best €3 hot meal in town (daily 11:00–21:00, Wengasse 4, tel. 09861/92417).

A **supermarket** is near Rödertor, just outside the wall (Mon–Sat 8:00–20:00, closed Sun, on left as you exit wall).

Beer Gardens and Discos

Rothenburg's beer gardens can be great fun, but they're only open when the weather is balmy.

Unter den Linden, a beer garden in the valley along the river, is worth the 20-minute hike on a pleasant evening (daily in season with decent weather, 10:00–22:00 and sometimes later, self-service food and good beer, call first to confirm it's open, tel. 09861/5909).

As it's in the valley on the river, it's cooler than Rothenburg; bring a sweater.

Gasthof Rödertor, just outside the wall through the Rödertor gate, is great for a rowdy crowd, cheap food, and good beer (May–Sept daily 17:00–24:00, look for wood gate, tel. 09861/2022). If the beer garden is closed, their indoor restaurant (described above) is a good value.

Two popular **discos** are just down the street: Black Out (Ansbacher Strasse 15, in alley next to Sparkasse bank, open Wed and Fri–Sat 22:00–3:00, closed Sun–Tue and Thu) and Club 23 (around corner from bank on Adam Hörber Strasse, open Thu–Sat from 22:00, closed Sun–Wed, tel. 09861/933-045).

Dessert

Eis Café D' Isep, with a pleasant interior, is the town's ice-cream parlor. They do fancy ice creams, cakes, and drinks on the only real pedestrian street in town (daily 11:00–22:00, closed during winter, 1 block off Market Square at Hafengasse 17).

Wine-Drinking in the Old Center

Trinkstube zur Hölle ("Hell") is dark and foreboding, offering a thick wine-drinking atmosphere. Unfortunately, it's become painfully touristic (simple menu served until late, daily 17:00–24:00, closed Sun Jan–March, a block past Medieval Crime and Punishment Museum on Burggasse, with devil hanging out front, tel. 09861/4229).

Mario's **Altfränkische Weinstube am Klosterhof** (see "Traditional Franconian Restaurants," page 167) is the liveliest place, and the clear favorite with locals for an atmospheric drink or late meal. When every other place is asleep, you're likely to find good food, drink, and liveliness here.

Eisenhut, behind the fancy hotel of the same name on Herrngasse, is a good bet for gentle and casual beer-garden ambience within the old center.

Restaurant Glocke, a *Weinstube* (wine bar) popular with locals, is run by Rothenburg's oldest wine-makers, the Thürauf family. The menu, which has a very extensive wine list, is in German only because the friendly staff wants to explain your options in person. Their €4.20 deal, which lets you sample five Franconian wines, is popular (€10–15 entrées, Mon–Sat 10:30–23:00, Sun 10:30–14:00, Plönlein 1, tel. 09861/958-990).

Meet the Locals

For a rare chance to mix it up with locals who aren't selling anything, bring your favorite slang and tongue twisters to the **English Conversation Club** at Mario's Altfränkische Weinstube am

Klosterhof (Wed 19:30–24:00, Anneliese from Friese shop and Hermann the German are regulars; see restaurant listed under "Traditional Franconian Restaurants," above). This group of intrepid linguists celebrated their 1,000th meeting in 2003. There are always local members there from 19:00. Consider coming early for dinner, or after 21:00, when the beer starts to sink in, the crowd grows, and everyone seems to speak that second language a bit easier.

TRANSPORTATION CONNECTIONS

From Rothenburg by Bus: The Romantic Road bus tour takes you in and out of Rothenburg each afternoon (April–Oct), heading to Munich, Frankfurt, or Füssen. See the schedule and tour description below.

By Train: A tiny train line connects Rothenburg to the outside world via **Steinach** (generally at :05 after each hour, 15 min). If you plan to arrive in Rothenburg by train, note that the last train to Rothenburg departs nightly from Steinach at 20:30. For those leaving Rothenburg by train, the first train to Steinach departs at 6:05, the last at about 20:00. If you plan on arriving in Steinach after 20:00 (the last train), note that the German government believes in providing public transport to its visitors, as well as its citizens; it subsidizes the taxi fare to Rothenburg. If you make an appointment with a participating taxi service (such at tel. 09861/2000) at least an hour in advance, they'll drive you from Steinach to Rothenburg for the train fare (€3.60/person) rather than the €22 regular fare. Other taxi companies: tel. 09861/7227 and 09861/95100.

From Steinach by Train to: Rothenburg (almost hrly, 15 min, last train at 20:00), **Würzburg** (hrly, 1 hr), **Nürnberg** (2/ hr, 1–1.5 hr, most change in Ansbach or Neustadt an der Aisch), **Munich** (hrly, 3 hrs, 2 changes), **Frankfurt** (hrly, 3 hrs, change in Würzburg), **Berlin** (3 hrs, 3 changes). Train connections in Steinach are usually within a few minutes (to Rothenburg generally from track 5). Train info: tel. 11861 (€0.50/min).

Route Tips for Drivers

The autobahn serves Würzburg, Rothenburg, and Dinkelsbühl very efficiently, making the drive from Frankfurt to Munich with these stops very fast. But if you have the time and inclination to meander, the Romantic Road—the small and carefully signposted road tracing the medieval trade route between the Rhine and the Roman road that went over the Alps south of Munich—is worth the effort.

Heading south from Rothenburg, get an early start to enjoy

the quaint hills and rolling villages of what was Germany's major medieval trade route. The views of Rothenburg from the west, across the Tauber Valley, are magnificent.

After a quick stop in the center of Dinkelsbühl, cross the baby Danube River (Donau) and continue south along the Romantic Road to Füssen. Drive by Neuschwanstein Castle just to sweeten your dreams before crossing into Austria to get set up at Reutte (see Bavaria and Tirol chapter).

If detouring past Oberammergau, you can drive through Garmisch, past Germany's highest mountain (Zugspitze), into Austria via Lermoos, and on to Reutte. Or you can take the small scenic shortcut to Reutte past Ludwig's Linderhof castle and along the windsurfer-strewn Plansee.

The Romantic Road

The Romantic Road (Romantische Strasse) winds you past the most beautiful towns and scenery of Germany's medieval heartland. Once Germany's medieval trade route, now it's the best way to connect the dots between Füssen, Munich, and Frankfurt (www.romantischestrasse.de).

Wander through quaint hills and rolling villages, and stop wherever the cows look friendly or a town fountain beckons. My favorite sections are from Füssen to Landsberg and Rothenburg to Weikersheim. (If you're driving with limited time, connect Rothenburg and Munich by autobahn.) Caution: The similarly promoted "Castle Road," which runs between Rothenburg and Mannheim, sounds intriguing but is nowhere near as interesting.

Throughout Bavaria, you'll see colorfully ornamented maypoles decorating town squares. Many are painted in Bavaria's colors, white and blue. The decorations that line each side of the pole symbolize the crafts or businesses of that community. Each May Day, they are festively replaced. Traditionally, rival communities try to steal each other's maypole. Locals guard their new pole night and day as May Day approaches. Stolen poles are ransomed only with lots of beer for the clever thieves.

Getting Around the Romantic Road
By Bus: The Deutsche Touring company runs buses daily between Frankfurt and Munich in each direction (April–Oct, tel. 069/790-350, www.romantic-road-coach.de). I used to heartily recommend this bus tour, but given its recent price spikes, increasingly inflexible schedule, and long travel times, it's no longer a good deal—take the train instead. However, if you'd like to see the Romantic Road the slow and scenic way, confirm departures and arrivals when you

Romantic Road Bus Schedule

The Romantic Road bus runs daily April through October. Every day, one bus goes north to south (Frankfurt to Munich), and another follows the same route south to north (Munich to Frankfurt). Along the way, both buses pass through towns and attractions such as Würzburg, Rothenburg, the Wieskirche, and Füssen. You can begin or end your journey at any of these stops. The following times are based on the 2005 schedule. Check www.euraide.de/ricksteves for any changes.

North to South
Depart Frankfurt 8:00
Depart Würzburg 10:00
Arrive Rothenburg 11:50
Depart Rothenburg. 12:10
Arrive Dinkelsbühl 12:50
Depart Dinkelsbühl. 13:30
Arrive Wieskirche 17.45
Depart Wieskirche 18:00
Arrive Füssen. 19:05
Depart Füssen 19:15
Arrive Munich 21:00

South to North
Depart Munich. 8:00
Depart Füssen 9:50
Arrive Wieskirche 11:00
Depart Wieskirche 11:15
Arrive Dinkelsbühl 16:05
Depart Dinkelsbühl. 16:25
Arrive Rothenburg 17:05
Depart Rothenburg. 17:30
Depart Würzburg 19:35
Arrive Frankfurt 21:00

buy your ticket—schedules aren't posted, and special events can temporarily change bus-stop locations and schedules.

Buses usually leave from train stations (in towns large enough to have one), but the stops are not well signed. The grim drivers usually hand out maps and brochures and play a tape-recorded narration of the journey highlights in English. Buses stop too briefly in Rothenburg (about 20 min) and Dinkelsbühl (about 30 min), and just long enough to use the WC at a few other attractions. You can join or leave the trip where you like (but if you choose to stay at a particular stop, you'll have to wait until tomorrow for the next bus—or find another way to your next destination). If you prefer urban sights and speedy trains, this can seem like a glorified

Greyhound ride with a beverage service (free coffee, €1 for cold drinks).

The ride from Frankfurt to Füssen costs €76 and takes 11 hours, and Frankfurt to Munich costs €95 and takes 13 hours (pay cash on the bus, luggage storage costs a few extra euros). Shorter segments cost less. Students and seniors—without a railpass—get a 10 percent discount.

You can get a 60 percent discount on your bus ticket if you have a German railpass, Eurailpass, or Eurail Selectpass (if Germany is one of your selected countries). As of 2005, you did not have to use a travel day of a flexipass to get this discount. Readers have reported that some bus drivers refuse to honor this discount, or insist on charging them a travel day. Set them straight.

Bus reservations are almost never necessary. But they are free and easy, and, technically, without one you can lose your seat to someone who has one (tel. 069/790-350 to reserve).

By Car: Follow the brown *Romantische Strasse* signs and the free tourist brochure (available all over the place) that describes the journey.

SIGHTS

Along the Romantic Road

These sights are listed from north to south.

Frankfurt—The northern terminus of the Romantic Road is in this country's Manhattan (covered in its own chapter on page 191).

Würzburg—With its fancy palace and chapel, historic Würzburg can make a good overnight stop (see next chapter).

Weikersheim—This untouristy town has a palace with fine Baroque gardens (luxurious picnic spot), a folk museum, and a picturesque town square.

▲Herrgottskapelle—This peaceful church is graced with Tilman Riemenschneider's greatest carved altarpiece (Easter–Oct daily 9:15–17:30, less off-season, tel. 07933/508). Across the street is the Fingerhut (thimble, literally "finger hat") museum (€2, April–Oct daily 9:00–18:00, less off-season, tel. 07933/370). The southbound Romantic Road bus stops here for 15 minutes, long enough to see one or the other. The church and museum are a mile south of Creglingen (TI tel. 07933/631, www.creglingen.de).

▲▲▲Rothenburg—See above for information on Germany's best medieval town.

▲Dinkelsbühl—Rothenburg's little sister is cute enough to merit a short stop. A moat, towers, gates, and a beautifully preserved medieval wall surround this town. Dinkelsbühl's history museum is meager and without a word of English. The Kinderzeche children's festival celebrates the success of the local children who

The Romantic Road

pleaded with the Swedish army during the Thirty Years' War, convincing them to spare the town. The festival turns Dinkelsbühl wonderfully on end for a week at the end of July. The helpful **TI** on the main street sells maps with a short walking tour and can help find rooms (Mon–Fri 9:00–18:00, Sat 10:00–13:00 & 14:00–16:00, Sun 10:00–13:00, shorter hours off-season, tel. 09851/90240, www.dinkelsbuehl.de).

Sleeping in Dinkelsbühl: Consider **Hotel Palmengarten,** run by the Danner-Bohl family (Sb-€34–46, Db-€62–76, Tb-€77–88, parking garage-€5, Untere Schmiedgasse 14, tel. 09851/57670,

fax 09851/7548, www.sonne-palmengarten.de, info@sonne
-palmengarten.de).

Nördlingen—Known for its 15-mile-wide valley that was carved by a meteor 15 million years ago, Nördlingen separates the Schwabian and Franconian Alps. (The town also gained fame as the "grain basket" because of its rich soil.) Apollo astronauts did research and field training here; if you visit the museum dedicated to the study of the meteor (Riesenkrater Museum), so can you (Tue–Sun 10:00–12:00 & 13:30–16:30, closed Mon, Eugene Shoemaker Platz 1, tel. 09081/273-8220).

Augsburg—Founded more than 2,000 years ago by Emperor Augustus, Augsburg enjoyed its heyday in the 15th and 16th centuries. Today, it's Bavaria's third largest city, and the place where the idea for the "Romantic Road" originated.

Röttenbuch—This nondescript village has an impressive church in a lovely setting. The bus stops here only on request.

Landsberg am Lech—Like many towns in this area, Landsberg (on the river Lech) has its roots in salt trade. Every four years, the town returns to its medieval roots and hosts the Ruethen Pageant. The town, founded the same year as Munich (1158), was shaped by the architect Dominikus Zimmerman (of Wieskirche fame). Adolf Hitler wrote *Mein Kampf* while serving his prison sentence here after the Beerhall Putsch of 1923 (when Hitler and his followers unsuccessfully attempted to take over the government of Bavaria).

▲▲Wieskirche—This is Germany's most glorious Baroque-rococo church, beautifully restored and set in a sweet meadow. Heavenly! Romantic Road buses from Füssen stop here for 15 minutes. (See page 102 of the Bavaria and Tirol chapter.)

Füssen—This town, three miles from the stunning Neuschwanstein Castle, is worth a stop on any sightseeing agenda. (See page 94 of the Bavaria and Tirol chapter for description and accommodations.)

WÜRZBURG

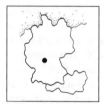

A historic city—though freshly rebuilt since World War II—Würzburg is worth a stop to see its impressive Prince Bishop's Residenz, the bubbly Baroque chapel (Hofkirche) next door, and the palace's sculpted gardens. Surrounded by vineyards and filled with atmospheric *Weinstuben*, this small, tourist-friendly town is easy to navigate by foot or streetcar. Today, 25,000 of its 130,000 residents are students—making the town feel young and very alive.

ORIENTATION

(area code: 0931)

Tourist Information

Würzburg's helpful TI is in the rococo Falken Haus on the Marktplatz (April–Dec Mon–Fri 10:00–18:00, Sat 10:00–14:00, May–Oct also Sun 10:00–14:00; Jan–March Mon–Fri 10:00–16:00, Sat 10:00–13:00, closed Sun, tel. 0931/372-398, www.wuerzburg .de). Their free *Visitor's Guide* pamphlet and map covers the tourist's Würzburg well. The TI also books rooms for free (in person only, not by phone) and sells detailed maps for biking through the local wine country. If you'll be continuing on the Romantic Road (see previous chapter), the TI also has the *Romantische Strasse* brochure and a list of car-rental options. The TI also sells the Würzburg Welcome Card, offering minimal discounts on a few sights and restaurants (€2/7 days).

Würzburg's Beginnings

The city was born centuries before Christ at an easy-to-ford part of the Main River under an easy-to-defend hill. A Celtic fort stood where the fortress stands today. Later, three Irish missionary monks came here to Christianize the local barbarians. In A.D. 686, they were beheaded, and their relics put Würzburg on the pilgrimage map. About 500 years later, since the town was the seat of a bishop, Holy Roman Emperor Frederick Barbarossa came here to get the bishop's OK to divorce his wife. The bishop said "No problem," and the HRE thanked him by giving him secular rule of the entire region of Franconia. From then on, the bishop was also a prince, and the Prince Bishop of Würzburg answered only to the Holy Roman Emperor.

Arrival in Würzburg

Würzburg's train station is user-friendly and filled with handy services (€2 lockers in main hall, WCs between main hall and tunnel to platforms). Walk out of the train station to the small square in front. A big **city map** board provides a quick orientation (on small building to the right). Farther right is the **post office** (Mon–Fri 8:00–18:00, Sat 9:00–12:00, closed Sun) and the **Romantic Road bus stop** (track 13, curb closest and parallel to station building, look for very small yellow Romantische Strasse sign and schedule).

From the cul-de-sac in front of the station, **trams** (#1, #3, #4, or #5) take you one stop to recommended hotels (except Hotel-Pension Spehnkuch near station) or two stops to Market Square and the TI. By **foot,** cross over the busy Röntgenring and head up the shop-lined Kaiserstrasse. For the **Residenz,** it's either a 15-minute walk or a short bus ride (on #14, #16, #20, #26, or #28).

Helpful Hints

Internet Access: Try the **Stadtbücherei** (library, a.k.a. *Stabü*) next to the TI (€3/hr, Mon–Fri 10:00–18:00, Thu until 19:00, Sat 10:00–14:00, closed Sun, wise to call for reservations, check in with info desk on 1st floor, Falken Haus, Marktplatz, tel. 0931/373-439).

Bike Rental: Fahrrad-Station at the train station rents good **bikes** (€6 from 13:00–18:30, or €10/24 hrs, no helmets, April–Oct Tue–Fri 9:30–18:30, Sat 9:30–14:30, closed Sun–Mon and Nov–March, passport number required, ask for a basket, tel. 0931/57445).

Festivals: Würzburg—ever clever with trade—schedules its three annual festivals (wine, Mozart, and the Kiliani-Volksfest) in rapid succession to keep things busy from June 1 through late July.

Local Guide: Maureen Aldenhoff, who grew up in Liverpool but has been married to a Würzburger for 30 years, gives good private walking tours (€78/2 hrs, €90/3 hrs, tel. 0931/52135, maureen.aldenhoff@web.de).

Getting Around Würzburg

You can easily walk to everything but the hill-top fortress. The single ticket (*Einzelfahrschein*, €2/good for 1 hr) is valid for all city bus or tram rides, including the bus to the fortress, as are the 24-hour passes (*Tageskarte Solo*, €4 for 1 person, or €8.10 for a *Tageskarte Familie* to cover 2 adults and kids under age 15). Either ticket can be bought on the bus from the driver or at a streetside machine, and tickets purchased on a Saturday are also good on Sunday. Note that tickets are only valid if stamped, so be sure to insert yours into the little box in the tram or bus. For transit info, tel. 0931/362-321, or visit the transit pavilion (Mon–Fri 7:30–18:00, closed Sat–Sun, exit the train station and the pavilion is on your right just before you cross the Röntgenring).

SELF-GUIDED WALK

Welcome to Würzburg

This brief walk gets you from the Residenz to the Old Main Bridge (Alte Mainbrücke) through the key old-town sights.

• *Begin at the fountain in front of the Residenz.*

Fountain of Franconia: In 1814, the Prince Bishop got the boot and Franconia was secularized. The region was given to Bavaria to be ruled by the Wittelsbach family, so Franconia is technically a part of Bavaria (which is like Ireland being part of Britain—never call a Franconian a Bavarian). This statue—a gift from the townspeople to their new royal family—turns its back to the palace and faces the town. It celebrates the artistic and intellectual genius of Franconia with statues of three great hometown boys (a medieval bard, the woodcarver Riemenschneider, and the painter Grünewald).

• *If Franconia hopped down and ran 300 yards ahead down Hofstrasse, she'd hit the red-spired cathedral. Meet her there.*

St. Kilian's Cathedral (Dom): This is the fourth-largest Romanesque cathedral in Germany. The building's core is

Romanesque (1040–1188), with Gothic spires and Baroque additions to the transepts. Enter through the back (end nearest you, on the right-hand side) and leave through the main entrance.

• *From here, you can make a quick stop at the brand-new Cathedral Museum (through passageway on your right-hand side).*

Cathedral Museum (Museum am Dom): The museum features a bizarre combination of old and new religious art. It pairs 11th- to 18th-century works with modern interpretations, sprinkles it all with a Christian theme, and wraps it in a shiny new building (€3 or €4.50 combo-ticket with Cathedral Treasury, April–Oct Tue–Sun 10:00–19:00, Nov–March Tue–Sun 10:00–17:00, closed Mon year-round, tel. 0931/3866-5600, www.museum-am-dom.de).

• *Upon leaving, you'll see Domstrasse leading down to the spire of the town hall and the Old Main Bridge (where this walk will end). On your left you'll see a sign for the Cathedral Treasury (Domschatz, €2.50 or €4.50 combo-ticket with Cathedral Museum, Tue–Sun 14:00–17:00, closed Mon, tel. 0931/386-261). But we're looping right. Go a block up Kurschner Hof. On your right, you'll pass the entrance to the...*

Neumünster Basilica: Like the Dom, this church has a Romanesque body with a Baroque face. Go up the stairs to take a look inside, then continue up the street. Notice the quiet of the pedestrian zone. Locals wouldn't have it any other way—electric trolleys, bikes, and pedestrians.

• *Enter the square with the two-tone church.*

Upper Market Square (Marktplatz): The fancy yellow-and-white rococo House of the Falcon once had three different facades. To fix it, the landlady gave a wandering band of stucco artists a chance to show their stuff and ended up with this (TI and library with Internet access).

• *Set your eyes on the church.*

Marienkapelle: The two-tone, late-Gothic church was the merchants' answer to the Prince Bishop's cathedral. Since Rome didn't bankroll the place, it's ringed with "swallow shops" (like swallows' nests cuddled up against a house)—enabling the church to run little businesses. The sandstone statues (replicas of Riemenschneider originals) are the 12 apostles and Jesus. Walk downhill along the church to the lower marketplace, where the city's **produce market** bustles daily except Sunday (May–Oct 8:00–16:00). The famous Adam and Eve statues (flanking the side entrance to the church) show off Riemenschneider's mastery of the body. Continue around the church to the west portal (main entrance), where the carved Last Judgment shows kings, ladies, and bishops—some going to heaven, others making up the chain gang bound for hell, via the monster's mouth. (This was commissioned by those feisty town merchants tired of snooty blue-bloods.) Continue around to the next entry to see the Annunciation, with a cute angel Gabriel telling Mary (who is a virgin, symbolized by the lilies) the good news. Notice how God whispers through a speaking tube as baby Jesus slips down and into her ear.

• *Head back around to the lower market (Adam-and-Eve side) and leave downhill toward the yellow building with the clock. Follow Langgasse left (past a public WC) to the fountain facing City Hall and the bridge.*

City Hall (Rathaus): Würzburg's City Hall is relatively humble because of the power of the Prince Bishop. A side room on the left holds the Gedenkraum 16. März (March) 1945—a memorial to the 20-minute Allied bombing that created a firestorm, destroying (and demoralizing) the town just six weeks before the end of World War II. Check out the sobering models, ponder the names (lining the ceiling) of those killed, and read the free English flier (City Hall free and always open).

• *Now, face the...*

Old Main Bridge (Alte Mainbrücke): This bridge, from 1133, is the second-oldest in Germany. The 12 statues lining the bridge are Würzburg saints and Prince Bishops. Walk to the St. Kilian statue (with the golden sword)—one of the three monks who were shown being beheaded in the Residenz Hofkirche Chapel. Stand so you can't see the white power-plant tower and enjoy the best view in town. Marienberg Fortress caps the hill (see below). Squint up at Kilian pointing to God...with his head on.

The hillside is blanketed with grapevines—destined to become the fine Stein Franconian wine. Johann Wolfgang von Goethe, the German Shakespeare, ordered 900 liters of this vintage annually. A friend once asked Goethe what he thought were the three most important things in life. He said, "Wine, women, and song." When asked if he had to give one up, which it would be, without hesitating, Goethe answered "Song." Then, when asked what he would choose if he had to give up a second, Goethe paused and said, "It depends on the vintage."

• *Your walking tour is over. From here, consider paying a visit to the fortress on the hill above you.*

SIGHTS

▲▲**Würzburg's Residenz**—This Franconian Versailles features grand rooms, 3-D art, and a massive fresco by Tiepolo. The fresco has been under restoration recently—obscuring part of it—though this project is supposed to be finished by May of 2006. When Tiepolo's masterful work is fully unveiled, the Residenz is a ▲▲▲ sight.

Cost, Hours, Location: €4.50, daily April–Oct 9:00–18:00, Nov–March 10:00–16:00, last entry 30 min before closing, no photos,

tel. 0931/355-170 or 0931/355-1712. Don't confuse the Residenz (a 15-min walk southeast of the train station) with Marienberg Fortress (on the hilltop). Easy parking is available in front of the Residenz (€1.50/1st hr, €1 every subsequent hour, pay at the machine before you leave your car).

Tours, Information, Services: English tours, offered May through October daily at 11:00 and 15:00, give you access to the normally closed South Wing rooms, including the Mirror Kabinett (45 min, call ahead or let the cashier know you want to join the English tour, covered in entry price, but tips are welcome if the guide is good). The €3 English guidebook is dry and lengthy. Few English descriptions are provided in the Residenz; follow the self-guided tour, below, for an overview. On the right as you exit the ticket office, you'll find free WCs and €1 storage lockers.

Residenz Grounds: The elaborate Hofkirche Chapel is next door (as you exit the palace, go left), and the entrance to the pic-nic-worthy garden is just beyond (for more on both, see below).

❍ Self-Guided Tour: The following self-guided tour gives you the basics to appreciate this fine palace.

• *Begin at the entrance.*

1. Vestibule: The grand circular driveway was just right for six-horse carriages to drop off their guests. The elegant stairway comes with low steps, enabling high-class ladies to glide gracefully up, heads tilted back to enjoy Europe's largest and grandest fresco opening up above them.

• *Ascend the stairs and look up at the...*

2. Tiepolo Fresco: In 1752, the Venetian master Tiepolo was instructed to make a grand fresco illustrating the greatness of Europe, Würzburg, and the Prince Bishop. And he did—in only 13 months. Find the four continents, each symbolized by a woman on an animal and pointing to the Prince Bishop in the medallion above Europe. America—desperately uncivilized—sits naked with feathers in her hair on an alligator among severed heads. She's being served hot chocolate, a favorite import and nearly a drug for Europeans back then. Africa sits on a camel in a land of trade and fantasy animals (based on secondhand reports). Asia rides her elephant in the birthplace of Christianity and the alphabet. And Europe is shown as the center of high culture—Lady Culture points her brush not at Rome, but at Würzburg. The Prince Bishop had a healthy ego. The ceiling features Apollo and a host of Greek gods, all paying homage to the PB (under partial restoration until May of 2006).

Würzburg

1. Sankt Josef Hotel
2. Hotel Schönleber
3. Hotel Barbarossa
4. Hostel
5. Hotel-Pension Spehnkuch
6. Weinhaus zum Stachel
7. Würzburger Ratskeller
8. Backöfele Restaurant
9. Martinsklause & Martinz
10. Café Two Jours
11. Wirtshaus zum Lämmle
12. Weinstube Maulaffenbäck
13. Weinstube Bürgerspital
14. Market Square: Café Schönborn & Café Michel
15. Romantic Road Bus Stop
16. Bike Rental
17. Marienkapelle

3. The White Hall: This hall, actually gray, was kept plain to punctuate the colorful rooms on either side. It's a rococo-stucco fantasy. (The word "rococo" comes from the Portuguese word for the frilly rocaille shell.)

• *Straight ahead is the palace gift shop. To see more of Tiepolo's work, cross through the gift shop to the* **Tiepolo Gallery,** *where you'll find a collection of his paintings and etchings (included in admission). Otherwise, continue to your left, following signs for* Rundgang.

4. The Imperial Hall: This hall is the ultimate example of Baroque: harmony, symmetry, illusion, and the bizarre; lots of light and mirrors facing windows; and all with a foundation of absolutism (a divine monarch, inspired by Louis XIV). Take a moment to marvel at all the 3-D tricks in the ceiling. Here's another trick: As you enter the room, look left and check out the dog in the fresco. When you get to the window, have another look...notice that he has gotten older and fatter while you were crossing the hall. The room features three scenes: On the ceiling, find Father Main (the local river) amusing himself with a nymph. The two walls tell more history. On one, the bishop presides over the marriage of a happy Barbarossa (whose bride was actually 12 years old, unlike the woman in the painting, who looks considerably older). The bishop's power is demonstrated through his oversized fingers (giving the benediction) and through the details of his hat, which—unlike his face—is not shown in profile. Opposite that is the pay-off: Barbarossa, now the Holy Roman Emperor, gives the bishop Franconia and the secular title of prince. From this point onward, the Prince Bishop rules. Before leaving the room, survey the garden (explained below) from the balcony.

5. The North Wing: This wing is a string of lavish rooms—evolving from fancy Baroque to fancier rococo—used for the Prince Bishop's VIP guests. It's a straight shot, with short English descriptions in each room to the Green Room in the corner.

6. The Green Lacquer Room: This room is named for its silver-leaf walls, painted green. The Escher-esque inlaid floor was painstakingly restored after WWII bombings. Have fun multiplying in the mirrors before leaving. The nearby hall shows photos of the city in rubble in 1945—and craftsmen bringing the palace back to its original splendor soon after.

▲▲**Hofkirche Chapel**—This sumptuous chapel was for the exclusive use of the Prince Bishop (private altar upstairs with direct entrance to his residence) and his court (ground floor). The decor and design is textbook Baroque. Architect Balthasar Neumann was stuck with the existing walls. His challenge was to bring in light and create symmetry—essential to any Baroque work. He did it with mirrors and hidden windows. All the gold is real—if paper-thin—gold leaf. The columns are "manufactured marble," which isn't marble at all but marbled plaster. This method was popular because it was cheap and the color could be controlled. Pigment was mixed into plaster, which was rolled onto the stone or timber core of the column. This half-inch veneer was then polished. You can tell if a "marble" column is real or fake by resting your hand on it. If it warms up...it's not marble. The faded painting high above the altar shows three guys in gold robes losing their heads (monks who were martyred; see "Würzburg's Beginnings," page 179). The two side paintings are by the great fresco artist Tiepolo. Since the plaster wouldn't dry in the winter, Tiepolo spent his downtime painting with oil (free, daily April–Oct 9:00–18:00, Nov–March 10:00–16:00, closed during Sun 10:00 Mass and on Catholic holidays; facing the palace, use separate entrance at far right just before garden entrance).

Residenz Garden—One of Germany's finest Baroque gardens is a delightful park (enter next to the chapel). The Italian section, just inside the gate, features statues of Greek gods, carefully trimmed 180-year-old yew trees, and an orangery (WCs in far right corner). The French section, directly behind the palace around to the left, is grand à la Versailles but uses terraces to create the illusion of spaciousness (since it was originally hemmed in by the town wall).

Marienberg Fortress (Festung Marienberg)—This 13th-century fortified retreat was the original residence of Würzburg's Prince Bishops. After being stormed by the Swedish army during the Thirty Years' War, the fortress was rebuilt in Baroque style. The fortress contains two museums: a **City History Museum** (Fürstenbaumuseum, €4, €5 combo-ticket for both museums, April–mid-Oct Tue–Sun 9:00–18:00, closed Mon and off-season, tel. 0931/355-1750) and the **Mainfränkisches Museum,** which highlights the work of Riemenschneider, Germany's top wood-carver and onetime mayor of Würzburg (€3, €5 combo-ticket for both museums, few English explanations, €3 audioguide, April–Oct Tue–Sun 10:00–17:00, Nov–March until 16:00, closed Mon year-round, tel. 0931/205-940, www.mainfraenkisches-museum .de; Riemenschneider fans will also find his work throughout Würzburg's many churches). The **fortress grounds** (free) provide fine city views. The gift shop sells a good €2.60 guide explaining the fortress' history, courtyard buildings, and museums. For restaurants at the fortress, see "Eating," below.

Getting to Marienberg Fortress: Take bus #9 (€2 one-way, covered by *Tageskarte* pass, runs daily 10:00–18:00 every 40 min, departs from Residenzplatz and Barbarossaplatz/Juliuspromenade). To walk, cross the Alte Mainbrücke and follow small Festung Marienberg signs to the right uphill for a heart-thumping 20 minutes (signs pointing left indicate a longer, more gradual path through vineyards).

SLEEPING

Würzburg's good-value hotels provide a stress-free first or last night when flying in or out of Frankfurt. Hourly trains connect the two cities in 90 minutes (see "Transportation Connections," page 19).

Sleep Code

(€1 = about $1.20, country code: 49, area code: 0931)
S = Single, **D** = Double/Twin, **T** = Triple, **Q** = Quad, **b** = bathroom,
s = shower only. Credit cards are accepted, English is spoken,
and breakfast is included.

To help you sort easily through these listings, I've divided
the rooms into three categories, based on the price for a standard double room with bath:

$$$ **Higher Priced**—Most rooms €85 or more.
 $$ **Moderately Priced**—Most rooms between €70–85.
  $ **Lower Priced**—Most rooms €70 or less.

Near Theaterstrasse

These hotels cluster within a block on Theaterstrasse (7-min walk from station: head up Kaiserstrasse to circular awning at Barbarossaplatz, angle left toward McDonald's for Theaterstrasse). Quieter rooms are in back, front rooms have street noise, and all are entertained by church bells.

$$$ Hotel Schönleber has 32 good rooms, but the two hotels listed below offer a better value (S–€40, Sb–€58–64, D–€58, Ds–€64–82, Db–€86–92, Tb–€105–111, elevator, Theaterstrasse 5, tel. 0931/304-8900, fax 0931/16012, www.hotel-schoenleber.de, reservierung@hotel-schoenleber.de).

$$ Hotel Barbarossa, tucked peacefully away on the fourth floor, rents 18 fresh and comfortable rooms (S–€30, Ss–€40, Sb–€50, Db–€80, Tb–€90, these discounted prices are promised through 2006 with this book and cash payment, elevator, across from McDonald's, Theaterstrasse 2, tel. 0931/321-370, fax 0931/321-3737, marchiorello@t-online.de, Martina Marchiorello).

Elsewhere in Würzburg

The first two listings are closer to the station; the third is across the river.

$$$ Sankt Josef Hotel has 33 sharp rooms and a pleasant breakfast room (Sb–€50, Db–€80–90 depending on size, non-smoking rooms, reserve ahead for parking–€8/day, left off Theaterstrasse to Semmelstrasse 28, tel. 0931/308-680, fax 0931/308-6860, www.hotel-st-josef.de, hotel.st.josef@t-online.de, Herr and Frau Casagrande speak some English). The hotel also has a restaurant (Thu–Tue from 17:00, Sat–Sun also open for lunch 11:00–14:30, closed Wed).

$ Hotel-Pension Spehnkuch is the best budget hotel near the station. Overlooking a busy street but quiet behind double-paned windows, it's friendly, simple, clean, and comfortable, but can be smoky (S-€29, D-€52, T-€75, cash only; if canceling, call 72 hours in advance; 3-min walk from station; exit station and take a right onto 1st street, walk 500 feet to Röntgenring 7, on 1st floor; tel. 0931/54752, fax 0931/54760, www.pension-spehnkuch.de, spehnkuch@web.de, Markus).

$ Würzburg's **hostel**, across the river, has 226 beds (€17 per bed in 4- to 10-bed rooms, includes sheets and breakfast, non-members-€3 extra, cash only, must be under age 27, family rooms, lunch and dinner available, 1:00 curfew, 20-min walk from station, cross Alte Mainbrücke and turn left on Saalgasse, Burkarderstrasse 44, tel. 0931/42590, jhwuerzburg@djh-bayern.de).

EATING

Zum Stachel, the town's oldest *Weinhaus*, originated as the town's tithe barn—where people deposited 10 percent of their produce as tax. In 1413, it began preparing the produce and selling wine. Today, it's a worthy splurge serving gourmet Franconian meals in an elegant stone-and-ivy courtyard and woody dining room. The ceiling depicts a medieval *Stachel* (mace) in deadly action (€20 entrées, daily 11:00–23:00, reservations smart for this dressy place, from Marktplatz head toward river, turn right on Gressengasse to intersection with Marktgasse, Gressengasse 1, tel. 0931/52770, www.weinhaus-stachel.de).

Backöfele is a fun hole-in-the-wall (literally) offering a rustic menu full of local specialties. Named "the oven" for its entryway, this place is a hit with Germans (€6–16 entrées, daily 12:00–24:00, reservations smart, with your back to town hall go straight on Augustinerstrasse, take 1st left onto Wolfhartsgasse and 1st right to Ursulinergasse 2, tel. 0931/59059).

At **Würzburger Ratskeller,** choose from three seating options: an inviting courtyard (weather permitting), a stately restaurant, or a cozy multiroom *Weinstube* below (€8–15 entrées, daily 11:30–24:00, reservations smart, next to town hall, Langasse 1, tel. 0931/13021).

At **Martinsklause,** a 12th-century cellar near the cathedral, the bar is an old confessional, and the booths are made from cut-up church pews. You'll find local wines and specialties on the menu (€6–12 entrées, Tue–Sun 17:00–24:00, closed Mon, Martinstrasse 21, tel. 0931/353-9290). Upstairs, **Martinz** serves a long list of sweet and savory pancakes *(Pfannkuchen)*, salads, steaks, and soups (€4–9 entrées, Mon 11:00–17:00, Tue–Sun 11:00–22:00). In good weather, try the *Biergarten* terrace.

Café Schönborn, in the shadow of the Marienkapelle on the Market Square, is a good place for a light lunch (soups and salads), a bottomless cup of coffee (virtually unheard of in Germany, served here until 11:00), people-watching, or a late-night drink with the hip crowd. The inside can be loud and smoky, but the outside seating is great (€3–8 light meals, Mon–Sat 8:00–24:00, Sun 10:00–24:00, live jazz on Thu nights, Marktplatz 30, tel. 0931/404-4818).

Café Michel, across the square, is a quieter, more family-oriented teahouse, serving soups, small sandwiches, cakes, tea, and coffee. This place has been around since 1911 (€2–5 plates, Mon–Sat 8:00–18:00, Sun 13:00–17:30, Marktplatz 11, tel. 0931/53776).

Café Two Jours, trendy with students, dishes up inexpensive soups, salads, and sandwiches while paying homage to pop-magazine culture (€4–6 plates, daily 9:00–24:00, Juliuspromenade 40, tel. 0931/571-003).

For a beer garden under the trees, consider **Wirtshaus zum Lämmle** behind the TI (€6–10 entrées, Mon–Sat 11:00–22:00, closed Sun, plenty of fish and meaty fare, Marienplatz 5, tel. 0931/54748). Half a block away, **Weinstube Maulaffenbäck** is a tiny and characteristic place for cheap Franconian meals and good wine (€5–7 entrées, April–Oct Mon–Sat 10:00–24:00, Nov–March Mon–Sat 16:00–23:00, closed Sun, Maulhardgasse 9, tel. 0931/52351).

Eating at Marienberg Fortress: A self-service cafeteria/*Biergarten* next to the Mainfränkisches Museum has typical sausage-and-pretzel fare (€4–8 meals). The fancier *Burggaststätte*, next to the City History Museum, is a lesser value (€6–10 meals, same hours as museum, closed Mon, tel. 0931/47012).

Wine-Drinking to Support the Needy

Würzburg has several large wineries that produce the area's distinctive, bulbous *Bocksbeutel* bottles. These institutions, originally founded as homes for the old and poor, began making wine to pay the bills. Today, these grand Baroque complexes, which still make wine and serve the needy, have restaurants, wine shops, and extensive wine cellars (for serious buyers only). After more than 600 years, the **Bürgerspital** now cares for about a hundred local seniors, funding its work by selling its wine. Its characteristic restaurant and wine bar are right downtown. The funky little **wine store** is a time warp, filled with locals munching B.Y.O. sandwiches while sipping a glass of wine (Mon–Fri 9:00–18:00, Sat 9:00–15:00, closed Sun, corner of Theaterstrasse and Semmelstrasse, Theaterstrasse 19, tel. 0931/350-3403, www.buergerspital.de). Its **Weinstube Bürgerspital** is a classy, candle-lit restaurant with a cloistered feel and gorgeous courtyard seating (€4–8 entrées, daily 10:00–24:00, Theaterstrasse 19, tel. 0931/352-880).

TRANSPORTATION CONNECTIONS

From Würzburg by Train to: Rothenburg (hrly, 1 hr, change in Steinach; the tiny Steinach–Rothenburg train often leaves from track 5 shortly after the Würzburg train arrives), **Frankfurt Airport** (hrly, 90 min), **Nürnberg** (2–3/hr, 1–1.25 hrs), **Munich** (hrly, 2.5 hrs, usually with 1 or 2 changes), **Köln** (hrly, 3.5 hrs), **Berlin** (hrly, 4 hrs, 1 change). Train info: tel. 11861 (€0.50/min).

FRANKFURT

Frankfurt, the northern terminus of the Romantic Road, offers a good look at today's no-nonsense, modern Germany. There's so much more to this country than castles and old cobbled squares. Cosmopolitan Frankfurt is a business hub of the united Europe, giving it a special sophistication and spice. Especially in the area around the train station, you'll notice the fascinating multiethnic flavor of the city. A third of its 650,000 residents carry foreign passports. For years, Frankfurt was a city to avoid...but today, it has a unique energy that makes it worth a look.

Planning Your Time

You might fly into or out of Frankfurt am Main, or at least pass through. Even two or three hours in Frankfurt leaves you with some powerful impressions. The city's great sights are 20 minutes from its train station, which is 12 minutes from its airport. At a minimum, wander the old town area (Römerberg) and head up to the top of the Main Tower for commanding city views. With more time or an overnight, Frankfurt has plenty of museums and other attractions to choose from.

World Cup Warning: Be warned that in June and July of 2006, all of Germany will be flooded by soccer fans attending matches for the World Cup (see sidebar on page 6). Frankfurt will be especially crowded when it hosts games on June 10, 13, 17, and 21, plus a quarterfinal match on July 1.

ORIENTATION

(area code: 069)

Frankfurt, a forest of skyscrapers perched on the banks of the Main (pronounced "mine") River, has been dubbed Germany's

"Mainhattan." The city is Germany's trade and banking capital, leading the country in skyscrapers (mostly bank headquarters)...and yet, a third of Frankfurt is green space.

Near the train station is the convention center (Messe), the red light district, and most of the skyscrapers. Beyond that zone (to the east) is Frankfurt's old town, with the Römerberg, or central market square, as its focal point. Across the river, the south bank of the Main is lined with Frankfurt's top museums, and beyond that is Sachsenhausen, the characteristic restaurant zone.

Tourist Information

Frankfurt has several TIs. The handiest is inside the train station's main entrance, offering an abundance of brochures and a free hotel-booking service (Mon–Fri 8:00–21:00, Sat–Sun 9:00–18:00, tel. 069/2123-8800, www.frankfurt-tourismus.de). Buy the city/subway map (the basic €0.50 version is fine—skip the detailed €1 map) and consider the *Frankfurt Welcome* brochure (€0.50). The TI sells the **Museum Ticket** (€12, valid 2 days, covers 25 museums) and Frankfurt Card (see below), and offers bus tours of the city (see below). You'll find other TIs on Römerberg's square (Mon–Fri 9:30–17:30, Sat–Sun until 16:00), on the pedestrian shopping street Zeil, and at the airport.

The **Frankfurt Card** gives you a transit pass (including connections to and from the airport), 50 percent off all major museums, and 25 percent off the city bus tour, which virtually pays for the pass (€8/1 day, €12/2 days, sold at TI). If you're touring like mad for a day, this card can be worthwhile. Note that most museums are closed Monday and most are open until 20:00 on Wednesday (confirm at any TI).

The basic **city bus tour** gives a 2.5-hour orientation to Frankfurt, including Römerberg, Goethe House, and (summer only) the Main Tower (€25, 25 percent discount with Frankfurt Card, recorded narration, April–Oct daily at 10:00 and 14:00, Nov–March daily at 14:00). The bus picks up at the Römerberg TI first, then 15 minutes later at the Frankfurt train station TI.

Local Guide: Elisabeth Lücke loves her city and shares it very well (€50/hr, reserve in advance, tel. 06196/45787, www.elisabeth -luecke.de, elisabeth.luecke@t-online.de).

Arrival in Frankfurt

By Train: The Frankfurt train station (Hauptbahnhof) bustles with travelers. The TI is in the main hall just inside the front door. Lockers and baggage check (€3/day, daily 6:00–20:00) are in the main hall across from the TI. More lockers are at track 24, across from the post office (Mon–Fri 7:00–19:30, Sat 8:00–16:00, closed Sun, does not accept packages, automatic stamp machine outside). WCs (€0.70) are under track 9/10. Inquire about train tickets in the Reisezentrum across from track 9 (daily 6:00–22:00). Pick up a snack at the fine food court across from tracks 4 and 5. Above the Reisezentrum is a peaceful lounge with a snack bar, clean WCs, telephones, and a children's play area (free entry with ticket or railpass, free coffee and juice in first-class lounge). The station is a five-minute walk from the convention center (Messe), a three-minute subway ride from the center, or a 12-minute shuttle train from the airport.

By Plane: See "Frankfurt's Airport," page 205.

Getting Around Frankfurt

By Subway: Frankfurt's subway is easy to use, but a 10-minute wait for a train can be normal. From the train station, follow signs for U-Bahn (U, blue) or S-Bahn (S, green). Buy your tickets *(Fahrkarten)* from an RMV machine. Find your destination on the chart, key in the number, choose your ticket type, then pay. Choose *Einzelfahrt* for a regular single ticket (€2), *Kurzstrecke* for a short ride (€1.15, 3 stops or less), or *Tageskarte* for an all-day pass (€4.80 without the airport, €7.30 with). A one-way ticket to the airport costs €3.30.

By Taxi: A taxi stand is just outside the main entrance of the train station to your left. An average ride to the Römerberg square should cost you €6 (more in slow traffic). To get to the airport from any of my recommended hotels, count on at least €22.

SELF-GUIDED WALK

Welcome to Frankfurt's Römerberg

This sightseeing walk focuses on Römerberg, Frankfurt's lively market square, and begins at the train station (because that's where you'll likely arrive in Frankfurt). Allow 30 to 60 minutes, depending on whether you walk to the square from the station.

• Start at the...

Frankfurt

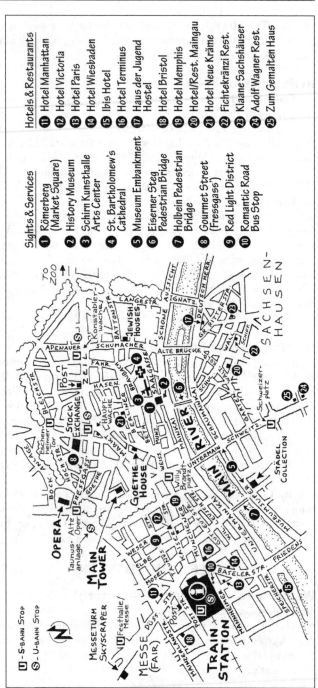

Sights & Services

1 Römerberg (Market Square)
2 History Museum
3 Schirn Kunsthalle Arts Center
4 St. Bartholomew's Cathedral
5 Museum Embankment
6 Eiserner Steg Pedestrian Bridge
7 Holbein Pedestrian Bridge
8 Gourmet Street (Fressgass')
9 Red Light District
10 Romantic Road Bus Stop

Hotels & Restaurants

11 Hotel Manhattan
12 Hotel Victoria
13 Hotel Paris
14 Hotel Wiesbaden
15 Ibis Hotel
16 Hotel Terminus
17 Haus der Jugend Hostel
18 Hotel Bristol
19 Hotel Memphis
20 Hotel/Rest. Maingau
21 Hotel Neue Kräme
22 Fichtekränzi Rest.
23 Klaane Sachshäuser
24 Adolf Wagner Rest.
25 Zum Gemalten Haus

Train Station: This is Germany's busiest train station: 350,000 travelers make their way to 25 platforms to catch 1,800 trains every day. While it was big news when it opened in the 1890s, it's a dead-end station, which, with today's high-speed trains, makes it outdated. In fact, the speedy ICE trains are threatening to bypass Frankfurt altogether unless it digs a tunnel to allow for a faster pass-through stop (a costly project is now in the discussion stage).

• *To get to Römerberg, it's a 20-minute walk (up Kaiserstrasse), a €6 taxi ride (without traffic), or three-minute subway ride. To take the subway, buy a ticket (see "Getting Around Frankfurt," above) and fol-low signs to U-4 (direction Seckbacher Landstrasse) or U-5 (direction Preungesheim). Choose the track with the closest Nächste Abfahrt (next departure) time and go two stops to Römerberg. Exit the station following Römerberg signs(not Domplatz). As you surface, you'll see the tall, red tower of St. Bartholomew's Cathedral behind you, where we'll end this walk. For now, walk around the building in front of you and downhill to...*

Römerberg: Frankfurt's market square, a ▲ sight, was the birthplace of the city. The town hall *(Römer)* houses the *Kaisersaal,* or Imperial Hall, where Holy Roman Emperors celebrated their coronations. Today, the *Römer* houses the city council and mayor's office. The cute row of half-timbered houses (rebuilt in 1983) opposite the *Römer* is typical of Frankfurt's quaint old center before World War II.

• *Walk past the red-and-white church downhill toward the river to Frankfurt's...*

History Museum (Historisches Museum): Most won't want to hike through the actual museum upstairs, which has two floors of artifacts, paintings, and displays—without a word of English (€4, Tue–Sun 10:00–17:00, Wed until 20:00, Sat 13:00–17:00, closed Mon, Saalgasse 19, tel. 069/2123-5599, www.historisches -museum.frankfurt.de). But the models in the ground-floor annex

are fascinating (€1, follow signs to *Altstadtmodelle,* English film and explanations). Study the maps of medieval Frankfurt. The wall sur-rounding the city was torn down in the early 1800s to make the ring of parks and lakes you see on your modern map. The long, densely packed row of houses on the eastern end of town was Frankfurt's Jewish ghetto from 1462 to 1796. The five original houses that survive comprise one of the city's two Jewish Museums. (Frankfurt is the birthplace of Anne Frank and the Rothschild banking family.) The big model in the middle of the room shows the town in the 1930s. Across from it, you can see the horror that befell the town in 1940, 1943, and on the "fatal night" of March 23, 1944. This last Allied bombing accomplished its goal of demoralizing the city. Find the facade of the destroyed city hall—where you just were. The film behind this model is a good 15-minute tour of Frankfurt through the ages (ask them to change the language for you—"*Auf Englisch, bitte?*"). At the model of today's Frankfurt, orient yourself, then locate the riverfront (a nice detour with a grassy park and fun Eiserner Steg pedestrian bridge, to the left as you leave this museum), and the long, skinny "pistol" (the Schirn arts exhibition center) pointing at the cathedral—where you're going next.

• *Leaving the museum, turn right to...*

Saalgasse: Literally "hall street," this lane of postmodern buildings echoes the higgledy-piggledy buildings that stood here until World War II. In the 1990s, famous architects from around the world were each given a ruined house of the same width and told to design a new building to reflect the building that stood there before the war. As you continue down the street, guess which one is an upside-down half-timbered house with the stars down below.

(Hint: Animals are on the "ground floor.") Saalgasse leads to some ancient Roman ruins in front of St. Bartholomew's Cathedral. The grid of stubs was the subfloor of a Roman bath (allowing the floor to be heated). The small monument in the middle of the ruins commemorates the 794 meeting of Charlemagne (king of the Franks and first Holy Roman Emperor) with the local bishop—the first official mention of a town called Frankfurt. When Charlemagne and the Franks fled from the Saxons, a white deer led them to the

easiest place to cross the Main—where the Franks could ford the river—hence, Frankfurt. The skyscraper with the yellow emblem in the distance is the tallest office block in Europe (985 feet). Next to it, with the red-and-white antenna, is the Main Tower (open to the public—highly recommended and described below).

• *Behind the Roman ruins is...*

St. Bartholomew's Cathedral (Kaiserdom): Ten Holy Roman Emperors were elected and crowned in this cathedral between 1562 and 1792. The church was destroyed in World War II, rebuilt, and reopened in 1955. Twenty-seven scenes from the life of St. Bartholomew (Bartholomäus in German) flank the high altar and ring the choir. Everything of value was moved to safety before the bombs came. But the delightful red sandstone chapel of Sleeping Mary (to the left of the high altar), carved and painted in the 15th century, was too big to move—so it was fortified with sandbags. The altarpiece and fine stained glass next to it survived the bombing (free, Sat–Thu 9:00–12:00 & 14:30–17:00, closed Fri, enter on side opposite river). In 2006, the newly restored tower may be open for tourists to climb.

• *From the cathedral, it's a short walk back to Römerberg or to the Zeil, Frankfurt's lively department store–lined pedestrian boulevard. Or you can explore more of Frankfurt's sights.*

SIGHTS

Between Römerberg and the Station

▲**Main Tower**—Finished in 2000, this tower houses the Helaba Bank and offers the best public viewpoint from a Frankfurt sky-scraper. A 45-second, ear-popping eleva-tor ride—and then 50 steps—takes you to the 55th floor, 650 feet above the city (€4.50, daily 10:00–21:00, Fri–Sat until 23:00, last entry 30 min before closing, enter at Neue Mainzer Strasse 52, near corner of Neue Schlesingerstrasse, tel. 069/365-4777). Here, from Frankfurt's ultimate viewpoint, survey the city circling clockwise, starting with the biggest skyscraper (with the yellow emblem).

1. Commerce Bank Building: Designed by Norman Foster (of Berlin Reichstag and London City Hall fame), the Commerce Bank building was finished in 1997. It's 985 feet high, with nine winter gardens spiraling up its core. Just to the left is Römerberg—the old town center. Look to the right (clockwise).

2. European Central Bank: The blue-and-gold euro sym-bol (€) decorates the front yard of the Euro Tower, home of the European Central Bank (a.k.a. "City of the Euro"). Its 1,000 employees administer the all-Europe currency from here. Typical of skyscrapers in the 1970s, it's slim—to allow maximum natural light into all workplaces inside. The euro symbol in the park was unveiled on January 1, 2002, the day the euro went into circulation in the 12 Eurozone countries.

The Museum Embankment lines Schaumainkai (see page 200) on the far side of the Main River, just beyond the Euro Tower.

3. Airport: The Rhine-Main Airport, in the distance, is the largest employment complex in Germany (62,000 workers). Frankfurt's massive train station dominates the foreground. From the station, the grand Kaiserstrasse cuts through the city to Römerberg.

4. Messe: The Frankfurt fair (Messe), marked by the skyscraper with the pointy top, is a huge convention center—the size of 40 soccer fields. It sprawls behind the skyscraper that looks like a classical column sporting a visor-like capital. (The protruding lip of the capital is heated so that icicles don't form, break off, and impale people on the street below.) Frankfurt's fair originated in 1240, when the emperor promised all participating merchants safe passage (www.messefrankfurt.com). The black twin towers of the Deutsche Bank in the foreground are typical of mid-1980s mirrored architecture.

5. West End and Good Living: The West End—with vast green spaces and the telecommunications tower—is Frankfurt's trendiest residential quarter. The city's "good-living spine" cuts from the West End to the right. Stretching from the classic-looking **Opera House** are broad and people-filled boulevards made to order for eating and shopping. Your skyscraper spin-tour is over. Why don't you go join them?

Opera House, Gourmet Street, and Zeil—From the Opera House to pedestrian boulevards, this is Frankfurt's good-living spine. The Opera House was finished in 1880 to celebrate high German culture and the newly created nation. With both Mozart and Goethe flanking the entrance, all are reminded that this is a house of both music and theater. The original opera house was destroyed in World War II. Over the objections of a mayor nicknamed "Dynamite Rudy," the city rebuilt it in the original style (U-Bahn: Alte Oper). Facing the opera, turn right and walk down a restaurant-lined boulevard (Grosse Bockenheimer) nicknamed "Gourmet Street" (Fressgass'). (Frankfurt's version of Fifth Avenue, lined with top fashion shops, is the parallel Goethe Strasse.) Gourmet Street leads to Zeil, a lively, tree-lined festival-of-life pedestrian boulevard and department-store strip.

▲Goethe House (Goethehaus)—Johann Wolfgang von Goethe (1749–1832), a scientist, minister, poet, lawyer, politician, and playwright, was a towering figure in the early Romantic age. His birthplace, now a fine museum, is a five-minute walk northwest of

Römerberg. It's furnished as it was in the mid-18th century, when the boy destined to become the German Shakespeare grew up here. Sixteen rooms on four floors tell his story: how his father dedicated his life and wealth to cultural pursuits, and how his mother told young Goethe fairy tales every night, stopping just before the ending so that the boy could exercise his own creativity. Goethe's family gave him all the money he needed to travel and learn. His collection of 2,000 books was sold off in 1795. Recently, 800 of these have been located and repurchased by the museum (you'll see them in the library). This building honors the man who inspired the Goethe Institute, dedicated to keeping the German language strong. It's no wonder, then, that there's not a word of English in the place—the €1.50 English booklet is essential (€5, covered by €12 Museum Ticket, €3 off with Frankfurt Card, pricey €4.50 audioguide, daily 10:00–17:30; 15-min walk from Hauptbahnhof up Kaiserstrasse, turn right on Am Salzhaus, Grosser Hirschgraben 23; tel. 069/138-800, www.goethehaus-frankfurt.de).

▲**Frankfurt's Red Light District**—A browse through Frankfurt's sleazy red light district offers a fascinating way to kill time between trains. From the station, Taunusstrasse leads two blocks to Elbestrasse, where you'll find a zone of 20 "eros towers"—each a five-story-tall brothel filled with prostitutes. Climbing through a few of these may be one of the more memorable experiences of your European trip (€25, daily). While hiking through the towers feels safe, the aggressive women at the neighboring strip shows can be pretty unsettling. Ever since the Middle Ages, Frankfurt's thriving prostitution industry has gone hand-in-hand with its trade fairs. Today, it thrives with the Messe. Prostitutes note that business varies with the theme of the trade show—while the auto show is boom time, they complain that Frankfurt's massive book fair is a bust. Frankfurt's prostitutes are legal and taxed. Since they pay taxes, they are organizing to get the same benefits that any other taxed worker gets. This area can be dangerous if you're careless. If you take a wrong turn, you'll find creepy streets littered with drug addicts. In 1992, Frankfurt began offering "pump rooms" to its hard-drug users. These centers provide clean needles and a safe and caring place for addicts to go to maintain their habit and get counseling. Ten years later, while locals consider the program a success, wasted people congregate in neighborhoods like this one.

Across the River

The Schaumainkai riverside promenade (across the river, over Eiserner Steg pedestrian bridge from Römerberg) is great for an evening stroll or people-watching on any sunny day. Keep your eyes peeled for nude sunbathers. On Saturdays, the museum strip street is closed off for a sprawling flea market.

Sachsenhausen District and Frankfurt's Culinary Specialties—Rather than beer-garden ambience, Frankfurt offers an apple-wine pub district. For a traditional eating-and-drinking zone with more than a hundred characteristic apple-wine pubs (and plenty of ethnic and other options), visit cobbled and cozy Sachsenhausen (wander to the east end of Schaumainkai, or from the train station take tram #16 to Schweizerplatz; also see "Eating," page 203). *Apfelwein*, drunk around here since Charlemagne's time 1,200 years ago, became more popular in the 16th century, when local grapes were diseased. It enjoyed another boost two centuries later, when a climate change meant that grapes grew poorly in the area. Apple wine is about the strength of beer (5.5 percent alcohol). It's served spiced and warm in winter, cold in summer. To complement your traditional drink with a traditional meal, order Frankfurt sausage or pork chops and kraut.

Frankfurt's Museum Embankment (Museumsufer)—The Museum Embankment features nine museums lining the Main River along Schaumainkai (mostly west of Eiserner Steg pedestrian bridge). In the 1980s, Frankfurt decided that it wanted to buck its "Bankfurt" and "Krankfurt" (*krank* means "sick") image. It went on a culture kick and devoted 11 percent of the city budget to the arts and culture. The result: Frankfurt has become a city of art. Today, locals and tourists alike enjoy an impressive strip of museums housed in striking buildings. These nine museums (including architecture, film, world cultures, and great European masters—the Städel Collection) and a dozen others are all well described in the TI's *Museumsufer* brochure (covered by €12 Museum Ticket sold at TI and participating museums, good for 2 days, most museums Tue–Sun 10:00–17:00, Wed until 20:00, closed Mon, www.kultur.frankfurt.de).

SLEEPING

Avoid driving or sleeping in Frankfurt, since the city's numerous trade fairs send hotel prices skyrocketing. In 2006, the busiest months for trade fairs are January, March, May, September, and November. July and December have almost none, and the rest of the months fall somewhere in between (an average of 7 days a month). Visit www.messefrankfurt.com (and select "Trade Fairs") for an exact schedule.

In addition to Frankfurt's usual crowds of businesspeople, the city will be playing host to soccer fans from around the world as it hosts World Cup matches on June 10, 13, 17, and 21, and on July 1. Book far ahead (or avoid the city entirely) on these dates.

Sleep Code

(€1 = about $1.20, country code: 49, area code: 069)
S = Single, **D** = Double/Twin, **T** = Triple, **Q** = Quad, **b** = bathroom,
s = shower only. Unless otherwise noted, credit cards are
accepted, English is spoken, and breakfast is included.

To help you sort easily through these listings, I've divided
the rooms into three categories, based on the price for a standard double room with bath:

$$$ **Higher Priced**—Most rooms €90 or more.
$$ **Moderately Priced**—Most rooms between €70–90.
$ **Lower Priced**—Most rooms €70 or less.

Near the Train Station

Pleasant Rhine or Romantic Road towns are just a quick drive or
train ride away. But if you must spend the night in Frankfurt, here
are some places within a few blocks of the train station (and its
fast and handy train to the airport; to sleep at the airport itself,
see "Frankfurt's Airport," page 205). This isn't the safest neighborhood; don't wander into seedy-feeling streets, and be careful after
dark.

For a rough idea of directions to hotels, stand with your back
to the main entrance of the station: Using a 12-hour clock, Hotel
Manhattan is across the street at 10:00, Hotel Victoria at 1:00,
Hotel Memphis and Hotel Terminus are at 2:00, Hotel Wiesbaden
at 4:00, Hotel Paris at 5:00, and Hotel Bristol at 7:00. The Ibis
Hotel is on a nicer street two blocks beyond Hotel Paris.

$$$ **Hotel Bristol** is a swanky new boutique hotel, run by
Michael Rosen, owner of the Manhattan and Memphis (see
below). The Bristol reflects a new generation of train-station hotels,
serving up style and flair, from its nod to Pacific Rim architecture
to its teak-furnished patio café called Summer Lounge. Thirsty?
Have a drink at the 24-hour bar downstairs. Just two blocks from
the station, it's surprisingly quiet (Sb-€90, Db-€105, free Internet
in lobby, huge breakfast buffet, elevator, Ludwigstrasse 15, tel.
069/242-390, fax 069/251-539, www.bristol-hotel.de, info@bristol
-hotel.de).

$$$ **Hotel Manhattan,** with 60 sleek, arty rooms, is beauti-
fully located across from the station. An unusual mix of warm and
accommodating staff with all the business-class comforts, it's a
good splurge on a first or last night in Europe (Sb-€87, Db-€102,
show this book to get a 10 percent break during non-convention times, further discount when really slow—including weekends, kids under 12 free, elevator, free Internet access in lobby,

Düsseldorfer Strasse 10, tel. 069/269-5970, fax 069/2695-97777, www.manhattan-hotel.com, manhattan-hotel@t-online.de, Herr Rosen).

$$$ Hotel Victoria, similarly friendly, is midway between the station and the old town on the grand Kaiserstrasse (75 rooms, Sb-€65–85, Db-€75–95, suite-€120, Kaiserstrasse 59, on corner with Elbestrasse, tel. 069/273-060, fax 069/2730-6100, www .victoriahotel.de, victoria-hotel@t-online.de).

$$$ Hotel Memphis, three long blocks from the station on a busy street, is not as stylish as its two siblings (Manhattan and Bristol, above), but the owner's philosophy carries through: It's clean and simple, committed to good service and value (Sb-€85, Db-€95, kids under 6 stay free, ask for a room on the quiet side—*ruhige Seite,* Münchener Strasse 15, tel. 069/242-6090, fax 069/2426-0999, www.memphis-hotel.de, memphis-hotel @t-online.de).

$$ Hotel Paris has 20 fine but worn rooms and a nice staff, making this a decent value (Sb-€60, Db-€80, Karlsruherstrasse 8, tel. 069/273-9963, fax 069/2739-9651, www.hotelparis.de, reservation@hotelparis.de).

$$ Hotel Terminus is a good choice if you aren't looking for style—just a clean, decent, business-class hotel, right across from the station (Sb-€50–70, Db-€70–90, Tb-€90–110, cheaper rates are for weekends, €8 parking, some non-smoking rooms, Münchenerstrasse 59, tel. 069/242-320, fax 069/237-411, www .hotel-terminus.de, hotel-terminus@euko.de).

$ Hotel Wiesbaden, though a bit run-down, with 39 faded, sometimes smoky rooms and unfortunate hallways, has kind management and feels safe (Sb-€49, Db-€66, Tb-€75, Qb-€88, elevator, breakfast next door at the more elegant Hotel National, Baseler Strasse 52, tel. 069/232-347, fax 069/252-845, hotelwiesbaden@web.de).

$ Ibis Hotel Frankfurt Friedensbrücke, a bargain-price chain hotel, is a super value, with 233 identical rooms on a quiet riverside street away from the station riffraff (Sb/Db-€59–72, €125 during fairs, Tb-€79–92, lower prices are for weekends, breakfast-€9 per person, non-smoking rooms, elevator, parking-€8/day, exit station to right and follow Baseler Strasse 3 blocks, before river turn right on Speicherstrasse to #4, tel. 069/273-030, fax 069/237-024, www.ibishotel.com, h1445@accor-hotels.com).

Away From the Station

Hotel Neue Kräme is near Römerberg, Hotel Maingau is in the Sachsenhausen District (see page 200), and the hostel is a bus ride away.

$$$ Hotel Neue Kräme is a quiet little oasis tucked away above the center of Frankfurt's downtown action, just steps from Römerberg and the restaurant-filled Fressgass'. Friendly Hermann, who lived in the U.S. and loves to revive his English, welcomes guests in this bright and cheerful little blue-and-white place. If you are just here for one night, stay at the station—but if you're in town for a few days and want a central base, you'll enjoy this location (Sb-€85, Db-€105, elevator, non-smoking rooms available, parking-€16/day, Neue Kräme 23, tel. 069/284-046, fax 069/296-288, hotel.neuekraeme@t-online.de).

$$ Hotel Maingau, located across the river in the museum- and pub-friendly Sachsenhausen District, is in a quiet, residential neighborhood facing a park. The hotel hallways are dark, but the rooms are bright. If you're looking for a little tranquility away from the station, stay here (Sb-€70, Db-€80, Tb-€95, fancy dinners at adjacent Maingau restaurant—see listing below, tel. 069/609-140, fax 069/620-790, Schiffer Strasse 38-40, www.maingau.de, hotel@maingau.de).

$ *Hostel:* The **Haus der Jugend** hostel is open to guests of any age (€20–24 per bed in 8- and 10-bed dorms, €24–28 in 3- to 4-bed dorms, Sb-€39–43, Db-€34–38, higher prices are for guests age 27 or older, includes daily hostel membership fee, sheets and breakfast, 470 beds, €4.80 for lunch or dinner, Internet access in lobby, laundry, 2:00 curfew, take bus #46 direction Mühlberg—goes 3/hr from station to Frankenstein Platz, Deutschherrnufer 12, tel. 069/610-0150, fax 069/6100-1599, www.jugendherberge -frankfurt.de, jugendherberge_frankfurt@t-online.de).

EATING

The Sachsenhausen District, an easy walk from Schweitzerplatz, abounds with traditional apple-wine pubs (see page 200). All the ones I've listed have both indoor and outdoor seating in a woodsy, rustic setting. Not just for tourists, these characteristic places are popular with Frankfurters, too. If you are craving *Leiterchen* ("ladders," or spare ribs), these are your best bet. Here are two more local specialties, available at most apple-wine bars, for the adventurous to try: Boiled eggs (or beef) and potatoes topped with a green sauce of seven herbs *(Grüne Sosse)*, or an aged, cylindrical, ricotta-like cheese served with onions and vinegar, called *Handkäse mit Musik* ("hand cheese with music").

Fichtekränzi offers the typical specialties (and some lighter fare) both in its cozy picnic-table and bench-filled beer hall, and outside under the trees. The staff is friendly and the atmosphere relaxed (€7–12 entrées, daily from 17:00, Wall Strasse 5, tel. 069/612-778).

Adolf Wagner is a traditional joint that serves a local constituency. It tends to get a little smoky, so try to score a table in the outside courtyard area (€7–11 entrées, daily 11:00–24:00, Schweizer Strasse 71, tel. 069/612-565).

Klaane Sachshäuser, owned by the same family for five generations, is popular with German tour groups and prides itself on its *Leiterchen* (€7–15 entrées, Mon–Sat from 16:00, closed Sun, Neuer Wall 11, tel. 069/615-983).

Zum Gemalten Haus, named for the wall murals that adorn the facade of the building, serves German cuisine and is deceptively mellow—it's rumored to get a little wild on the weekends (€10–20 entrées, Wed–Sun 10:00–24:00, closed Mon–Tue, Schweizer Strasse 67, tel. 069/614-559).

Irish pubs and salsa bars clutter the pedestrian zone around Rittergasse and Klappergasse, just north of the Affentor. The cobblestone streets and medieval buildings feel like Epcot Center, rather than historic Frankfurt, but if you're looking for a place to do a pub crawl, this is it.

Splurge at **Maingau** for a break from traditional German food and pubs. Repeatedly hailed as one of the best restaurants in Frankfurt, it boasts an extensive wine list, fancy tasting menus, recommended wine pairings, and an international lineup, including filet of venison and vegetarian options such as thyme-infused risotto. For less of an investment, indulge in a three-course lunch special. Don't be fooled by its modest exterior—this place is elegant inside (€13–20 entrées; tasting *menus* are €13–30 for lunch, €25–46 for dinner, more with wine pairings; Tue–Fri 11:30–15:00 & 17:00–22:30, Sat 18:00–22:30, Sun 11:30–15:00, closed Mon, call for reservations, tel. 069/610-752, Schiffer Strasse 38, www .maingau.de).

TRANSPORTATION CONNECTIONS

Frankfurt am Main

From Frankfurt by Train to: Rothenburg (hrly, 3 hrs, changes in Würzburg and Steinach; the tiny Steinach–Rothenburg train often leaves from track 5, shortly after the Würzburg train arrives), **Würzburg** (hrly, 2 hrs), **Nürnberg** (hrly, 2 hrs), **Munich** (hrly, 4 hrs, 1 change), **Baden-Baden** (2/hr, 1.5 hrs, transfer in Mannheim or Karlsruhe), **Bacharach** (hrly, 1.5 hrs, change in Mainz; first train to Bacharach departs at 6:00, last train at 20:45), **Freiburg** (hrly, 2 hrs, change in Mannheim), **Bonn** (hrly, 1.75 hrs direct), **Koblenz** (hrly, 1.5 hrs direct), **Köln** (almost hrly, 1.25 hrs direct; more with a transfer at Frankfurt's airport), **Berlin** (hrly, 6 hrs), **Amsterdam** (every 2 hrs, 4.5 hrs direct, more with a transfer in Utrecht), **Bern** (hrly, 4.5 hrs, changes in Mannheim and Basel), **Brussels** (hrly,

5 hrs, change in Köln), **Copenhagen** (6/day, 9 hrs, change in Hamburg), **London** (6/day, 8 hrs, 3 changes), **Milan** (hrly, 9 hrs, 2 changes), **Paris** (9/day, 6.5 hrs, up to 3 changes), **Vienna** (8/day, 8 hrs, 2 changes). Train info: tel. 11861 (€0.50/min).

Romantic Road Bus: I'd skip the bus (which has become an inefficient and unfriendly service over the years) and take the train instead. But if you're determined to take the bus, you can buy your ticket at the invariably unhelpful Deutsche Touring office (Mon–Fri 7:00–19:00, Sat 7:00–14:00, Sun 7:00–13:00, entrance at Mannheimer Strasse 15, follow signs to *Südausgang* about 100 yards—bus stop is to the right, Touring office is across street from stop, tel. 069/230-735 or 069/790-300, www.romantic-road-coach.de) or pay cash when you board the bus. While the company claims you're 90 percent safe without a reservation, you can book a seat for free by calling 069/790-350. The Frankfurt–Munich bus trip costs €95. Travelers with railpasses (German, Eurail, or Eurail Selectpass) get a 60 percent discount. The bus departs from in front of the Deutsche Touring office promptly at 8:00 (April–Oct, confirm time at TI, Deutsche Touring office, or www.euraide.de /ricksteves).

Frankfurt's Airport

The airport *(Flughafen)* is user-friendly. There are two separate terminals (know your terminal, call the airline). All trains and subways operate out of Terminal 1 (but taxis serve both). A skyline train connects the two terminals.

The airport offers showers (€6), a baggage-check desk (daily 6:00–22:00, €3.50 per bag/day), lockers (€3–5/24 hrs, depending on size), free Internet access (at the *e-lounge* by departures Terminal 1B), ATMs, fair banks with long hours, a grocery store (daily 6:30–21:30, Terminal 1, on level 0 between sectors A and B), a post office, a train station, a business lounge (Europe City Club—€16/4 hrs for anyone with a plane ticket, on departure level, daily 7:00–22:00), easy rental-car pickup, plenty of parking, an information booth, a pharmacy (7:00–21:30, Terminal 1/B), a medical clinic (Terminal 1C), a casino, and even McBeer. McWelcome to Germany.

If you're meeting someone, each terminal has a hard-to-miss "meeting point" near where those arriving pop out.

Airport Info (in English): For flight information, call 01805/372-4636 (www.frankfurt-airport.de) or contact the airlines directly during business hours (wait for an announcement in English): Lufthansa—tel. 01803-803-803 or 069/6969-4433, American Airlines—tel. 01803-242-324 or 069/6902-1781, Delta—tel. 01803-337-880 or 069/6902-8751, Northwest/KLM—tel. 01805-214-201 or 069/6902-1831. Pick up the free brochure *Your*

Airport-Assistant for a map and detailed information on airport services (available at the airport and at most Frankfurt hotels).

Getting Between the Airport and Downtown Frankfurt: The airport is a 12-minute train ride from Frankfurt's downtown train station (€3.30, 4/hr, ride included in €8 Frankfurt Card but not in €4.80 all-day *Tageskarte* transit pass). Figure around €25 for a taxi from any of my recommended hotels.

Trains: The airport has its own train station (Terminal 1). Train travelers can validate railpasses or buy tickets at the airport station.

From Frankfurt Airport by Train to: **Rothenburg** (hrly, 3 hrs, with transfers in Würzburg and Steinach), **Würzburg** (2/hr, 2 hrs), **Nürnberg** (hrly, 2 hrs), **Munich** (2/hr, 4 hrs, 1 change), **Baden-Baden** (every 2 hrs, 1.5 hrs direct, 2 hrs with a transfer in Mainz), **Köln** (at least hrly, 1 hr), **Koblenz** (hrly, 1.25 hrs, more with a transfer in Mainz), **Bacharach** (hrly, 1 hr, change in Mainz; first train to Bacharach departs at 6:00, last train at 21:00), and **international destinations** (such as Paris, London, Milan, Amsterdam, Vienna, and many more).

Flying Home from Frankfurt: Some of the trains from the Rhine stop at the airport on their way into Frankfurt (e.g., hrly 90-min rides direct from Bonn; hrly 90-min rides from Bacharach with a change in Mainz; earliest train from Bacharach to Frankfurt leaves about 5:40, last train at 21:30). By car, head toward Frankfurt on the autobahn and follow the little airplane signs to the airport.

Sleeping at Frankfurt Airport: You can sleep at the airport, but you'll pay a premium and miss out on seeing Frankfurt. Considering the ease of the shuttle train from Frankfurt (4/hr, 12 min), I don't advise it. But if you must, the airport **Sheraton** has 1,000 international business-class rooms (rates vary wildly depending on season and conventions, but Db usually around €200–250, about 25 percent discount with major corporate ID—try anything, AAA and senior discounts, kids up to age 18 free in the room, includes big breakfast, non-smoking rooms, fitness club, Terminal 1, tel. 069/69770, fax 069/6977-2351, www.sheraton.com/frankfurt, salesfrankfurt@sheraton.com).

The **Ibis** has cheaper rooms in the same neighborhood, but it isn't as handy and the staff is impersonal (Db-€80–100, breakfast-€9, Langer Kornweg 9a–11, Kelsterbach, tel. 06107/9870, fax 06107/987-444, www.ibishotel.com, h2203@accor-hotels.com).

Route Tips for Drivers

Frankfurt to Rothenburg: The three-hour autobahn drive from the airport to Rothenburg is something even a jet-lagged zombie can handle. It's a 75-mile straight shot to Würzburg on A-3; just follow the blue autobahn signs to Würzburg. While you can carry on to Rothenburg by autobahn, for a scenic back-road approach, leave the freeway at the Heidingsfeld–Würzburg exit. If going directly to Rothenburg, follow signs south to Stuttgart/Ulm/ Road 19, then continue to Rothenburg via a scenic slice of the Romantic Road. If stopping at Würzburg, leave the freeway at the Heidingsfeld–Würzburg exit and follow Stadtmitte, then Centrum and Residenz signs from the same freeway exit. From Würzburg, Ulm/Road 19 signs lead to Bad Mergentheim and Rothenburg.

Frankfurt to the Rhine: Driving from Frankfurt to the Rhine or Mosel takes 90 minutes (follow blue autobahn signs from airport, major cities are signposted).

The Rhine to Frankfurt: From St. Goar or Bacharach, follow the river to Bingen, then autobahn signs to Mainz, then Frankfurt, then Messe, and finally the Hauptbahnhof (train station). The Hauptbahnhof garage (€15/day) is under the station near all recommended hotels.

RHINE VALLEY

The Rhine Valley is storybook Germany, a fairytale world of legends and robber-baron castles. Cruise the most castle-studded stretch of the romantic Rhine as you listen for the song of the treacherous Loreley. For hands-on castle thrills, climb through the Rhineland's greatest castle, Rheinfels, above the town of St. Goar. Castle connoisseurs will enjoy the fine interior of Marksburg Castle. Spend your nights in a castle-crowned village, either Bacharach or St. Goar. With more time, mosey through the neighboring Mosel Valley (see next chapter).

Planning Your Time

The Rhineland does not take much time to see. The blitziest tour is an hour at Köln's cathedral (see Köln chapter, page 277) and an hour looking at the castles from your train window. But for a better look, cruise in, tour a castle or two, sleep in a medieval town, and take the train out. If you have limited time, cruise less and explore Rheinfels Castle.

Ideally, spend two nights here, sleep in Bacharach, cruise the best hour of the river (from Bacharach to St. Goar), and tour the Rheinfels Castle. Those with more time can ride the riverside bike path. With two days and a car, visit the Rhine and the Mosel. With two days by train, see the Rhine and Köln.

If you have all the time in the world, there are countless castles you could visit. But with limited time and energy, you need to be selective in your castle-going. After the Rheinfels Castle, my favorites are Burg Eltz (see page 251 in next chapter; medieval interior, well-preserved, lost in a romantic forest in the next valley over), Marksburg Castle (page 220; rebuilt medieval interior,

Rhine Overview

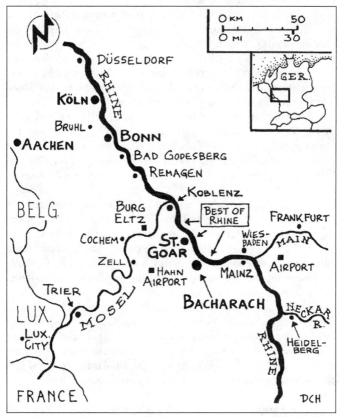

commanding Rhine setting), and Rheinstein Castle (page 223; 19th-century duke's hunting palace overlooking the Rhine).

The Rhine

Ever since Roman times, when this was the empire's northern boundary, the Rhine has been one of the world's busiest shipping rivers. You'll see a steady flow of barges with 1,000- to 2,000-ton loads. Tourist-packed buses, hot train tracks, and highways line both banks.

Many of the castles were "robber-baron" castles, put there by petty rulers (there were 300 independent little countries in medieval Germany, a region about the size of Montana) to levy tolls on passing river traffic. A robber baron would put his castle on, or even in, the river. Then, often with the help of chains and a tower on the opposite bank, he'd stop each ship and get his toll. There were 10 customs stops in the 60-mile stretch between Mainz and Koblenz alone (no wonder merchants were early proponents of the creation of larger nation-states).

Some castles were built to control and protect settlements, and others were the residences of kings. As times changed, so did the lifestyles of the rich and feudal. Many castles were abandoned for more comfortable mansions in the towns.

Most Rhine castles date from the 11th, 12th, and 13th centuries. When the pope successfully asserted his power over the German emperor in 1076, local princes ran wild over the rule of their emperor. The castles saw military action in the 1300s and 1400s, as emperors began reasserting their control over Germany's many silly kingdoms.

The castles were also involved in the Reformation wars, in which Europe's Catholic and Protestant dynasties fought it out using a fragmented Germany as their battleground. The Thirty Years' War (1618–1648) devastated Germany. The outcome: Each ruler got the freedom to decide if his people would be Catholic or Protestant, and one-third of Germany was dead. Production of Gummi bears ceased entirely.

The French—who feared a strong Germany and felt the Rhine was the logical border between them and Germany—destroyed most of the castles prophylactically (Louis XIV in the 1680s, the revolutionary army in the 1790s, and Napoleon in 1806). They were often rebuilt in neo-Gothic style in the Romantic age—the late 1800s—and today are enjoyed as restaurants, hotels, hostels, and museums.

These days, the Rhine Valley is in a bit of a rut. After the U.S. military pulled out of the region, tourism took a hit, and jobs became scarce. But there may be a silver lining for the tourist industry: Hahn Airport, once serving the American military, is now a hub for discount airlines (www.hahn-airport.de).

For information on Rhine castles, visit www.burgen-am -rhein.de. For more on the Rhine, visit www.loreleytal.com (heavy on hotels but has maps, photos, and a little history).

Getting Around the Rhine

While the Rhine flows north from Switzerland to Holland, the scenic stretch from Mainz to Koblenz hoards all the touristic charm. Studded with the crenellated cream of Germany's castles, it bustles with boats, trains, and highway traffic. Have fun exploring with a mix of big steamers, tiny ferries *(Fähre)*, trains, and bikes.

By Boat: While many travelers do the whole trip by boat, the most scenic hour is from St. Goar to Bacharach. Sit on the top deck with your handy Rhine map-guide (or the kilometer-keyed tour in this chapter) and enjoy the parade of castles, towns, boats, and vineyards.

There are several boat companies, but most travelers sail on the bigger, more expensive, and romantic Köln-Düsseldorfer (K-D) line (free with a consecutive-day Eurailpass or with dated Eurail Flexipass, Eurail Selectpass, or German railpass—but it uses up a day of any Flexipass, otherwise about €9 for the 1st hour, then progressively cheaper per hour; the recommended Bacharach–St. Goar trip costs €9 one-way, €11 round-trip; bikes cost €1.50; half-price days: Tue for bicyclists, Mon and Fri for seniors over 60, tel. 06741/1634 in St. Goar, tel. 06743/1322 in Bacharach, www .k-d.com). Boats run daily in both directions April through October, with no boats off-season. Complete, up-to-date schedules are posted in any station, Rhineland hotel, TI, or at www.euraide .de/ricksteves. Purchase tickets at the dock up to five minutes before departure. (Confirm times at your hotel the night before.) The boat is never full. Romantics will plan to catch the old-time *Goethe,* which sails each direction once a day (see "Rhine Cruise Schedule," page 214; confirm time locally).

The smaller Bingen-Rüdesheimer line is slightly cheaper than K-D (railpasses not valid, buy tickets on boat, tel. 06721/14140, www.bingen-ruedesheimer.com), with three two-hour round-trip St. Goar–Bacharach trips daily in summer (about €8.50 one-way, €10.50 round-trip; departing St. Goar at 11:00, 14:10, and 16:10; departing Bacharach at 10:10, 12:00, and 15:00).

By Car: Drivers have these options: 1) skip the boat; 2) take a round-trip cruise from St. Goar or Bacharach; 3) draw pretzels and let the loser drive, prepare the picnic, and meet the boat; 4) rent a bike, bring it on the boat for free, and bike back; or 5) take the boat one-way and return by train. When exploring by car, don't hesitate to pop onto one of the many little ferries that shuttle across the bridgeless-around-here river (see below).

By Ferry: While there are no bridges between Koblenz and Mainz, you'll see car-and-passenger ferries (usually family-run for generations) about every three miles. Ferries near St. Goar and Bacharach cross the river every 10 minutes daily in the summer from about 6:00 to 20:00, connecting Bingen–Rüdesheim, Lorch–Niederheimbach, Engelsburg–Kaub, and St. Goar–St.Goarshausen (adult-€1, car and driver-€3, pay on the boat). For a fun little jaunt, take a quick round-trip with some time to explore the other side.

By Bike: You can bike on either side of the Rhine, but for a designated bike path, stay on the west side, where a 35-mile path runs between Koblenz and Bingen. The six-mile stretch between St. Goar and Bacharach is smooth and scenic, but mostly along the highway. The bit from Bacharach to Bingen hugs the riverside and is road-free. Either way, biking is a great way to explore the valley.

Many hotels provide free or cheap bikes to guests; in St. Goar, Hotel am Markt rents bikes to guests for €5 per day. In Bacharach, anyone can rent bikes at Hotel Hillen (see below, €10/day for non-guests).

Consider taking a bike on the Rhine boats (free with ticket) and then biking back, or designing a circular trip using the fun and frequent shuttle ferries. A good target might be Kaub (where a tiny boat shuttles sightseers to the better-from-a-distance castle on the island) or Rheinstein Castle.

By Train: Hourly milk-run trains down the Rhine hit every town: St. Goar–Bacharach, 12 min; Bacharach–Mainz, 60 min; Mainz–Frankfurt, 45 min. Some train schedules list St. Goar but not Bacharach as a stop, but any schedule listing St. Goar also stops at Bacharach. Tiny stations are not staffed—buy tickets at the platform machines (user-friendly, takes paper). Prices are cheap (for example, €2.70 between St. Goar and Bacharach).

SELF-GUIDED TOUR

Der Romantische Rhein Blitz Zug/Schiff Fahrt

One of Europe's great train thrills is zipping along the Rhine enjoying this blitz tour, rated ▲▲▲. Or, even better, do it relaxing on the deck of a Rhine steamer, surrounded by the wonders of this romantic and historic gorge. Here's a quick and easy tour (you can cut in anywhere) that skips the syrupy myths filling normal Rhine guides. You can follow along on a train, bike, car, or boat. By train or boat, sit on the left (river) side going south from Koblenz. While nearly all the castles listed are viewed from this side, train travelers need to clear a path to the right window for the times I yell, "Cross over!"

You'll notice large black-and-white kilometer markers along the riverbank. I erected these years ago to make this tour easier to follow. They tell the distance from the Rhinefalls, where the Rhine leaves Switzerland and becomes navigable. Now the river-barge pilots have accepted these as navigational aids as well. We're tackling just 36 miles (58 kilometers) of the 820-mile-long (1,320 kilometer) Rhine. Your Rhine Blitz Tour starts at Koblenz and heads upstream to Bingen. If you're going the other direction, it still works. Just hold the book upside down.

Km 590—Koblenz: This Rhine blitz starts with Romantic Rhine thrills—at Koblenz. Koblenz is not a nice city (it was really hit hard in World War II), but its place as the historic *Deutsche Eck* (German corner)—the tip of land where the Mosel joins the Rhine—gives it a certain historic charm. Koblenz, from the Latin for "confluence," has Roman origins. Walk through the park, noticing the reconstructed memorial to the kaiser. Across the

Best of the Rhine

TO BONN & KÖLN

TO COCHEM & BURG ELTZ

EHRENBREIT-STEIN CASTLE

KOBLENZ 590

NOTE:
NUMBERS REFER
TO RIVERSIDE SIGNS
INDICATING KILOMETERS
NORTH OF THE RHINEFALLS

5 MILES
8 KM

N

LAHNECK 585 CASTLE

STOLZENFELS CASTLE

MARKSBURG 580 CASTLE

STERRENBERG & LIEBENSTEIN 567 CASTLE

BOPPARD 570

MAUS CASTLE 559

ST. GOARSHAUSEN

RHEINFELS CASTLE

KATZ CASTLE 556

ST. GOAR 557

LORELEY 554

KAUB

GUTENFELS 546 CASTLE

OBERWESEL 550

PFALZ CASTLE

SCHÖNBURG CASTLE

NIEDERWALD MONUMENT 528

LORCH 540

STAHLECK CASTLE

ASSMANNS-HAUSEN

BACHARACH 543

RÜDES-HEIM

SOONECK CASTLE 538

TO MAINZ

BINGEN

REICHENSTEIN CASTLE 534

MAUSETURM

EHRENFELS CASTLE 530

RHEINSTEIN CASTLE 533

L CASTLE
■ OTHER MONUMENT
● TOWN
··· CAR FERRIES

DCH

river, the yellow Ehrenbreitstein Castle now houses a hostel. It's a 30-minute hike from the station to the Koblenz boat dock.

Km 585—Lahneck Castle (Burg Lahneck): Above the modern autobahn bridge over the Lahn River, this castle *(Burg)* was built in 1240 to defend local silver mines; the castle was ruined by the French in 1688 and rebuilt in the 1850s in neo-Gothic style. Burg Lahneck faces another Romantic rebuild, the yellow Schloss Stolzenfels (out of view above the train, a 10-min climb from tiny parking lot, open for touring, closed Mon). Note that a *Burg* is a defensive fortress, while a *Schloss* is mainly a showy palace.

Rhine Cruise Schedule

Boats run May through September and on a reduced schedule for parts of April and October; no boats run November through March. These times are based on the 2005 schedule. Check www.euraide.de/ricksteves (boats heading from north to south) for any changes.

Koblenz	Boppard	St. Goar	Bacharach
—	9:00	10:15	11:25
*9:00	*11:00	*12:20	*13:35
11:00	13:00	14:15	15:25
—	14:00	15:15	16:15
14:00	16:00	17:15	18:25
13:10	11:50	10:55	10:15
14:10	12:50	11:55	11:15
—	13:50	12:55	—
—	—	**12:40	**12:00
18:10	16:50	15:55	15:15
*20:10	*18:50	*17:55	*17:15

*Riding the "Nostalgic Route," you'll take the 1913 steamer Goethe, with working paddle wheel and viewable engine room (departing Koblenz at 9:00 and Bacharach at 17:15).
**This boat is operated by a partner company.

Km 580—Marksburg Castle: This castle (black and white with the 3 modern chimneys behind it, just before town of Spay) is the best-looking of all the Rhine castles and the only surviving medieval castle on the Rhine. Because of its commanding position, it was never attacked. It's now open as a museum with a medieval interior second only to the Mosel's Burg Eltz (see self-guided tour of Marksburg Castle, page 220; for all the details on Burg Eltz, see page 251). The three modern smokestacks vent Europe's biggest car-battery recycling plant just up the valley. (If you haven't read the sidebar on river traffic on page 216, now's a good time.)

Km 570—Boppard: Once a Roman town, Boppard has some impressive remains of fourth-century walls. Notice the Roman towers and the substantial chunk of Roman wall near the train station, just above the main square.

If you visit Boppard, head to the fascinating church below the main square. Find the carved Romanesque crazies at the doorway. Inside, to the right of the entrance, you'll see Christian symbols from Roman times. Also notice the painted arches and vaults.

Originally most Romanesque churches were painted this way. Down by the river, look for the high-water *(Hochwasser)* marks on the arches from various flood years. (You'll find these flood marks throughout the Rhine and Mosel Valleys.)

Km 567—Sterrenberg Castle and Liebenstein Castle: These are the "Hostile Brothers" castles across from Bad Salzig. Take the wall between the castles (actually designed to improve the defenses of both castles), add two greedy and jealous brothers and a fair maiden, and create your own legend. Burg Liebenstein is now a fun, friendly, and affordable family-run hotel (9 rooms, Db-€98, suite-€120, giant king-and-the-family room-€195, easy parking, tel. 06773/308 or 06773/251, www.castle-liebenstein.com, hotel-burg -liebenstein@rhinecastles.com, Nickenig family).

Km 560: While you can see nothing from here, a 19th-century lead mine functioned on both sides of the river with a shaft actually tunneling completely under it.

Km 559—Maus Castle (Burg Maus): The Maus (mouse) got its name because the next castle was owned by the Katzenelnbogen family. (*Katz* means "cat.") In the 1300s, it was considered a state-of-the-art fortification...until Napoleon had it blown up in 1806 with state-of-the-art explosives. It was rebuilt true to its original plans around 1900. Today, the castle hosts a falconry show (€6.50, Tue–Sun at 11:00 and 14:30, closed Mon, 20-min walk up, tel. 06771/7669, www.burg-maus.de).

Km 557—St. Goar and Rheinfels Castle: Cross to the other side of the train. The pleasant town of St. Goar was named for a sixth-century hometown monk. It originated in Celtic times (really old) as a place where sailors would stop, catch their breath, send home a postcard, and give thanks after surviving the seductive and treacherous Loreley crossing. St. Goar is worth a stop to explore its mighty Rheinfels Castle. (For information, a guided castle tour, and accommodations, see page 234.)

Km 556—Katz Castle (Burg Katz): Burg Katz (Katzenelnbogen) faces St. Goar from across the river. Together, Burg Katz (built in 1371) and Rheinfels Castle had a clear view up and down the river, effectively controlling traffic. There was absolutely no duty-free shopping on the medieval Rhine. Katz got Napoleoned in 1806 and rebuilt around 1900.

Today, the castle is under a rich and mysterious ownership. In 1995, a wealthy and eccentric Japanese man bought it for about $4 million. His vision: to make the castle—so close to the Loreley that Japanese tourists are wild about—an exotic escape for his countrymen. But the town wouldn't allow his planned renovation of the historic (and therefore protected) building. Stymied, the frustrated investor just abandoned his plans. Today Burg Katz sits empty...the Japanese ghost castle.

Rhine River Trade and Barge-Watching

The Rhine is great for barge-watching. There's a constant parade of action, and each boat is different. Since ancient times, this has been a highway for trade. Today, the world's biggest port (Rotterdam) waits at the mouth of the river.

Barge workers are almost a subculture. Many own their own ships. The captain (and family) live in the stern. Workers live in the bow. The family car often decorates the bow like a shiny hood ornament. In the Rhine town of Kaub, there was a boarding school for the children of the Rhine merchant marine—but today it's closed, since most captains are Dutch, Belgian, or Swiss. The flag of the boat's home country flies in the stern (German; Swiss; Dutch—horizontal red, white, and blue; or French—vertical red, white, and blue). Logically, imports go upstream (Japanese cars, coal, and oil) and exports go downstream (German cars, chemicals, and pharmaceuticals). A clever captain manages to ship goods in each direction. Recently, giant Dutch container ships (which transport five times the cargo) are driving many of the traditional barges out of business, presenting the German economy with another challenge.

Tugs can push a floating train of up to five barges at once. Upstream it gets steeper and they can push only one at a time. Before modern shipping, horses dragged boats upstream (the faint remains of towpaths survive at points along the river). From 1873 to 1900, they laid a chain from Bonn to Bingen, and boats with cogwheels and steam engines hoisted themselves upstream.

Below the castle, notice the derelict grape terraces—worked since the eighth century, but abandoned only in the last generation. The Rhine wine is particularly good because the slate absorbs the heat of the sun and stays warm all night, resulting in sweeter grapes. Wine from the flat fields above the Rhine gorge is cheaper and good only as table wine. The wine from the steep side of the Rhine gorge—harder to grow and harvest—is tastier and more expensive.

About Km 555: A statue of the Loreley, the beautiful-but-deadly nymph (see next listing for legend), combs her hair at the end of a long spit—built to give barges protection from vicious icebergs that until recent years would rage down the river in the winter. The actual Loreley, a cliff (marked by the flags), is just ahead.

Km 554—The Loreley: Steep a big slate rock in centuries of legend and it becomes a tourist attraction, the ultimate Rhinestone. The Loreley (flags on top, name painted near shoreline), rising 450 feet over the narrowest and deepest point of the Rhine, has long

Today, 265 million tons travel each year along the 530 miles from Basel on the Swiss border to Rotterdam on the Atlantic.

Riverside navigational aids are of vital interest to captains who don't wish to meet the Loreley. Boats pass on the right unless they clearly signal otherwise with a large blue sign. Since downstream ships can't stop or maneuver as freely, upstream boats are expected to do the tricky do-si-do work. Cameras monitor traffic all along and relay warnings of oncoming ships by posting large triangular signals before narrow and troublesome bends in the river. There may be two or three triangles per signpost, depending upon how many "sectors," or segments, of the river are covered. The lowest triangle indicates the nearest stretch of river. Each triangle tells whether there's a ship in that sector. When the bottom side of a triangle is lit, that sector is empty. When the left side is lit, an oncoming ship is in that sector.

The **Signal and Riverpilots Museum,** located at the signal triangles at the upstream edge of St. Goar, explains how barges are safer, cleaner, and more fuel-efficient than trains or trucks (Wed and Sat 14:00–17:00, outdoor exhibits always open).

been important. It was a holy site in pre-Roman days. The fine echoes here—thought to be ghostly voices—fertilized the legendary soil.

Because of the reefs just upstream (at kilometer 552), many ships never made it to St. Goar. Sailors (after days on the river) blamed their misfortune on a *wunderbares Fräulein* whose long blonde hair almost covered her body. Heinrich Heine's *Song of Loreley* (the *Cliffs Notes* version is on local postcards) tells the story of a count who sent his men to kill or capture this siren after she distracted his horny son, causing him to drown. When the soldiers cornered the nymph in her cave, she called her father (Father Rhine) for help. Huge waves, the likes of which you'll never see today, rose from the river and carried Loreley to safety. And she has never been seen since.

But alas, when the moon shines brightly and the tour buses are parked, a soft, playful Rhine whine can still be heard from the Loreley. As you pass, listen carefully ("Sailors...sailors...over my bounding mane").

Km 552: Killer reefs, marked by red-and-green buoys, are called the "Seven Maidens." Okay, one more goofy legend: The prince of Schönburg Castle (*ober* Oberwesel) had seven spoiled daughters who always dumped men because of their shortcomings. Fed up, he invited seven of his knights up to the castle and demanded that his daughters each choose one to marry. But they complained that each man had too big a nose, was too fat, too stupid, and so on. The rude and teasing girls escaped into a riverboat. Just downstream, God turned them into the seven rocks that form this reef. While this story probably isn't entirely true, there's a lesson in it for medieval children: Don't be hard-hearted.

Km 550—Oberwesel: Cross to the other side of the train. Oberwesel was a Celtic town in 400 b.c., then a Roman military station. It now boasts some of the best Roman-wall and medieval-tower remains on the Rhine, and the commanding Schönburg Castle. Notice how many of the train tunnels have entrances designed like medieval turrets—they were actually built in the Romantic 19th century. Okay, back to the river side.

Km 546—Gutenfels Castle and Pfalz Castle, the Classic Rhine View: Burg Gutenfels (see white-painted *Hotel* sign) and

the shipshape Pfalz Castle (built in the river in the 1300s) worked very effectively to tax medieval river traffic. The town of Kaub grew rich as Pfalz raised its chains when boats came and lowered them only when the merchants had paid their duty. Those who didn't pay spent time touring its prison, on a raft at the bottom of its well. In 1504, a pope called for the destruction of Pfalz, but a six-week siege failed. Notice the overhanging outhouse (tiny white room—with faded medieval stains—between two wooden ones). Pfalz is tourable but bare and dull (€2 ferry from Kaub, €2.10 entry, April–Sept Tue–Sun 9:00–13:00 & 14:00–18:00, Oct–March until 17:00, last entry 60 min before closing, closed Mon and Dec, tel. 0172/262-2800).

In Kaub, on the riverfront directly below the castles, a green statue honors the German general Blücher. He was Napoleon's nemesis. In 1813, as Napoleon fought his way back to Paris after his disastrous Russian campaign, he stopped at Mainz—hoping to fend off the Germans and Russians pursuing him by controlling that strategic bridge. Blücher tricked Napoleon. By building the first major pontoon bridge of its kind here at the Pfalz Castle, he crossed the Rhine and outflanked the French. Two years later, Blücher and Wellington teamed up to defeat Napoleon once and for all at Waterloo.

Km 544—"The Raft Busters": Immediately before Bacharach, at the top of the island, buoys mark a gang of rocks notorious for busting up rafts. The Black Forest is upstream. It was poor, and wood was its best export. Black Foresters would ride log booms down the Rhine to the Ruhr (where their timber fortified coalmine shafts) or to Holland (where logs were sold to shipbuilders). If they could navigate the sweeping bend just before Bacharach and then survive these "raft busters," they'd come home reckless and likely horny, the German folkloric equivalent of American cowboys after payday.

Km 543—Bacharach and Stahleck Castle (Burg Stahleck): Cross to the other side of the train. The town of Bacharach is a great stop (see details and accommodations below). Some of the Rhine's best wine is from this town, whose name means "altar to Bacchus." Local vintners brag that the medieval Pope Pius II ordered Bacharach wine by the cartload. Perched above the town, the 13th-century Burg Stahleck is now a hostel.

Km 540—Lorch: This pathetic stub of a castle is barely visible from the road. Check out the hillside vineyards. These vineyards once blanketed four times as land as they do today, but modern economics have driven most of them out of business. The vineyards that do survive require government subsidies. Notice the small car ferry (3/hr, 10 min), one of several along the bridgeless stretch between Mainz and Koblenz.

Km 538—Sooneck Castle: Cross back to the other side of the train. Built in the 11th century, this castle was twice destroyed by people sick and tired of robber barons.

Km 534—Reichenstein Castle, and **Km 533—Rheinstein Castle:** Stay on the other side of the train to see two of the first castles to be rebuilt in the Romantic era. Both are privately owned, tourable, and connected by a pleasant trail. See listing on Rheinstein Castle on page 223.

Km 530—Ehrenfels Castle: Opposite Bingerbrück and the Bingen station, you'll see the ghostly Ehrenfels Castle (clobbered by the Swedes in 1636 and by the French in 1689). Since it had no view of the river traffic to the north, the owner built the cute little *Mäuseturm* (mouse tower) on an island (the yellow tower you'll see near the train station today). Rebuilt in the 1800s in neo-Gothic style, it's now used as a Rhine navigation signal station.

Km 528—Niederwald Monument: Across from the Bingen station on a hilltop is the 120-foot-high Niederwald monument, a memorial built with 32 tons of bronze in 1877 to commemorate "the reestablishment of the German Empire." A lift takes tourists to this statue from the famous and extremely touristy wine town of Rüdesheim.

From here, the Romantic Rhine becomes the industrial Rhine, and our tour is over.

SIGHTS

The following sights—Marksburg Castle, the Loreley Visitors Center, and Rheinstein Castle—are listed in the order you'd see them on the Rhine Blitz Tour, above.

Marksburg Castle

Thanks to its formidable defenses, invaders decided to give Marksburg a miss. This best-preserved castle on the Rhine, rated ▲▲, can be toured only with a guide, and tours are generally in German only (4/hr in summer, 1/hr in winter). Still, it's an awesome castle, and my self-guided walking tour (below) fits the 50-minute German-language tour (€4.50, family card-€12.50, daily April–Oct 10:00–18:00, last tour departs at 17:00, Nov–March 11:00–17:00, last tour at 16:00, tel. 02627/206, www.marksburg .de). Marksburg caps a hill above the Rhine town of Braubach (a short hike or shuttle train from the boat dock).

→ **Self Guided Tour:** Our tour starts inside the castle's first gate.

1. Inside the First Gate: While the dramatic castles lining the Rhine are generally Romantic rebuilds, Marksburg is the real McCoy—nearly all original construction. It's littered with bits of its medieval past, like the big stone ball that was swung on a rope to be used as a battering ram. Ahead, notice how the inner gate—originally tall enough for knights on horseback to gallop through—was made smaller, and therefore safer from enemies on horseback. Climb the Knights' Stairway carved out of slate rock and pass under the murder hole—handy for pouring boiling pitch on invaders. (Germans still say someone with bad luck "has pitch on his head.")

2. Coats of Arms: Colorful coats of arms line the wall just inside the gate. These are from the noble families who have owned the castle since 1283. In that year, financial troubles drove the first family to sell to the powerful and wealthy Katzenelnbogen family (who made the castle into what you see today). When Napoleon took this region in 1803, an Austrian family who sided with the French got the keys. When Prussia took the region in 1866, control passed to a friend of the Prussians who had a passion for medieval things—typical of this Romantic period. Then it was sold to the German Castles Association in 1900. Its offices are in the main palace at the top of the stairs.

3. Romanesque Palace: White outlines mark where the larger original windows were located, before they were replaced by easier-to-defend smaller ones. On the far right, a bit of the original plaster survives. Slate, which is soft and vulnerable to the elements, needs to be covered—in this case, by plaster. Because this is a protected historic building, restorers can use only the traditional plaster methods...but no one knows how to make plaster that works as well as the 800-year-old surviving bits.

4. Cannons: The oldest cannon here—from 1500—was back-loaded. This was advantageous, because many cartridges could be preloaded. But since the seal was leaky, it wasn't very powerful. The bigger, more modern cannons—from 1640—were one piece and therefore airtight, but had to be front-loaded. They could easily hit targets across the river from here. Stone balls were rough, so they let the explosive force leak out. The best cannonballs were stones covered in smooth lead—airtight and therefore more powerful and more accurate.

5. Gothic Garden: Walking along an outer wall, you'll see 160 plants from the Middle Ages—used for cooking, medicine, and witchcraft. The *Schierling* (hemlock, in the first corner) is the same poison that killed Socrates.

6. Inland Rampart: This most vulnerable part of the castle had a triangular construction to better deflect attacks. Notice the factory in the valley. In the 14th century, this was a lead, copper, and silver mine. Today's factory—Europe's largest car-battery recycling plant—uses the old mine shafts as vents (see the 3 modern smokestacks).

7. Wine Cellar: Since Roman times, wine has been the traditional Rhineland drink. Because castle water was impure, wine—less alcoholic than today's beer—was the way knights got their fluids. The pitchers on the wall were their daily allotment. The bellows were part of the barrel's filtering system. Stairs lead to the...

8. Gothic Hall: This hall is set up as a kitchen, with an oven designed to roast an ox whole. The arms holding the pots have notches to control the heat. To this day, when Germans want someone to hurry up, they say, "give it one tooth more." Medieval windows were made of thin alabaster or animal skins. A nearby wall is peeled away to show the wattle-and-daub construction (sticks, straw, clay, mud, then plaster) of a castle's inner walls. The iron plate to the left of the next door enabled servants to stoke the heater without being seen by the noble family.

9. Bedroom: This was the only heated room in the castle. The canopy kept in heat and kept out critters. In medieval times, it was impolite for a lady to argue with her lord in public. She would wait for him in bed to give him what Germans still call "a curtain lecture." The deep window seat caught maximum light for needlework and reading. Women would sit here and chat (or "spin a yarn") while working the spinning wheel.

10. Hall of the Knights: This was the dining hall. The long table is an unattached plank. After each course, servants could replace it with another preset plank. Even today, when a meal is over and Germans are ready for the action to begin, they say, "Let's lift up the table." The "action" back then was traveling minstrels who sang and told of news gleaned from their travels.

Notice the outhouse—made of wood—hanging over thin air. When not in use, its door was locked from the outside (the castle side) to prevent any invaders from entering this weak point in the castle's defenses.

11. Chapel: This chapel is still painted in Gothic style with the castle's namesake, St. Mark, and his lion. Even the chapel was designed with defense in mind. The small doorway kept out heavily armed attackers. The staircase spirals clockwise, favoring the sword-wielding defender (assuming he was right-handed).

12. Linen Room: Around 1800, the castle—with diminished military value—housed disabled soldiers. They'd earn a little extra money working raw flax into linen.

13. Two Thousand Years of Armor: Follow the evolution of armor since Celtic times. Because helmets covered the entire head, soldiers identified themselves as friendly by tipping their visor up with their right hand. This evolved into the military salute that is still used around the world today. Armor and the close-range weapons along the back were made obsolete by the invention of the rifle. Armor was replaced with breastplates—pointed (like the castle itself) to deflect enemy fire. This design was used as late as the start of World War I. A medieval lady's armor hangs over the door. While popular fiction has men locking their women up before heading off to battle, chastity belts were actually used by women as protection against rape when traveling.

14. The Keep: This served as an observation tower, a dungeon (with a 22-square-foot cell in the bottom), and a place of last refuge. When all was nearly lost, the defenders would bundle into the keep and burn the wooden bridge, hoping to outwait their enemies.

15. Horse Stable: The stable shows off bits of medieval crime and punishment. Cheaters were attached to stones or pillories. Shame masks punished gossipmongers. A mask with a heavy ball had its victim crawling around with his nose in the mud. The handcuffs with a neck hole were for the transport of prisoners. The pictures on the wall show various medieval capital punishments. Many times the accused was simply taken into a torture dungeon to see all these tools and, guilty or not, confessions spilled out of him. On that cheery note, your tour is over.

The Myth of the Loreley Visitors Center

This lightweight exhibit reflects on Loreley, traces her myth, and explores the landscape, culture, and people of the Rhine Valley. Displays in English describe the history well and a 3-D video adds to the experience. Maybe by the time you visit, the echo megaphones in the little theater will tell the legend in English rather than only German (€2.50, April–Oct daily 10:00–17:00, often closed Nov–March, tel. 06771/9100, www.loreley-touristik.de). From the exhibit, a five-minute walk (marked as 30 minutes) takes you to the impressive viewpoint overlooking the Rhine Valley from atop the famous rock. From there, it's a steep 15-minute hike down to the riverbank.

Hiking to the Visitors Center and Top of the Loreley: For a good two-hour hike from St. Goar up to the Loreley, catch the ferry across to the village of St. Goarshausen (€2 round-trip, 6/hr until 20:00, then 2/hr May–Oct until 23:00, Nov–April until 21:00). Then follow green *Burg Katz* (Katz Castle) signs up Burgstrasse under the train tracks to find steps on right *(Loreley über Burg Katz)* leading to the Katz Castle (now a private Japanese-owned hotel) and beyond. Traverse the hillside, always bearing right toward the river. You'll pass through a residential area, hike down a 50-yard path through trees, then cross a wheat field until you reach the Loreley Visitors Center (shops and restaurants, see above) and rock-capping viewpoint. From here, it's a steep 15-minute hike down to the river, where a riverfront trail takes you back to St. Goarshausen and the St. Goar ferry.

Rheinstein Castle (Schloss Burg Rheinstein)

This castle, a ▲▲ sight, seems to rule its chunk of the Rhine from a commanding position. While its 13th-century exterior is medieval-as-can-be, the interior is mostly a 19th-century duke's hunting palace. Visitors wander freely (with an English-language flier) among trophies, armor, and Romantic-era decor

Cost and Hours: €4, mid-March–mid-Nov daily 9:30–18:00; in off-season Mon–Thu 14:00–17:00, Sun 10:00–17:00, closed Fri–Sat; tel. 06721/6348, www.burg-rheinstein.de.

Getting There: This castle (at river kilometer marker #533, 2 km upstream from Trechtingshausen on the main highway, B9) is easy by **car** (small, free parking lot on B9, steep 5-min hike from there), or **bike** (great riverside bike path, 30 min upstream from Bacharach). It's less convenient by **boat** (no K-D stop nearby) or **train** (nearest stop in Trechtingshausen, 30-min walk away).

Bacharach

Once prosperous from the wine and wood trade, Bacharach (BAHKH-ah-rahkh, with a guttural *kh* sound) is now just a pleasant half-timbered village of a thousand people working hard to keep its tourists happy.

Tourist Information

The TI is on the main street in the Posthof courtyard next to the church (April–Oct Mon–Fri 9:00–17:00, Sat 10:00–14:00, Sun 10:00–14:00; Nov–March Mon–Fri 9:00–12:00, closed Sat–Sun; Internet access–€2/hr, Oberstrasse 45, from train station turn right and walk 5 blocks down main street with castle high on your left, tel. 06743/919-303, www.bacharach.de or www.rhein-nahe-touristik.de, Herr Kuhn and his team). The TI stores bags for day-trippers and provides ferry schedules. For accommodations, see "Sleeping," page 229.

Helpful Hints

Shopping: The Jost beer-stein stores carry most everything a shopper could want. One shop is across from the church in the main square, the other—which offers more porcelain and crystal...and discounts—is a block away at Rosenstrasse 16 (both shops open Mon–Sat 8:30–18:00, main square shop also open Sun 10:00–17:00, Rosenstrasse shop closed Sun, ships overseas, 10 percent discount with this book in 2006, tel. 06743/1224, www.phil-jost-germany.com).

Post Office: It's on Oberstrasse between the train station and the TI (Mon–Fri 9:00–12:00 & 15:00–18:00, Sat 9:00–12:00, closed Sun).

Bike Rental: While many hotels loan bikes to guests, the only real bike rental business in the town center is run by Erich at Hotel Hillen (see listing on page 230). He rents 25 new bikes daily from 9:00 until dark (€10/day for non-guests, €5/day for guests, with locks but no helmets, Langstrasse 18, tel. 06743/1287).

Local Guides and Walking Tours: Get acquainted with Bacharach by taking a walking tour. Charming Herr Rolf Jung, retired headmaster of the Bacharach school, is a superb English-speaking guide who loves sharing his town's story with Americans (€30, 90 min, call to reserve, tel. 06743/1519). Manuela Maddes is Herr Jung's back-up (tel. 06743/2759). If

Herr Jung or Manuela is not available, the TI has a list of other English-speaking guides, or take the self-guided walk, described below. On Saturdays at 11:00, the TI offers a walking tour (€4) primarily in German—but if you ask for English, you'll get it as well.

SELF-GUIDED WALK

Welcome to Bacharach

• *Start at the Köln-Düsseldorfer ferry dock (next to a fine picnic park).*

View the town from the parking lot—a modern landfill. The Rhine used to lap against Bacharach's town wall, just over the present-day highway. Every few years the river floods, covering the highway with several feet of water. The **castle** on the hill is a youth hostel. Two of the town's original 16 towers are visible from here (up to 5 if you look really hard). The huge roadside wine keg declares this town was built on the wine trade.

Reefs up the river forced boats to unload upriver and reload here. Consequently, Bacharach became the biggest wine trader on the Rhine. A riverfront crane hoisted huge kegs of prestigious "Bacharach" wine (which, in practice, was from anywhere in the region). The tour buses next to the dock and the flags of the biggest spenders along the highway remind you that today's economy is basically founded on tourism.

• *Before entering the town, walk upstream through the riverside park.*

This park was laid out in 1910 in the English style. Notice how the trees were planted to frame fine town views, highlighting the most picturesque bits of architecture. Until recently, stepping on the grass was *verboten*. The dark, sad-looking monument—its eternal flame long snuffed-out—is a war memorial. The German psyche is permanently scarred with memories of wars. Today, many Germans would rather avoid monuments like this, which revisit the dark periods before Germany became a nation of pacifists. Take a close look at the monument. Each panel honors sons of Bacharach who died for the Kaiser: in 1864 against Russia, in 1870 against France, in 1914 during World War I. The military Maltese Cross—flanked by classic German helmets—comes with a W, for Kaiser Wilhelm.

• *Continue to where the park meets the playground, and then cross the highway to the fortified riverside wall of the Catholic church—decorated with high-water marks recalling various floods.*

Check out the metal ring on the medieval slate wall. Before the 1910 reclamation project, the river extended out to here, and boats would use the ring to tie up. Upstream from here, there's a trailer park, and beyond that there's a campground. In Germany, trailer vacationers and campers are two distinct subcultures. Folks

Bacharach

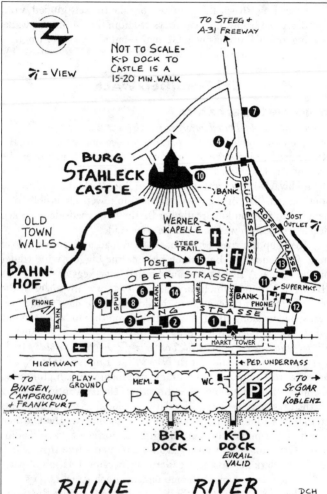

NOT TO SCALE-
K-D DOCK TO
CASTLE IS A
15-20 MIN. WALK

TO STEEG +
A-31 FREEWAY

= VIEW

BURG STAHLECK CASTLE

OLD TOWN WALLS

BAHN-HOF

WERNER KAPELLE

STEEP TRAIL

POST

BANK

JOST OUTLET

OBER STRASSE

PHONE

SPUR

KRAN.

BAUER

LANG

STRASSE

BANK

PHONE

SUPER MKT.

BLÜCHERSTRASSE

ROSEN STRASSE

MARKT TOWER

HIGHWAY 9

PLAY-GROUND

MEM.

PARK

WC

P

PED. UNDERPASS

TO BINGEN, CAMPGROUND, & FRANKFURT

TO St GOAR + KOBLENZ

B-R DOCK

K-D DOCK
EURAIL VALID

RHINE   RIVER

DCH

1 Hotel Rhein & Land Restaurant Stuber
2 Hotel/Rest. Kranenturm
3 Hotel Hillen & Bike Rental
4 Pension im Malerwinkel
5 Pension Binz
6 Pension Lettie
7 Pension Winzerhaus
8 Ursula Orth B & B

9 Irmgard Orth B & B
10 Jugendherberge Stahleck Hostel
11 Altes Haus Restaurant
12 Kurpfälzische Münze Restaurant
13 Bastian's Weingut zum Grüner Baum
14 Weingut Karl Heidrich
15 Old Posthof

who travel in trailers, like many retirees in the U.S., are a nomadic bunch, hauling around the countryside in their mobile homes and paying about €6 a night to park. Campers, on the other hand, tend to set up camp—complete with comfortable lounge chairs and even TVs—and stay put for weeks, even months. They often come back to the same plot year after year, treating it like their own private estate. These camping devotees have made a science out of relaxing.

• *At the church, go under the 1858 train tracks and hook right past the yellow floodwater yard stick and up the stairs onto the town wall. Atop the wall, turn left and walk under the long arcade. After a few steps, notice a well on your left. This is one of 40 such wells that, until 1900, provided water to the townsfolk. After passing the Hotel Rhein (see listing on page 229, hotel is before the Markt tower, which marks one of the town's 15 original 14th-century gates), descend, pass another well, and follow Markt street toward the town center, the two-tone church, and the town's main intersection.*

From here, Bacharach's main street (Oberstrasse) goes right to the half-timbered, red-and-white Altes Haus (from 1368, the oldest house in town) and left 400 yards to the train station. To the left (or south) of the church, a golden horn hangs over the old **Posthof** (TI, free WC upstairs in courtyard). The post horn symbolizes the postal service throughout Europe. In olden days, when the postman blew this, traffic stopped and the mail sped through. This post station dates from 1724, when stagecoaches ran from Köln to Frankfurt and would change horses here, Pony Express-style.

Step past the old-oak doors into the courtyard—once a carriage house and inn that accommodated Bacharach's first VIP visitors. Notice the fascist eagle (from 1936, on the left as you enter; a swastika once filled its center) and the fine view of the church and a ruined chapel above. The Posthof is on a charming square. Spin around to enjoy the higgledy-piggledy building style.

Two hundred years ago, Bacharach's main drag was the only road along the Rhine. Napoleon widened it to fit his cannon wagons. The steps alongside the church lead to the castle. Return to the church, passing the **Italian Ice Cream** café, where friendly Mimo serves his special invention: Riesling wine–flavored gelato (€0.60 per scoop, opposite Posthof at Oberstrasse 48).

Inside the church (daily 9:30–18:00, English info on table near door), you'll find Grotesque capitals, brightly painted in medieval style, and a mix of round Romanesque and pointed Gothic arches. Left of the altar, some medieval frescoes survive where an older Romanesque arch was cut by a pointed Gothic one.

• *Continue down Oberstrasse to the **Altes Haus.***

Notice the 14th-century building style—the first floor is made of stone, while upper floors are half-timbered (in the ornate style common in the Rhine Valley). Some of its windows still look medieval, with small flattened circles as panes (small because that's all that glass-blowing technology of the time would allow), pieced together with molten lead. Frau Weber welcomes visitors to enjoy the fascinating ground floor of her Altes Haus, with its evocative old photos and etchings (consider eating here later—see "Eating," page 232).

• *Keep going down Oberstrasse to the **old mint** (Münze), marked by a crude coin in its sign.*

Across from the mint, the wine garden of Bastian family is the liveliest place in town after dark (see page 233). Above you in the vineyards stands a lonely white-and-red tower—your destination.

At the next street, look right and see the mint tower, painted in the medieval style (illustrating that the Dark Ages weren't really *that* dark), and then turn left. Wander 30 yards up Rosenstrasse to the **well.** Notice the sundial and the wall painting of 1632 Bacharach with its walls intact. Climb the tiny-stepped lane behind the well up into the vineyard and to the tall, lonely tower. The slate steps lead to a small path through the vineyard that deposits you at a viewpoint atop the stubby remains of the old town wall. If the tower's open, hike to its top floor for the best view.

A grand medieval town spreads before you. When Frankfurt had 15,000 residents, medieval Bacharach had 4,000. For 300 years (1300–1600), Bacharach was big, rich, and politically powerful.

From this perch you can see the chapel ruins and six surviving **city towers.** Visually trace the wall to the castle. The castle was actually the capital of Germany for a couple of years in the 1200s. When Holy Roman Emperor Frederick Barbarossa went away to fight the Crusades, he left his brother (who lived here) in charge of his vast realm. Bacharach was home of one of seven electors who voted for the Holy Roman Emperor in 1275. To protect their own power, these elector-princes did their best to choose the weakest guy on the ballot. The elector from Bacharach helped select a two-bit prince named Rudolf von Hapsburg (from a no-name castle in Switzerland). The underestimated Rudolf brutally silenced the robber barons along the Rhine and established the mightiest dynasty in European history. His family line, the Hapsburgs, ruled much of Central Europe until 1918.

Plagues, fires, and the Thirty Years' War (1618–1648) finally did Bacharach in. The town, with a population of about a thousand, has slumbered for several centuries. Today, the castle houses commoners—40,000 overnights annually by youth hostelers.

In the mid-19th century, painters such as J. M. W. Turner and writers such as Victor Hugo were charmed by the Rhineland's romantic mix of past glory, present poverty, and rich legend. They put this part of the Rhine on the old "grand tour" map as the "Romantic Rhine." Victor Hugo pondered the ruined 15th-century chapel that you see under the castle. In his 1842 travel book, *Rhein Reise (Rhine Travels)*, he wrote, "No doors, no roof or windows, a magnificent skeleton puts its silhouette against the sky. Above it, the ivy-covered castle ruins provide a fitting crown. This is Bacharach, land of fairy tales, covered with legends and sagas." If you're enjoying the Romantic Rhine, thank Victor Hugo and company.

• *To get back into town, take the level path away from the river that leads along the once-mighty wall up the valley past the next tower. Then cross the street into the parking lot. Pass Pension Malerwinkel on your right, being careful not to damage the old arch with your head. Follow the creek past a delightful little series of half-timbered homes and cheery gardens known as "Painters' Corner"* (Malerwinkel). *Resist looking into some pervert's peep show (on the right) and continue downhill back to the village center. Nice work.*

SLEEPING

(country code: 49, area code: 06743)
See map on page 226 for locations. Ignore guest houses and restaurants posting *Recommended by Rick Steves* signs. If they're not listed in the current edition of this book, I do not recommend them.

$$$ Hotel Rhein, with 14 spacious and comfortable rooms, is classy, well-run, decorated with a modern flair, and overlooks the river. Since it's right on the train tracks, its river- and train-side rooms come with four-paned windows and air-conditioning (Db-€86 with this book and direct reservation in 2006, cheaper for 2 nights, half-board option, directly inland from the K-D boat dock at Landstrasse 50, tel. 06743/1243, fax 06743/1413, info@rhein-hotel-bacharach.de, www.rhein-hotel-bacharach.de). This place has been in the Stuber family for six generations. For a culinary splurge, consider dining here (see "Eating," page 232).

$$ Hotel Kranenturm, offering castle ambience without the climb, combines hotel comfort with *Zimmer* coziness right downtown. Run by hardworking Kurt Engel and his intense but friendly wife, Fatima, this hotel is actually part of the medieval fortification. Its former *Kran* (crane) towers are now round rooms. When the riverbank was higher, cranes on this tower loaded barrels of

Sleep Code

(€1 = about $1.20)
S = Single, **D** = Double/Twin, **T** = Triple, **Q** = Quad, **b** = bathroom, **s** = shower only. All hotels speak some English. Breakfast is included and credit cards are accepted unless otherwise noted.

To help you sort easily through these listings, I've divided the rooms into three categories, based on the price for a standard double room with bath:

$$$ **Higher Priced**—Most rooms €70 or more.
 $$ **Moderately Priced**—Most rooms between €50–70.
  $ **Lower Priced**—Most rooms €50 or less.

The Rhine is an easy place for cheap sleeps. *Zimmer* and *Gasthäuser* with €20 beds abound (and *Zimmer* normally discount their prices for longer stays). Rhine-area hostels offer €14 beds to travelers of any age. Each town's TI is eager to set you up, and finding a room should be easy any time of year (except for winefest weekends in Sept and Oct). Bacharach and St. Goar, the best towns for an overnight stop, are 10 miles apart, connected by milk-run trains, riverboats, and a riverside bike path. Bacharach is a much more interesting town, but St. Goar has the famous castle (see "St. Goar," page 233). Parking in Bacharach is simple along the highway next to the tracks (3-hour daytime limit is generally not enforced) or in the boat parking lot. Parking in St. Goar is tighter; ask at your hotel.

wine onto Rhine boats. While just 15 feet from the train tracks, a combination of medieval sturdiness, triple-paned windows, and included earplugs makes the riverside rooms sleepable (Sb-€40–44, Db-€55–62, bigger Db-€58–65, Db in huge tower rooms with castle and river views-€70–80, Tb-€80–95, honeymoon special-€90–105, lower price is for off-season or stays of at least 3 nights in high season, family deals, cash preferred, Rhine views come with ripping train noise, back rooms are quieter, kid-friendly, laundry service-€12.50, Langstrasse 30, tel. 06743/1308, fax 06743/1021, www.kranenturm.com, hotel-kranenturm@t-online.de). Kurt, a good cook, serves €6–18 dinners.

$$ Hotel Hillen, a block south of the Hotel Kranenturm, has a little less charm and similar train noise, with spacious rooms, good food, and friendly owners. They just installed new windows to minimize train noise, but to get a room on the quiet side ask for *ruhige Seite* (S-€25, Sb-€30, D-€35, Ds-€40, Db-€45, Tb-€60, Qb-€75, these special prices are for a 2-night minimum for those reserving directly with this book in 2006, 1-nighters pay €5 more, closed mid-Nov–March, family rooms, Langstrasse 18, tel. 06743/1287, fax 06743/1037, hotel-hillen@web.de, kind Iris speaks some English). The Hillen's Erich rents bikes (see page 224).

$$ Pension im Malerwinkel sits like a grand gingerbread house just outside the wall at the top end of town in a quiet little neighborhood so charming it's called "Painters' Corner" *(Malerwinkel)*. The Vollmer family's 20-room place is super-quiet and comes with a sunny garden on a brook and easy parking (Sb-€35, Db-€55–58 for 1 night, €53 for 2 nights, €50 for 3 nights, cash only, some rooms have balconies but most face parking lot, no train noise, bike rental-€6/day, from town center go uphill until you pass the old town gate and look left to Blücherstrasse 41, tel. 06743/1239, fax 06743/93407, www.im-malerwinkel.de, pension@im-malerwinkel.de).

$$ Pension Binz offers four large, bright rooms (Sb-€33, Db-€51, 3rd person-€18, apartment with 2-night minimum-€61, fine breakfast, Koblenzer Strasse 1, tel. 06743/1604, pension .binz@freenet.de, Carla speaks a little English).

$ At **Pension Lettie,** effervescent and eager-to-please Lettie offers four bright rooms. Lettie speaks English (she worked for the U.S. Army before they withdrew) and does laundry—€10.50 per load (Sb-€34, Db-€45, Tb-€62, Qb-€80, for 5b-€95, 6b-€105, studio apt-€50, prices valid with this book if you reserve direct rather than through TI, discount for 2-night stays, 6 percent more if paying with credit card, strictly non-smoking, buffet breakfast with waffles and eggs, no train noise, a few doors inland from Hotel Kranenturm, Kranenstrasse 6, tel. 06743/2115, fax 06743/947564, pension.lettie@t-online.de).

$ Pension Winzerhaus, a 10-room place run by friendly Sybille and Stefan, is 200 yards up the valley from the town gate, so the location is less charming, and the train noise is replaced by street noise. But the parking is easy, and rooms are simple, clean, and modern (Sb-€30, Db-€45, Tb-€60, Qb-€65, 10 percent off with this book, cash only, free bikes for guests, non-smoking rooms, Blücherstrasse 60, tel. 06743/1294, winzerhaus@compuserve.de).

$ *Orth* Zimmer: Delightful sisters-in-law run two fine little B&Bs across the lane from each other (from station walk down Oberstrasse, turn right on Spurgasse, look for Orth sign). **Ursula Orth** rents five rooms and speaks a smidge of English (Sb-€22, D-€31, Db-€34, Tb-€45, cash only, rooms 4 and 5 on ground floor, Spurgasse 3, tel. 06743/1557). **Irmgard Orth** rents two fresh rooms. She speaks even less English but is exuberantly cheery and serves homemade honey with breakfast (Sb-€20, Db-€34, cash only, Spurgasse 2, tel. 06743/1553). Their excellent prices assume you're booking direct, instead of with the TI.

$ Jugendherberge Stahleck hostel is a 12th-century castle on the hilltop—500 steps above Bacharach—with a royal Rhine view. Open to travelers of any age, this is a gem with eight beds and a private modern shower and WC in most rooms. A steep 20-minute climb on the trail from the town church, the hostel is warmly run by Evelyn and Bernhard Falke (FALL-keh), who serve hearty €6 all-you-can-eat buffet dinners. The hostel pub serves cheap local wine until midnight (€17 dorm beds with breakfast and sheets, €3.10 extra for non-members or in a double, couples can share one of five €44 Db, no smoking in rooms, open all day but 22:00 curfew, laundry machine, beds normally available but call and leave your name, they'll hold a bed until 18:00, tel. 06743/1266, fax 06743/2684, bacharach@diejugendherbergen.de). If driving, don't go in the driveway; park on the street and walk 200 yards.

EATING

Restaurants

You can easily find inexpensive (€10–15), atmospheric restaurants offering indoor and outdoor dining.

Hotel Rhein's **Land Restaurant Stuber** is Bacharach's best top-end choice. Chef Andreas Stuber is the sixth generation to prepare regional, seasonal plates, served on river- and track-side seating or indoors with a spacious wood-and-white-table-cloth elegance. Their William Turner *menu* is a pâté sampler plate worth considering (€9–15 entrées, closed Tue, call to reserve an outdoor table, facing the K-D boat dock just below the center of town, Landstrasse 50, tel. 06743/1243).

Altes Haus, the oldest building in town (see page 227), serves reliably good food with Bacharach's most romantic atmosphere (€9–15 entrées, Thu–Tue 12:00–15:30 & 18:00–21:30, closed Wed and Dec–Easter, dead center by the church, tel. 06743/1209). Find the cozy little dining room with photos of the opera singer who sang about Bacharach, adding to its fame.

Kurpfälzische Münze, while more expensive than Altes Haus, is a popular standby for lunch or a drink on its sunny terrace or in its pubby candlelit interior (€7–21 entrées, daily 11:00–22:00, in the old mint, a half-block down from Altes Haus, tel. 06743/1375).

Hotel Kranenturm is another good value, with hearty meals and good main-course salads. If you like trains, sit on their trackside terrace and trade travel stories with new friends over dinner, letting screaming trains punctuate your conversation. If you prefer charming old German decor, sit inside (see hotel listing on page 229).

Wine-Tasting

Bacharach is proud of its wine. Two places in town—rowdy and rustic Grüner Baum and sophisticated Weingut Heidrich—offer visitors an inexpensive chance to join in on the fun. Each place samples many varieties of wines in small glasses on spinning wine carousels.

At **Bastian's Weingut zum Grüner Baum,** groups of two to six people pay €13.50 for a wine carousel of 15 glasses—14 different white wines and one lonely rose—and a basket of bread. Your mission: Team up with others who have this book to rendezvous here after dinner. Spin the Lazy Susan, share a common cup, and discuss the taste. Doris Bastian insists: "After each wine, you must talk to each other." They offer soup and cold cuts, and good ambience indoors and out (Mon–Wed and Fri from 13:00, Sat–Sun from 12:00, closed Thu and Feb–mid-March, just past Altes Haus, tel. 06743/1208). To make a meal of a carousel, consider the *Kase Teller* (7 different cheeses, including *Spundekase,* the local soft cheese).

For a fun, family-run wine shop and *Stube* in the town center, visit **Weingut Karl Heidrich** (at Oberstrasse 16, directly in front of Hotel Kranenturm), where Markus proudly shares his family's wine while passionately explaining its fine points to travelers. They offer a variety of wine carousels with six wines (€10), which are ideal for the more sophisticated wine-taster.

St. Goar

St. Goar is a classic Rhine town—its hulk of a castle overlooking a half-timbered shopping street and leafy riverside park busy with sightseeing ships and contented strollers. From the boat dock, the main drag—a pedestrian mall without history—cuts through town before winding up to the castle. Rheinfels Castle, once the mightiest on the Rhine, is the single best Rhineland ruin to explore.

While the town of St. Goar itself isn't much more than a few hotels and restaurants, it makes a good base for hiking or biking the region. A tiny car ferry will shuttle you back and forth across the busy Rhine from here. (One of my favorite pastimes in St. Goar is chatting with friendly Heike at the K-D boat kiosk.)

Tourist Information

The helpful St. Goar TI, which books rooms and offers a free baggage-check service, is on the pedestrian street, three blocks from the K-D boat dock and train station (May–Sept Mon–Fri 9:00–12:30 & 13:30–18:00, Sat 10:00–12:00; Oct–April Mon–Fri until 16:30, closed Sat–Sun, from train station, go downhill around church and turn left on Heer Strasse, tel. 06741/383).

Helpful Hints

Picnics: St. Goar's waterfront park is hungry for a picnic. The small Edeka **supermarket** on the main street is great for picnic fixings. You can buy any quantity of produce—just push the photo or number on the scales (July–Sept Mon–Fri 8:00–18:00, Sat 8:00–13:00, usually closed Sun, shorter hours off-season).

Shopping: The friendly and helpful Montag family runs the Hotel Montag (Michael) and three **shops** (steins—Misha, Steiffs—Maria, and cuckoo clocks—Marion), all at the base of the castle hill road. The stein shop under the hotel has Rhine guides, fine steins, and copies of this year's *Rick Steves' Germany & Austria* guidebook. All three shops offer 10 percent off any of their souvenirs (including Hummels) for travelers with this book (€5 minimum purchase). On-the-spot VAT refunds cover about half your shipping costs (if you're not shipping, they'll give you VAT form to claim refund at airport).

Internet Access: Hotel Montag offers expensive coin-op access (see listing on page 241; €8/hr, disk-burning service, Heer Strasse 128, tel. 06741/1629).

Bike Rental: Try Hotel zur Loreley (€5/day, Heer Strasse 87, tel. 06741/1614).

SIGHTS

St. Goar's Rheinfels Castle

Sitting like a dead pit bull above St. Goar, this mightiest of Rhine castles rumbles with ghosts from its hard-fought past. Burg Rheinfels *was* huge—once the biggest castle on the Rhine (built in 1245). It withstood a siege of 28,000 French troops in 1692. But in 1797, the French revolutionary army destroyed it. The castle was used for ages as a quarry, and today—while still mighty—it's only a small fraction of its original size. This hollow but interesting shell offers your

St. Goar

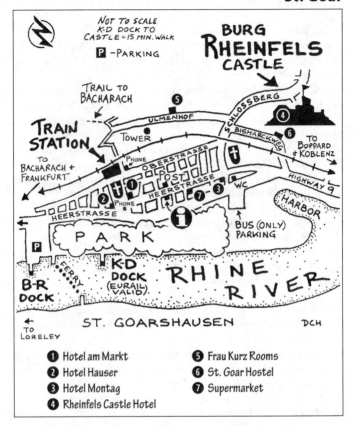

NOT TO SCALE
K·D DOCK TO
CASTLE = 15 MIN. WALK

P – PARKING

BURG RHEINFELS CASTLE

TRAIL TO BACHARACH

ULMENHOF

SCHLOSSBERG

TRAIN STATION

TOWER

BISMARCKWEG

TO BOPPARD & KOBLENZ

TO BACHARACH + FRANKFURT

PHONE

OBERSTRASSE

POST

HEERSTRASSE

PHONE

HEERSTRASSE

WC

HIGHWAY 9

P A R K

BUS (ONLY) PARKING

HARBOR

P

FERRY

K·D DOCK (EURAIL VALID)

B-R DOCK

R H I N E   R I V E R

← TO LORELEY

ST. GOARSHAUSEN

DCH

1. Hotel am Markt
2. Hotel Hauser
3. Hotel Montag
4. Rheinfels Castle Hotel
5. Frau Kurz Rooms
6. St. Goar Hostel
7. Supermarket

single best hands-on ruined-castle experience on the river.

Cost and Hours: €4, family card–€10, mid-March–Nov daily 9:00–18:00, last entry at 17:00, Dec–mid-March only Sat–Sun 11:00–17:00—weather permitting.

Tours and Information: Call in advance or gather 10 English-speaking tourists and beg to get an English tour—perhaps from Günther, the "last knight of Rheinfels" (tel. 06741/7753). Otherwise, follow my self-guided tour below. The castle map is mediocre; the English booklet is better, with history and illustrations (€2). If it's damp, be careful of slippery stones. A handy WC is in the castle courtyard under the stairs to the restaurant entry. Better yet, check out the guillotine urinals immediately across from the ticket booth (stand back when you pull to flush).

Let There Be Light: If planning to explore the mine tunnels, bring a flashlight, or do it by candlelight (museum sells candles with matches, €0.50).

Getting to the Castle: From St. Goar's boat dock or train station, take a steep 15-minute hike, a €5 taxi ride (tel. 06741/7011), or the kitschy "tschu-tschu" tourist train (€2 one-way, €3 round-trip, 7 min to the top, daily 9:30–18:00 but unreliable, 3/hr, runs from square between station and dock, also stops at Hotel Montag, complete with lusty music, tel. 06741/2030).

➲ **Self-Guided Tour:** Rather than wander aimlessly, visit the castle by following this tour: From the ticket gate, walk straight. Pass *Grosser Keller* on the left (where we'll end this tour) and walk through an internal gate past the *zu den gedeckten Wehrgängen* sign on the right (where we'll pass later) uphill to the museum (daily 10:00–12:30 & 13:00–17:30) in the only finished room of the castle.

❶ **Museum and Castle Model:** The seven-foot-tall carved stone immediately inside the door (marked *Keltische Säule von Pfalzfeld*)—a tombstone from a nearby Celtic grave—is from 400 years before Christ. There were people here long before the Romans...and this castle. Find the old wooden library chair near the tombstone. If you smile sweetly, the man behind the desk may demonstrate—pull the back forward and it becomes stairs for accessing the highest shelves.

The sweeping castle history exhibit in the center of the room is well described in English. The massive fortification was the only Rhineland castle to withstand Louis XIV's assault during the 17th century. At the far end of the room is a model reconstruction of the castle (not the one with the toy soldiers) showing how much bigger it was before French revolutionary troops destroyed it in the 18th century. Study this. Find where you are (hint: look for the tall tower). This was the living quarters of the original castle, which was only the smallest ring of buildings around the tiny central courtyard (13th century). The ramparts were added in the 14th century. By 1650, the fortress was largely complete. Ever since its destruction by the French in the late 18th century, it's had no military value. While no WWII bombs were wasted on this ruin, it served St. Goar as a quarry for generations. The basement of the museum shows the castle pharmacy and an exhibit of Rhine-region odds and ends, including tools and an 1830 loom. Don't miss the photos of ice-breaking on the Rhine. While once routine, ice-breaking hasn't been necessary here since 1963.

• *Exit the museum and walk 30 yards directly out, slightly uphill into the castle courtyard.*

❷ **Medieval Castle Courtyard:** Five hundred years ago, the entire castle circled this courtyard. The place was self-sufficient and ready for a siege with a bakery, pharmacy, herb garden, brewery, well (top of yard), and livestock. During peacetime, 300 to 600 people lived here; during a siege, there would be as many as 4,000. The walls were plastered and painted

St. Goar's Rheinfels Castle

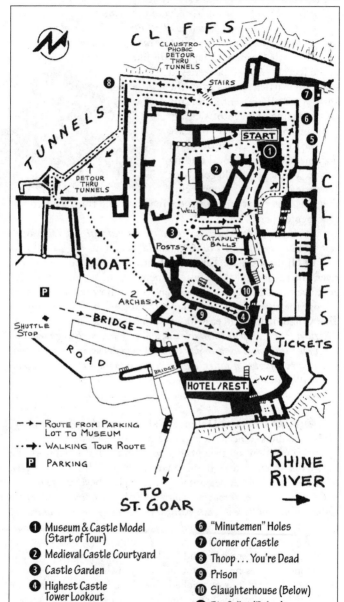

- **❶** Museum & Castle Model (Start of Tour)
- **❷** Medieval Castle Courtyard
- **❸** Castle Garden
- **❹** Highest Castle Tower Lookout
- **❺** Covered Defense Galleries
- **❻** "Minutemen" Holes
- **❼** Corner of Castle
- **❽** Thoop... You're Dead
- **❾** Prison
- **❿** Slaughterhouse (Below)
- **⓫** Big Cellar (Below)

white. Bits of the original 13th-century plaster survive.

• *Continue through the courtyard and out Erste Schildmauer, turn left into the next courtyard, and walk straight to the two old, wooden, upright posts. Find the pyramid of stone catapult balls on your left.*

❸ Castle Garden: Catapult balls like these were too expensive not to recycle—they'd be retrieved after any battle. Across from the balls is a well—essential for any castle during the age of sieging. Look in. Spit. The old posts are for the ceremonial baptizing of new members of the local trading league. While this guild goes back centuries, it's now a social club  that fills this court with a huge wine party the third weekend of each September.

• *If weary, skip to #5; otherwise, climb the cobbled path up to the castle's best viewpoint—up where the German flag waves.*

❹ Highest Castle Tower Lookout: Enjoy a great view of the river, the castle, and the forest. Remember, the fortress once covered five times the land it does today. Notice how the other castles (across the river) don't poke above the top of the Rhine canyon. That would make them easy for invading armies to see.

• *Return to the catapult balls, walk down the road, go through the tunnel, veer left through the arch marked* zu den gedeckten Wehrgängen, *go down two flights of stairs, and turn left into the dark, covered passageway (Covered Defense Galleries). From here, we will begin a rectangular walk taking us completely around (counterclockwise) the perimeter of the castle.*

❺ & ❻ Covered Defense Galleries with "Minutemen" Holes: Soldiers—the castle's "minutemen"—had a short commute: defensive positions on the outside, home in the holes below on the left. Even though these living quarters were padded with straw, life was unpleasant. A peasant was lucky to live beyond age 45.

• *Continue straight through the dark gallery and to the corner of the castle, where you'll see a white painted arrow at eye level. Stand with your back to the arrow on the wall.*

❼ Corner of Castle: Look up. A three-story, half-timbered building originally rose beyond the highest stone fortification. The two stone tongues near the top just around the corner supported the toilet. (Insert your own joke here.) Turn around and face the wall. The crossbow slits below the white arrow were once steeper. The bigger hole on the riverside was for hot pitch.

• *Follow that white arrow along the outside to the next corner. Midway you'll pass stairs on the right leading down* zu den Minengängen *(sign on upper left). Adventurers with flashlights can detour here (see*

"Optional Detour—Into the Mine Tunnels," page 240). You may come out around the next corner. Otherwise, stay with me, walking level to the corner. At the corner, turn left.

❽ **Thoop...You're Dead:** Look ahead at the smartly placed crossbow slit. While you're lying there, notice the stonework. The little round holes were for scaffolds used as they built up. They indicate this stonework is original. Notice also the fine stonework on the chutes. More boiling pitch...now you're toast, too.

• *Continue along the castle wall around the corner. At the grey railing, look up the valley and uphill where the sprawling fort stretched. Below, just outside the wall, is land where attackers would gather. The mine tunnels are under there, waiting to blow up any attackers (read below).*

Keep going along the perimeter, jog left, go down five steps and into an open field, and walk toward the wooden bridge. You may detour here into the passageway (on right) marked 13 Halsgraben. The "old" wooden bridge is actually modern. Angle left through two arches (before the bridge) and through the rough entry to the Verliess (prison) on the left.

❾ **Prison:** This is one of six dungeons. You walked through an entrance prisoners only dreamed of 400 years ago. They came and went through the little square hole in the ceiling. The holes in the walls supported timbers that thoughtfully gave as many as 15 residents something to sit on to keep them out of the filthy slop that gathered on the floor. Twice a day, they were given bread and water. Some prisoners actually survived longer than two years in here. While the town could torture and execute, the castle only had permission to imprison criminals in these dungeons. Consider this: According to town records, the two men who spent the most time down here—2.5 years each—died within three weeks of regaining their freedom. Perhaps after a diet of bread and water, feasting on meat and wine was simply too much.

• *Continue through the next arch, under the white arrow, then turn left and walk 30 yards to the Schlachthaus.*

❿ **Slaughterhouse:** Any proper castle was prepared to survive a six-month siege. With 4,000 people, that's a lot of provisions. The cattle that lived within the walls were slaughtered in this room. The castle's mortar was congealed here (by packing all the organic waste from the kitchen into kegs and sealing it). Notice the drainage gutters. "Running water" came through from drains built into the walls (to keep the mortar dry and therefore strong...and less smelly).

• *Back outside, climb the modern stairs to the left. A skinny, dark passage (yes, that's the one) leads you into the...*

⓫ **Big Cellar:** This *Grosser Keller* was a big pantry. When the castle was smaller, this was the original moat—you can see the rough lower parts of the wall. The original floor was 13 feet deeper.

The drawbridge rested upon the stone nubs on the left. When the castle expanded, the moat became this cellar. Halfway up the walls on the entrance side of the room, square holes mark spots where timbers made a storage loft, perhaps filled with grain. In the back, an arch leads to the wine cellar (sometimes blocked off) where finer wine was kept. Part of a soldier's pay was wine...table wine. This wine was kept in a single 180,000-liter stone barrel (that's 47,550 gallons), which generally lasted about 18 months.

The count owned the surrounding farmland. Farmers got to keep 20 percent of their production. Later, in more liberal feudal times, the nobility let them keep 40 percent. Today, the German government leaves the workers with 60 percent...and provides a few more services.

• *You're free. Climb out, turn right, and leave. For coffee on a terrace with a great view, visit the Rheinfels Castle Hotel, opposite the entrance (WC at base of steps).*

Optional Detour—Into the Mine Tunnels: Around 1600, to protect their castle, the Rheinfellers cleverly booby-trapped the land just outside their walls by building tunnels topped with thin slate roofs and packed with explosives. By detonating the explosives when under attack, they could kill hundreds of invaders. In 1626, a handful of underground Protestant Germans blew 300 Catholic Spaniards to—they figured—hell. You're welcome to wander through a set of never-blown-up tunnels. But be warned: It's 600 feet long, assuming you make no wrong turns; it's pitch-dark, muddy, and claustrophobic, with confusing dead-ends; and you'll never get higher than a deep crouch. It cannot be done without a light (flashlights available at entrance—see above). At stop #6 of the above tour, follow the stairs on the right leading down *zu den Minengängen* (sign on upper left).

The *Fuchsloch* sign welcomes you to the foxhole. Walk level (take no stairs) past the first steel railing (where you hope to emerge later) to the second steel railing. Climb down. The "highway" in this foxhole is three feet high. The ceiling may be painted with a white line indicating the correct path. Don't venture into the narrower side aisles. These were once filled with the gunpowder. After a small decline, take the second right. At the T-intersection, go right (uphill). After about 10 feet, go left. Take the next right and look for a light at the end of the tunnel. Head up a rocky incline under the narrowest part of the tunnel and you'll emerge at that first steel railing. The stairs on the right lead to freedom. Cross the field, walk under the bigger archway, and continue uphill toward the old wooden bridge. Angle left through two arches (before the bridge) and through the rough entry to the *Verliess* (prison) on the left. Rejoin the tour here at stop #8.

SLEEPING

(country code: 49, area code: 06741)

$$$ Hotel Montag, with 28 rooms, is on the castle end of town just across the street from the world's largest free-hanging cuckoo clock. Manfred and Maria Montag and their son Mike speak New Yorkish. Even though the hotel relies primarily on Contiki bus tours (mostly the "under 35" crowd...a.k.a. party animals), it's friendly, laid-back, and comfortable (Sb-€35–45, Db-€70–80, Tb-€90–100, 10 percent discount with this book in 2006, coin-op Internet access-€8/hr, disk-burning service, Heer Strasse 128, tel. 06741/1629, fax 06741/2086, hotelmontag@freenet.de). Check out their adjacent crafts shop (heavy on beer steins).

$$$ Rheinfels Castle Hotel is the town splurge. Actually part of the castle but an entirely new building, this luxurious 60-room place is good for those with money and a car (Db-€140–180 depending on river views and balconies, extra adult bed-€37, extra bed for kids ages 7–11—€25, kids under age 7 free, elevator, free parking, indoor pool and sauna, dress-up restaurant, Schlossberg 47, tel. 06741/8020, fax 06741/802-802, www.castle-hotel-rheinfels .com, info@burgrheinfels.de).

$$ Hotel am Markt, well-run by Herr and Frau Velich, is rustic, with all the modern comforts. It features a hint of antler with a pastel flair, 18 bright rooms, and a good restaurant where the son, Gil, is a fine chef (see "Eating," below). It's a good value and a stone's throw from the boat dock and train station (S-€35, Sb-€43, standard Db-€59, bigger riverview Db-€69, March-mid–April and Oct–mid-Nov Db-€50, Tb-€82, Qb-€88, closed mid-Nov–Feb, Am Markt 1, tel. 06741/1689, fax 06741/1721, www.hotelammarkt1 .de, hotel.am.markt@gmx.de). Rental bikes are available to guests (€5/day). They now also rent 10 rooms of equal quality (for the same price) in a smaller riverside hotel a block away.

$$ Hotel Hauser, facing the boat dock, is another good deal, warmly run by another Frau Velich. Its 12 rooms sit over a fine restaurant (S-€21.50, D-€45, Db-€50, great Db with Rhine-view balconies-€56, prices promised with this book and cash through 2006, Db cheaper off-season, costs more with credit card, Heer Strasse 77, tel. 06741/333, fax 06741/1464, www.hotelhauser.de, hotelhauser@t-online.de).

$ Frau Kurz offers St. Goar's best *Zimmer* deal, renting three delightful rooms with a breakfast terrace, garden, fine view, and homemade marmalade (S-€23, D-€40, Db-€44, 2-night minimum, cash only, no smoking, free and easy parking, confirm prices, honor your reservation or call to cancel, Ulmenhof 11, tel. & fax 06741/459, www.gaestehaus-kurz.de, jeanette.kurz@t-online.de, some English spoken). It's a steep five-minute hike from the train station (exit left from station, take immediate left at the yellow phone booth, pass under tracks to paved path, go up stairs and follow zigzag path to Ulmenhof, *Zimmer* is just past tower).

$ St. Goar Hostel, the big beige building under the castle (on road to castle, veer right just after railroad bridge), rents 14 doubles and piles of beds in 4- to 10-bed dorms. It has a well-run, strong, institutional atmosphere with a 22:00 curfew (but you can borrow the key) and hearty €6 dinners (D-€28, dorm beds-€14, includes breakfast, non-members pay €3 extra, all ages welcome, open all day, Bismarckweg 17, tel. 06741/388, fax 06741/2869, st-goar @diejugendherbergen.de).

EATING

Hotel am Markt serves tasty traditional meals with plenty of game and fish (try Chef Gil's specialties—roast wild boar and homemade cheesecake) at fair prices (daily specials, €5–16) with good atmosphere and service. For your Rhine splurge, walk, taxi, or drive up to **Rheinfels Castle Hotel** for its incredible view terrace in an elegant setting (€15–20 dinners, daily 18:30–21:15, reserve a table by the window, tel. 06741/8020, see hotel listing above). There are a couple of Italian places in town and plenty of ways to gather a picnic to enjoy on the riverside park. For plenty more options, take the quick train to Bacharach, leaving and returning hourly until very late (see below).

TRANSPORTATION CONNECTIONS

Milk-run trains stop at Rhine towns each hour starting as early as 6:00. Koblenz, Boppard, St. Goar, Bacharach, Bingen, and Mainz are each about 15 minutes apart. From Koblenz to Mainz takes 75 minutes. The St. Goar/Bacharach segment departs at about :20 after the hour in each direction (€2.60, buy tickets from the machine in the unmanned station). To get a faster big train, go to Mainz (for points east and south) or Koblenz (for points north, west, and along Mosel). Train info: tel. 11861 (€0.50/min).

From Mainz by Train to: **Bacharach/St. Goar** (hrly, 1 hr), **Cochem** (hrly, 2.5 hrs, change in Koblenz), **Köln** (3/hr, 90 min, change in Koblenz), **Baden-Baden** (hrly, 1.5 hrs), **Munich** (hrly, 4 hrs), **Frankfurt** (3/hr, 45 min), **Frankfurt Airport** (4/hr, 25 min).

From Koblenz by Train to: **Köln** (4/hr, 1 hr), **Berlin** (2/hr, 5.5 hrs, up to 2 changes), **Frankfurt** (3/hr, 1.5 hrs, 1 change), **Cochem** (2/hr, 50 min), **Trier** (2/hr, 2 hrs), **Brussels** (12/day, 4 hrs, change in Köln), **Amsterdam** (12/day, 4.5 hrs, up to 5 changes).

From Frankfurt by Train to: **Bacharach** (hrly, 1.5 hrs, change in Mainz; first train to Bacharach departs at 6:00, last train at 20:45), **Koblenz** (hrly, 1.5 hrs direct), **Rothenburg** (hrly, 3 hrs, transfers in Würzburg and Steinach), **Würzburg** (hrly, 2 hrs), **Nürnberg** (hrly, 2 hrs), **Munich** (hrly, 4 hrs, 1 change), **Amsterdam** (every 2 hrs, 4.5 hrs direct, more with transfer in Utrecht), **Paris** (9/day, 6.5 hrs, up to 3 changes).

From Bacharach by Train to: Frankfurt Airport (hrly, 1.5 hrs, change in Mainz, first train to Frankfurt airport departs about 5:40, last train 21:30).

MOSEL VALLEY

The misty Mosel is what some visitors hoped the Rhine would be—peaceful, sleepy, romantic villages slipped between the steep vineyards and the river; fine wine; a sprinkling of castles (Burg Eltz is tops); and lots of friendly *Zimmer*. Boat, train, and car traffic here is a trickle compared to the roaring Rhine. While the swan-speckled Mosel moseys 300 miles from France's Vosges mountains to Koblenz, where it dumps into the Rhine, the most scenic piece of the valley lies between the towns of Bernkastel-Kues and Cochem. I'd savor only this section. Cochem and Trier (see next chapter) are easy day trips from each other (1 hour by train, 55 miles by car). Cochem is the handiest home base unless you want the peace of Beilstein.

Throughout the region on summer weekends and during the fall harvest, wine festivals with oompah bands, dancing, and colorful costumes are powered by good food and wine. You'll find a wine festival in some nearby village any weekend, June through September. The tourist season lasts from April through October. Things close down tight through the winter.

Look for the booklet *The Castles of the Moselle* (€3.10, at local TIs), with information on castles from Koblenz to Trier (including Burg Eltz, Cochem, and Metternich in Beilstein). The booklet not only has historical and structural information, but also some drawings of what the now-ruined castles looked like originally.

Getting Around the Mosel Valley

By Train and Bus: The train zips you to Cochem, Bullay, or Trier in a snap. Bullay has bus connections with Zell (nearly hourly, 10 min) and with Beilstein (bus #711, Mon–Fri hourly 8:00–18:00, Sat–Sun 4/day, 35 min, get out at Ellenz Fähre and take ferry across). Cochem has more frequent bus connections with Beilstein (bus #716, Mon–Fri 9/day—including 3 before 7:00, Sat 5/day, Sun 3/day, 25 min, last bus departs Beilstein about 18:30, €3.15, buy tickets from driver, bus info: tel. 02671/8976). A one-way taxi from Cochem to Beilstein costs about €15. Pick up bus schedules at train stations or TIs.

By Boat: Daily departures on the Undine-Kolb Line allow you to cruise the most scenic stretch between Cochem, Beilstein, and Zell (tel. 02673/1515, www.kolb-mosel.de): between **Cochem and Zell** (1–2/day, May–Oct, but none on Fri and Mon May–June, 3 hrs, €15 one-way, €22 round-trip), between **Cochem and Beilstein** (5/day, 1 hr, €9 one-way, €12 round-trip), and between **Zell and Beilstein** (1–2/day May–Oct, but none on Fri and Mon May–June, 2 hrs, €12 one-way, €17 round-trip). You can also take the boat from **Cochem to Treis-Karden,** near Burg Eltz (3/day, daily mid-July–mid-Aug; Wed and Sat–Sun only May–mid-July and mid-Aug–Oct, 45 min, €7 one-way, €10 round-trip). To get from Treis-Karden to Burg Eltz, choose between a long hike (2 steep hours) or a taxi ride (see "Getting to Burg Eltz," page 253).

The KD (Köln-Düsseldorfer) line sails once a day in each direction, but only between **Cochem** and **Koblenz** (€21.80, mid-June–Sept daily, May–mid-June and early Oct Fri–Mon only, none in winter, Koblenz to Cochem 9:45–15:00, or Cochem to Koblenz 15:40–20:00; free with consecutive-day Eurailpass or a dated Eurail Flexipass, Eurail Selectpass, or German railpass—uses up a day of a Flexipass; tel. 02671/980-023, www.k-d.com). In early to mid-June, the locks close for 10 days of annual maintenance, and no boats run between Cochem, Koblenz, Beilstein, and Zell. With all the locks, Mosel cruises can be pretty slow.

By Car: The easygoing Mosel Wine Route turns anyone into a relaxed Sunday driver. Pick up a local map at a TI or service station. Koblenz and Trier are linked by two-lane roads that run along both riverbanks. While riverside roads are a delight, the river is very windy and shortcuts overland can save serious time—especially between Burg Eltz and Beilstein (see "Getting to Burg Eltz," page 253) and from the Mosel to the Rhine (note the Brodenback–Boppard shortcut). Koblenz, Cochem, and Trier have car-rental agencies.

By Bike: Biking along the Mosel is the rage among Germans. You can rent bikes in most Mosel towns (see village listings below). A fine bike path follows the river (with some bits still sharing the

Mosel Valley

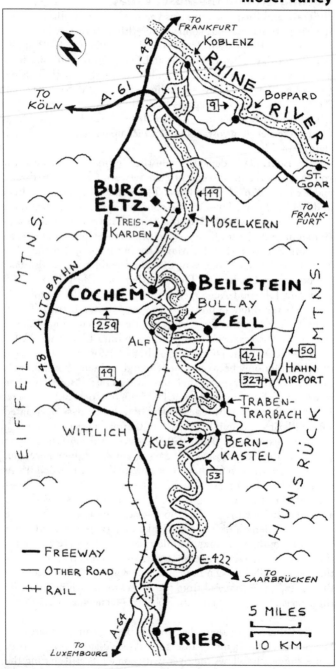

road with cars) from Koblenz to Zell. From Cochem, allow an hour to Beilstein and 2.5 hours for the full trip to Zell, and about 10 minutes from Bullay to Zell. Many pedal one way and relax with a return cruise.

By Ferry: About a dozen car-and-passenger ferries *(Fähre)* cross the Mosel between Koblenz and Trier. These are marked AF for auto and PF for pedestrian on the *Moselle Wine Road/Mosellauf* brochure.

Cochem

With a majestic castle and picturesque medieval streets, Cochem is the very touristic hub of this part of the river. Stroll pleasant paths along the idyllic riverbank, play life-size chess, or just grab a bench and watch Germany at play.

ORIENTATION

(area code:02671)

Tourist Information

The information-packed TI is by the bridge at the main bus stop. Most of the pamphlets (free map with town walk, town history flier) are kept behind the desk—ask. Their thorough 24-hour room listing in the window comes with a free phone connection. The TI also has information on special events, wine-tastings held by local vintners, public transportation to Burg Eltz, area hikes, and the informative €3 Mosellauf brochure or the cartoony €1 *Moselle Wine Road.* The *Tips and Information from A to Z* brochure (often out of stock and only in German) lists everything from car-rental agencies to saunas and babysitters (May–Oct Mon–Fri 9:00–17:00, Sat until 15:00, closed Sun; July–Oct also Sun 10:00–12:00; off-season closed weekends and at lunch, tel. 02671/60040, www.cochem.de, info@ferienland-cochem.de).

Arrival in Cochem

Make a hard right out of the train station (lockers available, €1.50–2.50/day, no WC) and walk about 10 minutes to the town center and TI (just past bus lanes on your left under bridge).

Drivers can park near the bridge. To get to the main square *(Markt)* and colorful medieval town center, continue under the bridge (€0.30 WC), then angle right and follow Bernstrasse.

Helpful Hints

Internet Access: Try COCbit-Kommunikation, on the street facing the river, across from the boat ticket booths (€5/hr,

Mon–Fri 10:00–12:00 & 14:00–18:00, Sat 10:00–13:00, closed Sun, Moselpromenade 7, tel. 02671/211).

Post Office: It's on Ravenestrasse, a five-minute walk from the TI toward the train station (Mon–Fri 9:00–17:00, Sat 9:00–12:00, closed Sun).

Supermarket: The supermarket is right across the street from the post office (Mon–Fri 8:30–18:30, Sat 8:00–15:00, closed Sun).

Bike Rental: The K-D boat kiosk at the dock rents bikes (€4/half-day, €7/day, May–Oct daily 9:30–18:00, closed in off-season, small selection). Radsport Schrauth, run by serious cyclists, has a good selection and helpful service (€3.50/half-day, €7/day, 30 percent more for mountain bikes, Mon–Fri 9:30–13:00 & 14:00–18:00, Sat 9:00–13:00, Sun 10:00–12:00, arrange weekend drop-off time, leave driver's license for deposit, Endertstrasse 41, right across from chairlift, tel. 02671/7974). Consider taking a bike on the boat or train and riding back.

Festival: Cochem's biggest wine festival is held the last weekend in August (Aug 26–27 in 2006). High season for wine aficionados lasts from August through October.

SIGHTS AND ACTIVITIES

Cochem Castle—This pointy castle is the work of overly imaginative 19th-century restorers (€4, mid-March–mid-Nov daily 9:00–17:00, closed mid-Nov–mid-Dec and Jan–mid-March, open last half of Dec, 20-min walk from Cochem, follow one of the frequent 40-min German-language tours while reading English explanation sheets or gather 12 English speakers and call a day ahead to schedule an English tour, tel. 02671/255, www.reichsburg-cochem.de). The resident falconer frequently shows off his flock; check the notice at the gate to see if the birds are in fine feather (€3, Tue–Sun at 11:00, 13:00, 14:30, 16:00, no shows Mon). A bus shuttles castle-seekers between the bridge near the TI and the road below the castle (€2 one-way, 2/hr, May–Oct only, walk last 10 min uphill to castle).

Chairlift and Hikes—For great views, you could ride the *Sesselbahn* chairlift (€4 one-way, €5.50 round-trip, open April–mid-Nov 10:00–18:00, www.cochemer-sesselbahn.de). Or you can scramble up the narrow path under the lift for 20 minutes of heart-pounding, aerobic excitement. Or hike up to the *Aussichtspunkt* (the Pinnerkreuz cross on the hill opposite the castle, find trailhead behind train station parking lot). For the best of all worlds, take the lift up and then follow the path to the *Bahnhof* down through the forest and then the vineyards to Weingut Rademacher.

Swimming, Tennis, and Golf—Cochem's Freizeit Zentrum offers an array of family-friendly activities: an indoor wave pool, an outdoor pool, a sauna, tennis courts, and mini-golf (€7.50/3 hrs for pools, extra for tennis and mini-golf, Tue–Fri 10:00–22:00, Sat–Sun 10:00–19:00, closed Mon, Moritzburger Strasse 1, tel. 02671/97990, www.moselbad.de).

Cruise—The Tanz Party mit Live Musik cruise is popular with German vacationers (€13, 20:15–22:30, nightly mid-July–Aug, May–mid-July Tue and Sat; Sept–Oct Tue, Thu, and Sat; 2-man schmaltzy band, tel. 02671/7387). For Mosel boat tours, see "Getting Around the Mosel Valley," above.

Sightseeing Train—A little yellow **train** leaves from under the bridge at the TI and does a sightseeing loop (€4.50, 2/hr, May–Oct 10:00–18:00, no train in off-season, 30 min, commentary only in German—ask for the flier in English).

SLEEPING

(country code: 49, area code: 02671)
August is very tight, with various festivals and generally inflated prices.

$$$ Rustic **Hotel Lohspeicher,** just off the main square on a street with tiny steps, is for those who want a real hotel—with high prices—in the thick of things. Its nine high-ceilinged rooms have modern comforts (Sb-€50, Db-€80–100, elevator, breakfast in a fine stone-and-timber room, restaurant, parking-€5/day, closed Feb, Obergasse 1, tel. 02671/3976, fax 02671/1772, www .lohspeicher.de, service@lohspeicher.de, Ingo).

$$$ **Hotel am Hafen,** across the river, offers views of Cochem, and some of the 20 rooms have balconies (Sb-€60–75, Db-€70–100, deluxe Db-€100–130—but not worth the extra

---

Sleep Code

(€1 = about $1.20)
S = Single, **D** = Double/Twin, **T** = Triple, **Q** = Quad, **b** = bathroom, **s** = shower only. Unless otherwise noted, credit cards are accepted, English is spoken, and breakfast is included.

To help you sort easily through these listings, I've divided the rooms into three categories based on the price for a standard double room with bath:

$$$ **Higher Priced**—Most rooms €70 or more.
  $$ **Moderately Priced**—Most rooms between €50–70.
    $ **Lower Priced**—Most rooms €50 or less.

money, all rooms €10 more for 1-night stays, staff can be uneven, air-con, Uferstrasse 3, tel. 02671/97720, fax 02671/977-227, www.hotel-am-hafen.de, hotel-am-hafen@t-online.de).

$ Weingut Rademacher rents six beautiful ground-floor rooms. Wedged between vineyards and train tracks, with a pleasant garden and a big common kitchen, it's a great value. Charming hostess Andrea and her husband Hermann give tours of their wine cellar when time permits (earlier is better); guests enter for free. If there's no tour, visitors are welcome to taste the wine (Sb-€27.50, Db on train side-€45, Db on vineyard side-€51, less for 3 nights, family deals, non-smoking, free parking, go right from station on Ravenestrasse, turn right on Pinnerstrasse, walk under tracks and curve right to Pinnerstrasse 10, tel. 02671/4164, fax 02671/91341).

$ Haus Andreas has 10 clean, modern rooms at fair prices (Sb-€23–30, Db-€36–40, Tb-€54, prices vary by length of stay, cash only, Schlossstrasse 9, reception is often across the street in shop at #16, tel. 02671/1370 or 02671/5155, fax 02671/1370, Frau Pellny speaks a little English). From the main square, take Herrenstrasse; after a block, angle right up the steep hill on Schlossstrasse.

$ *Hostel:* Cochem's hostel, just opened in 2003, is a huge, family-friendly complex with 146 beds, picnic tables, grill pit, playground, game room, bar, restaurant, and a sundeck over the Mosel (dorm bed-€17.50, Db-€46, more for nonmembers, includes sheets and breakfast, half- and full-board options available at extra cost, fills up Aug–Oct—reserve in advance, Klottenerstrasse 9, tel. 02671/8633, fax 02671/8568, www.diejugendherbergen.de, cochem@diejugendherbergen.de).

EATING

Zum Stüffje is a traditional half-timbered *Weinstube* with simple food and veggie options (Wed–Mon 11:30–14:00 & 17:30–21:00, closed Tue, Oberbachstrasse 14, tel. 02671/7260).

Gaststätte Noss, with fine food served inside or out, is open later than most other restaurants (€8–15 entrées, May–Oct Fri–Wed 10:00–22:00, Nov–April Fri–Wed 17:30–22:00, closed Thu year-round, Moselpromenade 4, tel. 02671/7067; don't confuse with hotel of the same name).

Locals go to "Arthur's place," officially named **Alte Gutschänke,** for a glass of wine in a cozy cellar seated at long, wooden get-to-know-your-neighbor tables (extensive wine list and basic food, Mon–Fri from 18:00, Sat–Sun from 14:00, open Easter–Oct, closed winter, just up the hill at Schlossstrasse 6, tel. 02671/8950).

TRANSPORTATION CONNECTIONS

From Cochem by Train to: Bullay (near Zell, hrly, 10 min), **Moselkern** (near Burg Eltz, hrly, 35 min), and **Trier** (hrly, 60 min). Train info: tel. 11861 (€0.50/min). Bus info: tel. 02671/8976.

Beyond the Mosel Valley: To get anywhere by train outside the valley, take a train to **Koblenz** (hrly, 60 min). From there, you can catch trains to **Frankfurt** (hrly, 60 min), **Köln** (every 10 min, 60 min), or **Remagen** (hrly, 40 min).

Burg Eltz

My favorite castle in all of Europe lurks in a mysterious forest. It's been left intact for 700 years and is furnished throughout as it was 500 years ago. Thanks to smart diplomacy and clever marriages, Burg Eltz was never destroyed. (It survived one 5-year siege.) It's been in the Eltz family for 820 years.

Eltz means "stream." The first *Burg* on the *Eltz* (castle on the stream) appeared in the 12th century to protect a trade route. By 1472, the castle looked like it does today, with the homes of three big landlord families gathered around a tiny courtyard within one formidable fortification. Today, the excellent 45-minute tour winds you through two of those homes, while the third remains the fortified quarters of the Eltz family. The elderly countess of Eltz—whose family goes back 33 generations here (you'll see a photo of her family)—enjoys flowers. Each week for 40 years, she's had grand arrangements adorn the public castle rooms.

It was a comfortable castle for its day: 80 rooms made cozy by 40 fireplaces and wall-hanging tapestries. Its 20 toilets were automatically flushed by a rain drain. The delightful chapel is on a lower floor. Even though "no one should live above God," this chapel's placement was acceptable because it fills a bay window, which floods the delicate Gothic space with light. The three families met—working out common problems as if sharing a condo—in the large "conference room." A carved jester and a rose look down

Burg Eltz Area

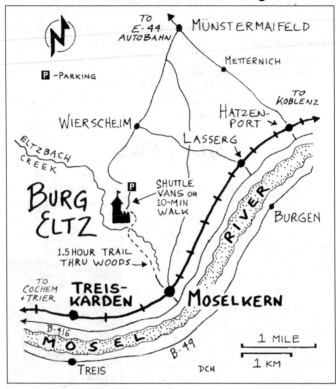

on the big table, reminding those who gathered that they were free to discuss anything ("fool's freedom"—jesters could say anything to the king), but nothing discussed could leave the room (the "rose of silence"). In the bedroom, have fun with the suggestive decor: the jousting relief carved into the canopy, and the fertile and phallic figures hiding in the lusty green wall paintings.

Near the exit, the €2.50 treasury fills the four higgledy-piggledy floors of a cellar with the precious, eccentric, and historic mementos of this family that once helped elect the Holy Roman Emperor and, later, owned a sizable chunk of Croatia (Hapsburg favors).

Cost, Hours, Information: €6 castle entry, plus €2.50 for treasury, April–Oct daily from 9:30, last tour departs at 17:30, closed Nov–March, tel. 02672/950-500, www.burg-eltz.de.

Tours: The only way to see the castle is with a 45-minute tour (included in entry price). German tours go constantly (with helpful English fact sheets, €0.50). Guides speak English and thoughtfully collect English speakers into their own tours—well worth waiting for (never more than 20 min). It doesn't hurt to call ahead to see if an English tour is scheduled—or organize your own by corralling 20 English speakers in the inner courtyard, then push the red button on the white porch and politely beg for an English guide.

Getting to Burg Eltz: By **train,** get off at the deserted Moselkern station midway between Cochem and Koblenz (hourly trains, no lockers, phones and taxis at station). Leaving the station, exit right and follow *Burg Eltz* signs for about 20 minutes up, down, and inland along a residential street (signs are sparse, but have faith and stay on the main road). Then take the marked trail (slippery when wet, slightly steep near end).

It's a pleasant 90-minute **hike** between the station and castle through a pine forest where sparrows carry crossbows, and maidens, disguised as falling leaves, whisper "watch out."

Alternatively, you can **taxi** from Cochem (30 min, €40 one-way for up to 4 people, Cochem taxi tel. 02671/8080) and then enjoy the hike downhill back to the train station in Moselkern. A cheaper taxi option is to train to either Moselkern or Treis-Karden, and have the taxi meet you there (15 min, €18 from Moselkern, €23 from Treis-Karden, taxi tel. 02672/1407, have your hotel call taxi ahead of time with train arrival time). If you have luggage, Treis-Karden is your best bet (there's no place to check baggage at Moselkern). At the Tries-Karden station, you can ask the staff in the little glass office (marked *Kf*) facing the tracks if you can leave your bags for a few hours. Or, if they can't and you're really desperate, ask at the elegant Schloss-Hotel Petry, a fine restaurant serving traditional food across from the station. They're often happy to oblige you—particularly if you're having lunch there (lunch daily 11:30–14:15, St. Castorstrasse 80, tel. 02672/9340, www.schloss -hotel-petry.de, info@schloss-hotel-petry.de).

A more romantic option is to take a **boat** from Cochem to Treis-Karden, then choose between a steep hike up to the castle (ask boat crew for hiking directions, allow 2 hours) or a taxi (see above).

The easiest option is by **car:** From Koblenz, leave the river at Hatzenport following the white Burg Eltz signs through the towns of Münstermaifeld and Wierschem. From Cochem, following the *Münstermaifeld* signs from Moselkern saves about 10 minutes. (Note that the *Eltz* signs at Moselkern lead to a trailhead for the hour-long hike to the castle. To drive directly to the castle, ignore the *Eltz* signs until you reach Münstermaifeld.) The castle parking lot (€1.50/day, daily 9:00–18:00) is 1.25 miles past Wierschem. From the lot, hike 10 minutes downhill to the castle or wait (maximum 10 min) for the red castle shuttle bus (€1.50 one-way). There are three Burg Eltz parking lots; only this lot (1.25 miles south of

Wierschem) is close enough for an easy walk. Another option is to park at the Moselkern station (free) and follow the park-and-walk signs (see above).

If driving from Burg Eltz to Beilstein or Zell, you'll save 30 minutes with this **shortcut:** From Eltz, cross the river at Treis-Karden, go through town, and bear right at the swimming pool (direction Bruttig-Fankel). This overland route deposits you in Bruttig, a scenic three-mile riverside drive from Beilstein (21 miles from Zell).

Beilstein

Upstream from Cochem is the quaintest of all Mosel towns. Cozy Beilstein (BILE-shtine) is Cinderella-land—extremely tranquil except for its territorial swans. Its 180 residents run 30 or so hotels and eateries. Beilstein has no real tourist office, but several cafés advertise that they have town info. Parking is free in any space you can find along the riverside road.

Herr Nahlen rents **bikes** for pleasant riverside rides (Bachstrasse 47, €6/day, reservations smart, tel. 02673/1840).

Getting to Beilstein: Beilstein lacks a train station. From Cochem, you can get to Beilstein by bus (#716, hourly, fewer buses on weekends, 15 min) or taxi (€15). If coming from Bullay, catch bus #711 (€4.55, bus info tel. 02671/8976) to Ellenz Fähre and, from there, take the ferry across the river to Beilstein (ferries run 9:24–19:24, Mon–Fri hourly, Sat–Sun every 2 hours).

SELF-GUIDED WALK

Welcome to Beilstein

Explore the narrow lanes, ancient wine cellar, resident swans, and ruined castle by following this short walk.

• *Stand where the village hits the river.*

1. Beilstein's Riverfront: In 1963, the big road and the Mosel locks were built, making the river so peaceful today. Before then, access to Beilstein was limited to a tiny one-way lane and the small ferry. The cables that tether the ferry once allowed the motorless craft to go back and forth powered only by the current and an angled rudder. Today, it shuttles people (€1), bikes, and cars constantly (Tue–Thu and Sat–Sun 9:00–12:00 & 13:00–18:00, Mon

11:40–18:00, Fri 10:30–18:00). The campground across the river is typical of German campgrounds—80 percent of its customers set up their trailers and tents at Easter and use them as summer homes until October, when the regular floods chase them away for the winter. If you stood where you are now through the winter, you'd have cold water up to your crotch five times. Look inland. The Earl of Beilstein—who ruled from his castle above town—built the Altes Zollhaus in 1634 to levy tolls from river traffic. Today, the castle is a ruin, the once-mighty monastery (see the big church high on the left) is down to one monk, and the town's economy is based only on wine and tourists.

Beilstein's tranquility is thanks to Germany's WWI loss. This war cost Germany the region of Alsace (now part of France). Before World War I, the Koblenz–Trier train line—which connects Alsace to Germany—was the busiest in Germany. It tunnels through the grape-laden hill across the river in what was the longest train tunnel in Germany. The construction of a supplemental line destined to follow the riverbank (like the lines that crank up the volume on the Rhine) was stopped in 1914 and, since Alsace went to France in 1918, the plans were scuttled.

Follow Bachstrasse into town. You'll notice blue plaques on the left marking the high-water *(Hochwasser)* points of historic floods.

At the first corner, Furst-Metternich Strasse leads left to the monastery (climb stairs marked the *Klostertreppe*). While its population is down to one Carmelite, Rome maintains an oversized-for-this-little-town church that runs a restaurant with a great view.

Bachstrasse—literally, "creek street"—continues straight through Beilstein, covering up the brook that once flowed through town providing a handy disposal service 24/7. Today, Bachstrasse is lined by wine cellars. The only way for a small local vintner to make any decent money these days is to sell his wine directly to customers in inviting little places like these.

• *Your first right leads to the...*

2. Market Square: For centuries, neighboring farmers sold their goods on Marktplatz. The *Zehnthaus* (tithe house) was the village IRS, where locals would pay one-tenth *(Zehnte)* of their produce to their landlord (either the Church or the earl). Pop into the Zehnthauskeller. Stuffed with peasants' offerings 400 years ago, it's now packed with vaulted medieval ambience. It's fun at night for candlelit wine-tasting, soup and cold cuts, and schmaltzy music (live Fri and Sat). The Bürgerhaus (above the fountain) had nothing to do with medieval fast food. First the village church, then the *Bürger's* (like a mayor) residence, today it's *the* place for a town party or wedding. Haus Lipmann (on the riverside, now a recommended hotel and restaurant—see "Sleeping," below) dates from 1727. It was built by the earl's family as a residence after the French destroyed his castle. Haus Lipmann's main dining hall was once the knights' hall.

• *The stepped lane leads uphill (past the Zehnthaus, follow signs for Burgruine Metternich) to...*

3. Beilstein's Castle: Beilstein once rivaled Cochem as the most powerful town on this part of the Mosel. Its castle (Burg Metternich) is a sorry ruin today, but those who hike up are rewarded with a postcard Mosel view and a chance to hike even higher to the top of its lone surviving tower (€2, April–Oct daily 9:00–18:30, closed Nov–March, closes earlier off-season, view café/restaurant, tel. 02673/936-39).

For more exercise and an even better view, continue up behind the castle and follow the road uphill. A hundred yards above the castle (take the left fork), you'll find the ultimate "castle–river bend–carpets of vineyards" photo stop. The derelict roadside vineyard is a sign of recent times—the younger generation is abandoning the family plots, opting out of all that hard winemaking work. A surprising sight—the most evocative Jewish cemetery *(Judenfriedhof)* this side of Prague—is 200 yards farther up the road.

During the 700 years leading up to 1942, Beilstein hosted a Jewish community. As in the rest of Europe, wealthy Jews could buy citizenship and enjoy all the protections afforded to residents. These *Schutzjuden*, or "protected Jews," were shielded from the often crude and brutal "justice" of the Middle Ages. In 1840, 25 percent of Beilstein's 300 inhabitants were Jewish. But no payment could shield this community from Hitler—so there are no Jews in today's Beilstein. (A small Jewish community in Koblenz maintains this lovely cemetery.)

• *From here, you can return to the castle gate, ring the bell (Klingel), and show your ticket to get back in and retrace your steps, or continue on the road, which curves and leads downhill (a gravel path at the next bend on the left leads back into town).*

SLEEPING

(country code: 49, area code: 02673)
Many of Beilstein's hotels shut down from mid-November through March.

$$$ Hotel Haus Lipmann is your chance to live in a medieval mansion with hot showers and TVs. A prizewinner for atmosphere, it's been in the Lipmann family for 200 years. The creaky wooden staircase and the elegant dining hall, with long wooden tables surrounded by antlers, chandeliers, and feudal weapons, will get you in the mood for your castle sightseeing, but the riverside terrace may mace your momentum (5 rooms, Sb-€75–85, Db-€85–95, cash only, closed Nov–April, Marktplatz 3, tel. 02673/1573, fax 02673/1521, www.hotel-haus-lipmann.com, hotel.haus.lipmann@t-online.de). The entire Lipmann family—Marion and Jonas, their hardworking son David, and his wife Anja—hustles for its guests.

Marion's brother Joachim Lipmann runs two hotels of his own: **$$$ Hotel Am Klosterberg** is a big modern place with 16 comfortable rooms at the extremely quiet top of town (Db-€60–80, Auf dem Teich 8, up the main street 200 yards inland, tel. 02673/1850, fax 02673/1287, www.hotel-lipmann.de, lipmann@t-online.de). The half-timbered, riverfront **$$ Altes Zollhaus Gästezimmer** packs all the comforts into eight tight, bright rooms (Sb-€45, Db-€60, deluxe Db-€80, cash only, closed Nov–March, same contact info as Hotel Am Klosterberg; adjoining restaurant Alte Stadtmauer open daily 10:30–22:00).

$$ Hotel Gute Quelle offers half-timbers, a good restaurant, and 13 inviting rooms, plus seven in an annex across the street (Sb-€35, D-€52, Db-€60, less for longer stays, closed Dec–March, Marktplatz 34, tel. 02673/1437, fax 02673/1399, www.hotel-gute-quelle.de, info@hotel-gute-quelle.de, helpful Susan speaks Irish).

$ The welcoming Gasthaus Winzerschenke an der Klostertreppe is a great value, right in the tiny heart of town (5 rooms, Db-€48, bigger Db-€58, cash only, discount for 2-night stays, closed Nov–Easter, go up main street and take 2nd left onto Furst-Metternich-Strasse, reception in restaurant, tel. 02673/1354, fax 02673/962-371, www.winzerschenke-beilstein.de, winzerschenke-beilstein@t-online.de, Frau Sausen and her son Christian).

EATING

You'll have no problem finding a characteristic dining room or a relaxing riverview terrace.

Restaurant Haus Lipmann serves good fresh food with daily specials on a glorious leafy riverside terrace (€10–15 entrées, daily 10:00–23:00).

The **Zehnthauskeller** on the Marktplatz is *the* place for wine-tasting with soup, cold plates, and lively *Schlager* (kitschy German folk-pop) while old locals on holiday sit under a dark medieval vault (Tue–Sun 11:00–23:00, closed Mon, off-season until 18:00).

Zell

Peaceful, with a fine riverside promenade, a pedestrian bridge over the water, and plenty of *Zimmer,* Zell makes a good overnight stop. Zell has a long pedestrian zone filled with colorful shops, restaurants, and *Weinstuben* (wine bars). A fun oompah folk band plays on weekend evenings on the main square, making evenings here a delight.

Getting to Zell: Trains go hourly from Cochem or Trier to Bullay, where the bus takes you to little Zell (€1.50, 2/hr, 10 min; bus stop is across street from Bullay train station, check yellow MB schedule for times, last bus at about 19:00). The central Zell stop is called Lindenplatz.

ORIENTATION

Tourist Information

The TI is just off the pedestrian street, four blocks downriver from the pedestrian bridge; at the fountain with the cat statue, walk away from the river (Mon–Fri 9:00–12:30 & 13:30–17:00, Sat 10:00–13:00, closed Sun, off-season also closed Sat, tel. 06542/96220, www.zellmosel.de).

Helpful Hints

Internet Access: Berliner Kaffe-Kännchen offers two terminals at €6.40 an hour (Mon–Tue and Thu–Fri 8:00–18:30, Sat until 18:00, Sun 14:00–18:00, closed Wed, across pedestrian bridge opposite bus stop at Balduinen Strasse 107, tel. 06542/5450).

Bike Rental: Frau Klaus rents bikes (€6/day, pick up 8:30–13:00, arrange return time, 1.25 miles out of town, toward Bullay at Hauptstrasse 5, tel. 06542/41087, no English spoken).

Views: For a village view, walk up to the medieval wall's gatehouse and through the cemetery to the old munitions tower.

SIGHTS

Mosel Museum—The little Wein und Heimatmuseum features Mosel history (Wed and Sat 15:00–17:00, in same building as TI).

Winery Tour—Locals know Zell for its Schwarze Katze (Black Cat) wine. Peter Weis runs the F. J. Weis winery and gives an entertaining and free tour of his 40,000-bottle-per-year wine cellar. The clever 20-minute tour starts at 17:00 (call ahead to reserve, open daily April–Nov 10:30–19:00, closed Dec–March but call and they might fit you in for a tasting, he also rents apartments—see below, tel. 06542/41398, f.j.weis@t-online.de); buy a bottle or two to keep this fine tour going. A blue flag marks his *Weinkeller* south of town, 200 yards past the bridge toward Bernkastel, riverside at Notenau 30.

SLEEPING

(country code: 49, area code: 06542)
Zell's hotels are a disappointment, but its private homes are a fine value. The owners speak almost no English and discount their rates if you stay more than one night. They don't take reservations long in advance for one-night stays; just call a day ahead.

$$$ Hotel zum Grünen Kranz is the place if you're looking for room service, a sauna, a pool, and an elevator (32 rooms, Sb-€45–60, Db-€86–120, non-smoking rooms, Balduinstrasse 13, tel. 06542/ 98610, fax 06542/986-180, www.zum-gruenen-kranz.de, info@zumgruenenkranz.de). In the annex across the street, they rent 10 immense apartments (prices on request).

$$$ Hotel Ratskeller, just off the main square on a pedestrian street, rents 14 sharp rooms with tile flooring and fair rates (Sb-€45, Db-€72, cheaper Nov–mid-April, above a pizzeria, Balduinstrasse 36, tel. 06542/98620, fax 06542/986-244, ratskeller -zellmosel@web.de, Gardi).

$$$ Hotel Weinhaus Mayer has 16 newly renovated rooms with top comforts, many with riverview balconies (Db-€84, tel. 06542/61169, fax 06542/61160, www.hotel-weinhaus-mayer.de, info@hotel-weinhaus-mayer.de).

$$$ Weinhaus Mayer, an old pension with 10 rooms, is perfectly central and has Mosel views. It's managed by the non-English-speaking parents of the daughter who runs the hotel listed directly above (Db-€70–72, cash only, Balduinstrasse 15, tel. 06542/4530, fax 06542/61160, info@hotel-weinhaus-mayer.de).

$$ Peter Weis Apartments, of the F. J. Weis winery (recommended above), rents two luxurious apartments (Db-€55, less for 2 or more nights, extra person-€10, he'll get breakfast for you-€10, or you can walk to bakery and buy it yourself, 200 yards beyond bridge on Bernkastel road, riverside at Notenau 30, tel. 06542/41398, fax 06542/961-178, www.weingut-fjweis.de, f.j.weis@t-online.de).

$ Gasthaus Gertrud Thiesen is classy, with a TV-living-breakfast room and a river view. The Thiesen house has four big, bright rooms and is on the town's first corner overlooking the Mosel from a great terrace (D-€40, cash only, closed Nov–Feb, Balduinstrasse 1, tel. 06542/4453).

$ Homey **Gästehaus am Römerbad,** near the church, rents six cheap and sleepable rooms (Sb-€21, Db-€41, cash only, Am Römerbad 5, tel. 06542/41602, Elizabeth Münster).

TRIER

Germany's oldest city lies at the head of the scenic Mosel Valley, near the Luxembourg border. An ancient Roman capital, Trier brags that it was inhabited by Celts for 1,300 years before Rome even existed. Today Trier is thriving and feels very young. A short stop here offers you a look at Germany's oldest Christian church, one of its most enjoyable market squares, and its best Roman ruins.

Founded by Augustus in 16 B.C., Trier served as the Roman town Augusta Treverorum for 400 years. When Emperor Diocletian (who ruled A.D. 285–305) divided his overextended Roman Empire into four sectors, he made Trier the capital of the west: roughly modern-day Germany, France, Spain, and England. For most of the fourth century, this city of 80,000, with a four-mile wall, four great gates, and 47 round towers, was the favored residence of Roman emperors. Emperor Constantine used the town as the capital of his fading Western Roman Empire. Many of the Roman buildings were constructed under Constantine before he left for Constantinople. In 480, Trier fell to the Franks. Today, Trier's Roman sights include the huge city gate (Porta Nigra), basilica, baths, and amphitheater.

ORIENTATION

(area code: 0651)

Tourist Information

Trier's small but helpful TI is just through the Porta Nigra. You can pay €1.50 for an easily readable map, but cheapskates and those with good eyes can squint at the free small-print map, which suffices for navigating Trier's key sights. They also sell a useful little guide to the city called *Trier: History and Monuments* (€4) as well as the *Holiday Region Trier* brochure (€1, lists opening hours of Trier's sights, info on city tours, Mosel boat excursions, events, leisure activities, and more). Consider also the booklet *Walking Tours through Trier* (€3), which has little information on sights

but a great map and proposed walking routes (Roman, medieval, Jewish, rainy day). The TI also offers tours (see "Tours," below) and a free room-booking service (May–Sept Mon–Sat 9:00–19:00, Sun 10:00–17:00; Oct–April Mon–Sat 10:00–17:00, Sun 10:00–13:00, tel. 0651/978-080, www.trier.de/english, info@tit.de).

Discount Cards: The **Trier Card** allows free use of city buses and discounts on city tours, museums, and Roman sights (€9, family-€15, valid for 3 days, sold at TI). Since the town is small and walkable, this is only a good deal if you'll be here for two or three days and plan to visit lots of sights. If you're visiting at least three Roman sights (including baths, Porta Nigra, and amphitheater, but not the Archaeological Museum), buy the **Roman sights combo-ticket** instead (a.k.a. "combination admission ticket," €6.20, family ticket-€14.80, available at participating sights).

Arrival in Trier

By Train: From the train station (lockers-€1.50–2.50/day, WC-€0.50), walk 15 boring minutes and four blocks up Theodor-Heuss-Allee to the big black Roman gate and turn left under the gate to find the TI. From here the main pedestrian mall (Simeonstrasse) leads into the town's charm: the Market Square and cathedral (a 5-min walk) and basilica (5 more min). The *Reisezentrum* at the station can answer your train-schedule questions and book tickets for you (Mon–Fri 7:00–19:00, Sat 8:30–17:15, Sun 10:30–18:15).

By Car: Drivers get off at Trier Verteilerkreis and follow signs to *Zentrum*. There is parking near the gate and TI.

Helpful Hints

Laundry: A well-maintained, self-service launderette is near Karl Marx's House (€8 for the works, English instructions, daily 8:00–22:00, Brückenstrasse 19).

Bike Rental: The local citizens' group called Bürgerservice rents out bikes for reasonable daily rates. Find them just off track 11 at the train station (€7.50/24 hrs, €2.50 extra for mountain bikes, leave €30 and ID as deposit, mid-April–Oct daily 9:00–19:00; Nov–mid-April Mon–Fri 10:00–18:00, closed Sat–Sun, tel. 0651/148-856, www.bues-trier.de, radstation@bues-trier.de).

TOURS

Walking Tours—The TI offers a €6 two-hour walking tour in English on Saturday at 13:30 (May–Oct only) and €70 private two-hour tours (tel. 0651/978-080).

Bus Tours—For a live guide and a big, air-conditioned bus, take the one-hour bus tour offered by the TI (€6, May–Oct daily at 13:00 in English).

Tourist Train—If you're tired and want a city overview, consider riding the hokey little red-and-yellow tourist train, the Römer-Express, for its 35-minute loop of Trier's major old-town sights (€6, daily April–Oct 2/hr 10:00–18:00, daily March and Nov hourly 11:00–17:00, recorded narration in English, departs from TI, buy tickets from driver or at TI, tel. 0651/9935-9525).

SELF-GUIDED WALK

Welcome to Trier

This fun walk, offering a taste of Trier old, new, and in-between, will take you to this historic city's top sights.

• *Start at the...*

Porta Nigra: Roman Trier was built as a capital. Its architecture mirrored the grandeur of the empire. Of the four-mile wall's four huge gates, only this north gate survives. This most impressive Roman fortification in Germany (worth ▲) was built without mortar—only iron pegs hold the sandstone blocks together. While the other three gates were destroyed by medieval metal and stone scavengers, this "black gate" (originally red sand-

stone, but darkened by time) survived because it became a church. Saint Simeon—a pious Greek recluse—lived inside the gate for seven years. After his death in 1035, the Saint Simeon monastery was established, and the gate was made into a two-story church—lay church on the bottom, monastery church on top. Napoleon had everything non-Roman about the structure destroyed in 1803, but the 12th-century Romanesque apse—the round part at the east end—survived. You can climb around the gate, but there's little to

Trier

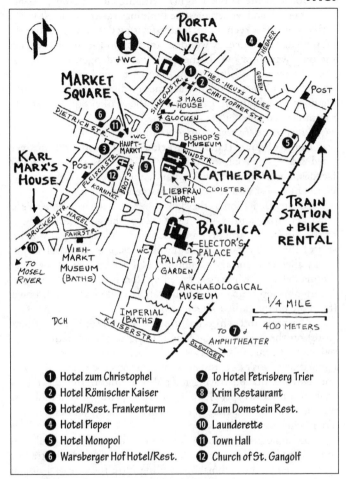

Trier

⓵ Hotel zum Christophel
⓶ Hotel Römischer Kaiser
⓷ Hotel/Rest. Frankenturm
⓸ Hotel Pieper
⓹ Hotel Monopol
⓺ Warsberger Hof Hotel/Rest.
⓻ To Hotel Petrisberg Trier
⓼ Krim Restaurant
⓽ Zum Domstein Rest.
⓾ Launderette
⓫ Town Hall
⓬ Church of St. Gangolf

see aside from a fine town view. Just inside the entrance, look for pictures of how the gate looked during various eras, including its church phase (€2.10, included in Roman sights combo-ticket, daily April–Sept 9:00–18:00, March and Oct until 17:00, Nov–Feb until 16:00).

Trier's main pedestrian drag, which leads away from the gate, is named for Saint Simeon. The arcaded courtyard and buildings of the monastery of Saint Simeon remain, and are now home to the TI and a city museum (museum closed through 2006 for renovation).

• As you walk to the Market Square, you'll glimpse—about halfway down on your left at Simeonstrasse 19—the...

House of the Three Magi (Dreikönigshaus): Now a restaurant, this colorful Venetian-style building was constructed in the 13th century as a keep. Look for the floating door a story above the present-day entrance. A wooden staircase to this door was once the only way in or out. If the town was in danger, the staircase could be burned or torn down, in order to fend off enemies and protect inhabitants. (Look for another medieval keep with a floating door—the Frankenturm—just off the Market Square, near the recommended hotel of the same name.)

• *Continue down the pedestrian street until you reach the...*

Market Square (Hauptmarkt): Trier's Hauptmarkt square— rated ▲▲—is a people-filled swirl of fruit stands, flowers, painted facades, and fountains (with a handy public WC). This is one of Germany's most in-love-with-life marketplaces.

For an orientation to the sights, go to the square's centerpiece, a market cross, and stand on the side of the cross (east) closest to the big stone cathedral a block away. This cathedral was the seat of the archbishop. In medieval times, the cathedral was its own walled city, and the archbishop of Trier was one of the seven German electors who chose the Holy Roman Emperor. This gave the archbishop tremendous political, as well as spiritual, power (for more on the cathedral, see below).

The pink-and-white building (now an H&M department store) on the corner of the lane leading to the cathedral was a **palace** for the archbishop. Notice the seal above the door: a crown flanked by a crosier, representing the bishop's ecclesiastical power, and a sword, demonstrating his political might. This did not sit well with the townspeople of Trier. The square you're standing in was the symbolic battlefield of a centuries-long conflict between Trier's citizens and the bishop.

The stone **market cross** (a replica of the A.D. 958 original, now in the City Museum—see above) next to you celebrates the trading rights given to the archbishop by King Otto the Great. This was a slap in the face to Trier's townspeople, since trading rights were usually reserved for free cities—which they wanted to become.

Look across the square from the lane to the cathedral, to the 15th-century **Town Hall (Steipe).** The people of Trier wanted a Town Hall, but the bishop wouldn't allow it—so they built this "assembly hall" instead, with a knight on each second-story corner. The knight on the left, facing the Market Square, has his mask up, watching over his people. The other knight, facing the cathedral and the bishop, has his mask down and his hand on his sword, ready for battle.

Tensions mounted 30 years later. Look to the left, at the tall white steeple with yellow trim. This is the Gothic tower of the **Church of St. Gangolf,** the medieval townspeople's church, and fire watchman's post. (From medieval times until the present day, a bell has rung nightly at 22:00, reminding local drunks to go home. When the automatic bell-ringer broke a few years ago, concerned locals flooded the mayor with calls.) In 1507, Trier's mayor built this new Gothic tower to make the people's church higher than the cathedral. A Latin Bible verse adorns the top in gold letters: "Stay awake and pray." In retaliation, the bishop raised one tower of his cathedral (all he could afford). He topped it with a threatening message of his own, continuing the Town Hall's verse: "For you never know the hour when the Lord will come."

Look farther to the left, to the Renaissance **St. Peter's Fountain** (1595). This fountain symbolizes thoughtful city government, with allegorical statues of justice (sword and scale), fortitude (broken column), temperance (wine and water), and prudence (snake and mirror—missing for generations). The ladies represent idealized cardinal virtues—but notice the rude monkeys hiding on the column behind them, showing the way things are really done.

Find the recommended **Zum Domstein** restaurant near the fountain. In Trier, you can't even put a rec room in your basement without tripping over Roman ruins. The owner of this restaurant discovered a Roman column in her cellar. Upstairs, she still sells traditional German food. Downstairs, you'll find the column, a mini-museum of Roman crockery, and expensive cuisine (€22–30) based on ancient Roman recipes (daily 12:00–14:00 & 18:00–21:00, or just sneak in for a peek, Am Hauptmarkt 5).

The rest of the square is a textbook of architectural styles. Notice the half-timbered houses at the north end of the square (toward Porta Nigra), marking Trier's 14th-century Jewish ghetto. Nearby, look for the Art Deco hotel that now houses a McDonald's (whose famous arches are dubbed by locals "the golden horn"). You'll also see the overpriced and uninspired **Toy Museum** (Spielzeugmuseum) recently relocated inside the Town Hall (€4, €10 family card for 2 adults and up to 5 kids, daily 11:00–18:00, Hauptmarkt 14, tel. 0651/75850, www .spielzeugmuseum-trier.de).

• *When you're finished on the square, head down the lane to the...*

Cathedral (Dom): This ▲▲ sight is the oldest church in Germany. St. Helena was the mother of Emperor Constantine (who legalized Christianity in the Roman Empire in A.D. 312) and an important figure in early Christian history. She allowed part of her palace to be used as the first church on this spot. In A.D. 326, to celebrate the 20th anniversary of his reign, Constantine began the construction of St. Peter's in Rome and this huge cathedral in Trier—also called St. Peter's. The Dom information center is on the courtyard across from the cathedral; ask if any excavations from the very first part of Constantine's cathedral are open for public viewing.

Begin your visit in the large front courtyard of the cathedral. As you face the cathedral, look in the corner behind you and to your left (near the pink palace); you'll see a large patch of light-colored bricks in an L shape in the ground. The original Roman cathedral was more than four times its present size; these light-colored bricks mark one corner of this massive "double cathedral." (The opposite corner was at the back of the smaller Liebfrau church, waaay across the courtyard.) The plaque by the corner shows the floor plan of the original Roman cathedral.

Enter the cathedral (free, April–Oct daily 6:30–18:00, Nov–March daily 6:30–17:30, €0.10 English info flyer, www.trierer-dom .de). You'll see many altars lining the nave, dedicated not to saints, but to bishops. These ornate funeral altars were a fashionable way for the powerful archbishop-electors to memorialize themselves. Even the elaborate black-and-white altar at the back of the church (where you entered) is not a religious shrine, but a memorial for a single rich bishop.

The "pilgrim's walk" (the stairway at the right front of the church) leads to the chapel holding the cathedral's most important relic, the Holy Robe of Christ, found by St. Helena on a pilgrimage to Jerusalem (rarely on view, but you can see its reliquary, look for photos of the actual robe after the first flight of stairs). The second flight of stairs leads to the **treasury** (Dom Schatzkammer), displaying huge bishops' rings, the sandal of St. Andrew (in a box topped with a golden foot), and a holy nail supposedly from the Crucifixion (€1.50, April–Oct Mon–Sat 10:00–16:45, Sun 14:00–16:45; Nov–March Mon–Sat 11:00–15:45, Sun 14:00–15:45). From the treasury, you can fight the crowds the last few stairs up to the chapel (same hours as treasury). Back down the stairs, the door on your left leads to the peaceful Domkreuzgang **cloister** between the Dom and the Liebfrau church. As you leave the cathedral the way you came in, notice the controversial modern (1972) paintings at the back of the church, representing the Alpha (Paradise/Creation, to the left) and the Omega (the Last Judgment, to the right).

If you want to visit the Bishop's Museum (described below), go right as you exit the cathedral's main door and turn down the first street on your right (Windstrasse). As you walk with the cathedral on your right, you'll be able to see the different eras of its construction. The big red cube that makes up the back half of the present-day cathedral is all that remains of the enormous original fourth-century Roman construction (at one time twice as tall as what you see here). Arched bricks in the facade show the original position of Roman windows and doors. Around this Roman nucleus, chunks were grafted on over a millennium and a half of architectural styles: the front half of the cathedral facing the big courtyard, added in the 11th century; the choir on the back, from the 12th century; and the transept and round Baroque shrine on the far back, from the 18th century.

If you look at the original Roman construction squarely, you'll see that it's not perfectly vertical. Locks were built along the Mosel River in the 1960s, depleting groundwater—which was the only thing preserving the church's original wooden foundation. The foundation disintegrated, and the walls began to sag. Architects competed to find a way to prevent the cathedral from collapsing, and the winner—a huge steel bracket above the main nave, holding the walls up with cables—seems to be working.

• *Just past the cathedral on Windstrasse to the left is the...*

Bishop's Museum (Bischöfliches Diözesanmuseum): This cathedral museum, rated ▲, offers exhibits on the history of the cathedral. Inside and to the right, find the small model of the original Roman church, and the bigger model showing some of the present-day excavations of its various pieces. Don't miss the pieced-together remains of fine ceiling frescoes (dating from A.D. 310–320) from a Roman palace. The palace was destroyed around 325, and the Dom was built over it. The 50,000 pieces of the frescoes were discovered while cleaning up from WWII bombs. The vivid reds, greens, and blues of the restored works depict frolicking cupids, bejeweled women, and a philosopher clutching his scroll (all described in German). A good €3.60 English book clearly explains the palace ceiling's elaborate structure and the fresco restoration process. Elsewhere in the museum, the stone capitals, gold chalices, vestments, and icons are meaningless to most, unless you can read German (€2, April–Oct Mon–Sat 9:00–17:00, Sun 13:00–17:00; Nov–March closed Mon, Windstrasse 6, tel. 0651/710-5255, www.museum.bistum-trier.de).

• *Connected to the cathedral's right side, on the southeast corner of the original Roman church site, is...*

Liebfrau Church: Claimed to be the oldest Gothic church in Germany (it dates from 1235), this church was built when Gothic was in vogue, so French architects were brought in—and paid with money borrowed from the bishop of Köln when funds ran dry. It's now filled with colorful, modern stained glass (daily April–Oct 7:30–18:00, Nov–March until 17:30).

• *From the church, head two blocks south (away from Market Square) to the 200-foot-by-100-foot...*

Basilica/Imperial Throne Room (Konstantin Basilica):
This building is the largest intact Roman structure outside of
Rome (worth ▲▲). It's best known

as a basilica, but it actually started
as a throne room. Go inside and
look up: Each of the squares in
the ceiling above you is 10 feet by
10 feet—as big as your hotel room.
Picture this throne room in ancient
times, decorated with golden mosaics, rich marble, colorful stucco,
and busts of Constantine and his
family filling the seven niches. The
emperor sat in majesty under a canopy on his altar-like throne. The
windows in the apse around him were smaller than the ones along
the side walls, making his throne seem even bigger.

The last emperor moved out in A.D. 395, and petty kings set
up camp in the building throughout the Middle Ages. By the
12th century, the bishops had taken it over and converted it to
a five-story palace. The building became a Lutheran church in
1856, and remains the only Lutheran church in Trier. It was badly
damaged by WWII bombs, and later partially restored. A good
€1.30 English booklet brings the near-empty shell to life (free,
April–Oct Mon–Sat 10:00–18:00, Sun 12:00–18:00, Nov–March
Tue–Sat 11:00–12:00 & 15:00–16:00, Sun 12:00–13:00, closed
Mon, tel. 0651/72468).

A rococo wing, the Elector's Palace, was added to the basilica
in the 18th century to house the archbishop-elector; today, it
houses local government offices (closed to the public).

• *The rococo wing faces a fragrant garden, which leads to three sights: an
interesting archaeological museum, the remains of a Roman bath, and a
25,000-seat amphitheater. We'll check out all three, starting with the...*

Archaeological Museum (Rheinisches Landesmuseum):
This is not only a ▲ museum, but also an active excavation and
research center. Upstairs, in the back and to the right, is a huge
model of Roman Trier (try to pick out the buildings you're visiting
today: cathedral, basilica, baths). Downstairs, explore the huge
funerary monuments. Once these were all painted like the replica
in the courtyard; today, they tell archaeologists volumes about daily
life in Roman times. Find the woman visiting a beauty salon. (Hint:
She's on the tallest monument.) The mosaics room is a highlight.
On the wall, find the mosaic of four horses surrounding the superstar charioteer Polydus (mosaic floors were the *Sports Illustrated*
covers of the Roman world), discovered intact at the Imperial
Baths (€5.50, May–Oct Mon–Fri 9:30–17:00, Sat–Sun 10:30–
17:00; Nov–April closed Mon, few English descriptions but good

audioguide free with entry, tel. 0651/97740, www.landesmuseum
-trier.de).

• *To reach the amphitheater and Imperial Baths, exit the Archaeological
Museum to the left and follow the stone wall for 200 yards to the busy
street. For the unexceptional **amphitheater** (€2.10, included in Roman
sights combo-ticket, April–Sept daily 9:00–18:00, Oct and March
until 17:00, Nov–Feb until 16:00, tel. 0651/73010), take the marked
pedestrian underpass, then follow Hermesstrasse another half-mile as it
curves up the hill (ignore signs pointing you to the right). To reach the
Imperial Bath ruins, go right through the opening in the wall.*

Imperial Baths (Kaiserthermen): Built by Constantine, this
is the biggest of Trier's three Roman baths and the most intricate
bath of the Roman world. Trier's cold northern climate, the size
of the complex, and the enormity of Constantine's ego meant that
these Imperial Baths required a two-story subterranean complex
of pipes, furnaces, and slave galleys to keep the water at a perfect
47 degrees Celsius (120 degrees Fahrenheit). Explore the underground tunnels (nearly a mile's worth), noticing the chest-high
holes in the walls that used to hold the floor (slaves above, pipes
below). It's an impressive complex—too bad the baths never quite
worked right and were left unfinished after Constantine left
(€2.10, included in Roman sights combo-ticket, April–Sept daily
9:00–18:00, Oct–March daily 9:00–17:00, tel. 0651/44262).

Another, less interesting Roman bath is a 10-minute walk
away: A modern glass box covers bath excavations at the **Viehmarkt
Museum.** Locals grouse that the ruins sat in the rain for years
before their tax money was used to build this expensive new house.
The red bricks in the marketplace outside show the intersection
of the original Roman roads, laid out as a grid (€2.10, included in
Roman sights combo-ticket, Tue–Sun 9:00–17:00, closed Mon,
last entry 30 min before closing, €1.50 English brochure, 10-min
walk from Market Square down Brotstrasse, right on Fahrstrasse
to Viehmarktplatz, tel. 0651/994-1057).

• *Our walk is over. From here, you can backtrack to the Market Square
for more of the food/flowers/fountains/people-watching; or (if the
Market Square's capitalism makes you see red), you can continue down
Fahrstrasse, turning right on Brückenstrasse for Karl Marx's House (see
below).*

SIGHTS

Karl Marx's House—Communists can lick their wounds at Karl
Marx's birthplace, where early manuscripts, letters, and photographs of the influential economist/philosopher fill several rooms.
Oblivious to their slide out of a shrinking middle class, people still
sneer (€3, includes free brochure, April–Oct Mon 13:00–18:00,

Tue–Sun 10:00–18:00; Nov–March daily 14:00–17:00, 15-min film in English at :20 after each hour, a reasonable amount of English description, or buy €7.50 book, tel. 0651/970-680, www .fes.de/marx). From the Market Square, it's a 10-minute walk down Fleischstrasse—which becomes Brückenstrasse—to the house at Brückenstrasse 10.

SLEEPING

For locations, see the map on page 263.

Near Porta Nigra

$$$ The classy **Hotel zum Christophel** offers top comfort in its 11 rooms, above a fine restaurant and with a kind owner (Sb-€55– 60, Db-€85–90, elevator, Am Porta Nigra Platz, Simeonstrasse 1, tel. 0651/979-4200, fax 0651/74732, www.zumchristophel.de, info@zumchristophel.de).

$$$ Hotel Römischer Kaiser, next door, is a lesser value, charging more for a polished lobby and 43 comparable rooms (Sb-€67–77, Db-€98–108, includes parking, elevator, Am Porta Nigra Platz, tel. 0651/97700, fax 0651/977-099, www.hotels-trier.de, rezeption@hotels-trier.de).

Near Market Square

$$ Hotel Frankenturm, decked out in modern style with track lighting and cheery color schemes, is above a lively saloon and next to a medieval keep of the same name. The six rooms with private baths are on the first floor up; the other six rooms are two floors up with a shared bath (S-€40, Sb-€60, D-€50, Db-€80, T-€60, Tb-€90, no elevator, Dietrichstrasse 3, tel. 0651/978-240, fax 0651/978-2449, www.hotel-frankenturm.de, frankenturm @t-online.de).

Sleep Code

(€1 = about $1.20, country code: 49, area code: 0651)
S = Single, **D** = Double/Twin, **T** = Triple, **Q** = Quad, **b** = bathroom, **s** = shower only. Unless otherwise noted, credit cards are accepted, English is spoken, and breakfast is included.

To help you sort easily through these listings, I've divided the rooms into three categories, based on the price for a standard double room with bath:

$$$ Higher Priced—Most rooms €85 or more.
$$ Moderately Priced—Most rooms between €50–85.
$ Lower Priced—Most rooms €50 or less.

$ Warsberger Hof, run by the local citizens' league, is clean and simple, with 150 beds and a restaurant, which is also open to the public, serving inexpensive food. This is your best value for cheap sleeps in town (€15 per bed in 3- to 6-bed dorms, sheets-€2.50, S-€25, D-€42, T-€60, Q-€76, showers down the hall, breakfast not included, a block off Market Square, Dietrichstrasse 42, tel. 0651/975-250, fax 0651/975-2540, www.warsberger-hof.de, info@warsberger-hof.de).

Not so near Market Square

$$ Hotel Petrisberg Trier is top-quality and ideal if you have a car or don't mind the pleasant 20-minute walk or €8 cab ride into town. It's situated on a hillside overlooking the city, exuding old-school elegance without being stuffy. The Pantenburg family takes great care to spoil all their guests; Helmut whips up tasty egg breakfasts while his granddaughter, a former wine pageant winner, works reception (Sb-€60–65, Db-€88–95, Sickingenstrasse 11–13, tel. 0651/4640, fax 0651/46450, www.hotel-petrisberg.de, info@hotel-petrisberg.de).

Near the Train Station

$$ Hotel Pieper is run by the friendly Becker family (he cooks and she keeps the books). They rent 21 comfortable rooms furnished with dark wood over a pleasant neighborhood restaurant (rack rates: Sb-€44, Db-€70, Tb-€88; special rates: Sb-€40, Db-€65, these prices good with this book and cash only through 2006; 8-min walk from station, 2 blocks off main drag, Thebäerstrasse 39, tel. 0651/23008, fax 0651/12839, www.hotel-pieper-trier.de, info@hotel-pieper-trier.de). From the station, follow Theodor-Heuss-Allee (toward Porta Nigra) to the second big intersection, angle right onto Göbenstrasse, and continue as the road curves and becomes Thebäerstrasse.

$$ Hotel Monopol, at the train station, has 35 older but clean rooms. It's dark but handy (S-€31–34, Sb-€39–47, D-€52–57, Db-€62–69, Tb-€93, Qb-€112, elevator, Bahnhofsplatz 7, tel. 0651/714-090, fax 0651/714-0910, www.hotel-monopol-trier.de, bernd.glatzel@hotel-monopol-trier.de).

EATING

Good eateries abound on the side streets leading away from the pedestrian drag of Simeonstrasse and the Market Square. On Dietrichstrasse, try the restaurants in the recommended hotels **Warsberger Hof** (€4–10 entrées, daily 11:30–22:00, outdoor courtyard seating, includes family-oriented, kid-friendly **Rautenstrauch Restaurant** and **Leonardy,** latter offers a €5 breakfast buffet

Sat–Sun until 11:00) or **Frankenturm** (€4–15 entrées, weekday lunch specials €7, Mon–Sat 11:30–24:00, Sun 18:00–24:00). Young locals enjoy trendy Mediterranean cuisine at **Krim,** also just off the Market Square (€4–13 entrées, daily 9:00–24:00, breakfast until 18:00, Glockenstrasse 7, tel. 0651/73943). The popular **Zum Domstein** serves pricey Roman fare in a cellar and cheaper German fare upstairs (daily 12:00–14:00 & 18:00–21:00, Am Hauptmarkt 5, tel. 0651/74490; see page 265).

TRANSPORTATION CONNECTIONS

From Trier by Train to: Cochem (hrly, 45 min), **Köln** (7/day, 3 hrs), **Koblenz** (hrly, 75 min), **Bullay** (with buses to Zell, hrly, 40 min), **St. Goar/Bacharach** (hrly, 2.5 hrs), **Baden-Baden** (hrly, long 4 hrs, with 1–2 changes). Train info: tel. 11861 (€0.50/min).

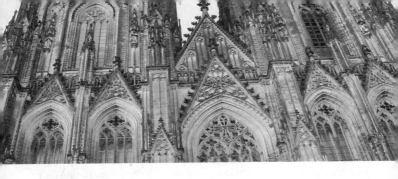

KÖLN AND THE
UNROMANTIC RHINE

Romance isn't everything. Köln is an urban Jacuzzi that keeps the Rhine churning. It's home to Germany's greatest Gothic cathedral and its best collection of Roman artifacts, a world-class art museum, and a healthy dose of German urban playfulness.

Peaceful Bonn, which offers good people-watching and fun pedestrian streets, used to be the capital of West Germany. The small town of Remagen had a bridge that helped defeat Hitler in World War II, and unassuming Aachen, near the Belgian border, was once the capital of Europe.

Köln

Germany's fourth-largest city, Köln ("Cologne" in English) has a compact, lively center. The Rhine was the northern boundary

of the Roman Empire and, 1,700 years ago, Constantine—the first Christian emperor—made Colonia the seat of a bishopric. Five hundred years later, under Charlemagne, Köln became the seat of an archbishopric. With 40,000 people within its walls, it was the largest German city and an important cultural and religious center throughout the Middle Ages. Today, the city is most famous for its toilet water. Eau de Cologne was first made here by an Italian chemist in 1709.

Even though WWII bombs destroyed 95 percent of Köln (population down from 800,000 to 40,000), it has become, after a remarkable recovery, a bustling commercial and cultural center, as well as a fun, colorful, and pleasant-smelling city.

Planning Your Time

Köln makes an ideal on-the-way stop; it's situated on a major rail line and its top sights are clustered near the train station. With an hour or two, you can toss your bag in a locker, zip through the cathedral, and head out of town. More time (or an overnight) allows you to delve into the city's many fine museums.

ORIENTATION

(area code: 0221)

Köln's old-town core, bombed out then rebuilt quaint, is traffic-free and includes a park and bike path along the river. From the cathedral/TI/train station, Hohe Strasse leads into the shopping action.

For a quick old-town ramble, stroll down Hohe Strasse and take a left at the city hall *(Rathaus)* to the river (where K-D Rhine cruises start). Enjoy the quaint old town and the waterfront park. The Hohenzollernbrücke, crossing the Rhine at the cathedral, is the busiest railway bridge in the world (30 trains per hour all day long).

World Cup Warning: The eyes of the world turn to Germany in June and July of 2006, as it puts on the World Cup soccer championships (see page 6). Köln (and its hotels) will be especially crowded when it hosts matches on June 11, 17, 20, 23, and 26.

Tourist Information

Köln's energetic TI, opposite the church entrance, has a basic €0.20 city map and several brochures (July–Aug Mon–Sat 9:00–22:00, Sun 10:00–18:00; Sept–June Mon–Sat 9:00–21:00, Sun 10:00–18:00; Unter Fettenhennen 19, tel. 0221/2213-0400, www.koelntourismus.de). They also offer a range of private guided tours, covering such topics as architecture, medieval Köln, and Romanesque churches (call TI to reserve). For information on Köln's museums, visit www.museenkoeln.de. Note that most museums are closed on Monday.

WelcomeCard: The card includes use of the city's transit system (which includes local trains to Bonn, but not the slick InterCity and Express trains), a 50 percent discount on major museums (Roman-Germanic Museum, Ludwig, Käthe Kollwitz, and Wallraf-Richartz), and smaller discounts on other attractions like the Chocolate Museum (€9/24 hrs, €14/48 hrs,

Köln

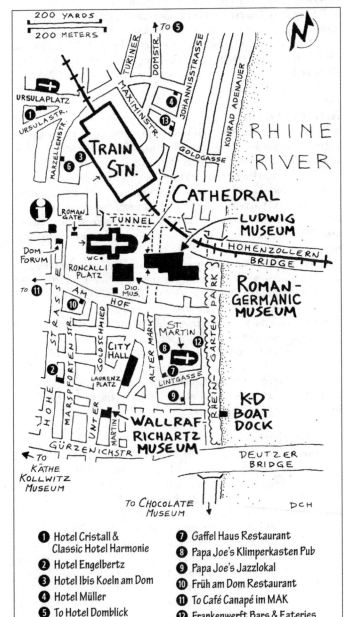

200 YARDS
200 METERS

N

RHINE RIVER

TRAIN STN.

CATHEDRAL

LUDWIG MUSEUM

HOHENZOLLERN BRIDGE

ROMAN-GERMANIC MUSEUM

K-D BOAT DOCK

DEUTZER BRIDGE

WALLRAF-RICHARTZ MUSEUM

CITY HALL

ST. MARTIN

TUNNEL

RONCALLI PLATZ

DOM FORUM

ROMAN GATE

URSULAPLATZ

GOLDGASSE

KONRAD ADENAUER

JOHANNISSTRASSE

DOMSTR.

TURINER

MAXIMINSTR.

URSULASTR.

MARZELLENSTR.

LAURENZ PLATZ

MARSPFORTEN STR.

GOLDSCHMIED

HOHE STRASSE

ALTER MARKT

LINTGASSE

RHEIN GARTEN PARK

GÜRZENICHSTR

UNTER MARTIN

AM HOF

DIO. MUS.

WC.

TO ⑤

TO ⑪

← TO KÄTHE KOLLWITZ MUSEUM

TO CHOCOLATE MUSEUM

DCH

① Hotel Cristall & Classic Hotel Harmonie
② Hotel Engelbertz
③ Hotel Ibis Koeln am Dom
④ Hotel Müller
⑤ To Hotel Domblick
⑥ Station Hostel
⑦ Gaffel Haus Restaurant
⑧ Papa Joe's Klimperkasten Pub
⑨ Papa Joe's Jazzlokal
⑩ Früh am Dom Restaurant
⑪ To Café Canapé im MAK
⑫ Frankenwerft Bars & Eateries
⑬ Deutsche Touring Office

€19/72 hrs; discounts for families or groups of 3 or more).

City Bus Tours: Two-hour German/English city bus tours leave daily from the TI (€14, discount with WelcomeCard, cash only, buy tickets from driver, April–Oct daily at 10:00, 12:30, and 15:00, plus a shorter version at 17:30 on Sat; Nov–March daily at 11:00 and 14:00; smart to reserve summer Sat tours, tel. 0221/979-2570 or 0221/979-2571).

Arrival in Köln

Köln couldn't be easier to visit—its three important sights cluster within two blocks of the TI and train station. This super pedestrian zone is a constant carnival of people.

Köln's bustling **train station** has everything you need: a drugstore, food court, juice bar, shopping mall with grocery store, pricey WC (€1), travel center (*Reisezentrum*, Mon–Fri 5:30–23:00, Sat–Sun 6:00–22:00), and lockers (€3/24 hrs, accepts coins and €5 and €10 bills, put money in and wait 30 seconds for door to open; next to *Reisezentrum*).

For questions about the Romantic Road bus, visit the Deutsche Touring office one block behind the station (Mon–Fri 9:00–18:00, closed Sat–Sun, Johanisstrasse 43-45, tel. 0221/759-8660).

Exiting the front of the station (the end near track 1), you'll find yourself smack-dab in the shadow of the cathedral (Dom). If your jaw drops, pick it up. Up the steps and to the right is the main entrance to the cathedral (TI across street). For hotels Müller and Domblick, leave the station from the back (the end near track 11).

If you **drive** to Köln, follow signs to *Zentrum*, then continue to the huge Parkhaus am Dom pay lot under the cathedral (€1.75/hr, €15/day).

Helpful Hints

Internet Access: Consider the **Weltcom Internet/Call Center** a block from the station at Marzellenstrasse 9 (€3/hour, also sells cheap phone cards, daily 8:00–24:00, tel. 0221/179-3110).

Bike Rental: You can rent bikes from the riverside Kölner Fahrradverleih, a 10-minute walk from the station (marked on TI map; €2/hr, €10/day, ask about recommended route, Sedanstrasse 27, tel. 0221/723-627). They also offer German-English guided **bike tours** of the city (€15, 3 hrs, daily April–Oct at 13:30, rain poncho provided just in case, max 10 people, reservations recommended, mobile 0171-629-8796). Consider biking the path along the Rhine River up past the convention center *(Messe)* and to the Rheinpark for a picnic.

Ticket Office: To get tickets to concerts, the opera, and the theater, stop by KölnMusik Ticket next to the Roman-Germanic

Museum (Mon–Fri 10:00–19:00, Sat 10:00–16:00, closed Sun, tel. 0221/2040-8160, can book ahead at www.koelnticket.de).

Festival: Köln's Lichter Festival lights up the sky on July 29, with fireworks, music, and lots of boats on the river (get details from TI or at www.koelner-lichter.de).

SIGHTS

Köln's Cathedral (Dom)

The neo-Gothic Dom—Germany's most exciting church, and easily worth ▲▲▲—looms immediately up from the train station.

Cost and Hours: Free, open daily 6:00–19:30; no tourist visits during church services daily 6:30–10:00 and at 18:30, Sun also at 12:00, 17:00, and 18:30; get schedule at Dom Forum office or www.koelner-dom.de).

Tours: The one-hour English-only tours are reliably excellent (€4, Mon–Sat at 10:30 and 14:30, Sun at 14:30, meet inside front door of Dom, tel. 0221/9258-4730). Your tour ticket also gives you free entry to the English-language 20-minute video in the Dom Forum directly following the tour (see "Dom Forum," page 281).

⊙ Self-Guided Tour: If you don't take the guided tour, follow this seven-stop walk (note that stops 3–7 are closed during confession Mon–Fri 7:45–9:00, Sat 14:00–18:00).

❶ Roman Gate and Cathedral Exterior: The square in front of the cathedral has been a busy civic meeting place since ancient times. A Roman temple stood where the cathedral stands today. The north gate of the Roman city, from A.D. 50, marks the start of Köln's 2,000-year-old main street.

Look for the life-size replica tip of a spire. The real thing is 515 feet above you. The cathedral facade, finished according to the original 13th-century plan, is "neo-Gothic" from the 19th century.

Postcards show the church after the 1945 bombing. The red brick building—off to your right as you face the church—is the Diocesan Museum. The Roman-Germanic Museum is between that and the cathedral, and the modern-art Ludwig Museum is behind that (all described below).

Step inside the church. Grab a pew in the center of the nave.

❷ Nave: If you feel small, you're supposed to. The 140-foot-tall ceiling reminds us of our place in the vast scheme of things. Lots of stained glass—enough to cover three football

Köln Cathedral

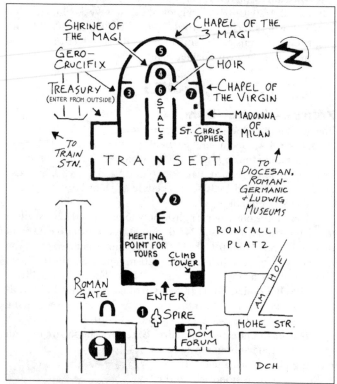

SHRINE OF THE MAGI

CHAPEL OF THE 3 MAGI

GERO-CRUCIFIX

CHOIR

TREASURY
(ENTER FROM OUTSIDE)

CHAPEL OF THE VIRGIN

STALLS

MADONNA OF MILAN

ST. CHRISTOPHER

TO TRAIN STN.

TRANSEPT

TO DIOCESAN, ROMAN-GERMANIC & LUDWIG MUSEUMS

NAVE

RONCALLI PLATZ

MEETING POINT FOR TOURS

CLIMB TOWER

ROMAN GATE

ENTER

AM HOF

SPIRE

HOHE STR.

DOM FORUM

DCH

fields—fills the church with light, representing God.

The church was begun in 1248. The choir—the lofty area from the center altar to the far end ahead of you—was finished in 1322. Later, with the discovery of America and routes to the Indies by sea, trade shifted away from inland ports like Köln. Funds dried up and eventually the building stopped. For 300 years, the finished end of the church was walled off and functioned as a church, while the unfinished torso (where you now sit) waited. For centuries, the symbol of Köln's skyline was a huge crane that sat atop the unfinished west spire.

With the rise of German patriotism in the early 1800s, Köln became a symbol of German unity. And the Prussians—the movers and shakers behind German unity—mistakenly considered Gothic a German style. They initiated a national tax that funded the speedy completion of this gloriously Gothic German church. Nearly 700 workers (compared to 100 in the 14th century) finished the church in just 38 years (1842–1880). The great train station was built in the shadow of the cathedral's towering spire.

The glass windows in the front of the church are medieval. The glass surrounding you in the nave is not as old, but it's precious nevertheless. The glass on the left is Renaissance. That on the right—a gift from Ludwig I, father of "Mad" King Ludwig of tourist fame—is 19th-century Bavarian.

While 95 percent of Köln was destroyed by WWII bombs, the structure of the cathedral survived fairly well. In anticipation of the bombing, the glass and art treasures were taken to shelters and saved. The new "swallow's nest" organ above you was installed to celebrate the cathedral's 750th birthday in 1998. Relics (mostly skulls) fill cupboards on each side of the nave. The guys in the red robes are cathedral cops, called *Schweizers* (after the Swiss guard at the Vatican); if a service is getting ready to start, they might hustle you out (unless you'd like to stay for the service).

❸ **Gero-Crucifix:** As you step through the gate into the oldest part of the church, look for the mosaic of the ninth-century church on the floor. It shows a saint holding the Carolingian Cathedral, which stood on this spot for several centuries before this one was built.

Ahead of you on the left, the Chapel of the Cross features the oldest surviving monumental crucifix from north of the Alps. Carved in 976 with a sensitivity 300 years ahead of its time, it shows Jesus not suffering and not triumphant—but with eyes closed...dead. He paid the price for our sins. It's quite a two-fer: great art and powerful theology in one. The cathedral has three big pilgrim stops: this crucifix, the Shrine of the Magi, and the *Madonna of Milan* (both coming up).

Continue to the front end of the church, stopping to look at the big golden reliquary in the glass case behind the high altar.

❹ **Shrine of the Magi:** Relics were a big deal in the Middle Ages. Köln's acquisition of the bones of the Three Kings in the 12th century put it on the pilgrimage map and brought in enough money to justify the construction of this magnificent place. By some stretch of medieval Christian logic, these relics also justified the secular power of the local king. This reliquary, made in about 1200, is the biggest and most splendid I've seen. It's seven feet of gilded silver, jewels, and enamel. Old Testament prophets line the bottom, and 12 New Testament apostles—with a wingless angel in the center—line the top.

Inside sit the bones of the Magi...three skulls with golden crowns. So what's the big deal about these three kings of

Christmas-carol fame? They were the first to recognize Jesus as the savior and the first to come as pilgrims to worship him. They inspired medieval pilgrims and countless pilgrims since. For a thousand years, a theme of this cathedral has been that life is a pilgrimage...a search for God.

❺ Chapel of the Three Magi: The center chapel, at the far end, is the oldest. It also features the church's oldest window (center, from 1265). The design is typical: a strip of Old Testament scenes on the left with a theologically and visually parallel strip of New Testament scenes on the right (such as, on bottom panels: to the left, the birth of Eve; to the right, the birth of Mary with her mother Anne on the bed).

Later, glass (which you saw lining the nave) was painted and glazed. This medieval window is actually colored glass, which is assembled like a mosaic. It was very expensive. The size was limited to what pilgrim donations could support. Notice the plain, budget design higher up.

❻ Choir: Peek into the center zone between the high altar and the carved wooden central stalls. (You can usually only get inside if you take the tour.) This is surrounded by 13th- and 14th-century art: carved oak stalls, frescoed walls, statues painted as they would have been, and original stained glass high above. Study the fanciful oak carvings. The woman cutting the man's hair is a Samson-and-Delilah warning to the sexist men of the early Church.

❼ Chapel of the Virgin: The nearby chapel faces one of the most precious paintings of the important Gothic School of Köln.

The Patron Saints of Köln was painted in 1442 by Stefan

Lochner. Notice the photographic realism and believable depth. There are literally dozens of identifiable herbs in the grassy foreground. During the 19th century, the city fought to have it in the museum. The Church went to court to keep it. The judge ruled that it could stay in the cathedral only as long as a Mass was said before it every day. For more than a hundred years, that happened at 18:30. Now, 21st-century comfort has trumped 19th-century law; in winter, services take place in the warmer Sacraments Chapel instead. (For more on the School of Köln art style, see "Wallraf-Richartz Museum," page 282.)

Overlooking the same chapel, the *Madonna of Milan* sculpture (1290), associated with miracles, was a focus of pilgrims for centuries.

As you head for the exit, find the statue of St. Christopher (with Jesus on his shoulder and the pilgrim's staff). Since 1470, pilgrims and travelers have looked up at him and taken solace in the hope that their patron saint is looking out for them. Go in peace.

More Cathedral Sights

Church Spire Climb—For 509 steps and €2, you can enjoy a fine city view from the cathedral's south tower (€5 combo-ticket also includes treasury, May–Sept daily 9:00–18:00, March–April and Oct until 17:00, Nov–Feb until 16:00). From the *Glockenstube* (only 400 steps up), you can see the Dom's nine huge bells, including "Dicke Peter" (24-ton Fat Peter), claimed to be the largest free-swinging church bell in the world.

Treasury—The treasury sits outside the cathedral's left transept (when you exit through the front door, turn right and continue right around the building to the gold pillar that reads *Schatzkammer*). The six dim, hushed rooms are housed in the cathedral's 13th-century stone cellar vaults (€4, €5 combo-ticket also includes spire, daily 10:00–18:00, last entry 30 min before closing, lockers at entry with €1 coin deposit, tel. 0221/1794-0300).

Spotlights shine on black cases filled with gilded chalices and crosses, medieval reliquaries (bits of chain, bone, cross, and cloth in gold-crusted glass capsules), and plenty of fancy bishop garb: intricately embroidered miters and vestments, rings with fat gem-stones, and six-foot gold crosiers. Displays come with brief English descriptions, but the little €4 book sold inside the cathedral shop provides extra information.

Dom Forum—This helpful visitors center, across from the entrance of the cathedral, is a good place to take a break (Mon–Fri 10:00–18:30, Sat 10:00–17:00, Sun 13:00–17:00, plenty of info, welcoming lounge with €0.70 coffee and juice, clean WC downstairs—free but donation requested, tel. 0221/9258-4720, www.domforum.de). They offer an English-language "multi-vision" video on the history of the church daily at 11:30 and 15:30 (starts slow but gets a little better, 20 min, €1.50 or included with church tour).

Diocesan Museum—This museum contains some of the cathedral's finest art (free, Fri–Wed 10:00–18:00, closed Thu, brick building to right of Roman Museum, Roncalliplatz 2, tel. 0221/257-7672, www.kolumba.de).

Near the Cathedral

▲▲Roman-Germanic Museum (Römisch-Germanisches Museum)—Germany's best Roman museum offers minimal English among its elegant and fascinating display of Roman artifacts: glassware, jewelry, and mosaics (€4.50, 50 percent discount with WelcomeCard, Tue–Sun 10:00–17:00, closed Mon,

Roncalliplatz 4, tel. 0221/2212-4590, www.museenkoeln.de/rgm). The permanent collection is downstairs and upstairs; temporary exhibits are on the ground floor.

Budget travelers can view the museum's prize piece, a fine mosaic floor, free from the front window. Once the dining-room floor of a rich merchant, this is actually its original position (the museum was built around it). It shows scenes from the life of Dionysus...wine and good times, Roman-style. The tall monument over the Dionysus mosaic is the mausoleum of a first-century Roman army officer. Upstairs, you'll see a reassembled, arched original gate to the Roman city with the Roman initials for the town, CCAA, still legible, and incredible glassware that Roman Köln was famous for producing. The gift shop's €0.50 brochure provides too little information, and the €12 book too much (detailed descriptions for this museum and about Roman artifacts displayed in other German cities).

▲▲**Ludwig Museum**—Next door and more enjoyable, this museum—in a slick and modern building—offers a stimulating trip through the art of the last century and American Pop and post-WWII art. Artists include German and Russian expressionists, the Blue Rider school, and Picasso. The floor plan is a mess. Just enjoy the art. The *Agfa History of Photography* exhibit is three rooms with no English; look for the pigeon with the tiny vintage camera strapped to its chest (€7.50, often more due to special exhibitions, 50 percent discount with WelcomeCard, Tue–Sun 10:00–18:00, closed Mon, last entry 30 min before closing, must check large bags, exhibits are fairly well described in English; classy but pricey cafeteria—€5–9 salads, pastas, sandwiches, and soups; Bischofsgartenstrasse 1, tel. 0221/2212-6165, www.museum-ludwig.de).

Hohe Strasse—The Roman arch in front of the cathedral reminds us that even in Roman times, this was an important trading street and a main road through Köln. In the Middle Ages, when Köln was a major player in the heavyweight Hanseatic Trading League, two major trading routes crossed here. This high street thrived. Following its complete destruction in World War II, it emerged once again as an active trading street—the first pedestrian shopping mall in Germany. Today it remains a wonderful place to stroll and shop.

Farther from the Cathedral
These museums are several blocks south of the cathedral.

▲▲**Wallraf-Richartz Museum**—Housed in a cinderblock of a building near the city hall, this minimalist museum features a world-class collection of old masters, from medieval to northern Baroque and Impressionist. You'll see the best collection anywhere

of Gothic School of Köln paintings (1300–1550), offering an intimate peek into those times. Included is German, Dutch, Flemish,
and French art by masters such as Dürer, Rubens, Rembrandt,
Hals, Steen, van Gogh, Renoir, Monet, Munch, and Cézanne
(€5.80, often more due to special exhibitions, 50 percent discount
with WelcomeCard, Tue 10:00–20:00, Wed–Fri 10:00–18:00,
Sat–Sun 11:00–18:00, closed Mon, English descriptions and good
€2.50 audioguide for permanent exhibit, Martin Strasse 39, tel.
0221/2212-1119, www.museenkoeln.de/wrm).

Imhoff-Stollwerck Chocolate Museum—Chocoholics love this
place, cleverly billed as the "MMMuseum." You'll take a well-

described-in-English tour following the origin of the cocoa bean to
the finished product. You can see
displays on the culture of chocolate
and watch treats trundle down the
conveyor belt in the functioning
chocolate factory, the museum's
highlight. The top-floor exhibit
of chocolate advertising is fun.
Sample sweets from the chocolate
fountain, or take some home from
the fragrant, choc-full gift shop (€6, discount with WelcomeCard,
Tue–Fri 10:00–18:00, Sat–Sun 11:00–19:00, closed Mon, last entry
1 hour before closing, Rheinauhafen 1a, tel. 0221/931-8880, www
.schokoladenmuseum.de).

The museum is a 10-minute walk south on the riverfront
between Deutzer and Severins bridges. Or take the handy Schoko-
Express tourist train from Roncalliplatz (€2 each way, 2/hr, pick-up
point changes depending on events on the church square—either
by TI or by the Ticket Office, confirm location at TI).

Käthe Kollwitz Museum—This contains the largest collection
of the artist's powerful expressionist art, welling from her experiences living in Berlin during the tumultuous first half of the last
century (€3, 50 percent discount with WelcomeCard, Tue–Fri
10:00–18:00, Sat–Sun 11:00–18:00, closed Mon, Neumarkt 18–24,
tel. 0221/227-2899, www.kollwitz.de). From Hohe Strasse, go west
on Schildergasse for about 10 minutes; go past Neumarkt Gallerie to
Neumarkt Passage, enter Neumarkt Passage, and walk to the glass-
domed center courtyard. Take the glass elevator to the fifth floor.

SLEEPING

Köln is *the* convention town in Germany. (In addition, remember
that the city is hosting World Cup soccer matches on June 11, 17,
20, 23, and 26.) Consequently, the town is either jam-packed with

---

Sleep Code

(€1 = about $1.20, country code: 49, area code: 0221)
S = Single, **D** = Double/Twin, **T** = Triple, **Q** = Quad, **b** = bathroom,
s = shower only. Unless otherwise noted, credit cards are
accepted, English is spoken, and breakfast is included.

To help you sort easily through these listings, I've divided
the rooms into three categories, based on the price for a standard double room with bath:

$$$ Higher Priced—Most rooms €100 or more.
$$ Moderately Priced—Most rooms between €75–100.
$ Lower Priced—Most rooms €75 or less.

---

hotels in the €180 range, or empty and hungry. Unless otherwise
noted, prices listed are the non-convention weekday rates. You'll
find that prices are much higher during conventions, but soft on
weekends (always ask) and for slow-time drop-ins. Outside of convention times, the TI can always get you a discounted room in a
business-class hotel (for a €3 fee).

In 2006, conventions are scheduled for these dates: Jan 16
through 22, Jan 29 through Feb 3, Feb 9 through 11, Feb 13 through
19, March 5 through 8, March 30 through April 2, April 4 through
7, May 10 through 13, May 19 through 21, May 30 through June 1,
June 8 through 10, July 29 (Köln's Lichter Festival), Aug 8 through
10, Sept 3 through 5, Sept 8 through 17, Sept 19 through 24, Sept
26 through Oct 1, Oct 11 through 15, Oct 20 through 22, Oct 24
through 28, Nov 1 through 12, Nov 23 through 26, Dec 1 through 3.
For an update, visit www.koelnmesse.de. Unlisted smaller conventions can lead to small price increases. Big conventions in nearby
Düsseldorf can also fill up rooms and raise rates in Köln.

Classy Hotels on Ursulaplatz

For locations, see map on page 275.

Two good business-class splurge hotels stand side-by-side a
five-minute walk northwest of the station (exit straight out, near
track 1, then turn right on Marzellenstrasse, up to Ursulaplatz).
These can be pricey but are an excellent value on non-convention
weekends.

$$$ Classic Hotel Harmonie is all class, striking a perfect
balance between modern and classic. Its 72 rooms include some
luxurious "superior" rooms (with hardwoods and swanky bathrooms, including a foot-warming floor) that become affordable on
weekends. So *this* is how the other half lives (Sb-€75–95, Db-€115,
€20 less on non-convention weekends if you ask, some rooms have

train noise so request quiet room, non-smoking rooms, air-con, elevator, Ursulaplatz 13–19, tel. 0221/16570, fax 0221/165-7200, www.classic-hotel-harmonie.de, harmonie@classic-hotels.com).

$$$ Hotel Cristall is a modern "designer hotel" with 84 cleverly appointed rooms (enjoy the big easel paintings and play human chess on the carpet). The deeply-hued breakfast room and lounge are so hip that German rock stars have photo shoots here (Sb-€72, Db-€95 but drops to €89 on weekends, rack rates can be higher, request quiet room to escape street and train noise, non-smoking rooms, air-con, elevator, Ursulaplatz 9–11, tel. 0221/16300, fax 0221/163-0333, www.hotelcristall.de, info@hotelcristall.de).

Near the Pedestrian Zone
These moderately priced places, centrally located along the pedestrian zone, are more convenient than charming.

$$ Hotel Engelbertz is a fine, family-run, 40-room place an eight-minute walk from the station and cathedral at the end of the pedestrian mall (specials for readers with this book in 2006 who request a discount during non-convention times: Sb-€52 and Db-€68 if you call to reserve on same day or day before, Sb-€64 and Db-€85 if you reserve in advance; regular rate Sb-€70 and Db-€100, convention rate Db-€190, elevator, just off Hohe Strasse at Obenmarspforten 1-3, tel. 0221/257-8994, fax 0221/257-8924, www.hotel-engelbertz.de, info@hotel-engelbertz.de).

$$ Hotel Ibis Koeln am Dom, a huge budget chain with a 71-room modern hotel right at the train station, offers all the comforts in a tidy, affordable package (Sb-€77, Db-€89; convention rate: Sb-€109, Db-€121; breakfast-€9, non-smoking rooms, air-con, elevator, Hauptbahnhof, entry across from station's *Reisezentrum*, tel. 0221/912-8580, fax 0221/9128-58199, www.ibishotel.com, h0739@accor.com).

Budget Options behind the Station
Affordable, family-run hotels line Domstrasse and Brandenburger Strasse behind (northeast of) the train station in a quieter neighborhood. To reach these hotels, exit the station away from the cathedral (the end near track 11).

$ Hotel Müller, run with great pride by enthusiastic Frau Müller, has 15 recently renovated rooms offering three-star quality at two-star prices (because it doesn't have an elevator). Enjoy the outdoorsy basement breakfast room/bar and the courtyard terrace (Sb-€45, Db-€65, prices can double during big conventions, Internet in lobby; exit behind station to Breslauer Platz, walk up Johannisstrasse 2 blocks, left on Brandenburger Strasse to #20; tel. 0221/912-8350, fax 0221/9128-3517, www.hotel-mueller-koeln.de, hotel-mueller-koeln@t-online.de).

$ Hotel Domblick, a lesser value, offers 23 basic but well-maintained rooms behind a creepy eye-plus-Dom logo—are we looking at the cathedral, or is it looking at us (Sb-€60, Db-€75, elevator; exit behind station to Breslauer Platz, walk left 2 blocks, turn right on Domstrasse, and walk 2 blocks up to #28; tel. 0221/123-742, fax 0221/125-736, www.hotel-dom-blick.de, hotel-domblick@t-online.de)?

$ Station Hostel, with 60 beds, is a two-minute walk from the train station (dorm bed-€16–19, S-€28, Sb-€35, D-€42, Db-€50, Tb-€66, includes sheets, key deposit-€10, kitchen, small breakfast-€3, no curfew, free Internet in lobby, laundry-€4.50, tel. 0221/912-5301, fax 0221/912-5303, exit station on Dom side, walk straight 1 block, turn right on Marzellenstrasse to #44-56, www.hostel-cologne.de, station@hostel-cologne.de).

EATING

Kölsch is both the dialect spoken here and the city's distinct type of beer (pale, hoppy, and highly fermented). You'll find plenty of places to enjoy both in the streets around Alter Markt (2 blocks off the river, near city hall), as well as along Lintgasse and the waterfront area called the Frankenwerft.

Gaffel Haus serves good local food (€10 meals, daily until 24:00, near Lintgasse at Alter Markt 20–22, tel. 0221/257-7692).

Papa Joe's Klimperkasten, in a dark pub packed with memorabilia and nightly live jazz (piano only, €4–8 meals, open daily for lunch and dinner, Alter Markt 50–52, tel. 0221/258-2132), and its rowdier sibling, **Papa Joe's Jazzlokal** (nightly from 20:00, Buttermarkt 37, tel. 0221/257-7931, www.papajoes.de for jazz schedule), win the atmosphere award.

Touristy **Früh am Dom,** closer to the cathedral and train station, offers three floors of drinking and dining options (€7–16 meals, daily 8:00–24:00, Am Hof 12–14, tel. 0221/261-3211).

Café Canapé im MAK, with sophisticated locals enjoying light fare, is a good option for a non-*Bräuhaus* lunch (€3–7 meals, Tue–Sun 11:00–17:00, closed Mon, just across Hohe Strasse from the cathedral in Museum of Applied Arts—or Museum für Angewandte Kunst—at An der Rechtschule 1, inside front door and down the stairs, smoky inside, courtyard seating outside, tel. 0221/2212-6721).

TRANSPORTATION CONNECTIONS

From Köln by Train to: Bonn (6/hr, 20 min), **Remagen** (2/hr, 30–60 min), **Aachen** (2/hr, 30–60 min), **Frankfurt Airport** (at least hrly, 1 hr), **Koblenz** (4/hr, 1 hr), **Bacharach** or **St. Goar** (hrly,

1.5 hrs, transfer in Koblenz), **Cochem** (every 2 hrs direct, 1.75 hrs; more with a transfer in Koblenz, 2 hrs), **Trier** (hrly, 2.75 hrs direct; more with a transfer in Koblenz, 2.75 hrs), **Paris** (7/day, 4 hrs), **Amsterdam** (every 2 hrs direct, 3 hrs; more with a transfer in Utrecht). Train info: tel. 11861 (€0.50/min).

The Unromantic Rhine

Highlights
▲**Bonn**—Bonn was chosen for its sleepy, cultured, and peaceful nature as a good place to plant Germany's first post-Hitler government. After Germany became one again, Berlin took over its position as capital.

Today, Bonn is sleek, modern, and, by big-city standards, remarkably pleasant and easygoing. The pedestrian-only old town stretching out from the station will make you wonder why the United States can't trade in its malls for real, people-friendly cities. The market square and Münsterplatz—filled with street musicians—are a joy. People-watching doesn't get much better, though the actual sights are disappointing. There's a sparse exhibit at Beethoven's House (€4; April–Oct Mon–Sat 10:00–18:00, Sun 11:00–18:00; Nov–March Mon–Sat 10:00–17:00, Sun 11:00–17:00; last entry 30 min before closing, free English brochure, tel. 0228/981-7525, www.beethoven-haus-bonn.de). The TI is a five-minute walk from the station (Mon–Fri 9:00–18:30, Sat 9:00–16:00, Sun 10:00–14:00, room-finding service-€2, go straight on Windechstrasse, next to Karstadt department store, tel. 0228/775-000).

The Unromantic Rhine

▲**Remagen**—Midway between Koblenz and Köln are the scant remains of the Bridge at Remagen, of WWII (and movie) fame. But the memorial and the bridge stubs are enough to stir the emotions of Americans who remember when it was the only bridge that remained, allowing the Allies to cross the Rhine and race to Berlin in 1945. A small museum tells the bridge's fascinating story in English. It was built during World War I to help supply the German forces on the Western Front—ironic that this was the bridge Eisenhower said was worth its weight in gold for its service against Germany. Hitler executed four generals for their failure to blow it up. Ten days after U.S. forces arrived, the bridge did collapse, killing 28 American soldiers. Today you can pay your respects at the bridge and visit its "Peace Museum" (€3.50, March–mid-Nov daily 10:00–17:00, May–Oct until 18:00, closed mid-Nov–Feb; it's on the Rhine's west bank, south side of Remagen town, follow *Brücke von Remagen* signs, www.bruecke-remagen .de). Remagen TI: tel. 02642/20187.

▲**Aachen (Charlemagne's Capital)**—This city was the capital of Europe in A.D. 800, when Charles the Great (Charlemagne) called it Aix-la-Chapelle. The remains of his rule include an impressive Byzantine/Ravenna–inspired church with his sarcophagus and throne. See the headliner newspaper museum and great fountains, including a clever arrange-'em-yourself version.

Lowlights

Heidelberg—This famous old university town attracts hordes of Americans. Any surviving charm is stained almost beyond recognition by commercialism. It doesn't make it into Germany's top three weeks.

Mainz, Wiesbaden, and Rüdesheim—These towns are all too big or too famous. They're not worth your time. Mainz's Gutenberg Museum is also a disappointment.

NÜRNBERG

Nürnberg (sometimes spelled Nuremberg in English), Bavaria's second city, is packed with interesting sights. At one of Europe's most important medieval trading crossroads, and with a large imperial castle marking it as a stronghold of the Holy Roman Empire, Nürnberg was one of Europe's leading cities around 1500. Today the red sandstone Gothic buildings in its charming old town make the city feel far smaller than its population of 500,000. Nürnberg is known for its glorious medieval architecture, its important Germanic history museum, its tragic Nazi past, its famous Christmas market (Germany's biggest), and its little bratwurst (Germany's tiniest).

Planning Your Time

Nürnberg is a handy stop between other German destinations, and an easy add-on to any itinerary that includes Munich, Würzburg, or Rothenburg. In fact, a brand-new express train now connects Nürnberg to Munich in just an hour (hourly departures). For the quickest visit to Nürnberg, toss your bag in a locker at the station and head directly to the Nazi Documentation Center. With more time, stroll through the old town from the train station up to the castle (following the route described under "Sights and Activities" on page 291). On the way back to the station (or your hotel), stop off at the Germanic National Museum.

World Cup Warning: Germany hosts the World Cup in June and July of 2006 (see page 6), including several matches in Nürnberg (on June 11, 15, 18, 22, and 25). On and near these dates, expect the city and its hotels to be packed.

ORIENTATION

(area code: 0911)

Nürnberg's old town (containing all the non-Nazi sights) is surrounded by its three-mile-long wall and moat, and beyond that, a ring road. Just south of the ring is the train station, and inside the ring, the medieval Frauentor gate. From the Frauentor, sights cluster along a straight line (Königstrasse) downhill to the small Pegnitz River, then back uphill through the market square (Hauptmarkt) to the castle (Kaiserburg). The Nazi Documentation Center—at the former Nazi Rally Grounds—is southeast of the center (easily accessible by tram or S-Bahn; see "Nazi Sites," page 301).

Tourist Information

Nürnberg's handy and helpful TI is in the modern building just inside the Frauentor (Mon–Sat 9:00–19:00, closed Sun, across ring road from station at Bahnhofplatz, tel. 0911/233-6131, www .tourismus.nuernberg.de). Pick up the free city map (with updated sight hours and prices on the back) and get information about bus and walking tours. The TI also offers free Internet access, books rooms (no fee), and sells transit passes and the Nürnberg Card (see below). The TI's second branch is at the Hauptmarkt (Mon–Sat 9:00–18:00, May–Oct and during Christmas Market also Sun 10:00–16:00).

Nürnberg Card: The Nürnberg Card covers all of your local transportation and admission to all of Nürnberg's museums, plus a few other discounts (€18/2 days, sold at TI). The catch: It's available only to those who spend at least one night in Nürnberg. The "Take Five" ticket (below) is a much better deal for most sightseers.

"Take Five" Ticket: Nürnberg's "Take Five" ticket is a good deal for busy sightseers. For €16, you get five entrances into your choice of seven different museums (including Albrecht Dürer House, City Museum, Nazi Documentation Center, and Nürnberg Trials Courtroom; sold at participating sights and at TI). The ticket is shareable, so two people can use it to each get in free to two different museums (and have 1 additional entrance left over).

Arrival in Nürnberg

Nürnberg's stately old Hauptbahnhof—with a shiny new interior—is conveniently located at the southern edge of the city center, just outside the old city walls and ring road. The station has WCs, lockers, ATMs, and lots of shops. You can get train information and buy tickets at the *Reisezentrum* in the main hall (center of building).

To reach the Frauentor (the medieval city's southern gate)—which is near most recommended hotels and is also the starting point for exploring the old town—follow signs for *Ausgang/City* in the underpass, then signs to *Königstor/Fraventor* and *Altstadt* (old town). When you emerge, the TI is on your right and the Frauentor tower (a.k.a. Königstor) is on your left.

To go directly to the Nazi Documentation Center from the station, leave through the exit by McDonald's and catch tram #9 (direction Doku-Zentrum).

Getting Around Nürnberg

Most of Nürnberg's sights are in the strollable old town, but the Nazi sites are beyond easy walking distance. Nürnberg's public transportation network, run by VGN, has trams, buses, U-Bahns (subways), and S-Bahns (faster suburban trains). All work on the same tickets, which you can buy at the TI, vending machines, or on board (buses only). A single ticket costs €1.40 (good for 90 min of travel in one direction, including transfers). A day ticket is €3.60 (*TagesTicket Solo*, good for one calendar day or Sat and Sun; the €6.20 *TagesTicket Plus* covers 2 adults and up to 4 children; www.vgn.de).

TOURS

Walking Tours—Tours of Nürnberg's old town in English leave from the Hauptmarkt every day May through October at 13:00 (€7.50 plus castle admission, kids under 14 free, 2.5 hrs, book in advance at TI or just show up and pay guide). This is the only way to see the sights in the castle interior with an English-speaking guide (see "Imperial Castle" on page 299).

Bus Tours—The tours, which include some walking, leave daily at 9:30 May through October from the Old Granary at Hallplatz, two blocks up from the Frauentor TI (€11, buy ticket on bus or at TI, 2.5 hrs, in German and English, tel. 0911/202-2910).

Tourist Train—For a lower-key tour, hop on the little train that makes the rounds in the old town (€4, 30 min, leaves Hauptmarkt about hourly 10:30–16:00).

Private Guide—For a good local guide, call Doris Ritter (€88/2 hrs, €20/hr after that, tel. 0911/518-1719, doris.ritter@nuernberg -tours.de).

SELF-GUIDED WALK

Welcome to Nürnberg's Old Town

Nürnberg's best sights are conveniently clustered along a straight-line thoroughfare connecting the Hauptbahnhof with the market

Central Nürnberg

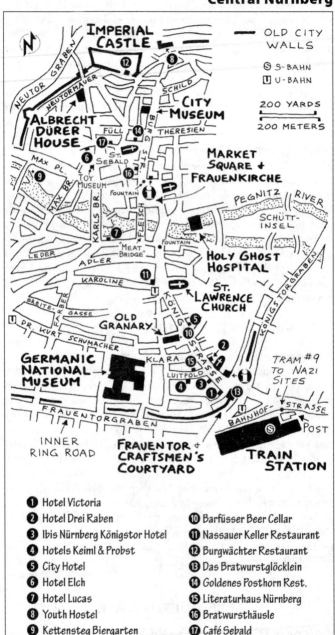

OLD CITY WALLS

Ⓢ S-BAHN
Ⓤ U-BAHN

200 YARDS
200 METERS

IMPERIAL CASTLE

CITY MUSEUM

ALBRECHT DÜRER HOUSE

MARKET SQUARE + FRAUENKIRCHE

ST. SEBALD

TOY MUSEUM

PEGNITZ RIVER

SCHÜTT-INSEL

MEAT BRIDGE

HOLY GHOST HOSPITAL

ST. LAWRENCE CHURCH

OLD GRANARY

GERMANIC NATIONAL MUSEUM

TRAM #9 TO NAZI SITES

FRAUENTORGRABEN

INNER RING ROAD

FRAUENTOR + CRAFTSMEN'S COURTYARD

TRAIN STATION

POST

❶ Hotel Victoria
❷ Hotel Drei Raben
❸ Ibis Nürnberg Königstor Hotel
❹ Hotels Keiml & Probst
❺ City Hotel
❻ Hotel Elch
❼ Hotel Lucas
❽ Youth Hostel
❾ Kettensteg Biergarten
❿ Barfüsser Beer Cellar
⓫ Nassauer Keller Restaurant
⓬ Burgwächter Restaurant
⓭ Das Bratwurstglöcklein
⓮ Goldenes Posthorn Rest.
⓯ Literaturhaus Nürnberg
⓰ Bratwursthäusle
⓱ Café Sebald

square (Hauptmarkt) and the castle (Kaiserburg). For a good orientation, take the following self-guided stroll. Plan on an hour, not including stops.

• *Begin at the Frauentor (where you emerge from the Hauptbahnhof underpass).*

Frauentor: This tower guards one of the four medieval entrances to Nürnberg's old town. Nürnberg did not have abundant natural resources or a navigable waterway, so its people made their living through trade and crafts (such as making scientific instruments, weapons, and armor). The German emperors took note of this industrious little town, and granted it economic privileges by naming it a "Free Imperial City" in the 13th century (giving it the right to answer directly to the Holy Roman Emperor himself). This started a boom for Nürnberg that eventually led to the construction of these walls. Of the three miles of wall that once surrounded the city, 90 percent is still intact. Many Central European cities of this size (such as Vienna) tore down their walls to make way for expansion in the 1800s, and Nürnberg nearly did the same. Now they're glad they didn't—it's better for tourism.

• *Between the walls just next to the gate, you'll see the entrance to the...*

Craftsmen's Courtyard (Handwerkerhof): This hokey collection of half-timbered houses was built in 1971 to celebrate craftsmanship and to honor the 500th birthday of Nürnberg's famous resident Albrecht Dürer. (Dürer, arguably Germany's best painter, was considered the ultimate craftsman.) The proud medieval tradition of craftsmanship continues today, as the city is home to some of Germany's top goldsmiths and glassblowers.

While a bit kitschy, this courtyard gives tourists a medieval vibe as they enter the old town from the station. The courtyard is packed with replicas of medieval shops, where artisans actually make—and, of course, sell—leather, pottery, and brass goods. (There's also a good place to sample the tiny local Bratwurst—see "Das Bratwurstglöcklein," page 310.) In the Middle Ages, this area between the walls was not a medieval mall but *Passkontrolle*—a customs and security checkpoint zone where all visitors had to register before they could enter the town.

• *When you're finished poking around the courtyard, head into town (with the train station at your back) on...*

Königstrasse: Though it had always been one of the four primary entrances to Nürnberg, this street became the city's main drag only after the train station was built in the early 20th century. It's lined with key sights, several recommended hotels and restaurants, and some wonderful Gothic and neo-Gothic architecture.

Nürnberg hit its peak in the 14th century, when the Golden Bull law (1356) regularized the election of the Holy Roman Emperor. From then throughout the Middle Ages, German emperors were elected in Frankfurt, crowned in Aachen, and had their first Imperial Diet (a gathering of German nobles and VIPs) right here in Nürnberg.

Nürnberg's low point came during World War II. By the end of the war, 90 percent of the old town was destroyed—the only German city hit worse was Dresden. If a building was only damaged, it was repaired in the original Gothic style—check out the building with the Peschke shop on the right. But some buildings were completely destroyed. Instead of rebuilding these exactly as they were, or replacing them with modern-style buildings, Nürnbergers compromised, creating a style that was at once modern and traditional. Look down the street at #71. The design is modern, but it incorporates Gothic elements and uses the same distinctive red sandstone as older buildings.

Ahead, on the left, is the small Clara Church (Klarakirche). In the Middle Ages, Nürnberg had nine monasteries like this one. When the Reformation hit, Nürnberg turned Lutheran, and most of the monasteries were torn down. As they fell, so did Nürnberg's importance; the city was now Lutheran, but its emperors were still Catholic. The ever-important Imperial Diet—once Nürnberg's claim to fame—moved to more Catholic-friendly Regensburg.

Across the street from Clara Church, look for Mary on the second-story corner. You'll see statues like this—blessing houses—all over Nürnberg.

• *Continue down Königstrasse to Hallplatz and the Old Granary (where the pedestrian stretch begins). If you want to visit the excellent Germanic National Museum (described on page 301) now, turn left at Hallplatz and walk 200 yards. Otherwise, check out the...*

Old Granary (Mauthalle): Medieval Nürnberg had 11 of these huge granaries to ensure that they'd have enough food in case of famine or siege. The grain was stored up above in the attic (behind all of those little dormer windows). Today the cellar is home to a lively beer hall, Barfüsser (see "Eating," page 309).

Continue down pedestrians-only Königstrasse. This drag used to have more cars and trams than any other street in town. But when the U-Bahn came in the 1970s, this part of the street became traffic-free.

• *After another two blocks, you'll see...*

St. Lawrence Church (Lorenzkirche): The church, a ▲▲ sight, is a massive house of worship, but it's not a cathedral—because Nürnberg never had a bishop (a fact locals were very proud of...a bishop would just order them around, and they prized their independence). The name of Königstrasse ("King's Street")—where you've been walking—is misleading. When most royals came to town, they actually preferred to come through the west gate—so they could approach this masterful facade head-on. Stand in front of the church's main door. Flip around and imagine the Holy Roman Emperor coming down the "Imperial Way," which dead-ended at this magnificent Oz-like church.

Study the **facade** (completed c. 1360). Adam and Eve flank the doors. In the first row above the left door, you'll see two scenes: Jesus' birth on top, and the visit from the Magi on the bottom (with the starfish of Bethlehem shining from above). Over the right door, you'll see the slaughter of the innocents (with a baby skewered by a Roman sword—classic medieval subtlety), and below that, the presentation of Jesus in the temple and the flight to Egypt. Above those scenes is the Passion story (from lowest to highest: trial, scourging, carrying the cross, Crucifixion, deposition, entombment, Resurrection, and people coming out of their graves for Judgment Day). The saved (Peter and company) are on the left, and the sorry chain gang of the damned (including kings and bishops) are shuttled off to Hell on the right. Above it all stands the triumphant resurrected Christ, with the sun and moon at his feet, flanked by angels tooting alphorns.

It's worth a few minutes to step inside (enter around right side, €1 donation requested, €5 for a pass to take photos, Mon–Sat 9:00–17:00, Sun 13:00–16:00).

The **interior** wasn't completely furnished until more than a century after the church was built—just in time for the Reformation (so the Catholic decor suddenly adorned a now-Lutheran church). Most of the decorations inside were donated by wealthy Nürnbergers trying to cut down on their time in purgatory. Over the centuries, this art survived three separate threats: the iconoclasm of the Reformation, the whitewashing of the Baroque age, and the bombing of World War II. While Nürnberg was the first "Free Imperial City" to break with the Catholic Church and become Lutheran, locals didn't go wild (like Swiss Protestants did) in tearing down the rich, Mary-oriented decor of their fine churches. Luther told the iconoclasts, "Tear the idols out of your heart, and you'll understand that these statues are only pieces of wood."

Suspended over the altar, the woodcarving called **The Annunciation** is by one of medieval Germany's best woodcarvers (and Nürnberg citizen), Veit Stoss. Carved in 1517, it shows the angel Gabriel telling Mary she'll be giving birth to the Messiah. Startled, she drops her prayer book. This is quite Catholic (notice the rosary setting with beads, and a circle of roses with a medallion depicting the "Joys of Mary"). The dove sits on Mary's head, and God the Father—looking as powerful as a Holy Roman Emperor—looks down. The figures are carved from linden trees. This survived the Reformation covered in a sack, revealed only on special occasions. Around back, enjoy more details—Mary's cascading hair, and the sun and the moon. Nearby, the altar painting at the very front of the church (behind the altar) shows the city of Nürnberg in 1483.

To the left of the altar, the frilly **tabernacle** tower is the "house of sacraments" that stored the consecrated Communion wafer. After the Mass, leftovers needed a worthy—even heavenly—home...and this was it. The cupboard behind the gold grate was the appropriate receptacle for "the body of Christ." The theme of the carving is the Passion. The scenes ascend in chronological

order: Last Supper, Judas' kiss, arrest, Crucifixion, and so on. Everything is carved of stone except for the risen Christ. He was living, and so was this...it's made of wood. The man holding the tabernacle on his shoulders is the artist who created it, Adam Kraft. In the Middle Ages, artists were faceless artisans, no more important than a blacksmith or a stonemason. But in the 1490s, when this was made, the Renaissance was in the air, and artists like Kraft began putting themselves into their works. Kraft's contemporary, the painter Albrecht Dürer, actually signed his works—an incredible act in Germany at that time (see "Albrecht Dürer House," page 300).

Adam Kraft is looking up at a **plaque** honoring the American philanthropist who donated nearly a million Deutschmarks in 1950 to help rebuild the church. Though the church was devastated by WWII bombs, everything movable was hidden away in bunkers, including the stained glass you see today. The plaque is in English but hard to read—written in the Gothic *Fraktur* font so popular back then. In the back of the church, a silent **video** (with dates in the upper corner) shows the preparations in anticipation of WWII bombs, the destruction, and the reconstruction.

As you leave, notice that the church has many **side chapels**—employing an innovative trick of expanding the nave out so the buttresses are actually inside the church.

From St. Lawrence Church to the River: Back outside, find the castle-like building on the corner across from the church facade. This is the only remaining **tower house** in Nürnberg. It was built in 1200, when there was no city wall, and the locals had to fend for themselves. It's basically a one-family castle. (In the basement, you'll find an appropriately medieval restaurant—complete with suits of armor—called the Nassauer Keller; see "Eating," page 309.)

Continue downhill to the river. American moralists might shield their eyes from the kinky **Fountain of the Seven Virtues.** Otherwise, play a game: Circle the sprightly fountain and try to identify the classic virtues by the symbolism: justice (on top), faith, love, hope (anchor), courage (lion), temperance (moderation), patience. Are any birds sipping?

• *When you get to the bridge, look to the right.*

Holy Ghost Hospital (Heilig-Geist-Spital): This river-spanning hospital was donated to Nürnberg in the 14th century by the city's richest resident, eager to do his part to help the poor...

and hopefully skip purgatory altogether. (A statue of him hangs out on the second-story corner of the Spital Apotheke, the first building after the bridge.) He funded this very scenic hospital to care for ill, disabled, and elderly Nürnbergers. The wing over the river dates from the 16th century. Beneath the middle window under the turret, find the dove—symbol of the Holy Ghost, the hospital's namesake.

If you look in the distance to the right—beyond the hospital and the next two bridges—you'll see a half-timbered fragment of the town wall. The big white building to the right of that is Germany's biggest multiplex, with 21 screens (most underground).

Cross to the other side of the bridge, and look at the next bridge over (the "Meat Bridge"). Look familiar? It's based on Venice's Rialto Bridge. This is the narrowest point of the river, and flooding was a big concern. Since this bridge doesn't have any piers, there's less chance of a collapse. When this was built in 1596, it was considered an engineering feat—the most high-tech bridge in Central Europe. The river once powered the town's medieval water mills.

Continue across the bridge, jogging left at the fork, and study the monument depicting characters from a 15th-century satire called *The Ship of Fools (Das Narrenschiff)*. It's adapted to follies that plague modern society—violence, technology, and apathy. Hey, how about the quiet, people-friendly ambience created by making this big city traffic-free in the center? Do a slow 360-degree spin and imagine this back home.

• *Now enter the...*

Market Square (Hauptmarkt): When Nürnberg boomed in the 13th century, it consisted of two distinct walled towns separated by the river. As the towns grew and it became obvious that the two should merge, the middle wall came down. This market square (rated ▲▲), built by the Holy Roman Emperor Charles IV, became the center of the newly united city. Though Charles is more often associated with Prague (he's the namesake for the Charles Bridge and Charles University), he also loved Nürnberg—visiting 60 times during his reign.

The **Frauenkirche** church on the square is located on the site of a former synagogue (inside, there's a Star of David on the floor). When Nürnberg's towns were separate, Jewish residents were required to live in this swampy area close to the river and outside the walls. When the towns merged and the land occupied by the Jewish quarter became valuable, Charles IV allowed his subjects to force out the Jews—and 600 were killed in the process...a somber reminder that anti-Semitism predates the Nazis.

Year-round, the market square is lively with fruit, flower, and souvenir stands. For a few weeks before Christmas, it hosts Germany's largest **Christmas market** (*Christkindlmarkt,* over 2 million visitors annually).

• *Walk across the square to the pointy, gold...*

Beautiful Fountain (Schöner Brunnen): Medieval tanneries, slaughterhouses, and the hospital you just saw dumped their byproducts into the river. So this fountain brought clean drinking water into the square. Of course, it's packed with allegorical meaning. The outermost figures ringing the bottom represent the arts (such as philosophy, music, and astronomy). On the pillars just above them are the four church fathers and the four evangelists, showing that religion is higher than the arts. On the column itself, the lowest figures are the seven electors of the Holy Roman Emperor and nine heroes—three Christian (like King Arthur and Charlemagne); three Jewish (like King David); and three heathen (like Julius Caesar). At the very top are eight prophets, hovering above—and granting legitimacy to—worldly power. On the side of the fountain facing the river, you'll probably see tourists fussing over a gold ring. If you believe in such silly tour-guide tales, spinning this ring three times brings good luck...okay, go ahead and spin it. The black ring opposite (nearest the stork bearing a baby) brings fertility. Civic marriage ceremonies that take place at the adjacent City Hall often end up here for photos.

• *Leave the square straight uphill from the fountain, heading for the castle. Along the way, you'll pass St. Sebald (Sebaldkirche), Nürnberg's second great Gothic church. Beyond that on the left, you'll see the...*

City Museum (Stadtmuseum Fembohaus): This museum, packed with information about the city, is worth a visit primarily for the three interesting models of historic Nürnberg on the fourth floor. Request an English version of the 15-minute audio program that explains the 1930s town model and illustrates the effects of the WWII bombing with a slide show (€1 for models only, €5 for whole museum, Tue–Fri 10:00–17:00, Sat–Sun 10:00–18:00, closed Mon, Burgstrasse 15, tel. 0911/231-2595).

• *Now huff the rest of the way up to the imperial castle. At its base, the cobbled path forks. The right fork leads to the youth hostel, and the left leads to the castle courtyard (see big, round tower high above) and over the Burgwächter restaurant (see page 310). If you want to head straight into the castle, take the left fork and skip to "Imperial Castle," below (you'll circle counterclockwise, eventually returning to this spot). For a scenic detour, take the right fork, and go on a brief...*

Castle Garden Walk: Before entering the main complex, pop behind the castle (to the right) into the Castle Garden (Burggarten) for views of the north end of the town fortifications (16th-century bastions) and into the moat. From here you have access to the city walls, which lead down to the river (a 15-min walk along the park-like path past roses and other gardens).

• *After your walk, enter the castle courtyard, pausing under the tall tower for a superb city view.*

Imperial Castle (Kaiserburg): In the Middle Ages, Holy Roman Emperors stayed here when they were in town. This huge complex has 45 buildings. The part on the right, which used to house the stables and store grain, is now a youth hostel (see page 308).

The castle interior and museum are standard fare and rated ▲. The most interesting bits here are the so-called Deep Well (which, at 165 feet, is...well, deep) and the Romanesque double-decker chapel (higher nobility in the upper chapel, lower nobility down below, plus a special balcony for the emperor). The tower climb offers only a higher city view.

Unfortunately, you must see these sights with a German tour (castle grounds free; entry to buildings only with German tours: €5 for 1-hr tour of museum, palace, and chapel, €6 also includes tour of well and climbing the tower on your own; €3 to climb tower on your own and join a German tour only for the well; tickets sold at

top end of courtyard; daily April–Sept 9:00–18:00, Oct–March 10:00–16:00, tel. 0911/244-6590). The only alternative is to go with the TI's English tour of the entire old town, which includes the castle (see "Tours," page 291). Deep Well visits (about 4/hr), even with the German guide, are simple, quick, and fun: You'll see water poured way, waaay down—into an incredible hole dug in the 14th century. Then a small candle table is lowered until it almost disappears into the water table.

• *After you leave the castle, consider a stroll to one of Nürnberg's oldest neighborhoods. Facing downhill, leave the castle to the right, then take the lower fork. In a couple of blocks, you'll reach Tiergärtnertorplatz. Near the top of the square, you'll see a huge rabbit. While it looks like roadkill with mice gnawing at it, it's actually a modern interpretation of one of the best-known paintings by medieval Nürnberg artist Albrecht Dürer,* The Hare *(the original painting is in Vienna).*

The rabbit faces a half-timbered building at the bottom of the square. That's the...

Albrecht Dürer House (Albrecht-Dürer-Haus): Nürnberg's most famous local lived in this house (rated ▲) for the last 20 years of his life. Albrecht Dürer (1471–1528) was a contemporary of Michelangelo who studied in Venice and brought the Renaissance to stodgy medieval Germany. He did things that were unthinkable to other northern European artists of his time—such as signing his works, or painting things like hares simply for study (not on commission).

Nothing in the museum is original (all of the paintings are replicas—the only Dürer originals in Nürnberg are in the Germanic National Museum, described below). But it does a fine job of capturing the way that Dürer actually lived, including a replica of the workshop where he printed his woodcuts with a working printing press. A 17-minute movie plays continuously (in English on your headphones). The top floor is a gallery with copies of Dürer's most famous paintings and woodcuts. On Saturdays at 14:00, you can meet Dürer's wife, Agnes, who speaks English and takes you through their house (€5, includes Agnes-led audioguide, live Agnes tour-€2.50 extra, €1.50 English brochure also available, Tue–Sun 10:00–17:00, Thu until 20:00, closed Mon, Albrecht-Dürer-Strasse 39, tel. 0911/231-2568).

• *You've walked from the southern gate of Nürnberg to the northern gate, and your tour is over. If heading from here to the Nazi sites (see below), a taxi is your best bet. Or, for more old-town sightseeing on your way back to the Frauentor, consider a detour to two more museums, listed under "Sights" below.*

SIGHTS

Toy Museum (Spielzeugmuseum)—Nürnberg is famous for woodworking. You can see some examples of this local craft—and lots more—at this entertaining, interactive collection of toys from across the ages (€5 per adult, €0.50 more for unlimited kids,

Tue–Fri 10:00–17:00, Sat–Sun 10:00–18:00, closed Mon except during Christmas Market, Karlstrasse 13-15, 0911/231-3164).

▲▲**Germanic National Museum (Germanisches National-museum)**—This sweeping museum is dedicated to the cultural history of the German-speaking world. Entering, you walk along the "Way of Human Rights." Designed by an Israeli artist, its pillars trumpet each right protected by the United Nations' Universal Declaration of Human Rights.

The museum's highlights are currently gathered in a marvelous one-hall exhibit called "Allure of the Masterpiece" (Faszination Meisterwerk, on display through Jan 2007). While heavy on the Dürer, Rembrandt, and Riemenschneider, it contains 200 treasures of fine and decorative arts from the 16th through the 18th centuries, giving visitors a chance to savor the aura of 300 years of German masterpieces. Highlights are the early globe (since it dates from 1492, the Americas are conspicuously missing), seven works by Dürer (the only originals in town), and the sumptuous *Nürnberg Madonna* (1515). More delicate and intimate than a Riemenschneider, this anonymous carving of the favorite hometown girl was the symbol of the city during the Romantic Age (19th century).

And there's plenty to see in the rest of the museum. Entering the main section, you'll stand before a wall of street signs from East Berlin dating from the time when the main drag in many towns was called Strasse der Befreiung—"Street of the Liberation" (by the U.S.S.R., from the Nazis and capitalism). You'll see an awesome collection of historical musical instruments, arms and armor, historic toys, stained glass, Bauhaus pottery, and 20th-century German art and culture. In room 219, don't miss the "approved Nazi art," a small collection that promoted the ideals of Nazism. The fashion section lights up as you walk through it to protect the fine fabrics through the ages (€5, free Wed 18:00–21:00, free English tours every other Sun at 14:00, open daily 10:00–18:00, Wed until 21:00, 2 blocks west of Königstrasse at Kartäusergasse 1, entrance on far side of building, tel. 0911/13310, www.gnm.de).

Nazi Sites

Today's Nürnberg is coming to terms with its Nazi past. Though the city tries to recast itself as the "City of Human Rights," its reputation as Hitler's favorite place for a big rally will be hard to shake. For WWII-history buffs, Nürnberg offers an excellent museum—the Nazi Documentation Center—at the heart of the chilling remains of Hitler's vast Rally Grounds (now Luitpoldhain park).

Nazi Sites in Nürnberg

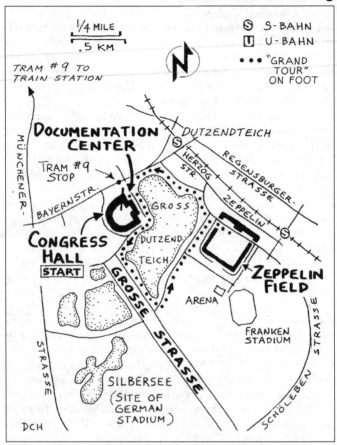

TRAM #9 TO
TRAIN STATION

1/4 MILE

.5 KM

Ⓢ S-BAHN
Ⓤ U-BAHN
••• "GRAND
TOUR"
ON FOOT

DOCUMENTATION
CENTER

DUTZENDTEICH

MÜNCHENER-

TRAM #9
STOP

BAYERNSTR.

GROSS

HERZOG
STR.

REGENSBURGER-
STRASSE

ZEPPELIN

CONGRESS
HALL

START

DUTZEND-
TEICH

ARENA

ZEPPELIN
FIELD

GROSSE STRASSE

STRASSE

FRANKEN
STADIUM

SCHÖLEBEN STRASSE

SILBERSEE
(SITE OF
GERMAN
STADIUM)

DCH

▲▲▲Nazi Documentation Center (Dokumentations-zentrum)—Visitors to Europe's Nazi and Holocaust sites inevitably ask the same haunting question: How could this happen? This superb museum does its best to provide an answer. It meticulously traces the evolution of the National Socialist (Nazi) movement, focusing on how it both energized and terrified the German people (the exhibit's official title is "Fascination and Terror"). Special attention is paid to Nürnberg's role in the Nazi movement, including the construction and use of the Rally Grounds, where Hitler's largest demonstrations took place. This is not a World War II or Holocaust museum; those events are almost an afterthought. Instead, the Center frankly analyzes the Nazi phenomenon, to understand how it happened—and to prevent it from happening again.

The museum is housed in Hitler's unfinished Party Congress

Hall, planned to host the mammoth annual Nazi Party gatherings. Today it's symbolically sliced open by its modern entryway to show the guts and brains of the Nazi movement.

The exhibit is a one-way walk. Allow two hours just for the fine videos you can see along the way. Nazi history buffs should allow an extra hour for the two movies that play continuously in the Kino at the start of the exhibit, offering excellent insights into the mass hypnosis of the German nation (interviews and old footage with English subtitles). Once you're in the exhibit, the included audioguide gives everything meaning and works well (turns on automatically at video presentations, you dial room numbers for overviews and specific numbers for details of displays—if rushed, listen to the overviews only). You'll see parts of Leni Riefenstahl's brilliant 1934 propaganda classic *Triumph of the Will*, and just before the end, footage of the Nürnberg Trials. The last stop (before the long ramp back to the start) is a catwalk giving you a look into the core of what would have been a Congress Hall filled with 50,000 cheering Nazis (an artist's sketch is on a nearby wall).

Cost, Hours, Information: €5, includes audioguide, €2 English guidebook is a must, €6 combo-ticket includes Nürnberg Trials Courtroom (see below), Mon–Fri 9:00–18:00, Sat–Sun 10:00–18:00, Bayernstrasse 110, tel. 0911/231-5666, www.museen.nuernberg.de.

Getting to the Nazi Documentation Center and Rally Grounds: The museum is located in one small wing of Hitler's cavernous, unfinished Congress Hall—the largest surviving example of Nazi architecture. The Nazi Documentation Center and Rally Grounds are near Dutzendteich, southeast of the old town. From the Hauptbahnhof, you have two easy options: tram or S-Bahn. Tram #9 leaves from in front of the McDonald's at the train station every 10 minutes (direction Doku-Zentrum, trip takes about 15 min, check return times upon arrival); the last stop is at the doorstep of the Documentation Center. S-Bahn #2 is slightly faster (10 min, stop Dutzendteich), but less frequent (every 20 min), and it drops you off a long 10-minute walk from the museum but closer to the Rally Grounds. From the Hauptmarkt or City Hall, you can also hop on the made-for-tourists bus #36. All three options cost the same (€1.40 one-way, covered by €3.60 transit day ticket).

▲**Rally Grounds (Reichsparteitagsgelände)**—Albert Speer, Hitler's favorite architect, designed this immense complex of

Nazis in Nürnberg

It's no coincidence that Nürnberg appealed to Hitler. For one thing, it was convenient: Nürnberg is centrally located in Germany, making it a handy meeting point for Nazi supporters. Hitler also had a friend here, Julius Streicher (a.k.a. the "Franconian Führer"), who fanned the flames of Nazism and anti-Semitism though his inflammatory newspaper *Der Stürmer (The Storm Trooper).*

But of far greater importance, Nürnberg was steeped in German history. Long before the rise of Nazism, the city—one-time home of Dürer and the Holy Roman Emperor, packed with buildings in the quintessential German Gothic style—was nicknamed the "most German of German cities." As one of the most important cities of medieval Europe, Nürnberg appealed to Hitler as a way to legitimize his Third Reich by invoking Germany's glorious past. Hitler loved the idea of staging his rallies within sight of the imposing Kaiserburg castle, a symbol of the First Reich (the Holy Roman Empire).

When Hitler took power in 1933, he made Nürnberg the site of his *Reichsparteitage*—**Nazi Party Rallies.** Increasingly elaborate celebrations of Nazi culture, ideology, and power took place here annually for the next six years. The chilling images from Leni Riefenstahl's documentary *Triumph of the Will* were filmed at the 1934 rallies. At the 1935 rallies, the Nazis devised the first laws—which came to be known as the **Nürnberg Laws**—that legally defined Jews as second-class citizens.

Hitler and his favorite architect, Albert Speer, designed staggeringly massive buildings (such as a stadium seating 400,000 spectators) to host the proceedings. The **Rally Grounds** were the ultimate example of Hitler's preferred architecture style: stark, huge, and neoclassical. Only a few of the plans were completed before World War II broke out in 1939, forcing the construction budget to be reassigned to the war effort. Today it's possible to walk around the still-unfinished remains of Hitler's megalomaniacal super-structures (see "Rally Grounds" on page 303).

As the war drew to a close, the world puzzled over what to do with the Nazi officers who had overseen some of the most gruesome atrocities in the history of humankind. It was finally decided that they should be tried as war criminals by an international tribunal (spearheaded by the U.S. and based on the Anglo-American code of law). These trials took place right here in the Nürnberg Trials Courtroom (see page 306). The **Nürnberg Trials**—the first ever such war-crimes tribunal—brought about a new concept of international law, which continues today in The Hague, Netherlands.

buildings (over 4 square miles) for the Nazi rallies. You'll get the best sense of the Rally Grounds simply from the exhibits inside the Documentation Center. Not much of Hitler's ambitious plans were completed, and to visit the surviving fragments, you'll have to make quite a hike. At a minimum, walk the 10 minutes from the Documentation Center to Zeppelin Field. For a more in-depth visit, the "Grand Tour" described below gives a sense of the mind-boggling scale of what Hitler and Speer planned (figure an hour round-trip from the Documentation Center—see map).

To get to Zeppelin Field directly from the Documentation Center, simply follow the lake for 10 minutes (with the lake on your right).

Zeppelin Field (Zeppelinwiese): This was the site of the Nazis' biggest rallies, including those famously filmed by Leni

Riefenstahl. You can actually climb up on the grandstand and stand on the platform in front of the Zeppelin Tribune, where Hitler stood to survey the masses (up to 250,000 people at a time). The Tribune is based on the design of the ancient Greek Pergamon altar (now in Berlin's Pergamon Museum); it was originally topped by a towering swastika, which was detonated by the Allies soon after the end of the war. Clowning around on the speaking platform with any Nazi gestures is illegal and taken seriously by the police.

Grand Tour: To hike the entire area, begin at the Nazi Documentation Center, in the **Congress Hall** (Kongresshalle). This huge building—big enough for an audience of 50,000—was originally intended to be topped with a roof and skylight. As you leave the Documentation Center, turn right and walk along the side of the building. When you get to the end, turn right again and continue walking with the Congress Hall on your right. Continue past the end of the building, and then turn left (under the *Kommen Sie gut nach Hause* sign) onto the Great Road. The lights you see in the distance hover above the Franken Stadium (a soccer field before Hitler, then used for Nazi rallies, and now used for soccer once again—for the 2006 World Cup).

As you walk along the **Great Road** (Grosse Strasse), with a lake on either side, consider the gigantic scale of this complex. At 200 feet wide, the Great Road was big enough to be used as a run-way by the Allies after the war. The road points toward Nürnberg's imperial palace, Kaiserburg—Hitler's symbolic connection to the Holy Roman Empire (the First Reich).

Near the end of the lake, ahead and to the right, was to be the site of the **German Stadium** (Deutsches Stadion)—the biggest in the world (with 400,000 seats). They got as far as digging a foundation before funding was redirected to the war effort. Today, the site of the stadium is a park surrounding the big Silbersee lake—which was the hole for the never-built stadium's foundation.

If you'd like to detour to the German Stadium site, you can—but it's time-consuming, without much to see. Instead, walk down the first lakeside path on your left as you reach the end of the Great Road. Continue along the lake for a good 15 minutes until you dead-end into the parking lot. To your right is the huge Zeppelin Field (described above).

From Zeppelin Field, hike along the lake (with the lake on your left) back toward the Congress Hall. When you dead-end at the busy road, the S-Bahn station is to the right, and the tram stop is in front of the museum to your left.

Nürnberg Trials Courtroom (Nürnberger Prozesse)—In 1945, in courtroom *(Saal)* #600 of Nürnberg's Palace of Justice (Justizgebäude), 21 Nazi war criminals stood trial before an international tribunal of judges appointed by the four victorious countries. After a year of trials and deliberations, 12 Nazis were sentenced to death by hanging, three were acquitted, and the rest were sent to prison. One of the death sentences was for Hitler's right-hand man, Hermann Göring. He wanted to be shot by firing squad—a proper military execution—but his request was denied. Instead, two hours before his scheduled hanging, Göring committed suicide with poison he had smuggled into his cell, infuriating many who thought that this death was too easy for him.

While this historic courtroom is still in active use, you can tour it on weekends (€2.50, €6 combo-ticket includes Nazi Documentation Center, tours Sat–Sun 13:00–16:00 at the top of each hour, not all tours in English—call ahead to confirm schedule, west of center at Fürther Strasse 110, enter on Bärenschanzstrasse, take U-1 to Bärenschanze, it's just behind *Pit Stop* sign, tel. 0911/231-5666).

SLEEPING

The most crowded days of 2006 in Nürnberg will be June 11, 15, 18, 22, and 25, when the city hosts World Cup soccer matches. You can also expect higher prices during major conventions in the spring and fall (around 25 percent increase for most conventions, but as much as 75 percent for the huge toy fair—Feb 2–7 in 2006). Prices also go up in December, especially weekends, when the Christmas market is going on. Aside from the World Cup commotion, the months of July and August are generally low season and come with the lowest prices.

EATING

Nürnberg is famous for its pinkie-sized Bratwurst (called, like local residents, *Nürnberger*). Nürnbergers—the people—insist that size doesn't matter; they maintain that *in der Kürze liegt die Würze:* in the shortness lies the tastiness. For a quick snack, eat these tiny Brats three at a time, side-by-side, in a bun (sold at kiosks on the street). Restaurant menus often offer them in 6-, 8-, or 10-weenie servings with *Beilagen,* which means your choice of a side dish (generally potato salad or kraut).

Nürnberg is packed with atmospheric old places to try this or other regional specialties. For convenience, I've listed restaurants that are on (or near) Königstrasse, the main drag connecting the station to the castle. Only the last two places are away from this tourist zone—buried in the west end of the old town, and known only to locals.

Barfüsser Beer Cellar fills the basement of the old grain storehouse *(Mauthalle)* with jovial Germans munching meat-on-the-bone (from pork knuckle to duck) and swilling beer. This is good, smoky, German fun. On hot nights, the cellar's empty and their tables spill out onto Königstrasse (€5–8 meals, daily 11:00–24:00, Hallplatz 2, tel. 0911/204-242).

Nassauer Keller is a snug and classy 13th-century vaulted cellar filled with suits of armor, happy eaters, and traditional food. A small door leads down steep steps into a dressy dining room—popular for roast shoulder of pork and other traditional fare. It's a little pricey but worth the extra euros. Avoid this place on hot days (€10–14 plates, Mon–Sat 12:00–15:00 & 18:00–24:00, closed Sun, across from St. Lawrence Church at Karolinenstrasse 2–4, tel. 0911/225-967).

Goldenes Posthorn is the most elegant of the Behringer restaurant empire (see below for its sister restaurants, Bratwurstglöcklein and Bratwursthäusle). While no longer in its original historic location, this institution is supposedly the oldest *Weinstube* in Germany and, once upon a time, Albrecht Dürer's favorite hangout. Come here to enjoy everything from Franconian specialties and Bratwurst to daily fish and vegetarian plates, either in the warm, light-wood interior or on the patio in the shadow of St. Sebald Church (€6–10 meals, non-smoking section, cash only, daily 11:00–23:00, Glöckleingasse 2, tel. 0911/225-153, fax 0911/227-645, www.goldenes-posthorn.de).

Literaturhaus Nürnberg, run by the local book club, is popular for readings. It serves trendy breakfasts (daily until 15:00) and creative international dishes for €5 to €9. Locals like to order several varied little plates, or just enjoy its inviting café ambience for drinks and sweets (daily 9:00–24:00, 2 blocks from Frauentor just off Königstrasse at Luitpoldstrasse 6, tel. 0911/234-2658).

Burgwächter serves up German cuisine—either in its cozy restaurant, or on its covered patio, with big, rustic picnic tables. It's just under the castle and gets a mix of tourists and local clientele (€5–10 plates, good salads, daily 11:00–24:00, Am Ölberg 10, tel. 0911/222-126).

Das Bratwurstglöcklein is touristy for its location—in the middle of the Craftsmen's Courtyard, just inside the Frauentor. But locals enjoy the food, too. It's a convenient place to sample Nürnberg's famous Bratwurst surrounded by ye olde half-timbered decor—indoors and out (cheaper take-out, Mon–Sat 10:30–21:30, closed Sun, Im Handwerkerhof, tel. 0911/227-625).

Bratwursthäusle is a high-energy, woody-yet-mod place with a leafy terrace (enjoyable people-watching) and a cozy interior. It serves little more than Bratwurst, but they're all made in-house by the *Häusle's* own butcher and served with the style of a fine restaurant. Chat up the owner, friendly Herr Behringer, and he'll be happy to tell you about Bratwurst Saints (open long hours daily, midway between Market Square and the castle on the main drag, Rathausplatz 1, tel. 0911/227-695).

Café Sebald is a Bratwurst-free bistro serving well-presented "creative Euro-Asian" cuisine in a classy indoor/outdoor setting. They're friendly, stylish, and into good music. The local clientele appreciates their €8 to €12 daily blackboard specials (plates up to €20, daily 11:00–22:00, 2 blocks behind—west of—St. Sebald Church towards the wall at Geiersberg 11, tel. 0911/381-303).

Kettensteg Biergarten is a hip jumble of picnic tables under trees overlooking the city's river and medieval wall. Its youthful energy and big flames give it a tribe-like ambience in the evening. Don't bother eating indoors here—this is for leafy, cobbled outdoor dining surrounded by happy locals and in-the-know foreign students (€8–10 meals, strong German cuisine with a few modern surprises and decent salads, daily in summer 11:00–23:00, west of Market Square where the river hits the wall, Maxplatz 35, tel. 0911/221-081). They have a cool riverside bar, if you just want a slow, hard drink.

TRANSPORTATION CONNECTIONS

From Nürnberg by Train to: Rothenburg (at least hrly, 1.25–2 hrs, change in Steinach), **Würzburg** (2–3/hr, 1 hr), **Munich** (hrly, 1 hr), **Frankfurt** (2/hr, 2 hrs), **Rothenburg** (hrly, 1.5 hrs), **Salzburg** (hrly with change in Munich, 3.5 hrs). Train info: tel. 11861 (€0.50/min).

DRESDEN

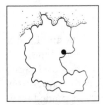

Dresden, the capital of Saxony, surprises visitors with fine Baroque architecture and impressive museums. It's historical, intriguing, and fun—especially in 2006, when the town celebrates its 800th birthday. While the city is packed with tourists, 85 percent of them are German. Until Americans rediscover Dresden's Baroque glory, you'll feel like you're in on a secret.

At the peak of its power in the 18th century, the capital of Saxony ruled most of present-day Poland and Eastern Germany from the bank of the Elbe River. Dresden's "Louis XIV" was Augustus the Strong. As both prince elector of Saxony and king of Poland, he imported artists from all over Europe, peppering his city with stunning Baroque buildings. Dresden's grand architecture and dedication to the arts—along with the gently rolling hills surrounding the city—earned it the nickname "Florence on the Elbe."

Sadly, these days Dresden is better known for its destruction in World War II. American and British pilots firebombed the city on the night of February 13, 1945. More than 25,000 people were killed, and 75 percent of the historical center was destroyed. American Kurt Vonnegut, who was a POW in Dresden during the firebombing, later memorialized the event in his novel *Slaughterhouse-Five.*

When Germany was divvied up at the end of World War II, Dresden wound up in the Soviet sector. Forty years of communist rule left the city in an economic hole—even today, Saxony's unemployment rate hovers around 19 percent. Some older Dresdeners feel nostalgia for the Red old days, when "everyone had a job." But in the decade and a half since the Berlin Wall fell, Dresden has made real progress in getting back on its feet—and most locals are enjoying capitalism with gusto. Today's Dresden is a young and vibrant city, crawling with happy-go-lucky students who barely remember communism.

Under the communists, Dresden patched up some of its damaged buildings, left many others in ruins, and replaced even more with huge, modern, pedestrian-unfriendly sprawl. But today, Dresden seems all about rebuilding. Circa-1946 photos are on walls everywhere, and the city's most important and beautiful historic buildings in the Old Town have been restored. Across the river, the New Town was missed by the bombs. While well-worn, it retains its prewar character and is emerging as the city's fun and lively people zone. Most tourists never cross the bridge away from the famous Old Town museums...but a visit to Dresden isn't complete without a wander through the New Town.

Planning Your Time

Dresden, conveniently located halfway between Prague and Berlin, is well worth even a quick stop. If you're short on time, Dresden's top sights can be seen in a midday break on your Berlin–Prague train ride (it's about 2.5 hrs from both). Catch the early train, throw your bag in a locker at the station (€2), follow my self-guided walk (page 315), and visit some museums before taking an evening train out.

If you have more time, Dresden merits an overnight stay. The city is a handy home base for getting back to nature at Saxon Switzerland National Park (see page 327) or side-tripping to the town of Görlitz for its intriguing mix of rich architecture and culture (see next chapter).

ORIENTATION

(area code: 0351)
Dresden is big, with half a million residents. Its city center hugs a curve on the Elbe River. Despite the city's size, virtually all of its sights are within easy strolling distance along the south bank of the Elbe in the Old Town (Altstadt). South of the Old Town (a 5-min tram ride or 15-min walk away) is the main train station (Hauptbahnhof). North of the Old Town, across the river, you'll find the residential-feeling New Town (Neustadt). While the New Town boasts virtually no sights, it's lively, colorful, and fun to explore—day or night—and has some recommended hotels and restaurants.

Dresden

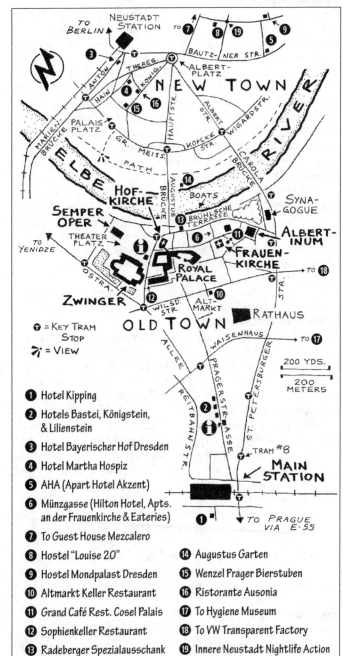

To Berlin

Neustadt Station

To ⑦ ⑧ ⑲ ⑨ ⑤

Bautz-Ner Str.

③

Albert-Platz

New Town

River

Elbe

④ ⑮ ⑯

Palais Platz

Gr. Meiss.

Path

Hof-Kirche

⑭ **Boats**

Synagogue

Semper Oper

Brühlsche Terrasse

⑬ ⑪

Albertinum

To Yenidze

Theater Platz

ℹ️ ⑥

Frauen-Kirche

Royal Palace

To ⑱

Ostra-

Zwinger

⑫ **Wilsd. Str.** **Alt-Markt** ⑩

Old Town

Rathaus

To ⑰

🚋 = Key Tram Stop

🔭 = View

Allee

Waisenhaus

Reitbahn Str.

Prager Strasse

St. Petersburger

200 Yds.

200 Meters

① Hotel Kipping

② Hotels Bastei, Königstein, & Lilienstein

③ Hotel Bayerischer Hof Dresden

④ Hotel Martha Hospiz

⑤ AHA (Apart Hotel Akzent)

⑥ Münzgasse (Hilton Hotel, Apts. an der Frauenkirche & Eateries)

⑦ To Guest House Mezcalero

② ℹ️

Tram #8

Main Station

①

To Prague via E-55

⑧ Hostel "Louise 20"

⑨ Hostel Mondpalast Dresden

⑩ Altmarkt Keller Restaurant

⑪ Grand Café Rest. Cosel Palais

⑫ Sophienkeller Restaurant

⑬ Radeberger Spezialausschank

⑭ Augustus Garten

⑮ Wenzel Prager Bierstuben

⑯ Ristorante Ausonia

⑰ To Hygiene Museum

⑱ To VW Transparent Factory

⑲ Innere Neustadt Nightlife Action

Tourist Information

Dresden has two TIs (both open Mon–Fri 10:00–18:00, Sat 10:00–16:00, closed Sun, general TI tel. 0351/491-920, www .dresden-tourist.de): in the heart of the Old Town at **Theaterplatz** (in neoclassical Schinkelwache building, next to Zwinger), and in a freestanding kiosk at the train-station end of **Prager Strasse,** near the Mercure Hotel. Both TIs book rooms (€3/person), sell concert and theater tickets, and operate travel agencies. Ask about what's new in fast-changing Dresden, especially in this monumental year (see "Helpful Hints," below). Get the handy, free one-page city map with a listing of key sights, hours, and prices on the back. For live entertainment and cultural events, study the monthly *Theater Konzert Kunst* (free, in German only).

The **Dresden City Card** (sold at both TIs) gives you admission to all of Dresden's top museums, discounts on some lesser museums, and unlimited use of the city's transit system (€19/48 hrs, €29 for 72-hr "Regional" version that includes outlying areas). If you're only here for the day, skip it—instead, buy a one-day museum pass, called a *Tageskarte* (€10, covers all state museums, including most listed in this chapter; available at participating museums). The Web site for all Dresden state museums is www.skd-dresden.de.

Arrival in Dresden

Dresden has two major train stations. If you're coming for the day and want easiest access to the sights, use the **Hauptbahnhof** (main train station), just south of the Old Town. Exit the station following signs for the city, taxis, and trams. To take a **tram** into the center, cross the tram tracks at Wiener Platz and veer right to find tram #8 or #11 (departing to your left), which zips you to the historical center (Theaterplatz or Postplatz). The 15-minute **walk** to the Old Town offers an insightful glimpse of the communist era as you stroll down Prager Strasse (described on page 325; from the station, continue straight through Wiener Platz, under and past the towering Mercure Hotel).

The **Neustadt** station serves the New Town north of the river, near some recommended hotels. From the Neustadt station, tram #11 runs to Am Zwingerteich, a park in the center of the Old Town right next to the sights.

Trains run between the Hauptbahnhof and Neustadt station every 10 minutes (€1.70, 10-min ride, most trains stop at each station—ask; the stations are also connected by slower tram #3).

Helpful Hints

Festivals: Dresden celebrates its 800th birthday in 2006. Expect a whole slew of events throughout the year. Highlights include the week-long Stadtfestwoche (City Festival Week,

July 14–23); a parade re-enacting the history of the Wettin family, complete with costumes and knights on horseback (Historischer Festumzug, Aug 27); and the re-opening of the full collection of the historic Green Vault in September. For more details, see www.dresden.de/800.

Sightseeing Schedules: Many of Dresden's museums (including all Zwinger museums and Watchman's Tower) are closed on Monday. The Royal Palace and Albertinum are closed on Tuesday. The Hofkirche hosts free pipe-organ concerts twice a week (April–Dec on Wed and Sat at 11:30).

Local Guide: Maren Koban is a genteel local woman who loves sharing the story of her hometown, as she has since 1991 (€100/half-day, tel. 0351/311-1315).

Getting Around Dresden

Dresden's slick new trams and buses work well for the visitor. Buy tickets at the machines on the platforms or in the trams (€1.70 per ride or €1 for a *Kurzstrecke*—short stretch—of fewer than 4 stops; most machines accept coins only). A day ticket *(Tageskarte)* is good until 4:00 the next morning (the 1-zone, €4.50 version works for sightseeing within the city). Free use of public transit is included with the City Card (see above). Taxis are handy and generally honest (€2 to start, then €1.10 per kilometer). The Hilton Hotel (across from the Frauenkirche) rents bikes to guests and non-guests (€8/5 hrs, €12/day, leave credit-card number for security deposit).

SELF-GUIDED WALK

Do-It-Yourself Dresden Baroque Blitz Tour

Dresden's major sights are conveniently clustered along a delightfully strollable promenade next to the Elbe. Get to know this sightseeing zone by taking this ▲▲▲ walk. Though the city has a long and colorful history, we'll focus on the three eras that have shaped it the most: Dresden's Golden Age in the mid-18th century under Augustus the Strong; the city's destruction by firebombs in World War II; and the communist regime that took over at the war's end and continued until 1989.

The following walk laces together Dresden's top sights in about an hour, not counting museum stops. Unless otherwise noted, Dresden's museums are light on English information (no audioguides) but heavy on sightseeing value.

Theaterplatz: Begin at Theaterplatz (convenient drop-off point for tram #8 from Hauptbahnhof). Face the equestrian statue (King John, an unimportant mid-19th-century ruler) in the middle of the square. In front of you, behind the statue, is the Saxon State Opera House—nicknamed the **Semper Oper** after its architect,

Central Dresden

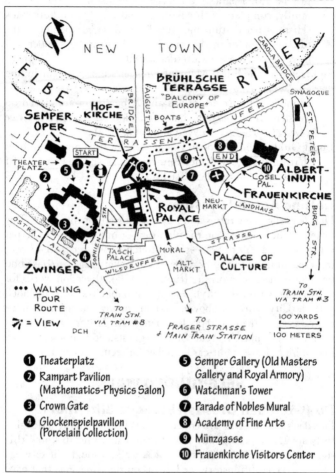

❶ Theaterplatz
❷ Rampart Pavilion (Mathematics-Physics Salon)
❸ Crown Gate
❹ Glockenspielpavillon (Porcelain Collection)
❺ Semper Gallery (Old Masters Gallery and Royal Armory)
❻ Watchman's Tower
❼ Parade of Nobles Mural
❽ Academy of Fine Arts
❾ Münzgasse
❿ Frauenkirche Visitors Center

Gottfried Semper (visits only with a tour, see page 324).

When facing the Opera House, on your left stands the neo-classical Schinkelwache (Guard-house, houses the TI). The big building behind it and to the right is the Semper Gallery, the east wing of the Zwinger (your next stop). Across the square from the Opera House is the Hofkirche, with its distinctive open-work steeple, and behind that is the sprawling Royal Palace

(both described below). All the buildings you see here—Dresden's Baroque treasures—are replicas. The originals were destroyed by American and British bombs in a single night. For over 60 years, Dresden has been rebuilding—and there's lots more work to do.

• *Walk through the passageway into the Zwinger courtyard (to your left as you face the Opera House), noticing the Crown Gate on the opposite side lowering majestically into view. Stop in the middle of the courtyard, where we'll survey all four wings.*

The Zwinger: This palace complex, worth ▲▲, is a Baroque masterpiece—once the pride and joy of the Wettin dynasty, and today filled with fine museums. The Wettins ruled Saxony for over 800 years, right up until the end of the First World War. Saxony

wasn't ruled by a king, but by a prince elector—one of a handful of nobles who elected the Holy Roman Emperor. The prince elector of Saxony was one of Germany's most powerful people, and the 18th century was Saxony's Golden Age. Friedrich Augustus I, prince elector of Saxony, wheeled and dealed—and converted from his Saxon Protestantism to a more Polish-friendly Catholicism—to become King Augustus II of Poland. Legends paint Augustus as a macho, womanizing, powerful, ambitious, properly Baroque man—a real Saxon superstar. A hundred years after his death, historians dubbed him "the Strong." Today tour guides love to impart silly legends about Augustus, who supposedly fathered 365 children and could break a horseshoe in half with his bare hands. Like most Wettins, Augustus the Strong was unlucky at war, but a clever diplomat and a lover of the arts. We can thank Augustus and the rest of the Wettins—and the nobles who paid them taxes—for Dresden's rich architectural and artistic heritage.

"Zwinger" means the no-man's land just outside the city wall. Gradually this empty space evolved into the complex of buildings you see today. By Augustus' time, the Zwinger was used for celebrations of Saxon royalty. Imagine an over-the-top royal wedding in this complex.

Let's get oriented. Face the north wing (with the Crown Gate on your left). You're looking at the **Rampart Pavilion** (Wallpavillon), the first wing of the palace—an orangery built for Augustus' fruit trees. Stairs lead to a fine Zwinger view from the terrace above. This wing of the Zwinger houses the fun **Mathematics-Physics Salon** (see page 324). Turn to the left, facing

the **Crown Gate** (Kronentor). The gate's golden crown is topped by four eagles, symbolizing Polish royalty (remember that Augustus was also king of Poland). Turn again to the left to see the **Glockenspielpavillon.** The glockenspiel near the top of the gate has 40 bells made of Meissen porcelain (bells chime every 15 min and play melodies at 11:15, 14:15, and 17:15). Above the glockenspiel stands Hercules, with the Earth on his back—a fitting symbol for Augustus the Strong. This wing of the Zwinger also houses Augustus the Strong's **Porcelain Collection** (see page 324). Turn once more to the left (with the Crown Gate behind you) to see the **Semper Gallery.** This Zwinger wing was added to the original courtyard a hundred years later by Gottfried Semper (of Opera House fame). It houses Dresden's best museum, the **Old Masters Gallery,** as well as the **Royal Armory** (see page 324).

Throughout the city, you'll see the local sandstone looking really sooty. Locals claim that it's not pollution, but natural oxidation that turns the stone black in about 30 years.

Take time to enjoy some of the Zwinger's excellent museums. Ponder this: Anticipating WWII bombs, Dresdeners preserved their town's art treasures by storing them in underground mines and cellars in the countryside. This saved these great works from Allied bombs...but not from the Russians. Nearly all of the city's artwork ended up in Moscow until after Stalin's death in 1953, when the art was returned by the communist regime to win over their East German subjects.

When you're finished with the museums, exit the Zwinger through the Glockenspielpavillon (south gate). Halfway through the corridor, look for the timelines telling the history of the Zwinger in German: to the right, its construction, and to the left, its destruction and reconstruction. Notice the Soviet spin: On May 8, 1945, the Soviet army liberated Dresden from "fascist tyranny" *(faschistischen Tyrannei)*, and from 1945 to 1964, the Zwinger was rebuilt with the "power of the workers and peasants" *(Arbeiter- und Bauern-Macht).*

• *As you exit the corridor, jog to the left, cross the street and the tram tracks, and walk down the perpendicular Taschenberg Strasse with the yellow Taschenberg Palace on your right (ruined until 1990, today the city's finest 5-star hotel). Go under the passageway between the Royal Palace and the yellow palace. Ahead of you and to the right, the blocky modern building is the...*

Palace of Culture (Kulturpalast): This theater, built by the communist government in 1969, is still used for concerts today. Notice the mural depicting communist themes: workers; strong women; care for the elderly; teachers and students; and, of course, the red star and the seal of former East Germany. Such symbolism is rare in post-communist Germany, and many believe it's only a matter of time before this mural disappears.

• *Now turn left (with the Palace of Culture behind you). Walk toward the tallest tower ahead on the left (the climbable Watchman's Tower). On your left is the east wing of the sprawling...*

Royal Palace (Residenzschloss): The palace is still being repaired from the WWII firebombing; the farther you walk,

the more destruction you'll see. Its reconstruction is expected to last until 2010, when the Royal Palace will house civic offices and the city's massive art collection—only a third of which is currently in museums. Much of the palace is already open, with a fine collection—consider stopping in now to see the sumptuous **Green Vault** (Grünes Gewölbe; see page 325).

Just before you reach the big passageway, look for the bombed-out gap in the wall to your left. This was the palace's **Great Courtyard.** Across the courtyard, you see the black-and-white decoration on the inside of the western wing. These images, called sgraffito, are scratched into plaster over charcoal. Look halfway up the **Watchman's Tower** at the tourists, enjoying the best viewpoint in town (see page 325). Because of ongoing renovation, the location of the entrance to this tower changes regularly; for the latest on how to get up there, ask at the info desk at the Green Vault.

• *Continue through the passageway into the **Palace Square**. Ahead of you and to the left is the...*

Hofkirche (Cathedral): Why does Dresden, a stronghold of local-boy Martin Luther's Protestant Reformation, boast such a beautiful Catholic cathedral? When Augustus the Strong died, his son wanted to continue as king of Poland, like his father. The pope would allow it only if Augustus Junior built a Catholic church in Dresden. Thanks to Junior's historical kissing-up, the mere 5 percent of locals who are Catholic get to enjoy this fine church. The elevated passageway connecting the church with the palace allowed the royal family to avoid walking in the street with commoners.

Step inside (free, enter through side door facing palace,

Mon–Thu 9:00–17:00, Fri 13:00–17:00, Sat 10:30–16:00, Sun 12:00–16:00, tel. 0351/484-4712, www.kathedrale-dresden.de). The fine Baroque pulpit—hidden by locals in the countryside during World War II—is carved out of linden wood. The glorious 3,000-pipe organ filling the back of the nave is played for the public on Wednesdays and Saturdays at 11:30 (free, April–Dec only).

The Memorial Chapel (facing the rear of the church, on the left) is dedicated to those who died in the WWII firebombing and to all victims of violence. Its evocative *pietà* altarpiece was made in 1973 of Meissen porcelain. Mary offers the faithful the crown of thorns, as if to remind us that Jesus—on her lap, head hanging lifeless on the left—died to save humankind. The altar (freestanding, in front) shows five flaming heads. It seems to symbolize how Dresdeners suffered...in the presence of their suffering savior. The dates on the altar (30-1-33 and 13-2-45) mark the dark period between Hitler's rise to power and the night Dresden was destroyed.

The basement houses the royal crypt, including the heart of the still-virile Augustus the Strong—which, according to legend, still beats when a pretty woman comes near (crypt only open for one 45-min German tour each day).

• *As you leave the Hofkirche, look back at the palace. To the left, next to the palace's main entrance, you'll see a long, yellow mural called the...*

Parade of Nobles (Fürstenzug): This mural—worth ▲—is painted on 24,000 tiles of Dresden porcelain. Longer than a football field, it illustrates 700 years of Saxon royalty. It was built to commemorate Saxon history and heritage after Saxony became a part of Germany in 1871. The artist carefully studied armor and clothing through the ages, allowing you to accurately trace the evolution of weaponry and fashions for seven centuries. (This is great for couples—try this for a switch: men watch the fashions, women the weaponry.)

The very last figure (or the first one you see, coming from this direction) is the artist himself, Wilhelm Walther. Then come commoners (miner, farmer, carpenter, teachers, students, artists), and then the royals, with 35 names and dates marking over 700 years of Wettin rule. Stop at 1694. That's August II (Augustus the Strong), the most important of the Saxon kings. He stomps on the rose (symbol of Martin Luther, the Protestant movement, and the Lutheran church today) to gain the Polish crown. The first Saxon royal is Konrad der Grosse ("the Great"). And waaay up at the very

front of the parade, an announcer with a band and 12th-century cheerleaders excitedly herald the arrival of this wondrous procession. The porcelain tiles, originals from 1907, survived the bombing. When created, they were fired three times at 2,400 degrees Fahrenheit...and then fired again during the 1945 firestorm at only 1,800 degrees.

• *When you're finished looking at the mural, return to the Palace Square, face the river, and climb the big staircase on your right, up to the...*

Brühlsche Terrasse: This so-called "Balcony of Europe," a delightful ▲▲ promenade, was once Dresden's defensive rampart. Look ahead along the side of the terrace facing the river to see

openings for cannons and other weapons. But by Baroque times, fortresses were no longer necessary, and this became one of Europe's most charming promenades. Stroll and enjoy the leafy canopy of linden trees. Past the first fountain and the café, belly up to the railing facing the Elbe River.

Dresden claims to have the world's largest and oldest fleet of historic **paddleboat steamers:** nine riverboats from the 19th century (some of which still have plaques promising a "10-year warranty"). The hills in the distance (to left) are home to Saxon vineyards, producing Germany's northernmost wine. Because only a small amount of the land is suitable for vineyards, Saxon wine is expensive and enjoyed mostly by locals.

Below you to the left is the **Augustus Bridge** (Augustusbrücke), connecting Dresden's Old Town with the New Town. During the massive floods of August, 2002, water filled about two-thirds of the arches. Notice how the raging floodwaters actually cleaned the sandstone inside the bridge's arches. At the far end of the Augustus Bridge, look for the golden equestrian statue, a symbol of Dresden. It's Augustus the Strong, the **Goldene Reiter** (Golden Rider), facing east to his kingdom of Poland.

The area across the bridge is the **New Town** (Neustadt). While three-quarters of Dresden's Old Town was decimated by Allied firebombs, much of the New Town survived. The 18th-century apartment buildings here were restored—giving the area a Baroque look instead of the blocky Soviet style predominant on the Old Town side of the river. The New Town is a trendy district today, and well worth exploring (see page 326). The **Three Kings Church** (Dreikönigskirche, steeple visible above the Goldene Reiter) marks a neighborhood with some recommended restaurants (see page 333).

The interesting **mosque-shaped building** in the distance to the far left (marked Yenidze), originally a tobacco factory designed to advertise Turkish cigarettes, is now an office building with restaurants and nightclubs. A few steps to your left is the recommended Radeberger Spezialausschank café—the best place for a drink or meal with a river view (see page 332).

Continue walking along the Brühlsche Terrasse. Ahead on the right, you'll see the glass domes of the **Academy of Fine Arts**.

(Locals call the big dome on the right "the lemon juicer.") At the modern globe sculpture on the terrace, go down the stairs on your right and head toward the huge rebuilt Frauenkirche. You'll walk along **Münzgasse,** lined with trendy restaurants (see page 332). This street re-creates the lively café scene of prewar Dresden. With the newly rebuilt Frauenkirche (ahead of you) as a centerpiece, this district will soon teem with more restaurants and cafés like these.

• *At the end of Münzgasse, you'll see the reconstructed...*

Frauenkirche (Church of Our Lady): This church, rated ▲▲, is the heart and soul of the city. Augustus the Strong grew jealous of the mighty Catholic domes of Venice and London, and demanded that a proper Lutheran church be built in Dresden. Completed in 1743, this was Germany's biggest Protestant church (310 feet high). Its unique central stone cupola design gave it the nickname "handbell church."

While it's a great church, this building garners the world's attention primarily because of its tragic history. On the night of February 13, 1945, the firebombs came. When the smoke cleared the next morning, the Frauenkirche was still standing. It burned for two days before finally collapsing. After the war, the Frauenkirche was kept in rubble as a peace monument and the site of many memorial vigils.

In 1992, the reconstruction of the church began. The restorers used as many of the church's original stones as possible, fitting it together like a giant jigsaw puzzle. About a third of the church is original stones (notice the dark ones, placed in their original spots), and new pieces were custom-made to fill in the gaps. The reconstruction has cost more than €100 million, 90 percent of which came from donors around the world.

Since its consecration in October of 2005, the church interior is open to visitors (free but donation requested, Mon–Fri 10:00–12:00 & 13:00–18:00, closed Sat–Sun, www.frauenkirche-dresden.de). Inside you'll find the tangled, battered original cross that stood at the top of the dome until 1945. The copy capping the new church was built by an English coppersmith whose father actually dropped bombs on the church during that fateful night. Those feeling energetic can get a great view over the city by climbing the stairs to the top of the dome (€8, daily 10:00–18:00, follow signs to *Kuppelaufstieg*).

Though the church itself has re-opened, the nearby **Frauenkirche Visitors Center** will likely remain open to tell the story of the bombing and rebuilding (Mon–Fri 10:00–18:00, Sat–Sun 10:00–17:00, grayish-green building beyond yellow palace at Georg-Treu-Platz 3, tel. 0351/656-0680).

• *Your tour is over. Enjoy the bustle of Münzgasse, and consider taking in more museums, such as the nearby **Albertinum** (sculpture and modern art—see page 325).*

SIGHTS

In the Zwinger

All museums in the Zwinger palace complex have the same hours: Tuesday through Sunday 10:00 to 18:00, closed Monday (tel. 0351/491-4619). All of these sights are covered by the €10 *Tageskarte* museum pass (buy at any sight), or you can pay individually for each museum (prices listed below).

▲▲▲Old Masters Gallery (Gemäldegalerie Alte Meister)— Dresden's best museum features works by Raphael, Titian, Rembrandt, Rubens, Vermeer, and more. It's particularly enjoyable for its "quality, not quantity" approach to showing off great art. Locals remember the Old Masters Gallery as the first big public building reopened after the war, in 1956.

Entering, you'll pass a small room with portraits of the Wettin kings who patronized the arts and founded this collection. The next room shows five cityscapes of Dresden, painted during its Golden Age by Canaletto. These paintings of mid-18th-century Dresden—showing the Hofkirche (still under construction) and the newly completed Frauenkirche—offer a great study of the city. Next you enter a world of Rubens and Belgian Baroque. This high-powered Catholic art is followed by humbler, quieter Protestant art of the Dutch Masters, including a fine collection of Rembrandts (don't miss his jaunty self-portrait—with Saskia on his lap and a glass of ale held aloft) and a pristine Vermeer *(Girl at a Window Reading a Letter)*. The German late Gothic/early Renaissance rooms include exquisite canvases by Cranach and Dürer. Farther on, the Venetian masters include a sumptuous *Slumbering Venus* by Giorgione (1510). He died while still working on this, so Titian stepped in to finish it. Giorgione's idealized Venus isn't asleep, but deeply restful—at peace with the plush nature.

The collection's highlight: Raphael's masterful *Sistine Madonna*. The portrait features the Madonna and Child, two early Christian martyrs (Saints Sixtus and Barbara), and wispy angel faces in the clouds. Mary is in motion, offering the savior to a needy world. But recently, the stars of this painting are the pair of whimsical angels in the foreground. These lovable tykes—of T-shirt and poster fame—are bored...just hanging out, oblivious to the exciting arrival of the Messiah just behind them. They connect the heavenly world of the painting with you and me (€6, includes Royal Armory entry, no English explanations so consider the good €13 English guidebook, in Zwinger's Semper Gallery, tel. 0351/491-4619).

Royal Armory (Rüstkammer)—One big room packed with swords and suits of armor, the armory is especially interesting for its tiny children's armor and the jousting exhibit in the back (€3 alone, or included with €6 ticket to Old Masters Gallery, across passage from Old Masters Gallery).

Mathematics-Physics Salon (Mathematisch-Physikalischer Salon)—This fun collection features globes, lenses, and clocks from the 16th–19th centuries (€3, north end of Zwinger courtyard).

▲Porcelain Collection (Porzellansammlung)—Every self-respecting European king had a porcelain works, and the Wettins had the most famous: Meissen. The Saxon prince electors went beyond producing, and also collected other porcelain—from France to Japan and China. Augustus the Strong was obsessed with this stuff... he liked to say he had "porcelain sickness." Here you can enjoy some of his symptoms, under chandeliers in elegant galleries (€5, good English descriptions, south end of Zwinger courtyard).

More Sights in the Old Town

These sights are listed in the order you'll encounter them on my self-guided walking tour (above).

Semper Opera—Three opera houses have stood in this spot: The first was destroyed by a fire in 1869, the second by firebombs in 1945. The rebuilt Semper Oper continues to be a world-class venue, and tickets for the Saxon State Orchestra (the world's oldest) are hard to come by (on sale a year in advance; box office in Schinkelwache TI across the square, Mon–Fri 10:00–18:00, Sat 10:00–16:00, closed Sun, tel. 0351/491-1705, fax 0351/491-1700, www.semperoper.de).

The opulent opera house is great for concerts and performances, but not for touring. It can only be visited with a German-speaking guide and English handouts (€6, €2 ticket to take photos, 1 hr, tour schedule depends on rehearsal schedule, enter on right side, tel. 0351/491-1496).

▲▲**Royal Palace (Residenzschloss)**—This Renaissance palace was once the residence of the Saxon prince elector. Formerly one of the finest Renaissance buildings in Germany, it's slowly being rebuilt after the destruction of World War II. In 2006, the grand halls and audience chambers of Augustus the Strong will be re-opened. Until then, it holds a coin collection, a print collection, and the lavish Green Vault treasure chamber.

The famed **Green Vault** (Grünes Gewölbe), which finally returned to the palace in 2004, is a glittering treasury collection conceived as a Baroque synthesis of the arts by Augustus the Strong in the early 1700s. It evolved as the royal family's extravagant treasure-trove of ivory, silver, and gold knickknacks. Gawk at the incredibly elaborate diorama of the Delhi Court birthday celebration of a mogul (a thinly veiled stand-in for Augustus the Strong). In 2006, the entire collection should be on display in the historic rooms on the ground floor of the west wing (€6, covered by €10 *Tageskarte* museum pass, Wed–Mon 10:00–18:00, closed Tue).

▲**Watchman's Tower (Hausmannsturm)**—This tower is worth the 160 steps for a panoramic view of Dresden. On the way up, you'll see exhibits (in German, but with interesting photos and blueprints) about the tower's construction, destruction, and reconstruction (€2.50 for tower, if just going up for the view don't buy the €5 ticket for tower and temporary exhibit, covered by €10 *Tageskarte* museum pass, April–Oct Wed–Mon 10:00–18:00, last entry 17:30, closed Tue and Nov–March, tel. 0351/491-4563). Due to renovation at the palace, the location of the tower entrance is unpredictable; ask at the nearby Green Vault for information (listed above).

Albertinum—This historic building houses the **Sculpture Collection** (Skulpturensammlung) and the **New Masters Gallery** (Gemäldegalerie Neue Meister), which features works by 19th- and 20th-century greats such as Renoir, Rodin, van Gogh, Degas, and Klimt. Don't miss Otto Dix's moving triptych *War* (painted between the World Wars), Gustav Klimt's *Buchenwald,* and a Rodin *Thinker* at the top of the main stairwell (€6, covered by €10 *Tageskarte* museum pass, Wed–Mon 10:00–18:00, closed Tue, at far end of Brühlsche Terrasse, tel. 0351/491-4619).

Away from the Old Town

Prager Strasse—This communist-built pedestrian mall, connecting the train station and the historic center, was ruins until the 1960s. Even today, "Prague Street" reflects Soviet ideals: big, blocky, functional buildings without extraneous ornamentation. As you stroll down Prager Strasse, imagine these buildings without any of the color or advertising. (Stores "advertised" with simple signs reading *Milk, Bread,* or simply *Products.*) Today, the street is filled with corporate logos, shoppers with lots of choices, and a fun

summertime food circus. When all the construction is finished, this will be an impressive people zone.

▲**New Town (Neustadt)**—A big sign across the river from the old center declares, "Dresden continues here." This seems directed at tourists who visit the city and stay exclusively in the Old Town. Don't be one of them—make a point to explore Dresden's New Town, too.

While there are no famous sights in the New Town, it's the only part of Dresden that predates World War II. Today it's thriving with cafés, shops, clubs, and—most important—just regular people. I've listed several hotels and restaurants worth considering in the neighborhood (see "Sleeping" and "Eating," below).

Hygiene Museum (Deutsches Hygiene Museum)—This museum, a highly conceptual compilation of vaguely health-related exhibits, is one of those sights that's virtually impossible to describe. The exterior fresco—by German Expressionist painter Otto Dix—sets the tone for the unsettling interior. The museum was founded in 1911, and the current location opened its doors in 1930, when its administration still embraced the idea of eugenics (genetic engineering). Since then, the museum has produced and collected models from the 16th century to the present, including little wooden anatomical figures with removable parts (complete with strategically placed fig leaves), X-ray machines from the 1930s, and graphic wax models of venereal diseases. The exhibit is divided into weirdly themed sections (Life and Death, Disease, Physiology, Reproduction, and Grooming). There are some English explanations, or you can rent the €1 audioguide, but most of the exhibits speak (or shriek) for themselves. Perhaps a reflection of the typically German pragmatism toward sexuality, this place is usually filled with school groups or families with young kids. With the right attitude, it's easy to get a kick out of this highly interactive museum, but those easily disturbed should stay away (€6, Tue–Sun 10:00–18:00, closed Mon; take tram #1, #2, #4, or #12 to Zirkusstrasse and follow signs, or take tram #10 or #13 to Hygiene Museum, www.dhmd.de). If you still have an appetite, there's a nice restaurant in the lobby.

Volkswagen Transparent Factory (Gläserne Manufaktur)—
Car buffs will make a pilgrimage to this new VW factory on
the southeastern edge of town. You don't have to custom-order
a luxury-model Phaeton to see how they're manufactured. Two
floors of this fascinating, transparent building are open to visitors
interested in the assembly of one of VW's high-end cars. (If you do
buy a car, you can bring a folding chair, park yourself on the platform, and follow it through every moment of the 36-hour "birth"
process.) The parts are delivered to the logistics plant just on the
edge of town, then transported to this manufacturing plant by
public tram. The informative, high-tech touchscreen displays are
in English, so you don't need the guided tour (which they encourage you to take, but is technically optional). It's smart to contact
them in advance to reserve a time (free, daily 8:00–20:00, can be
closed on short notice for special events, Lennestrasse 1, take tram
#4 from Theaterplatz or Prager Strasse, tel. 01805/896-268, www
.glaesernemanufaktur.de, infoservice@glaesernemanufaktur.de).

Near Dresden: Saxon Switzerland National Park

Consider a break from big-city sightseeing to spend a half day taking a *wunderbar* hike through this scenic national park.

Twenty miles southeast of Dresden (an easy 45-min S-Bahn
ride away), the Elbe River cuts a scenic swath through the beech
forests and steep cliffs of Saxon Switzerland (Sächsische Schweiz)
National Park. You'll share the trails with serious rock climbers
and equally serious Saxon grandmothers. Allow five hours (including lunch) to enjoy this day trip.

Take the S-Bahn line 1 from either the Hauptbahnhof or
the Neustadt station (a €9 *Verbundraum Tageskarte*—regional day
ticket—covers the whole trip, direction Schandau, departs hourly).
Get off at the Kurort Rathen stop, follow the road downhill five
minutes through town to the dock, and take the ferry across the
Elbe (€1.30 round-trip, buy on board, crossing takes 2 min, runs
continuously). When the ferry docks on the far (north) side of the
river, turn your back on the river and walk 100 yards through town,
with the little creek on your right. Turn left after the Sonniges Eck
Restaurant (tasty lunch option, check out the 2002 flood photos
in their front dining room) and walk up the lane. The trail begins
with stairs on your left just past Hotel Amselgrundschlösschen
(follow *Bastei* signs).

A 45-minute walk uphill through the woods leads you to
the Bastei Bridge and stunning views of gray sandstone sen-
tries rising several hundred feet from forest ridges. Elbe Valley
sandstone was used to build Dresden's finest buildings (including the Frauenkirche and Zwinger), as well as Berlin's famous
Brandenburg Gate. The multiple-arch bridge looks straight out

of Oz—built in 1851 specifically for Romantic Age tourists, and scenic enough to be the subject of the first landscape photos ever taken in Germany. Take the time to explore the short 50-yard spur trails that reward you with classic views down on the Elbe 900 feet below. Watch the slow-motion paddle steamers leave V-shaped wakes as they chug upstream toward the Czech Republic, just around the next river bend. If you're not afraid of heights, explore the maze of catwalks through the scant remains of the Neue Felsenberg, a 13th-century Saxon fort once perched precariously on the bald stony spires (€1.50, entrance 50 yards before Bastei Bridge).

Just a five-minute uphill hike beyond the bridge is the Berg Hotel Panorama Bastei, with a fine restaurant, a quick snack bar, and memorable views. Return back down to the Elbe ferry via the same trail.

NIGHTLIFE

To really connect with Dresden as it unfolds, you need to go to the **Innere Neustadt** ("Inner New Town," a 10-min walk from Neustadt train station). This area was not bombed in World War II, and after 1989 it sprouted the first entrepreneurial cafés and bistros. While eateries are open long hours, the action picks up after 22:00. The clientele is young, hip, pierced, and tattooed.

Rather than seek out particular places in this continuously evolving scene, I'd just get to the epicenter (corner of Görlitzer Strasse and Louisenstrasse) and wander. Pop through the Kunsthofpassage, a Hundertwasser-type apartment block with some fun spots (Görlitzer Strasse 23). At Bohmischestrasse 34 (a half block off Lutherplatz), a Russian-flavored *Kneipe* has an imported beach, giving it a Moscow/Maui ambience. The Carte Blanche Transvestite Bar is a hoot for some (€25, most nights from 20:00, Priessnitzstrasse 10, tel. 0351/204-720).

For more sedate entertainment, stroll along the New Town's riverbank after dark for fine floodlit views of the Old Town.

SLEEPING

Dresden is packed with big, conference-style hotels. Characteristic, family-run places are harder to come by. (The communists weren't fans of quaint.) The TI has a room-booking service (€3/person). Peak season for big business-class hotels is May, June, September,

---

Sleep Code

(€1 = about $1.20, country code: 49, area code: 0351)
S = Single, **D** = Double/Twin, **T** = Triple, **Q** = Quad, **b** = bathroom,
s = shower only. All of these places speak English and accept
credit cards. Unless otherwise noted, breakfast is included.

    To help you sort easily through these listings, I've divided
the rooms into three categories, based on the price for a standard double room with bath:

  $$$ **Higher Priced**—Most rooms €120 or more.
    $$ **Moderately Priced**—Most rooms between €80–120.
     $ **Lower Priced**—Most rooms €80 or less.

---

and October. Peak season for hostels is July and August (especially
weekends).

For hotel locations, please see the map on page 313.

In the Old Town

$$$ Hilton Dresden has 340 luxurious rooms (some with views
of the Frauenkirche) in the heart of the Old Town, one block from
the river. Complete with porters, fitness club, pool, and several res-
taurants, it's everything you'd expect from a four-star chain hotel
(Sb-€155–190, Db-€170–205, breakfast-€19, An der Frauenkirche
5, tel. 0351/864-2725, fax 0351/864-2889, www.hilton.de, info
.dresden@hilton.com).

$$ Hotel Kipping, with 20 tidy rooms a hundred yards
behind the Hauptbahnhof, is professionally run by the friendly and
proper Kipping brothers (Rainer and Peter). The building was one
of few in this area to survive the firebombing—in fact, people took
shelter here during the attack (Sb-€70–95, Db-€85–115, 1-person
suite-€115–130, 2-person suite-€130–145, child's bed-€20; higher
prices are for weekends, May–June, and Sept–Oct; elevator, free
parking, Winckelmannstrasse 6, tram #8 whisks you to the Old
Town, tel. 0351/478-500, fax 0351/478-5090, www.hotel-kipping
.de, reception@hotel-kipping.de). Their restaurant serves international cuisine and Saxon specialties (€9–12 entrées, Mon–Sat
18:00–22:30, closed Sun).

$$ Apartments an der Frauenkirche rents 36 new units just
above all the restaurant action on Münzgasse. Designed for longer
stays but welcoming to one-nighters, these modern, comfortable
apartments come with kitchens and the lived-in works (Db-
€80–95, extra bed-€15, breakfast not included, cheaper for longer
stays and off-season, parking at nearby garage-€8/day, Münzgasse

10, tel. 0351/438-1111, www.dresden-tourismus.de, info@dresden -tourismus.de).

$ Hotels Bastei, Königstein, and **Lilienstein** are cookie-cutter members of the Ibis chain, goose-stepping single-file up Prager Strasse (listed in order from the station to the center). Each is practically identical, with 360 rooms (newly renovated Bastei is a couple euros more in high season). Though utterly lacking in charm, they are an excellent value in a convenient location between the Hauptbahnhof and the Old Town (Sb-€59–69, Db-€71–78, apartment-€84 for a family of 3–4, breakfast-€9/person, air-con, elevator, Internet in lobby, parking-€6.50/day, can't miss them on Prager Strasse; Bastei reservation tel. 0351/4856-6661, fax 0351/4856-5555, hotel-bastei@ibis-dresden.de; Königstein reservation tel. 0351/4856-6662, fax 0351/4856-6666, hotel-koenigstein@ibis -dresden.de; Lilienstein reservation tel. 0351/4856-6663, fax 0351/4856-7777, hotel-lilienstein@ibis-dresden.de; Web site for all three: www.ibis-hotel.de). Skip their overpriced hotel restaurants. Instead, eat at the nearby Hotel Kipping (see above) or in the Old Town (see "Eating," page 332).

In the New Town

The first two hotels are fancy splurges in a tidy residential neighborhood surrounding the Neustadt train station. The rest are cheap and funky, buried in the trendy, newly happening café-and-club zone called the Innere Neustadt ("Inner New Town," about a 10-min walk from Neustadt station—see page 328).

$$$ Hotel Bayerischer Hof Dresden, a hundred yards toward the river from the Neustadt train station, offers 50 rooms and elegant and inviting public spaces in a grand old building (Sb-€85–95, Db-€110–130, pricier suites, non-smoking rooms, elevator, free parking, Antonstrasse 33–35, yellow building across from station, tel. 0351/829-370, fax 0351/801-4860, www.bayerischer-hof -dresden.de, info@bayerischer-hof-dresden.de).

$$ Hotel Martha Hospiz, with 50 rooms near the recommended restaurants on Königstrasse, is bright and cheery. The two old buildings that make up the hotel have been smartly renovated and connected in back with a glassed-in winter garden and an outdoor breakfast terrace in a charming garden. It's a 10-minute walk to the historical center, and a five-minute walk to the Neustadt station (S-€54, Sb-€72–84, Db-€102–118, extra bed-€26, elevator; leaving Neustadt station, turn right on Hainstrasse, left on Theresenstrasse, and then right on Nieritzstrasse to #11; tel. 0351/81760, fax 0351/8176-222, www.vch.de/marthahospiz .dresden, marthahospiz .dresden@vch.de).

$$ AHA (Apart Hotel Akzent), on a big, noisy street, has a homey and welcoming ambience. The 29 simple but neat apartments all come with kitchens; most (except the top floor) have balconies. It's a bit farther from the center—10 minutes by foot east of Albertplatz, a 20-minute walk or a quick ride on tram #11 from the center—but its friendliness, coziness, and good value make it a winner (Sb-€60–65, Db-€70–90, small Db about €10 cheaper, twins about €10 more, request back side to avoid street noise, non-smoking rooms, elevator, Bautzner Strasse 53, tel. 0351/800-850, fax 0351/8008-5114, www.ahahotel-dresden.de, kontakt@ahahotel -dresden.de).

$ Guest House Mezcalero, decorated Mexican from top to bottom, is a 22-room place a 10-minute walk from the Neustadt station at the edge of the lively Innere Neustadt zone. It feels classy and comfy, with an adobe ambience (S-€30, Sb-€45, D-€50, Db-€60, dorm bed-€17, breakfast-€5, from either station catch tram #7 to Bischofsweg, Königsbrücker Strasse 64, tel. 0351/810-770, fax 0351/810-7711, www.mezcalero.de, info@mezcalero.de).

$ Hostel "Louise 20" rents 83 beds in the heart of the Innere Neustadt. Though located in the wild-and-edgy nightlife district, it feels safe, solid, clean, and comfy. The newly furnished rooms, guests' kitchen, cozy common room, and friendly staff make it the best place in town for cheap beds (S-€30, D-€42, small dorm-€17/bed, 20-bed dorm-€12.50/bed, €2.50 less if you have sheets, breakfast extra, no lockers, generally booked up on summer weekends, Louisenstrasse 20, tel. 0351/8894-894, www.louise20.de, info@louise20.de).

$ Hostel Mondpalast Dresden is young and hip, in the heart of the Innere Neustadt above a cool bar. It's good for backpackers with little money and an appetite for late-night fun (S-€29, Sb-€39, D-€37, Db-€50, dorm bed-€13.50, one-time fee of €1.50 for sheets, breakfast-€5, lockers, kitchen, lots of facilities, tram #7 from Hauptbahnhof or #11 from Neustadt station, near Kamenzer Strasse at Louisenstrasse 77, tel. 0351/563-4050, www.mondpalast .de, info@mondpalast.de).

EATING

Dresden's ancient beer halls were destroyed in the firebombing and not replaced by the communists. As the city comes back to life, nearly every restaurant seems bright, shiny, and modern. While Old Town restaurants are touristy, the prices are reasonable, and it's easy to eat for €10 to €15 just about anywhere. For cheaper prices and authentic local character, leave the famous center, cross the river, and wander through the New Town.

The special local dessert is *Dresdner Eierschecke*, an eggy cheesecake with vanilla pudding, raisins, and almond shavings sold all over town.

In the Old Town

Münzgasse, the busy and touristy street that connects the Brühlsche Terrasse promenade and the Frauenkirche, is the liveliest street in the Old Town, with a fun selection of eateries. Choose from tapas, Aussie, goulash, crêpes, and even antiques (Kunst Café Antik scatters its tables among a royal estate sale of fancy furniture and objets d'art). Service is a necessary evil, the clientele is international, and the action spills out onto the cobbled pedestrian lane on balmy evenings. Towering high above you is the newly rebuilt Frauenkirche.

Altmarkt Keller, a few blocks farther from the river on Altmarkt square, is a festive beer cellar that serves nicely presented Saxon and Bohemian food and has good Czech beer on tap. The lively crowd, cheesy music (live Fri–Sat from 20:00), and jolly murals add to the fun. While the on-square seating is fine, the vast-but-stout air-conditioned cellar offers your best memories. The giant mural inside the entryway—representing the friendship between Dresden and Prague—reads, "The sunshine of life is drinking and being happy" (€8–10 entrées, daily 11:00–24:00, Altmarkt 4, to the right of McDonald's, tel. 0351/481-8131).

Grand Café Restaurant Cosel Palais serves Saxon and French cuisine in the shadow of the newly rebuilt Frauenkirche. This is a Baroque, chandeliered dining experience with fine courtyard seating—great for an elegant meal or tea and pastries (€10–15 meals, daily specials, open daily 10:00–24:00, An der Frauenkirche 12, tel. 0351/496-2444).

Erlebnisgastronomie *(Experience Gastronomy):* All the rage among Dresdeners (and German tourists in Dresden) is *Erlebnisgastronomie.* Elaborately decorated theme restaurants have sprouted next to the biggest-name sights around town, with over-the-top theme-park decor and historically costumed waitstaff. These can offer a fun change of pace and aren't the bad value you might suspect. The best is **Sophienkeller.** It does its best to take you to the 18th century and the world of Augustus the Strong. The king himself, along with his countess, musicians, and magicians, stroll and entertain, while court maidens serve traditional Saxon food from a "ye olde" menu. Read their colorful brochure to better understand the place. It's big (400 seats), and even has a rotating carousel table with suspended swing-chairs you sit in while you eat (€10–15 plates, daily 11:00–24:00, under the 5-star Taschenberg Palace Hotel, Taschenberg 3, tel. 0351/497-260, www.sophienkeller -dresden.de).

With a River View: **Radeberger Spezialausschank** is dramatically situated on the Brühlsche Terrasse promenade with a rampart-hanging view terrace and three levels taking you down to river level. For river views from the "Balcony of Europe," this is your spot. The inviting-yet-simple menu includes daily Saxon specials and cheap wurst and kraut. The cool river-level bar comes with big copper brewery vats and good beer (daily 10:00–24:00, reservations smart for view terrace, Terrassenufer 1, tel. 0351/484-8660).

In the New Town

Venture to these eateries—across Augustus Bridge from the Old Town—for lower prices and a more local scene. I've listed them nearest to farthest from the Old Town.

Just across Augustus Bridge

Augustus Garten is a lazy, crude-yet-inviting beer garden with super-cheap self-service food (pork knuckle, kraut, cheap beer, and lots of mustard). You'll eat among big bellies—and no tourists— with a fun city-skyline-over-the-river view (daily 11:00–24:00, good weather only, Wiesentorstrasse 2, tel. 0351/404-5854). Walk across the bridge from the Old Town, and it's on your immediate right.

On Königstrasse

For trendy elegance without tourists, have dinner on Königstrasse. After crossing the Augustus Bridge, hike five minutes up the obviously communist-built main drag of the New Town, then turn left to find this charming Baroque street. As this is a fast-changing area, you might survey the other options on and near Königstrasse before settling down.

Wenzel Prager Bierstuben serves country Bohemian cuisine in a woodsy bar that spills out into an airy, glassed-in gallery—made doubly big by its vast mirror (€8–10 entrées, daily 11:00–24:00, Königstrasse 1, tel. 0315/804-2010).

Ristorante Ausonia, with Italian cuisine, comes with fine outdoor seating. Luigi Murolo and his family will give you a break from mustard and kraut (€7–9 pizza or pasta, daily 11:30–23:30, Königstrasse 9, tel. 0351/803-3123). While you're here, the breezy beer garden in the churchyard across the street is worth a look.

TRANSPORTATION CONNECTIONS

From Dresden by Train to: Görlitz (hrly, 1.5 hrs), **Bautzen** (about hrly, 30–45 min; Bautzen-bound trains continue on to Görlitz), **Zittau** (better from Neustadt, hrly, 1.5–2 hrs), **Berlin** (every 2 hrs, 2.25 hrs), **Prague** (7/day, 3 hrs), **Munich** (every 2 hrs, 7 hrs, transfer in Leipzig, Nürnberg, or Fulda), **Frankfurt** (every 2 hrs, 4.5 hrs), **Nürnberg** (every 2 hrs, 4.5 hrs), **Vienna** (1/day, 7 hrs), **Budapest** (1/day, 9 hrs). There are overnight trains from Dresden to Zürich, the Rhineland, and Munich. Train info: tel. 11861 (€0.50/min).

GÖRLITZ

Tucked away in Germany's easternmost corner, the surprisingly beautiful town of Görlitz is a treasure-trove of architecture and one of this country's best-kept secrets.

During the Middle Ages, Görlitz was a major European crossroads, at the intersection of trade routes from Moscow to Barcelona and from the Baltic Sea to Venice. Trade in cloth and beer made the city flourish. Görlitz's rich cultural tapestry was gradually enhanced as the centuries passed, leaving it a delightful collage of architectural styles. The town escaped most of World War II's bombs, but soon after was split down the middle along its river—with half of the town in Germany, the other half in Poland. Görlitz's historic buildings were preserved by the East German government, saving it from the unsightly communist-era blemishes that mark most former East German towns.

Since the Wall fell, Görlitz has sprung back to life and is busily polishing its gorgeous facades. The town offers a unique opportunity to venture to the eastern fringes of Germany, sample Silesian culture and cuisine, and appreciate some breathtaking architecture and stay-a-while squares. Best of all, it's virtually undiscovered by foreign tourists.

Planning Your Time

Although Görlitz is an ideal day trip from Dresden (hourly 1.5-hour trains), the city's subtle charm warrants an overnight stay. Görlitz opens up on long summer nights, as pubs and cafés spill out into the cobbles. Get lost and wander the back streets and alleys.

Görlitz

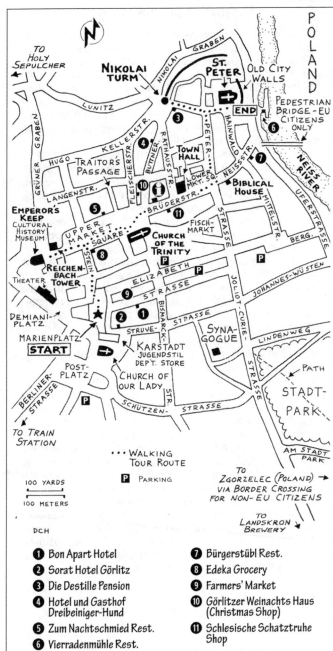

TO HOLY SEPULCHER

NIKOLAI TURM

ST. PETER

OLD CITY WALLS

END

POLAND

PEDESTRIAN BRIDGE – EU CITIZENS ONLY

NEISSE RIVER

NIKOLAI GRABEN

LUNITZ

KELLERSTR.

RATHAUSSTR.

BÜTTNER

TOWN HALL

PETER-

HAINWALD

NEISSSTR.

UFERSTRASSE

GRÜNER GRABEN

HUGO

TRAITOR'S PASSAGE

LANGENSTR.

FLEISCHERSTR.

BRÜDERSTR.

LOWER MKT. SQ.

BIBLICAL HOUSE

MITTELSTR.

EMPEROR'S KEEP

CULTURAL HISTORY MUSEUM

UPPER MARKET SQUARE

STEIN

FISCH-MARKT

STRASSE

BERG.

REICHEN-BACH TOWER

THEATER

ELIZABETH

STRASSE

CHURCH OF THE TRINITY

BISMARCK-

JOLIOT-CURIE-STRASSE

JOHANNES-WÜSTEN

DEMIANI-PLATZ

STRUVE-

STRASSE

SYNA-GOGUE

LINDENWEG

MARIENPLATZ

START

POST-PLATZ

KARSTADT JUGENDSTIL DEPT. STORE

CHURCH OF OUR LADY

STR.

SCHÜTZEN- STRASSE

PATH

STADT-PARK

BERLINER STRASSE

TO TRAIN STATION

AM STADT PARK

••• WALKING TOUR ROUTE

P PARKING

TO ZGORZELEC (POLAND) → VIA BORDER CROSSING FOR NON-EU CITIZENS

TO LANDSKRON BREWERY

100 YARDS

100 METERS

DCH

❶ Bon Apart Hotel

❷ Sorat Hotel Görlitz

❸ Die Destille Pension

❹ Hotel und Gasthof Dreibeiniger-Hund

❺ Zum Nachtschmied Rest.

❻ Vierradenmühle Rest.

❼ Bürgerstübl Rest.

❽ Edeka Grocery

❾ Farmers' Market

❿ Görlitzer Weinachts Haus (Christmas Shop)

⓫ Schlesische Schatztruhe Shop

Görlitz: A Silesian Brew

Görlitz is a city with an identity crisis, much like the entire region of Silesia. Silesia, which has never been a "country" of its own, encompasses parts of Germany (where it's called "Schlesien"), Poland ("Śląsk"), and the Czech Republic ("Slezsko"). Silesians are proud of this diversity, and of their pragmatic ability to work and live peacefully with each other despite the borders that separate them. Just like the Silesians themselves, their cuisine, folk art, and customs are a mish-mash of German, Czech, and Polish.

Although founded as the village of Gorelec in 1071 by Slavic Sorbs, Görlitz came under the German sphere of cultural influence in the 12th century and has been predominantly German ever since. For most of its early existence, the city technically belonged to Bohemia, but was ceded to Saxony after the Peace of Prague in 1635. In 1815, Görlitz fell into Prussian hands at the Congress of Vienna and became the largest city in the province of Lower Silesia.

The city's unusual experience in World War II made it the unique place it is today: While Görlitz almost miraculously escaped destruction (only its bridge was bombed), it was split in two by the Potsdam Agreement in 1945. This treaty determined the Neisse River—which runs through the center of Görlitz—to be the border between Germany and Poland. The following year, Poland expelled all Germans from its country, which included booting them out of Silesia and, therefore, out of the Polish side of Görlitz.

This expulsion created two ethnically distinct halves: the German town of Görlitz on the west side of the river, and the Polish town of Zgorzelec, which is still part of Poland on the east. Although most German Silesians have long since abandoned any hope of re-establishing their lost homeland, they have gone to great efforts to stress the unity between Silesians of all ethnic backgrounds—Poles, Czechs, and Germans—by re-establishing cultural connections across the rivers and mountains. Czechs and Poles are strong participants at all city festivals. After German, the most common languages you'll hear spoken in the streets and see on signs in Görlitz are Polish and Czech. German Görlitz and Polish Zgorzelec recently completed construction of the bridge across the Neisse, destroyed during the war. Locals like to think this largely symbolic gesture makes Görlitz the most European city in Europe.

German tourists fill Görlitz on weekends during the summer, but since Americans haven't discovered Görlitz yet, it is a great chance to enjoy a real Back Door experience.

ORIENTATION

(area code: 03581)
With a population of about 66,000, Görlitz is the largest city in what's left of German Silesia. While Görlitz lost a third of its population to Poland in 1945, the historic center and most sights of interest to travelers remains in Germany. The compact Old Town (Altstadt), and almost everything to see and do, is an easy stroll roughly between Marienplatz and the western bank of the Neisse River. The focal point of the Old Town are the twin market squares, Upper (Obermarkt) and Lower (Untermarkt).

Tourist Information

The TI, called Görlitzinformation, sells maps (€1) and can book you a room (for a €3 fee). Information in English is sometimes sporadic (open Mon–Fri 9:00–18:30, Sat 10:00–16:00, Sun 10:00–14:00, closed Sun Jan–Feb, between Obermarkt and Untermarkt at Brüderstrasse 1, tel. 03581/475-723, www.eurotour.goerlitz.de). Pick up the €7 *Görlitz Town Guide,* a small but informative do-it-yourself walking tour. The handy, indispensable *Architectural Guide Through the Old Town of Görlitz* (€7) describes almost every building in the Old Town in a convenient flip-out format. To arrange for a guided tour in English, call 03581/475-728.

Arrival in Görlitz

Görlitz's train station, about a half-mile southwest of the city center, is a sight in itself. Built in 1901, the main hall is a pearl of Prussian *Jugendstil,* while the building itself is neoclassical. Follow Berlinerstrasse into town (15-min walk) or take tram #2 or #3 (€1.10, 5 min) to Demianiplatz.

Getting Around Görlitz

The communists left little Görlitz with a highly developed and efficient public transportation system (€1.10 per ride). All buses and trams converge at Demianiplatz. The Old Town is compact, so unless you're planning to visit the Holy Sepulcher or go out to the Landskron mountain, you'll probably only use public transit to get from the train station into the city center.

SELF-GUIDED WALK

Welcome to Görlitz

The joy of Görlitz is simply wandering the Old Town and appreciating the architecture. Begin this orientation walk at Marienplatz, the small square right outside the former city walls.

Marienplatz: The unique *Jugendstil* department store **Karstadt** (completed in 1911) has a richly decorated facade concealing an ornate glass-domed interior with intricate staircases and galleries. Behind Karstadt is the **Church of our Lady** (Frauenkirche), a 15th-century, late-Gothic church built near the hospital and poorhouse outside the city walls. To the north, the **Fat Tower** (Dicker Turm) is the second oldest tower in the city's defensive network. Although the tower itself is Gothic (from 1270), it's topped by a copper Renaissance cupola. The tower was attached to the so-called Women's Gate (Frauen Tor) in 1477. It's decorated with a sandstone relief of the Görlitz city coat of arms, featuring a Bohemian lion and a Silesian black eagle—representing Görlitz as an independent and free city.

• *Walk down Steinstrasse and onto the...*

Upper Market Square (Obermarkt): This square dates from the 13th century, and is lined with mainly Baroque houses. The **Reichenbach Tower** dominates the western end of the square.

The tower formed the western city wall and dates from the 13th century, although the cylindrical portion was added in 1485 and is topped with a Baroque cupola from 1782. The tower housed city guards and watchmen—who among other things kept a lookout for fires— until the last "tower family" moved out in 1904. Inside is an impressive collection of armaments and an interesting exhibit on the daily lives of the tower's occupants (€3.50, ticket also includes Emperor's Keep, Tue–Sun 10:00–17:00, closed Mon, Platz des 17. Juni, tel. 03581/671-355). The view from the top is worth the 165 steps.

In 1490, Görlitz strengthened its city fortifications by building a circular bastion outside Reichenbach Tower. The structure came to be known as the **Emperor's Keep** (Kaisertruz) when the Swedish troops made their last stand against the Imperial Saxon army during the Thirty Years' War. Since then, the Emperor's Keep has been used as an archive and today houses the Cultural History Museum. The museum is worth a visit for a look at the historical models of Görlitz that show the intact city walls (€3.50, ticket also includes Reichenbach Tower, Tue–Sun 10:00–17:00, closed Mon).

Görlitz Architecture

Although no bombs fell on Görlitz during World War II, the city didn't escape partial destruction during the Thirty Years' War and the ravages of three great city fires. Each wave of devastation allowed Görlitz to rebuild in the architectural style of the time. The results are an astonishing collection of exemplary buildings from every architectural era: Gothic, Renaissance, Baroque, *Gründerzeit* (late 19th century), and *Jugendstil*. The East German government placed the entire city under a protection order, rescuing it from the bleak communist aesthetic of the late 20th century. More than 3,700 buildings are registered historical monuments. This, combined with energetic reconstruction, makes Görlitz the gem that it is today.

In 1245, Franciscan monks consecrated the **Church of the Trinity** (Dreifaltigkeitskirche) at the southeast side of Obermarkt. Although originally a Romanesque structure, renovations in 1380 gave the church its current late-Gothic appearance. The church houses some interesting furniture, ornately carved choir stalls, and a large carved Gothic altar triptych (free, daily 9:00–18:00, tel. 03581/311-311). When the Reformation took hold in Silesia in 1563, the monks were forced to surrender the keys to the Church of the Trinity.

The church's **tower** is unusually thin (the locals call it the *Mönch*, or "Monk"). The clock doesn't keep very good time, thanks to one in a series of Cloth-Maker Rebellions. In the Middle Ages, Görlitz was run by the powerful guilds of the cloth trade and the brewers, who neglected the rights of their workers and forbade non-members from practicing their trades. Finally, in the early 16th century, the workers rose up against the corrupt city council, who allowed the guilds to continue their unfair practices. The rebels ended their meetings punctually at midnight to avoid the night watchmen who would be on the other side of town at that hour. But the city council was one step ahead: They ordered the church bell to chime seven minutes before midnight to fool the conspirators out onto the street and into the waiting arms of the guard. Fourteen of the conspirators were executed, and 25 more banished from the city. To this day, the bell chimes seven minutes early.

Across the square is the **Traitor's Passage** (Verrätergasse), a dark and sinister passageway used by the instigators of the rebellion to sneak in and out of the main marketplace.

• *To leave Obermarkt, walk down...*

Brüderstrasse: This street, connecting Obermarkt and Untermarkt, is home to one of the finest collections of Renaissance houses in Europe. The orange-and-gray house at the end of Brüderstrasse (#8) claims to be Germany's oldest Renaissance civic building (from 1526). As you pass Schwarzestrasse, look left. The street's flying buttresses are typical of Görlitz's Old Town. These two are remnants of a series of brick barriers used to keep insurgents out of the inner city during the Cloth-Maker Rebellions.

• *At the end of Brüderstrasse, you'll reach...*

Lower Market Square (Untermarkt): The remarkably well-preserved Untermarkt is one of Germany's most impressive squares. Typical of Central European squares, it's built up in the

middle to make maximum use of this prime real estate. The square shows just how prosperous the cloth trade made Görlitz.

The building at #14 (east end of the square) housed the city **scales** and was one of the most important commercial buildings in the city since, at its peak, over 1,000 wagons per day entered the

city. Everything had to be weighed and duties paid here. The late-Gothic ground floor, which housed the scales, is topped off with three Renaissance levels. The column-topping busts are a virtual Who's Who of the town's masons and scale-masters.

Around the corner from the scales, on the northern edge of the square, the city established a **commodity exchange** at the beginning of the 18th century. The building was also a kind of department store used to drive simple street vendors away from the financial center. With the rabble banished, the Baroque building with adorning portal was a favored place for merchants to meet and deal.

Diagonally across the market on the corner of Peterstrasse is the **City Apothecary** (Ratsapotheke). The owner attempted

to transform a Gothic building into a Renaissance masterpiece, but ended up only incorporating the two styles. The two sundials on the southern facade were added in 1550. The left one (Solarium) displays the time using the Arabic, local, Roman, and Babylonian clocks. The dial on the right (Arachne, "spider" in Greek) displays the position of the planets and the signs of the

zodiac. The City Apothecary houses one of the city's best cafés.

• *Untermarkt is dominated by the tall Gothic tower of the...*

Town Hall: Görlitz had no town hall until 1350, when the city purchased this building from a prominent citizen. The tower was extended to 195 feet in 1368. A lightning strike blew the top off the tower on July 9, 1742, prompting the addition of the current Baroque turret. The tower houses two clocks. The upper clock measures day, month, and phase of the moon, while the lower clock tells the time. The warrior's head used to stick out his tongue every hour, but now just seems to open his mouth. The date inscribed on the clock, 1584, commemorates the year when Bartholomäus Sculteus, an astronomer and mathematician, first divided the clock into 12 points. Sculteus also helped develop the Gregorian calendar. The city honored Sculteus, a Görlitz native, by being the first city in Germany to adopt the new calendar and clock. The Town Hall stairs represent the height of Görlitz Renaissance sculpture and lead from the street level to the building's then-main entrance. City officials used the balcony to make public announcements and decrees. If you look closely at the statue of Justice (1591), she's not blindfolded—the city, in other words, is the highest authority.

• *For evidence that Görlitz is definitely a Protestant town, head down Neissstrasse to #29. There you'll find the...*

Biblical House: Since the Church banned religious depictions on secular buildings, the carvings on the Biblical House made it clear that the Reformation had come to stay. The houses in the Neissstrasse all burned to the ground in 1526. Hanz Heinz, a cloth trader, purchased this house and rebuilt it completely in the Renaissance style. The house is named after the sandstone reliefs decorating the facade between the first and second floor parapets. The top level represent the New Testament, with (from left to right) the Annunciation, birth of Jesus, Jesus' baptism, the Last Supper, and the Crucifixion. The bottom row depicts the creation of Eve, the fall of man, Isaac's sacrifice, Moses receiving the Ten Commandments, and Moses banishing serpents.

• *Backtrack to Untermarkt and hang a left onto...*

Peterstrasse: This is yet another impressive street. Look inside #14—the staircase seems to hang in mid-air. The house at #6 is a perfect example of renovations gone wrong: The building is Renaissance, with Gothic doors and windows, ionic columns, and Baroque decorations—the mishmash doesn't really work, does it?

At the end of Peterstrasse, you can turn either right or left. Left leads to the **Nikolaiturm.** The oldest of Görlitz's towers marks site of the original village of Gorelec. The Nikolaiturm, like all of the city-wall towers, got a facelift that replaced its pointy top with its current round dome in the 18th century. The city walls and gates were destroyed in 1848—the stones were used to build the Jägerkaserne, a barracks off in the distance to the left

of the Nikolaiturm. The only remaining section of the city wall is now a pleasant park that curves around from the base of the Nikolaiturm to the back of the Church of St. Peter. Alternatively, to the right of the park entrance, a small alleyway (Karpfengurnd) snakes its way back to the Peterstrasse.

• *If you turn right at the end of Peterstrasse, you'll reach the...*

Church of St. Peter (Peterskirche): The church was completed—after many setbacks, landslides, and Hussite invasions—in 1457, and renovated after fire destroyed the interior in 1691. The spires were added in 1890. The facade looks like a thousand other Gothic churches, but it's what's inside that counts: The Silesian-Italian Eugenio Casparini's **Sun Organ** (Sonnenorgel) is a spectacular, one-of-a-kind musical instrument and the center of Görlitz's musical life since 1701. The organ gets its name not from the golden sun at the center (which spins when air is pushed through the pipe), but for the circularly arranged pipes that shoot out like the sun's rays. Take in a free concert Thursday or Sunday at noon (Nov–March Sun only). The colorful baptistery, from 1617, is also worth a look.

• *Your walk is finished. Consider visiting some of Görlitz's other sights (described below), or relax with a local Landskron beer.*

SIGHTS

▲Synagogue—Görlitz had a modest Jewish community from the Middle Ages until the mid-1930s, but the Jews all but disappeared by 1945. The synagogue's impressive rectangular tower rises above a saddled roof. The *Jugendstil* prayer hall is spanned by a shallow cupola. The interior of the structure was damaged during the *Kristallnacht* pogrom, but the building remained standing not only due to the strength of the reinforced concrete structure, but because the Nazi leader of Görlitz lived next door and feared his own house would catch fire. The unused building is currently being renovated and will be used as a pan-European house of learning and understanding (Otto-Müllerstrrasse 6).

▲▲▲Holy Sepulcher (Heiliges Grab)—One of Görlitz's most unique and interesting sights, this is the only complete and relatively accurate replica of the garden of Gethsemane and the holy places in Jerusalem, as they appeared in the 15th century. After making a pilgrimage to Jerusalem, Georg Emmerich commissioned this site as an offering to those who could not make such a journey themselves (built 1480–1503). The first building is the two-story Chapel of the Holy Cross. Reflecting the traditional belief that Christ was crucified on the site of Adam's grave, the crypt represents the tomb of Adam with the Golgotha Chapel above. Next door is the Salbhaus, a tiny chapel with a statue of Mary anointing Jesus' dead body. Finally, the Church of the Holy Sepulcher is a much smaller version of the original, but nonetheless a fabulous fusion of Middle Eastern and European architecture. Medieval pilgrims to this site purchased a *Görlitzer Scheckel*—gold, silver, or pewter, according to their means—as payment to the church and symbol of their pilgrimage. To this day entry to the shrine is technically free, but you're expected to buy a *Scheckel* (Mon–Fri 10:00–16:00, Sun 11:00–16:00, closed Sat, Heilige-Grab-Strasse 79, tram #1, #2, or #3 to Heilige Grab, www.heiligesgrab-goerlitz.de).

▲▲**Landskron Brewery**—Beer has been brewed in Görlitz since the 12th century. The last remaining (and best) brewery is Landskron. The brewery offers tours in German, but the staff tries to be accommodating to English-speakers. In the end, it's all about the taste samples anyway. There are two versions: the ".33l Tour" (€5, 1.5 hrs) or the ".5l Tour" (€8, 2.5 hrs). Contact the brewery in advance to check the tour schedule and reserve (An der Landskronbrauerei 116, tel. 03581/246-121, www.landskron.de, besichtigung@landskron.de). In the summer, the brewery hosts a myriad of concerts and other events.

▲**Landskrone**—On the outskirts of the city is a dormant volcano that stretches 1,376 feet above sea level. The city of Görlitz purchased the Landskrone from the aristocracy and incorporated it into the city in 1440. The volcano provided wood for building (especially for rebuilding the town after fire) and basalt for cobblestones, and gave the city a commanding view over the area to defend against marauding robber-barons. The observation tower on top came in the 18th century, and a small restaurant in 1844 (although the current version was rebuilt in 1951). The entire area is a park, ideal for short hikes to the top. To get here, take tram #2 to the stop Biesnitz/Landeskrone.

Near Görlitz

Three Silesian towns near Görlitz offer an interesting and diverse glimpse into this unique crossroads of cultures.

▲▲▲**Zgorzelec**—When everything east of the Neisse River (and, farther north, the Oder River) became a part of Poland, Görlitz lost its eastern suburb. By 1946, Poles transplanted from Belarus and the Ukraine eliminated all traces of the German past and created the city of Zgorzelec. On both sides of the river, government and citizenry are making great strides to glue the city back together (at least culturally) in a united Europe. A walk across the bridge into Poland is an interesting experience and offers a stark contrast to wonderfully restored Görlitz. Zgorzelec is the obviously the less wealthy part of the city, but offers a fine collection of patrician and burgher houses (along ulica Warszawska), albeit in desperate need of repair. Once across the bridge, turn to the right and up the hill to reach the Upper Lusatian Memorial Hall (nowadays the Dum Kultury, or Civic House of Culture), a memorial to Kaiser Wilhelm I.

Important Note: The bridge near the end of the Neisstrasse is only for citizens of the European Union. Everybody else has to cross farther south, down the river, at the main bridge crossing point. This is better for you anyway, since the main part of Zgorzelec is closer to that border. Americans and Canadians need a passport, but no visa, to cross into Poland.

Zittau and Oybin Castle (Burg Oybin)—Although Zittau is a splendid city in its own right, with pretty squares and a Town Hall by Schinkel, the real reason to come here is to take the narrow-gauge railroad to the castle ruins at Oybin. Bohemian Emperor Charles IV built the fortress and monastery Burg Oybin in the 14th century. The structure fell into disuse by the 16th century and was repeatedly struck by lightning in the 18th and 19th centuries. The ruins are huge and fun to poke around, and the views into the unique geological formations of the Zittau Mountains are grand (castle entry-€3.50, daily April–Oct 9:00–18:00, Nov–March 10:00–16:00, www.burgundkloster-oybin.de).

Bautzen/Budyšin—This town, about halfway between Dresden and Görlitz, is the cultural capital of the Sorbs (or "Wends," as they are known in the U.S.). The Sorbs—not to be confused with the Serbs of the former Yugoslavia, much farther south—are of Slavic descent, and still speak a distinct language that's a hybrid of Polish and Czech. About 20,000 Sorbs live in Germany, making up the country's only indigenous ethnic minority.

Bautzen's dual language signs and slightly Mediterranean feel of spacious squares and public fountains, combined with intact city walls and a tower that's more off-center than Pisa's, make this town a perfect stopover between Dresden and Görlitz. Bautzen is also home to Germany's only Simultaneous Church, a house of worship shared by Catholics on one side and Protestants on the other. Germany's best spicy mustard comes from Bautzen. For more information on the town, see www.bautzen.de.

SHOPPING

Görlitzer Weinachts Haus celebrates Christmas all year long. Stop here for good deals on traditional crafts such as nutcrackers, incense burners shaped like smoking men, and nativity scenes.

Big draws are traditional paper stars from Herrnhut, hand-blown Sorb glass eggs, and Thuringian glass (Mon–Fri 10:00–18:00, Sat 10:00–14:00, closed Sun, Fleischerstrasse 19, just off Obermarkt—look for the huge nutcracker out front).

Schlesische Schatztruhe is one-stop shopping for all your Silesian souvenir needs: books, posters, maps, cookbooks, and more. This is the first place to stop for Silesian ceramics and "Polish pottery" from Bolesławiec (Bunzlau in German). Their *Streusselkuchen* pastry seems to stay fresh forever (Mon–Fri 9:00–19:00, Sat 10:00–19:00, Sun 10:00–18:00, Brüderstrasse 13, tel. 03581/410-956, www.schlesien-heute.de).

SLEEPING

\$\$ Bon Apart is a comfortable hotel with an eclectic interior design that can only be described as "Gothic meets Baroque." It's a great value, with the best breakfast buffet in town. The rooms and suites have kitchens, and they brew their own beer (Sb-€60–90, Db-€70–90, 1-person suite-€110, 2-person suite-€130, family suites-€170-225, Elisabethstrasse 41, tel. & fax 03581/48080, www.bon-apart.de, info@bon-apart.de).

\$\$ Sorat Hotel Görlitz offers good, basic rooms for a fair price in a *Jugendstil* villa built in 1901 (Sb-€66–76, Db-€86–96, includes champagne breakfast buffet, Struvestrasse 1, near Marienplatz behind Karstadt department store, tel. 03581/406-577, fax 03581/406-579, www.sorat-hotels.com).

\$ Die Destille (literally, "The Distillery") is a clean, friendly, family-run pension with well-apportioned rooms near the Nikolaiturm. A good breakfast is left in the refrigerator near your room, allowing you to have breakfast whenever you want. During renovation of the building in the 1990, workers discovered a *mikveh* (ritual Jewish bath) in the basement (Sb-€46, Db-€65, cash only,

---

Sleep Code

(€1 = about \$1.20, country code: 49, area code: 03581)
S = Single, **D** = Double/Twin, **T** = Triple, **Q** = Quad, **b** = bathroom, **s** = shower only. Unless otherwise noted, credit cards are accepted, English is spoken, and breakfast is included.

To help you sort easily through these listings, I've divided the rooms into three categories, based on the price for a standard double room with bath:

\$\$ Higher Priced—Most rooms €70 or more.
\$ Lower Priced—Most rooms less than €70.

Nikolaistrasse 6, tel. & fax 03581/405-302, www.destille-goerlitz .de).

$ Hotel und Gasthof Dreibeiniger-Hund (literally "Three-Legged Dog"), down the street from Die Destille, is a small, meticulously restored 14th-century pension offering 13 cozy and romantic rooms (Sb-€47, Db-€67, cash only, book ahead in summer, Büttnerstrasse 13, 03581/423-980, www.dreibeinigerhund.de).

EATING

Silesians are a hearty people, and their cooking combines German, Polish, and Czech elements into one of Germany's most interesting regional cuisines. The Silesian specialty is *Schlesisches Himmelreich* (literally "Silesian Heaven"), a mix of pork roast and ham with stewed fruit in a white sauce served with dumplings. For dessert, try Silesian *Streusselkuchen,* a yummy crumb cake available everywhere. Landskron is Görlitz's ubiquitous brew and one of the best pilsners in Germany.

Zum Nachtschmied offers solid Silesian food at good prices in a neat village-blacksmith atmosphere. There's been a restaurant in this location since the 13th century. Try one of the excellent *Pfannen* dishes, served in a cast-iron skillet. This is one of the few places in Görlitz that has the rare, but out-of-this-world, Landskron Hefeweizen on tap (daily 11:00–15:00 & 18:00–23:00, Obermarkt 18, tel. 3581/411-657).

The **Dreibeiniger-Hund** (see "Sleeping," above) has a personal and homey restaurant. Regional cuisine with fresh and seasonal specialties make the "Dog" a must. In summer, sit outside under the sprawling oak tree (daily 11:00–23:00, Büttnerstrasse 13, tel. 03581/423-980).

Die Destille (also recommended under "Sleeping," above) is a delightful restaurant with a friendly staff and great views of the Nikolaiturm. They excel at extremely traditional Silesian dishes, including the best *Schlesisches Himmelreich* in Görlitz (daily 12:00–23:00, Nikolaistrasse 6, tel. 03581/405-302).

Vierradenmühle, Germany's easternmost restaurant, is the perfect place to ponder the division and reunification of Europe. The restaurant sits on top of a water filtration station and former power plant (with museum) in the Neisse River, so the eastern foundation wall is actually the German-Polish border. Don't let the historical aside distract you from the wonderful Silesian cooking and fresh Landskron (Mon–Sat 11:00–24:00, Sun 10:00–22:00, at the end of Neissestrasse at Hotherstrasse 20, tel. 03581/406-661, www.vierradenmuehle.de).

Good eateries abound on **Neisstrasse,** stretching from Untermarkt to the river. Almost every building on the street was once a brewery. The pick of the litter is the **Bürgerstübl** (#27), which was recently renovated with the help of the Landskron brewery and has a secret beer-garden in the back.

Picnic Supplies: The only grocery store in the city center is the **Edeka,** at the corner of Steinstrasse and Obermarkt (Mon–Fri 8:00–18:30, Sat 8:00–16:00, closed Sun). For fresh fruit and produce, try the **Farmer's Market,** on Elisabethstrasse across from the Bon-Apart Hotel (Mon–Fri 6:00–18:00, Sat 6:00–12:00, closed Sun).

TRANSPORTATION CONNECTIONS

From Görlitz by Train to: Zittau (hrly, 45 min), **Bautzen** (about hrly, 30–45 min; Bautzen-bound trains continue on to Dresden), **Dresden** (hrly, 1.5 hrs), **Berlin** (hrly, 2.5 hrs, transfer in Cottbus). Train info: tel. 11861 (€0.50/min).

BERLIN

No tour of Germany is complete without a look at its historic and reunited capital. Over the last decade, Berlin has been a construction zone. Standing over ripped-up tracks and under a canopy of cranes, visitors witnessed the rebirth of a great European capital. Today, as we enjoy the thrill of walking over what was the Wall and through the well-patched Brandenburg Gate, it's clear that history is not contained in some book, but an exciting story that we are a part of. Historians find Berlin exhilarating.

Berlin had a tumultuous 20th century. After the city was devastated in World War II, it was divided by the Allied powers: The American, British, and French sectors became West Berlin, and the Soviet sector, East Berlin. That division was set in stone in 1961 when the Soviets boxed in the East by building the Berlin Wall. The Wall lasted 28 years. In 1990, less than a year after the Wall fell, the two Germanys officially became one. When the dust settled, Berliners from both sides of the once-divided city faced the monumental challenge of reunification.

While the work's far from over, a new Berlin has emerged. Berliners joke they don't need to go anywhere because their city's always changing. Spin a postcard rack to see what's new. A five-year-old guidebook on Berlin covers a different city.

Reunification has had its negative side, and locals are fond of saying, "the Wall survives in the minds of some people." Some "Ossies" (impolite slang for Easterners) miss their security. Some "Wessies" miss their easy ride (military deferrals, subsidized rent, and tax breaks). For free spirits, walled-in West Berlin was a citadel of freedom within the East.

The city government has been eager to charge forward with

little nostalgia for anything that was Eastern. Big corporations and the national government have moved in, and the dreary swath of land that was the Wall and its notorious "death strip" has been transformed. City planners are boldly taking Berlin's reunification and the return of the national government as a good opportunity to make Berlin a great capital once again.

Today Berlin feels like the nuclear fuel rod of a great nation. It's so vibrant with youth, energy, and an anything-goes-and-anything's-possible buzz that Munich feels spent in comparison. Berlin is both extremely popular and surprisingly affordable. As a booming tourist attraction, the year 2005 was, by far, its best year yet. And 2006 promises to be even better.

Planning Your Time

Because of Berlin's inconvenient location, try to enter and/or leave by either night train or plane. On a three-week trip through Germany and Austria, I'd give Berlin at least two days and spend them this way:

Day 1: Begin your day getting oriented to this huge city: Either take the 10:00 "Discover Berlin" guided walking tour offered by Original Berlin Walks (see page 356); or follow my "Do-It-Yourself Orientation Tour" by bus to the Reichstag (page 360), then continue by foot down Unter den Linden (page 370). Focus on sights along Unter den Linden, including the Reichstag dome (most crowded 10:00–16:00; best to visit 8:00–9:00 or 21:00–22:00) and Museum Island (with the Pergamon and Egyptian museums).

Day 2: Today concentrate on the sights in central Berlin, and in eastern Berlin south of Unter den Linden. Spend the morning lost in the paintings at the Gemäldegalerie. After lunch, hike via Potsdamer Platz to the Topography of Terror exhibit and along the surviving Zimmerstrasse stretch of Wall to the Museum of the Wall at Checkpoint Charlie. If you're not museum-ed out yet, swing by the magnificent Jewish Museum. Finish your day in the lively East—particularly the once glum, then edgy, now fun-loving and trendy Prenzlauer Berg district.

If you're maximizing your sightseeing, you could squeeze a hop-off, hop-on bus tour into Day 1. Remember that the Reichstag dome and the Museum of the Wall are open late.

Berlin merits additional time if you have it. There's much more in the city. And the concentration camp at Sachsenhausen and the palace at Potsdam are both worth side-trips.

World Cup Warning: Germany hosts the World Cup soccer championships in 2006 (see page 6)—and Berlin will be at the center of the action. In addition to hosting matches on June 13, 15, 20, 23, and 30, Berlin is the site of the kick-off celebration on June

Berlin Sightseeing Modules

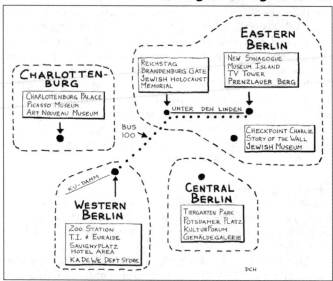

8 and the final championship match on July 9. If you'll be in Berlin in June or July, plan for a packed city.

ORIENTATION

(area code: 030)

Berlin is huge, with 3.4 million people. But the tourist's Berlin can be broken into four digestible chunks:

1. Eastern Berlin: The former East Berlin has the highest concentration of worthwhile sights and colorful neighborhoods. Near the famous Brandenburg Gate, you'll find the Reichstag building, Pariser Platz, and the new Holocaust Memorial. From the Brandenburg Gate, the famous Unter den Linden boulevard runs east through eastern Berlin, passing Museum Island (Pergamon Museum, Egyptian Museum, and Berlin Cathedral) on the way to Alexanderplatz (TV Tower). The intersection of Unter den Linden and Friedrichstrasse is emerging as the new center of the city. South of Unter den Linden, you'll find the delightful Gendarmenmarkt square, most Nazi sites (including the Topography of Terror exhibit), the Jewish Museum, the best Wall-related sights (Museum of the Wall at Checkpoint Charlie and East Side Gallery), and the colorful Turkish neighborhood of Kreuzberg. North of Unter den Linden are these worth-a-wander neighborhoods: around Oranienburger Strasse (Jewish Quarter and New Synagogue), Hackescher Markt, and Prenzlauer Berg (several recommended hotels and a very lively restaurant/nightlife zone).

2. Central Berlin: Potsdamer Platz, Kulturforum (Gemäldegalerie, New National Gallery, Museum of Arts and Crafts, Musical Instruments Museum, and Philharmonic Concert Hall), and the giant Tiergarten park.

3. Western Berlin: This is the area around the Bahnhof Zoo (Zoo Train Station) and the grand Kurfürstendamm Boulevard, nicknamed "Ku'damm" (transportation hub, tours, information, shopping, and recommended hotels). The East is all the rage. But the West, while staid, is still vibrant, with lots of big-name stores and destination restaurants that keep Berliners coming back. During the Cold War, this "Western Sector" was the hub for Western visitors. Capitalists visited the West, with a nervous side-trip behind the Wall into the grim and foreboding East. (Cubans, Russians, Poles, and Angolans stayed in and did their sightseeing in the East.) Remnants of this Iron Curtain-era Western focus have left today's visitors with a stronger focus on the Ku'damm and Bahnhof Zoo than the district really deserves.

4. Charlottenburg Palace Area: The palace and nearby museums (Picasso and Art Nouveau), on the western edge of the city center. This area is of least interest to a visitor on a tight schedule.

Tourist Information

Berlin's TIs are run by a for-profit agency working for the city's big hotels, which colors the information they provide. The main TI is five minutes from Bahnhof Zoo, in the once-impressive **Europa Center** (with Mercedes symbol on top, enter outside to left at Budapester Strasse 45, Mon–Sat 10:00–19:00, Sun 10:00–18:00, tel. 030/250-025, www.berlin-tourist-information.com). Smaller TIs are in the **Brandenburg Gate** (daily 10:00–18:00, longer in summer) and at the base of the TV Tower at **Alexanderplatz** (daily 10:00–18:00, longer in summer).

The TIs sell a good city map (€1), the "*Schaulust*" Museumspass (described below), and various local publications, including the *Berlin Calendar* (see below). They also offer a €3 room-finding service (but only to hotels that give them kickbacks—many don't). Most hotels have free city maps.

"*Schaulust*" *Museumspass:* This €15, three-day combo-ticket covers many of Berlin's national museums (including the Pergamon, Egyptian Museum, and Gemäldegalerie) as well as several others (such as the Jewish Museum). Entry to most of these museums costs €5–8, so the Museumspass pays for itself if you visit at least three of the included museums (not valid for special exhibitions, purchase at TI or participating museums). Note that if a museum is closed on one of the days of your Museumspass, you have access to that museum on the fourth day to make up for lost time. Also be aware that the national museums covered by this pass are different from the private attractions and sights covered by the transit-and-discount WelcomeCard (see "Getting Around Berlin," below).

Alternative Tourist Information: EurAide's information office, located in the Bahnhof Zoo Reisezentrum (in front of train station, by taxi stand), provides an excellent service. They have answers to all your questions about Berlin or train travel around Europe. It's staffed by Americans (so communication is simple), and they have a knack for predicting your needs, then publishing free fliers to serve you (Mon–Fri 9:00–12:30 & 13:30–17:00, closed Sat–Sun and all Jan, great opportunity to get future train and *couchette* reservations nailed down ahead of time, Prague Excursion passes available—see page 410, www.euraide.com). EurAide also gives out a good, free city map and sells all public-transit tickets (including the €5.80 day pass) and the Welcome Card (see "Getting Around Berlin," page 355)—making a trip to the TI probably unnecessary. To get the most out of EurAide, have your questions ready before your visit.

Local Publications: Various magazines can help make your time in Berlin more productive (all available at the TI and most newsstands). **Berlin Programm** is a comprehensive German-language monthly that lists upcoming events and museum hours (€1.60, www.berlin-programm.de). The German-English, bimonthly, TI-produced **Berlin Calendar** magazine offers timely features on Berlin and a partial calendar of events (also €1.60). **Exberliner Magazine** is the only real English-language monthly (mostly for expat Americans, but also helpful for curious travelers). It has an edgy, youthful focus and gives a fascinating insider's look at this fast-changing city (€2, www.exberliner.com). Or pick up the free, informative magazines that promote the upstart tour companies **New Berlin Walks** and **Insider Tours** (described on page 357).

Arrival in Berlin

By Train: Berlin's long-range plans are clear: Before long, virtually all international trains will arrive at Europe's biggest train station, the mostly underground **Lehrter Bahnhof** (a.k.a. Berlin Hauptbahnhof-Lehrter Bahnhof). Berliners are already calling it the "transfer station," where the national train system meets the city train system. And, as there's really nothing a human being could want to do in the Lehrter neighborhood—except transfer—that's exactly what you'll do here. Upon arrival, you'll hop on the U-Bahn or S-Bahn and finish your trip into Berlin; if you have a train ticket or valid railpass, you can ride the S-Bahn—but not the U-Bahn—to your final destination for free. The push is to get the

Lehrter Bahnhof up and running in time for the World Cup (June and July of 2006).

If you arrive at Lehrter Bahnhof and you'd rather get to Bahnhof Zoo (where many of my recommended hotels are), simply catch any subway train west for three stops (more details on Bahnhof Zoo below). If you're sleeping in the Prenzlauer Berg neighborhood, take the S-Bahn from Lehrter Bahnhof east for two stops to Hackescher Markt, then catch the M1 tram north.

The main station in western Berlin is **Bahnhof Zoo** (a.k.a. Bahnhof Zoologischer Garten). Until Lehrter Bahnhof is finished, those coming from Western Europe will probably land at Zoo (rhymes with "toe"). It's small, well-organized, and handy (lockers and baggage check available in back of station). But, as Lehrter Bahnhof takes over, Bahnhof Zoo will soon go from being a grand train hub to just an oversized subway station.

Upon arrival by train at Bahnhof Zoo, orient yourself like this: Inside the station, follow signs to Hardenbergplatz. Step into this busy square filled with city buses, taxis, the transit office, and derelicts. The Original Berlin Walks start from the curb immediately outside the station at the top of the taxi stand (see "Tours," page 356). Between you and the McDonald's across the street is the stop for bus #100 (departing to the right for my "Do-It-Yourself Orientation Tour," page 360). Turn right and tiptoe through the riffraff to the eight-lane highway, Hardenbergstrasse. Walk to the median strip and stand with your back to the tracks. Ahead you'll see the black, bombed-out hulk of the Kaiser Wilhelm Memorial Church and the Europa Center (Mercedes symbol spinning on roof), which houses the main TI. Just ahead on the left, amid the traffic, is the BVG transport information kiosk (where you can buy a €5.80 day pass covering the subway and buses, and pick up a free subway map). If you're facing the church, my recommended western Berlin hotels are behind you to your right (see page 399).

By Plane: For information on Berlin's airports, see "Transportation Connections," page 409.

Helpful Hints

Medical Help: If you need to see a doctor, dial "Call a Doc" at tel. 01804-2255-2362 (www.calladoc.com), a non-profit referral service designed for tourists. Payment is arranged between you and the doctor, and is likely far more affordable than similar care in the U.S.

Museum Hours: Many major Berlin museums are closed on Monday. All national museums, including the Pergamon and Gemäldegalerie (plus others as noted in "Sights," page 363), are free for the last four hours on Thursdays (that is, if it closes at 18:00, it's free from 14:00 on; www.museen-berlin.de).

Monday Activities: Since many museums are closed on Monday, save the day for Berlin Wall sights, the Reichstag dome, my "Do-It-Yourself Orientation Tour" and strolling Unter den Linden (described below), walking/bus tours, the Jewish Museum, churches, the zoo, or shopping along Kurfürstendamm (Ku'damm) Boulevard or at the Kaufhaus des Westens (KaDeWe) department store. Be warned that when Monday is a holiday—as it is several times a year—museums are open then and closed Tuesday.

Addresses: Many Berlin streets are numbered with odd and even numbers on the same side of the street, often with no connection to the other side (for example, Ku'damm #212 can be across the street from #14). To save steps, check the white street signs on curb corners; many list the street numbers covered on that side of the block.

Internet Access: You'll find cheap, fast Internet access 24/7 at several **easyInternetcafé** outlets. Handy locations include: Hardenbergplatz 2 (across from Bahnhof Zoo, next to McDonald's), Ku'damm 224 (10-min walk from Bahnhof Zoo), and Rathaus-Passagen (on Alexanderplatz). Buy a ticket at the self-service machines and follow the English instructions. Unused time can be used at any locale for up to a week.

Bookstore: Berlin Story, a big, fun-loving bookshop, has the best selection anywhere in town of English-language books on Berlin. They also have a fascinating and free little museum in the back with a model of Unter den Linden from 1930 and a room showing a good 25-minute Berlin history video (in English). The shop has a knowledgeable staff and stocks an amusing mix of knickknacks and East Berlin nostalgia souvenirs (daily 10:00–19:00, Unter den Linden 40, www.berlinstory.de).

Laundry: Schnell und Sauber Waschcenter is a handy launderette near my recommended western Berlin hotels (€5–9 wash and dry, daily 6:00–23:00, Leibnizstrasse 72, 4 blocks west of Savignyplatz, near intersection with Kantstrasse). Near my recommended hotels in Prenzlauer Berg, try **Holly's Wasch-Theke** (€5–9 wash and dry, includes detergent, daily 7:00–23:00, last load in at 21:30, attached café, Kollwitzstrasse 93, tel. 030/443-9210).

Travel Agency: Last Minute Flugbörse can help you find a flight in a hurry (next to TI in Europa Center, Mon–Sat 10:00–20:00, closed Sun, tel. 030/2655-1050, www.lastminuteflugboerse.de). **American Express** is near Unter den Linden, at Friedrichstrasse 172 (Mon–Fri 9:00–19:00, Sat 10:00–13:00, closed Sun, travel agency tel. 030/201-7400; for traveler's checks, call tel. 0800-185-3100).

Getting Around Berlin

Berlin's sights spread far and wide. Right from the start, commit yourself to the fine public-transit system.

By Subway and Bus: The U-Bahn (*Untergrund-Bahn*, Berlin's subway), S-Bahn (*Schnell-Bahn*, or "fast train," mostly above ground and with fewer stops), *Strassenbahn* (streetcars), and all buses are consolidated into one "BVG" system that uses the same tickets. *Erwachsener* means "adult"—anyone 14 or older. Here are your options:

• A basic ticket *(Einzel Fahrschein)* for two hours of travel in one direction on buses or subways—€2.10. It's easy to make this ticket stretch to cover several rides...as long as they're all in the same direction.

• A cheap short-ride ticket *(Kurzstrecke)* for a single short ride of six bus stops or three subway stations, with one transfer—€1.30.

• A day pass *(Tageskarte)* covering zones A and B, the city proper—€5.80 (good until 3:00 the morning after). To get out to Potsdam, you need a ticket covering zone C—€6. (For longer stays, a 7-day *Tageskarte* is also available—€25, or €30 including zone C; or buy 2 WelcomeCards, described below.)

• The Berlin/Potsdam **WelcomeCard** gives you transportation in zones A, B, and C, and 25-percent discounts on lots of minor and a few major museums (including Checkpoint Charlie), sightseeing tours (including the recommended Original Berlin Walks), and music and theater events (€16/48 hrs, €22/72hrs; valid for an adult and up to 3 kids younger than 14). If you plan to cover a lot of ground during a two- or three-day visit, this is usually the best transit deal.

Buy your U- or S-Bahn tickets from machines at stations. (They are also sold at BVG pavilions at train stations and airports, the TI, and EurAide.) Don't be afraid of the automated machines: First select the type of ticket you want, then load in the coins or paper bills. As you board the bus or tram, or enter the subway system, punch your ticket in a red or yellow clock machine to validate it (or risk a €40 fine). The double-decker buses are a joy (can buy ticket on bus), and the subway is a snap. The S-Bahn (but not U-Bahn) is free with a validated Eurailpass (but it starts use of a flexi-day).

Sections of the U- or S-Bahn sometimes close temporarily for repairs. In this situation, a bus route often replaces the train (*Ersatzverkehr*, or "replacement transportation").

By Taxi: Taxis are easy to flag down, and taxi stands are common. A typical ride within town costs €10–16, and a cross-town trip (for example, Bahnhof Zoo to Alexanderplatz) will run you around €25. A local law designed to help people get safely and affordably home from their subway station late at night is handy for tourists any time of day: A short ride of no more than two kilometers (1.25 miles) is a flat €3. (Ask for "*Kurzstrecke, drei euro, bitte.*") To get this cheap price, you must hail a cabbie on the street rather than go to a taxi stand (from a stand, it's a minimum €5 charge). Cabbies aren't crazy about the law, so insist on the price and be sure to keep the ride short.

By Bike: Be careful—in Berlin, motorists don't brake for bicyclists (and bicyclists don't brake for pedestrians). Fortunately, some roads and sidewalks have special red-painted bike lanes. Just don't ride on the regular sidewalk—it's *nicht erlaubt* (not allowed).

In western Berlin, you can rent good bikes at the **Bahnhof Zoo** left-luggage counter, next to the lockers at the back of the station (daily 6:15–21:00, €10/day, €23/3 days, €35/7 days, requires passport and €50 cash deposit; bikes come with lock, air pump, and mounted basket; there's a limited supply of bikes and they've been known to run out). In the east, **Fahrradstation** near the Friedrichstrasse S-Bahn station has a huge number of bikes (€15/24 hrs, daily 9:00–19:00, closed Sun in winter, Dorotheenstrasse 30, tel. 030/2045-4500).

TOURS

Walking Tours

Berlin is an ideal city to get to know with a walking tour—it's a ▲▲▲ experience. The city is a battle zone of extremely competitive and creative walking tour companies, all offering employment to American and British expats and students and cheap, informative tours to visiting travelers. The Original Berlin Walks was, as its name implies, the original. Smelling a business opportunity, some of its former guides and others spliced guerilla business tactics into O.B.W.'s established model and started their own walking tour companies. All give variations on the same themes: general introductory walk, Hitler and Nazi sites walk, communism walk, and day trips to Potsdam and the Sachsenhausen Concentration Camp. The youth-oriented outfits also do nightly pub crawls. By next year, there will likely be other companies with guides on street corners handing out fliers to promote their tours (for which they are not paid, but rely on tips). For details, see the various Web sites. Here's my take on the current situation.

The Original Berlin Walks—This is the most established operation, with the most serious tours aiming at a clientele with a longer attention span. They don't offer "free tours" or pub crawls. I've enjoyed the help of O.B.W.'s high-quality, high-energy guides for many years, and routinely hire them when my tour groups are in town. I've always been impressed with the caliber of the guides that founder Nick Gay has assembled. Tours generally cost €12

(€9 with the WelcomeCard or if you're under 26). Readers of this book get an additional €1 discount on their first tour in 2006. For any of these tours, just show up at the taxi stand in front of Bahnhof Zoo. Many tours have a second departure point 30 minutes later in eastern Berlin's Hackescher Markt S-Bahn station, outside Häagen-Dazs.

The Original Berlin Walks' itineraries include the following: **Discover Berlin** introductory walk (daily year-round at 10:00, April–Oct also daily at 14:30); **Infamous Third Reich Sites** (May–Sept Wed at 10:00, Sat–Sun at 10:00 and 14:30; departs from Bahnhof Zoo meeting point only); **Jewish Life in Berlin** (Mon at 10:00 May–Sept); and **Potsdam** (€15, inquire about schedule, see page 395). Many of the Third Reich and Jewish history sights are difficult to pin down without these excellent walks. Also consider their six-hour trip to the **Sachsenhausen Concentration Camp,** intended "to provide a challenging history lesson with universal applications" (€15; May–Sept Tue, Thu, Fri, Sat, and Sun at 10:15; March–April and Oct Tue and Sun at 10:15; departs from Bahnhof Zoo meeting point only, requires transit day ticket with zone C—or buy from guide, call office for specifics). Confirm tour schedules at EurAide or by phone with Nick or his wife and partner, Serena (tel. 030/301-9194, www.berlinwalks .de, info@berlinwalks.de). As you pay for Original Berlin Walks up front, tipping is not expected. Nick can also arrange private guides (€130/3 hrs, e-mail him for details).

Insider Tours and New Berlin Walks—Unlike other European cities, there are no regulations controlling who can give tours in Berlin. Lots of upstart companies come and go, but these two feisty and aggressive newcomers are well-established. They target a younger crowd and offer free intro tours. Their guides make their money off of tips, cross-selling their specialty tours, and the hugely successful pub crawls (with profit supplemented by featured bars). Each company publishes a wonderful, free Berlin guide magazine (distributed all over town and worth grabbing for the sightseeing information even if you're not taking their walks). They offer essentially the same itineraries as Original Berlin Walks and roughly this formula: You take their introductory walk for free, then choose—if you wish—to take any of their other walks (€10–12 each). For all the details, see their magazines or visit www .insidertour.com or www.newberlintours.com.

Insider Tours and New Berlin Walks each offer €10 pub crawls (or some would say, "pub brawls"). They leave from Hackescher Markt at 20:30 or 21:00, generally visit four bars and two clubs, and are a great way to get drunk with new English-speaking friends from around the world while getting a peek at the Berlin bar scene...invaded by 50 loud tourists.

Berlin at a Glance

▲▲▲**Reichstag** Germany's historic Parliament building, topped with a striking dome you can ascend. **Hours:** Daily 8:00–24:00, last entry 22:00. Long lines—go very early (8:00) or late (after 21:00).

▲▲▲**Museum of the Wall at Checkpoint Charlie** Moving museum near the former site of the famous border checkpoint between the American and Soviet sectors, with stories of brave escapes during the Cold War and the gleeful days when the wall fell. **Hours:** Daily 9:00–22:00.

▲▲▲**Jewish Museum Berlin** User-friendly museum celebrating Jewish culture, in a highly conceptual building. **Hours:** Daily 10:00–20:00, Mon until 22:00.

▲▲▲**Gemäldegalerie** Germany's top collection of 13th- through 18th-century European paintings, featuring Dürer, van Eyck, Rubens, Titian, Raphael, Caravaggio, and more. **Hours:** Tue–Sun 10:00–18:00, Thu until 22:00, closed Mon.

▲▲**Berlin Wall** Mostly gone, but parts of the wall are still visible—including the East Side Gallery, the Documentation Center at Nordbahnhof, and a chunk near the Topography of Terror (former SS and Gestapo headquarters). **Hours:** Always open.

▲▲**Brandenburg Gate** One of Berlin's most famous landmarks, a multi-arched gateway, at the former border of East and West. **Hours:** Always open.

▲▲**Memorial to the Murdered Jews of Europe** New Holocaust memorial featuring nearly 3,000 symbolic pillars, plus an exhibition about the Jewish victims of Hitler. **Hours:** Memorial always open; exhibition open Tue–Sun 10:00–20:00, closed Mon.

▲▲**Unter den Linden** Leafy boulevard through the heart of former East Berlin, lined with some of the city's top sights. **Hours:** Always open.

▲▲**Pergamon Museum** World-class museum of classical antiquities on Museum Island (just off Unter den Linden), featuring the fantastic second-century B.C. Greek Pergamon Altar. **Hours:** Tue–Sun 10:00–18:00, Thu until 22:00, closed Mon.

▲▲**Egyptian Museum** Proud home (on Museum Island) of the exquisite 3,000-year-old bust of Queen Nefertiti. **Hours:** Daily 10:00–18:00, Thu until 22:00.

▲▲**Gendarmenmarkt** Inviting square bounded by twin churches (one with a fine German history exhibit), a chocolate shop, and a concert hall. **Hours:** Always open.

▲▲**New Synagogue** Largest prewar synagogue in Berlin, destroyed in WWII, with a facade that has since been rebuilt. **Hours:** May–Aug Sun–Mon 10:00–20:00, Tue–Thu 10:00–18:00, Fri 10:00–17:00, closed Sat; Sept–April Sun–Thu 10:00–18:00, Fri 10:00–14:00, closed Sat.

▲**Prenzlauer Berg** One of Berlin's most colorful and lively neighborhoods, worth exploring. **Hours:** Always bustling.

▲**Potsdamer Platz** The "Times Square" of old Berlin, long a postwar wasteland, now rebuilt with huge glass skyscrapers, an underground train station, and—covered with a huge canopy—the Sony Center mall with eateries. **Hours:** Always open.

▲**Musical Instruments Museum** Impressive collection of historic instruments. **Hours:** Tue–Fri 9:00–17:00, Sat–Sun 10:00–17:00, closed Mon.

▲**Kaiser Wilhelm Memorial Church** Evocative destroyed church in the heart of the former West Berlin, with a modern annex. **Hours:** Church open Mon–Sat 10:00–16:00, closed Sun, annex open daily 9:00–19:00.

▲**Käthe Kollwitz Museum** Features the black-and-white art of the local artist who conveyed the suffering of Berlin's stormiest century. **Hours:** Wed–Mon 11:00–18:00, closed Tue.

▲**Kaufhaus des Westens (KaDeWe)** The "Department Store of the West"—the biggest on the Continent—is where East Berliners flocked when the wall came down. **Hours:** Mon–Fri 10:00–20:00, Sat 9:30–20:00, closed Sun.

▲**Charlottenburg Palace** Baroque Hohenzollern palace, on the edge of town. **Hours:** Tue–Sun 10:00–17:00, closed Mon.

▲**Berggruen Collection** Notable works by Picasso, Matisse, van Gogh, Cézanne, and Paul Klee. **Hours:** Tue–Sun 10:00–18:00, closed Mon.

▲**Bröhan Museum** Collection of Art Nouveau and Art Deco furnishings. **Hours:** Tue–Sun 10:00–18:00, closed Mon.

Brewer's Berlin Tours—For a more exhaustive (or, for some, exhausting) walking tour of Berlin, consider Brewer's Berlin Tours. These are run by Terry, a former British embassy worker in East Berlin, and his well-trained staff. Their All-Day Berlin tours are legendary for their length, and best for those with a long attention span and a serious interest in Berlin (€12, tour lasts 8 hrs or more, departs daily at 10:00 from Kaiser Wilhelm Memorial Church near Bahnhof Zoo, or 30 min later from Australian Ice Cream Shop at Friedrichstrasse U- and S-Bahn station, tel. 030/2248-7435, mobile 0177-388-1537, www.brewersberlintours.com).

City Bus Tours

For bus tours, the old, sedate Severin & Kühn company dominates. You have two options.

1. Full-blown bus tours: Severin & Kühn offers a long list of bus tours in and around Berlin; their three-hour "Big Berlin Tour" is a good introduction (€22, daily at 10:00 and 14:00, live guides in 2 languages, from Ku'damm 216, tel. 030/880-4190, www.severin -kuehn-berlin.de). Their office on Karl-Liebknecht-Strasse is across from the TV Tower in eastern Berlin.

2. Hop-on, hop-off circle tours: Several companies make a circuit of the city (City-Circle Sightseeing is good, offered by Severin & Kühn). The TI has all the brochures. The tours offer unlimited hop-on, hop-off privileges for their routes (about 14 stops) with a recorded commentary (€19, daily 10:00–18:00, last bus leaves from Ku'damm at 16:00, 2–4/hr, 2-hr loop). Just hop on where you like and pay the driver. On a sunny day when some double-decker buses go topless, these are a photographer's delight, cruising slowly by just about every major sight in town.

SELF-GUIDED TOUR

Do-It-Yourself Orientation Tour: Bus #100 from Bahnhof Zoo to the Reichstag

This tour narrates the route of convenient bus #100, which connects my recommended hotel neighborhood in western Berlin with the sights in eastern Berlin. If you have the €19 and two hours for a hop-on, hop-off bus tour (described above), take that instead. But this short €2.10 bus ride is a fine city introduction. Bus #100 is a sightseer's dream, stopping at Bahnhof Zoo, Europa Center/Hotel Palace, Victory Column (Siegessäule), Reichstag, Brandenburg Gate, Unter den Linden, Pergamon Museum, and ending at Alexanderplatz. While you could ride it to the end, it's more fun to get out at the Reichstag and walk down Unter den Linden at your own pace (using my commentary on page 370). When combined with the self-guided walk down Unter den Linden,

Berlin

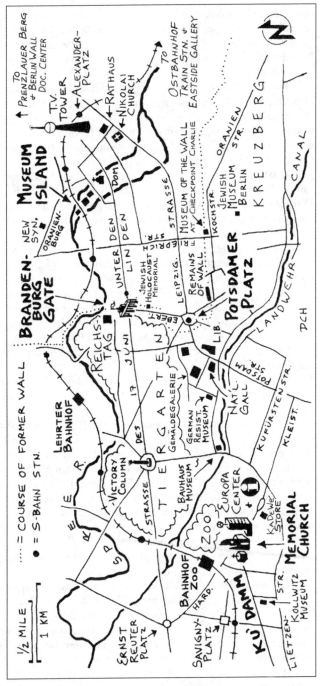

this tour merits ▲▲▲. Before you take this bus into eastern Berlin, consider checking out the sights in western Berlin (see page 391). Note that as Berlin adjusts itself around its new mega-station, Lehrter Bahnhof, bus #100 will likely swing farther north to this station before reaching the Reichstag.

The Tour Begins: Buses start from Hardenbergplatz in front of the Bahnhof Zoo. Buses come every 10 minutes, and single tickets are good for two hours—so take advantage of hop-on-and-off privileges. Climb aboard, stamp your ticket (giving it a time), and grab a seat on top. This is about a 10-minute ride. The upcoming stop will light up on the reader board inside the bus.

➋ On your left and then straight ahead, before descending into the tunnel, you'll see the bombed-out hulk of the **Kaiser Wilhelm Memorial Church,** with its postwar sister church (described on page 391) and the **Europa Center.** This is the "West End" shopping district, a bustling people zone with big department stores nearby. When the Wall came down, East Berliners flocked to this area's department stores (especially KaDeWe, described on page 393). Soon after, the biggest, swankiest new stores were built in the East. Now the West is trying to win those shoppers back by building even bigger and better shopping centers around Europaplatz. Across from the Zoo station, the under-construction Zoofenster tower will be taller than all the buildings you see here.

Emerging from the tunnel, on your immediate right you'll see the Berlin tourist information office.

➋ At the stop in front of Hotel Palace: On the left, the elephant gates mark the entrance to the **Berlin Zoo** and its aquarium (described on page 393).

➋ Driving down Kurfürstenstrasse, you'll pass several Asian restaurants—a reminder that, for most, the best food in Berlin is not German. Turning left, with the huge Tiergarten park in the distance ahead, you'll cross a canal and see the famous **Bauhaus Archive** (an off-white, blocky building) behind the trees on the right. The Bauhaus movement ushered in a new age of modern architecture that emphasized function over beauty, giving rise to the blocky steel-and-glass skyscrapers in big cities around the world. On the left is Berlin's new embassy row. The big turquoise wall marks the communal home of all five Nordic embassies. This building is perfectly "green," run entirely by solar power.

➋ The bus enters a 400-acre park called the **Tiergarten,** packed with cycling paths, joggers, and—on hot days—nude sunbathers. Straight ahead, the **Victory Column** (Siegessäule, with the gilded angel, described on page 387) towers above this vast city park that was once a royal hunting grounds, now nicknamed the "green lungs of Berlin."

⊃ On the left, a block after leaving the Victory Column: The 18th-century, late-rococo **Bellevue Palace** is the German White House. Formerly a Nazi VIP guest house, it's now the residence of the federal president (whose power is mostly ceremonial). If the flag's out, he's in.

⊃ Driving along the Spree River: This park area was a residential district before World War II. Now, on the left-hand side, it's filled with the buildings of the **national government.** The huge brick "brown snake" complex was built to house government workers—but it didn't sell, so now its apartments are available to anyone. A metal Henry Moore sculpture entitled *Butterfly* floats in front of the slope-roofed House of World Cultures (Berliners have nicknamed this building "the pregnant oyster"). The modern tower (next on left) is a carillon with 68 bells (1987).

Somewhere around here, the bus may detour north to the new **Lehrter Bahnhof.** Stick with it, and you'll veer back south towards the Reichstag.

⊃ Leap out at the Platz der Republik stop. (While you could continue on bus #100, it's better on foot from here.) Through the trees on the left you'll see Germany's new and sprawling **Chancellory.** Started during the more imperial rule of Helmut Kohl, it's now considered overly grand. The big park is the **Platz der Republik,** where the Victory Column stood until Hitler moved it. The gardens were recently dug up to build underground train tracks serving the Lehrter Bahnhof (across the field between the Chancellory and the Reichstag). Watch your step—excavators found a 250-pound, undetonated American bomb.

⊃ Just down the street stands an old building with a new dome...the **Reichstag.**

SIGHTS

Eastern Berlin
I've arranged the following sights in the order of a convenient self-guided orientation walk, picking up where my "Do-It-Yourself Orientation Tour" (above) leaves off. Allow a comfortable hour for this walk from the Reichstag to Alexanderplatz, including time for lingering (but not museum stops).

Near the Brandenburg Gate
▲▲▲**Reichstag Building**—The parliament building—the heart of German democracy—has a short but complicated and emotional history. When it was inaugurated in the 1890s, the last emperor, Kaiser Wilhelm II, disdainfully called it the "house for chatting." It was from here that the German Republic was proclaimed in 1918. In 1933, this symbol of democracy nearly burned

down. While the Nazis blamed a Communist plot, some believe that Hitler himself (who needed what we'd call today a "new Pearl Harbor") planned the fire, using it as a handy excuse to frame the Communists and grab power. As World War II drew to a close, Stalin ordered his troops to take the Reichstag from the Nazis by

May 1 (the workers' holiday). More than 1,500 Nazis made their last stand here—extending World War II by two days. On April 30, 1945, it fell to the Allies. It was hardly used from 1933 to 1999. For the building's 101st birthday in 1995, the Bulgarian-American artist Christo wrapped it in silvery-gold cloth. It was then wrapped again in scaffolding, rebuilt by British architect Lord Norman Foster, and turned into the new parliamentary home of the Bundestag (Germany's lower house). To many Germans, the proud resurrection of the Reichstag symbolizes the end of a terrible chapter in German history.

The **glass cupola** rises 155 feet above the ground. Its two sloped ramps spiral 755 feet to the top for a grand view. Inside the dome, a cone of 360 mirrors reflects natural light into the legislative chamber below. Lit from inside at night, this gives Berlin a memorable night-light. The environmentally friendly cone also helps with air circulation, drawing hot air out of the legislative chamber and pulling in cool air from below.

Hours: Free, daily 8:00–24:00, last entry 22:00, most crowded 10:00–16:00 (wait in line to go up—good street musicians, metal detectors, no big luggage allowed, some hour-long English tours when parliament is not sitting, tel. 030/2273-2152, www.bundestag .de).

Crowd-Beating Tips: Berlin is now Germany's biggest tourist attraction. Lines here can be terrible. If possible, visit before 9:00 or after 21:00. Pick up the English-language flier just before the security checkpoint to have something to read as you wait. Those with table reservations at the Dachgarten rooftop restaurant don't wait in the long lines. Go straight to the front and tell them you have a reservation. Reserve in advance by phone or e-mail (€15–26 entrées with a view, daily 9:30–16:30 & 18:30–24:00, tel. 030/2262-9933, kaeferreservierung.berlin@feinkost-kaefer.de).

⊘ Self-Guided Tour: As you approach the building, look above the door, surrounded by stone patches from WWII bomb damage, to see the motto and promise: *Dem Deutschen Volke* ("To the German People"). The open, airy lobby towers 100 feet high, with 65-foot-tall colors of the German flag. See-through glass doors show the **central legislative chamber.** The message: There will be no secrets in government. Look inside. The seats are "Reichstag blue," a lilac-blue color designed by the architect to brighten the otherwise gray interior. The German eagle (a.k.a. the "fat hen") spreads his wings behind the podium. Notice the doors marked "Yes," "No," and "Abstain"...the Bundestag's traditional "sheep jump" way of counting votes (for critical and close votes, all 669 members leave and vote by walking through the door of their choice).

Ride the elevator to the base of the glass **dome.** Take time to study the photos and read the circle of captions—an excellent exhibit telling the Reichstag story. Then study the surrounding architecture: a broken collage of new on old, like Germany's history. Notice the dome's giant and unobtrusive sun-screen that moves as necessary with the sun. Peer down through the sky-light to look over the shoulders of the elected representatives at work.

For Germans, the best view from here is down—keeping a close eye on their government.

Start at the ramp nearest the elevator and wind up to the top of the **double ramp.** Take a 360-degree survey of the city as you hike: First, the big park is the **Tiergarten,** the "green lungs" of Berlin. Beyond that is the **Teufelsberg,** or Devil's Hill (built of rubble from the destroyed city in the late 1940s and famous during the Cold War as a powerful ear of the West—notice the telecommunications tower on top). Knowing the bombed-out and bulldozed story of their city, locals say, "You have to be suspicious when you see the nice, green park." Find the **Victory Column** (Seigessäule, moved by Hitler in the 1930s from in front of the Reichstag to its present position in the Tiergarten). Next, scenes of the new Berlin spiral into your view—**Potsdamer Platz,** marked by the conical glass tower that houses Sony's European headquarters. The yellow building to the right is the Berlin Philharmonic Concert Hall, marking the museums at the Kulturforum. Continue circling left, and find the green chariot atop the **Brandenburg Gate.** A monument to Roma (Gypsy) victims of the Holocaust will be built between the Reichstag and Brandenburg Gate. (The Roma, as disdained by the Nazis as were the Jews, lost the same percentage of their population to Hitler.) The new **Jewish Holocaust Memorial** stretches south of Brandenburg Gate. Next, you'll see **former East Berlin** and the city's next huge construction zone, with a forest of 300-foot-tall skyscrapers in the works. Notice the TV Tower (with the Pope's Revenge—explained on page 378), the Berlin Cathedral's massive dome, the red tower of the city hall, the golden dome of the New Synagogue, and the Reichstag's **Dachgarten Restaurant** (see above). Follow the train tracks in the distance to the left toward Berlin's huge, new central train station, **Lehrter Bahnhof**. Just in front of it, alone in a field, is the Swiss Embassy. This used to be surrounded by buildings, but now it's the only one left. Complete your spin tour with the blocky **Chancellory,** nicknamed by Berliners "the washing machine." It may look like a pharaoh's tomb, but it's the office and home of Germany's most powerful person, the chancellor (currently Angela Merkel).

Memorial to Politicians Who Opposed Hitler—As you leave the Reichstag, look for the row of slate slabs imbedded in the ground by the park across from the main entry (looks like a fancy slate bicycle rack). This is a memorial to the 96 politicians (the equivalent of our congressmen) who were murdered and persecuted because their politics didn't agree with Chancellor Hitler's. They were part of the weak and ill-fated attempt at post-WWI democracy in Germany, the Weimar Republic. These were the people who could have stopped Hitler...so they became his first victims. Each slate slab remembers one man—his name, party (mostly KPD, or Communists, and SPD, or Socialists), and date and location of death—generally in concentration camps. (*KZ* means concentration camp.) They are honored here because it's in front of the building in which they worked.

To the Brandenburg Gate: Let's continue our walk and cross what was the Berlin Wall. Leaving the Reichstag, follow the busy road to the left, around the building. At the rear of the building (across the street, at the edge of the park) is a small **memorial to East Berliners** who died trying to cross the wall. Look at the faces of these exceptionally free spirits. The wall was built on August 13, 1961. These people died within months—mostly by trying to swim the river.

The Brandenburg Gate is ahead. Stay on the park side of the street for a better view of the gate. The road construction is an American taxpayer-funded project. As the U.S. Embassy needs a buffer zone from traffic for security concerns, the road is being moved back in order to be replaced by a bigger pedestrian zone.

As you cross at the light, notice the double row of **cobblestones**—this goes all around the city, marking where the Wall used to stand. (You could go directly to the Jewish Holocaust Memorial from here, but we'll go through the Brandenburg Gate first, then reach the memorial through Pariser Platz.)

▲▲Brandenburg Gate (Brandenburger Tor)—The historic Brandenburg Gate (1791) was the grandest, and is the last survivor, of 14 gates in Berlin's old city wall (this one led to the neighboring

The Berlin Wall

The 100-mile "Anti-Fascist Protective Rampart," as it was called by the East German government, was erected almost overnight in 1961 to stop the outward flow of people (3 million leaked out between 1949 and 1961). The 13-foot-high Wall *(Mauer)* had a 16-foot tank ditch, a no-man's-land (or "death strip") that was 30 to 160 feet wide, and 300 sentry towers. During its 28 years, there were 1,693 cases when border guards fired, 3,221 arrests, and 5,043 documented successful escapes (565 of these were East German guards).

The carnival atmosphere of those first years after the Wall fell is gone, but hawkers still sell "authentic" pieces of the Wall, DDR (East German) flags, and military paraphernalia to gawking tourists. When it fell, the Wall was literally carried away by the euphoria. What managed to survive has been nearly devoured by a decade of persistent "Wall peckers."

Americans—the Cold War victors—have the biggest appetite for Wall-related sights, and a few bits and pieces remain for us to seek out. Berlin's single best Wall-related sight is the Museum of the Wall at Checkpoint Charlie (see page 381). Actual fragments of Wall that are close to the center include the short stretch at Zimmerstrasse/Wilhelmstrasse (near the Topography of Terror exhibit; see page 382), and the longer East Side Gallery (near the Ostbahnhof; see page 384). Farther afield is the Berlin Wall Documentation Center along Bernauer Strasse (near S-Bahn: Nordbahnhof; see page 386).

For a tour along a mostly nonexistent chunk of the former Wall, you can rent a *Hear We Go* audioguide about the Wall at Checkpoint Charlie. The audioguide leads you from the checkpoint along Zimmerstrasse to Potsdamer Platz, and then brings you back via Leipziger Strasse and Mauerstrasse (€7.50, 80 min).

city of Brandenburg). The gate was the symbol of Prussian Berlin... and later the symbol of a divided Berlin. It's crowned by a majestic four-horse chariot with the Goddess of Peace at the reins.

Napoleon took this statue to the Louvre in Paris in 1806. After the Prussians defeated Napoleon and got it back (1813), she was renamed the Goddess of Victory.

The gate sat unused, part of a sad circle dance called the Wall, for more than 25 years. Now postcards all over town show the ecstatic day—November 9, 1989—

The Brandenburg Gate, Arch of Peace

Two hundred years ago, the Brandenburg Gate was designed as an arch of peace, crowned by the Goddess of Peace and showing Mars sheathing his sword. The Nazis misused it as a gate of triumph and aggression. Today a Room of Silence is dedicated to the peaceful message of the original Brandenburg Gate (daily 11:00–18:00). As you enter the room and consider the history of Berlin—which is carefully not dedicated to any particular religion—you may be inspired to read the prayer of the United Nations:

"Oh Lord, our planet Earth is only a small star in space. It is our duty to transform it into a planet whose creatures are no longer tormented by war, hunger, and fear, no longer senselessly divided by race, color, and ideology. Give us courage and strength to begin this task today so that our children and our children's children shall one day carry the name of man with pride."

when the world enjoyed the sight of happy Berliners jamming the gate like flowers on a parade float. Pause a minute and think about struggles for freedom—past and present. (There's actually a special room built into the gate for this purpose—see above.) Around the gate, look at the information boards with pictures of how much this area changed throughout the 20th century. The latest chapter: The shiny white gate was completely restored in 2002 (but you can still see faint patches marking war damage). The TI within the gate is open daily from 10:00 to 18:00.

The Brandenburg Gate, the center of old Berlin, sits on a major boulevard running east to west through Berlin. The western segment, called Strasse des 17 Juni (named for a workers' uprising against the DDR government in the 1950s), stretches for four miles from the Brandenburg Gate and Victory Column (past the flea market—see page 387) to the Olympic Stadium. But we'll follow this city axis in the opposite direction, east, walking along what is known as Unter den Linden—into the core of old imperial Berlin and past what was once the palace of the Hohenzollern family who ruled Prussia and then Germany. The palace—the reason for just about all you'll see—is a phantom sight, long gone (though some Berliners hope to rebuild it). Alexanderplatz, which marks the end of this walk, is near the base of the giant TV Tower hovering in the distance.

Ponder the fact that you're standing in what was the so-called "death strip." Now cross through the gate, into...

▲**Pariser Platz**—"Paris Square," so named after the Prussians defeated Napoleon in 1813, was once filled with important government buildings—all bombed to smithereens in World War II. For decades, it was an unrecognizable, deserted no-man's-land. But now, sparkling new banks, embassies (the French Embassy rebuilt where it was before WWII), a palace of coffee (Starbucks), and a swanky hotel have filled in the void. The winners of World War II got prime real estate: The American, French, British, and Soviet (now Russian) embassies are all on or near this square.

Face the gate and look to your left. The **U.S. Embassy** once stood here, and a new one will stand in the same spot (due to be completed in 2008). This new embassy has been controversial; for safety's sake, Uncle Sam wanted it away from other buildings, but the Germans preferred it in its original location. A compromise was reached, building the embassy by the gate—but rerouting several major roads (at the expense of American taxpayers) to reduce the security risk. And, for good measure, there will be no front door to fortify. Throughout the world, American embassies are the most fortified buildings in town. Taking fortification one step further, the U.S. Embassy in Berlin will be reached by a tunnel that visitors will enter from the park across the big street opposite the Brandenburg Gate.

Just to the left, the **DZ Bank building** is by Frank Gehry, the unconventional American architect famous for Bilbao's organic Guggenheim Museum, Prague's Dancing House, Seattle's EMP, Chicago's Millennium Park, and Los Angeles' Walt Disney Concert Hall. Gehry fans might be surprised at the DZ Bank building's low profile. Structures on Pariser Platz are expected to be bland so as not to draw attention away from the Brandenburg Gate. (The glassy facade of the Academy of Arts, next to Gehry's building, is controversial for that very reason.) For your fix of the good old Gehry, step into the lobby and check out its undulating interior. It's a fish—and you feel like you're both inside and outside of it. Gehry's vision is explained on a nearby plaque.

The **Academy of Arts** (Akademie der Kunst), with its controversial glass facade, is next door. Its doors lead to a mall (daily 10:00–22:00), which leads directly to the vast...

▲▲Memorial to the Murdered Jews of Europe (Denkmal für die Ermordeten Juden Europas)—The new Holocaust memorial, consisting of 2,711 gravestone-like pillars and completed in 2005, is an essential stop for any visit to Berlin. This is the first formal German government-sponsored Holocaust memorial. Jewish-American architect Peter Eisenman won the competition for the commission (and built it on time and on budget—€27 million). It's controversial for the focus—just Jews. The government promises to make memorials to the other groups targeted by Hitler.

The pillars are made of hollow concrete, each chemically coated for easy removal of graffiti. The number of pillars, symbolic of nothing, is simply how many fit on the provided land.

Is it a labyrinth...symbolic cemetery...intentionally disorienting? The meaning is entirely up to the visitor to derive. The idea is for you to spend time pondering this horrible chapter in human history.

The pondering takes place under the sky. For the learning, you go under the field of concrete pillars to the state-of-the-art exhibition area. This studies the Nazi system of extermination, humanizes the victims, traces stories of individual families and collects vivid personal accounts, and lists 200 different places of genocide (all well-explained in English, free, Tue–Sun 10:00–20:00, closed Mon, www.stiftung-denkmal.de).

The location—where the Wall once stood—is coincidental. It's just a place where lots of people will experience it. The bunker of Nazi propagandist Joseph Goebbels was discovered during the work and left buried (under the northeast corner of the memorial). Hitler's bunker is just 200 yard away, under a nondescript parking lot. Such Nazi sites are intentionally left hidden to discourage neo-Nazi elements from creating a shrine.

Now backtrack to Pariser Platz, and begin strolling...

Along Unter den Linden

Unter den Linden is the heart of former East Berlin. In Berlin's good old days, Unter den Linden was one of Europe's grand boulevards. In the 15th century, this carriageway led from the palace to the hunting grounds (today's big Tiergarten). In the 17th century, Hohenzollern princes and princesses moved in and built their palaces here so they could be near the Prussian emperor.

Named centuries ago for its thousand linden trees, this was the most elegant street of Prussian Berlin before Hitler's time and the main drag of East Berlin after his reign. Hitler replaced the venerable trees—many 250 years old—with Nazi flags. Popular discontent actually drove him to replant linden trees. Today, Unter den Linden is no longer a depressing Cold War cul-de-sac, and its pre-Hitler strolling café ambience is returning.

As you walk toward the giant TV Tower, the big building you see jutting out into the street on your right is the **Hotel Adlon.** It hosted such notables as Charlie Chaplin, Albert Einstein, and Greta Garbo. This was where Garbo said, "I want to be alone," during the filming of *Grand Hotel*. And, perhaps fresher in your memory, this is where Michael Jackson shocked millions by dangling his little baby over the railing (2nd balcony up, center of facade). Destroyed by Russians just after World War II, the grand Adlon was rebuilt in 1996. See how far you can get inside.

The Unter den Linden S-Bahn station ahead of you is one of Berlin's former **ghost subway stations.** During the Cold War,

Unter den Linden

① Pariser Platz
② U.S. Embassy
③ Memorial to the Murdered Jews of Europe
④ Hotel Adlon
⑤ Russian Embassy
⑥ Komische Oper
⑦ Neustadtische Kirchstrasse
⑧ Berlin Story Bookstore
⑨ Frederick II Statue
⑩ Bebelplatz
⑪ Book Burning Memorial
⑫ Humboldt University
⑬ Neue Wache Memorial
⑭ German History Museum
⑮ Pergamon Museum
⑯ Egyptian Museum & Old National Gallery
⑰ Berlin Cathedral
⑱ Palace of the Republic
⑲ Marien Church
⑳ City Hall
㉑ TV Tower
㉒ Alexanderplatz
㉓ Gendarmenmarkt
㉔ German Cathedral
㉕ Hotel Unter den Linden

most underground train tunnels were simply blocked at the border. But a few Western lines looped through the East. To make a little hard Western cash, the Eastern government rented the use of these tracks to the West, but the stations (which happened to be in East Berlin) were strictly off-limits. For 28 years, the stations were unused, as Western trains slowly passed through, seeing only eerie DDR (East German) guards and lots of cobwebs. Literally within days of the fall of the Wall, these stations were reopened, and today they are a time warp (looking essentially as they did when built in 1931, with dreary old green tiles and original signage). Go down into the station, walk along the track (the walls are lined with historic photos of the Reichstag through the ages), and exit on the other side, following signs to *Russische Botschaft...* the Russian Embassy.

The **Russian Embassy** was the first big postwar building project in East Berlin. It's built in the powerful, simplified, neo-classical style Stalin liked. While not as important now as it was a few years ago, it's immense as ever. It flies the Russian white, red, and blue. Find the hammer-and-sickle motif decorating the window frames—a reminder of the days when this was the embassy of the U.S.S.R.

Continuing past the Aeroflot Airline offices, look across the street to the right to see the back of the **Komische Oper** (Comic Opera; program and view of ornate interior posted in window). While the exterior is ugly, the fine old theater interior—amazingly missed by WWII bombs—survives.

Across from Aeroflot is **Neustadtische Kirchstrasse.** This

street is a commercial waste-land—the fate of any street unlucky enough to host the U.S. Embassy. While cars are *verboten*, pedestrians are welcome to wander through. When the U.S. Ambassador moves into his impressive new digs by the Brandenburg Gate in 2008, this street will spring back to life.

Back on the main drag, next to Einstein Café (at #40), is a great bookstore, **Berlin Story.** In addition to a wide range of English-language books, this shop has a free museum (with a model of 1930s Unter den Linden) and a 25-minute English film about the history of Berlin (daily 10:00–19:00; for more details, see page 354). This is also a good opportunity to pick up some nostalgic knickknacks from the Cold War. The West lost no time in consuming the East; consequently, some are feeling a wave of nostalgia—or *Ost*-algia—for the old days of East Berlin. In recent local elections, nearly half of East Berlin's voters—and 6 percent of West Berliners—voted for the old Communist Party.

One symbol of that era has been given a reprieve. As you continue to Friedrichstrasse, look at the DDR-style pedestrian lights, and you'll realize that someone had a sense of humor back then. The perky red and green men—*Ampelmännchen*—were under threat of replacement by the far less jaunty Western signs. Fortunately, the DDR signals will be kept after all.

At **Friedrichstrasse,** look right. Before the war, the Unter den Linden/Friedrichstrasse intersection was the heart of Berlin. In the 1920s, Berlin was famous for its anything-goes love of life. This was the cabaret drag, a springboard to stardom for young and vampy entertainers like Marlene Dietrich. (Born in 1901, Dietrich starred in the first German "talkie" and then headed straight to

Hollywood.) Over the last few years, this boulevard—lined with super department stores (such as Galeries Lafayette, with its cool marble and glass waste-of-space interior, Mon–Sat 9:30–20:00, closed Sun; belly up to its amazing ground-floor viewpoint, or have lunch in its cafeteria—see page 408) and big-time hotels (such as the Hilton and Regent)—has slowly begun to replace Ku'damm as the grand commerce and café boulevard of Berlin. (More recently, the West is retaliating with some new stores of its own.) Across from Galeries Lafayette is American Express (handy for any train-ticket needs—see page 354).

If you continued down Friedrichstrasse, you'd wind up at the sights listed in "South of Unter den Linden," below—including the Museum of the Wall at Checkpoint Charlie (a 10-min walk from here). But for now, continue along Unter den Linden. You'll notice big, colorful **water pipes** around here, and throughout Berlin. As long as the city remains a big construction zone, it will be laced with these drainage pipes—key to any building project. Berlin's high water table means any new basement comes with lots of pumping out.

Continue down Unter den Linden a few more blocks, past the large equestrian statue of Frederick III ("the Great"), and turn right into the square called **Bebelplatz.** Stand on the glass window in the center.

Frederick the Great—who ruled from 1740 to 1786—established Prussia as a military power. This square was the center of the "new Rome" Frederick envisioned. His grand palace was just down the street (long since destroyed, but there's talk of rebuilding it—explained below).

Look down through the glass you're standing on (center of Bebelplatz): The room of empty bookshelves is a memorial to the notorious Nazi **book burning.** It was on this square in 1933 that staff and students from the university threw 20,000 newly forbidden books (like Einstein's) into a huge bonfire on the orders of the Nazi propaganda minister Joseph Goebbels. A memorial plaque nearby reminds us of the prophetic quote by the German Jewish philosopher Heinrich Heine. In 1820, he said, "When you start by burning books, you'll end by burning people." A century later, his books were among those that went up in flames on this spot.

Bebelplatz is bounded by great buildings. The **German State Opera** was bombed in 1941, rebuilt to bolster morale and to celebrate its centennial in 1943, and bombed again in 1945. The former **state library** is where Vladimir Lenin studied much of his exile away. If you climb to the second floor of the library and go through the door opposite the stairs, you can see a stained-glass window depicting Lenin's life's work with almost biblical reverence. On the ground floor is a great little student café with light food, Tim's

Canadian Deli (student prices—€2 plates, garden seating, Mon–Sat 7:00–20:00, closed Sun). The round, Catholic **St. Hedwig's Church**—nicknamed the "upside-down teacup"—was built to placate the subjects of Catholic lands Frederick added to his empire. (Step inside to see the cheesy DDR government renovation.)

Humboldt University, across Unter den Linden, was one of Europe's greatest. Marx and Lenin (not the brothers or the sisters) studied here, as did Grimm (both brothers) and more than two dozen Nobel Prize winners. Einstein, who was Jewish, taught here until taking a spot at Princeton in 1932 (smart guy).

Continue down Unter den Linden. The next square on your right holds the **Opera House**. The Opernpalais, preening with fancy prewar elegance, hosts a number of pricey restaurants. Its Operncafé, with the best desserts and the longest dessert bar in Europe, is popular with Berliners for their *Kaffee und Kuchen* (see page 407).

On the university side, the Greek temple-like building set in the small, chestnut tree-filled park is the **Neue Wache** (the emperor's "New Guardhouse," from 1816). When the Wall fell,

this memorial to the victims of fascism was transformed into a new national memorial. Look inside, where a replica of the Käthe Kollwitz statue, *Mother with Her Dead Son,* is surrounded by thought-provoking silence. This marks the tombs of Germany's unknown soldier and the unknown concentration camp victim. The inscription in front reads, "To the victims of war and tyranny." Read the entire statement in English (on wall, right of entrance). The memorial, open to the sky, incorporates the elements—sunshine, rain, snow—falling on this modern-day *pietà*.

After the Neue Wache, the next building you'll see is Berlin's pink-yet-formidable Zeughaus, or arsenal. Dating from 1695, it's considered the oldest building on the boulevard. It houses the **German History Museum** (Deutsches Historisches Museum, €2, daily 10:00–18:00, tel. 030/203-040, www.dhm.de). It's a two-part affair: the old, pink arsenal building (under renovation, but soon to open) and its new I. M. Pei–designed annex (temporary exhibits, now open). Beginning in 2007, the main building will house the permanent collection, with two huge rectangular floors packed with artifacts telling the story of Berlin—making this the top history museum in town. But for now, the big attraction is the far-out Pei architecture. Walk through the old arsenal to get to the new annex. From the old building (with the Pei glass canopy over its courtyard), you take a tunnel to the new wing, emerging under a striking glass spiral staircase that unites four floors with surprising views and lots of light. It's here that you'll experience why Pei—famous for his glass pyramid at Paris' Louvre—is called the "perfector of classical modernism," "master of light," and a magician of uniting historical buildings with new ones. (If you can't get in through the arsenal, venture down the street—Hinter dem Giesshaus—to the left of the museum to see the Pei annex.)

Next, Unter den Linden crosses the **Spree River.** Just before the bridge, wander left along the canal through a tiny but color-ful arts-and-crafts market (weekends only; a larger flea market is just outside the Pergamon Museum—see below). Canal tour boats leave from here (€7, 1 hr, departures on the half-hour, tour in German only but so lame it hardly matters). Then go back out to the main road and cross the bridge to...

Museum Island (Museumsinsel)

This island, home of Germany's first museums, is gradually being renovated to consolidate the art collections of East and West Berlin. Today it plays host to three great museums: the Pergamon (classical antiquities), the Altes Museum (housing the Egyptian Museum, with the bust of Queen Nefertiti), and the Old National Gallery (19th-century German Romantic painting). All of these museums are covered by the €15 Museumspass (see page 351) or a single €12 Museum Island ticket. Individual admissions are €8 each. Visit any of these museums, and other Museum Island attractions, before continuing our walk. Once you're finished, skip down to "Museum Island to Alexanderplatz," below, to resume the self-guided tour.

For 300 years, the island's big central square, the **Lustgarten,** has flip-flopped between being a military parade ground and a people-friendly park, depending upon the political tenor of the time. In 1999, it was made into a park again (read the history posted in corner opposite church). On a sunny day, it's packed with relaxing locals and is one of Berlin's most enjoyable public spaces.

▲▲**Pergamon Museum**—This world-class museum, part of Berlin's Collection of Classical Antiquities (Antikensammlung), stars the fantastic Pergamon Altar. From a second-century B.C. Greek temple, the altar shows the Greeks under Zeus and Athena beating the giants in a dramatic pig pile of mythological mayhem. Check out the action spilling onto the stairs. The Babylonian Ishtar Gate (glazed blue tiles from the 6th century B.C.) and many ancient Greek and Mesopotamian treasures are also impressive (€8, or €12 Museum Island ticket, or €15 Museumspass, free Thu after 18:00, open Tue–Sun 10:00–18:00, Thu until 22:00, closed

Mon, courtyard café, Am Kupfergraben, tel. 030/2090-5577). The excellent audioguide (free with admission, but €4 during free Thu extended hours) covers the museum's highlights. Don't mind the scaffolding. Renovation projects (due to last until 2008) may cause small sections of the museum to close temporarily in 2006, but the museum will remain open.

▲▲**Egyptian Museum (Ägyptisches Museum)**—Showing off one of the world's top collections of Egyptian art, this wonderfully presented new museum fills the second floor of Berlin's Altes Museum (Old Museum), facing the grassy Lustgarten park (€8, or €12 Museum Island ticket, or €15 Museumspass, free Thu after 18:00, open daily 10:00–18:00, Thu until 22:00, tel. 030/343-5730).

The curator welcomes you on the included audioguide and encourages a broader approach to the museum than just seeing its claim to fame, the bust of Queen Nefertiti (described below). The fine audioguide celebrates new knowledge about ancient Egyptian civilization and offers fascinating insights into work-a-day Egyptian life as it describes the vivid papyrus collection, slice-of-life artifacts, and dreamy wax portraits decorating mummy cases.

But let's face it: The main reason to visit is to enjoy one of the great thrills in art appreciation—gazing into the still-young and beautiful face of 3,000-year-old Queen Nefertiti, the wife of King Akhenaton. This bust of Queen Nefertiti (c. 1340 B.C.) is the

most famous piece of Egyptian art in Europe. Discovered in 1912, Nefertiti—with all the right beauty marks: long neck, symmetrical face, and just the right makeup—is called "Berlin's most beautiful woman." The bust never left its studio, but served as a master model for all other portraits of the queen. (That's probably why the left eye was never inlaid.) Buried for over 3,000 years, she was found in the early 1900s by a German team who, by agreement with the Egyptian government, got to take home any workshop models they found. Although this bust is not particularly representative of Egyptian art in general, it has become a symbol for Egyptian art by popular acclaim.

Old National Gallery (Alte Nationalgalerie)—This gallery, behind the Egyptian Museum/Altes Museum, shows 19th-century German Romantic art: man against nature, Greek ruins dwarfed in enchanted forests, medieval churches, and powerful mountains (€8, or €12 Museum Island ticket, or €15 Museumspass, free Thu after 18:00, open Tue–Sun 10:00–18:00, Thu until 20:00, closed Mon, tel. 030/2090-5801).

Berlin Cathedral (Berliner Dom)—This century-old church towers over Museum Island (€5 includes access to dome gallery, Mon–

Sat 9:00–20:00, Sun 12:00–20:00, until 19:00 in winter, www.berliner-dom.de; many organ concerts offered each week, ticket office on Lustgarten side, daily 10:00–18:00, tel. 030/2026-9136). Inside, the great reformers (Luther, Calvin, and company) stand around the brilliantly restored dome like stern saints guarding their theology. Frederick I rests in an ornate tomb (right transept, near entrance to dome). The 270-step climb to the outdoor dome gallery is tough, but offers pleasant, breezy views of the city at the finish line (last entry 45 min before closing). The crypt downstairs is not worth a look.

Across Unter den Linden (with the copper-tinted windows) is the decrepit...

Palace of the Republic—A symbol of the communist days, this was East Berlin's parliament building and futuristic entertainment complex. Although it officially has a date with the wrecking ball, its future is uncertain. Much of Frederick the Great's earlier palace (which stood where the Palace of the Republic stands today) actually survived World War II but was torn down by the communists since it symbolized the imperialist past. Now some Berliners want to rebuild Frederick's palace from scratch, exactly as it once was. Other Berliners insist that what's done is done. The current, Soviet-style building may be gone in 2006. But as of late 2005, there were still East Berliners and artists camping in it, insisting that it is part of the local heritage and should be saved.

Museum Island to Alexanderplatz

Continue walking down Unter den Linden. Before crossing the bridge (and leaving Museum Island), look right. The pointy twin spires of the 13th-century Nikolai Church mark the center of medieval Berlin. This Nikolai-Viertel (district) was restored by the DDR and was trendy in the last years of socialism. Today it's a lively-at-night riverside restaurant district.

As you cross the bridge, look left in the distance to see the gilded **New Synagogue dome,** rebuilt after WWII bombing (see page 385). Across the river to the left of the bridge is the giant SAS Radisson Hotel and new shopping center with a huge aquarium in the center. The elevator goes right through the middle of an undersea world (you can see it from the Radisson lobby). Here in the center of the old communist capital, it seems capitalism has settled in with a spirited vengeance.

Across the street, in the park, are grandfatherly statues of Marx and Engels (nicknamed by locals "the old pensioners"). Surrounding them are stainless-steel monoliths depicting the struggles of the workers of the world. Walk toward **Marien Church** (from 1270, interesting but very faded old *Dance of Death* mural inside door) at the base of the TV Tower. The big, red-brick building past the trees on the right is the **City Hall,** built after the revolution of 1848 and arguably the first democratic building in the city.

The 1,200-foot-tall **TV Tower** (Fernsehturm) offers a fine view from halfway up (€7.50, daily March–Oct 9:00–1:00 in the morning, Nov–Feb 10:00–24:00, tel. 030/242-3333). The tower offers a handy city orientation and an interesting view of the flat, red-roofed sprawl of Berlin—including a peek inside the city's many courtyards *(Höfe)*. Consider a kitschy trip to the observation deck for the view and lunch in its revolving restaurant (mediocre food, €12 plates, horrible lounge music, reservations smart for dinner, same phone number). It's very retro and somewhat trendy these days, so expect a line if you ascend. Built (with Swedish know-how) in 1969, the tower was meant to show the power of the atheistic state at a time when DDR leaders were having the crosses removed from church domes and spires. But when the sun shined on their tower, the greatest spire in East Berlin, a huge cross was reflected on the mirrored ball. Cynics called it "The Pope's Revenge." East Berliners dubbed the tower the "Big Asparagus." They joked that if it fell over, they'd have an elevator to the West.

Farther east, pass under the train tracks into **Alexanderplatz.** This area—especially the Kaufhof department store—was the commercial pride and joy of East Berlin. Today, it's still a landmark, with a major U- and S-Bahn station.

Our orientation stroll is finished. For a ride through workaday eastern Berlin, with its Lego-hell apartments (dreary even with their new face-lifts), hop back on bus #100 from here. It loops five minutes to the end of the line and then, after a couple minutes' break, heads on back. (This bus retraces your route, finishing at Bahnhof Zoo.) Or consider extending this foray into eastern Berlin, to...

Karl-Marx-Allee

The buildings along Karl-Marx-Allee in East Berlin (just beyond Alexanderplatz) were completely leveled by the Red Army in 1945. When Stalin decided this main drag should be a showcase street, he had it rebuilt with lavish Soviet aid and named it Stalin Allee. Today this street, done in the bold "Stalin Gothic" style so common in Moscow in the 1950s, has been restored, re-named after Karl Marx, and lined with "workers' palaces"—providing a rare

Eastern Berlin

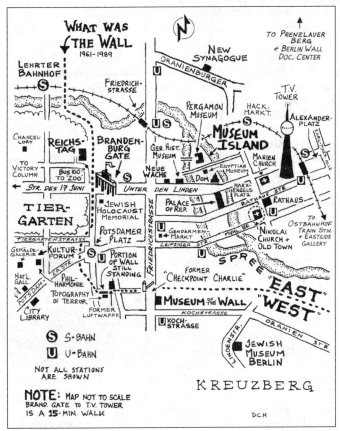

WHAT WAS THE WALL 1961-1989

LEHRTER BAHNHOF

FRIEDRICH-STRASSE

NEW SYNAGOGUE

ORANIENBURGER

TO PRENZLAUER BERG & BERLIN WALL DOC. CENTER

T.V. TOWER

PERGAMON MUSEUM

HACK. MARKT.

ALEXANDER-PLATZ

CHANCEL-LORY

REICHS-TAG

BRANDEN-BURG GATE

GER. HIST. MUSEUM

MUSEUM ISLAND

MARIEN CHURCH

TO VICTORY COLUMN

BUS 100 TO ZOO

NEUE WACHE

EGYPTIAN MUSEUM

DOM

STR. DES 17 JUNI

UNTER DEN LINDEN

MARX ENGELS PLATZ

RATHAUS STR.

RATHAUS

TIER-GARTEN

JEWISH HOLOCAUST MEMORIAL

PALACE OF REP.

TO OSTBAHNHOF TRAIN STN. & EASTSIDE GALLERY

TIERGARTENSTRASSE

POTSDAMER PLATZ

GENDARMEN-MARKT

MÜHL. BR.

NIKOLAI CHURCH & OLD TOWN

SPREE

GEMÄLDE-GALLERIE

KULTUR-FORUM

EBERT STR.

LEIPZIGER STR.

PORTION OF WALL STILL STANDING

NAT'L. GALL.

PHIL-HARMONIE

POTSDAM. STR.

TOPOGRAPHY OF TERROR

FORMER "CHECKPOINT CHARLIE"

FORMER LUFTWAFFE

"EAST" "WEST"

CITY LIBRARY

MUSEUM OF THE WALL

KOCHSTRASSE

ORANIEN STR.

KOCH-STRASSE

LINDENSTR.

JEWISH MUSEUM BERLIN

FRIEDRICHSTRASSE

KREUZBERG

Ⓢ S-BAHN

Ⓤ U-BAHN

NOT ALL STATIONS ARE SHOWN

NOTE: MAP NOT TO SCALE BRAND. GATE TO T.V. TOWER IS A **15**-MIN. WALK

DCH

look at Berlin's communist days. Distances are a bit long for convenient walking, but you can cruise Karl-Marx-Allee by taxi, or ride the U-Bahn to Strausberger Platz and walk to Frankfurter Tor. Notice the Social Realist reliefs on the buildings and the lampposts, which incorporate the wings of a phoenix (rising from the ashes) in their design.

The **Café Sibylle,** just beyond the Strausberger Platz U-Bahn station, is a fun spot for a coffee, traditional DDR ice-cream treats, and a look at its free, informal museum that tells the story of the most destroyed street in Berlin. While the humble exhibit is nearly all in German, it's fun to see the ear and half a moustache from what was the largest statue of Stalin in Germany (the centerpiece of the street until 1961) and a few intimate insights into apartment life in a DDR flat. The café is popular for its good coffee and *Schwedeneisbecher mit Eierlikor*—an ice-cream sundae with a shot of liquor, popular among those nostalgic for communism (daily 10:00–20:00, Karl-Marx-Allee 72, at intersection with Koppenstrasse, a block from U-Bahn: Strausberger Platz, tel. 030/2935-2203).

Heading out to Karl-Marx-Allee (just beyond the TV Tower), you're likely to notice a giant colorful **mural** decorating a blocky communist-era skyscraper. This was the Ministry of Education, and the mural is a tile mosaic trumpeting the accomplishments of the DDR's version of "No Child Left Behind."

South of Unter den Linden

The following sights—heavy on Nazi and Wall history—are listed roughly north to south (as you reach them from Unter den Linden).

▲▲**Gendarmenmarkt**—This delightful and historic square is bounded by twin churches, a tasty chocolate shop, and the Berlin Symphony's concert hall (designed by Schinkel, the man who put the neoclassical stamp on Berlin). In summer, it hosts a few outdoor cafés, *Biergarten*s, and sometimes concerts. The name of the square—part French and part German—reminds us that in the 17th century, a fifth of all Berliners were French émigrés,

Protestant Huguenots fleeing Catholic France. Back then, tolerant Berlin was a magnet for the persecuted. The émigrés vitalized the city with new ideas and know-how.

The German Cathedral (described below) on the square has an exhibit worthwhile for history buffs. The French Cathedral (Französischer Dom) offers a humble museum on the Huguenots and a chance to climb 254 steps to the top for a grand city view (€1.50, daily 9:00–19:00).

Fassbender & Rausch, on the corner near the German Cathedral, claims to be Europe's biggest chocolate store. After 150 years of chocolate-making, this family-owned business proudly displays its sweet delights—250 different kinds—on a 55-foot-long buffet. Truffles are sold for about €0.50 each (Mon–Fri 10:00–20:00, Sat 10:00–18:00, Sun 12:00–18:00, corner of Mohrenstrasse at Charlottenstrasse 60, tel. 030/2045-8440).

Gendarmenmarkt is buried in what has recently emerged as Berlin's new "Fifth Avenue" shopping district. For the ultimate in top-end shops, find the corner of Jägerstrasse and Französische Strasse and wander through the Quartier 206 (Mon–Fri 10:30–19:30, Sat 10:00–18:00, closed Sun, www.quartier206.com).

German Cathedral (Deutscher Dom)—This cathedral, bombed flat in the war and rebuilt only in the 1980s, houses the thought-provoking *Milestones, Setbacks, Sidetracks (Wege, Irrwege, Umwege)* exhibit, which traces the history of the German parliamentary system. The exhibit—while light on actual historical artifacts—is well done and more interesting than it sounds. It takes you quickly from the revolutionary days of 1848 to the 1920s, and then more deeply through the tumultuous 20th century. There are no English descriptions, but you can follow the essential, excellent, and free 90-minute English-language audioguide or buy the wonderfully detailed €10 guidebook. If this museum seems to be an attempt by the German government to develop a more sophisticated and educated electorate in the interest of stronger democracy, you're exactly right. Germany knows (from its own troubled history) that a dumbed-down electorate, manipulated by clever spin-meisters and sound-bite media blitzes, is a dangerous thing (free; June–Aug Tue–Sun 10:00–19:00, Tue until 22:00, closed Mon; Sept–May Tue–Sun 10:00–18:00, Tue until 22:00, closed Mon; on Gendarmenmarkt just off Friedrichstrasse, tel. 030/2273-0431).

▲▲▲**Museum of the Wall at Checkpoint Charlie (Mauermuseum Haus am Checkpoint Charlie)**—While the famous border checkpoint between the American and Soviet sectors is long gone, its memory is preserved by one of Europe's most interesting

museums. During the Cold War, the House at Checkpoint Charlie stood defiantly—spitting distance from the border guards—showing off all the clever escapes over, under, and through the Wall. Today, while the drama is over and hunks of the Wall stand like victory scalps at its door, the museum still tells a gripping history of the Wall, recounts the many ingenious escape attempts (early years—with a cruder wall—saw more escapes), and includes plenty of video coverage of those heady days when people-power tore down the Wall (€9.50, assemble 10 tourists and get in for €5.50 each, €3 audioguide, discount with WelcomeCard but not covered by Museumspass, cash only, daily 9:00–22:00, U-6 to Kochstrasse or—better from Zoo—U-2 to Stadtmitte, Friedrichstrasse 43–45, tel. 030/253-7250, www.mauermuseum.de). If you're pressed for time, this is a good after-dinner sight. With extra time, consider the "Hear We Go" audioguide about the Wall that takes you outside the museum (€7.50, 80 min).

Where Checkpoint Charlie once stood, notice the thought-provoking post with larger-than-life posters of a young American soldier facing east and a young Soviet soldier facing west. Around you are reconstructions of the old checkpoint. It's not named for a person, but because it was checkpoint number three—as in Alpha (at the East–West German border, a hundred miles west of here), Bravo (as you enter Berlin proper), and Charlie (the most famous because it was the only one where foreigners could pass). A few yards away (on Zimmerstrasse), a glass panel describes the former checkpoint. From there, a double row of cobbles in Zimmerstrasse traces the former path of the Wall (these innocuous cobbles run throughout the city, even through some modern buildings). Follow the cobbles one very long block to Wilhelmstrasse, a surviving stretch of Wall, and the...

Topography of Terror (Topographie des Terrors)—The park behind the Zimmerstrasse/Wilhelmstrasse bit of Wall marks the site of the command center of Hitler's Gestapo and SS. Because of the horrible things planned here, the rubble of these buildings will always be left as rubble. The SS, Hitler's personal bodyguards, grew to become a state-within-a-state, with its talons in every corner of German society. Along an excavated foundation of the building, an exhibit tells the story of National Socialism and its victims in Berlin (free, info booth open daily May–Sept 10:00–20:00, Oct–April 10:00–18:00 or until dark, tel. 030/2548-6703, www.topographie.de). The free English-language audioguide is essential (available only until 18:45 in summer), as everything printed is in German.

Across the street (facing the Wall) is the **German Finance Ministry** (Bundesministerium der Finanzen). Formerly the headquarters of the Nazi Luftwaffe (Air Force), this is the only major Hitler-era government building that survived the war's bombs. The communists used it to house their—no joke—Ministry of Ministries. Walk up Wilhelmstrasse (to the north) to see an entry gate (on your left) that looks much like it did when Germany occupied nearly all of Europe. On the north side of the building (farther up Wilhelmstrasse, at corner with Leipziger Strasse) is a wonderful example of communist art. The mural (from the 1950s) is classic Social Realism, showing the entire society—industrial laborers, farm workers, women, and children—all happily singing the same patriotic song. This was the communist ideal. For the reality, look at the ground in the courtyard in front of the mural to  see an enlarged photograph from a 1953 uprising here against the communists—quite a contrast.

Hitler and the Third Reich

While many come to Berlin to see Hitler sites, these are essentially invisible. The German Resistance Museum is in German only and difficult for the tourist to appreciate (see page 387). The Topography of Terror (SS and Gestapo headquarters) is a fascinating exhibit but—again—only in German, and all that remains of the building is its foundation (see page 382). (Both museums have helpful audioguides in English.) Hitler's bunker is completely gone (near Potsdamer Platz). Your best bet for "Hitler sites" is to take the Infamous Third Reich Sites walking tour offered by Original Berlin Walks (see "Tours," page 356). EurAide has a good flier listing and explaining sites related to the Third Reich.

▲▲▲**Jewish Museum Berlin (Jüdisches Museum Berlin)**—This museum is one of Europe's best Jewish sights. The highly con-

ceptual building is a sight in itself, and the museum inside—an overview of the rich culture and history of Europe's Jewish community—is excellent. The Holocaust is appropriately remembered, but it doesn't overwhelm this celebration of Jewish life.

Designed by American architect Daniel Libeskind (who is redeveloping New York City's World Trade Center site), the zinc-walled building's zigzag shape is pierced by voids symbolic of the irreplaceable cultural loss caused by the Holocaust. Enter through the 18th-century Baroque building next door, then go through an underground tunnel to reach the museum interior.

Before you get to the exhibit, your visit starts with three

memorial spaces. Underground, follow the Axis of Exile to a disorienting slanted garden with 49 pillars. Then the Axis of Holocaust leads to an eerily empty tower shut off from the outside world. A detour near the bottom of the long stairway leads to the "Memory Void," a thought-provoking space of "fallen leaves":

heavy metal faces that you walk on, making un-human noises with each step.

Finally, climb the stairs to the top of the museum, from where you stroll chronologically through the 2,000-year story of Judaism in Germany. The exhibit, on two floors, is engaging. Interactive bits (for example, spell your name in Hebrew) make it lively for kids. English explanations interpret both the exhibits and the design of the very symbolic building. Even though the museum is in a nondescript residential neighborhood (a 10-min walk from the Hallesches Tor U-Bahn station or the Checkpoint Charlie museum), it's well worth the trip (€5, covered by Museumspass, discount with WelcomeCard, daily 10:00–20:00, Mon until 22:00, last entry 1 hr before closing, closed on Jewish holidays, tight security includes bag check and metal detectors; U-Bahn line 1, 6, or 15 to Hallesches Tor, take exit marked *Jüdisches Museum*, exit straight ahead, then turn right on Franz-Klühs-Strasse, museum is 5 min ahead on your left at Lindenstrasse 9; tel. 030/2599-3300, www.juedisches-museum-berlin.de). The museum has a good café/restaurant (€9 daily specials, lunch 12:00–16:00, snacks at other times, tel. 030/2593-9760).

East Side Gallery—The biggest remaining stretch of the Wall is now "the world's longest outdoor art gallery." It stretches for nearly a mile and is covered with murals painted by artists from around the world. The murals are routinely whitewashed so new ones can be painted. This segment of the Wall makes a poignant walk. For a quick look, take the S-Bahn to Ostbahnhof station (follow signs to *Stralauerplatz* exit; once outside, TV Tower will be to your right; go left and at next corner look to your right—Wall is across the busy street). The gallery only survives until a land-ownership dispute can be solved, when it will likely be developed like the rest of the city. (Given the recent history, imagine the complexity of finding rightful owners of all this suddenly-very-valuable land.) If you walk the entire length of the East Side Gallery, you'll find a small Wall souvenir shop at the end and a bridge crossing the river to a subway station at Schlesisches Tor (in Kreuzberg).

Kreuzberg—This district—once abutting the dreary Wall and inhabited mostly by poor Turkish guest laborers and their families—is still run-down, with graffiti-riddled buildings and plenty of student and Turkish street life. It offers a gritty look at melting-pot Berlin, in a city where original Berliners are as rare as old buildings. Berlin is the fourth-largest Turkish city in the world, and Kreuzberg is its "downtown." But to call it a "little Istanbul" insults the big one. You'll see *döner kebab* stands, shops decorated with spray paint, and mothers wrapped in colorful scarves looking like they just got off a donkey in Anatolia. But lately, an influx of immigrants from many other countries has diluted the

Turkish-ness of Kreuzberg. Berliners come here for fun ethnic eateries. For a dose of Kreuzberg without getting your fingers dirty, joyride on bus #129 (catch it near Jewish Museum). For a colorful stroll, take the U-Bahn to Kottbusser Tor and wander—ideally on Tuesday and Friday between 12:00 and 18:00, when the Turkish Market sprawls along the Maybachufer riverbank.

North of Unter den Linden

While there are few major sights to the north of Unter den Linden, this area has some of Berlin's trendiest, most interesting neighborhoods.

▲▲**New Synagogue (Neue Synagogue)**—A shiny gilded dome marks the New Synagogue, now a museum and cultural center on Oranienburger Strasse. Only the dome and facade have been restored—a window overlooks the vacant field marking what used to be the synagogue. The largest and finest synagogue in Berlin before World War II, it was desecrated by Nazis on "Crystal Night" (Kristallnacht) in 1938, bombed in 1943, and partially rebuilt in 1990. Inside, past tight security, there's a small but moving exhibit on the Berlin Jewish community through the centuries with some good English descriptions (ground floor and 1st floor). On its facade, the *Vergesst es nie* message—added by East Berlin Jews in 1966—means "Never forget." East Berlin had only a few hundred Jews, but now that the city is united, the Jewish community numbers about 12,000 (€3; May–Aug Sun–Mon 10:00–20:00, Tue–Thu 10:00–18:00, Fri 10:00–17:00, closed Sat; Sept–April Sun–Thu 10:00–18:00, Fri 10:00–14:00, closed Sat; last entry 30 min before closing, U-Bahn: Oranienburger Tor, Oranienburger Strasse 28/30, tel. 030/8802-8300 and press 1, www.cjudaicum.de).

A block from the synagogue, walk 50 yards down Grosse Hamburger Strasse to a little park. This street was known for 200 years as the "street of tolerance" because the Jewish community donated land to Protestants so that they could build a church. Hitler turned it into the "street of death" *(Todes Strasse)*, bulldozing 12,000 graves of the city's oldest Jewish cemetery and turning a Jewish nursing home into a deportation center. Note the two memorials—one erected by the former East Berlin government, the other built later by the city's unified government. With the small but persistent neo-Nazi element still a problem in Berlin, a plainclothes police officer keeps watch over this park somewhere nearby.

▲**Oranienburger Strasse**—Berlin is developing so fast, it's impossible to predict what will be "in" next year. The area around Oranienburger Strasse is definitely trendy (but is being challenged by hip Friedrichshain, farther east, and Prenzlauer Berg, described below). While the area immediately around the synagogue is dull,

100 yards away things get colorful. The streets behind Grosse Hamburger Strasse flicker with atmospheric cafés, *Kneipen* (pubs), and art galleries. At night (from about 20:00), techno-prostitutes line Oranienburger Strasse. Prostitution is legal here, but there's a big debate about taxation. Since they don't get unemployment insurance, why should they pay taxes?

Hackescher Markt—This neighborhood, near Oranienburger Strasse, is worth exploring. A block in front of the Hackescher Markt S-Bahn station is **Hackesche Höfe,** with eight courtyards bunny-hopping through a wonderfully restored 1907 *Jugendstil* building (www.hackesche-hoefe.com). Berlin's apartments are organized like this—courtyard after courtyard leading off the main roads. This complex is full of trendy restaurants (including a good Turkish place, Hasir—see page 408), theaters, and cinema (playing movies in their original languages). This is a wonderful example of how to make huge city blocks livable.

▲Prenzlauer Berg—Young, in-the-know locals agree that this is one of Berlin's most colorful neighborhoods (roughly between Helmholtzplatz and Kollwitzplatz and along Kastanienallee, U-Bahn: Senefelderplatz and Eberswalder Strasse; or take the S-Bahn to Hackescher Markt and catch the M1 tram north). This part of the city was largely untouched during World War II, but its buildings slowly rotted away under the communists. Since the Wall fell, it's been overrun with laid-back hipsters, energetic young families, and clever entrepreneurs who are breathing life back into its classic old apartment blocks, deserted factories, and long-forgotten breweries. While no longer "up-and-coming," and on the road to gentrification, Prenzlauer Berg is a celebration of life and a joy to stroll through. The area feels strangely wholesome and family-friendly, as former ruffians with tattoos, piercings, and an appetite for the cutting-edge life are now responsible young parents. Though it's a few blocks farther out than the neighbor-hoods described above, it's a fun area to explore and have a meal (see page 408) or spend the night (see page 402).

Natural History Museum (Museum für Naturkunde)—This museum is worth a visit just to see the largest dinosaur skeleton ever assembled (actually, unassembled until 2007). While you're there, meet "Bobby" the stuffed ape (€3.50, Tue–Fri 9:30–17:00, Sat–Sun 10:00–18:00, closed Mon, last entry 30 min before clos-ing, U-Bahn line 6 to Zinnowitzer Strasse, Invalidenstrasse 43, tel. 030/2093-8591).

Berlin Wall Documentation Center (Dokumentationszentrum Berliner Mauer)—The last surviving complete "Wall system" (with both parts of its Wall and its no-man's-land, or "death strip," all still intact) is now part of a sober little memorial and "Doku-Center." While it's really directed at German-speakers and far from other sights, it's handy enough to the S-Bahn that any Wall aficionado will find it worth a quick visit. The Documentation Center has a photo gallery and rooftop viewpoint (accessible by elevator), from which you can view the "Wall system." It's poignantly located where a church was destroyed to make way for the Wall; today a memorial chapel has been built where the church once stood (free, April–Oct Tue–Sun 10:00–18:00, Nov–March until 17:00, closed Mon year-round, Bernauer Strasse 111, tel. 030/464-1030, www .berliner-mauer-dokumentationszentrum.de). Take the S-Bahn to Nordbahnhof and walk 200 yards along Bernauer Strasse, which is still lined with a long chunk of Wall.

Central Berlin

Tiergarten Park

Berlin's "Central Park" stretches two miles from Bahnhof Zoo to the Brandenburg Gate.

Victory Column (Siegessäule)—The Tiergarten's centerpiece, the Victory Column, was built to commemorate the Prussian defeat of France in 1870. The pointy-helmeted Germans rubbed it in, decorating the tower with French cannons and paying for it all with francs received as war reparations. The three lower rings commemorate Bismarck's victories. I imagine the statues of Moltke and other German military greats—which lurk in the trees nearby—goose-stepping around the floodlit angel at night. Originally standing at the Reichstag, the immense tower was actually moved to this position by Hitler in 1938 to complement his anticipated victory parades. Streets leading to the circle are flanked by surviving Nazi guardhouses—built in the bold style that fascists loved. At the memorial's first level, notice how WWII bullets chipped the fine marble columns. Climbing its 285 steps earns you a breathtaking Berlin-wide view and a close-up look at the gilded angel made famous in the U2 video (€2.20; April–Sept Mon–Thu 9:30–18:30, Fri–Sun 9:30–19:00; Oct–March daily 9:30–17:30; closes in the rain, WCs for paying guests only, no elevator, bus #100, tel. 030/8639-8560). From the tower, the grand Strasse des 17 Juni leads east to the Brandenburg Gate.

Flea Market—A colorful flea market with great antiques, more than 200 stalls, collector-savvy merchants, and fun German fast-food stands thrives weekends beyond the Victory Column on Strasse des 17 Juni (S-Bahn: Tiergarten).

German Resistance Memorial (Gedenkstätte Deutscher Widerstand)—This memorial and museum, just south of the Tiergarten, tells the story of the German resistance to Hitler. The Bendlerblock was a military headquarters where an ill-fated attempt to assassinate Hitler was plotted (the actual attempt occurred in Rastenburg, eastern Prussia). Stauffenberg and his co-conspirators were shot here in the courtyard. While posted explanations are in German only, the spirit that haunts the place is multilingual (free, Mon–Fri 9:00–18:00, Thu until 20:00, Sat–Sun 10:00–18:00, free and good English audioguide with passport, €3 printed English translation, no crowds, near Kulturforum at Stauffenbergstrasse 13, enter in courtyard, door on left, main exhibit is on 3rd floor, bus #M29, tel. 030/2699-5000).

Potsdamer Platz

The "Times Square" of Berlin, and possibly the busiest square in Europe before World War II, Potsdamer Platz was cut in two by the Wall and left a deserted no-man's-land for 40 years. Today,

this immense commercial/ residential/entertainment center, sitting on a futuristic transportation hub, is home to the European corporate headquarters of several big-league companies.

The new Potsdamer Platz was a vision begun in 1991, when it was announced that Berlin would resume its position as capital of Germany. Sony, Daimler-Chrysler, and other major corporations have turned the square once again into a center of Berlin. Like great Christian churches were built upon pagan holy grounds, Potsdamer Platz— with its corporate logos flying high and shiny above what was the Wall—trumpets the triumph of capitalism.

While Potsdamer Platz tries to give Berlin a common center, the city has always been—and remains—a collection of towns. Locals recognize 28 distinct neighborhoods that may have grown together but still maintain their historic orientation. While Munich has the single dominant Marienplatz, Berlin will always have Charlottenburg, Savignyplatz, Kreuzberg, Prenzlauer Berg, and so on. In general, Berliners prefer these characteristic neighborhoods. They're unimpressed by the grandeur of Potsdamer Platz, and consider it simply a good place for movies with over-priced, touristy restaurants.

While most of the complex just feels big (the arcade is like any huge, modern, American mall), the entrance to the complex and Sony Center Platz are worth a visit.

For an overview of the new construction, and a scenic route to Sony Center Platz, start at the Bahnhof Potsdamer Platz (east end of Potsdamer Strasse, S- and U-Bahn: Potsdamer Platz). Find the green hexagonal clock tower with the traffic lights on top. This is a replica of the first automatic **traffic light** in Europe, which once stood at the six-street intersection of Potsdamer Platz. On either side of Potsdamer Strasse, you'll see enormous cubical entrances to the brand-new underground Potsdamer Platz train station. Near these entrances, notice the slanted **glass cylinders** sticking out of the ground. The mirrors on the tops of the tubes move with the sun to collect light and send it underground. Notice the slabs of the Wall re-erected where the Wall once stood. The single slab marks the spot where the first piece was cut out (see photo and history on nearby panel). Now go in one of the train station entrances and follow signs to Sony Center. (While you're down there, look for the other ends of the big glass tubes.)

You'll come up the escalator into **Sony Center** under a grand canopy. At night, multicolored floodlights play on the underside

of this tent. Office workers and tourists eat here by the fountain, enjoying the parade of people. The modern Bavarian Lindenbrau beer hall—the Sony boss wanted a *Bräuhall*—serves traditional food (€5–16, big salads, 3-foot-long taster boards of 8 different beers, daily 11:00–24:00, tel. 030/2575-1280). The adjacent Josty Bar is built around a surviving bit of a venerable hotel that was a meeting place for Berlin's rich and famous before the bombs (daily 9:00–24:00, tel. 030/2575-9702). You can browse the futuristic Sony Style Store, visit the Filmhaus (Film Museum Berlin, with an exhibit on Marlene Dietrich and a rare cinema that plays movies in their original language—without German dubbing), and pop into the Zoon Center (where the VW "my first car" exhibit prepares kids for the exciting day that they get their license and they, too, can enjoy Germany's beloved autobahns).

Across Potsdamer Strasse, you can ride what's billed as "the fastest elevator in Europe" to skyscraping rooftop views at the **Panaromapunkt.** You'll travel at nearly 30 feet per second to the top of the 300-foot-tall Kollhoff tower. Its sheltered but open-air view deck provides a fun opportunity to survey Berlin's ongoing construction from above (€3.50, daily 11:00–20:00, last lift 19:30, closed Mon in winter, in red-brick building at Potsdamer Platz 1, tel. 030/2529-4372, www .panoramapunkt.de).

Kulturforum

Just west of Potsdamer Platz, with several top museums and Berlin's concert hall, is the city's cultural heart (admission to all Kulturforum sights covered by a single €8 combo-ticket or the €15 Museumspass; phone number for all museums: tel. 030/266-2951). Of its sprawling museums, only the Gemäldegalerie is a must. To reach the Kulturforum, take the S- or U-Bahn to Potsdamer Platz, then walk along Potsdamer Platz and Potsdamer Strasse. From the Zoo station, you can also take bus #200 to Philharmonie. Across Potsdamer Strasse from the Kulturforum is the huge National Library (free English periodicals).

▲▲▲**Gemäldegalerie**—Germany's top collection of 13th-through 18th-century European paintings (more than 1,400 canvases) is beautifully displayed in a building that's a work of art in itself. Follow the excellent free audioguide. The North Wing starts with German paintings of the 13th to 16th centuries, including eight by Dürer. Then come the Dutch and Flemish—Jan Van Eyck, Brueghel, Rubens, Van Dyck, Hals, and Vermeer. The wing finishes with German, English, and French 18th-century art, such as Gainsborough and Watteau. An octagonal hall at the end features an impressive stash of Rembrandts. The South Wing is saved for the Italians—Giotto, Botticelli, Titian, Raphael, and Caravaggio (€8 Kulturforum ticket or €15 Museumspass, free Thu after 18:00, open Tue–Sun 10:00–18:00, Thu until 22:00, closed Mon, clever little loaner stools, great salad bar in cafeteria upstairs, Matthäikirchplatz 4).

New National Gallery (Neue Nationalgalerie)—This features 20th-century art, with ever-changing special exhibits (€8 Kulturforum ticket or €15 Museumspass, open Tue–Fri 10:00–18:00, Thu until 22:00, Sat–Sun 11:00–18:00, closed Mon, café downstairs).

Museum of Arts and Crafts (Kunstgewerbemuseum)—Wander through a thousand years of applied arts—porcelain, fine *Jugendstil* furniture, Art Deco, and reliquaries. There are no crowds and no English descriptions (€8 Kulturforum ticket or €15 Museumspass, free Thu after 14:00, open Tue–Fri 10:00–18:00, Sat–Sun 11:00–18:00, closed Mon).

▲**Musical Instruments Museum (Musikinstrumenten Museum)**—This impressive hall is filled with 600 exhibits from the 16th century to modern times. Wander among old keyboard instruments and funny-looking tubas. There's no English, aside from a €0.10 info sheet, but it's fascinating if you're into pianos (€8 Kulturforum ticket or €15 Museumspass, Tue–Fri 9:00–17:00, Sat–Sun 10:00–17:00, closed Mon, low-profile white building east of the big, yellow Philharmonic Concert Hall, tel. 030/254-810).

Poke into the lobby of Berlin's **Philharmonic Concert Hall** and see if there are tickets available during your stay (ticket office open Mon–Fri 15:00–18:00, Sat–Sun 11:00–14:00, must purchase tickets in person, box office tel. 030/2548-8132).

Western Berlin

Throughout the Cold War, Western travelers learned to think of Berlin's "West End" as the heart of the city. But it no longer is. With the huge changes the city has undergone since 1989, the real "city center" is now, once again, Berlin's historic center (around Unter den Linden and Friedrichstrasse). While the West End has long had the best infrastructure to support your visit, and still works well as a home base, it's no longer the obvious base from which to explore Berlin. As Lehrter Bahnhof puts the Bahnhof Zoo essentially out of business in 2006, this change will be become even more pronounced. Having said all that, there still are a few interesting sights within an easy walk of the recommended West End hotels and Bahnhof Zoo.

▲**Kurfürstendamm**—West Berlin's main drag, Kurfürstendamm boulevard (nicknamed "Ku'damm"), starts at Kaiser Wilhelm Memorial Church and does a commercial cancan for two miles. In the 1850s, when Berlin became a wealthy and important capital, her new rich chose Kurfürstendamm as their street. Bismarck made it Berlin's Champs-Elysées. In the 1920s, it became a chic and fashionable drag of cafés and boutiques. During the Third Reich, as home to an international community of diplomats and journalists, it enjoyed more freedom than the rest of Berlin. Throughout the Cold War, economic subsidies from the West made sure that capitalism thrived on Ku'damm. And today, while much of the old charm has been hamburgerized, Ku'damm is still a fine place to enjoy elegant shops (around Fasanenstrasse), department stores, and people-watching.

▲**Kaiser Wilhelm Memorial Church (Gedächtniskirche)**—This church was originally a memorial to the first emperor of Germany. Reliefs and mosaics show great events in the life of Germany's favorite kaiser, from his coronation in 1871 to his death in 1888. The church's bombed-out ruins have been left standing as a memorial to the destruction of Berlin in World War II. Under a neo-Romanesque mosaic ceiling, a small exhibit features interesting photos about the bombing and before-and-after models of the church (free, Mon–Sat 10:00–16:00, closed Sun, www.gedaechtniskirche.com).

Western Berlin

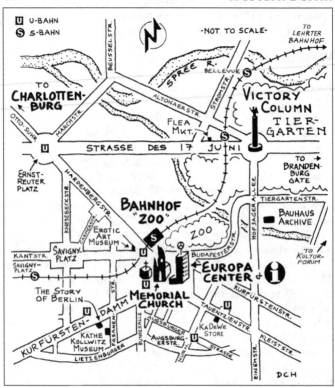

After the war, some Berliners wanted to tear the church down and build it anew. Instead, it was decided to keep the ruin as a memorial, and stage a competition to design a modern add-on section. The winning selection—the short, modern building (1961) next to the church—offers a world of 11,000 little blue windows (free, daily 9:00–19:00). The blue glass was given to the church by the French as a reconciliation gift. For more information on both churches, pick up the English booklet (€2.60).

The lively square between the churches and the Europa Center (a once-impressive, shiny high-rise shopping center built as a showcase of Western capitalism during the Cold War) usually attracts street musicians.

The Story of Berlin—Filling most of what seems like a department store right on Ku'damm, this sprawling history exhibit is a business venture making money off of telling the stormy 800-year story of Berlin in a creative way. While there are almost no real historic artifacts, the exhibit does a good job of cobbling together many dimensions of the life and tumultuous times of this great city. The highlight is the included 30-minute tour of a circa 1972 radiation-proof bomb shelter—designed to house 3,500 for 14 days (€9.50, daily 10:00–20:00, last entry 18:00, well-described in English, upon arrival confirm time of next English-language bunker tour, Kurfürstendamm 207, at corner of Uhlandstrasse, in the Ku'damm Karree Mall, tel. 030/8872-0100).

▲**Käthe Kollwitz Museum**—This local artist (1867–1945), who experienced much of Berlin's stormiest century, conveys some powerful and mostly sad feelings about motherhood, war, and suffering through the stark faces of her art (€5, €1 pamphlet has English explanations of a few major works, Wed–Mon 11:00–18:00, closed Tue, a block off Ku'damm at Fasanenstrasse 24, tel. 030/882-5210, www.kaethe-kollwitz.de).

▲**Kaufhaus des Westens (KaDeWe)**—The "Department Store of the West," with a staff of 2,100 to help you sort through its vast selection of 380,000 items, claims to be the biggest department store on the Continent. You can get everything from a haircut and train ticket (basement) to souvenirs (3rd floor). The theater and concert box office on the sixth floor charges an 18 percent booking fee, but they know all your options (cash only). The sixth floor is a world of gourmet taste treats. The biggest selection of deli and exotic food in Germany offers plenty of classy opportunities to sit down and eat. Ride the glass elevator to the seventh floor's glass-domed Winter Garden self-service cafeteria—fun but pricey (Mon–Fri 10:00–20:00, Sat 9:30–20:00, closed Sun, U-Bahn: Wittenbergplatz, tel. 030/21210, www.kadewe.de). The Wittenbergplatz U-Bahn station (in front of KaDeWe) is a unique opportunity to see an old-time station. Enjoy its interior.

Berlin Zoo—More than 1,400 different kinds of animals call Berlin's famous zoo home—or so the zookeepers like to think. Germans enjoy seeing the pandas at play (straight in from the entrance). I enjoy seeing the Germans at play (€11 for zoo or world-class aquarium, €16.50 for both, children half price, daily 9:00–18:30, Nov–Feb until 17:00, aquarium closes 30 min earlier; feeding times—*Fütterungszeiten*—posted on map just inside entrance, the best feeding show is the sea lions—generally at 11:00, 13:30, and 15:15; enter near Europa Center in front of Hotel Palace or opposite Bahnhof Zoo on Hardenbergplatz, Budapester Strasse 34, tel. 030/254-010).

Erotic Art Museum—This offers two floors of graphic art (especially Oriental), old-time sex toy knickknacks, and a special exhibit on the queen of German pornography, the late Beate Uhse. This amazing woman, a former test pilot for the Third Reich and groundbreaking purveyor of condoms and sex ed in the 1950s, was the female Hugh Hefner of Germany and CEO of a huge chain of porn shops (€5, daily 9:00–24:00, last entry 23:00, hard-to-beat gift shop, at corner of Kantstrasse and Joachimstalerstrasse, a block from Bahnhof Zoo, tel. 030/886-0666). If you just want to see sex, you'll see much more for half the price in a private video booth next door.

Charlottenburg Palace Area

The Charlottenburg district—with a cluster of museums across the street from a grand palace—is a popular side-trip from downtown. But the palace isn't much to see, and in 2005 the Egyptian Museum (with the bust of Queen Nefertiti—see page 376) moved downtown and took with it the main reason I'd go all the way out to Charlottenburg. The former Egyptian Museum may reopen as a Museum of Surreal Art in 2007. To get here, ride U-2 to Sophie-Charlotte Platz and walk 10 minutes up the tree-lined boulevard Schlossstrasse (following signs to *Schloss*), or—much faster—catch bus #145 (direction Spandau) direct from Bahnhof Zoo.

For a Charlottenburg lunch, the **Luisen Bräu** is a comfortable brewpub restaurant with a copper and woody atmosphere, good local "microbeers" (*dunkles* means "dark," *helles* is "light"), and traditional German grub (€5–8 meals, daily 9:00–24:00, fun for groups, across from palace at Luisenplatz 1, tel. 030/341-9388).

▲**Charlottenburg Palace (Schloss Charlottenburg)**—If you've seen the great palaces of Europe, this Baroque Hohenzollern palace comes in at about number 10 (behind Potsdam, too). It's even more disappointing since the main rooms can be toured only with a German guide (€8 includes 50-min tour, €2 to see just upper floors without tour, €7 to see palace grounds excluding tour areas, last tour 1 hr before closing, cash only, Tue–Sun 10:00–17:00, closed Mon, tel. 030/320-911).

The **Knöbelsdorff Wing** features a few royal apartments. Go upstairs and take a substantial hike through restored-since-the-war, gold-crusted white rooms (€5 depending on special exhibitions, free English audioguide, Tue–Fri 10:00–18:00, Sat–Sun 11:00–18:00, closed Mon, last entry 1 hr before closing, when facing the palace walk toward the right wing, tel. 030/3209-1442).

▲**Berggruen Collection: Picasso and His Time**—This tidy little museum is a pleasant surprise. Climb three floors through a fun and substantial collection of Picassos. Along the way, you'll see plenty of notable works by Matisse, van Gogh, and Cézanne. Enjoy a great chance to meet Paul Klee (€6, covered by Museumspass, free Thu after 14:00, open Tue–Sun 10:00–18:00, closed Mon, Schlossstrasse 1, tel. 030/326-9580).

▲**Bröhan Museum**—Wander through a dozen beautifully furnished *Jugendstil* and Art Deco living rooms, a curvy organic world of lamps, glass, silver, and posters. English descriptions are posted on the wall of each room on the main floor. While you're

Charlottenburg Palace Area

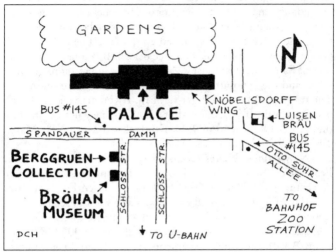

there, look for the fine collection of Impressionist paintings by Karl Hagemeister (€4–8 depending on special exhibits, covered by Museumspass excluding special exhibits, Tue–Sun 10:00–18:00, closed Mon, Schlossstrasse 1A, tel. 030/3269-0600, www.broehan -museum.de).

Near Berlin

▲**Potsdam Palaces**—Featuring a lush park strewn with the extravagant whimsies of Frederick the Great, the sleepy town of Potsdam has long been Berlin's holiday retreat. Frederick's super-rococo Sanssouci Palace is one of Germany's most dazzling. His equally extravagant New Palace, built to disprove rumors that Prussia was running out of money after the costly Seven Years' War, is on the other side of the park (it's a 30-min walk between palaces). The Potsdam **TI** is a good source of information (April–Oct Mon–Fri 9:00–19:00, Sat–Sun 10:00–16:00, less off-season, 5-min walk from Potsdam S-Bahn station, walk straight out of station and take first right onto An der Orangerie, Friedrich-Ebert Strasse 5, tel. 0331/275-5850).

Your best bet for seeing Sanssouci Palace is to take the Potsdam TI tour (see below). Otherwise, to make sense of all the ticket and tour options for the two palaces, stop by the palaces' information office (across the street from windmill near Sanssouci entrance, helpful English-speaking staff, tel. 0331/969-4202).

Sanssouci Palace: Even though *sans souci* means "without a care," it can be a challenge for an English speaker to have an enjoyable visit. The palaces of Vienna, Munich, and even Würzburg offer equal sightseeing thrills with far fewer headaches. While the grounds are impressive, the interior of Sanssouci Palace can be visited only by a one-hour tour in German (with a borrowed English text), and these tours get booked up quickly. The only English option is the Potsdam TI's tour (see below). If you take a German tour of Sanssouci, you must be at the palace in person to get your ticket and the appointment time for your tour. In the summer, if you arrive by 9:00, you'll get right in. If you arrive after 10:00, plan on a wait. If you arrive after 12:00, you may not get in at all (€8; April–Oct Tue–Sun 9:00–17:00, closed Mon; Nov–March Tue–Sun 9:00–16:00, closed Mon).

New Palace (Neues Palais): Use the English texts to tour Frederick's New Palace (€5, plus €1 for optional live tour in German; April–Oct Sat–Thu 9:00–17:00, closed Fri; Nov–May Sat–Thu 9:00–16:00, closed Fri). If you also want to see the king's apartments, you must take a required 45-minute tour in German (€6, offered May–Oct daily at 11:00, 13:00, and 15:00). Off-season (Nov–April), the king's apartments are closed, and you can visit the rest of the New Palace only on a German tour (€5); it can take up to an hour for enough people to gather.

Walking Tours: The Potsdam TI's handy walking tour includes Sanssouci Palace, offering the only way to get into the palace with an English-speaking guide (€26 covers walking tour, palace, and park, at 11:00 daily except Mon, 3.5 hrs, departs from Film Museum across from TI—walk straight out of Potsdam S-Bahn station and take first right onto An der Orangerie, reserve by phone, in summer reserve at least 2 days in advance, tel. 0331/275-5850).

A "Discover Potsdam" walking tour (which doesn't include Sanssouci Palace) is offered by Original Berlin Walks. The tour leaves from Berlin's Zoo station at 9:45 every Sunday, May through September (€15, or €11.20 if under age 26 or with WelcomeCard, meet at taxi stand at Zoo station, public transportation not included but can buy ticket from guide, no booking necessary, tel. 030/301-9194). The guide takes you to Cecilienhof Palace (site of postwar Potsdam conference attended by Churchill, Stalin, and Truman), through pleasant green landscapes to the historic heart of Potsdam for lunch, and to Sanssouci Park.

What to Avoid: Potsdam's much-promoted Wannsee boat rides are torturously dull.

Getting to Potsdam: Potsdam is easy to reach from Berlin (17 min on direct Regional Express/RE trains from Bahnhof Zoo every 30 min, or 30 min direct on S-Bahn line 7 from Bahnhof Zoo to Potsdam station; round-trip covered by €6 transit day pass with zones A, B, and C). If you're taking the Potsdam TI's tour, walk to the Film Museum from the Potsdam S-Bahn stop (see "Walking Tours," above). If not taking the TI tour, catch bus #695

Greater Berlin

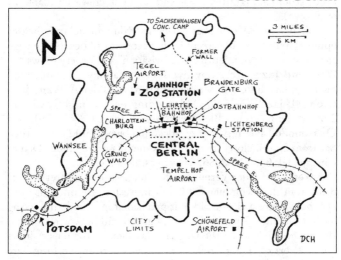

from the Potsdam station to the palaces (3/hr, 20 min). Use the same bus #695 to shuttle between the sights in the park. For a more scenic approach, take tram #96 or #X98 from the Potsdam station to Luisenplatz, then walk 15 minutes through the park and enjoy a classic view of Sanssouci Palace.

Other Day Trips—EurAide has researched and printed a *Get Me Outta Here* flier describing good day trips to small towns and another flier on the nearby Sachsenhausen Concentration Camp (which many consider as interesting as Dachau; a Sachsenhausen day trip is also offered by Original Berlin Walks—see page 356).

NIGHTLIFE

Berlin is a happening place for nightlife—whether it's nightclubs, pubs, jazz music, cabaret, hokey-but-fun German variety shows, theater, or concerts. Tourists stroll the Ku'damm after dark.

Sources of Entertainment Info: *Berlin Programm* lists a non-stop parade of concerts, plays, exhibits, and cultural events (€1.60, in German, www.berlin-programm.de); *Exberliner Magazine* (€2, www.exberliner.com) and the TI-produced *Berlin Calendar* (€1.60) have less information, but are in English (all sold at kiosks and TIs). For the young and determined sophisticate, *Zitty* and *Tip* are the top guides to alternative culture (in German, sold at kiosks). Also pick up the free schedules *Flyer* and *030* in bars and clubs. The free magazines by walking-tour companies such as New Berlin Walks (www.newberlintours.com) and Insider Tours (www.insidertour.com) are also good, providing the English-language inside scoop on nightlife, cheap eats, and pub crawls (available all over town).

Visit KaDeWe's ticket office for your music and theater options (sixth floor, 18 percent fee but access to all tickets; see page 393). Ask about "competitive improvisation" and variety shows.

West End Jazz—To enjoy live music near my recommended Savignyplatz hotels in western Berlin, consider **A Trane Jazz Club** (all jazz, €7–15 cover depending on act, nightly 21:00–2:00 in the morning, Bleibtreustrasse 1, tel. 030/313-2550) and **Quasimodo Live** (mix of jazz, rock, and blues, €5–12 cover, Tue–Sat from 22:00, closed Sun-Mon, Kantstrasse 12a, under Delphi Cinema, tel. 030/312-8086, www.quasimodo.de).

Cabaret—Bar Jeder Vernunft offers modern-day cabaret a short walk from the recommended hotels in western Berlin. This variety show under a classic old tent perched atop a modern parking lot is a hit with German speakers, but can still be worthwhile for those who don't speak the language (as some of the music shows are in a sort of "Dinglish"). Even some Americans perform here periodically. Tickets are generally around €15, and shows change regularly (performances start at 20:30, closed Sun, seating can be a bit cramped, south of Ku'damm at Schaperstrasse 24, tel. 030/883-1582, www.bar-jeder-vernunft.de).

German Variety Show—To spend an evening enjoying Europe's largest revue theater, consider Revue Berlin at the Friedrichstadt Palast. The show basically depicts the history of Berlin, and is choreographed in a funny and musical way that's popular with the Lawrence Welk–type German crowd. It's entertaining for your entire English-speaking family (€13–51, Tue–Sat 20:00, also Sat–Sun at 16:00, no shows Mon, U-Bahn: Oranienburger Tor, tel. 030/284-8830, www.friedrichstadtpalast.de).

Nightclubs and Pubs—Oranienburger Strasse's trendy scene (page 385) is being eclipsed by the action at Friedrichshain (farther east). To the north, you'll find the hip Prenzlauer Berg neighborhood, packed with everything from smoky pubs to small art bars and dance clubs (best scene is around Helmholtzplatz, U-Bahn: Eberswalder Strasse; see page 386).

Pub Crawls—Various walking-tour companies offer €10 pub crawls providing an opportunity to drink heavily in a series of bars and clubs with several dozen new English-speaking friends. For details, see page 357.

SLEEPING

When in Berlin, I sleep in the former West, on or near Savignyplatz. While Bahnhof Zoo and Ku'damm are no longer the center of Berlin, the trains, TI, and walking tours are all still handy to Zoo.

Sleep Code

(€1 = about $1.20, country code: 49, area code: 030)
S = Single, **D** = Double/Twin, **T** = Triple, **Q** = Quad, **b** = bathroom,
s = shower only. Unless otherwise noted, credit cards are
accepted, English is spoken, and breakfast is included.

To help you sort easily through these listings, I've divided
the rooms into three categories, based on the price for a standard double room with bath:

$$$ **Higher Priced**—Most rooms €125 or more.
  $$ **Moderately Priced**—Most rooms between €85–125.
    $ **Lower Priced**—Most rooms €85 or less.

And the streets around the tree-lined Savignyplatz (a 10-min walk
behind the station) have a neighborhood charm. While towering
new hotels are being built in the new center, simple, small, friendly,
good-value places abound here. My listings are generally located
a couple of flights up in big, run-down buildings. Inside, they're
clean, quiet, and spacious enough so that their well-worn character
is actually charming. Rooms in back are on quiet courtyards.

As an alternative, I've also listed some suggestions in eastern Berlin's youthful and increasingly popular Prenzlauer Berg
neighborhood, as well as a couple other possibilities elsewhere.

Berlin is packed and hotel prices go up on holidays, including
Green Week in mid-January, Easter weekend, the first weekend
in May, Ascension weekend in May, the Love Parade (mid-July),
German Unity Day (Oct 3), Christmas, and New Year's. Note that
with Germany hosting the World Cup in 2006, cities throughout
the country will be jammed and charging top dollar for rooms
from about June 8 through July 9. The World Cup kick-off celebration takes place in Berlin on June 8, and the city is hosting matches
on June 13, 15, 20, 23, and 30, as well as the final match on July 9.

During slow times, the best values are actually business-class
rooms on the push list booked through the TI. But as the world
rediscovers what a great destination Berlin is, a rising tide of tourists will cause these deals to fade away.

Western Berlin

Near Savignyplatz and Bahnhof Zoo

These hotels and pensions are a 5- to 15-minute walk from Bahnhof
Zoo (or take S-Bahn to Savignyplatz). Asking for a quieter room
in back gets you away from any street noise. The area has an artsy
charm going back to the cabaret days in the 1920s, when it was the
center of Berlin's gay scene. Of the accommodations listed in this

Savignyplatz Neighborhood

- ① Hotel Askanischerhof
- ② Hecker's Hotel
- ③ Hotel Carmer 16
- ④ Hotel Astoria
- ⑤ Hotel-Pension Funk
- ⑥ Hotel Bogota
- ⑦ Pension Peters
- ⑧ Hotel Pension Alexandra
- ⑨ Pension Alexis
- ⑩ Dicke Wirtin Pub
- ⑪ Die Zwölf Apostel Rest.
- ⑫ Ristorante San Marino
- ⑬ Zillemarkt Restaurant
- ⑭ Technical University Mensa
- ⑮ To Weyers Café Rest.
- ⑯ Quasimodo Live
- ⑰ A Trane Jazz Club
- ⑱ To Launderette
- ⑲ Ullrich Supermarkt
- ⑳ The Story of Berlin
- ㉑ Käthe Kollwitz Museum

area, Pension Peters offers the best value for budget travelers.

$$$ Hotel Askanischerhof is the oldest *Zimmer* in Berlin, posh as can be with 16 sprawling, antique-furnished living rooms you can call home. Photos on the walls brag of famous movie-star guests. Frau Glinicke offers Old World service and classic Berlin atmosphere (Sb-€95–110, Db-€117–145, extra bed-€25, free parking, non-smoking rooms, elevator, Ku'damm 53, tel. 030/881-8033, fax 030/881-7206, www.askanischer-hof.de, info@askanischer -hof.de).

$$$ Hecker's Hotel is an ultramodern, four-star business hotel with 69 rooms and all the sterile Euro-comforts (Sb-€125, Db-€150, all rooms €200 during conferences but generally only €100 July–Aug—except during World Cup games, breakfast-€15, non-smoking rooms, elevator, parking-€9–12/day, between Savignyplatz and Ku'damm at Grolmanstrasse 35, tel. 030/88900, fax 030/889-0260, www.heckers-hotel.com, info@heckers-hotel.com).

$$ Hotel Carmer 16, with 30 bright, airy rooms, feels like a big, professional hotel with all the comfy extras (Db-€93, ask for a Rick Steves discount, extra person-€20, some rooms have balconies, elevator and a few stairs, beauty parlor and mini-spa upstairs, Carmerstrasse 16, tel. 030/3110-0500, fax 030/3110-0510, www.hotel-carmer16.de, info@hotel-carmer16.de).

$$ Hotel Astoria is a friendly, three-star, business-class hotel with 32 comfortably furnished rooms and affordable summer and weekend rates (high season Db-€117; prices drop to Db-€94 during low season of July–Aug, Nov–Feb; breakfast-€10 extra, non-smoking floors, elevator, free Internet in lobby, parking-€14/day, around corner from Bahnhof Zoo at Fasanenstrasse 2, tel. 030/312-4067, fax 030/312-5027, www.hotelastoria.de, info@hotelastoria.de).

$$ Hotel-Pension Funk, the former home of a 1920s silent-movie star, is delightfully quirky. Kind manager Herr Michael Pfundt offers 14 elegant old rooms with rich Art Nouveau furnishings (S-€34–57, Ss-€41–72, Sb-€52–82, D-€52–82, Ds-€72–93, Db-€82–113, extra person-€23, prices guaranteed through 2006 with this book, cash preferred, Fasanenstrasse 69, a long block south of Ku'damm, tel. 030/882-7193, fax 030/883-3329, www.hotel-pensionfunk.de, berlin@hotel-pensionfunk.de).

$$ Hotel Bogota is a once-elegant old slumbermill renting 125 rooms in a sprawling old maze of a building that once housed the Nazi Chamber of Culture. Today pieces of the owner's modern-art collection lurk around every corner (S-€44, Ss-€57, Sb-€72, D-€69, Ds-€77, Db-€98, extra bed-€20, children under 12 free, non-smoking rooms, elevator, bus #109 from Bahnhof Zoo to Schlüterstrasse 45, tel. 030/881-5001, fax 030/883-5887, www.hotelbogota.de, hotel.bogota@t-online.de).

$ Pension Peters, run by a German-Swedish couple, is sunny and central, with a cheery breakfast room. Decorated sleek Scandinavian, with every room renovated, it's a winner (S-€36, Ss-€47, Sb-€58, D-€51, Ds-€68, Db-€78–83, extra bed-€10, prices guaranteed through 2006 with this book, kids under 12 free, family room, cash preferred, Internet in lobby, 10 yards off Savignyplatz at Kantstrasse 146, tel. 030/3150-3944, fax 030/312-3519, www.pension-peters-berlin.de, penspeters@aol.com, Annika and Christoph). The same family also runs a larger hotel just outside of Berlin (see Hotel Pankow on page 405) and rents apartments in Prenzlauer Berg (ideal for small groups and longer stays).

$ Hotel Pension Alexandra has 11 pleasant rooms on a tree-lined street between Savignyplatz and Ku'damm. Expect the usual high ceilings and marble entryway found in these turn-of-the-century buildings, but with added touches—most rooms and the elegant breakfast room are decorated with original antique furniture (Ss-€45, Sb-€59, Ds-€65, Db with small bed-€70, standard Db-€85, extra bed-€30, Wielandstrasse 32, tel. 030/881-2107, fax 030/885-7780, www.hotelalexandra.de, Frau Kuhn).

$ Pension Alexis is a classic Old World four-room pension in a stately 19th-century apartment run by Frau and Herr Schwarzer (who speak just enough English). The shower and toilet facilities are old and cramped, but this, more than any other Berlin listing, has you feeling at home with a faraway aunt (S-€43, D-€65, T-€97, Q-€128, €5 extra for 1-night stay, cash only, big rooms, Carmerstrasse 15, tel. 030/312-5144).

Eastern Berlin

Prenzlauer Berg

If you want to sleep in the former East Berlin, set your sights on the youthful, colorful, fun Prenzlauer Berg district. After decades of neglect, this corner of the East has quickly come back to life. Gentrification has brought Prenzlauer Berg great hotels, tasty ethnic and German eateries (see page 408), and a happening nightlife scene. All the graffiti is just some people's way of saying they care. The huge and impersonal concrete buildings are now enlivened with a street fair of fun little shops and eateries. Prenzlauer Berg is about a mile and a half north of Alexanderplatz, roughly between Kollwitzplatz and Helmholtzplatz, and to the west, along Kastanienallee (known affectionately as "Casting Alley" for its extra share of beautiful people). The closest U-Bahn stops are Senefelderplatz at the south end of the neighborhood and Eberswalder Strasse at the north end. For more on Prenzlauer Berg, see page 386. Or, for less walking, take the S-Bahn to Hackescher Markt, then catch the M1 tram north.

$$$ Myer's Hotel is a boutique-hotel splurge renting 41 simple, small, but elegant rooms. The gorgeous public spaces include a patio and garden. Details done right and impeccable service set this place apart. This peaceful hub—off a quiet courtyard and tree-lined street, just a 10-minute walk from Kollwitzplatz or the nearest U-Bahn stop (Senefelderplatz)—makes it hard to believe you're in a capital city (Sb-€85–135, Db-€110–175, price depends on size of room, Metzer Strasse 26, tel. 030/440-140, fax 030/4401-4104, www.myershotel.de, info@myershotel.de).

$$ Hotel Jurine (yoo-REEN) is a pleasant 53-room business-style hotel whose friendly staff aims to please. Enjoy the breakfast buffet surrounded by modern art, or relax in the lush backyard (Sb-€75, Db-€100, Tb-€130, extra bed-€35, prices can double during conventions, breakfast-€13, parking garage-€12/day, 10-min walk

Prenzlauer Berg Neighborhood

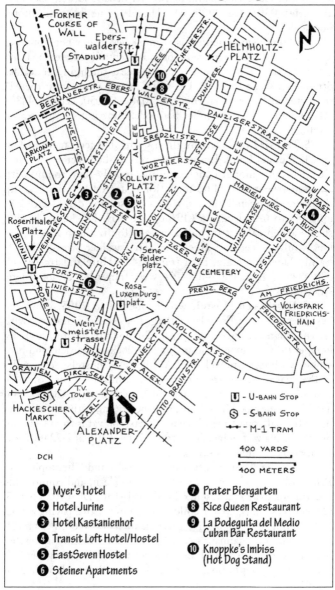

1. Myer's Hotel
2. Hotel Jurine
3. Hotel Kastanienhof
4. Transit Loft Hotel/Hostel
5. EastSeven Hostel
6. Steiner Apartments
7. Prater Biergarten
8. Rice Queen Restaurant
9. La Bodeguita del Medio Cuban Bar Restaurant
10. Knoppke's Imbiss (Hot Dog Stand)

to U-Bahn: Senefelderplatz, Schwedter Strasse 15, tel. 030/443-2990, fax 030/4432-9999, www.hotel-jurine.de, mail@hotel-jurine.de).

$$ Hotel Kastanienhof is a simple, less classy hotel offering 35 fine but slightly overpriced rooms. It's centrally located, making getting around Berlin a cinch, and it's near the hip Eberswalder Strasse bar scene (Sb-€78, Db-€103, just 40 yards from the M1 tram stop at Kastanienallee 65, tel. 030/443-050, fax 030/4430-5111, www.hotel-kastanienhof-berlin.de, info@hotel-kastanienhof-berlin.de).

$ Transit Loft is technically a hostel, but feels more like an upscale budget hotel. Located in a refurbished factory, it offers clean, bright, modern, new-feeling, mostly-blue rooms with an industrial touch. The reception—staffed by friendly, hip Berliners—is open 24 hours, with a bar serving drinks all night long (4- to 6-bed dorms-€19/bed, Sb-€59, Db-€69, Tb-€90, sheets and breakfast included, no age limit, cheap Internet in lobby, fully wheelchair-accessible, Greifswalder Strasse 219; U-Bahn: Alexanderplatz, then tram M4 to Hufelandstrasse; tel. 030/4849-3773, fax 030/4405-1074, www.transit-loft.de, loft@hotel-transit.de).

$ EastSeven Hostel, which opened in 2005, rents the best cheap beds in Prenzlauer Berg. It's sleek and modern, with all the hostel services and more: 24-hour reception, inviting lounge, fully equipped guests' kitchen, lockers, garden, and bike rental. Children are welcome. While most hostels—especially in Prenzlauer Berg—are annoyingly youthful to anyone over 30, easygoing people of any age are comfortable here (S-€30, D-€44, T-€57, €16 for a bed in a 4-, 5-, or 6-bed dorm, bathrooms always down the hall, one-time €3 fee for sheets, 100 yards from U-Bahn: Senefelderplatz at Schwedter Strasse 7, tel. 030/9362-2240, www.eastseven.de, info@eastseven.de).

$ Steiner Apartments, run by Annika and Christoph from Pension Peters, are seven well-located, modern, and comfortable apartments near Hackescher Markt (Sb-€50, Db-€70, Tb-€75, Qb-€80, cash only, up to 2 children sleep free with 2 paying adults, fully equipped as if you live there, Linienstrasse 60, near intersection with Gormannstrasse, 350 yards from S-Bahn: Hackescher Markt, even closer to U-Bahn: Rosenthaler Platz, www.pension-peters-berlin.de; to book, contact Pension Peters, described on page 401).

On Unter den Linden

$$ Hotel Unter den Linden is ideal for those nostalgic for the days of Soviet rule—although nowadays, at least the management tries to be efficient and helpful. Formerly one of the best hotels in the DDR, this huge, blocky landmark, right on Unter den Linden in the heart of what was East Berlin, is reasonably comfortable and fairly priced. Built in 1966, with prison-like corridors and curiously skinny doors, it has 331 modern, plain, and comfy rooms (Sb-€67–87, Db-€109–123, deals for drop-ins and those who book on their Web site, non-smoking rooms, Unter den Linden 14, at intersection with Friedrichstrasse, tel. 030/238-110, fax 030/2381-1100, www.hotel-unter-den-linden.de, reservation@hotel-unter-den-linden.de).

Away from the Center

$ Hotel Pankow is a fresh, colorful 43-room place run by Annika and Christoph (from the Pension Peters, page 401). It's a 30-minute commute north of downtown but a good value (S-€31, Sb-€46, D-€41, Db-€61, T-€51, Tb-€71, Q-€61, Qb-€81, family rooms, 2 children under 16 free in room with parents, elevator, Internet in lobby, free parking in lot or €3/day in garage, tram in front of hotel takes you to the center in 30 min, Pasewalker Strasse 14-15, tel. 030/486-2600, fax 030/4862-6060, www.hotel-pankow-berlin.de, hotelpankow@aol.com).

Hostels

Berlin is known among budget travelers for its fun, hip hostels. Here are three good bets: **$ Studentenhotel Meininger 10** (€13 dorm beds, D-€46, includes sheets and breakfast, cash only, no curfew, elevator, free parking, near City Hall on JFK Platz, Meiningerstrasse 10, U-Bahn: Rathaus Schoneberg, tel. 030/7871-7414, www.meininger-hostels.de), **$ Mitte's Backpacker Hostel** (€15 dorm beds, S-€30–35, D-€46–56, T-€63, Q-€80, sheets-€2.50, no breakfast, could be cleaner, no curfew, Internet in lobby, laundry, bike rental, English newspapers, U-Bahn: Zinnowitzerstrasse, Chauseestrasse 102, tel. 030/2839-0965, fax 030/2839-0935, www.backpacker.de, info@backpacker.de), or **$ Circus** (€15–18 dorm beds, S-€32, D-€48, Db-€60, T-€60, Q-€72, 2-person apartment with kitchen-€75, 4-person apartment-€130, sheets-€2, breakfast-€5, cash only, no curfew, Internet in lobby, 2 locations, U-Bahn: Rosa-Luxemburg Platz, Rosa-Luxemburg Strasse 39, or U-Bahn: Rosenthaler Platz, Weinbergsweg 1a, both tel. 030/2839-1433, fax 030/2839-1484, www.circus-berlin.de, info@circus-berlin.de).

EATING

Don't be too determined to eat "Berlin-style." The city is known only for its mildly spicy sausage. Still, there is a world of restaurants in this ever-changing city to choose from. Your best approach may be to choose a neighborhood, rather than a particular restaurant.

For quick and easy meals, colorful pubs—called *Kneipen*—offer light meals and the fizzy local beer, *Berliner Weiss*. Ask for it *mit Schuss* for a shot of fruity syrup in your suds. If the kraut is getting wurst, try one of the many Turkish, Italian, or Balkan restaurants. Eat cheap at *Imbiss* snack stands, bakeries (sandwiches), and falafel/kebab counters. Bahnhof Zoo has several bright and modern fruit-and-sandwich bars and a grocery (daily 6:00–24:00).

Western Berlin

Near Savignyplatz

Several good restaurants are on or within 100 yards of Savignyplatz, near my recommended western Berlin hotels. Take a walk and survey these; continue your stroll along Bleibtreustrasse to discover many trendier, more creative little eateries.

Dicke Wirtin is a smoky pub with traditional old-Berlin *Kneipe* atmosphere and good, solid home cooking at reasonable prices—such as their famously cheap *Gulaschsuppe*. While their interior is fun and pubby, their streetside tables are also inviting (€6–10 daily specials, open daily from 12:00 with dinner served from 18:00, just off Savignyplatz at Carmerstrasse 9, tel. 030/312-4952).

Die Zwölf Apostel (literally "The Twelve Apostles") is trendy for good Italian food. Choose between indoors with candlelit ambience, on a sun-dappled patio, or overlooking the parade on its pedestrian street. A dressy local crowd packs this restaurant for €10 pizzas and €15–30 meals (open 24 hrs daily, cash only, outside seating in summer until 22:00, immediately across from Savignyplatz S-Bahn entrance, Bleibtreustrasse 49, tel. 030/312-1433).

Ristorante San Marino, on the square, is another good Italian eatery, serving cheaper pasta and pizza. It's more kid-friendly (daily 11:00–1:00 in the morning, Savignyplatz 12, tel. 030/313-6086).

Zillemarkt Restaurant, which feels like an old-time Berlin beer garden, serves traditional Berlin specialties in the garden or in the rustic candlelit interior. Their *Berliner Allerlei* is a fun way to sample a bit of nearly everything (€10 meals, daily 10:00–24:00, near the S-Bahn tracks at Bleibtreustrasse 48a, tel. 030/881-7040).

Technical University Mensa, a student cafeteria with impossibly cheap prices, puts you in a modern university scene with fine food and good indoor or streetside seating (general public entirely welcome, Mon–Fri 11:00–15:30, closed Sat–Sun, cheap coffee bar downstairs with Internet access, just north of Uhlandstrasse at Hardenbergstrasse 34).

Weyers Café Restaurant, serving quality international and German cuisine, is a great value and worth the 15-minute walk from Savignyplatz. It's sharp, with white tablecloths, but not stuffy. On a sunny day, its patio is packed with natives (€10 dinner plates, daily 8:00–2:00 in the morning, seating indoors or outside on the leafy square called Ludwigkirchplatz, Pariser Strasse 16, reservations smart after 20:00, tel. 030/881-9378). Even though this restaurant is farther away, it gets you into a real neighborhood scene without a tourist in sight.

Ullrich Supermarkt is the neighborhood grocery store (Mon–Sat 9:00–22:00, closed Sun, Kantstrasse 7, under the tracks near Bahnhof Zoo). There's plenty of fast food near Bahnhof Zoo and on Ku'damm.

Near Bahnhof Zoo

Self-Service Cafeterias: The top floor of the famous department store, **KaDeWe,** holds the Winter Garden Buffet view cafeteria, and its sixth-floor deli/food department is a picnicker's nirvana. Its arterials are clogged with more than 1,000 kinds of sausage and 1,500 types of cheese (Mon–Fri 10:00–20:00, Sat 9:30–20:00, closed Sun, U-Bahn: Wittenbergplatz). **Wertheim** department store, a half-block from Kaiser Wilhelm Memorial Church, has cheap food counters in the basement and a city view from its self-service cafeteria, Le Buffet, located up six banks of escalators (Mon–Sat 9:30–20:00, closed Sun, U-Bahn: Ku'damm). **Marche,** a chain that's popped up in big cities all over Germany, is another inexpensive, self-service cafeteria within a half block of Kaiser Wilhelm Memorial Church (Mon–Thu 8:00–22:00, Fri–Sat 8:00–24:00, Sun 10:00–22:00, plenty of salads, fruit, made-to-order omelets, Ku'damm 14, tel. 030/882-7578).

Eastern Berlin

Along Unter den Linden

These eateries are listed as you'll reach them as you walk along Unter den Linden from west to east.

At the Opera House (Opernpalais): The **Operncafé** is perhaps the classiest coffee stop in Berlin, with a wide selection of decadent desserts (daily 8:00–24:00, across from university and war memorial at Unter den Linden 5, tel. 030/202-683). The beer and tea garden in front has a cheap food counter (from 10:00, depending on weather).

Near the Pergamon Museum: **Deponie3** is a trendy Berlin *Kneipe* usually filled with students from nearby Humboldt University. Garden seating in the back is nice if you don't mind the noise of the S-Bahn passing directly above you. The interior is a cozy, wooden wonderland of a bar with several inviting spaces. They serve basic sandwiches, salads, traditional Berlin dishes, and hearty daily specials (€3–7 breakfasts, €5–11 lunches and dinners, sometimes with live music, open daily from 9:00, Georgenstrasse 5, 1 block from Pergamon under S-Bahn tracks, tel. 030/2016-5740).

Georgenstrasse is home to other good restaurants, including a branch of Die Zwölf Apostel (daily until 24:00, described under "Near Savignyplatz," above).

In the Heart of Old Berlin's Nikolai Quarter: During the Cold War, the Nikolai Quarter was the cute, cobbled, and characteristic old town of East Berlin. Today the district feels pretty soulless but is a popular restaurant zone at night. **Bräuhaus Georgbrau** is a thriving beer hall sitting on a picturesque courtyard overlooking the Spree River. Eat in the lively and woody but mod-feeling interior, or outdoors with fun riverside seating (cheap plates, 3-foot-long sampler board with a dozen small glasses of beer, daily 10:00–24:00, 2 blocks south of Berlin Cathedral and across the river at Spreeufer 4, tel. 030/242-4244).

South of Unter den Linden, near Gendarmenmarkt

The twin churches of Gendarmenmarkt seem to be surrounded by people in love with food. The lunch and dinner scene is thriving with upscale restaurants serving good cuisine at highly competitive prices to local professionals. If in need of a quick-yet-classy lunch, stroll around the square and along Charlottenstrasse. Consider **Lutter & Wegner Restaurant,** well-known for its Austrian cuisine (*Schnitzel* and *Sauerbraten*) and popular with businesspeople. It's dressy, with fun sidewalk seating or a dark and elegant interior (2-course lunch with wine-€15, gourmet dinner *menu*-€34, daily 12:00–15:00 & 18:00–22:00, Charlottenstrasse 56, tel. 030/202-9540). **Galeries Lafayette Food Circus** is a festival of fun eateries in the basement of the landmark department store (Mon–Sat 10:00–20:00, closed Sun, U-Bahn: Französische Strasse).

Turkish Cuisine North of Unter den Linden, near Hackescher Markt

As Berlin is one of the world's largest Turkish cities, it's no wonder you can find some good Turkish restaurants here. While most think of Turkish food as fast and cheap, **Hasir Turkish Restaurant** is your chance to dine with candles, hardwood floors, and happy Berliners as snappy Turkish waiters bring plates piled high with meaty Anatolian specialties. The restaurant, in a courtyard of the Hackesche Höfe shopping complex (see page 386), offers indoor and outdoor tables filled with an enthusiastic local crowd (€13 plates, huge and splittable portions, daily from 11:30 until late, a block from the Hackescher Markt S-Bahn station at Oranienburger Strasse 4, tel. 030/2804-1616).

In Prenzlauer Berg

Prenzlauer Berg is packed with fine restaurants—German, ethnic, and everything in between. (For more on this district, see page 386.) Before making a choice, I'd spend half an hour strolling and browsing through this bohemian wonderland of creative eateries. Ideally, ride the U-Bahn to Rosenthaler Platz, check out that zone, then hike up Kastanienallee, which takes you past the recommended Prater Biergarten and side streets lined with impromptu outdoor tables. Kastanienallee dead-ends at Eberswalder Strasse, where you'll find Knoppke's Imbiss and, within a half block, Rice Queen and La Bodeguita del Medio.

Prater Biergarten offers a mellow outdoor ambience. Berlin's oldest beer garden is a family-friendly delight. It has two zones: the restaurant (serious traditional *Biergarten* cuisine, huge indoor area, and a few tables outside) and the vast self-service beer garden under the trees (with a much simpler menu and an intriguing selection of munchies). This isn't the typical yodeling-and-lederhosen Bavarian beer garden—in addition to the wurst and beer are fine wine and snacks like olives, nuts, and pickles (Mon–Sat 18:00–24:00, Sun 10:00–24:00, Kastanienallee 7, tel. 030/448-5688).

Rice Queen Restaurant is crisp and casual, with a fruity minimalist decor. They serve cheap yet delicious South Asian dishes from a fun menu that makes you glad you're hungry (€6 plates, daily 17:00–24:00, 1 block from U-Bahn: Eberswalder Strasse at Danziger Strasse 13, tel. 030/4404-5800).

La Bodeguita del Medio Cuban Bar Restaurant is purely fun-loving Cuba—Christmas lights, graffiti-caked walls, Che Guevara posters, animated staff, and an ambience that makes you want to dance. Come early to eat or late to drink. It seems the waiters know the regulars' drinks (daily from 18:00, 1 block from U-Bahn: Eberswalder Strasse at Lychener Strasse 6, tel. 030/4171-4276). This restaurant has been here for over a decade—and in fast-changing Prenzlauer Berg, that's an eternity.

Knoppke's Imbiss, a super-cheap German-style hot dog stand, has been a Berlin institution for over 70 years—it was family-owned even during DDR times. Berliners say Knoppke's cooks up the best *Currywurst* (grilled hot dog with curry-infused ketchup) in town. There are a few tables under a nearby tent for sit-down wurst-munching (Mon–Fri 6:00–20:00, Sat 12:00–19:00, closed Sun; Kastanienallee dead-ends at the elevated train tracks, and under them you'll find Knoppke's at Schönhauser Allee 44A). Don't be fooled by the Currystation at the foot of the stairs coming out of the station; Knoppke's is actually across the street, under the tracks.

TRANSPORTATION CONNECTIONS

Berlin has long had several major train stations. But now, with **Lehrter Bahnhof** (officially, Berlin Hauptbahnhof-Lehrter Bahnhof) emerging as the single, massive central station, all the others are wilting into glorified subway stations. Until Lehrter is finished (sometime in 2006), **Bahnhof Zoo**—which was the West Berlin train station—will still serve Western Europe: Frankfurt, Munich, Hamburg, Paris, and Amsterdam. The **Ostbahnhof** (formerly East Berlin's main station) still faces east, serving Prague, Warsaw, Vienna, and Dresden. The **Lichtenberg Bahnhof** (eastern Berlin's top U- and S-Bahn hub) also handles a few eastbound trains. Expect exceptions. All stations are conveniently connected by subway and even faster by train. When the age of Lehrter begins, think of it as a transfer station—centrally located, but not really near anything of interest. Most new arrivals will immediately transfer to the U- or S-Bahn to get to their ultimate Berlin destination.

From Berlin by Train to: Dresden (every 2 hrs, 2 hrs), **Frankfurt** (hrly, 4 hrs), **Munich** (14/day, 6 hrs, 8 hrs overnight), **Köln** (hrly, 6 hrs), **Amsterdam** (3/day, 7 hrs), **Budapest** (3/day, 13 hrs; 2 go via Czech Republic and Slovakia, so Eurailpass is not valid), **Copenhagen** (4/day, 6.5 hrs, change in Hamburg; also consider the direct overnight train-plus-ferry route to Malmö, Sweden, which is just 20 min from Copenhagen; this trip is covered by a railpass that includes either Germany or Sweden—but you don't need to have both countries), **London** (4/day, 15 hrs, but you're generally better off flying cheap on easyJet or Air Berlin—see below), **Paris** (4/day, 13 hrs, change in Köln, 1 direct 12-hr night train), **Zürich** (6/day, 10 hrs, 1 direct 12-hr night train), **Prague** (5/day, 5 hrs, no overnight trains), **Warsaw** (4/day, 6 hrs, 1 night train from Lichtenberg station; reservations required on all Warsaw-bound trains), **Kraków** (2/day, 10 hrs), **Vienna** (3/day, 12 hrs via Czech Republic; for second-class ticket, Eurailers pay an extra €40; otherwise, take the Berlin–Vienna via Passau train—nightly at 20:00). It's smart to reserve in advance for any train to or from Amsterdam or Prague. Train info: tel. 11861 (€0.50/min).

Eurailpasses don't cover the Czech Republic. The **Prague Excursion pass** picks up where Eurail leaves off, getting you from any border into Prague and then back out to Eurail country again within seven days (first class-€50, second class-€40, youth second class-€35, buy from EurAide at Berlin's Bahnhof Zoo or Munich's Hauptbahnhof and get reservations—€3—at the same time).

There are **night trains** from Berlin to these cities: Munich, Köln, Brussels, Paris, Vienna, Budapest, Kraków, Warsaw, Basel, and Zürich. There are no night trains from Berlin to anywhere in Italy or Spain. A *Liegeplatz,* or berth (€13–36), is a great deal; inquire at EurAide at Bahnhof Zoo for details. Beds cost the same whether you have a first- or second-class ticket or railpass. Trains are often full, so reserve your bed a few days in advance from any travel agency or major train station in Europe.

The **Berlin-Paris night train** goes through Belgium. If you're using a railpass, either the pass must include Benelux, or you'll have to pay extra for the Belgian segment of the trip.

Berlin's Two Airports

Allow €20 for a taxi ride to or from either of Berlin's airports. **Tegel Airport** handles most flights from the United States and Western Europe (4 miles from center, catch the faster bus #X9 to Bahnhof Zoo, or bus #109 to Ku'damm and Bahnhof Zoo for €2; bus TXL goes to Alexanderplatz in East Berlin). Flights from the east and discount airlines usually arrive at **Schönefeld Airport** (12.5 miles from center, short walk to S-Bahn station where you catch the regional express into the city, railpass valid). The central telephone number for both airports is 01805-000-186. For British Air, tel. 01805-266-522; Delta, tel. 01803-337-880; SAS, tel. 01803-234-023; or Lufthansa, tel. 01803-803-803.

Berlin, the New Discount Airline Hub: Berlin is now the continental European hub for easyJet (with lots of flights to Spain, Italy, Eastern Europe, the Baltics, and more—book long in advance to get the incredible €30-and-less fares, www.easyjet.com). Ryanair (www.ryanair.com) and Air Berlin (www.airberlin.com) are also making the London-Berlin trip (and other routes) dirt cheap. Consequently, in the last year, British visits to Berlin are up over 50 percent. All discount airlines use Berlin's Schönefeld Airport.

AUSTRIA

AUSTRIA

(Österreich)

During the grand old Hapsburg days, Austria was Europe's most powerful empire. Its royalty built a giant kingdom (Österreich means "Eastern Empire") of more than 60 million people by making love, not war—having lots of children and marrying them into the other royal houses of Europe.

Today this small, landlocked country does more to cling to its elegant past than any other nation in Europe. The waltz is still the rage. Austrians are very sociable; it's important to greet people in the breakfast room and those you pass on the streets or meet in shops. The Austrian version of "Hi" is a cheerful *"Grüss Gott"* ("May God greet you"). You'll get the correct pronunciation after the first volley—listen and copy.

While they speak German and talked about unity with Germany long before Hitler ever said *Anschluss,* the Austrians cherish their distinct cultural and historical traditions. They are not Germans. Austria is mellow and relaxed compared to Deutschland. *Gemütlichkeit* is the local word for this special

Austria

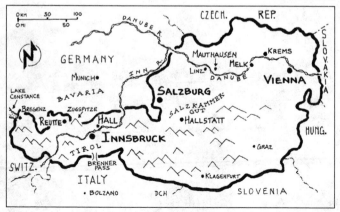

Austria Almanac

Official Name: Republik Öesterreich ("Eastern Empire") or simply Öesterreich.

Population: Austria's 8 million people (similar to the state of Georgia) are 90 percent ethnic Austrian, plus 4 percent from the former Yugoslavia. Three out of four Austrians is Catholic; one in 20 is Muslim. German is the dominant language, but some provinces recognize other official languages for their Slavic- and Hungarian-descended people.

Latitude and Longitude: 47°N and 13°E. The latitude is the same as Minnesota or Washington state.

Area: With 32,700 square miles, Austria is similar in size to South Carolina or Maine.

Geography: The northeast is flat and well populated; the less-populated southwest is mountainous, with Alps rising up to the 12,450-foot Grossglockner. The 1,770-mile-long Danube River meanders west-to-east through the upper part of the country, passing through Vienna.

Biggest Cities: One in four Austrians lives in the capital of Vienna (1.6 million in the city; 2 million in the greater metropolitan area). Graz has 220,000, and Linz has 185,000.

Economy: Located at the crossroads of Europe and bordered by eight countries, Austria is well integrated into the EU economy. The Gross Domestic Product is $255 billion (similar to Washington state's). It has a GDP per capita of $31,000—among Europe's highest. One of its biggest money-makers is tourism. Austria produces wood, paper products (nearly half the land is forested)...and Red Bull Energy Drink. The country faces an aging population who collects social security—a situation that will increasingly strain the national budget in years to come.

Government: Chancellor Wolfgang Schüssel—head of a center-right coalition government—faces re-election in the parliamentary elections scheduled for fall of 2006. Two minority parties make news beyond their numbers—the liberal Greens (10 percent) and the conservative BZÖ, headed by "yuppie fascist" Jörg Haider. Austria has been officially neutral since 1955.

Flag: Three horizontal bands of red (top), white, and red.

The Average Austrian: A typical Austrian is 40 years old, has 1.36 children, and will live to be 79. He or she inhabits a 900-square-foot home, and spends the majority of his or her leisure time with a circle of a few close friends.

Austrian cozy-and-easy approach to life. It's good living—whether engulfed in mountain beauty or bathed in lavish high culture. The people stroll as if every day were Sunday, topping things off with a cheerful visit to a coffee or pastry shop.

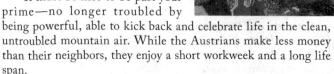

It must be nice to be past your prime—no longer troubled by being powerful, able to kick back and celebrate life in the clean, untroubled mountain air. While the Austrians make less money than their neighbors, they enjoy a short workweek and a long life span.

Prices in Austria are lower than in Germany. Shops are open from 8:00 to 17:00 or 18:00.

Austrians eat on about the same schedule we do. Treats include Wiener schnitzel (breaded veal cutlet), *Knödel* (dumplings), *Apfelstrudel,* and fancy desserts like the *Sachertorte,* Vienna's famous chocolate cake. Bread on the table sometimes costs extra (if you eat it). Service is included in restaurant bills, but it's polite to leave a little extra (about 5 percent).

In Austria, all cars must have a **Vignette** toll sticker stuck to the inside of their windshield to legally drive on the freeways. These are sold at all border crossings (24 hours a day), big gas stations near borders, and car-rental agencies. Stickers cost €8 for 10 days (€22 for 2 months). Not having one earns you a stiff fine.

In the following section, I'll cover Austria's top destinations *except* for Reutte, in Tirol. For this book, Reutte has been annexed by Germany. You'll find it in the Bavaria and Tirol chapter.

VIENNA

(Wien)

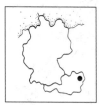

Vienna is a head without a body. For 640 years the capital of the once-grand Hapsburg Empire, she started and lost World War I, and with it her far-flung holdings. Today, you'll find an elegant capital of 1.6 million people (one-fifth of Austria's population) ruling a small, relatively insignificant country. Culturally, historically, and from a sightseeing point of view, this city is the sum of its illustrious past. The city of Freud, Brahms, Maria Theresa's many children, a gaggle of Strausses, and a dynasty of Holy Roman Emperors ranks right up there with Paris, London, and Rome.

Vienna has always been the easternmost city of the West. In Roman times, it was Vindobona, on the Danube facing the Germanic barbarians. In the Middle Ages, Vienna was Europe's bastion against the Ottoman Turks—a Christian breakwater against the riding tide of Islam (hordes of up to 200,000 Turks were repelled in 1529 and 1683). During this period, as the Turks dreamed of conquering what they called "the big apple" for their sultan, Vienna lived with a constant fear of invasion (and the Hapsburg court ruled from safer Prague). You'll notice none of Vienna's great palaces were built until after 1683, when the Turkish threat was finally over. While Vienna's old walls held out the Turks, World War II bombs destroyed nearly a quarter of the city's buildings. In modern times, neutral Austria took a big bite out of the U.S.S.R.'s Warsaw Pact buffer zone. And today, Vienna is a springboard for newly popular destinations in Eastern Europe.

The truly Viennese person is not Austrian, but a second-generation Hapsburg cocktail, with grandparents from the distant corners of the old empire—Hungary, the Czech Republic,

Greater Vienna

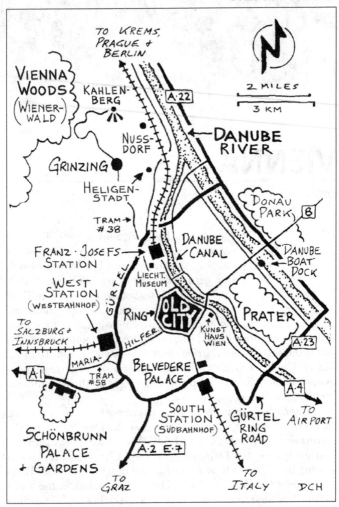

Slovakia, Poland, Slovenia, Croatia, Bosnia, Serbia, Romania, and Italy. Vienna is the melting-pot capital of a now-collapsed empire that, in its heyday, consisted of 60 million people—only eight million of whom were Austrian.

In 1900, Vienna's 2.2 million inhabitants made it the world's fifth-largest city (after New York, London, Paris, and Berlin). But these days—with dogs being the preferred "child" and the average Viennese mother having only 1.3 children—the population is down to around 1.6 million.

The Hapsburgs, who ruled the enormous Austrian Empire

from 1273 to 1918, shaped Vienna. Some ad agency has convinced Vienna to make Elisabeth, wife of Emperor Franz Josef—with her narcissism and struggles with royal life—the darling of the local tourist scene. You'll see "Sissy" all over town. But stay focused on the Hapsburgs who mattered: Maria Theresa (r. 1740–1780, see page 448) and Franz Josef (r. 1848–1916, see page 442).

After the defeat of Napoleon and the Congress of Vienna in 1815 (which shaped 19th-century Europe), Vienna enjoyed its violin-filled belle époque, which shaped our romantic image of the city: fine wine, chocolates, cafés, and waltzes.

Planning Your Time

For a big city, Vienna is pleasant and laid-back. Packed with sights, it's worth two days and two nights on the speediest trip. To be grand-tour efficient, you could sleep in and sleep out on the train (Berlin, Kraków, Venice, Rome, the Swiss Alps, Paris, and the Rhine Valley are each handy night trains away). But then you'd miss the Danube and Melk. I'd come in from Salzburg via Hallstatt, Melk, and the Danube and spend two days this way:

Day 1: 9:00–Circle the Ring by tram, following my self-guided tour (page 425); 10:00–Drop by the TI for any planning and ticket needs, then see the sights in Vienna's old center (using my self-guided commentary)—Monument Against War and Fascism, Kaisergruft crypt, Kärntner Strasse, St. Stephen's Cathedral, and Graben; 12:00–Finger sandwiches for lunch at Buffet Trzesniewski; 13:00–Tour the Hofburg and treasury; 16:00–Hit one more museum, or shop, browse, and people-watch; 19:30–Choose classical music (concert or opera), House of Music museum, or *Heuriger* wine garden.

Day 2: Morning—choose between Schönbrunn Palace (arrive at 9:00, return to central Vienna by noon) or Lipizzaner stallions' morning practice (10:00–12:00); 12:00–Have lunch at Naschmarkt or Rosenberger Markt; 13:00–Tour the Opera; 14:00–Kunsthistorisches Museum; 16:00–Your choice of the many sights left to see in Vienna; Evening–See Day 1 evening options.

For efficient sightseeing, drivers should note that Schönbrunn Palace is conveniently on the way out of town toward Salzburg.

The year 2006 is a good time to visit Vienna, as the city celebrates the 250th birthday of Wolfgang Amadeus Mozart. For details on all the festivities, see page 470.

ORIENTATION

(area code: 01)

Vienna—Wien in German (pronounced "veen")—sits between the Vienna Woods (Wienerwald) and the Danube (Donau). To the southeast is industrial sprawl. The Alps, which arc across Europe from Marseille, end at Vienna's wooded hills, providing a popular playground for walking and sipping new wine. This greenery's momentum carries on into the city. More than half of Vienna is parkland, filled with ponds, gardens, trees, and statue-maker memories of Austria's glory days.

Think of the city map as a target. The bull's-eye is St. Stephen's Cathedral, the first circle is the Ringstrasse, and the second is the Gürtel outerbelt. The old town—snuggling around towering cathedral south of the Danube—is bound tightly by the Ringstrasse, marking what used to be the city wall. The Gürtel, a broader ring road, contains the rest of downtown.

Addresses start with the district, or *Bezirk,* followed by street and building number. The Ring circles the first *Bezirk*. Any address higher than the ninth *Bezirk* is beyond the Gürtel, far from the center. The middle two digits of Vienna's postal codes show the *Bezirk*. The address "7, Lindengasse 4" is in the seventh district, #4 on Linden Street. Its postal code would be 1070.

Nearly all your sightseeing will be done in the core first district or along the Ringstrasse. As a tourist, concern yourself only with this compact old center. When you do, sprawling Vienna suddenly becomes manageable.

Tourist Information

Vienna's one real tourist office is a block behind the Opera House at Albertinaplatz (daily 9:00–19:00, tel. 01/24555, press 2 for English info, www.vienna.info). Confirm your sightseeing plans and pick up the free and essential city map with a list of museums and hours (also available at most hotels), the monthly program of concerts (called *Wien-Programm*—includes daily calendar and information on the contemporary cultural scene, including live music, jazz, walks, expositions, and evening museum options), the biannual city guide *(Vienna Journal)*, and the youth guide *(Vienna Hype)*. The TI also books rooms for a €2.90 fee. While hotel and ticket-booking agencies at the train stations and airport can answer questions and give out maps and brochures, I'd rely on the official TI if possible.

Consider the TI's handy €3.60 *Vienna from A to Z* booklet. Every important building sports a numbered flag banner that keys into this guidebook. *A to Z* numbers are keyed into the TI's city map. When lost, find one of the "famous-building flags" and match its number to your map. If you're at a famous building, check the map to see what other key numbers are nearby, then check the *A to Z* book description to see if you want to go in. This system is especially helpful for those just wandering aimlessly among Vienna's historic charms.

The much-promoted €17 **Vienna Card** might save the busy sightseer a few euros. It gives you a 72-hour transit pass (worth €12) and discounts of 10 to 50 percent at the city's museums. (Seniors and students will do better with their own discounts.)

Arrival in Vienna

By Train at the West Station (Westbahnhof): Train travelers arriving from Munich, Salzburg, and Melk land at the Westbahnhof. The *Reisebüro am Bahnhof* books hotels (for a €4.50 fee), has maps, answers questions, and has a train info desk (daily 7:30–21:00). The Westbahnhof also has a grocery store (daily 5:30–23:00), ATMs, Internet access, change offices, and storage facilities. Airport buses and taxis wait in front of the station.

To get to the city center (and most likely, your hotel), take the U-Bahn on the U-3 line (buy your ticket or transit pass—described under "Getting Around Vienna," below—from a *Tabak* shop in the station or from a machine). Blue *U-3* signs lead down to the tracks (direction Simmering for Mariahilfer Strasse hotels or the center). If your hotel is along Mariahilfer Strasse, your stop is on this line (see page 480). If you're sleeping in the center or just sightseeing, ride five stops to Stephansplatz, escalate in the exit direction Stephansplatz, and you'll hit the cathedral. The TI is a five-minute stroll down the busy Kärntner Strasse pedestrian street.

By Train at the South Station (Südbahnhof): Those arriving from Italy and Prague will probably land here. The Südbahnhof has all the services, left luggage, and a TI (daily 9:00–19:00). To reach Vienna's center, follow the S (Schnellbahn) signs to the right and down the stairs, and take any train in the direction Floridsdorf; transfer in two stops (at Landsstrasse/Wien Mitte) to the U-3 line, direction Ottakring, which goes directly to Stephansplatz and Mariahilfer Strasse hotels. Tram D also goes to the Ring, and bus #13A goes to Mariahilfer Strasse.

By Train at Franz Josefs Station: If you're coming from Krems (in the Danube Valley), you'll arrive at Vienna's Franz Josefs station. From here, take tram D into town. Better yet, get off your train at Spittelau (the stop before Franz Josefs) and use its handy U-Bahn station.

By Plane: Vienna International Airport is 12 miles from the center (airport code: VIE, tel. 01/7007-22233, www.viennaairport .com). It's connected to the very central Wien-Mitte station by S-Bahn (S-7 yellow, €3, 2/hr, 24 min). A speedier new City Airport Train (CAT) connects the airport to Wien-Mitte (green signs, €9, 2/hr, 16 min, www.cityairporttrain.com). Express airport buses (parked immediately in front of the arrival hall, €6, 2/hr, 30 min, buy tickets from drivers) go conveniently to Schwedenplatz, Westbahnhof, and Südbahnhof, from which it's easy to continue by public transportation. Taxis into town cost about €35 (including €10 airport surcharge). Hotels arrange for fixed-rate car service to the airport (€30, 30-min ride).

Some budget carriers—especially SkyEurope—fly into **Bratislava Airport,** in the nearby capital of Slovakia (Letisko Bratislava, airport code: BTS, www.letiskobratislava.sk). This airport is marketed as "Vienna-Bratislava" (thanks to its proximity to both capitals). To reach Vienna, there are several buses (€10–15, trip takes about 90 min), or take a taxi (figure €60-90, depending on whether you use a Slovak or an Austrian cab). SkyEurope's Web site has more details: www.skyeurope.com.

Helpful Hints

Money: ATMs are everywhere. Banks are open weekdays roughly from 8:00 to 15:00 (until 17:30 on Thu). After hours, you can change money at train stations, the airport, post offices, or the American Express office (Mon–Fri 9:00–17:30, Sat 9:00–12:00, closed Sun, Kärntner Strasse 21-23, tel. 01/5124-0040).

Internet Access: The TI has a list of Internet cafés. BigNet is the dominant outfit (www.bignet.at), with lots of stations at Kärntner Strasse 61 (daily 10:00–24:00) and Hoher Markt 8–9 (daily 10:00–24:00). Surfland Internet Café is near the Opera (daily 10:00–23:00, Krugerstrasse 10, tel. 01/512-7701).

Post Offices: Choose from the main post office (Postgasse in center, open 24 hrs daily, handy metered phones), Westbahnhof (Mon–Fri 7:00–22:00, Sat–Sun 9:00–20:00), Südbahnhof (daily 7:00–22:00), or near the Opera (Mon–Fri 7:00–19:00, closed Sat–Sun, Krugerstrasse 13).

English Bookstores: Consider the **British Bookshop** (Mon–Fri 9:30–19:30, Sat 9:30–18:00, closed Sun, at corner of Weihburggasse and Seilerstätte, tel. 01/512-1945; same hours at branch at Mariahilfer Strasse 4, tel. 01/522-6730) or **Shakespeare & Co.** (Mon–Sat 9:00–19:00, closed Sun, north of Hoher Markt square, Sterngasse 2, tel. 01/535-5053).

Travel Agency: Intropa is convenient, with good service for flights and train tickets (Mon–Fri 9:00–18:00, Sat 10:00–13:00, closed Sun, Neuer Markt 8, tel. 01/513-4000). Train tickets come with a €2 service charge when purchased from an agency rather than at the station—but the convenience is worth this modest cost.

Getting Around Vienna

By Public Transportation: Take full advantage of Vienna's simple, cheap, and super-efficient transit system, which includes trams, buses, subway (U-Bahn), and faster suburban trains (S-Bahn).

I use the tram mostly to zip around the Ring (tram #1 or #2) and take the U-Bahn to outlying sights or hotels. Numbered lines (such as #38) are trams, and numbers followed by an *A* (such as #38A) are buses. The smooth, modern trams are Porsche-designed, with "backpack technology" locating the engines and mechanical hardware on the roofs for a lower ride and easier entry. Lines that begin with U (e.g., U-3) are U-Bahn lines (designated by the end-of-the-line stops). Blue lines are the speedier S-Bahns. Take a moment to study the eye-friendly city-center map on station walls to internalize how the transit system can help you. The free tourist map has essentially all the lines marked, making the too-big €1.50 transit map unnecessary (information tel. 01/790-9105).

Trams, buses, the U-Bahn, and the S-Bahn all use the same tickets. Buy your tickets from *Tabak* shops, station machines, *Vorverkauf* offices in the station, or on board (just on trams, single tickets only, more expensive). You have lots of choices:

- Single tickets (€1.50, €2 if bought on tram, good for 1 journey with necessary transfers);
- 24-hour transit pass (€5);
- 72-hour transit pass (€12);
- 7-day transit pass (*Wochenkarte,* €12.50, pass always starts on Mon); or
- 8-day card (*Acht Tage Karte),* covering eight full days of free transportation for €24 (can be shared—for example, 4 people for 2 days each). With a per-person cost of €3/day (compared to €5/day for a 24-hour pass), this can be a real saver for groups. Kids under 15 travel free on Sundays and holidays.

Stamp a time on your ticket as you enter the Metro system, tram, or bus (stamp it only the first time for a multiple-use pass). Cheaters pay a stiff €44 fine if caught—and then they make you buy a ticket. Rookies miss stops because they fail to open the door. Push buttons, pull latches—do whatever it takes. Study the excellent wall-mounted street map before you exit the U-Bahn station. Choosing the right exit—signposted from the moment you step off the train—saves lots of walking.

By Taxi: Vienna's comfortable, civilized, and easy-to-flag-down taxis start at €2.50. You'll pay about €8 to go from the Opera to the Westbahnhof. Pay only what's on the meter—any surcharges (other than the €2 fee added to fares when you telephone them, or €10 for the airport) are just crude cabbie rip-offs.

By Car with Driver: Consider the luxury of having your own car and driver. Johann (a.k.a. John) Lichtl is a kind, honest, English-speaking cabbie who can take up to four passengers in his car (€25/1 hr, €20/hr for 2 or more hours, mobile 0676-670-6750). Consider hiring Johann for a day trip to the Wachau Valley (see previous chapter, €110, up to 8 hrs), or to drive you to Salzburg with Wachau sightseeing en route (€190, up to 12 hrs; other trips by negotiation).

By Bike: Vienna is a great city for biking—*if* you own a bike. Bike rental is a hassle (get list at TI). There are no bike-rental options in the center; the nearest is out at Prater Park (see page 469). The bikes you'll see parked in public racks all over town are part of a loaner system that is only workable for locals with mobile phones. The bike path along the Ring is wonderfully entertaining.

By Buggy: Rich romantics get around by traditional horse and buggy. These buggies, called *Fiakers,* clip-clop visitors on tours lasting 20 minutes (€40—old town), 40 minutes (€65—old town and the Ring), or one hour (€95—all of the above, but more thorough). You can share the ride and cost with up to five people. Because it's a kind of guided tour, before settling on a carriage, talk to a few drivers and pick one who's fun and speaks English.

TOURS

Walking Tours—The TI's *Walks in Vienna* brochure describes Vienna's many guided walks. The basic 90-minute "Vienna First Glance" introductory walk is offered daily throughout the summer (€12, leaves at 14:00 from near the Opera, in English and German, tel. 01/894-5363, www.wienguide.at).

Bus Tours—Vienna Sightseeing operates hop-on, hop-off tours covering 13 predictable sightseeing stops (departures from Opera at top of each hour 10:00–17:00, recorded commentary). Given Vienna's excellent public transportation and this outfit's meager one-bus-per-hour frequency, I'd take this not to hop on and off, but only to get the narrated orientation drive through town (€20 for 24-hr ticket, or €12 if you stay on for the full 60-min circular ride—skipping the hop-on, hop-off privileges). Their 3.5-hour Vienna city sights tour includes a visit to Schönbrunn Palace and a bus tour around town (€34; April–Oct 3/day—9:45, 10:30, and 14:45; Nov–March 2/day—9:45 and 14:00; call 01/7124-6830 to book this or get info on other tours). These leave from the Opera or, 30 minutes later, from the Südbahnhof.

Local Guides—The tourist board Web site (www.vienna.info) has a long list of local guides with specialties and contact informa-tion. Lisa Zeiler is a good English-speaking guide (2-hr walks for €125—if she's booked up, she can set you up with another guide, tel. 01/402-3688, lisa.zeiler@gmx.at). Ursula Klaus, an art scholar specializing in turn-of-the-century Vienna, enjoys tailoring tours to specific interests (especially music, art, architecture). She does two-hour tours for €120 (tel. 01/522-8556, mobile 0676-421-4884, ursula.klaus@aon.at).

Vienna

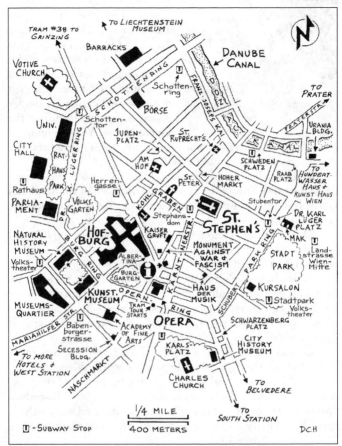

TRAM #38 TO GRINZING

↖ TO LIECHTENSTEIN MUSEUM

BARRACKS

VOTIVE CHURCH

DANUBE CANAL

TO PRATER

SCHOTTEN RING

Schotten-ring

FRANZ JOSEFS KAI

BÖRSE

URANIA BLDG.

UNIV.

Schotten-tor

LÜGERING

JUDEN-PLATZ

ST. RUPRECHT'S

CITY HALL

RAT-HAUS

AM HOF

SCHWEDEN PLATZ

RAAB PLATZ

TO HUNDERT-WASSER HAUS & KUNST HAUS WIEN

Rathaus

Herren-gasse

HOHER MARKT

ST. PETER

PARK

Stubentor

PARLIA-MENT

VOLKS-GARTEN

KOHL GRABEN

Stephans-dom

ST. STEPHEN'S

DR. KARL LÜGER PLATZ

NATURAL HISTORY MUSEUM

HOF-BURG

Kaiser Gruft

MAK

Land-strasse Wien-Mitte

Volks-theater

BURG RING

KÄRNERSTR.

MONUMENT AGAINST WAR & FASCISM

STADT PARK

ALBER-TINA

BURG-GARTEN

HAUS DER MUSIK

KURSALON

MUSEUMS-QUARTIER

KUNST-MUSEUM

Stadtpark Volks-theater

MARIAHILFER STR.

Baben-burger-strasse

ACADEMY OF FINE ARTS

OPERA

OPERN-RING

SCHUBER RING

SCHWARZENBERG PLATZ

TRAM TOUR STARTS

CITY HISTORY MUSEUM

Secession BLDG.

KARLS-PLATZ

TO MORE HOTELS & WEST STATION

NASCHMARKT

CHARLES CHURCH

TO BELVEDERE

TO SOUTH STATION

¼ MILE

400 METERS

Ⓤ - SUBWAY STOP

DCH

SELF-GUIDED TRAM TOUR

Around the Ringstrasse

In the 1860s, Emperor Franz Josef had the city's ingrown medieval wall torn down and replaced with a grand boulevard 190 feet wide. The road, arcing nearly three miles around the city's core, predates all the buildings that line it—so what you'll see is very "neo": neo-classical, neo-Gothic, and neo-Renaissance. One of Europe's great streets, the Ringstrasse is lined with many of the city's top sights. Trams #1 and #2 and a great bike path circle the whole route—and so should you.

This self-guided tram tour, rated ▲▲, gives you a fun orientation and a ridiculously quick glimpse of the major sights as you glide by (€1.50, €2 if bought on tram, 30-min circular tour). Tram

#1 goes clockwise; tram #2, counterclockwise. Most sights are on the outside, so use tram #2 (sit on the right, ideally in the front seat of the front car; or—for maximum view and minimum air—sit in the bubble-front seat of the second car). Start immediately across the street from the Opera House. You can jump on and off as you go (trams come every 5 min). Read ahead and pay attention—these sights can fly by. Let's go:

❂ Immediately on the left: The city's main pedestrian drag, Kärntner Strasse, leads to the zigzag roof of **St. Stephen's Cathedral.** This tram tour makes a 360-degree circle around the cathedral, staying about this same distance from it.

❂ At first bend (before first stop): Look right, toward the tall fountain and the guy on a horse. Schwarzenberg Platz shows off its **equestrian statue** of Prince Charles Schwarzenberg, who fought Napoleon. Behind that is the Russian monument (behind the fountain), which was built in 1945 as a forced thanks to the Soviets for liberating Austria from the Nazis. Formerly a sore point, now it's just ignored. Beyond that (out of sight, on tram D route) is Belvedere Palace (see page 465).

❂ Going down Schubertring, you reach the huge **Stadtpark** (City Park) on the right, which honors many great Viennese musicians and composers with statues. At the beginning of the park, the gold-and-cream concert hall behind the trees is the **Kursalon,** opened in 1867 by the Strauss brothers, who directed many waltzes here. The touristy Strauss concerts are held in this building (see "Music Scene," page 469).

❂ Immediately after next stop, look right: In the same park, the gilded statue of "Waltz King" **Johann Strauss** holds a violin as he did when he conducted his orchestra, whipping his fans into a three-quarter-time frenzy.

❂ At next stop at end of park: On the left, a green statue of **Dr. Karl Lüger** honors the popular man who was mayor of Vienna until 1910.

❂ At next bend: On the right, the quaint white building with military helmets decorating the windows was the **Austrian ministry of war**—back when that was a big operation. Field Marshal Radetzky, a military big shot in the 19th century under Franz Josef, still sits on his high horse. He's pointing toward the post office, the only Art Nouveau building facing the Ring. Locals call the architecture along the Ring "**historicism**" because it's all neo-this and neo-that—generally fitting the purpose of the particular building (for example, farther along the Ring, we'll see the neo-Gothic City Hall—recalling when medieval burghers ran the city government in Gothic days; a neoclassical parliament building—celebrating ancient Greek notions of democracy; and a neo-Renaissance opera house—venerating the high culture filling it).

◐ At next corner: The white-domed building over your right shoulder as you turn is the Urania, Franz Josef's 1910 **observatory.** Lean forward and look behind it for a peek at the huge red cars of the giant 100-year-old Ferris wheel in Vienna's Prater Park (fun for families, described on page 469).

◐ Now you're rolling along the **Danube Canal.** This "Baby Danube" is one of the many small arms of the river that once made up the Danube at this location. The rest have been gathered together in a mightier modern-day Danube, farther away. This neighborhood was thoroughly bombed in World War II. The buildings across the canal are typical of postwar architecture (1960s). They were built on the cheap, and are now being replaced by sleek, futuristic buildings. This was the site of the original Roman town, Vindobona. In three long blocks, on the left (opposite the BP station, be ready—it passes fast), you'll see the ivy-covered walls and round Romanesque arches of St. Ruprecht's, the oldest church in Vienna (built in the 11th century on a bit of Roman ruins). Remember, medieval Vienna was defined by that long-gone wall that you're tracing on this tour. Across the river is an OPEC headquarters, where oil ministers often meet to set prices. Relax for a few stops until the corner.

◐ Leaving canal, turning left up Schottenring, at first corner: A block down on the right, you can see a huge red-brick **castle**— actually a high-profile barracks built here at the command of a nervous Emperor Franz Josef (who found himself on the throne as an 18-year-old in 1848, the same year people's revolts against autocracy were sweeping across Europe).

◐ At next stop: On the left, the orange-and-white, neo-Renaissance temple of money—the **Börse**—is Vienna's stock exchange.

◐ Next stop, at corner: The huge, frilly, neo-Gothic church on the right is a "**votive church,**" built as a thanks to God when an 1853 assassination attempt on Emperor Franz Josef failed. Ahead on the right (in front of tram stop) is the **Vienna University** building (established in 1365, it has no real campus as the buildings are scattered around town). It faces (on the left, behind a gilded angel across the Ring) a chunk of the old **city wall.**

◐ At next stop, on right: The neo-Gothic **City Hall** (Rathaus), flying the flag of Europe, towers over Rathaus Platz. This square is a festive site in summer, with a huge screen showing outdoor movies, operas, and concerts and a thriving food circus (see page 487—if you're hungry and it's thriving, hop off now). In the winter, the City Hall becomes a huge Advent calendar, with 24 windows opening—one each day—as Christmas approaches. Immediately across the street (on left) is the **Burgtheater,** Austria's national theater.

⊖ At next stop, on right: The neo-Greek temple of democracy houses the **Austrian Parliament.** The lady with the golden helmet is Athena, goddess of wisdom. The big construction mess is for the restoration of the building's grand ramp. Across the street (on left) is the imperial park called the **Volksgarten.**

⊖ After the next stop on the right is the **Natural History Museum,** the first of Vienna's huge twin museums. It faces the **Kunsthistorisches Museum,** containing the city's greatest collection of paintings. The **MuseumsQuartier** behind them completes the ensemble with a collection of mostly modern-art museums. A hefty statue of Empress Maria Theresa squats between the museums, facing the grand gate to the **Hofburg,** the emperor's palace (on left, across the Ring). Of the five arches, only the center one was used by the emperor. (Your tour is essentially finished. If you want to jump out here, you're at many of Vienna's top sights.)

⊖ Fifty yards after the next stop, on the left through a gate in the black-iron fence, is a statue of Mozart. It's one of many charms in the **Burggarten,** which until 1918 was the private garden of the emperor. Vienna had more than its share of intellectual and creative geniuses. A hundred yards farther (on left, just out of the park), the German philosopher Goethe sits in a big, thought-provoking chair playing trivia with Schiller (across the street on your right). Behind the statue of Schiller is the **Academy of Fine Arts.**

⊖ Hey, there's the **Opera** again. Jump off the tram and see the rest of the city.

SELF-GUIDED WALK

Welcome to Vienna

This walk connects the top three sights in Vienna's old center: the Opera, St. Stephen's Cathedral, and the Hofburg Palace. Along the way, you'll get a glimpse of Vienna past and present. The total trip takes about an hour, not counting sightseeing stops (which could be lengthy).

• *Begin by standing on the square in front of Vienna's landmark Opera.*

Opera: This is regarded by music-lovers as one of the planet's premier houses of music. If you're a fan, consider taking a guided tour of the Opera, or spring for a performance (standing-room tickets are surprisingly cheap; for information on all your Opera options, see page 434). The U-Bahn station in front of the Opera is actually a huge underground shopping mall with fast food, newsstands, lots of pickpockets, and even an Opera Toilet Vienna experience (€0.50, *mit Musik*).

• *Walk behind the Opera to find the famous...*

Sacher Café: This is the home of every chocoholic's fantasy, the *Sachertorte*. While locals complain that the cakes have gone downhill (and many tourists are surprised how dry they are), a coffee and slice of cake here can be €8 well invested. For maximum elegance, sit inside (daily 8:00–23:30, Philharmoniker Strasse 4, tel. 01/51456).

• *Near the Sacher Café (turn right as you exit) is a square called Albertinaplatz, where you'll find the TI, as well as the evocative...*

Monument Against War and Fascism: This powerful, thought-provoking four-part statue merits ▲. The split white monument, *The Gates of Violence*, remembers victims of all wars and violence, including the 1938–1945 Nazi rule of Austria. A montage of wartime images—clubs and WWI gas masks, a dying woman birthing a future soldier, chained slave laborers—sits on a pedestal of granite cut from the infamous quarry at Mauthausen Concentration Camp (see page 501). The hunched-over figure on the ground behind is a Jew forced to wash anti-Nazi graffiti off a street with a toothbrush. The statue with its head buried in the stone (Orpheus entering the underworld) reminds Austrians of the consequences of not keeping their government on track. Behind that, the 1945 declaration of Austria's second republic—with human rights built into it—is cut into the stone. This monument stands on the spot where several hundred people were buried alive while hiding in the cellar of a building demolished in a WWII bombing attack (see photo to right of park).

Austria was pulled into World War II by Germany, which annexed the country in 1938, saying Austrians were wannabe Germans anyway. But Austrians are not Germans—never were, never will be. They're quick to tell you that while Austria was founded in the 10th century, Germany wasn't born until 1870. For seven years during World War II (1938–1945), there was no Austria. In 1955, after 10 years of joint occupation by the victorious Allies, Austria regained total independence on the condition that it would be forever neutral (and never join NATO or the Warsaw Pact). To this day, Austria is outside of NATO (and Germany).

• *Across the square from the TI is the...*

Albertina Museum: Overlooking Albertinaplatz is what looks like a big terrace. This was actually part of Vienna's original defensive rampart. Later, it was the home to Empress Maria Theresa's daughter Maria Christina. And today, it's topped by a sleek, controversial titanium canopy (called the "diving board" by critics) that welcomes visitors into a recently restored museum. For details on the Albertina Museum, see page 447.

Adolf Loos
(1870–1933)

Adolf Loos—Vienna's answer to Frank Lloyd Wright—famously condemned needless ornamentation, declaring, "Decoration is a crime." You can see three good examples of his work (all c. 1900 and described in this chapter) as you stroll the old center. Just off Kärntner Strasse is the Loos American Bar (Kärntnerdurchgang 10). On the Graben, you can descend into the finest public toilets in town. And facing Michaelerplatz, in front of the Hofburg entrance, is the Loos House (a.k.a. the "house without eyebrows").

• *Across Albertinaplatz from the Albertina Museum is the street called Tegetthoffstrasse. Walk down this street a block to the square called Neuer Markt. Fronting the square is the...*

Kaisergruft: This church houses the remains of the Hapsburgs (not as gruesome as it sounds—it's basically a bunch of fancy coffins labeled with names you might recognize). Before moving on, consider paying your respects here (described on page 449).

• *After visiting the Kaisergruft, cross Neuer Markt and turn left down...*

Kärntner Strasse: This grand, mall-like street (traffic-free since 1974) is the people-watching delight of this in-love-with-life city. While it's mostly a crass commercial pedestrian mall with its famed elegant shops now long gone, locals know it's the same road crusaders marched down as they headed off for the Holy Land in the 12th century. Its name indicates that it points south, in the direction of the region of Kärnten (Carinthia, today divided between Austria and Slovenia).

Along this drag, you'll find lots of action—shops, street music, the city casino (at #41), the venerable Lobmeyr Crystal shop (#26), American Express (#21), the Loos American bar (dark, plush, small, great €8 cocktails, no shorts, Kärntnerdurchgang 10, tel. 01/512-3283), and then, finally, the cathedral. Where Kärntner Strasse hits Stephansplatz (at #3), the Equitable Building (filled with lawyers, bankers, and insurance men) is a fine example of historicism from the turn of the century. Step in, climb the stairs, and imagine how slick the courtyard must have felt in 1900.

• *At the end of Kärntner Strasse, you'll wander into...*

Stephansplatz: Vienna's fun and colorful main square is also home to its cathedral, St. Stephen's. Now's the time to visit this massive church (see page 435).

• *When you're finished on Stephansplatz, head for the Hofburg. At the bottom of the square (near the start of Kärntner Strasse) is the street called...*

Graben: This was once a *Graben*, or ditch—originally the moat for the Roman military camp. In the middle of this pedestrian zone (at the intersection with Bräuner Strasse), top-notch street entertainers dance around an extravagant **plague monument.** In the Middle Ages, people didn't understand the causes of plagues, and figured they were a punishment from God. It was common for survivors to bribe or thank God with a monument like this one (c. 1690). Find Emperor Leopold, who ruled during the plague and made this statue in gratitude. (Hint: The typical inbreeding of royal families left him with a gaping under bite.) Below Leopold,  Faith (with the help of a disgusting little cupid) tosses old naked women—symbolizing the plague—into the abyss.

Just before the plague monument is Dorotheergasse, leading to the Dorotheum auction house (see page 460). Just beyond the monument, you'll pass a fine set of **public WCs.** Around 1900, a local chemical maker needed a publicity stunt. He purchased two wine cellars under the Graben and hired Adolf Loos to design classy WCs in the Modernist style (complete with chandeliers and finely crafted mahogany) to prove that his chemicals really got things clean. The restrooms remain clean to this day—in fact, they're so inviting that they're used for poetry readings. Locals and tourists happily pay €0.50 for a quick visit.

• *The Graben dead-ends at the aristocratic supermarket Julius Meinl am Graben (see "Eating," page 486). At the end of Graben, turn left onto...*

Kohlmarkt: This is Vienna's most elegant shopping street (except for "American Catalog Shopping" at #5, 2nd floor), with the emperor's palace at the end. Strolling Kohlmarkt, daydream about the edible window displays at **Demel** (#14, daily 10:00–19:00). Demel is the ultimate Viennese chocolate shop. During the summer, when the tables are moved outside, a room is filled with Art Nouveau boxes of Empress Sissy's choco-dreams come true: *Kandierte Veilchen* (candied violet petals), *Katzenzungen* (cats' tongues), and so on. The cakes here are moist (compared to the dry *Sachertortes*). The delectable window displays change about weekly, reflecting current happenings in Vienna. Inside, an impressive cancan of cakes is displayed to tempt visitors into springing for the €10 cake-and-coffee deal (point to the cake you want). You

Vienna at a Glance

▲▲▲Opera Dazzling, world-famous opera house. **Hours:** Visit by guided 45-min tour only, daily in English; July–Aug at 11:00, 13:00, 14:00, 15:00, and often at 10:00 and 16:00; Sept–June fewer tours, afternoon only; call ahead to confirm tour times.

▲▲▲Hofburg Treasury The Hapsburgs' collection of jewels, crowns, and other valuables—the best on the Continent. **Hours:** Wed–Mon 10:00–18:00, closed Tue.

▲▲▲Kunsthistorisches Museum World-class exhibit of the Hapsburgs' art collection, including Raphael, Titian, Caravaggio, Bosch, and Brueghel. **Hours:** Tue–Sun 10:00–18:00, Thu until 21:00, closed Mon.

▲▲▲Schönbrunn Palace Spectacular summer residence of the Hapsburgs, similar in grandeur to Versailles. **Hours:** Daily July–Aug 8:30–18:00, April–June and Sept–Oct 8:30–17:00, Nov–March 8:30–16:30, reservations recommended.

▲▲St. Stephen's Cathedral Enormous, historic Gothic cathedral in the center of Vienna. **Hours:** Church doors open Mon–Sat 6:00–22:00, Sun 7:00–22:00, officially only open for tourists Mon–Sat 8:30–11:30 & 13:00–16:30, Sun 13:00–16:30.

▲▲Hofburg Imperial Apartments Lavish main residence of the Hapsburgs. **Hours:** Daily 9:00–17:00.

▲▲Hofburg New Palace Museums Uncrowded collection of armor, musical instruments, and ancient Greek statues, in the elegant halls of a Hapsburg palace. **Hours:** Wed–Mon 10:00–18:00, closed Tue.

▲▲Albertina Museum Hapsburg residence with decent apartments and world-class permanent and temporary exhibits. **Hours:** Daily 10:00–18:00, Wed until 21:00.

▲▲Kaisergruft Crypt for the Hapsburg royalty. **Hours:** Daily 9:30–16:00.

▲▲Haus der Musik Modern musuem with interactive exhibits on Vienna's favorite pastime. **Hours:** Daily 10:00–22:00.

▲▲**Belvedere Palace** Elegant palace of Prince Eugene of Savoy, with a collection of 19th- and 20th-century Austrian art (including Klimt). **Hours:** Tue–Sun 10:00–18:00, closed Mon.

▲**Monument Against War and Fascism** Powerful four-part statue remembering victims of the Nazis. **Hours:** Always open.

▲**Lipizzaner Museum** Displays dedicated to the regal Lipizzaner Stallions; horse-lovers should check out their practice sessions. **Hours:** Museum open daily 9:00–18:00; stallions practice across the street roughly Feb–June and Sept–Oct Tue–Sat 10:00–12:00 when the horses are in town—call to confirm.

▲**Augustinian Church** Hapsburg marriage church, now hosting an 11:00 Sunday Mass with wonderful music. **Hours:** Open long hours daily.

▲**Imperial Furniture Collection** Eclectic collection of Hapsburg furniture. **Hours:** Tue–Sun 10:00–18:00, closed Mon.

▲**Naschmarkt** Sprawling, lively, people-filled outdoor market. **Hours:** Mon–Fri 6:00–18:30, Sat 6:00–17:00, closed Sun, closes earlier in winter.

▲**Natural History Museum** Big building facing Kunsthistorisches Museum, featuring the ancient *Venus of Willendorf*. **Hours:** Wed–Mon 9:00–18:30, Wed until 21:00, closed Tue.

▲**Dorotheum** Vienna's highbrow auction house. **Hours:** Mon–Fri 10:00–18:00, Sat 9:00–17:00, closed Sun.

▲**Academy of Fine Arts** Small but exciting collection with works by Bosch, Botticelli, Rubens, Guardi, and Van Dyck. **Hours:** Tue–Sun 10:00–18:00, closed Mon.

▲**Liechtenstein Museum** Baroque art collection of the family that governs one of Europe's tiniest nations. **Hours:** Wed–Mon 9:00–20:00, closed Tue.

▲**KunstHausWien** Modern art museum dedicated to zany local artist/environmentalist Hundertwasser. **Hours:** Daily 10:00–19:00.

can sit inside, with a view of the cake-making, or outside, with the street action. Shops like this boast "K. u. K."—good enough for the *König und Kaiser* (king and emperor—same guy).

Just beyond Demel and across the street, at #1152, you can pop into a charming little Baroque **carriage courtyard,** with the surviving original carriage garages.

• *Kohlmarkt ends at...*

Michaelerplatz: In the center of this square, a scant bit of Roman Vienna lies exposed. On the left are the fancy Loden Plankl shop, with traditional formal wear, and the stables of the Spanish Riding School. Study the grand entry facade to the Hofburg Palace—it's neo-Baroque from around 1900. The four heroic giants illustrate Hercules wrestling with his great challenges (much like the Hapsburgs, I'm sure). Opposite the facade, notice the modern Loos House (now a bank), which was built at about the same time. It was nicknamed the "house without eyebrows" for the simplicity of its windows. An anti–Art Nouveau statement (inspired by Frank Lloyd Wright and considered Vienna's first "modern" building), this was actually shocking at the time. To quell some of the outrage, the architect added flower boxes.

• *You've made it to the Hofburg Palace. To get to the sights inside, simply walk through the gate, under the dome, and into the first square (In der Burg). For details on all the sights here, see page 437.*

SIGHTS

For a self-guided walk connecting these first three landmark sights, see page 428.

Opera (Staatsoper)

The Opera, facing the Ring and near the TI, is a central point for any visitor—easily worth ▲▲▲. While the critical reception of the building 130 years ago led the architect to commit suicide, and though it's been rebuilt since being destroyed by WWII bombs, it's still a sumptuous place.

Tours: Unless you're attending a performance, you can enter the Opera only with a guided 45-minute tour (€4.50, daily in English; July–Aug at 11:00, 13:00, 14:00, 15:00, and often at 10:00 and 16:00; Sept–June fewer tours, afternoon only). Tours are often canceled for rehearsals and shows, so check the posted schedule or call 01/514-442-606.

Performances: The Vienna State Opera—with musicians provided by the Vienna Philharmonic Orchestra in the pit—is one of the world's top opera houses. There are 300 performances a year, but in July and August the singers rest their voices. Since there are different operas nearly nightly, you'll see big trucks out back and constant action backstage—all the sets need to be switched each day. Even though the expensive seats normally sell out long in advance, the opera is perpetually in the red and subsidized by the state.

To **buy tickets** in advance, call 01/513-1513 (phone answered daily 10:00–21:00, www.wiener-staatsoper.at). If seats aren't sold out, last-minute tickets (for pricey seats—up to €100) are sold for €40 from 9:00 to 14:00 only the day before the show.

Unless Placido Domingo is in town, it's easy to get one of 567 **standing-room tickets** (*Stehplätze*, €2 at the top or €3.50 downstairs). While the front doors open one hour before the show starts, a side door (on the Operngasse side, the door under the portico nearest the fountain) is open an hour and a half before curtain time, giving those in the know an early grab at standing-room tickets. Just walk in straight, then head right until you see the ticket booth marked *Stehplätze* (tel. 01/5144-42419). If fewer than 567 people are in line, there's no need to line up early. If you're one of the first 160 in line, try for the "Parterre" section and you'll end up directly under the Emperor's Box. You can even buy standing-room tickets after the show has started—in case you want only a little taste of opera. Dress is casual (but do your best) at the standing-room bar. Locals save their spot along the rail by tying a scarf to it.

Rick's Crude Tip: For me, three hours is a lot of opera. But just to see and hear the Opera House in action for half an hour is a treat. You can buy a standing-room spot and just drop in for part of the show. Ushers don't mind letting tourists with standing-room tickets in for a short look. Ending time is posted in the lobby—you could stop by for just the finale. If you go at the start or finish, you'll see Vienna dressed up.

St. Stephen's Cathedral (Stephansdom)

This massive church is the Gothic needle around which Vienna spins. Today worth ▲▲, it has survived Vienna's many wars and symbolizes the city's freedom.

Cost: Entering the church is free, but going up the towers costs €3 (by stairs, south tower) or €4 (by elevator, north tower). For more information, see "Towers" below.

Hours: The church doors are open Mon–Sat 6:00–22:00, Sun 7:00–22:00, but it's officially only open for tourists Mon–Sat 8:30–11:30 & 13:00–16:30, Sun 13:00–16:30. During services, you can't enter the main nave (unless you're attending

Mass), but you can go into the back of the church to reach the north tower elevator (daily 8:30–17:30, Nov–March until 16:30). The stairs up to the south tower (enter from outside) are open daily 9:00–17:30.

Tours: The €4 tours in English are entertaining (daily April–Oct at 15:45, check information board inside entry to confirm schedule).

❍ **Self-Guided Tour:** This is the third church to stand on this spot. The church survived the bombs of World War II, but, in the last days of the war, fires from the street fighting between Russian and Nazi troops leapt to the rooftop. The original timbered Gothic rooftop burned, and the cathedral's huge bell crashed to the ground. With a financial outpouring of civic pride, the roof was rebuilt in its original splendor by 1952. The ceramic tiles are purely decorative (locals who contributed to the postwar reconstruction each "own" one for their donation).

The **grounds** around the church were a cemetery until Josef II emptied it as an "anti-plague" measure. (Inside, a few of the most important tombstones decorate the church walls.) You can still see the footprint of the old cemetery church in the pavement, today ignored by the human statues. Remains of the earlier Virgil Chapel (dating from the 13th century) are immediately under this (on display in the U-Bahn station).

Study the church's **main entrance** (west end). You can see the original Romanesque facade (c. 1240) with classical Roman statues embedded in it. Above are two stubby towers nicknamed "pagan towers" because they're built with Roman stones (flipped over to hide the inscriptions and expose the smooth sides). Two 30-foot-tall columns flank the main entry. If you stand back and look at the tops, you'll see that they symbolize creation (one's a penis, the other's a vagina).

Go inside. Find the dramatic photos of **WWII damage** (with bricks neatly stacked and ready) in glass cases 20 yards opposite the south entrance (on the wall near 3a).

The nave is ringed with **chapels.** The church once had over a hundred. This was typical of Catholic churches, as each guild and leading family had their own chapel. The Tupperware-colored glass windows date from 1950. Before WWII, the entire church was lit with windows like the ones behind the altar. Those, along with the city's top art treasures, were hidden safely from the Nazis in salt mines. The altar painting of the stoning of St. Stephen is early Baroque, painted on copper.

St. Stephen's is proud to be Austria's national church. A **plaque** explains how each region contributed to the rebuilding after World War II: windows from Tirol, furniture from Vorarlberg, the floor from Lower Austria, and so on.

The Gothic sandstone **pulpit** in the middle of the nave (on left) is a realistic masterpiece carved from three separate blocks (find the seams). A spiral stairway winds up to the lectern, surrounded and supported by the four Latin Church fathers: Saints Ambrose, Jerome, Gregory, and Augustine. The railing leading up swarms with symbolism: lizards (animals of light) and battle toads (animals of darkness). The "Dog of the Lord" stands at the top,

making sure none of those toads pollutes the sermon. Below the toads, wheels with three parts (the Trinity) roll up, while wheels with four parts (the four seasons, symbolizing mortal life) roll down. This work, by Anton Pilgram, has all the elements of the Flamboyant Gothic style in miniature. Gothic art was done for the glory of God. Artists were anonymous. But this was around 1500, and the Renaissance was going strong in Italy. While Gothic persisted in the North, the Renaissance spirit had already arrived. In the more humanist Renaissance, man was allowed to shine—and artists became famous. So Pilgram included a rare self-portrait bust in his work (the guy with sculptor's tools, in the classic "artist observing the world from his window" pose under the stairs).

Towers: You can ascend both towers, the south (outside right transept, by spiral staircase) and the north (via crowded elevator inside on the left). The 450-foot-high south tower, called St. Stephen's Tower, offers the far better view, but you'll earn it by hiking 343 tightly wound steps up the spiral staircase (€3, daily 9:00–17:30, this hike burns about 1 *Sachertorte* of calories). From the top, use your *Vienna from A to Z* to locate the famous sights. The north tower shows you a mediocre view and a big bell: the 21-ton Pummerin, cast from the cannon captured from the Turks in 1683, and supposedly the second biggest bell in the world that rings by swinging (locals know it as the bell that rings in the Austrian New Year; €4, daily 8:30–17:30, Nov–March until 16:30).

Cathedral Museum (Dom Museum): This forlorn museum (outside left transept past horses) gives a close-up look at piles of religious paintings, statues, and a treasury (€5, Tue–Sat 10:00–17:00, closed Sun–Mon, Stephansplatz 6, tel. 01/515-523-560).

Hofburg Palace

The complex, confusing, and imposing Imperial Palace, with 640 years of architecture, demands your attention. This first Hapsburg residence grew with the family empire from the

Sissy
(1837–1898)

Empress Elisabeth—Franz Josef's mysterious, narcissistic, and beautiful wife—is in vogue. Sissy was mostly silent. Her main goals in life seem to have been preserving her reputation as a beautiful empress, maintaining her Barbie Doll figure, and tending to her fairytale, ankle-length hair. In spite of severe dieting and fanatic exercise, age took its toll. After turning 30, she allowed no more portraits to be painted and was generally seen in public with a delicate fan covering her face (and bad teeth). Complex and influential, she was adored by Franz Josef, whom she respected. Her personal mission and political cause was promoting Hungary's bid for nationalism. Her personal tragedy was the death of her son Rudolf, the crown prince, by suicide. Disliking Vienna and the confines of the court, she traveled more and more frequently. Over the years, the restless Sissy and her hardworking husband became estranged. In 1898, while visiting Geneva, Switzerland, she was murdered by an Italian anarchist.

Sissy has been compared to Princess Diana because of her beauty, bittersweet life, and tragic death. Her story is wonderfully told in the new Sissy Museum, now part of the Hofburg Imperial Apartments tour.

13th century until 1913, when the last "new wing" opened. The winter residence of the Hapsburg rulers until 1918, it's still the home of the Spanish Riding School, the Vienna Boys' Choir, the Austrian president's office, 5,000 government workers, and several important museums.

Rather than lose yourself in its myriad halls and courtyards, focus on three sections: the Imperial Apartments, Treasury, and Neue Burg (New Palace).

Orientation from In der Burg: Begin at the square called In der Burg (enter through the gate from Michaelerplatz). The statue is of Emperor Franz II, grandson of Maria Theresa, grandfather of Franz Josef, and father-in-law of Napoleon. Behind him is a tower with three kinds of clocks (the yellow disk shows the stage of the moon tonight). On the right, a door leads to the Imperial Apartments. Franz faces the oldest part of the palace. The colorful gate, which used to have a drawbridge, leads to the 13th-century Swiss Court (named for the Swiss mercenary guards once stationed here), the Treasury (Schatzkammer), and the Imperial Chapel (Hofburgkapelle, where the Boys' Choir sings the Mass—see page 470). For the Heroes' Square and the New Palace, continue opposite the way you entered In der Burg, passing through the

Vienna's Hofburg Palace

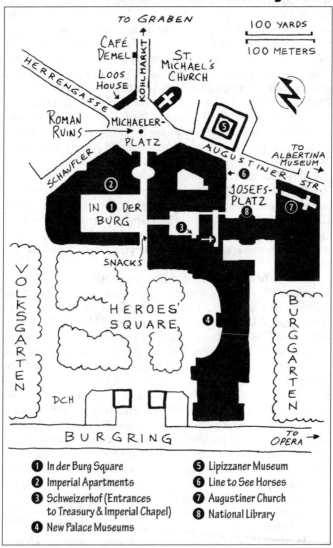

1 In der Burg Square

2 Imperial Apartments

3 Schweizerhof (Entrances to Treasury & Imperial Chapel)

4 New Palace Museums

5 Lipizzaner Museum

6 Line to See Horses

7 Augustiner Church

8 National Library

left-most tunnel (with a tiny but handy sandwich bar—Hofburg Stüberl, Mon–Fri 7:00–18:00, Sat–Sun 10:00–16:00, your best bet if you need a bite or drink before touring the Imperial Apartments). Note that Hapsburg sights not actually inside the Hofburg (including the Lipizzaner Stallions, the Augustinian Church, and the Albertina Museum) are covered on page 445.

▲▲▲Imperial Apartments (Kaiserappartements)—These lavish, Versailles-type, "wish-I-were-God" royal rooms are the downtown version of the grander Schönbrunn Palace. If you're rushed and have time for only one palace, do this (€8.90, daily 9:00–17:00, last entry 16:30, from courtyard through St. Michael's Gate, just off Michaelerplatz, tel. 01/533-7570). Palace visits are a one-way romp through 20 rooms. You'll find some helpful posted English information, and, with that and the following description, you won't need the €7.50 *Imperial Apartments and Sissy* museum guidebook. The included audioguide brings the exhibit to life. Tickets also get you into the royal silver and porcelain collection *(Silberkammer)* near the turnstile. If touring the silver and porcelain, do it first to save walking.

❍ Self-Guided Tour: Get your ticket, tour the silver and porcelain collection, climb the stairs, go through the turnstile, study the family tree tracing the Hapsburgs from 1273 to their messy WWI demise, and use the big model of the palace complex to understand the complex lay of the imperial land. Then head into the...

Sissy Museum: The first six rooms tell the life story of Empress Elisabeth's fancy world—her luxury homes and fairytale existence. While Sissy's life story is the perfect stuff of legends, the exhibit tries to keep things from getting too giddy, and doesn't add to the sugary, kitschy image that's been created. The exhibit starts with her assignation and traces the development of her legend, analyzing how her fabulous but tragic life could create a 19th-century Princes Diana from a rocky start (when she was disdained for abandoning Vienna and her husband, the venerable Emperor Franz Josef). You'll read bits of her poetic writing, catch snatches of movies made about her, see exact copies of her now-lost jewelry, and learn about her escapes, dieting mania, and chocolate bills. Admire Sissy's hard-earned thin waist (20 inches at age 16, 21 inches at age 50...after giving birth to 4 children). The black statue in the dark room represents the empress after the suicide of her son—aloof, thin, in black, with her back to the world.

After the Sissy rooms, a one-way route takes you through a series of royal rooms.

Waiting Room for the Audience Room: A map and mannequins from the many corners of the Hapsburg realm illustrate the multi-ethnicity of the vast empire. Every citizen had the right to meet privately with the emperor. Three huge paintings entertained guests while they waited. They were propaganda, showing crowds of commoners enthusiastic about their Hapsburg royalty. On the right: an 1809 scene of the emperor returning to Vienna, celebrating news that Napoleon had begun his retreat. Left: the return of the emperor from the 1814 Peace of Paris, the treaty that ended the

Napoleonic wars. (The 1815 Congress of Vienna that followed was the greatest assembly of diplomats in European history. Its goal: to establish peace through a "balance of power" among nations. While rulers ignored nationalism in favor of continued dynastic rule, this worked for about 100 years, until a colossal war—World War I—wiped out the Hapsburgs and the rest of Europe's royal families.) Center: Less important, the emperor makes his first public appearance to adoring crowds after recovering from a life-threatening illness (1826). The chandelier—considered the best in the palace—is Baroque, made of Bohemian crystal.

Audience Room: Suddenly, you were face-to-face with the emp. The portrait on the easel shows Franz Josef in 1915, when he was over 80 years old. Famously energetic, he lived a spartan life dedicated to duty. He'd stand at the high table here to meet with commoners, who came to show gratitude or make a request. (Standing kept things moving.) On the table, you can read a partial list of 56 appointments he had on January 3, 1910 (family name and topic of meeting).

Conference Room: The emperor presided here over the equivalent of cabinet meetings. After 1867, he ruled the Austro-Hungarian Empire, so Hungarians sat at these meetings. The paintings on the wall show the military defeat of a popular Hungarian uprising...subtle.

Emperor Franz Josef's Study: The desk was originally between the windows. Franz Josef could look up from his work and see his lovely, long-haired, tiny-waisted Empress Elisabeth's reflection in the mirror. Notice the trompe l'oeil paintings above each door, giving the believable illusion of marble relief. Notice also all the family photos—the perfect gift for the dad/uncle/hubby who has it all.

The walls between the rooms are wide enough to hide servants' corridors (the door to his valet's room is in the back left corner). The emperor lived with a personal staff of 14: "three valets, four lackeys, two doormen, two manservants, and three chambermaids."

Emperor's Bedroom: This features his famous no-frills iron bed and portable washstand (necessary until 1880, when the palace got running water). While he had a typical emperor's share of mistresses, his dresser was always well-stocked with photos of Sissy. Franz Josef lived here after his estrangement from Sissy. An etching shows the empress—a fine rider and avid hunter—riding sidesaddle while jumping a hedge. The big, ornate stove in the corner was fed from behind. Through the 19th century, this was a standard form of heating.

Small Salon: This is dedicated to the memory of the assassinated Emperor Maximilian of Mexico (bearded portrait, Franz

Emperor Franz Josef
(1830–1916)

Franz Josef I—who ruled for 68 years (1848–1916)—was the embodiment of the Hapsburg Empire as it finished its six-century-long ride. Born in 1830, Franz Josef had a stern upbringing that instilled in him a powerful sense of duty and—like so many men of power—a love of things military.

His uncle, Ferdinand I, was a dimwit, and, as the revolutions of 1848 were rattling royal families throughout Europe, the Hapsburgs replaced him, putting 18-year old Franz Josef on the throne. FJ put down the revolt with bloody harshness and spent the first part of his long reign understandably paranoid as social discontent simmered.

FJ was very conservative. But worse, he figured wrongly that he was a talented military tactician, leading Austria into disastrous battles against Italy (which was fighting for its unification and independence) in the 1860s. His army endured severe, avoidable casualties. It was clear: FJ was a disaster as a general.

Wearing his uniform to the end, he never saw what a dinosaur his monarchy was becoming, and never thought it strange that the majority of his subjects didn't even speak German. He had no interest in democracy and pointedly never set foot in Austria's parliament building. But, like his contemporary Queen Victoria, he was the embodiment of his empire—old-fashioned but sacrosanct. His passion for low-grade paperwork earned him the nickname "Joe Bureaucrat." Mired in these petty details, he missed the big picture. He helped start a Great War that ultimately ended the age of monarchs. The year 1918 marked the end of Europe's big royal families: Hohenzollerns (Prussia), Romanovs (Russia), and Hapsburgs (Austria).

Josef's brother, killed in 1867). This was also a smoking room—necessary in the early 19th century, when smoking was newly fashionable (but only for men—never in the presence of women). Left of the door is a small button the emp had to buzz before entering the quarters of his estranged wife. You can go right in.

Empress' Bedroom and Drawing Room: This was Sissy's, refurbished neo-rococo in 1854. She lived here—the bed was rolled in and out daily—until her death in 1898.

Sissy's Dressing/Exercise Room: Servants worked two hours a day on Sissy's famous hair here. She'd exercise on the wooden structure. While she had a tough time with people, she did fine with animals. Her favorite dogs hang adorably on the wall.

Sissy's Bathroom: Detour into the behind-the-scenes palace.

In the narrow passageway, you'll walk by Sissy's hand-painted-porcelain, dolphin-head WC (on the right). In the main bathroom, you'll see her huge copper tub (with the original wall coverings behind it). Sissy was the first Hapsburg to have running water in her bathroom (notice the hot and cold faucets). You're walking on the first linoleum ever used in Vienna—from around 1880. Next, enter the servants' quarters, with tropical scenes painted by Bergl in 1766. As you leave these rooms and re-enter the imperial world, look back to the room on the left.

Empress' Great Salon: The room is painted with Mediterranean escapes, the 19th-century equivalent of travel posters. The statue is of Elisa, Napoleon's oldest sister (by the neo-classical master, Canova). Turn the corner and pass through the anterooms of Alexander's apartments.

Red Salon: The Gobelin wall hangings were a 1776 gift from Marie Antoinette and Louis XVI in Paris to their Viennese counterparts.

Dining Room: It's dinnertime, and Franz Josef has called his extended family together. The settings are modest...just silver. Gold was saved for formal state dinners. Next to each name card was a menu with the chef responsible for each dish. (Talk about pressure.) While the Hofburg had tableware for 4,000, feeding 3,000 was a typical day. The cellar was stocked with 60,000 bottles of wine. The kitchen was huge—50 birds could be roasted on the hand-driven spits at once.

Through the shop, you're back on the street. Two quick lefts take you back to the palace square (In der Burg), where you can pass through the black, red, and gold gate and to the treasury.

▲▲▲**Treasury (Weltliche und Geistliche Schatzkammer)**— This "Secular and Religious Treasure Room" contains the best jewels on the Continent. Slip through the vault doors and reflect on the glitter of 21 rooms filled with scepters, swords, crowns, orbs, weighty robes, double-headed eagles, gowns, gem-studded bangles, and an eight-foot-tall, 500-year-old unicorn horn (or maybe the tusk of a narwhal)—which was considered incredibly powerful in the old days, giving its owner the grace of God. These were owned by the Holy Roman Emperor—a divine monarch (€8, Wed–Mon 10:00–18:00, closed Tue, follow *Schatzkammer* signs to the Schweizerhof, tel. 01/52524).

○ Self-Guided Tour: The well-produced, €2 audioguide provides a wealth of information. Here are the highlights.

Room 2: The personal crown of Rudolf II has survived since 1602—it was considered too well-crafted to cannibalize for other crowns. It's a big deal because it's the adopted crown of the Austrian Empire, established in 1806 after Napoleon dissolved the Holy Roman Empire (an alliance of Germanic kingdoms so named because it tried to be the continuation of the Roman Empire). Pressured by Napoleon, the Austrian Francis II—who had been Holy Roman Emperor—became Francis I, Emperor of Austria. Francis I/II (the stern guy on the wall, near where you entered) ruled from 1792 to 1835. Look at the crown. Its design symbolically merges the typical medieval king's crown and a bishop's miter.

Rooms 3 and 4: These contain some of the coronation vestments and regalia needed for the new Austrian emperor.

Room 5: Ponder the Throne Cradle. Napoleon's son was born in 1811 and made king of Rome. The little eagle at the foot is symbolically not yet able to fly, but glory-bound. Glory is symbolized by the star, with dad's big *N* raised high.

Room 11: The collection's highlight is the 10th-century crown of the Holy Roman Emperor. The imperial crown swirls with symbolism "proving" that the emperor was both holy and Roman. The jeweled arch over the top is reminiscent of the parade helmet of ancient Roman emperors whose successors the HRE claimed to be. The cross on top says the HRE ruled as Christ's representative on earth. King Solomon's portrait (on the crown, right of cross) is Old Testament proof that kings can be wise and good. King David (next panel) is similar proof that they can be just. The crown's eight sides represent the celestial city of Jerusalem's eight gates. The jewels on the front panel symbolize the 12 apostles.

The nearby 11th-century Imperial Cross preceded the emperor in ceremonies. Encrusted with jewels, it carried a substantial chunk of *the* cross and *the* holy lance (supposedly used to pierce the side of Jesus while on the cross; both items displayed in the same glass case). This must be the actual holy lance, as Holy Roman Emperors actually carried this into battle in the 10th century. Look behind the cross to see how it was actually a box that could be clipped open and shut. You can see bits of the "true cross" anywhere, but this is a prime piece—with the actual nail hole.

The other case has jewels from the reign of Karl der Grosse (Charlemagne), the greatest ruler of medieval Europe. Notice Charlemagne modeling the crown (which was made a hundred years after he died) in the tall painting adjacent.

Room 12: The painting shows the coronation of Maria Theresa's son Josef II in 1764. He's wearing the same crown and royal garb you've just seen.

Room 16: Most tourists walk right by perhaps the most exquisite workmanship in the entire treasury, the royal vestments (15th century). Look closely—they're painted with gold and silver threads.

▲Heroes' Square (Heldenplatz) and the New Palace (Neue Burg)—This last grand addition to the palace, from the early 20th century, was built for the Hapsburg heir Franz Ferdinand (it was

tradition for rulers not to move into their predecessor's quarters). But—while he was waiting politely for his long-lived uncle, Emperor Franz Josef, to die so he could move into his new digs—Franz Ferdinand was murdered in Sarajevo in 1914, sparking the beginning of World War I. The rest, as they say...

The palace's grand facade arches around **Heroes' Square.** Notice statues of two great Austrian heroes on horseback: Prince Eugene of Savoy (who defeated the Turks that had earlier threatened Vienna) and Archduke Charles (first to beat Napoleon in a battle, breaking Nappy's image of invincibility and heralding the end of the Napoleonic age). The frilly spires of Vienna's neo-Gothic City Hall break the horizon, and a line of horse-drawn carriages await their customers.

▲▲**New Palace Museums: Armor, Music, and Ancient Greek Statues**—The Neue Burg—technically part of the Kunsthistorisches Museum across the way—houses three fine museums (same ticket): an armory (with a killer collection of medieval weapons), historical musical instruments, and classical statuary from ancient Ephesus. The included audioguide brings the exhibits to life and lets you actually hear the fascinating old instruments in the collection being played. An added bonus is the chance to wander all alone among those royal Hapsburg halls, stairways, and painted ceilings (€8, Wed–Mon 10:00–18:00, closed Tue, almost no tourists, tel. 01/5252-4484). This place should be open throughout 2006 (after being renovated last fall), but if you're traveling early in the year, call to make sure it's open.

More Hapsburg Sights near the Hofburg

Central Vienna has plenty more sights associated with the Hapsburgs. With the exception of the last one (on Mariahilfer Strasse), these are all near the Hofburg. Remember that the biggest Hapsburg sight of all, Schönbrunn Palace, makes a great half-day trip (4 miles from the center—see page 466).

Palace Garden (Burggarten)—This greenbelt, once the back yard of the Hofburg and now a people's park, welcomes people to loiter on the grass. On nice days, it's lively with office workers enjoying a break. The statue of Mozart facing the Ringstrasse is popular. The iron-and-glass pavilion now houses the recommended Palmenhaus Restaurant (see page 487) and a small but fluttery butterfly exhibit (€5; April–Oct Mon–Fri 10:00–16:45, Sat–Sun 10:00–18:15; Nov–March daily 10:00–15:45). The

butterfly zone is delightfully muggy on a brisk off-season day, but trippy any time of year. If you tour it, notice the butterflies hanging out on the trays with rotting slices of banana. They lick the fermented banana juice as it beads, and then just hang out there in a stupor...or fly in anything but a straight line.

▲**Lipizzaner Museum**—A must for horse-lovers, this tidy museum in the Renaissance Stallburg Palace shows (and tells in English) the 400-year history of the famous riding school. Lipizzaner fans have a warm spot in their hearts for General Patton, who, at the end of World War II—knowing that the Soviets were about to take control of Vienna—ordered a raid on the stable to save the horses and ensure the survival of their fine old bloodlines. Videos show the horses in action on TVs throughout the museum. The "dancing" originated as battle moves: *pirouette* (quick turns) and *courbette* (on hind legs to make a living shield for the knight). The 45-minute movie in the basement theater also has great horse footage (showings alternate between German and English). These are very special horses—you'll notice they actually have "surnames," as all can be traced to the original six 16th-century stallions (€5, daily 9:00–18:00, between Josefsplatz and Michaelerplatz at Reitschulgasse 2, tel. 01/5252-4583, www.lipizzaner.at). Any time of day, you can see the horses prance on video in the museum's window. Video cameras allow visitors to "peek in" on the horses lives.

Seeing the Lipizzaner Stallions: Seats for performances by Vienna's prestigious Spanish Riding School book up months in advance, but standing room is often available the same day (tickets-€45–160, standing room-€28, March–June and Sept–Oct Sun at 11:00, sometimes also Fri at 18:00, tel. 01/533-9031, www.srs.at). Luckily for the masses, training sessions with music in a chandeliered Baroque hall are open to the public (€12 at the door, roughly Feb–June and Sept–Oct Tue–Sat 10:00–12:00—but only when the horses are in town). Tourists line up early at Josefsplatz, gate 2. Save money and avoid the wait by buying the €15 combo-ticket that covers both the museum and the training session (and lets you avoid that ticket line). Or, better yet, simply show up late. If you want to hang out with Japanese tour groups, get there early and wait for the doors to open at 10:00. But almost no one stays for the full two hours—except for the horses. As people leave, new tickets are printed continuously, so you can just waltz in with no wait at all. If you arrive at 10:45, you'll see the best action as one group of horses finishes and two more perform before they call it a day.

▲**Augustinian Church (Augustinerkirche)**—This is the Gothic and neo-Gothic church where the Hapsburgs latched, then buried, their hearts (weddings took place here, and the royal hearts are in the vault). Don't miss the exquisite, tomb-like Canova memorial (neoclassical, 1805) to Maria Theresa's favorite daughter, Maria Christina, with its incredibly sad white-marble procession. The church's 11:00 Sunday Mass is a hit with music-lovers—both a Mass and a concert, often with an orchestra accompanying the choir. To pay, contribute to the offering plate and buy a CD afterwards. Programs are available at the table by the entry all week (church open long hours daily, Augustinerstrasse 3).

The church faces Josefsplatz, with its statue of the great reform emperor Josef II. The **National Library** (€5, Tue–Sun 10:00–18:00, Thu until 21:00, closed Mon, next to the Augustinian Church) is worth a look.

▲▲**Albertina Museum**—This building, at the southern tip of the Hofburg complex (near the Opera), was the residence of Maria Teresa's favorite daughter: Maria Christina, who was the only one allowed to marry for love rather than political strategy. Her many sisters were jealous. (Marie Antoinette had to marry the French king...and lost her head over it.) Maria Christina's husband, Albert of Saxony, was a great collector of original drawings. He amassed an enormous assortment of works by Dürer, Rembrandt, Rubens, and others. Today the Albertina presents wonderful exhibitions of these fine works and allows visitors to tour its elegant state rooms and enjoy temporary exhibits of other artists (€9, price can vary based on special exhibits, €3.50 audioguide also available for both permanent and temporary exhibits, daily 10:00–18:00, Wed until 21:00, overlooking Albertinaplatz across from TI and Opera House, tel. 01/534-830, www.albertina.at).

The Albertina consists of three components. First, stroll through the Hapsburg state rooms (French classicism—lots of white marble). Top-quality facsimiles of the collection's greatest pieces hang in these rooms. Then browse the modern gallery, featuring special exhibitions. From March 15 until August 27, 2006, the Albertina devotes this space to a specially designed Mozart installation, celebrating the composer's 250th birthday. (For more "Year of Mozart" events, see page 470.) Finally, the Albertina also displays selections from its own spectacular collection of works by Michelangelo, Rubens, Rembrandt, and Raphael, plus a huge sampling of precise drawings by Albrecht Dürer. Of Dürer's 400

Empress Maria Theresa (1717–1780) and Her Son, Emperor Josef II (1741–1790)

Maria Theresa was the only woman to officially rule the Hapsburg Empire in that family's 700-year reign. She was a strong and effective empress (r. 1740–1780). People are quick to remember Maria Theresa as the mother of 16 children (10 survived). Imagine that the most powerful woman in Europe either was pregnant or had a newborn for most of her reign. Maria Theresa ruled after the Austrian defeat of the Turks, when Europe recognized Austria as a great power. (Her rival, the Prussian emperor, said, "When at last the Hapsburgs get a great man, it's a woman.")

The last of the Baroque imperial rulers, and the first of the modern rulers of the Age of Enlightenment, Maria Theresa marked the end of the feudal system and the beginning of the era of the grand state. She was a great social reformer. During her reign, she avoided wars and expanded her empire by skillfully marrying her children into the right families. For instance, after daughter Marie Antoinette's marriage into the French Bourbon family (to Louis XVI), a country that had been an enemy became an ally. (Unfortunately for Marie, her timing was off. Arriving in time for the Revolution, she lost her head.)

Maria Theresa was a great reformer and in tune with her age. She taxed the Church and the nobility, provided six years of obligatory education to all children, and granted free health care to all in her realm. Maria Theresa also welcomed the boy genius Mozart into her court.

The empress' legacy lived on in her son, **Josef II,** who ruled as emperor himself for a decade (1780–1790). He was an even more avid reformer, building on his mother's accomplishments. An enlightened monarch, Josef mothballed the too-extravagant Schönbrunn Palace, secularized the monasteries, established religious tolerance within his realm, freed the serfs, made possible the founding of Austria's first general hospital, and promoted relatively enlightened treatment of the mentally ill. Josef was a model of practicality (for example, reusable coffins à la *Amadeus,* and no more than 6 candles at funerals)—and very unpopular with other royals. But his policies succeeded in preempting the revolutionary anger of the age, enabling Austria to avoid the turmoil that shook so much of the rest of Europe.

original drawings that survived, Albert collected 300 of them. Most were sold or stolen over the ages, and today the collection is down to about 100. Since these fragile sketches and exquisite drawings are very sensitive to light, they're kept mostly in darkness and shown only rarely, in rotation. The collection is vast, so you'll always see exciting originals, thoughtfully described in English.

▲▲**Kaisergruft, the Remains of the Hapsburgs**—Visiting the imperial remains is not as easy as you might imagine. These original organ donors left their bodies—about 150 in all—in the unassuming Kaisergruft (Capuchin Crypt), their hearts in the Augustinian Church (described above; church open long hours daily, but to see the goods you'll have to talk to a priest), and their entrails in the crypt below St. Stephen's Cathedral. Don't tripe.

Upon entering the Kaisergruft (€4, daily 9:30–16:00, last entry 15:40, behind Opera on Neuer Markt), buy the €0.50 map with a Hapsburg family tree and a chart locating each coffin.

The double coffin of **Maria Theresa** (1717–1780) and her husband, **Franz I** (1708–1765), is worth a close look for its artwork. Maria Theresa outlived her husband by 15 years—which she spent in mourning. Old and fat, she installed a special lift enabling her to get down into the crypt to be with her dear, departed Franz (even though he had been far from faithful). The couple recline—Etruscan style—atop their fancy lead coffin. At each corner are the crowns of the Hapsburgs—the Holy Roman Empire, Hungary, Bohemia, and Jerusalem. Notice the contrast between the rococo splendor of Maria Theresa's tomb and the simple box holding her more modest son, **Josef II** (at his parents' feet; for more on Maria Theresa and Joe II, see the sidebar on page 448).

Franz Josef (1830–1916) is nearby, in an appropriately austere military tomb. Flanking Franz Josef are the tombs of his son, the archduke **Rudolf**, and Empress Elizabeth. Rudolf and his teenage love committed suicide together in 1889 and—since the Church figured he forced her and was therefore a murderer—it took considerable legal hair-splitting to win Rudolf this spot (after examining his brain, it was determined that he was physi-cally retarded and therefore incapable of knowingly killing himself and his girl). *Kaiserin* Elisabeth (1837–1898), a.k.a. **Sissy,** always gets the "Most Flowers" award.

In front of those three is the most recent Hapsburg tomb. **Empress Zita** was buried in 1989. Her burial procession was probably the last such Old Regime event in European history. The monarchy died hard in Austria.

While it's fun to chase down all these body parts, remember that the real legacy of the Hapsburgs is the magnificence of this city. Step outside. Look up. Watch the clouds glide by the ornate gables of Vienna.

▲**Imperial Furniture Collection (Kaiserliches Hofmobilien-depot)**—Bizarre, sensuous, eccentric, or precious, this is your peek at the Hapsburgs' furniture—from grandma's wheelchair to the emperor's spittoon—all thoughtfully described in English. The Hapsburgs had many palaces, but only the Hofburg was permanently furnished. The rest were furnished on the fly—set up and taken down by a gang of royal roadies called the "Depot of Court Movables" (Hofmobiliendepot). When the monarchy was dissolved in 1918, the state of Austria took possession of the Hofmobiliendepot's inventory—165,000 items. Now this royal storehouse is open to the public in a fine, new, sprawling museum. Don't go here for the *Jugendstil* furnishings. The older Baroque, rococo, and Biedermeier pieces are the most impressive and tied most intimately to the royals. Combine a visit to this museum with a stroll down the lively shopping boulevard, Mariahilfer Strasse (€7, Tue–Sun 10:00–18:00, closed Mon, Mariahilfer Strasse 88, tel. 01/5243-3570).

Kunsthistorisches Museum

This exciting museum, across the Ring from the Hofburg Palace, is worth ▲▲▲. It showcases the grandeur and opulence of the

Hapsburgs' collected artwork in a grand building (built as a museum in 1888). There are European masterpieces galore, all well-hung on one glorious floor, plus a fine display of Egyptian, classical, and applied arts.

Cost, Hours, Location: €10, audioguide-€2, Tue–Sun 10:00–18:00, Thu until 21:00, closed Mon, on the Ringstrasse at Maria Theresien-Platz, U-2 or U-3: Volkstheater/Museumsplatz, tel. 01/525-240, www.khm.at.

◉ **Self-Guided Tour:** Thanks to Gene Openshaw for writing the following tour.

The Kunsthistorwhateveritis Museum—let's just say "Koonst"—houses some of the most beautiful, sexy, and fun-loving art from two centuries (c. 1450–1650). The collection reflects the *joie de vivre* of Austria's luxury-loving Hapsburg rulers. At their peak of power in the 1500s, the Hapsburgs ruled Austria, Germany, northern Italy, the Netherlands, and

Kunsthistorisches Museum

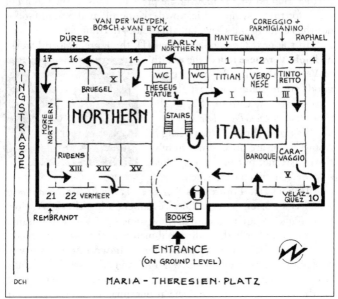

Spain—and you'll see a wide variety of art from all these places and beyond.

Of the museum's many exhibits, we'll tour only the Painting Gallery (Gemäldegalerie) on the first floor. Climb the main staircase, featuring Antonio Canova's statue of *Theseus Clubbing the Centaur.* Italian Art is in the right half of the building (as you face Theseus), and Northern Art to the left. Notice that the museum labels the largest rooms with Roman numerals (Saal I, II, III), and the smaller rooms around the perimeter with Arabic (Rooms 1, 2, 3).

• *Enter Saal I and walk right into the High Renaissance.*

Venetian Renaissance (1500–1600)—Titian, Veronese, Tintoretto: Around the year 1500, Italy had a Renaissance, or "rebirth," of interest in the art and learning of ancient Greece and Rome. In painting, that meant that ordinary humans and Greek gods joined saints and angels as popular subjects.

Saal I spans the long career of **Titian** the Venetian (that rhymes)—from creamy Madonnas to down-to-earth portraits to erotic Greek myths. *Nymph and Shepherd,* a late work, creates a misty landscape where a flute-playing shepherd ogles a naked nymph while fingering his instrument. In *Ecce Homo,* a crowd mills about, when suddenly there's a commotion. They nudge each other and start to point. Follow their gaze diagonally up the stairs to a battered figure entering way up in the corner. "Ecce Homo!" says

Pilate. "Behold the man." And he presents Jesus to the mob. For us, as for the unsympathetic crowd, the humiliated Son of God is not the center of the scene, but almost an afterthought.

In the next large gallery (Saal II), the large, colorful works by **Paolo Veronese** reflect the wealth of Venice, the funnel where luxury goods from the exotic East flowed into Northern Europe. So, in the *Adoration of the Magi (Die Anbetung der Könige)*, these-Three-Kings-from-Orient-are dressed not in biblical costume, but in the imported silks of Venetian businessmen.

In Saal III, **Tinoretto's** *Susanna and the Elders (Susanna im Bade)* is an often-painted Old Testament story that gave pious Christians a religious excuse to show some skin. Virtuous Susanna is spied on in her bath by dirty old men who then wrongly accuse her to hide their own hypocrisy. We're drawn into the story by Susanna's beauty—and by the wall of flowers that stretches almost straight back, making the painting an extension of where we stand. At the far end, an old man leers at Susanna. Tintoretto places us at the near end, looking at Susanna through the picture frame... making us peeping Toms, as well.

• *Find the following paintings in Rooms 1–4, the smaller rooms that adjoin Saals I, II, and III.*

Italian Renaissance and Mannerism: Mantegna's *St. Sebastian (Der hl. Sebastian)*, shot through with arrows, was an early Christian martyr, but he stands like a Renaissance statue—on a pedestal, his weight on one foot, and displaying his Greek-god anatomy. Mantegna places the three-dimensional "statue" in a three-dimensional setting, using floor tiles and roads that recede into the distance to create the illusion of depth.

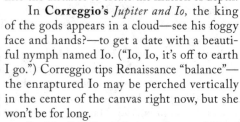

In **Correggio's** *Jupiter and Io,* the king of the gods appears in a cloud—see his foggy face and hands?—to get a date with a beautiful nymph named Io. ("Io, Io, it's off to earth I go.") Correggio tips Renaissance "balance"—the enraptured Io may be perched vertically in the center of the canvas right now, but she won't be for long.

In his *Self-Portrait in a Convex Mirror (Selbstbildnis im Konvexspiegel)*, 21-year-old **Parmigianino** (like the cheese) gazes into a convex mirror and perfectly reproduces the curved reflection on a convex piece of wood. Amazing.

The 22-year-old **Raphael** (roff-eye-EL) captured the spirit of the High Renaissance, combining symmetry, grace, beauty and emotion. His *Madonna of the Meadow (Die Madonna im Gruben)* is a mountain of motherly love—Mary's head is the summit and her flowing robe is the base—enfolding baby Jesus and John the Baptist. The geometric perfection, serene landscape, and Mary's adorable face make this a masterpiece of sheer grace...but then

you get smacked by an ironic fist: The cross the little tykes play with foreshadows their gruesome deaths.

• *Find Caravaggio in Saal V.*

Caravaggio: Caravaggio (karra-VAH-jee-oh) shocked the art world with brutally honest reality. Compared with Raphael's super-sweet *Madonna of the Meadow*, Caravaggio's *Madonna of the Rosary (Die Rosenkranzmadonna)* looks perfectly ordinary, and the saints kneeling around her have dirty feet.

In *David with the Head of Goliath (David mit dem Haupt des Goliath)*, Caravaggio turns a third-degree-interrogation light on a familiar Bible story. David shoves the dripping head of the slain giant right in our noses. The painting, bled of color, is virtually a black-and-white crime-scene photo, slightly overexposed. Out of the deep darkness shine only a few crucial details. This David is not a heroic Renaissance Man like Michelangelo's famous statue, but a homeless teen that Caravaggio paid to portray God's servant. And the severed head of Goliath is none other than Caravaggio himself, an in-your-face self-portrait.

• *Find Room 10, in the corner of the museum.*

Velázquez: When the Hapsburgs ruled both Austria and Spain, cousins kept in touch through portraits of themselves and their kids. Diego Velázquez (vel-LOSS-kes) was the greatest of Spain's "photo-journalist" painters: heavily influenced by Caravaggio's realism, capturing his subjects without passing judgment, flattering, or glorifying them.

Watch little Margarita Hapsburg grow up in three different *Portraits of Margarita Theresa (Die Infantin Margarita Teresa)* from age two to age nine. Margarita was destined from birth to marry her Austrian cousin, the future Emperor Leopold I. Pictures like these, sent from Spain every few years, let her pen-pal/fiancé get to know her. Also see a portrait of Margarita's little brother, *Philip Prospero*, looking like a tiny priest. The kids' oh-so-serious faces, regal

poses, and royal trappings are contradicted by their cuteness. No wonder Velázquez was so popular.

• *Complete the Italian Art wing by passing through several rooms of Baroque art, featuring large, colorful canvases showcasing over-the-top emotions and the surefire mark of Baroque art—pudgy winged babies.*

Northern Art is in the east wing, opposite the Titian room.

Early Northern Art: The Northern "Renaissance," brought on by the economic boom of Dutch and Flemish trading, was more secular and Protestant than Catholic-funded Italian art. We'll see fewer Madonnas, saints, and Greek gods and more peasants, landscapes, and food. Paintings are smaller and darker, full of down-to-earth objects. Northern artists sweated the details, encouraging the patient viewer to appreciate the beauty in everyday things.

In Room 14, **Rogier Van Der Weyden**'s *Triptych: The Crucifixion (Kreuzinungsaltar)* strips the Crucifixion down to the essential characters, set in a sparse landscape. The agony is understated,

seen in just

a few solemn faces and dramatically creased robes. **Hieronymous Bosch**'s *Christ Carrying the Cross (Kreutzragning)* is crammed with puny humans, not supermen. And in the painstakingly detailed *Portrait of Cardinal Niccolo Albergati*, **Jan Van Eyck** refuses to airbrush out the jowls and wrinkles, showcasing the quiet dignity of an ordinary man.

• *Room X contains the largest collection of Bruegels in captivity. Linger. If you like it, linger longer.*

Pieter Bruegel (c. 1525–1569)—Norman Rockwell of the 16th Century: The undisputed master of the slice-of-life village scene was Pieter Bruegel the Elder. (His name is pronounced "BROY-gull," and is sometimes spelled *Brueghel*. Don't confuse Pieter Bruegel the Elder with his sons, Pieter Brueghel the Younger and Jan Brueghel, who added luster and an "h" to the family name.) Despite his many rural paintings, Bruegel was actually an urban metrosexual who liked to wear peasants' clothing to observe country folk at play (a trans-fest-ite?). He celebrated their simple life, but he also skewered their weaknesses—not to single them out as hicks, but as universal examples of human folly.

The Peasant Wedding (Bauernhochfest), Bruegel's most famous

work, is less about the wedding than the food. It's a farmers' feeding frenzy as the barnful of wedding guests scramble to get their share of free eats. Two men bring in the next course, a tray of fresh pudding. The bagpiper pauses to check it out. A guy grabs bowls and passes them down the table, taking our attention with them. Everyone's going at it, including a kid in an oversized red cap who licks the bowl with his fingers. In the middle of it all, look who's been completely forgotten—the demure bride sitting in front of the blue-green cloth. (One thing: The guy carrying the front end of the food tray—is he stepping

forward with his right leg, or with his left, or with... all three?)

Speaking of two left feet, Bruegel's *Peasant Dance (Bauerntanz)* shows peasants happily clogging to the tune of a lone bagpiper who wails away while his pit crew keeps

him lubed with wine. The three Bruegel landscape paintings are part of an original series of six "calendar" paintings, depicting the

seasons of the year. *The Gloomy Day* opens the cycle, as winter turns to spring...slowly. The snow has melted, flooding the distant river, the trees are still leafless, and the villagers stir, cutting wood and mending fences. We skip ahead to autumn *(The Return of the Herd)*—still sunny, but winter's storms are fast approaching.

We see the scene from above, emphasizing the landscape as much as the people. Finally, in *The Hunters in Snow (Die Jäger im Schnee)* it's the dead of winter, and three dog-tired hunters with their tired dogs trudge along with only a single fox to show for their efforts. As they crest the hill, the grove of bare trees opens up to a breathtaking view—they're almost home, where they can join their mates playing hockey. Birds soar like the hunters' rising spirits—emerging from winter's work and looking ahead to a new year.

• *Linger among the Breugels, then exit into the adjoining Room 16.*

Albrecht Dürer: As the son of a goldsmith and having traveled to Italy, Dürer (DEW-rer) combined meticulous Northern detail with Renaissance symmetry. So

his *Landaeur Altarpiece of the Trinity (Allerheiligenbild)* may initially look like a complex pig-pile of saints and angels, but it's perfectly geometrical. The crucified Christ forms a triangle in the center, framed by triangular clouds and flanked by three-sided crowds of people—appropriate for a painting about the Trinity. Dürer practically invented the self-portrait as an art form, and he included himself, the lone earthling in this heavenly vision (bottom right), with a plaque announcing that he, Albrecht Dürer, painted this in 1511.

• *Locate these paintings scattered through Rooms 17–21.*

More Northern Art: Contrast Dürer's powerful Renaissance Christ with **Lucas Cranach**'s all-too-human *Crucifixion (Die Kreuznigung)*—twisted, bleeding, scarred and vomiting blood, as the storm clouds roll in.

Albrecht Altdorfer's garish *Resurrection (Die Anferstehung Christi)* looks like a poster for a bad horror film—"EASTER SUNDAY III. He's back from the dead... and he's ticked!" A burning Christ ignites the dark cave, tingeing the dazed guards.

Hans Holbein painted *Jane Seymour,* wife number III of the VI wives of Henry VIII. The former lady in waiting—timid and modest—poses stiffly, trying very hard to look the part of Henry's queen. Next.

Giuseppe Arcimboldo's *Summer*—a.k.a "Fruit Face"—is one of four paintings the Hapsburg court painter did showing the seasons (and elements) as people. With a pickle nose, pear chin, and corn-husk ears, this guy literally is what he eats.

In *The Big Flower Bunch (Der Grosse Blumentraub),* **Jan Brueghel,** the son of the famous Bruegel, puts meticulously painted flowers from different seasons together in one artfully arranged vase.

• *Leaving the simplicity of Northern Art—small canvases, small themes, attention to detail—re-enter the big-canvased, bright-colored world of Baroque in Saals XIII and XIV.*

Peter Paul Rubens: Stand in front of Rubens' *Self-Portrait*

(Selbstbildnis) and admire the darling of Catholic-dominated Flanders (Belgium) in his prime: famous, wealthy, well-traveled, the friend of kings and princes, an artist, diplomat, man about town, and—obviously—confident. Rubens' work runs the gamut, from realistic portraits to lounging nudes, Greek myths to altarpieces, from pious devotion to violent sex. But, can we be sure it's Baroque? Ah yes, I'm sure you'll find a pudgy winged baby somewhere.

The 53-year-old Rubens married Hélène Fourment *(The Little Fur,* or *Das Pelszchen),* this dimpled girl of 16. She pulls the fur around her ample flesh, simultaneously covering herself and exalting her charms. Rubens called both this painting and his young bride "The Little Fur." Hmm. Hélène's sweet cellulite was surely an inspiration to Rubens—many of his female figures have Helene's gentle face and dimpled proportions.

In the large *Ildefonso Altarpiece,* a glorious Mary appears (with her entourage of p.w.b.'s) to reward the grateful Spanish saint with a chasuble (priest's smock). How could Rubens paint all these enormous canvases—this one alone is 130 square feet—in one lifetime? He didn't. He kept a workshop of assistants busy painting backgrounds and minor figures, working from Rubens' small sketches (often displayed alongside). Then the master stepped in to add the finishing touches.

· *Continue into Saal XIV, turn right, and find Room 21.*

Rembrandt van Rijn: Rembrandt got wealthy painting portraits of Holland's upwardly-mobile businessmen, but his great-

est subject was himself. In *The Large Self-Portrait (Das Grosse Selbstbildnis)* we see the hands-on-hips, defiant, open-stance determination of a man who will do what he wants, and if they don't like it, tough.

In typical Rembrandt style, most of the canvas is a dark, smudgy brown, with only the side of his face glowing from the darkness. (Remember Caravaggio? Rembrandt did.) Unfortunately, the year this was painted, Rembrandt's for-

tunes changed. Looking at the *Small Self-Portrait 1657 (Kleines Selbstbildnis 1657)*, consider Rembrandt's last years. His wife died, his children died young, and commissions for paintings dried up as his style veered from the common path. He had to auction off paintings to pay debts and died a poor man. Rembrandt's numerous self-portraits painted from youth till old age show a man always changing—from wide-eyed youth, to successful portraitist to this disillusioned but still defiant old man.

· *Complete your Kunst visit in the adjoining Room 22.*

Jan Vermeer: In his small canvases, the Dutch painter Jan Vermeer quiets the world down to where we can hear our own heartbeat, letting us appreciate the beauty in common things.

The curtain opens and we see *The Artist's Studio (Allegorie der Malerei)*, a behind-the-scenes look at Vermeer at work. He's painting a model dressed in blue, starting with her laurel-leaf headdress. The studio is its own little doll-house world framed by a chair in the foreground and the wall in back. Then Vermeer fills this space with the few gems he wants us to focus on—the chandelier, the map, the painter's costume. Everything is lit by a crystal-clear light, letting us see these everyday items with fresh eyes.

The painting is subtitled *An Allegory of Painting*. The model has the laurel leaves, trumpet, and book that

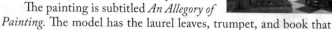

symbolize fame. The artist—his back to the public—earnestly tries to capture fleeting fame with a small sheet of canvas.

The Rest of the Kunst: We've seen only the "Kunst" (art) half of the Kunst-"Historisches" (history) Museum. The collections on the ground floor are among Europe's best, filled with ancient rubble and medieval curios. Highlights include a statue of the Egyptian pharaoh Thutmosis III and the Gemma Augustea, a Roman cameo. Sadly, one of the jewels in the museum's crown is now missing. Cellini's *Salt Cellar,* a divine golden salt bowl valued at €50 million, was stolen in 2003 by expert thieves—to the anguish of the Vienna art world.

Near the Kunsthistorisches Museum

▲**Natural History Museum**—In the twin building facing the Kunsthistorisches Museum, you'll find moon rocks, dinosaur stuff, and the fist-sized *Venus of Willendorf*—at 30,000 years old, the world's oldest sex symbol, found in the Danube Valley. This museum is a hit with children (€8, Wed–Mon 9:00–18:30, Wed until 21:00, closed Tue, tel. 01/521-770).

MuseumsQuartier—The vast grounds of the former imperial stables now corral several impressive, cutting-edge museums.

Walk into the complex from the Hofburg side, where the main entrance (with visitors center) leads to a big courtyard with cafés, fountains, and ever-changing "installation lounge furniture," all surrounded by the quarter's various museums (behind Kunsthistorisches Museum, U-2 or U-3: Volkstheater/Museumsplatz).

Various combo-tickets are available for those interested in more than just the Leopold and Modern Art museums (visit www.mqw.at).

The **Leopold Museum** features modern Austrian art, including the largest collection of works by Egon Schiele (1890–1918) and a few drawings by Kokoschka and Klimt (€9, €2.50 audioguide, Wed–Mon 10:00–19:00, Thu until 21:00, closed Tue, tel. 01/525-700, www.leopoldmuseum.org). Note that for these three artists, you'll do better in the Belvedere Palace (described below).

The **Museum of Modern Art** (Museum Moderner Kunst Stiftung Ludwig, a.k.a. "Mumok") is Austria's leading modern-art gallery. It's the striking lava-paneled building—three stories tall and four stories deep, offering seven floors of far-out art encased in very young stone. This huge, state-of-the-art museum displays revolving exhibits showing off art of the last generation—including

Klee, Picasso, and Pop (€8, Tue–Sun 10:00–18:00, Thu until 21:00, closed Mon, tel. 01/525-001-440, www.mumok.at).

Rounding out the sprawling MuseumsQuartier are an architecture museum, Transeuropa, Electronic Avenue, children's museum, and the Kunsthalle Wien—an exhibition center for contemporary art (€7.50, Thu–Tue 10:00–19:00, Thu until 22:00, closed Wed).

Central Vienna, inside the Ring

▲▲**Haus der Musik**—Vienna's House of Music has a small first-floor exhibit on the Vienna Philharmonic, and upstairs you'll enjoy fine audiovisual exhibits on each of the famous hometown boys (Haydn, Mozart, Beethoven, Strauss, and Mahler). But the museum is unique for its effective use of interactive touch-screen computers and headphones to actually explore the physics of sound. You can twist, dissect, and bend sounds to make your own musical language, merging your voice with a duck's quack or a city's traffic roar. Wander through the "sonosphere" and marvel at the amazing acoustics—I could actually hear what I thought only a piano tuner could hear. Pick up a virtual baton to conduct the Vienna Philharmonic Orchestra (each time you screw up, the musicians put their instruments down and ridicule you). A computer will help you compose your own waltz by throwing dice. Really experiencing the place takes time. It's open late and makes a good evening activity (€10, daily 10:00–22:00, last entry 75 min before closing, 2 blocks from Opera at Seilerstatte 30, tel. 01/51648, www.hdm.at).

▲**Vienna's Auction House, the Dorotheum**—For an aristocrat's flea market, drop by Austria's answer to Sotheby's, the Dorotheum. Its five floors of antique furniture and fancy knickknacks have been put up either for immediate sale or auction, often by people who inherited old things they don't have room for (Mon–Fri 10:00–18:00, Sat 9:00–17:00, closed Sun, classy little café on 2nd floor, between Graben and Hofburg at Dorotheergasse 17, tel. 01/515-600, www.dorotheum.com). Fliers show schedules for actual auctions, which you are welcome to attend.

Judenplatz Memorial and Museum—The square called Judenplatz marks the location of Vienna's 15th-century Jewish community, one of Europe's largest at the time. The square, once filled with a long-gone synagogue, is now dominated by a blocky memorial to the 65,000 Austrian Jews killed by the Nazis. The memorial—a library turned inside out—symbolizes Jews as "people of the book" and causes one to ponder the huge loss of

culture, knowledge, and humanity that took place between 1938 and 1945.

The Judenplatz Museum, while sparse, has displays on medieval Jewish life and a well-done video re-creating community scenes from five centuries ago. Wander the scant remains of the medieval synagogue below street level—discovered during the construction of the Holocaust memorial. This was the scene of a medieval massacre. Since Christians weren't allowed to lend money, Jews were Europe's moneylenders. As so often happened in Europe, when Christian locals fell too deeply into debt, they found a convenient excuse to wipe out the local ghetto—and their debts at the same time. In 1421, 200 of Vienna's Jews were burned at the stake. Others who refused a forced conversion committed mass suicide in the synagogue (€3, €7 combo-ticket includes a synagogue and Jewish Museum of the City of Vienna—see page 468, Sun–Thu 10:00–18:00, Fri 10:00–14:00, closed Sat, Judenplatz 8, tel. 01/535-0431).

Near Karlsplatz

These sights cluster around Karlsplatz, just southeast of the Ringstrasse (U-1, U-2, or U-4: Karlsplatz).

Karlsplatz—This fine and picnic-friendly square, with its Henry Moore sculpture in the pond, is ringed with sights. The Art Nouveau station pavilions—from the 19th-century municipal train system—are textbook *Jugendstil* by Otto Wagner (steel frame and decorative marble slabs with painted gold ornaments). One of Europe's first subway systems, it was built with a military purpose in mind: to move troops quickly in time of civil unrest—specifically, out to Schönbrunn Palace.

Charles Church (Karlskirche)—Charles Borromeo, a 16th-century bishop from Milan, was an inspiration during plague times. This "votive church" was dedicated to him in 1713, when an epidemic spared Vienna. The church offers the best Baroque in Vienna, with a unique combination of columns (showing scenes from the life of Charles Borromeo, à la Trajan's Column in Rome), a classic pediment, and an elliptical dome. But it's especially worthwhile for the chance (probably through 2006) to see restoration work in progress and up close (€6 includes a skippable 1-room museum, audioguide, and visit to renovation site; Mon–Sat 9:00–12:30 & 13:00–18:00, Sun 13:00–18:00, last entry 30 min before closing). The entry fee may seem steep, but remember that it funds the restoration.

Visitors ride the industrial lift to a platform at the base of the dome. (Consider that the church was built and decorated with a scaffolding system essentially the same as this one.) Once up there, you'll climb stairs to the steamy lantern at the extreme top of the church. At that dizzying height, you're in the clouds with cupids and angels. Many details that appear smooth and beautiful from ground level—such as gold leaf, rudimentary paintings, and fake marble—look rough and sloppy up close. It's surreal to observe the 3-D figures from an unintended angle. Faith, Hope, Charity, and Borromeo triumph and inspire—while Protestants

and their stinkin' books are trashed. Borromeo lobbies heaven for plague relief. At the very top, you'll see the tiny dove representing the Holy Ghost, surrounded by a cheering squad of nipple-lipped cupids.

Historical Museum of the City of Vienna (Wien Museum Karlsplatz)—This under-appreciated museum walks you through the history of Vienna with fine historic artifacts. You'll work your way up, chronologically: The ground floor exhibits Roman artifacts and original statues from St. Stephen's Cathedral (c. 1350), with various Hapsburgs showing off the slinky hip-hugging fashion of the day. The first floor features old city maps, booty from a Turkish siege, and an 1850 city model showing the town just before the wall was replaced by the Ring. Finally, the second floor displays a city model from 1898 (with the new Ringstrasse), sentimental Biedermeier paintings and objets d'art, and early-20th-century paintings (including some by Gustav Klimt). The museum is worth the €4 admission (free Sun and Fri morning, open Tue–Sun 9:00–18:00, closed Mon, www.wienmuseum.at).

▲Academy of Fine Arts (Akademie der Bildenden Künste)— This small but exciting collection includes works by Bosch, Botticelli, and Rubens (quick, sketchy cartoons used to create his giant canvases); a Venice series by Guardi; and a self-portrait by a 15-year-old van Dyck. It's all magnificently lit and well-described by the €2 audioguide, and comes with comfy chairs (€5, Tue–Sun 10:00–18:00, closed Mon, 3 blocks from Opera at Schillerplatz 3, tel. 01/5881-6225, www.akademiegalerie.at). The fact that this is a working art academy gives it a certain realness. As you wander the halls of the academy, ponder how history might have been different if Hitler—who applied to study architecture here but was rejected—had been accepted as a student. Before leaving, peek into the ground floor's central hall—textbook historicism, the Ringstrasse style of the late 1800s.

The Secession—This little building, behind the Academy of Fine Arts, is nicknamed the "golden cabbage" today (and "a temple for bullfrogs" when it was first built around the turn of the 20th century). It was created by the Vienna Secession movement, a group

Art Nouveau Sights

Vienna gave birth to its own curvaceous brand of Art Nouveau around the early 1900s: *Jugendstil* ("youth style"). The TI has a brochure laying out Vienna's 20th-century architecture. The best of Vienna's scattered *Jugendstil* sights: the gilded, cabbage-domed Secession building at the Ring end of the Naschmarkt (see below); the Belvedere Palace collection; and the clock on Hoher Markt (which does a musical act at noon).

of non-conformist artists led by Gustav Klimt, Otto Wagner, and friends. The Secession, whose slogan was "To each age its art, and to art its liberty," first exhibited their "liberty-style" art here in 1897. The young trees carved into the walls and its bushy "cabbage" rooftop are symbolic of renewal cycle. Today, the Secession continues to showcase cutting-edge art, as well as one of Gustav Klimt's most famous works, the *Beethoven Frieze* (€6, Tue–Sun 10:00–18:00, Thu until 20:00, closed Mon, Friedrichstrasse 12, tel. 01/587-5307, www.secession.at).

While the staff hopes you take a look at the temporary exhibits (and the ticket includes this whether you like it or not), most

tourists head directly for the basement, home to a small exhibit about the history of the building and the museum's highlight: Klimt's classic *Beethoven Frieze* (a.k.a. the "Searching Souls"). One of the masterpieces of Viennese Art Nouveau, this 105-foot-long fresco was a centerpiece of a 1902 "homage to Beethoven" exhibition. Sit down and read the free flier, which explains Klimt's still-powerful work. The theme, inspired by Beethoven's *Ninth Symphony,* features floating female figures "yearning for happiness." They drift and weave and search—like most of us do—through internal and external temptations and forces, falling victim to base and ungodly temptations, and losing their faith. Then, finally, they become fulfilled by poetry, music, and art as they reach the "Ideal Kingdom" where "True Happiness, Pure Bliss and Absolute Love" are found in a climactic embrace.

▲**Naschmarkt**—In 1898, the city decided to cover up its Vienna River. The long, wide square they created was filled with a lively produce market that still bustles most days (closed Sun). From near the Opera, the Naschmarkt (roughly, "Munchies Market") stretches along Wienzeile Street. This "Belly of Vienna" comes with two parallel lanes—one lined with fun and reasonable eateries, and the other featuring the town's top-end produce and gourmet goodies. This is where top chefs like to get their ingredients. At the gourmet vinegar stall, you sample the vinegar like perfume—with a drop on your wrist. Farther from the center, the Naschmarkt becomes likeably seedy and surrounded by sausage stands, Turkish *döner kebab* stalls, cafés, and theaters. Each Saturday, it's infested by a huge flea market where, in olden days, locals would come to hire a monkey to pick little critters out of their hair (Mon–Fri 6:00–18:30, Sat 6:00–17:00, closed Sun, closes earlier in winter, U-4: Kettenbruckengasse). For a picnic park, pick up your grub here and walk over to Karlsplatz (described above).

Beyond the Ring

▲**Liechtenstein Museum**—The noble Liechtenstein family (who own only a tiny country, but whose friendship with the Hapsburgs goes back generations) amassed an incredible private art collection. Their palace was long a treasure for Vienna art lovers. Then, in 1938—knowing Hitler was intent on plundering artwork to create an immense "Führer Museum"—the family fled to their tiny homeland with their best art. Only in March of 2004 was the collection re-established in Vienna, and opened again to the adoring public. The Liechtensteins' "world of Baroque pleasures" includes the family's rare French rococo carriage (which was used for their grand entry into Paris; it had to be carted to the edge of town and assembled, as nearly all such carriages were destroyed in the French Revolution), a plush Baroque library, an inviting English Garden, and an impressive collection of paintings including a complete cycle of early Rembrandts (€10, €4 audioguide, Wed–Mon 9:00–20:00, closed Tue, tram D to Bauernfeldplatz, Fürstengasse 1, tel. 01/319-5767-252, www.liechtensteinmuseum.at).

▲**KunstHausWien: Hundertwasser Museum**—This "make yourself at home" museum is a hit with lovers of modern art. It mixes the work and philosophy of local painter/environmentalist Friedensreich Hundertwasser (1928–2000). Stand in front of the colorful checkerboard building and consider Hundertwasser's style. He was against "window racism": Neighboring houses allow only one kind of window, but 100H$_2$O's windows are each different—and he encouraged residents to personalize them. He recognized "tree tenants" as well as human tenants. His buildings are spritzed with a forest and topped with dirt and grassy little parks—close to nature,

good for the soul. Floors and sidewalks are irregular—to "stimulate the brain" (although current residents complain it just causes wobbly furniture and sprained ankles). Thus 100H$_2$O waged a one-man fight—during the 1950s and 1960s, when concrete and glass ruled—to save the human soul from the city. (Hundertwasser claimed that "straight lines are godless.") Inside the museum, start with his interesting biography. His fun-loving paintings are half *Jugendstil* ("youth style") and half just kids' stuff. Notice the photographs from his 1950s days as part of Vienna's bohemian scene. Throughout the museum, notice the fun philosophical quotes from an artist who believed, "If man is creative, he comes nearer to his creator" (€9 for Hundertwasser Museum, €12 combo-ticket includes special exhibitions, half-price on Mon, open daily 10:00–19:00, extremely fragrant and colorful garden café, U-3: Landstrasse, Weissgerberstrasse 13, tel. 01/712-0491, www.kunsthauswien.com).

The KunstHausWien provides by far the best look at Hundertwasser. For an actual lived-in apartment complex by the green master, walk five minutes to the one-with-nature **Hundertwasserhaus** (free, at Löwengasse and Kegelgasse). This complex of 50 apartments, subsidized by the government to provide affordable housing, was built in the 1980s as a breath of architectural fresh air in a city of boring, blocky apartment complexes. While not open to visitors, it's worth visiting for its fun-loving and colorful patchwork exterior and the Hundertwasser festival of shops across the street. Don't miss the view from Kegelgasse to see the "tree tenants" and the internal winter garden residents enjoy.

Hundertwasser detractors—of which there are many—remind visitors that 100H$_2$O was a painter, not an architect. They describe the Hundertwasserhaus as a "1950s house built in the 1980s," and colorfully painted with no real concern about the environment, communal living, or even practical comfort. Nearly all the original inhabitants got fed up with the novelty and moved out.

▲▲**Belvedere Palace**—This is the elegant palace of Prince Eugene of Savoy (1663–1736), the still-much-appreciated conqueror of the Turks. Eugene, a Frenchman considered too short and too ugly to be in the service of Louis XIV, offered his services to the Hapsburgs. While he was short and ugly indeed, he became the greatest military genius of his age. When you conquer cities, as Eugene did, you get really rich. He had no heirs, so the state got his property and Emperor Josef II established the Belvedere as Austria's first great public art gallery. Today, his palace boasts sweeping views and houses the Austrian gallery of 19th- and 20th-century art (€7.50, €2.50 audioguide, Tue–Sun 10:00–18:00, closed Mon, entrance at Prinz-Eugen-Strasse 27, tel. 01/7955-7134, www.belvedere.at). To get here from the center, catch tram D at the

Opera (direction Südbahnhof, it stops at the palace gate).

Belvedere means **"beautiful view."** Sit at the top palace and look over the Baroque gardens, the mysterious sphinxes (which symbolized solving riddles and the finely educated mind of your host, Eugene), the lower palace, and the city. The spire of St. Stephen's Cathedral is 400 feet tall, and no other tall buildings are allowed inside the Ringstrasse. The hills—covered with vineyards—are where locals love to go to sample the new wine. (You can see Kahlenberg, from where you can walk down to several recommended *Heurigen* beyond the spire—see page 473.) These are the first of the Alps, which stretch from here all the way to Marseilles, France. The square you're overlooking was filled with people on May 15, 1955, as local leaders stood on the balcony of the Upper Palace (behind you) and proclaimed Austrian independence following a decade-long Allied occupation after World War II.

The **Upper Palace** was Eugene's party house. Today, like the Louvre in Paris (but much easier to enjoy), this palace contains a fine collection of paintings. The collection is arranged chronologically: on the first floor, you'll find historicism, Romanticism, Impressionism, Realism, tired tourism, Expressionism, Art Nouveau, and early modernism. Each room tries to pair Austrian works from that period with much better-known European works. It's fun to see the work of artists like van Gogh, Munch, and Monet hung with their lesser-known Austrian contemporaries. As Austria becomes a leader in art around 1900, the collection gets stronger, with fine works by Gustav Klimt, Oskar Kokoschka, and Egon Schiele. The Klimt room shows how even in his early work, the face was vivid and the rest dissolved into decor. During his "golden period," this background became his trademark gold leaf studded with stones. The corner room shows a small exhibit on Prince Eugene, Archduke Franz Ferdinand, and the signing of the state treaty in 1955. Don't miss the poignant Schiele family portrait from 1918—his wife died while he was still working on it. (Schiele and his child were soon taken by the influenza epidemic that swept through Europe after WWI.)

The upper floor shows off early-19th-century Biedermeier paintings (hyper-sensitive, super-sweet, uniquely Viennese Romanticism—the poor are happy, things are lit impossibly well, and folk life is idealized). Your ticket also includes the Austrian Baroque and Gothic art in the Lower Palace. Prince Eugene lived in that palace, but he's long gone and I wouldn't bother to visit.

Schönbrunn Palace (Schloss Schönbrunn)

Among Europe's palaces, only Schönbrunn rivals Versailles. Worth ▲▲▲, this summer residence of the Hapsburgs is located four miles from the center. It's big (1,441 rooms), but don't worry—only

40 rooms are shown to the public. (Today the families of 260 civil servants rent simple apartments in the rest of the palace.)

Getting There: Take tram #58 from the Westbahnhof directly to the palace, or ride U-4 to Schönbrunn and walk 400 yards. The main entrance is in the left side of the palace as you face it.

Royal Apartments—While the exterior is Baroque, the interior was finished under Maria Theresa in let-them-eat-cake rococo. The chandeliers are either of hand-carved wood with gold-leaf gilding or of Bohemian crystal. Thick walls hid the servants as they ran around stoking the ceramic stoves from the back, and attending to other behind-the-scenes matters. Most of the public rooms are decorated in neo-Baroque, as they were under Franz Josef (r. 1848–1916). When WWII bombs rained on the city and the palace grounds, the palace itself took only one direct hit. Thankfully, that bomb, which crashed through three floors—including the sumptuous central ballroom—was a dud.

Cost: The admission price is based on which route you select (each one includes an audioguide): the **Imperial Tour** (22 rooms, €8.90, 35 min, Grand Palace rooms plus apartments of Franz Josef and Elisabeth—mostly 19th-century and therefore least interesting) or the **Grand Tour** (40 rooms, €11.50, 50 min, adds apartments of Maria Theresa—18th-century rococo). A combo-ticket called the **Schönbrunn Pass Classic** includes the Grand Tour, as well as other sights on the grounds: the Gloriette viewing terrace, maze, privy garden, and court bakery—complete with *Apfelstrudel* demo and tasting (€15, available April–Oct only). I'd go for the Grand Tour.

Hours: Daily July–Aug 8:30–18:00, April–June and Sept–Oct 8:30–17:00, Nov–March 8:30–16:30. Information: www .schoenbrunn.at.

Crowd-Beating Tips: Schönbrunn suffers from crowds. It's busiest from 9:30 to 11:30, especially on weekends and in July and August; it's least crowded from 12:00 to 14:00 and after 16:00. To avoid the long delays in summer, make a reservation by telephone (tel. 01/8111-3239, answered daily 8:00–17:00). You'll get an appointment time and a ticket number. Check in at least 30 minutes early. Upon arrival, go to the group desk, give your number, pick up your ticket, and jump in ahead of the masses. If you show up in peak season without calling first, you deserve the frustration. (In this case, you'll have to wait in line, buy your ticket, and wait until the listed time to enter—which could be tomorrow.) If you have any time to kill, spend it exploring the gardens or Coach Museum.

Palace Gardens—After strolling by the Hapsburgs tucked neatly into their crypts, a stroll through the emperor's garden with countless commoners is a celebration of the evolution of civilization from autocracy into real democracy. As a civilization, we're doing well.

The park itself is free (daily sunrise to dusk, entrance on either side of the palace). Inside are several other sights, including a **palm house** (€3.50, daily May–Sept 9:30–18:00, Oct–April 9:30–17:00), Europe's oldest **zoo** (*Tiergarten,* built by Maria Theresa's husband for the entertainment and education of the court in 1752; €12, May–Sept daily 9:00–18:30, less off-season, tel. 01/877-9294), and—at the end of the gardens—the **Gloriette,** a purely decorative monument celebrating an obscure Austrian military victory and offering a fine city view (viewing terrace-€2, included in €15 Schönbrunn Pass Classic, daily April–Sept 9:00–18:00, July–Aug until 19:00, Oct until 17:00, closed Nov–March). A touristy choo-choo train makes the rounds all day, connecting Schönbrunn's many attractions.

Coach Museum Wagenburg—The Schönbrunn coach museum is a 19th-century traffic jam of 50 impressive royal carriages and sleighs. Highlights include silly sedan chairs, the death-black hearse carriage (used for Franz Josef in 1916, and most recently for Empress Zita in 1989), and an extravagantly gilded imperial carriage pulled by eight Cinderella horses. This was rarely used other than for the coronation of Holy Roman Emperors, when it was disassembled and taken to Frankfurt for the big event (€4.50; April–Oct daily 9:00–18:00; Nov–March Tue–Sun 10:00–16:00, closed Mon; last entry 30 min before closing, 200 yards from palace, walk through right arch as you face palace, tel. 01/877-3244).

"Honorable Mentions": More Vienna Museums

There's much, much more. The city map lists everything. If you're into Esperanto, undertakers, tobacco, clowns, firefighting, Freud, or the homes of dead composers, you'll find them all in Vienna.

These good museums try very hard but are submerged in the greatness of Vienna: **Jewish Museum of the City of Vienna** (€5, or €7 combo-ticket includes synagogue and Judenplatz Museum—described on page 460, Sun–Fri 10:00–18:00, Thu until 20:00, closed Sat, Dorotheergasse 11, tel. 01/535-0431, www.jmw .at), **Folkloric Museum of Austria** (Tue–Sun 10:00–17:00, closed Mon, Laudongasse 15, tel. 01/406-8905), and **Museum of Military History,** one of Europe's best if you like swords and shields (Heeresgeschichtliches Museum, €5.10, includes audioguide, Sat–Thu 9:00–17:00, closed Fri, Arsenal district, Objekt 18, tel. 01/795-610).

The vast **Austrian Museum of Applied Arts** (Österreichisches Museum für Angewandte Kunst, or "MAK") is Vienna's answer to London's Victoria and Albert collection. The museum shows off the fancies of local aristocratic society, including a fine *Jugendstil* collection (€8, free on Sat, open Tue–Sun 10:00–18:00, Tue until 24:00, closed Mon, Stubenring 5, tel. 01/711-360, www.mak.at).

ACTIVITIES

People-Watching and Strolling

These activities allow you to take it easy and enjoy the Viennese good life.

▲**City Park (Stadtpark)**—Vienna's City Park is a waltzing world of gardens, memorials to local musicians, ponds, peacocks, music in bandstands, and locals escaping the city. Notice the *Jugendstil* entrance at the Stadtpark U-Bahn station. The Kursalon, where Strauss was the violin-toting master of waltzing ceremonies, hosts daily touristy concerts in three-quarter time.

▲**Prater**—Since the 1780s, when the reformist Emperor Josef II gave his hunting grounds to the people of Vienna as a public park, this place has been Vienna's playground. While tired and a bit run-down these days, Vienna's sprawling amusement park still tempts visitors with its huge 220-foot-tall, famous, and lazy Ferris wheel *(Riesenrad)*, roller coaster, bumper cars, Lilliputian railroad, and endless eateries. Especially if you're traveling with kids, this is a fun, goofy place to share the evening with thousands of Viennese (daily 9:00–24:00 in summer, but quiet after 22:00, U-1: Praterstern). For a local-style family dinner, eat at Schweizerhaus (good food, great beer) or Wieselburger Bierinsel.

Sunbathing—Like most Europeans, the Austrians worship the sun. Their lavish swimming centers are as much for tanning as swimming. To find the scene, follow the locals to their "Danube Sea" and a 20-mile, skinny, man-made beach along Danube Island. It's traffic-free concrete and grass, packed with in-line skaters and bikers, with rocky river access and a fun park (easy U-Bahn access on U-1 to Donauinsel).

A Walk in the Vienna Woods (Wienerwald)—For a quick side-trip into the woods and out of the city, catch the U-4 to Heiligenstadt, then bus #38A to Kahlenberg, where you'll enjoy great views and a café overlooking the city. From there, it's a peaceful 45-minute downhill hike to the *Heurigen* of Nussdorf or Grinzing to enjoy some new wine (see "Vienna's Wine Gardens," page 473).

Naschmarkt—Vienna's busy produce market is a great place for people-watching (see page 463).

EXPERIENCES

Music Scene

As far back as the 12th century, Vienna was a mecca for musicians—both sacred and secular (troubadours). The Hapsburg emperors of the 17th and 18th centuries were not only generous supporters of music, but fine musicians and composers themselves.

2006: The Year of Mozart (Mozartjahr)

Mozart, born in 1756, would be 250 years old in 2006 if he had taken better care of himself. Everyone in Salzburg (where he was born, but largely ignored until the late 19th century—when someone figured out how well he could be marketed) and Vienna (where he spent the last 10 years of his life) is eager to lay claim to one of the world's most celebrated musicians. Starting with his birthday on January 27, you'll find a veritable Mozartpalooza: concerts, opera performances, exhibits about his life and work, and plenty of modern compositions inspired by his genius (www.wienmozart2006.at).

Everyone from the marionettes to the Vienna Boys' Choir is busy rehearsing Mozart-inspired programs. The **Vienna State Opera** will perform Mozart's most popular operas (his complete opera repertoire will be performed in Salzburg). From March 15 to August 27, the **Albertina Museum** hosts an installation on Mozart. The **Mozart Haus** (also known as the "Figaro Haus" because he wrote *The Marriage of Figaro* while living here) is expected to re-open in January after extensive restorations (just off of Stephansplatz, behind St. Stephen's Cathedral at Domgasse 5, www.mozarthausvienna.at).

(Maria Theresa played a mean double bass.) Composers like Haydn, Mozart, Beethoven, Schubert, Brahms, and Mahler gravitated to this music-friendly environment. They taught each other, jammed together, and spent a lot of time in Hapsburg palaces. Beethoven was a famous figure, walking—lost in musical thought—through Vienna's woods. In the city's 19th-century belle époque, "Waltz King" Johann Strauss and his brothers kept Vienna's 300 ballrooms spinning.

This musical tradition continues into modern times, leaving some prestigious Viennese institutions for today's tourists to enjoy: the Opera (see page 434), the Boys' Choir, and the great Baroque halls and churches, all busy with classical and waltz concerts.

Vienna is Europe's music capital. It's music *con brio* from October through June, reaching a symphonic climax during the Vienna Festival each May and June. Sadly, in July and August, the Boys' Choir, the Opera, and many more music companies are—like you—on vacation. But Vienna hums year-round with live classical music. Except for the Boys' Choir, the musical events listed below are offered in summer.

Vienna Boys' Choir—The boys sing (from a high balcony, where they are heard but not seen) at the 9:15 **Sunday Mass** from September through March in the Hofburg's Imperial Chapel (Hofburgkapelle; entrance at Schweizerhof, from Josefsplatz go through tunnel). Reserved seats must be booked two months in advance (€5–29, reserve by fax, e-mail, or mail: fax from the U.S. 011-431-533-992-775, hmk@aon.at, or write Hofmusikkapelle, Hofburg-Schweizerhof, 1010 Wien; call 01/533-9927 for information only—they can't book tickets at this number). Much easier, standing room inside is free and open to the first 60 who line up. Even better, rather than line up early, you can simply swing by and stand in the narthex just outside, where you can hear the boys and see the Mass on a TV monitor. Boys' Choir **concerts** (on stage at the Musikverein) are also given Fridays at 16:00 in May, June, September, and October (€35–48, standing room goes on sale at 15:30 for €15, Karlsplatz 6, U-1, U-2, or U-4: Karlsplatz, tel. 01/5880-4141). They're nice kids, but, for my taste, not worth all the commotion. Remember, many churches have great music during Sunday Mass. Just 200 yards from the Boys' Choir chapel, Augustinian Church has a glorious 11:00 service each Sunday (see page 447).

Touristy Mozart and Strauss Concerts—If the music comes to you, it's touristy—designed for flash-in-the-pan Mozart fans. Powdered-wig orchestra performances are given almost nightly in grand traditional settings (€25–50). Pesky wigged-and-powdered Mozarts peddle tickets in the streets. They rave about the quality of the musicians, but you'll get second-rate chamber orchestras, clad in historic costumes, performing the greatest hits of Mozart and Strauss. These are casual, easygoing concerts with lots of tour groups. While there's not a local person in the audience,  the tourists generally enjoy the evening. To sort through all your options, check with the ticket office in the TI (same price as on the street, but with all venues to choose from). Savvy locals suggest getting the cheapest tickets, as no one seems to care if cheapskates move up to fill unsold pricier seats. Critics explain that the musicians are actually very good (often Hungarians, Poles, and Russians working a season here to fund an entire year of music studies back home), but that they haven't performed much together so aren't "tight." The Mozarthaus is a small room richly decorated in Venetian Renaissance style with intimate chamber-music concerts (€29–35, almost nightly at 19:30, near St. Stephen's Cathedral at Singerstrasse 7, tel. 01-911-9077).

Strauss Concerts in the Kursalon—For years, Strauss concerts have been held in the Kursalon, where the "Waltz King" himself directed wildly popular concerts 100 years ago (€36–49, 4 concerts nightly April–Oct, 1 concert nightly other months, tel. 01/512-5790). Shows are a touristy mix of ballet, waltzes, and a 15-piece orchestra in wigs and old outfits. For the cheap option, enjoy a summer-afternoon coffee concert (free if you buy a drink, weekends and maybe also weekdays July–Aug 15:00–17:00).

Serious Concerts—These events, including the Opera, are listed in the monthly *Wien-Programm* (available at TI). Tickets run from €36 to €75 (plus a stiff 22 percent booking fee when booked in advance or through a box office like the one at the TI). While it's easy to book tickets online long in advance, spontaneity is also workable, as there are invariably people with tickets they don't need selling them at face value or less outside the door before concert time. If you call a concert hall directly, they can advise you on the availability of (cheaper) tickets at the door. Vienna takes care of its starving artists (and tourists) by offering cheap standing-room tickets to top-notch music and opera (1 hr before show time).

Summer of Music Festival (a.k.a. "KlangBogen")—This annual festival assures that even from June through September, you'll find lots of great concerts, choirs, and symphonies (special *KlangBogen* brochure at TI; get tickets at Wien Ticket pavilion off Kärntner Strasse next to Opera House, or go directly to location of particular event; Summer of Music tel. 01/42717, www.klangbogen.at).

Musicals—The Wien Ticket pavilion sells tickets to contemporary American and British musicals done in German language (€10–95 with €2.50 standing room), and offers these tickets at half price from 14:00 until 17:00 the day of the show. Or you can reserve (full-price) tickets for the musicals by calling up to one day ahead (call combined office of the 3 big theaters at tel. 01/58885).

Films of Concerts—To see free films of great concerts in a lively, outdoor setting near City Hall, check "Nightlife," page 475.

Classical Music to Go—To bring home Beethoven, Strauss, or the Wiener Philharmonic on a top-quality CD, shop at Gramola on the Graben, Emi on Kärntner Strasse, or Virgin Megastore on Mariahilfer Strasse.

Vienna's Cafés

In Vienna, the living room is down the street at the neighborhood coffeehouse. This tradition is just another example of Viennese expertise in good living. Each of Vienna's many long-established (and sometimes even legendary) coffeehouses has its individual character (and characters). These classic cafés are a bit tired, with a shabby patina and famously grumpy waiters who treat you like an uninvited guest invading their living room. Still, it's a welcoming place. They offer newspapers, pastries, sofas, quick and light workers' lunches, elegance, smoky ambience, and "take all the time you want" charm for the price of a cup of coffee. Order it *melange* (like a cappuccino), *brauner* (strong coffee with a little milk), or *schwarzer* (black). Americans who ask for a latte are mistaken for Italians and given a cup of hot milk. Rather than buy the *Herald Tribune* ahead of time, spend the money on a cup of coffee and read it for free, Vienna-style, in a café.

These are my favorites:

Café Hawelka has a dark, "brooding Trotsky" atmosphere, paintings by struggling artists who couldn't pay for coffee, a saloon-wood flavor, chalkboard menu, smoked velvet couches, an international selection of newspapers, and a phone that rings for regulars (Wed–Mon 8:00–2:00, Sun from 16:00, closed Tue, just off Graben, Dorotheergasse 6).

Café Central features *Jugendstil* decor and great *Apfelstrudel* (high prices and stiff staff, Mon–Sat 8:00–22:00, Sun 10:00–18:00, Herrengasse 14, tel. 01/533-376-326).

Café Sperl dates from 1880, and is still furnished identically to the day it opened—from the coat tree to the chairs (Mon–Sat 7:00–23:00, Sun 15:00–20:00 except closed Sun July–Aug, just off Naschmarkt near Mariahilfer Strasse, Gumpendorfer 11, tel. 01/586-4158).

If **Starbucks** seems big in Vienna, it's because the Seattle-based coffee empire has decided to test the Euro-waters here. Apparently, they figured that Vienna—with its love of fine coffee—would be a tough market to crack...and if they could succeed here, they could take Europe. Locals report that Starbucks is popular with teenagers and tourists, but the coffee is overpriced, and "flavored" coffee is nonsense to Viennese connoisseurs. Even so, the "coffee to go" trend has been picked up by many bakeries and other joints.

Vienna's Wine Gardens (*Heurigen*)

The *Heuriger* is a uniquely Viennese institution. When the Hapsburgs let Vienna's vintners sell their own new wine (called *Sturm*) tax-free, several hundred families opened *Heurigen* (wine-garden restaurants clustered around the edge of town)—and a tradition was born. Today they do their best to maintain the old-village atmosphere, serving the homemade new wine (the last vintage, until November 11, when a new vintage year begins) with light meals and strolling musicians. Most *Heurigen* are decorated with enormous antique presses from their vineyards. Wine gardens might be closed on any given day; always call ahead to confirm, if you have your heart set on a particular place. (For a near-*Heuriger* experience right downtown, drop by Gigerl Stadtheuriger—see page 485.)

At any *Heuriger,* fill your plate at a self-serve cold-cut buffet

(€6–9 for dinner). Food is sold by the *"10 dag"* unit. (A *dag* is a decigram, so *10 dag* is 100 grams...about a quarter pound.) Dishes to look for...or look out for: *Stelze* (grilled knuckle of pork), *Fleischlaberln* (fried ground-meat patties), *Schinkenfleckerln* (pasta with cheese and ham), *Schmalz* (a spread made with pig fat), *Blunzen* (black pudding...sausage made from blood), *Presskopf* (jellied brains and innards), *Liptauer* (spicy cheese spread), *Kornspitz* (whole-meal bread roll), and *Kummelbraten* (crispy roast pork with caraway). Waitresses will then take your wine order (€2.20 per quarter liter, about 8 oz). Many locals claim it takes several years of practice to distinguish between *Sturm* and vinegar.

There are more than 1,700 acres of vineyards within Vienna's city limits, and countless *Heuriger* taverns. For a *Heuriger* evening, rather than go to a particular place, take a tram to the wine-garden district of your choice and wander around, choosing the place with the best ambience.

Getting to the Heurigen: You have three options: a 15-minute taxi ride, trams and buses, or a goofy tourist train.

Trams make a trip to the Vienna Woods quick and affordable. The fastest way is to ride U-4 to its last stop, Heiligenstadt, where trams and buses in front of the station fan out to the various neighborhoods. Ride tram D to its end point for Nussdorf. Ride bus #38A for Grinzing and on to the Kahlenberg viewpoint—#38A's end station. (Note that tram #38—different from bus #38A—starts at the Ring and finishes at Grinzing). To get to Neustift am Walde, ride U-6 to Nussdorfer Strasse and catch bus #35A. Connect Grinzing and Nussdorf with bus #38A and tram D (transfer at Grinzingerstrasse).

The **Heurigen Express** train is tacky but handy and relaxing, chugging you on a hop-on, hop-off circle from Nussdorf through Grinzing and around the Vienna Woods with a light narration (€7.30, buy ticket from driver, 60 min, daily April–Oct 12:00–19:00, departs from end station of tram D in Nussdorf at the top of every hr, tel. 01/479-2808).

Here are a couple good *Heuriger* neighborhoods:

Grinzing: Of the many *Heuriger* suburbs, Grinzing is the most famous, lively...and touristy. Many people precede their visit to Grinzing by riding tram #38 from Schottentor (on the Ring) to its end (up to Kahlenberg for a grand Vienna view), and then ride 20 minutes back into the *Heuriger* action. From the Grinzing tram stop, follow Himmelgasse uphill toward the onion-top dome. You'll pass plenty of wine gardens—and tour buses—on your way up. Just past the dome, you'll find the heart of the *Heurigen*.

Heiligenstadt (Pfarrplatz): Between Grinzing and Nussdorf, this area features several decent spots, including the famous and touristy Mayer am Pfarrplatz (a.k.a **Beethovenhaus**, Mon–Sat

16:00–23:00, Sun 11:00–23:00, bus #38A stop: Fernsprechamt/ Heiligenstadt, walk 5 min uphill on Dübling Nestelbachgasse to Pfarrplatz 2, tel. 01/370-1287). This place has a charming inner courtyard with an accordion player and a sprawling backyard with a big children's play zone. Beethoven lived—and composed his *Sixth Symphony*—here in 1817. He hoped the local spa would cure his worsening deafness. **Weingut and Heuriger Werner Welser,** a block uphill from Beethoven's place, is lots of fun, with music nightly from 19:00 (open daily 15:30–24:00, Probusgasse 12, tel. 01/318-9797).

Nussdorf: A less-touristy district—characteristic and popular with locals—Nussdorf has plenty of *Heuriger* ambience. Right at the end station of tram D, you'll find three long and skinny places side by side: **Schübel-Auer Heuriger** (Tue–Sat 16:00–24:00, closed Sun–Mon, Kahlenbergerstrasse 22, tel. 01/370-2222) is my favorite. Also consider **Heuriger Kierlinger** (daily 15:30–24:00, Kahlenbergerstrasse 20, tel. 01/370-2264) and **Steinschaden** (daily 15:00–24:00, Kahlenbergerstrasse 18, tel. 01/370-1375). Walk through any of these and you pop out on Kahlenbergerstrasse, where a walk 20 yards uphill takes you to some more eating and drinking fun: **Bamkraxler** (literally, "Tree Jumper"), the only beer garden amid all these vineyards. It's a fun-loving, youthful place with fine keg beer and a regular menu—traditional, ribs, veggie, kids' menu—rather than the *Heuriger* cafeteria line (€6–10 meals, kids' playground, Tue–Sat 16:00–24:00, Sun 11:00–24:00, closed Mon, Kahlenbergerstrasse 17, tel. 01/318-8800).

Sirbu Weinbau Heuriger is actually in the vineyards, high above Vienna with great city and countryside views, a top-notch buffet, a glass veranda, and a traditional interior for cool weather. This place is a bit more touristy, since it's more upmarket and famous as "the ultimate setting" (April–Oct from 15:00, closed Sun, big children's play zone, Kahlenbergerstrasse 210, tel. 01/320-5928). It's high above regular transit service, but fun to incorporate into a little walking. Ideally, ride bus #38A to the end at Kahlenberg, and ask directions to the *Heuriger* (a 20-min walk downhill).

NIGHTLIFE

If old music and new wine aren't your thing, Vienna has plenty of alternatives. For an up-to-date rundown on fun after dark, get the TI's free *Vienna Hype* booklet.

Open-Air Cinema and Food Circus at City Hall—A thriving people scene erupts each evening in July and August at the park in front of the City Hall (Rathaus) on the Ring. A huge screen is set up with top-end speakers to show films of great concerts.

While it's not live, the quality is excellent and it's free. Classical, opera, or jazz—there's a different concert every night. Go early to enjoy dinner in the park, as there are countless (mostly ethnic) stalls serving fun and cheap meals to the youthful gang (daily from 11:00 until late in July and Aug). Single locals know this is the best pick-up place in town. Film schedules are at the TI.

Bermuda Triangle (Bermuda Dreieck)—The area known as the "Bermuda Triangle"—north of St. Stephen's Cathedral, between Rotenturmstrasse and Judengasse—is the hot local nightspot. You'll find lots of music clubs and classy pubs, or *Beisl* (such as Krah Krah, Salzamt, Bermuda Bräu, and First Floor—for cocktails with live fish). The serious-looking guards have nothing to do with the bar scene—they're guarding the synagogue nearby.

Gürtel—The Gürtel is Vienna's outer ring road. The arches of a lumbering viaduct (which carries a train track) are now filled with trendy bars, dance clubs, antique shops, and restaurants. To experience—or simply see—the latest scene in town, head out here. The people-watching—the trendiest kids on the block—makes the trip fun even if you're looking for exercise rather than a drink. Ride U-6 to Nussdorfer Strasse or Thaliastrasse and hike along the viaduct.

English Cinema—Two great theaters offer three or four screens of English movies nightly (€6–9): **English Cinema Haydn,** by my recommended hotels on Mariahilfer Strasse (Mariahilfer Strasse 57, tel. 01/587-2262, www.haydnkino.at); and **Artis International Cinema,** right in the town center a few minutes from the cathedral (Schultergasse 5, tel. 01/535-6570).

SLEEPING

As you move out from the center, hotel prices drop. My listings are in the old center (figure at least €100 for a decent double), along the likeable Mariahilfer Strasse (around €80), and near the Westbahnhof (around €60). While few accommodations in Vienna are air-conditioned (they are troubled by the fact that, per person, Las Vegas expends more energy keeping people cool than arctic Norway does to keep people warm), you can generally get fans on request. Places with elevators often have a few stairs to climb, too.

These hotels loose big and you pay more if you find a room through Internet booking sites. Book direct by phone, fax, or e-mail and save.

Sleep Code

(€1 = about $1.20, country code: 43, area code: 01)
S = Single, **D** = Double/Twin, **T** = Triple, **Q** = Quad, **b** = bathroom, **s** = shower only. English is spoken at each place. Unless otherwise noted, credit cards are accepted and breakfast is included.

To help you sort easily through these listings, I've divided the rooms into three categories, based on the price for a standard double room with bath:

$$$ **Higher Priced**—Most rooms €115 or more.
$$ **Moderately Priced**—Most rooms between €75–115.
$ **Lower Priced**—Most rooms €75 or less.

Within the Ring, in the Old City Center

You'll pay extra to sleep in the atmospheric old center, but if you can afford it, staying here gives you the best classy Vienna experience.

$$$ **Pension Pertschy** circles an old courtyard and is bigger and more hotelesque than the others listed here. Its 50 rooms are huge, but well-worn and a bit musty. Those on the courtyard are quietest (Sb-€87, small Db-€119, large Db-€172, cheaper off-season, extra bed-€32, non-smoking rooms, elevator, U-1 or U-3: Stephansplatz, Habsburgergasse 5, tel. 01/534-490, fax 01/534-4949, www.pertschy.com, pertschy@pertschy.com).

$$$ **Pension Neuer Markt** is family-run, with 37 quiet, comfy, old-feeling rooms in a perfectly central locale (Ss-€85, Sb-€90–110, smaller Ds-€96, Db-€100–130, prices vary with season and room size, extra bed-€20, elevator, Seilergasse 9, tel. 01/512-2316, fax 01/513-9105, www.hotelpension.at/neuermarkt, neuermarkt@hotelpension.at).

$$$ **Pension Aviano** is another peaceful place, with 17 comfortable rooms on the fourth floor above lots of old center action (Sb-€92, Db-€132–152 depending on size, 15 percent cheaper Nov–March, extra bed-€30, elevator, non-smoking rooms, between Neuer Markt and Kärntner Strasse at Marco d'Avianogasse 1, tel. 01/512-8330, fax 01/5128-3306, www.pertschy.com, aviano@pertschy.com).

$$$ **Hotel Schweizerhof** is classy, with 55 big rooms, all the comforts, and a more formal ambience. It's centrally located midway between St. Stephen's Cathedral and the Danube canal (Sb-€84–95, Db-€109–140, Tb-€131–160, low prices are for July–Aug and slow times, with cash and this book get your best price and then claim a 10 percent discount in 2006, can be noisy on weekends, elevator, Bauernmarkt 22, U-1 or U-3: Stephansplatz, tel. 01/533-1931, fax

Hotels and Restaurants in Central Vienna

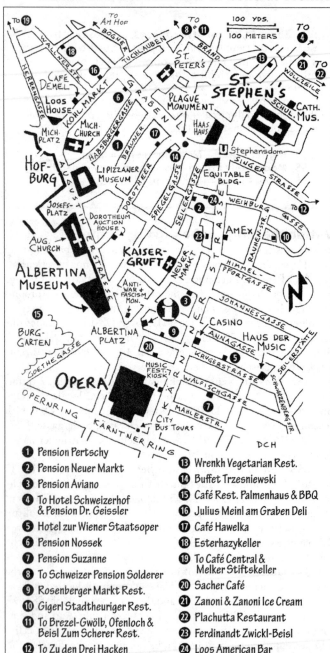

1. Pension Pertschy
2. Pension Neuer Markt
3. Pension Aviano
4. To Hotel Schweizerhof & Pension Dr. Geissler
5. Hotel zur Wiener Staatsoper
6. Pension Nossek
7. Pension Suzanne
8. To Schweizer Pension Solderer
9. Rosenberger Markt Rest.
10. Gigerl Stadtheuriger Rest.
11. To Brezel-Gwölb, Ofenloch & Beisl Zum Scherer Rest.
12. To Zu den Drei Hacken
13. Wrenkh Vegetarian Rest.
14. Buffet Trzesniewski
15. Café Rest. Palmenhaus & BBQ
16. Julius Meinl am Graben Deli
17. Café Hawelka
18. Esterhazykeller
19. To Café Central & Melker Stiftskeller
20. Sacher Café
21. Zanoni & Zanoni Ice Cream
22. Plachutta Restaurant
23. Ferdinandt Zwickl-Beisl
24. Loos American Bar

01/533-0214, www.schweizerhof.at, office@schweizerhof.at).

\$\$\$ Hotel zur Wiener Staatsoper, the Schweizerhof's sister hotel, is quiet and rich. Its 22 tight rooms come with high ceilings, chandeliers, and fancy carpets on parquet floors—ideal for people whose hotel tastes are a cut above mine. The singles are tiny, with beds too short for anyone over six feet tall (Sb-€84–95, Db-€109–140, Tb-€131–160, extra bed-€22, cheaper prices are for July–Aug and Dec–March, fans on request, elevator, U-1, U-2, or U-4: Karlsplatz, a block from Opera at Krugerstrasse 11, tel. 01/513-1274, fax 01/513-127-415, www.zurwienerstaatsoper.at, office @zurwienerstaatsoper.at, manager Claudia).

\$\$ At Pension Nossek, an elevator takes you above any street noise into Frau Bernad's and Frau Gundolf's world, where the children seem to be placed among the lace and flowers by an interior designer. With 30 rooms right on the wonderful Graben, this is a particularly good value (S-€46–54, Ss-€58, Sb-€69–73, Db-€110, €26 extra for sprawling suites, extra bed-€35, Internet in lobby, cash only, elevator, U-1 or U-3: Stephansplatz, Graben 17, tel. 01/5337-0410, fax 01/535-3646, www.pension-nossek.at, reservation@pension-nossek.at).

\$\$ Pension Suzanne, as Baroque and doily as you'll find in this price range, is wonderfully located a few yards from the Opera. It's small, but run with the class of a bigger hotel; the 25 rooms are packed with properly Viennese antique furnishings. Streetside rooms come with some noise (Sb-€76, Db-€94–115 depending on size, 4 percent discount with cash, extra bed-€30, spacious apartment for up to 6 also available, discounts in winter, fans on request, elevator, a block from Opera, U-1, U-2, or U-4: Karlsplatz and follow signs for Opera exit, Walfischgasse 4, tel. 01/513-2507, fax 01/513-2500, www.pension-suzanne.at, info@pension-suzanne.at, manager Michael).

\$\$ Schweizer Pension Solderer has been family-owned for three generations. The current owner, Anita, runs an extremely tight ship, offering 11 homey rooms, parquet floors, and lots of tourist info (S-€38–42, Sb-€55–65, D-€58–65, Db-€78–87, Tb-€102–109, Qb-€126–131, prices depend on season and room size, cash only, entirely non-smoking, elevator, laundry-€14/load, U-2 or U-4: Schottenring, Heinrichsgasse 2, tel. 01/533-8156, fax 01/535-6469, www.schweizerpension.com, schweizer.pension@chello.at).

\$\$ Pension Dr. Geissler has 23 comfortable rooms on the eighth floor of a modern building about 10 blocks northeast of St. Stephen's, near the canal (S-€48, Ss-€68, Sb-€76, D-€65, Ds-€77, Db-€95, 20 percent less in winter, elevator, U-1 or U-4: Schwedenplatz, Postgasse 14, tel. 01/533-2803, fax 01/533-2635, www.hotelpension.at/dr-geissler, dr.geissler@hotelpension.at).

Hotels and Pensions along Mariahilfer Strasse

Lively Mariahilfer Strasse connects the Westbahnhof (West Train Station) and the city center. The U-3 line, starting at the Westbahnhof, goes down Mariahilfer Strasse to the cathedral. This very Viennese street is a tourist-friendly and vibrant area filled with local shops and cafés. Most hotels are within a few steps of a U-Bahn stop, just one or two stops from the Westbahnhof (direction from the station: Simmering). The nearest place to do laundry is **Schnell & Sauber Waschcenter** (wash-€6 for small load or €9 for large load, plus a few euros to dry, daily 9:00–21:00, a few blocks north of Westbahnhof on Urban-Loritz-Platz).

$$$ NH Hotels, a Spanish chain, runs two stern, passionless business hotels a few blocks apart on Mariahilfer Strasse. Both rent ideal-for-families suites, each with a living room, two TVs, bathroom, desk, and kitchenette (rack rate: Db suite-€155, going rate usually closer to €100, plus €14 per person for optional breakfast, apartments for 2–3 adults, kids under 12 free, non-smoking rooms, elevator). The 78-room **NH Atterseehaus** is at Mariahilfer Strasse 78 (U-3: Zieglergasse, tel. 01/5245-6000, fax 01/524-560-015, nhatterseehaus@nh-hotels.com), and the **NH Wien** has 106 rooms at Mariahilfer Strasse 32 (U-3: Neubaugasse, tel. 01/521-720, fax 01/521-7215, nhwien@nh-hotels.com). The Web site for both is www.nh-hotels.com.

$$ Pension Corvinus is bright, modern, and warmly run by a Hungarian family: Miklós, Judit, and Zoltan. Its eight comfortable rooms are spacious, with small, compact bathrooms (Sb-€58, Db-€91, Tb-€105, extra bed-€26, non-smoking rooms, portable air-con-€10/day, elevator, free Internet in lobby, parking garage-€11/day, on the 3rd floor at Mariahilfer Strasse 57–59, tel. 01/587-7239, fax 01/587-723-920, www.corvinus.at, hotel@corvinus.at).

$$ Pension Mariahilf offers a clean, aristocratic air in an affordable and cozy pension package. Its 12 rooms are spacious but outmoded, with an Art Deco flair (Sb-€59–66, Db-€95–102, Tb-€124, lower prices are for longer stays, may be under new management in 2006, elevator, U-3: Neubaugasse, Mariahilfer Strasse 49, tel. 01/586-1781, fax 01/586-178-122, www.mariahilf-hotel.at, penma@inode.at).

$$ Haydn Hotel, in the same building as the Pension Corvinus (listed above), is big, fancy, and dark, with 50 spacious rooms. Most rooms have been remodeled (Sb-€65–90, Db-€90–100, 10 percent discount with cash and this book in 2006, suites and family apartments, extra bed-€30, air-con, non-smoking rooms, elevator, free Internet in lobby, Mariahilfer Strasse 57–59, tel. 01/587-44140, fax 01/586-1950, www.haydn-hotel.at, info@haydn-hotel.at, Nouri).

$$ Hotel Admiral is huge, quiet, and practical, with 80 large, comfortable rooms (Sb-€66, Db-€91, extra bed-€23, manager

Hotels and Restaurants outside the Ring

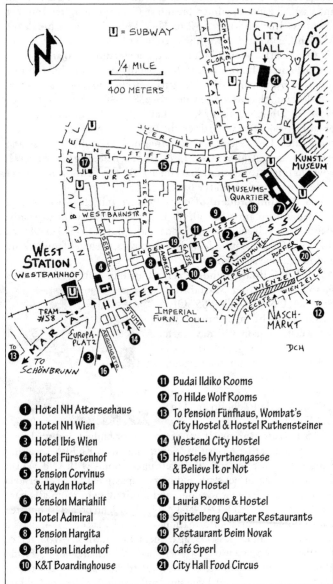

1 Hotel NH Atterseehaus
2 Hotel NH Wien
3 Hotel Ibis Wien
4 Hotel Fürstenhof
5 Pension Corvinus & Haydn Hotel
6 Pension Mariahilf
7 Hotel Admiral
8 Pension Hargita
9 Pension Lindenhof
10 K&T Boardinghouse
11 Budai Ildiko Rooms
12 To Hilde Wolf Rooms
13 To Pension Fünfhaus, Wombat's City Hostel & Hostel Ruthensteiner
14 Westend City Hostel
15 Hostels Myrthengasse & Believe It or Not
16 Happy Hostel
17 Lauria Rooms & Hostel
18 Spittelberg Quarter Restaurants
19 Restaurant Beim Novak
20 Café Sperl
21 City Hall Food Circus

Alexandra promises these prices through 2006 with this book and cash, cheaper in winter, breakfast-€5 per person, free Internet in lobby, free parking, U-2 or U-3: Volkstheater, a block off Mariahilfer Strasse at Karl Schweighofer Gasse 7, tel. 01/521-410, fax 01/521-4116, www.admiral.co.at, hotel@admiral.co.at).

$ Pension Hargita rents 24 generally small, bright, and tidy rooms (mostly twins) with Hungarian decor. This spick-and-span, well-located place is a fine value (S-€38, Ss-€45, Sb-€55, D-€52, Ds-€58, Db-€66, Ts-€73, Tb-€80, Qb-€110, extra bed-€12, breakfast-€4, reserve with credit card but pay with cash to get these rates, U-3: Zieglergasse, corner of Mariahilfer Strasse and Andreasgasse, Andreasgasse 1, tel. 01/526-1928, fax 01/526-0492, www.hargita.at, pension@hargita.at). As the pension has street noise, request a room in the back.

$ Pension Lindenhof rents 19 worn but clean rooms and is filled with plants (S-€30, Sb-€37, D-€51, Db-€67, cash only, elevator, U-3: Neubaugasse, Lindengasse 4, tel. 01/523-0498, fax 01/523-7362, pensionlindenhof@yahoo.com, Gebrael family, Zara and Keram speak English).

$ K&T Boardinghouse rents four big, comfortable rooms  facing the bustling Mariahilfer Strasse (Db-€65, Tb-€85, Qb-€105, 2-night minimum, no breakfast, air-con-€10/day, cash only, non-smoking, free Internet in lobby, 3 flights up, no elevator, Mariahilfer Strasse 72, tel. 01/523-2989, fax 01/522-0345, www.kaled.at, kaled@chello.at, Tina and Kaled).

$ Private Rooms: If you're on a tight budget and wish you had a grandmother to visit in Vienna, stay with English-speaking **Budai Ildiko.** She rents high-ceilinged rooms with Old World furnishings out of her dark and homey apartment. Two cavernous rooms, which sleep two to four, and a skinny twin room all share one bathroom (S-€32, D-€45, T-€64, Q-€79, no breakfast but free coffee, lots of tourist information, cash only, laundry-€4, classic old elevator, Lindengasse 39, apartment #5, tel. 01/523-1058, tel. & fax 01/526-2595, www.wienwien.at, budai@hotmail.com). **$ Hilde Wolf,** with the help of her grandson, Patrick, shares her apartment with travelers. Her four huge but stuffy rooms are like old libraries (S-€33, D-€50, T-€70, Q-€90, breakfast-€4, cash only, U-2: Karlsplatz, 3 blocks below Naschmarkt at Schleifmühlgasse 7, tel. 01/586-5103, fax 01/689-3505, www.schoolpool.at/bb). There's no sign or name at the street—she's on the first floor.

Near the Westbahnhof (West Station)

$$ Hotel Ibis Wien, a modern high-rise hotel with American charm, is ideal for anyone tired of quaint old Europe. Its 340 cookie-cutter rooms are bright, comfortable, and modern, with all the conveniences (Sb-€71, Db-€86, Tb-€101, €5 cheaper in July, breakfast-€9, non-smoking rooms, air-con, elevator, parking garage-€10/day, exit Westbahnhof to the right and walk 400 yards, Mariahilfer Gürtel 22-24, tel. 01/59998, fax 01/597-9090, h0796@accor.com).

$$ Hotel Fürstenhof, right across from the station, rents 58 spacious but borderline-musty rooms. This venerable hotel has an Old World maroon-velvet feel (S-€46, Sb-€69–94, D-€65, Db-€110, Tb-€120, Qb-€128, 10 percent cheaper if you book online, ask for quiet side—*ruhige Seite*, elevator, Internet in lobby, Europaplatz 4, tel. 01/523-3267, fax 01/523-326-726, www.hotel-fuerstenhof.com, reception@hotel-fuerstenhof.com).

$ Pension Fünfhaus is big, clean, and stark—almost institutional. The neighborhood is run-down (with a few ladies loitering late at night) and the staff can be grouchy, but this 47-room place is sill a decent value (S-€32, Sb-€40, D-€44, Db-€52, T-€66, Tb-€78, 4-person apartment-€90, prices promised with this book in 2006, cash only, closed mid-Nov–Feb, Sperrgasse 12, tel. 01/892-3545 or 01/892-0286, fax 01/892-0460, www.pension5haus.at, pension5haus@tiscali.at, Frau Susi Tersch). Half the rooms are in the fine main building and half are in the annex, which has good rooms but is near the train tracks and a bit scary on the street at night. From the station, ride tram #52 or #58 two stops down Mariahilfer Strasse away from center to the Kranzgasse stop, then backtrack two blocks to Sperrgasse.

Cheap Dorms and Hostels near Mariahilfer Strasse

$ Believe It or Not is a tiny, basic hostel with about the cheapest bunk beds in town in two coed rooms for up to 10 travelers. Hardworking and friendly Heny requires a minimum two-night stay and warns that this place is appropriate only for the young at heart (bed-€13.50, €10.50 Nov–Easter, cash only, locked up 10:00–12:30, no curfew, kitchen facilities, Myrthengasse 10, ring apt. #14, tel. 01/526-4658, www.believe-it-or-not-vienna.at, believe_it_or_not_vienna@hotmail.com).

$ Jugendherberge Myrthengasse is a well-run youth hostel (260 beds, €15–19 each in 3- to 6-bed rooms, includes sheets and breakfast, non-members pay €3.50 extra, always open, no curfew, lockers and lots of facilities, Myrthengasse 7, tel. 01/523-6316, fax 01/523-5849, hostel@chello.at).

$ Westend City Hostel, just a block from the Westbahnhof and Mariahilfer Strasse, is well-run and well-located, with 180 beds in 4- to 12-bed dorms (€17–25 per person, depending on how many in the room; includes sheets, breakfast, and locker; cash only, laundry, Internet in lobby, Fügergasse 3, tel. 01/597-6729, fax 01/597-672-927, www.westendhostel.at, westendcityhostel@aon.at).

$ Happy Hostel rents five ramshackle yet homey apartments for two to five people beautifully located on a quiet street a couple blocks from the Westbahnhof and Mariahilfer Strasse (€25/person, S-€35, Sb-€40, Db-€50–70, no breakfast, Aegidigasse 19, tel. 01/208-2618, www.happyhostel.at, info@happyhostel.at).

$ Lauria Rooms and Hostel is a creative little place run by friendly Gosha, with two 10-bed dorms (boys and girls mixed, with lockers) and several other rooms sleeping two to six each (€13.50 dorm beds, around €24 per person in other rooms, Kaiserstrasse 77, tram #5 or a 10-min walk from Westbahnhof, tel. 01/522-2555).

$ *More Hostels:* Other hostels with €16 beds and €40 doubles near Mariahilfer Strasse are **Wombat's City Hostel** (Grangasse 6, tel. 01/897-2336, www.wombats-hostels.com, office@wombats-vienna.at) and **Hostel Ruthensteiner** (Robert-Hamerling-Gasse 24, tel. 01/893-4202, www.hostelruthensteiner.com, info@hostelruthensteiner.com).

EATING

The Viennese appreciate the fine points of life, and right up there with waltzing is eating. The city has many atmospheric restaurants. As you ponder the Eastern European specialties on menus, remember that Vienna's diverse empire may be gone, but its flavor lingers.

While cuisines are routinely named for countries, Vienna claims to be the only *city* with a cuisine of its own: Vienna soups come with fillings (semolina dumpling, liver dumpling, or pancake slices). *Gulasch* is a beef ragout of Hungarian origin (spiced with onion and paprika). Of course, Viennese schnitzel (Wiener Schnitzel) is traditionally a breaded and fried veal cutlet (though pork is more common these days). Another meat specialty is boiled beef *(Tafelspitz)*. While you're sure to have *Apfelstrudel*, try the sweet cheese strudel, too (*Topfenstrudel*—wafer-thin strudel pastry filled with sweet cheese and raisins).

On nearly every corner, you can find a colorful *Beisl*. These uniquely Viennese taverns are a characteristic cross between an English pub and a French brasserie—filled with poetry teachers and their students, couples loving without touching, housewives on their way home from cello lessons, and waiters who enjoy serving hearty food and good drink at an affordable price. Ask at your hotel for a good *Beisl*.

Wherever you're eating, some vocabulary helps. Try the *grüner Veltliner* (dry white wine), *Traubenmost* (a heavenly grape juice—alcohol-free but on the verge of wine), *Most* (the same thing but lightly alcoholic), and *Sturm* (stronger than *Most*, autumn only). The local red wine (called *Portugieser*) is pretty good. Since the Austrian wine is often sweet, remember the word *trocken* (dry). You can order your wine by the *Viertel* (quarter liter, 8 oz) or *Achtel* (eighth liter, 4 oz). Beer comes in a *Krügel* (half liter, 17 oz) or *Seidel* (0.3 liter, 10 oz). The *dag* you see in some prices stands for "decigram" (10 grams). Therefore, *10 dag* is 100 grams, or about a quarter pound.

Near St. Stephen's Cathedral

All of these eateries are within a five-minute walk of the cathedral.

Gigerl Stadtheuriger offers a near-*Heuriger* experience (à la Grinzing— see "Vienna's Wine Gardens," page 473), often with accordion or live music, without leaving the city center. Just point to what looks good. Food is sold by the weight; 100 grams *(10 dag)* is about a quarter pound (cheese and cold meats cost about €3 per 100 grams, salads are about €2 per 100 grams; price sheet is posted on the wall to right of buffet line). They also have menu entrées, along with spinach strudel, quiche, *Apfelstrudel*, and, of course, casks of new and local wines. Meals run €7–11 (daily 15:00–24:00, indoor/outdoor seating, behind cathedral, a block off Kärntner Strasse, a few cobbles off Rauhensteingasse on Blumenstock, tel. 01/513-4431).

Am Hof Eateries: The square called Am Hof (U-3: Herrengasse) is surrounded by a maze of atmospheric medieval lanes; the following places are all within a block of the square. **Restaurant Ofenloch** serves good, old-fashioned Viennese cuisine with friendly service, both indoors and out. This 300-year-old eatery, with great traditional ambience, is central but not overrun with tourists (€12–18 main dishes, Tue–Sat 11:30–24:00, Mon 18:00–24:00, closed Sun, Kurrentgasse 8, tel. 01/533-8844). **Brezel-Gwölb**, a wonderfully atmospheric wine cellar with outdoor dining on a quiet square, serves delicious light meals, fine *Krautsuppe* (cabbage soup), and old-fashioned local dishes. It's ideal for a romantic late-night glass of wine (daily 11:30–1:00, leave Am Hof on Drahtgasse, then take first left to Ledererhof 9, tel. 01/533-8811). Around the corner, **Beisl "Zum Scherer"** is just as untouristy and serves traditional plates for €10. Sitting outside, you'll face a stern Holocaust memorial. Inside comes with a soothing woody atmosphere and intriguing decor (Mon–Sat 11:30–24:00, food until 22:00, closed Sun, Judenplatz 7, tel. 01/533-5164). Just below Am Hof, the ancient and popular **Esterhazykeller** has traditional fare deep underground or outside on a delightful square (Mon–Fri

11:00–23:00, Sat–Sun 16:00–23:00, self-service buffet in lowest cellar or from menu, Haarhof 1, tel. 01/533-3482).

Wine Cellars: These wine cellars are fun and touristy but typical, in the old center, with reasonable prices and plenty of smoke: **Melker Stiftskeller,** less touristy, is a *Stadtheuriger* in a deep and rustic cellar with hearty, inexpensive meals and new wine (Tue–Sat 17:00–24:00, closed Sun–Mon and most of July, between Am Hof and Schottentor U-Bahn stop at Schottengasse 3, tel. 01/533-5530). **Zu den Drei Hacken** is famous for its local specialties (€10 plates, Mon–Sat 11:00–23:00, closed Sun, indoor/outdoor seating, Singerstrasse 28, tel. 01/512-5895).

Ferdinandt Zwickl-Beisl is an inviting little pub with a user-friendly menu featuring the classic traditional *Beisl* plates, plus salads and vegetarian dishes. Choose between Old World, woody indoor seating and pleasant streetside seating (€9–15 plates, daily 9:00–24:00, a block off the Kärntner Strasse mob scene at Neuer Markt 2, tel. 01/513-8991).

Wrenkh Vegetarian Restaurant and Bar is popular for its high vegetarian cuisine. Chef Wrenkh offers daily €8 to €10 lunch *menus* and €8 to €13 dinner plates in a bright, mod bar or in a dark, smoke-free, fancier restaurant (Mon–Sat 11:30–23:00, closed Sun, July–Aug also closed Sat, Bauernmarkt 10, tel. 01/533-1526).

Buffet Trzesniewski is an institution—justly famous for its elegant and cheap finger sandwiches and small beers (€0.80 each). Three different sandwiches and a *kleines Bier (Pfiff)* make a fun, light lunch. Point to whichever delights look tasty (or grab the English translation sheet and take time to study your options). Pay for your sandwiches and a drink. Take your drink tokens to the lady on the right. Sit on the bench and scoot over to a tiny table when a spot opens up (Mon–Fri 8:30–19:30, Sat 9:00–17:00, closed Sun, 50 yards off Graben, nearly across from brooding Café Hawelka, Dorotheergasse 2, tel. 01/512-3291). This is a good opportunity (in the fall) to try the fancy grape juices—*Most* or *Traubenmost* (described above).

Julius Meinl am Graben, a posh supermarket right on the Graben, has been famous since 1862 as a top-end delicatessen with all the gourmet fancies. Along with the picnic fixings on the shelves, there's a café with light meals and great outdoor seating, a stuffy and pricey restaurant upstairs, and a take-away counter (shop open Mon–Fri 8:30–19:30, Sat 9:00–18:00, closed Sun; restaurant open Mon–Sat until 24:00, closed Sun; Am Graben 19, tel. 01/532-3334).

Akakiko Sushi: If you're just schnitzeled out, this small chain of Japanese restaurants with an easy sushi menu may suit you. The bento box meals are tasty. Three locations have no charm but are fast, reasonable, and convenient (€7–10 meals, all open daily

10:30–23:30): Singerstrasse 4 (a block off Kärntner Strasse near the cathedral), Heidenschuss 3 (near other recommended eateries just off Am Hof), and Mariahilfer Strasse 42–48 (5th floor of Kaufhaus Gerngross, near many recommended hotels).

Plachutta Restaurant, with a stylish green-and-crème, elegant-but-comfy interior and breezy covered terrace, is famous for the best beef in town. You'll find an enticing menu with all the classic Viennese beef dishes, fine deserts, attentive service, and an enthusiastic local clientele. They've developed the art of beef to the point of producing popular cookbooks (€15–20 meals, daily 11:30–23:00, U-3: Stubentor, 10-min walk from St. Stephen's Cathedral, Wollzeile 38, tel. 01/512-1577).

Ice Cream!: **Zanoni & Zanoni** is a very Italian *gelateria* run by an Italian family. They're mobbed by happy Viennese hungry for their huge €2 cones to go. Or, to relax, lick your gelato at their fun outdoor seating (daily 7:00–24:00, 2 blocks up Rotenturmstrasse from cathedral at Lugeck 7, tel. 01/512-7979).

Near the Opera

Café Restaurant Palmenhaus, overlooking the Palace Garden (Burggarten—see page 445), tucked away in a green and peaceful corner two blocks behind the Opera in the Hofburg's back yard, is a world apart. If you want to eat modern Austrian cuisine with palm trees rather than tourists, this is it. And, since it's at the edge of a huge park, it's great for families (€8 2-course lunches available Mon–Fri, €15–18 entrées, open daily 10:00–2:00 in the morning, serious vegetarian dishes, fish, extensive wine list, indoors in greenhouse or outdoors, tel. 01/533-1033). While nobody goes to the Palmenhaus for good prices, the **Palmenhaus BBQ,** a cool parkside outdoor pub just below that uses the same kitchen, is a wonderful value with more casual service (summer Thu–Sat from 20:00, closed Sun–Wed, open in good weather only, informal with €8–10 BBQ and meals posted on chalkboard).

Rosenberger Markt Restaurant is my favorite for a fast, light, and central lunch. Just a block toward the cathedral from the Opera, this cafeteria—while not cheap—is brilliant. Friendly and efficient, with special theme rooms for dining, it offers a fresh, smoke-free, and healthy cornucopia of food and drink (daily 10:30–23:00, lots of fruits, veggies, fresh-squeezed juices, addictive banana milk, ride the glass elevator downstairs, Maysedergasse 2, tel. 01/512-3458). You can stack a small salad or veggie plate into a tower of gobble for €2.90.

City Hall (Rathaus) Food Circus: During the summer, scores of outdoor food stands and hundreds of picnic tables are set up in the park in front of the City Hall. Local mobs enjoy mostly ethnic meals on disposable plates for decent-but-not-cheap prices. The fun thing here is the energy of the crowd, and a feeling that you're truly eating as the locals do...not schnitzel and quaint traditions, but trendy "world food" with people out having pure and simple fun in a fine Vienna park setting (July–Aug daily from 11:00 until late, in front of City Hall on the Ringstrasse).

Spittelberg Quarter

A charming cobbled grid of traffic-free lanes and Biedermeier apartments has become a favorite neighborhood for Viennese wanting a little dining charm between the MuseumsQuartier and Mariahilfer Strasse (handy to many recommended hotels; take Stiftgasse from Mariahilfer Strasse, or wander over here after you close down the Kunsthistorisches or Leopold Museum). Tables tumble down sidewalks and into breezy courtyards filled with appreciative locals enjoying dinner or a relaxing drink. Stroll Spittelberggasse, Schrankgasse, and Gutenberggasse and pick your favorite place. Don't miss the vine-strewn wine garden at Schrankgasse 1. **Amerlingbeisl,** with a casual atmosphere both on the cobbled street and in its vine-covered courtyard, is a great value (€7 plates, €6–8 daily specials, salads, veggie dishes, traditional specialties, daily 9:00–24:00, Stiftgasse 8, tel. 01/526-1660). The neighboring **Plutzer Bräu** is also good (ribs, burgers, traditional dishes, Tirolean beer from the keg, daily 11:00–2:00, food until 22:30, Schrankgasse 4, tel. 01/526-1215). For traditional Viennese cuisine with tablecloths, consider the classier **Witwe Bolte** (daily 11:30–15:00 & 17:30–23:30, Gutenberggasse 13, tel. 01/523-1450).

Near Mariahilfer Strasse

Mariahilfer Strasse is filled with reasonable cafés serving all types of cuisine.

Restaurant Beim Novak serves tasty and well-presented Viennese cuisine away from the modern rush. While this small and intimate place, thoughtfully run by Maximilian, has no outdoor seating, the charming back room offers a relaxing atmosphere (€7 lunch specials, €10–15 plates, Mon–Fri 11:30–15:00 & 18:00–22:00, open Sat for dinner Sept–March, closed Sun and in Aug, a block down Andreasgasse from Mariahilfer Strasse at Richtergasse 12, tel. 01/523-3244).

Naschmarkt (described on page 463) is Vienna's best Old World market, with plenty of fresh produce, cheap local-style eateries, cafés, *döner kebab* and sausage stands, and the best-value sushi in town (Mon–Fri 6:00–18:30, Sat 6:00–17:00, closed Sun, closes earlier in winter, U-4: Kettenbrückengasse). Survey the lane of eateries at the end of the market nearest the Opera. The circa-1900 pub is inviting. Picnickers can buy supplies at the market and eat on nearby Karlsplatz (plenty of chairs facing Charles Church).

TRANSPORTATION CONNECTIONS

Vienna has two main train stations: the Westbahnhof (West Station), serving Munich, Salzburg, Melk, and Budapest; and the Südbahnhof (South Station), serving Budapest, Prague, Poland, Slovenia, Croatia, and usually Italy (though some Italy-bound trains go from the Westbahnhof). A third station, Franz Josefs, serves Krems and the Danube Valley (but Melk is served by the Westbahnhof). There are exceptions, so always confirm which station your train leaves from. Metro line U-3 connects the Westbahnhof with the center, tram D takes you from the Südbahnhof and the Franz Josefs station to downtown, and tram #18 connects West and South stations. Train info: tel. 051-717 (to get an operator, dial 2, then 1).

From Vienna by Train to: Melk (hrly, 1–2 hrs, sometimes change in St. Pölten), **Krems** (hrly, 1 hr), **Salzburg** (hrly, 3 hrs), **Innsbruck** (every 2 hrs, 5.5 hrs), **Bratislava** (about hrly, 1 hr), **Budapest** (6/day, 3 hrs), **Prague** (6/day, 4.5 hrs), **Český Krumlov** (5/day, 6–7 hrs, up to 3 changes), **Munich** (hrly, 5.25 hrs, change in Salzburg, a few direct trains), **Berlin** (2/day, 10 hrs, longer on night train), **Zürich** (3/day, 9 hrs), **Ljubljana** (7/day, 6–7 hrs, convenient early-morning direct train, others change in Villach or Maribor), **Zagreb** (8/day, 6.5–10.5 hrs, 3 direct, others with up to 3 changes including Villach and Ljubljana), **Kraków** (4/day, 6.5–9 hrs, 2 direct including a night train departing at about 22:00, arriving around 6:00), **Warsaw** (4/day, 7.5–10 hrs, 2 direct including a night train), **Rome** (1/day, 13.5 hrs), **Venice** (3/day, 7.5 hrs, longer on night train), **Frankfurt** (4/day, 7.5 hrs), **Amsterdam** (1/day, 14.5 hrs).

Excursions by Car with Driver: Those wishing they had wheels may consider hiring Johann (see page 423) for Danube excursions from Vienna or en route to Salzburg (particularly economic for groups of 3–4).

To Eastern Europe: Vienna is the springboard for a quick trip to Prague and Budapest—three hours by train from Budapest (€40 one way, €50 round-trip if you stay 4 days or less; covered by any railpass that includes both Austria and Hungary) and four hours from Prague (€42 one way, €84 round-trip, €53 round-trip with Eurailpass). Americans and Canadians do not need visas to enter the Czech Republic or Hungary. Purchase tickets at most travel agencies. Eurail passholders bound for Prague must pay to ride the rails in the Czech Republic; for details, see page 410 of the Berlin chapter.

Route Tips for Drivers

Driving in and out of Vienna: Navigating in Vienna isn't bad. Study the map. As you approach from Krems, you'll cross the North Bridge and land on the Gürtel, or outer ring. You can continue along the Danube canal to the inner ring, called the Ringstrasse (clockwise traffic only). Circle around either thoroughfare until you reach the "spoke" street you need.

Vienna West to Munich, Salzburg, and Hall in Tirol: To leave Vienna, follow the signs past the Westbahnhof to Schloss Schönbrunn (Schönbrunn Palace), which is directly on the way to the West A-1 autobahn to Linz. Leave the palace by 15:00 and you should beat rush hour.

DANUBE VALLEY

From the Black Forest in Germany to the Black Sea in Romania, the Danube flows 1,770 miles through a dozen countries. Western Europe's longest river (the Rhine is only half as long), it's also the only major river flowing west to east, making it invaluable for commercial transportation.

The Danube is at its romantic best just west of Vienna. Mix a cruise with a bike ride through the Danube's Wachau Valley, lined with ruined castles, beautiful abbeys, small towns, and vineyard upon vineyard. After touring the glorious Melk Abbey, douse your warm, fairy-tale glow with a bucket of Hitler at the Mauthausen concentration camp.

Planning Your Time

For a day trip from Vienna, catch the early train to Melk, tour the Abbey, eat lunch, and take an afternoon trip along the river from Melk to Krems. Note that the boat goes much faster downstream (east, from Melk to Krems) than vice versa. From Krems, catch the train back to Vienna. Try a boat/bike combination or consider Austria Rail's convenient Kombi-ticket. This special package includes the train trip from Vienna to Melk, entry to the Melk Abbey, a boat cruise to Krems, and the return train trip to Vienna for a total of €39.50 (buy at any train station, or for more help and better English, get it at the DDSG office in Vienna: Mon–Fri 9:00–18:00, closed Sat–Sun, Friedrichstrasse 7, tel. 01/58880, www.ddsg-blue-danube.at). While this region is a logical day trip from Vienna, with good train connections to both Krems and Melk, spending a night in Melk is a convenient detour from the main Munich/Salzburg/Vienna train line

Danube Valley

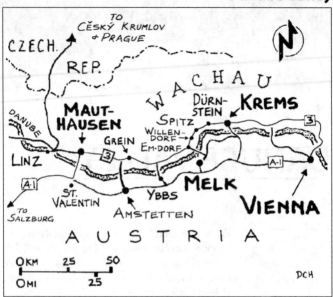

(from Salzburg to Vienna, transfer in Amstetten or Linz).

Mauthausen, farther away, should be seen en route to or from Vienna. On a three-week trip, I'd see only one concentration camp. Mauthausen is more powerful than the more-convenient Dachau, and worthwhile if you have a car.

Cruising the Danube's Wachau Valley

By car, bike, or boat, the 24-mile stretch of the Danube between Krems and Melk is as pretty as they come. You'll cruise the Danube's wine road, passing wine gardens all along the river. Those hanging out a wreath of straw or greenery are inviting you in to taste. In local slang, someone who's feeling his wine is "blue." (Blue Danube?) Note that in German, Danube is *Donau,* as you'll see by the signs.

By Boat: Two different companies run boats between Melk and Krems: **DDSG** (3/day in each direction May–Sept, 1/day April and Oct, tel. 01/58880, www.ddsg-blue-danube.at) and **Brandner** (2/day in each direction May–Sept, 1/day weekdays and 2/day weekends second half of April and Oct, tel. 07433/529-021, www.brandner.at). Both charge the same amount: €17 one-way, €22 round-trip ticket allowing stopovers (bikes ride free). In peak season (May–Sept), boats depart daily from Melk at 8:25, 11:00, 13:50 (2 different boats), and 16:15 (90-min ride downstream).

Boats depart from Krems at 10:10, 10:15, 13:00, 15:40, and 15:45 (because of the 6-knot flow of the Danube, the same ride upstream takes twice as long—3 hrs). The 16:15 departure from Melk and the 15:45 departure from Krems require an easy transfer in Spitz; the rest are direct. Confirm these times by calling the boat companies (see above), the Melk TI (see hours below), or the Krems TI (see listing on page 498). For a longer cruise, some boats start or end in Vienna.

By Bike: See the "Melk-to-Krems Danube Valley Bike Ride" described on page 497. Ask any local TI or your hotel for the latest on bike-rental options. Some hotels rent or loan bikes; in Melk, try Hotel zur Post (€7/half-day, €10/day, free for guests) or Gasthof Goldener Stern (€7/day for guests). Wachau Touristik Bernhardt has bike-rental depots at the Melk boat dock and by the train station at Spitz. For a €2 service fee, you can pick up your bike at one station and leave it at the other (€9/half-day, €12/day, June–Oct daily 10:00–16:30 at Melk, 9:00–16:30 at Spitz, returns until 18:00, best to call ahead, ID for deposit—they make a copy so you have the drop-off option, Melk tel. 0664/222-2070, Spitz tel. 02713/2222).

By Bus: The bus between Melk and Krems is a good budget or rainy-day alternative to the boat (€7, 60 min; Melk to Krems: Mon–Fri 3/day, Sat 2/day, none Sun; Krems to Melk: Mon–Fri 5/day, Sat 3/day, none Sun; catch bus at train station, buy ticket on bus; for best views, sit on the driver's side from Melk to Krems or the non-driver's side from Krems to Melk, bus info tel. 02752/5232-1350).

By Train: Hourly trains connect Vienna with Krems and with Melk. Trains to Melk depart from Vienna's Westbahnhof. Trains for Krems depart from Vienna's Franz Josefs Bahnhof. If you're starting or ending your visit to the Danube Valley with Krems, consider departing from or arriving at Vienna's Spittelau (the train's first stop after the Franz Josefs Bahnhof) instead of the Bahnhof itself, because Spittelau has a U-Bahn station and Franz Josefs Bahnhof does not.

While tiny, one-car, milk-run trains chug along from village to village up the river, they don't stop at Melk (which affects bicyclists; see "Melk-to-Krems Danube Valley Bike Ride" on page 497).

Melk

Sleepy and elegant under its huge abbey, which seems to police the Danube, the town of Melk offers a pleasant stop.

ORIENTATION

Tourist Information

The TI, run by helpful Manfred Baumgartner, is a block off the main square (look for green signs) and has info on nearby castles, the latest on bike rental, specifics on bike rides along the river, a free town map with a self-guided walking tour, and a list of Melk hotels and *Zimmer* (May–Sept Mon–Fri 9:00–12:00 & 14:00–18:00, Sat–Sun 10:00–12:00 & 16:00–18:00, off-season closed Sat afternoon and Sun, good picnic garden with WC behind TI, Babenbergerstrasse 1, tel. 02752/5230-7410). For accommodations, see "Sleeping," page 499.

Arrival in Melk

Walk straight out of the station (lockers-€2–3.50) for several blocks; at the curve, keep straight and go down the stairs, following the cobbled alley that dumps you into the center of the village. Access to Melk Abbey is up on your right, and the TI is a block off the end of the square to your right (follow signs to *Zum Stift* or *Fussweg Stift Melk*). If you arrive by boat, turn right as you leave the boat dock and follow the canalside bike path toward the big yellow abbey (the village is beneath its far side). In about five minutes, you'll come to a flashing light (at intersection with bridge); turn left and you're steps from downtown.

To reach the boat dock from Melk, leave the town toward the river, with the abbey on your right. Turn right when you get to the busy road and follow the canal (at the fork, it's quicker to jog left onto the bike path than to follow the main road). Follow signs for *Linienschifffahrt-Scheduled Trips-Wachau*.

SIGHTS AND ACTIVITIES

▲▲**Melk Abbey (Benediktiner-stift)**—Melk's newly restored abbey, beaming proudly over the Danube Valley, is one of Europe's great sights. Established as a fortified Benedictine abbey in the 11th century, it was destroyed by fire. What you see today is 18th-century Baroque. Architect Jakob Prandtauer made the building one with nature.

Melk

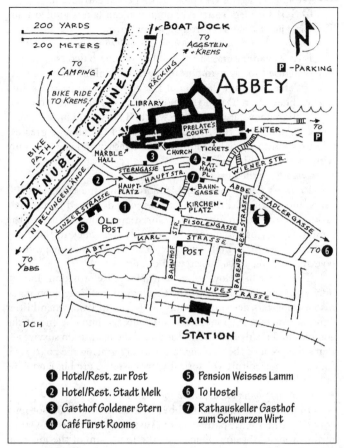

1 Hotel/Rest. zur Post
2 Hotel/Rest. Stadt Melk
3 Gasthof Goldener Stern
4 Café Fürst Rooms
5 Pension Weisses Lamm
6 To Hostel
7 Rathauskeller Gasthof zum Schwarzen Wirt

The abbey church, with its 200-foot-tall dome and symmetrical towers, dominates the complex—emphasizing its sacred purpose.

Freshly painted and gilded throughout, it's a Baroque dream, a lily alone. The grand restoration project—financed in part by the sale of the abbey's Gutenberg Bible to Harvard—was completed by 1996 to celebrate the 1,000th anniversary of the first reference to a country named Österreich (Austria).

Cost, Hours, Information: €7, includes entrance to Abbey Park, daily May–Sept 9:00–18:00, April and Oct 9:00–17:00, last entry one hour before closing; Nov–March the abbey is open only for tours in German with a little English at 11:00 and 14:00; tel. 02752/555-232, www.stiftmelk.at.

Tours: English tours of the abbey are offered daily (April–Oct at 14:55, €8.80 includes tour and admission, a private guide can be reserved in advance for €40 plus €7 per-person entrance fee).

⮕ **Self-Guided Tour:** Although you can take a guided tour, it's easiest just to wander through on your own.

• *Go through the first passageway and approach the grand entry to the...*

East Facade: Imagine the abbot on the balcony greeting you as he used to greet important guests. Flanking him are statues of Peter and Paul (leaders of the apostles and patron saints of the abbey church) and the monastery's coat of arms (crossed keys). High above are the Latin words "Glory only in the cross" and a huge copy of the Melk Cross (one of the abbey's greatest treasures—the original is hiding in the treasury and viewable only with special permission).

• *Pass into the main courtyard.*

Prelate's Courtyard: This is more than a museum. For 900 years, monks of St. Benedict have lived and worked here. Their task: bringing and maintaining Christianity and culture to the region. (Many of the monks live outside the abbey in the community.) They run a high school with about 800 students, a small boarding school, and a busy retreat center.

There have been low points. During the Reformation (1500s), only eight monks held down the theological fort. Napoleon made his headquarters here in 1805 and 1809. And in 1938, when Hitler annexed Austria, the monastery was squeezed into one end of the complex and nearly dissolved. But today, the institution survives—that's the point of the four modern frescoes gracing the courtyard, funded by agriculture (historically, monasteries are big landowners) and your visit.

• *In the far left-hand corner, climb the stairs to...*

Imperial Corridor and Abbey Museum: This 640-foot-long corridor, lined with paintings of Austrian royalty, is the spine of the Abbey Museum. Duck into the first room of the museum (on the left, near beginning of hall). Art treasures and a recently updated exhibit (with creepy sound and light effects) fill several rooms.

• *Continue through the museum—running parallel to the corridor—and go through the room at the end with the big rotating model of the abbey.*

Marble Hall: While the door frames are real marble, most of this large dining room/ballroom is stucco. The treasure here is the ceiling fresco (by Tirolean Paul Troger, 1731). Notice three themes: 1) The Hapsburgs liked to be portrayed as Hercules; 2) Athena, the goddess of wisdom, is included, because the Hapsburgs were smart as well as strong; and 3) The Hapsburgs were into art and culture. This is symbolized by angels figuratively reining in the forces of evil, darkness, and brutality so—through this wise moderation—goodness, beauty, art, and science can rule.

Balcony: Here, we enjoy dramatic views of the Danube Valley, the town of Melk, and the facade of the monastery church. The huge statue above everything shows the risen Christ, cross in hand and victorious over death—the central message of the entire place.

Library: The inlaid bookshelves, matching bindings, and another fine Troger fresco combine harmoniously to provide for the Marble Hall's thematic counterpart. This room celebrates not wise politics, but faith. The ceiling shows a woman surrounded by the four cardinal virtues (wisdom, justice, fortitude, and recycling)—natural traits that lead to a supernatural faith. The statues flanking the doors represent the four traditional university faculties (law, medicine, philosophy, and theology). The globes show a 17th-century view of the earth and heavens. Many of the monastery's 100,000 volumes fill the shelves (some of the oldest and most precious are in the glass display case).

Church: The finale is the church, with its architecture, ceiling frescoes, stucco marble, grand pipe organ, and sumptuous chapels combining in full Baroque style to make the theological point: A just battle leads to victory. The ceiling shows St. Benedict's triumphant entry into Heaven (on a fancy carpet). In the front, above the huge papal crown, saints Peter and Paul shake hands before departing for their final battles and ultimate victory. And, high above, the painting in the dome shows that victory: the Holy Trinity, surrounded

by saints of particular importance to Melk, happily in heaven.

Other Abbey Sights—Near the entrance (and exit) to the abbey, you'll find the Abbey Park (included in abbey ticket, or €3 for just the park, May–Oct daily 9:00–18:00, closed Nov–April)—home to a picturesque Baroque pavilion housing some fine Bergl frescoes and a café. Nearby, in the former orangery, is the abbey's expensive restaurant.

Danube Valley

▲▲Melk-to-Krems Danube Valley Bike Ride—The three-hour pedal from Melk to Krems takes you through the Wachau Valley—steeped in tradition, blanketed with vineyards, and ornamented with cute villages. Bicyclists rule here, and you'll find all the amenities that make this valley so popular with Austrians on two wheels. For bike-rental info in Melk, see page 493.

Bike routes are clearly marked with green *Donau-Radwanderweg* signs. The local TIs give out a free *Donau Radweg* brochure with a helpful if basic route map. As you study it, note the north bank has the best and most popular trail; it's paved all the way, winds through picturesque villages, and runs near, though not on, the river. But consider the south bank, which has less car traffic; although the bike trail merges with the actual road about half the time, it comes with better river views. (Note: The bike-in-a-red-border signs mean "no biking.")

Pedal downstream toward Krems to enjoy a gradual slope in your favor. While catching the boat back makes for a much longer day (it's slow upstream), cute one-car milk-run trains rattle up the valley stopping at most towns along the way (about hourly, 60 min from Krems to Emmersdorf opposite Melk, bike rack at rear of train—carry bike up the stairs to reach rack). If you prefer, you can go half-and-half by cruising to Spitz—a good midway point—and then hopping on a bike (or vice versa). Spitz has a boat station and train station (the bike path between Spitz and Krems is more interesting than between Melk and Spitz). Little ferries shuttle bikers and vacation-goers regularly across the river at three points.

A good day-plan from Melk (though your times may vary depending on when you rent the bike): Depart Melk at 8:00, bike the valley, lunch in Krems or picnic on train, and catch the 13:00 train from Krems back to Emmersdorf (across the river, 3 miles from Melk). If you run out of steam or time, you can catch a train at most towns en route.

Krems—This is a gem of a town. From the boat dock, walk a few blocks north and east to the TI and pick up a town map. Then stroll the traffic-free, shopper's-wonderland old town. If nothing else, it's a pleasant 20-minute walk from the dock to the train station (Krems–Vienna trains hrly, 60 min). The local **TI** can find you a bed in a private home (D-€40, Db-€50) if you decide to side-trip into Vienna from this small-town alternative (TI open Mon–Fri 8:30–18:00, Sat 10:00–12:00 & 13:00–17:00, Sun 10:00–12:00 & 13:00–16:00, Undstrasse 6, tel. 02732/82676).

Sleeping in Krems: **$$ Melanie Stasny's Gästezimmer** is a super place to stay (€23 per person in Db, Tb, or Qb, friendly with a proud vineyard and wine cellar, 300 yards from dock at Steiner Landstrasse 22, tel. 02732/82843, fax 02732/83141); when they're booked, they send travelers to their son's place down the street.

Dürnstein—This touristic flypaper lures hordes of visitors with its traffic-free quaintness and its one claim to fame (and fortune): Richard the Lionhearted was imprisoned here in 1193. You can probably sleep in his bedroom. The ruined castle above can be reached by a good hike with great river views.

Willendorf—This is known among art buffs as the town where the oldest piece of European art was found. There's a tiny museum in the village center (free, limited hours). A block farther uphill (follow the signs to Venus, just under tracks follow stairs to right) you can see the monument where the well-endowed, 30,000-year-old fertility symbol, the *Venus of Willendorf,* was discovered. (The fist-sized original is now in Vienna's Natural History Museum—see page 459.)

SLEEPING

Melk makes a fine overnight stop. Except during August, you shouldn't have any trouble finding a good room at a reasonable rate. The TI has a long list of people renting rooms for about €20 per person. Most of these are a few miles from the center.

$$$ Hotel zur Post is Melk's most modern-feeling hotel—professional and well-run by the Ebner family, with 28 comfy and tidy rooms over a good restaurant (Sb-€55–60, Db-€88–98 depending on size, Tb-€121–126, 8 percent discount with cash and this book, closed Jan–mid-Feb, elevator, Linzer Strasse 1, tel. 02752/52345, fax 02752/234-550, www.hotelpost-melk.at, info@hotelpost-melk.at). Hotel zur Post has free bikes for guests and rents them to others (€7/half-day, €10/day).

$$$ Hotel Stadt Melk, a block below the main square, has pink halls and drab, outmoded rooms. The moderately priced choices (below) offer better rooms for lower prices, but this will do in a pinch (Sb-€50–60, Db-€85, Hauptplatz 1, tel. 02752/52475, fax 02752/524-7519, www.hotelstadtmelk.com, hotel.stadtmelk@netway.at).

$$ Gasthof Goldener Stern's 11 rooms have recently been redone, with barn-flavored elegance and flowers on every pillow. The pricier canopy-bed rooms are very romantic. This lively place buzzes with locals eating in the atmospheric old restaurant—and

---

Sleep Code

(€1 = about $1.20, country code: 43, area code: 02752)
S = Single, **D** = Double/Twin, **T** = Triple, **Q** = Quad, **b** = bathroom, **s** = shower only. Breakfast is included, credit cards are accepted unless otherwise noted, and everyone speaks at least some English.

To help you sort easily through these listings, I've divided the rooms into three categories, based on the price for a standard double room with bath:

$$$ **Higher Priced**—Most rooms €75 or more.
$$ **Moderately Priced**—Most rooms between €40–75.
$ **Lower Priced**—Most rooms €40 or less.

with Regina and Kurt Schmidt's five children. It's on the small alley that veers off the main square above the twin turrets (D-€42–50, Db-€58–70, Db suite-€100, prices depend on room size, rooms for up to 5 also available, cash only, €7/day bike rental for guests, Sterngasse 17, tel. 02752/52214, fax 02752/522-144, www .sternmelk.at, goldenerstern.melk@aon.at).

$$ Café Fürst rents 10 clean, recently renovated rooms over its creaky restaurant. Run by the Madar family, it's right on the traffic-free main square, with a fountain outside the door and the Melk Abbey hovering overhead (Sb-€40, small Db-€58–60, big Db-€74, Tb-€75, cash only, Rathausplatz 3-5, tel. 02752/52343, fax 02752/523-434, cafe.madar@netway.at).

$ Pension Weisses Lamm has the cheapest beds in the center—and absentee management. All but two of the seven of its worn-but-clean rooms have bathrooms (Sb-€25, Db-€40, Tb-€60, cash only, Linzer Strasse 7, tel. 0664/231-5297, fax 02752/51224).

$ Hostel: The modern, institutional **youth hostel** is a 10-minute walk from the station; turn right at the post office (25 quad rooms, beds-€16.20, plus one-time €2 hotel tax, non-members-€3 extra, includes sheets and breakfast, closed 12:00–16:00 and Nov–March, Abt-Karl-Strasse 42, tel. 02752/52681, fax 02752/54257, melk@noejhw.at).

EATING

The recommended hotels **Gasthof Goldener Stern** and **Café Fürst** also have restaurants with fine, inexpensive local cuisine (both open daily).

Hotel Restaurant zur Post, classier and pricier, is worth the few extra euros (good local dishes, courtyard and fine streetside seating with an abbey view, daily 11:30–21:30, closed Jan–mid-Feb, Linzer Strasse 1, tel. 02752/52345). Downstairs is a fun and atmospheric wine cellar, with both local and international wines.

Melk's most elegant meals are served at **Hotel Restaurant Stadt Melk** (delicate nouvelle cuisine–type *menus*-€55–75 for standard or 8-course blowout, €20 entrées, terrace seating, reservations smart, daily 18:30–22:00, Hauptplatz 1, tel. 02752/52475).

Locals swear by the food at **Rathauskeller Gasthof zum Schwarzen Wirt,** with good Austrian and West African dishes. It's run by the Ghanese-Austrian Addo family (€8 for most meals, Mon–Sat 8:00–24:00, Sun 9:00–22:00, lunch specials, West African food only in the evening, Rathausplatz 13, tel. 02752/52257).

TRANSPORTATION CONNECTIONS

Melk is on the autobahn and just off the Salzburg–Vienna train line.

From Melk by Train to: Vienna's Westbahnhof (hrly, 1–2 hrs, some with transfer in St. Pölten), **Salzburg** (hrly, 2 hrs, transfer in Amstetten or Linz), **Mauthausen** (nearly hrly, 75 min, transfer at St. Valentin).

Mauthausen Concentration Camp

More powerful and less tourist-oriented than Dachau, this slave-labor and death camp functioned from 1938 to 1945 for the exploitation and extermination of Hitler's opponents. More than half of its

206,000 quarry-working prisoners died here, mostly from starvation or exhaustion. Mauthausen has a strangely serene setting, located next to the Danube above an overgrown quarry (€2, daily 9:00–17:30, last entry 1 hour before closing time, closed mid-Dec–Jan, some exhibits are at new visitors center—but tickets for the camp must be purchased inside camp at ticket booth, for directions to camp, see "Transportation Connections," page 502, tel. 07238/2269, TI tel. 07238/3860). You can borrow a free, tape-recorded 24-minute tour by leaving your ID. The excellent €3 English guidebook covers the site very well (bookshop just inside the visitors center entrance, closed 12:30–13:00). A graphic 45-minute movie is shown at the top of each hour between 9:00 and 16:00. There are several film rooms. Check in at the visitors center to request an English showing. Allow two hours to tour the camp completely. The camp barracks house a worthwhile museum at the far end of the camp on the right (no English).

The most emotionally moving rooms and the gas chamber are downstairs. The spirits of the victims of these horrors can still be felt. Back outside the camp, each victim's country has

erected a gripping memorial. Many yellowed photos have fresh flowers. Find the barbed-wire memorial overlooking the quarry and the "stairway of death" *(Todesstiege)* and walk at least halfway down (very uneven path). Return to the parking lot via the upper wall for a good perspective over the camp.

By visiting a concentration camp and putting ourselves through this emotional wringer, we heed and respect the fervent wish of the victims of this fascism—that we "never forget." Many people forget by choosing not to know.

SLEEPING AND EATING

Near Mauthausen

Just off the autobahn, less than four miles southwest of Mauthausen and 62 miles west of Vienna, Enns calls itself Austria's oldest town. **$$ Hotel zum Goldenen Schiff,** facing Enns' delightful main square, is a decent value, with 20 comfy rooms and a quaint location (Sb-€45, Db-€65, cash only, family rooms, free parking, Hauptplatz 23, tel. 07223/86086, fax 07223/860-8615, www .tiscover.at/hotel.brunner, wolfgang.brunner@liwest.at).

Moststub 'n Frellerhof, a farmhouse 50 yards below the Mauthausen parking lot, offers (weekends only) a refreshing, peaceful break after your visit. They serve *Most* (grape juice ready to become wine), homemade schnapps, and light, farm-fresh meals (May–Sept Sat–Sun from 13:00, closed Oct–April, playground, tel. 07238/2789).

TRANSPORTATION CONNECTIONS

Most trains stop at St. Valentin, midway between Salzburg and Vienna, where sporadic trains make the 15-minute ride to the Mauthausen station (get map from station attendant, camp is #9 on map, luggage check-€2.25).

Getting to Mauthausen Camp from Mauthausen Station: To cover the three miles between the camp and station, you can **hike** (1 hr, follow signs to *Ehemaliges KZ-Gedenkstätte Lager*) or **taxi** (minibus taxis available, about €10 one-way, ask taxi to pick you up in 2 hrs, share the cost with other tourists, tel. 07238/2439). Train info: tel. 07238/2207 or 051-717 (to get an operator, dial 2 then 1).

From Vienna by Train to Mauthausen: You can reach Mauthausen direct from Vienna's Franz Josefs Bahnhof or faster from the Westbahnhof with a transfer in St. Valentin.

From St. Valentin by Train to: Salzburg (hrly, 2 hrs), **Vienna** (hrly, 2 hrs).

Route Tips for Drivers

Hallstatt to Vienna, via Mauthausen, Melk, and Wachau Valley (210 miles): Leave Hallstatt early. Follow the scenic Route 145 through Gmunden to the autobahn and head east. After Linz, take exit #155, Enns, and follow the signs for Mauthausen (5 miles from freeway). Go through Mauthausen town and follow the *Ehemaliges KZ-Gedenkstätte Lager* signs. From Mauthausen, it's a speedy 60 minutes to Melk via the autobahn, but the curvy and scenic Route 3 along the river is worth the nausea. At Melk, signs to *Stift Melk* lead to the Benediktinerstift (Benedictine Abbey). Other Melk signs lead into the town.

The most scenic stretch of the Danube is the Wachau Valley between Melk and Krems. From Melk (get a Vienna map at the TI), cross the river again (signs to Donaubrücke) and stay on Route 3. After Krems, it hits the autobahn (A-22), and you'll barrel right into Vienna's traffic. (See "Route Tips for Drivers" in the Vienna chapter for details, page 490.)

SALZBURG

Salzburg is forever smiling to the tunes of Mozart and *The Sound of Music*. Thanks to its charmingly preserved old town, splendid gardens, Baroque churches, and Europe's largest intact medieval fortress, Salzburg feels made for tourism. It's a museum city with class. Vagabonds wish they had nicer clothes.

But even without Mozart and the von Trapps, Salzburg is steeped in history. In about A.D. 700, Bavaria gave Salzburg to Bishop Rupert for his promise to Christianize the area. Salzburg remained an independent state until Napoleon came (around 1800). Thanks in part to its formidable fortress, Salzburg managed to avoid the ravages of war for 1,200 years...until World War II. Much of the city was destroyed by WWII bombs (mostly around the train station), but the historic old town survived.

Eight million tourists crawl its cobbles each year. That's a lot of Mozart balls—and all that popularity has led to a glut of businesses hoping to catch the tourist dollar. Still, Salzburg is both a must and a joy.

This year marks the 250th birthday of Salzburg's beloved and most marketable son, Mozart. Be prepared for crowds, inflated hotel prices, and Mozart Mania starting as early as January. Ambitious concert schedules include performances of his complete operatic works; be sure to book in advance (check www.mozart2006.net for events).

Planning Your Time

While Vienna measures much higher on the Richter scale of sightseeing thrills, Salzburg is simply a touristy, stroller's delight. If you're going into the nearby Salzkammergut lake country (see next chapter), skip the *Sound of Music* tour—if not, allow half a day for it. The *S.O.M.* tour kills a nest of sightseeing birds with one ticket (city overview, *S.O.M.* sights, and a fine drive through the lakes). You'll probably need two nights for Salzburg—nights are important for swilling beer in atmospheric local gardens and attending concerts in Baroque halls and chapels. Seriously consider one of Salzburg's many evening musical events (a few are free, some are as low as €12, and most average €30–40). While the sights are mediocre, the town is an enjoyable Baroque museum of cobbled streets and elegant buildings. And to get away from it all, bike down the river or hike across the Mönchsberg.

The town of Hallstatt provides the best glimpse at the nearby Salzkammergut lake district (see next chapter). A day trip from Salzburg to Hallstatt is doable, but involves about five hours of travel time and makes for a very long day (skip it in winter, when Hallstatt is pretty dead).

ORIENTATION

(area code: 0662)
Salzburg, a city of 150,000 (Austria's 4th largest), is divided into old and new. The old town, sitting between the Salzach River and the 1,600-foot-high hill called Mönchsberg, holds nearly all the charm and most of the tourists.

Tourist Information
Salzburg has three helpful TIs (main tel. 0662/8898-70, www .salzburg.info). There's one at the **train station** (daily May–June

and Sept 8:30–20:00, July–Aug until 21:00, Oct–April until 19:30, tel. 0662/8898-7340). Another is on **Mozartplatz** in the old center (daily 9:00–18:00, July–Aug until 19:00, sometimes closed Sun in winter, tel. 0662/8898-7330). And another is at the **Salzburg Süd park-and-ride** (generally open Mon–Sat 10:00–18:00, opens at 9:00 July–Aug, closed Mon–Tue in May, closed Mon in June, and always closed Sun, Nov, and Jan–March, tel. 0662/8898-7360).

At any TI, you can pick up a free city-center map (the €0.70 map has a broader coverage and more information on sights, but probably isn't necessary), the *Salzburg Card* brochure (listing sights with current hours and prices), and a bimonthly schedule of events. Book a concert upon arrival. The TIs also book rooms for a fee.

Salzburg Card: The TI sells the Salzburg Card, which covers all your public transportation (including elevator and funicular) and admission to all the city sights (including Hellbrunn Castle). The card is pricey (€22/24 hrs, €29/48 hrs, €34/72 hrs, €3 less Oct–May), but if you'd like to pop into all the sights without concern for the cost, this can save money and enhance your experience. Get this, feel the financial pain once, and the city's all yours.

Arrival in Salzburg

By Train: The little Salzburg station is user-friendly. The TI is at track 2A. Downstairs at street level, you'll find a place to store your luggage, buy tickets, and get train information. Bike rental is nearby (see "Getting Around Salzburg," below). The bus station is across the street (where buses #1, #5, #6, #25, and #51 go to the old center; get off at the first stop after you cross the river for most sights and city center hotels, or just before the bridge for Linzergasse hotels). Figure €7 for a taxi to the center. To walk downtown (15 min), leave the station ticket hall to the left, and walk straight down Rainerstrasse, which leads under the tracks past Mirabellplatz, turning into Dreialtigkeitsgasse. From here, you can turn left onto Linzergasse for many of the recommended hotels, or cross the Staatsbrücke bridge for the old town (and more hotels). For a more dramatic approach, leave the station the same way but follow the tracks to the river, turn left, and walk the riverside path toward the fortress.

By Car: Follow *Zentrum* signs to the center, and park short-term on the street or longer under Mirabellplatz. Ask at your hotel for suggestions. (For more details, see "Transportation Connections," page 540.)

Helpful Hints

Internet Access: Readers of this book can get online free at the Panorama Tours terminal on Mirabellplatz through 2006.

Post Office: A full-service post office is located in the heart of town in the New Residenz (Mon–Fri 7:00–18:30, Sat 8:00–10:00, closed Sun).

Laundry: The launderette at the corner of Paris-Lodron Strasse and Wolf-Dietrich Strasse, near my recommended Linzergasse hotels, is handy (€10 self-service, €15 same-day full-service, Mon–Fri 7:30–18:00, Sat 8:00–12:00, closed Sun, tel. 0662/876-381).

American Express: AmEx has travel-agency services, but doesn't sell train tickets (Mon–Fri 9:00–17:30, closed Sat–Sun, Mozartplatz 5, tel. 0662/843-8400).

Getting Around Salzburg

By Bus: Single-ride tickets for central Salzburg *(Einzelkarte-Kernzone)* are sold on the bus for €1.80. At machines and *Tabak/Trafik* shops, you can buy cheaper single-ride tickets or a €3.40 day pass *(Tageskarte,* good for 24 hours, €4.20 if you buy it on the bus). To signal the driver you want to get off, press the buzzer on the pole. Bus info: tel. 0662/4480-6262.

By Bike: Salzburg is fun for cyclists. The following two bike-rental shops offer 20 percent off with a valid train ticket or Eurailpass; ask for it. **Top Bike** rents bikes from two outlets—at the river side of the train station (leave left and walk 50 yards); and on the river next to Staatsbrücke bridge (€6/2 hrs, €10/4 hrs, €15/24 hrs, usually daily April–June and Sept–Oct 10:00–17:00, July–Aug 9:00–19:00, closed Nov–March, tel. 06272/4656, mobile 0676-476-7259, www.topbike.at, Sabine). **Velo-Active** rents bikes on Residenz Platz, across from the American Express office in the old town (€4/hr, €12/24 hrs; mountain bikes-€6/hr, €18/24 hrs; daily 9:00–18:00 but hours unreliable—often you'll have to call or let the Panorama Tours man nearby help you, shorter hours off-season and in bad weather, passport number for security deposit, tel. 0662/435-595, mobile 0676-435-5950).

By Funicular and Elevator: The old town is connected to the top of the Mönchsberg mountain (and great views) via funicular and elevator (Web site for both: www.stadtbus.at). The **funicular** *(FestungsBahn)* whisks you up to the imposing Hohensalzburg Fortress (for prices, see page 520). The **elevator** *(MönchsbergAufzug)* on the east side of the old town propels you to the recommended Gasthaus Stadtalm café (see page 533 of "Sleeping," and page 538 of "Eating"), the Museum of Modern Art (see page 522), and wooded paths (€1.80 one-way, €2.90 round-trip, daily Sept–June 8:00–17:00, July–Aug 8:00–24:00).

By Taxi: Meters start around €3 (from train station to your hotel, allow about €8). As always, small groups can taxi for about the same price as riding the bus.

By Boat: Salzburg's **Salzach River Cruises** runs a basic 40-min round-trip cruise with recorded commentary (€12, April–Sept 8/day). For a longer cruise, ride to Hellbrunn and return by bus (€15, April–Sept 1–2/day). Boats leave from the old-town side of the river just downstream of the Staatsbrücke bridge (tel. 0662/8257-6912).

By Buggy: The horse buggies *(Fiaker)* that congregate at the Residenz Platz charge €35 for a 25-minute trot around the old town (www.fiaker-salzburg.at).

TOURS

Walking Tours—The tourist office offers two-language, one-hour guided walks of the old town. They are informative, but you'll be listening to a half hour of German (€8, daily at 12:15, start at TI on Mozartplatz, tel. 0662/8898-7330—just show up and pay the guide). To save that money (and avoid all that German), you can easily do it on your own using my "Welcome to Salzburg's Old Town" walk (see page 510).

Local Guides—**Christiana Schneeweiss** (literally, "Snow White"), a hardworking young guide with a passion for fitting local history into the big picture, gives spirited private tours (€75/1 hr, €129/2 hrs, €150/3 hrs, tel. 0664/340-1757, www.kultur -tourismus.com, info@kultur-tourismus.com). **Bärbel Schalber**, one of Salzburg's senior guides, offers a two-hour walk packed with information and spicy opinions for €75 (tel. 0662/632-225, baxguide@utanet.at). Salzburg has many other good guides (to book, call tel. 0662/840-406).

▲▲Sound of Music Tour—I took this tour skeptically (as part of my research chores) and liked it. It includes a quick but good general city tour, hits the *S.O.M.* spots (including the stately home, flirtatious gazebo, and grand wedding church), and shows you a lovely stretch of the Salzkammergut lake district. This is worthwhile for *S.O.M.* fans and those who won't otherwise be going into the Salzkammergut. Warning: Many think rolling through the Austrian countryside with 30 Americans singing "Doe, a Deer" is pretty schmaltzy. Local Austrians don't understand all the commotion. For more on *S.O.M.*, see "*Sound of Music* Debunked" sidebar on page 526.

Of the many companies doing the tour, consider Bob's Special Tours (usually uses a more intimate mini-bus) and the Panorama tours (more typical, professional big bus). Each one provides essentially the same tour (in English with a live and lively guide, 4 hours, free hotel pick-up) for the same price. The *S.O.M.* tour for each company costs €35, but you'll get a €5 discount from either if you book direct, mention Rick Steves, and pay cash. Getting a spot is simple—just call and make a reservation. Note: Your hotel will be eager to call to reserve for you—to get their commission—but if you let them do it, you will not get the discount I've negotiated.

Minibus Option: Ninety percent of **Bob's Special Tours** use an eight-seat mini-bus and therefore have better access for old-town sights, promote a more casual feel, and spend less time waiting and picking up (buses leave from Bob's office along the river just east of Mozartplatz at Rudolfskai 38, daily at 9:00 and 14:00 year-round, tel. 0662/849-511, mobile 0664-541-7492, www.bobstours.com).

Salzburg

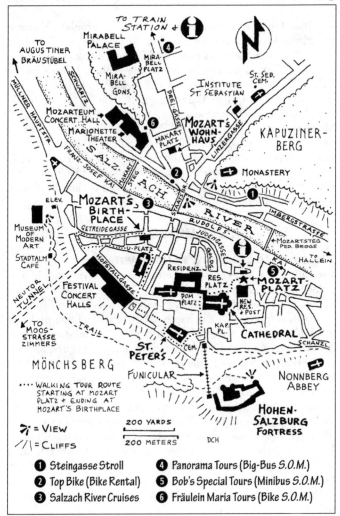

① Steingasse Stroll
② Top Bike (Bike Rental)
③ Salzach River Cruises
④ Panorama Tours (Big-Bus S.O.M.)
⑤ Bob's Special Tours (Minibus S.O.M.)
⑥ Fräulein Maria Tours (Bike S.O.M.)

Nearly all of Bob's tours stop for the luge ride when the weather is dry (mountain bobsled–€4 extra, confirm beforehand). Some travelers looking for Bob's tours at Mozartplatz have been hijacked by other companies...have Bob's pick you up at your hotel or meet the bus at their office.

Big-Bus Option: Salzburg Panorama Tours depart from their smart new kiosk at Mirabellplatz daily at 9:30 and 14:00 year-round (book by calling 0662/874-029 or online at www .panoramatours.com). Many travelers appreciate their more business-like feel, roomier buses, and slightly higher vantage point.

Bike Option: Alternatively, you can meet **Fräulein Maria** at the Mirabellgarten (behind the Hotel Bristol) for a *S.O.M.* bike tour. Main attractions include the Mirabell Gardens, the horse pond, St. Peter's Cemetery, Nonnberg Abbey, Leopoldskron Palace and, of course, the gazebo (€22 includes bike, daily at 9:30, allow 3 hours, mid May–Aug only, family-friendly, tel. 0650/342-6297, www.mariasbicycletours.com).

More Tours—Both Bob's and Panorama Tours also offer an extensive array of other day trips from Salzburg (Berchtesgaden Eagle's Nest, salt mines, and Salzkammergut lakes and mountains are the most popular, with the same discount—€5 off with this book, book direct and pay cash), all explained in their brochures, which litter hotel lobbies all over town.

SELF-GUIDED WALKS

Welcome to Salzburg's Old Town

I've linked the best sights in the old town into this handy self-guided orientation walk, rated ▲▲▲.

• *Begin in the heart of town, just up from the river, near the TI on...*

Mozartplatz: All the happy tourists around you probably wouldn't be here if not for the man honored by the statue here—Mozart (erected in 1842). Mozart spent much of his first 25 years (1756–1777) in Salzburg, the greatest Baroque city north of the Alps. But the city's much older. The Mozart statue actually sits on bits of Roman Salzburg. And the pink church of St. Michael overlooking the square is from A.D. 800. The first Salzburgers settled right around here. Near you are the American Express office and the tourist information office (with a concert box office). Just around the downhill corner is a pedestrian bridge leading over the Salzach River to the quiet, most medieval street in town, Steingasse (see page 519).

• *Walk toward the cathedral and into the big square with the huge fountain.*

Residenz Platz: Important buildings ringed this square when it was the ancient Roman forum...and they still do. Salzburg's energetic Prince-Archbishop Wolf Dietrich (who ruled from 1587–1612) was raised in Rome, counted the Medicis as his buddies, and had grandiose Italian ambitions for Salzburg. After a convenient fire destroyed the cathedral, he set about building "the Rome of the North." This square, with his new cathedral and palace, was the centerpiece of his Baroque dream city. A series of interconnecting squares—like you'll see nowhere else—lead from here through the old town.

For centuries, Salzburg's leaders were both important church officials *and* princes of the Holy Roman Empire, hence the title "prince-archbishop"—mixing sacred and secular authority. But Wolf Dietrich misplayed his hand, losing power and spending his last five years imprisoned in the Salzburg castle.

The fountain is as Italian as can be, with a Triton matching Bernini's famous Triton Fountain in Rome. Lying on a busy trade route to the south, Salzburg was well aware of the exciting things going on in Italy. Things Italian were respected (as in colonial America, when a bumpkin would "stick a feather in his cap and call it macaroni"). Local artists even Italianized their names in order to raise their rates.

Residenz: Dietrich's skippable palace is connected to the cathedral by a skyway. A series of ornately decorated rooms and an art gallery are open to visitors with time to kill (€8 includes both palace and gallery with audioguide for staterooms, daily 10:00–17:00, gallery closed Mon except July–Aug, tel. 0662/8042-2690).

Opposite the old Residenz is the new Residenz, which has long been a government administration building. Today it houses the central post office and the Heimatwerk, a fine shop showing off all the best local handicrafts (Mon–Fri 9:00–18:00, Sat 9:00–13:00, closed Sun). In 2006, Salzburg's grand history and art museum will open in this building, featuring a *Viva Mozart* exhibit about the famed composer. The show will cover his life, his work, his genius, and his relationship with women (€7, daily 9:00–18:00, Thu until 20:00, tel. 0662/6208-08123).

• *Atop the new Residenz rings the famous...*

Glockenspiel: This bell tower has a carillon of 35 17th-century bells (cast in Antwerp) that chimes throughout the day and plays tunes (appropriate to the month) at 7:00, 11:00, and 18:00. There was a time when Salzburg could afford to take tourists to the top of the tower to actually see the big barrel with adjustable tabs turn (like a giant music-box mechanism)...pulling the right bells in the right rhythm. Notice the ornamental top: an upside-down heart in flames surrounding the solar system (symbolizing that God loves all of creation).

Look back, past Mozart's statue, to the 4,220-foot-high Gaisberg—the forested hill with the television tower. A road leads to the top for a commanding view. Its summit is a favorite destination for local nature-lovers and kids learning to ski.

• *Walk under the prince-archbishop's skyway and step into Cathedral Square (Domplatz), where you'll find the...*

Salzburg Cathedral: This ▲▲ sight was one of the first Baroque buildings north of the Alps. It was finished in 1628, during the Thirty Years' War. (Pitting Roman Catholics against Protestants, this war devastated much of Europe and brought

Salzburg at a Glance

▲▲**Salzburg Cathedral** Glorious, harmonious, Baroque main church of Salzburg. **Hours:** May–Oct Mon–Sat 9:00–18:30, Sun 13:00–18:30, Nov–April Mon–Sat 10:00–17:00, Sun 13:00–17:00.

▲▲**Getreidegasse** Picturesque old shopping lane with characteristic wrought-iron signs. **Hours:** Always open.

▲▲**Mozart's Wohnhaus** Restored house where the composer lived, with the best Mozart exhibit in town. **Hours:** Daily 9:00–18:00, July–Aug until 19:00.

▲▲*Sound of Music* **Tour** Cheesy but fun tour through the *S.O.M.* sights of Salzburg and the surrounding Salzkammergut lake district, by minibus or big bus. **Hours:** Various options daily at 9:00, 9:30, and 14:00.

▲**Mozart's Birthplace** House where Mozart was born in 1756, featuring his instruments and other exhibits. **Hours:** Daily July–Aug 9:00–19:00, Sept–June 9:00–18:00.

▲**Mirabell Gardens and Palace** Beautiful palace complex with fine views, Salzburg's best concert venue, and *Sound of Music* memories. **Hours:** Gardens—always open; concerts—free in the park May–Aug Sun at 10:30 and Wed at 20:30, in the palace nearly nightly at 19:30, 20:00, or 20:30.

▲**Steingasse** Historic cobbled lane with trendy pubs, a tranquil,

most grand construction projects to a halt.) Experts differ on what motivated the builders: to emphasize Salzburg's commitment to the Roman Catholic cause and the power of the Church here, or to show that there could be a peaceful alternative to the religious strife that was racking Europe at the time. Salzburg's archbishop was technically the top papal official north of the Alps, but the city managed to stay out of the war. With its rich salt production, it had enough money to rise above the battling parties and didn't need papal money.

The dates on the iron gates refer to milestones in the church's history: In 774, the previous church (long since destroyed) was founded by St. Virgil, to be replaced in 1628 by the church you see today. In 1959, the reconstruction was completed after a WWII bomb blew through the dome.

Step inside (donation requested, May–Oct Mon–Sat 9:00–18:30, Sun 13:00–18:30, Nov–April Mon–Sat 10:00–17:00, tourist-free section of old Salzburg. **Hours:** Always open.

▲**St. Sebastian Cemetery** Baroque cemetery with graves of Mozart's wife and father, and other Salzburg VIPs. **Hours:** Daily April–Oct 9:00–18:30, Nov–March 9:00–16:00.

▲**Hohensalzburg Fortress** Imposing castle capping the Mönchsberg mountain overlooking town, with tourable grounds, impressive interior, commanding views, and good evening concerts. **Hours:** June–Aug 9:00–19:30, May and Sept 9:00–19:00, Oct–April 9:00–17:30. Concerts occur nearly nightly at 19:30, 20:00, or 20:30.

▲**Hellbrunn Castle** Palace on the outskirts of town featuring gardens with trick fountains. **Hours:** Daily May–June and Sept 9:00–17:30, July–Aug until 18:00 with palace tour or until 22:00 with fountain-only tour, April and Oct until 16:30, closed Nov–March. Last tour one hour before closing.

St. Peter's Cemetery Atmospheric old cemetery with mini-gardens overlooked by cliff face with monks' caves. **Hours:** Cemetery—daily April–Sept 6:30–19:00, Oct–March 6:30–18:00; caves—May–Sept Tue–Sun 10:30–17:00, closed Mon, less off-season.

St. Peter's Church Romanesque church with rococo decor. **Hours:** Long hours daily.

Sun 13:00–17:00). Enter the cathedral as if part of a festival procession—drawn toward the resurrected Christ by the brightly lit area under the dome, and cheered on by ceiling paintings of the Passion. Sit under the dome and imagine all four organs playing, each balcony filled with 14 musicians...glorious surround-sound. Mozart, who was the organist here for two years, would advise you that the acoustics are best in pews immediately under the dome. Study the symbolism of the decor all around you—intellectual, complex, and cohesive. Think of the altar in Baroque terms, as the center of a stage, with sunrays as spotlights in this dramatic and sacred theater.

Built in just 14 years (1614–1628), the church boasts harmonious architecture. When Pope John Paul II visited in 1998, 5,000 people filled the cathedral (330 feet long and 230 feet tall). The baptismal font (dark bronze, left of the entry) is from the previous cathedral (c. 1320). Mozart was baptized here ("Amadeus" means "beloved by God"). Concert and Mass schedules are posted at the entrance; the Sunday Mass at 10:00 is famous for its music.

The **Cathedral Museum** (Dom Museum) has a rich collection of church art (entry at portico, €5; mid-May–Oct and Dec Mon–Sat 10:00–17:00, Sun 11:00–18:00; closed Nov and Jan–mid-May, tel. 0662/844-189).

Under the skyway, a stairway leads down to the *Domgrabungen*—an excavation site under the church with a few second-century Christian Roman mosaics, and the foundation stones of the eighth-century church that stood here first (€2, daily 9:00–17:00, July–Aug only, tel. 0662/845-295).

From Cathedral Square to St. Peter's Cemetery: Cathedral Square is surrounded by "ecclesiastical palaces." The **statue of Mary** (1771) is looking away from the church, but if you stand in the rear of the square immediately under the middle arch, you'll see that she's positioned to be crowned by the two angels on the church facade.

From the cathedral, walk toward the fortress into the next square (passing the free underground public WCs and the giant chessboard), and head for the pond. This was a **horse bath,** the 18th-century equivalent of a car wash. Notice the puzzle above it—the artist wove the date of the structure into a phrase. It says, "Leopold the Prince Built Me," using the letters LLDVICMXVXI, which total 1732 (add it up...it works)—the year it was built. A small road (back by the chessboard) leads uphill to the fortress (and fortress lift). The stage is set up for the many visiting choirs who are unable to line up a gig. They are welcome to sing here anytime at all. With your back to the cathedral, leave the square through a gate on the right that reads *St. Peter*. It leads to a waterfall and St. Peter's Cemetery.

The **waterfall** is part of a canal system that has brought water into Salzburg from Berchtesgaden, 16 miles away, since the 13th century. Climb uphill a few steps to feel the medieval water power. The stream, divided from here into smaller canals, was channeled through town to provide fire protection, to flush out the streets (Sat morning was flood-the-streets day), and to power factories (there were more than 100 watermill-powered firms as late as the 19th century). There's a good view of the funicular climbing up to the castle from here. Drop into the fragrant and traditional **bakery** at the waterfall. It's hard to beat their rocklike *Roggenbrot* (various fresh rolls for less than €1, Thu–Tue 7:00–17:30, Sat until 12:00, closed Wed).

• *Now step into...*

St. Peter's Cemetery: This collection of lovingly tended mini-gardens abuts the Mönchberg's rock wall (free, silence is requested, daily April–Sept 6:30–19:00, Oct–March 6:30–18:00). Walk in about 50 yards to the intersection of lanes at the base of the cliff (marked by a stone ball). You're surrounded by three churches, each founded in the sixth century atop a pagan Celtic holy site. Look back toward the entry. The early-Gothic-style church was built in 1491—during the late Gothic period. (The old-school Gothic, rather then Baroque, implied allegiance to the Holy Roman Empire.) St. Peter's Church is closest to the stone ball. Notice the fine Romanesque stonework on the chapel nearest you, and the fancy rich guys' Renaissance-style tombs decorating its walls.

Wealthy as those guys were, they ran out of caring relatives. The graves surrounding you are tended by relatives. In Austria, grave sites are rented, not owned. Rent bills are sent out every 10 years. If no one cares enough to make the payment, you're gone. Notice that iron crosses were much cheaper than stone tombstones. While the cemetery where the von Trapp family hid out in *The Sound of Music* was actually in Hollywood, it was inspired by this one.

Look up the cliff. Legendary medieval hermit monks are said to have lived in the hillside—but "catacombs" they're not. For €1, you can climb lots of steps to see a few old caves, a chapel, and some fine views (May–Sept Tue–Sun 10:30–17:00, closed Mon, less off-season).

• *Continue downhill through the cemetery and out the opposite end. Just outside, hook right and drop into...*

St. Peter's Church: Just inside, enjoy a carved Romanesque welcome. An arcade of palm trees leads to a fine tympanum showing Jesus on a rainbow flanked by Peter and Paul over a stylized tree of life and under a Latin inscription reading, "I am the door to life, and only through me can you find eternal life." Enter the nave and notice how the once purely Romanesque vaulting has since been iced with a sugary rococo finish. Up the right side aisle is the tomb of St. Rupert, with a painting showing Salzburg in 1750 (one bridge, salt ships sailing the river, and angels hoisting barrels of salt to heaven as St. Rupert prays for his city). On pillars farther up the aisle are faded bits of 13th-century Romanesque frescos.

Leaving the church, notice the Stiftskeller St. Peter restaurant (on the left—described on page 537 and in "Mozart Dinner Concert" listing, page 528). Charlemagne ate here in A.D. 803—allowing locals to claim it's the oldest restaurant in Europe. Opposite where you entered the square, you'll see St. Rupert waving you into the next square (early-20th-century Bauhaus style, dorms for student monks), with a modern crucifix (1926) on the far wall. To the right of the crucifix (at #8), press the red button on the bronze door, enter, and see an unforgettable Expressionist-carved crucifix (also from the 1920s, free, open long hours daily).

• *The next square is...*

Toscanini Hof: This square faces the 1925 Festival Hall. The hall's three theaters seat 5,000. This is where the nervous Captain von Trapp waited before walking onstage (in the movie, he sang "Edelweiss"), just before he escaped with his family. On the left is the city's 1,500-space, inside-the-mountain parking lot; ahead, behind the *Felsenkeller* sign, is a tunnel (generally closed) leading to the actual concert hall; and to the right is the backstage of a smaller hall where carpenters are often building stage sets (door open on hot days).

• *Walk downhill through Max Reinhardt Platz (a mess today, but expecting a major renovation for the 2006 "Mozart Year" celebrations), to the right of the church and past the public WC into...*

Universitätsplatz: This square hosts a busy open-air produce market—Salzburg's liveliest (mornings Mon–Sat, best on Sat). Locals are happy to pay more here for the reliably fresh and top-quality produce (half of Austria's produce is now grown organically). The market really bustles on Saturday mornings, when the farmers are in town. Public marketplaces have fountains for washing fruit and vegetables. The fountain here (notice the little ones for smaller dogs and bigger dogs)—a part of the medieval water system—plummets down a hole and to the river. The sundial (over the water hole) is accurate (except for the daylight savings hour) and two-dimensional, showing both the time (obvious) and the date (less obvious). The fanciest facade overlooking the square is the backside of Mozart's Birthplace (described below).

• *Continue past the fountain to the end of the square, passing several characteristic and nicely arcaded medieval tunnels (on right) that connect the square to Getreidegasse. Cross the big road for a look at the giant horse troughs, adjacent the prince's stables. Paintings show the various*

breeds and temperaments of horses in his stable. Like Vienna, Salzburg had a passion for the equestrian arts. Take two right turns and you're at the start of...

Getreidegasse: This street, worth ▲▲, was old Salzburg's busy, colorful main drag. (*Schmuck* means "jewelry.") Famous for its old wrought-iron signs (best viewed from this end), the street still looks much as it did in Mozart's day—though the elegant shops are mostly gone, replaced by chain outlets. On the right at #39, Sporer serves up homemade spirits (€1.30 per shot). *Nuss* is nut, *Marille* is apricot (typical of this region), and *Edle Brande* are the stronger schnapps. Austrian wines are sold by the *Achtel* (eighth of a liter). Notice the old doorbells—one per floor. At #40, Eisgrotte serves good ice cream. Across from Eisgrotte, a tunnel leads to Bosna Stand, the local choice for the very best sausage in town (see page 538). Farther along, you'll pass McDonald's (with low-key medieval golden arches) and the Nordsee Restaurant (which was an even more controversial addition to this street than McDonald's). The knot of excited tourists and salesmen hawking goofy gimmicks mark the home of Salzburg's most famous resident.

Mozart's Birthplace (Geburtshaus): Mozart was born here in 1756. It was in this building—the most popular Mozart sight in town and worth ▲—that he composed most of his boy-genius works. For fans, it's almost a pilgrimage. The place is filled with scores of scores, portraits, his first violin (picked up at age 5), the clavichord (a predecessor of the piano, with simple teeter-totter keys that played very softly) upon which he composed *The Magic Flute* and the *Requiem*, and a relaxing video concert hall. Exhibits explain the life of Wolfgang on the road and tell about Salzburg in Mozart's day (including a furnished middle-class apartment). It's all well-described in English (€6, or €9 for combo-ticket that includes Mozart's Wohnhaus, daily July–Aug 9:00–19:00, Sept–June 9:00–18:00, last entry 30 min before closing, Getreidegasse 9, tel. 0662/844-313). Note that Mozart's Wohnhaus, across the river, provides a more informative visit than this more-visited site (see page 519).

• *When you're finished enjoying Getreidegasse and Mozart's Birthplace, you can continue this walk across the river (see below). To get there from Mozart's house, head for the river, jog left (past the fast-fish restaurant and free WCs), and climb to the top of the Makartsteg pedestrian bridge.*

Across-the-River Walk

This walk covers sights on the northern side of Salzburg, across the river from Salzburg's Old Town.

• *Begin at the Makartsteg pedestrian bridge, where you can survey the...*

Salzach River: Salzburg's river is called "salt river" not because it's salty, but because of the precious cargo it once carried—the salt mines of Hallein are just nine miles upstream. Salt could be transported from here all the way to the Danube, and on to Russia. The riverbanks and roads were built when the river was regulated in the 1850s. Before that, the Salzach was much wider and slower-moving. Houses opposite the old town fronted the river with docks and "garages" for boats. The grand buildings just past the bridge were built on reclaimed land in the late 19th century in the historicist style of Vienna's Ringstrasse.

Scan the cityscape. Notice all the churches. Salzburg, nicknamed the "Rome of the North," has 38 Catholic churches (plus 2 Protestant churches and a synagogue). Find the five streams gushing into the river. These date from the 13th century, when a river was split into five canals running through the town to power its mills. Hotel Stein (upstream, just left of next bridge) has a popular new roof-terrace café. Downstream, notice the Museum of Modern Art atop Mönchsberg, with a view café and a faux castle (actually a water reservoir). The Romanesque bell tower with the copper dome in the distance is the Augustine church, marking the best beer hall in town (the Augustiner Bräustübl—see page 539).

• *Cross the bridge, pass the Café Bazar (a fine place for a drink—see page 540), walk a block inland, and take a left past the heroic statues into...*

Mirabell Gardens and Palace (Schloss): The bubbly gardens laid out in 1730 for the prince-archbishop have been open to the public since 1850 (thanks to Emperor Franz Josef, who was rattled by the popular revolutions of 1848). The gardens are free, worth ▲, and open until dusk. The palace is only open as a concert venue (see below). The statues and the arbor (far left) were featured in *The Sound of Music.* Walk through the gardens to the palace. Look back, enjoy the garden/cathedral/castle view, and imagine how the prince-archbishop must have reveled in a vista that reminded him of all his secular and religious power. Then go to the right side of the palace and find the horse.

The rearing Pegasus statue (rare and very well-balanced) is the site of a famous *Sound of Music* scene where the kids all danced before lining up on the stairs (with Maria just beyond). The steps lead to a small mound in the park (made of WWII rubble, and today a rendezvous point for Salzburg's gay community). With your back to the palace, climb the stairs and find two tough dwarfs (early volleyball players with spiked mittens) welcoming you to Salzburg's Dwarf Park. Cross the elevated walk (noticing the city's fortified walls) to meet statues of a dozen actual dwarfs who served the prince-archbishop—modeled after real people with real fashions in about 1600. This was Mannerist art, from the hyper-realistic age that followed the Renaissance.

There's plenty of **music,** both in the park and in the palace. A brass band plays free park concerts (May–Aug Sun at 10:30 and Wed at 20:30). To properly enjoy the lavish Mirabell Palace—once the prince-archbishop's summer palace, and now the seat of the mayor—get a ticket to a Schlosskonzerte (my favorite venue for a classical concert—see page 528).

• *You could end the walk here, but if you want to visit one more Mozart sight, go a long block southeast to Makartplatz, where you'll find...*

Mozart's Wohnhaus: This reconstruction of Mozart's second home (his family moved here when he was 17) is the most informative Mozart sight in town, a ▲▲ sight. The English-language audioguide (included with admission, 90 min) provides a fascinating insight into Mozart's life and music, with the usual scores, old pianos, and an interesting 30-minute-long film (#17 on your audioguide for soundtrack) that runs continuously (€6, or €9 for combo-ticket that includes Mozart's Birthplace in the old town, daily 9:00–18:00, July–Aug until 19:00, last tickets sold 60 min before closing, allow 1 hr minimum for visit, Makartplatz 8, tel. 0662/8742-2740).

• *From here, you can walk a few blocks from the sights near Linzergasse (see "Sights and Activities," below), or you can head back over the river to enjoy some of the sights up on Salzburg's little mountain, Mönchsberg (see "Above the Old Town," below).*

SIGHTS AND ACTIVITIES

Across the River, near Linzergasse

▲**Steingasse**—This street, a block in from the river, was the only street in the Middle Ages going south to Hallein. Today, it's wonderfully tranquil and free of Salzburg's touristy crush (if coming from Mozartplatz, cross the river via the Mozartsteg pedestrian bridge, cross the busy Imbergstrasse, jog left and go a block farther inland to a quiet cobbled lane, and turn left).

Stroll down this peaceful chunk of old Salzburg—once the only road on this side of the river. Just after the Maison de Plaisir at #24 (for centuries, a town brothel—open from 24:00), you'll find a magnificent view of the fortress across the river. Notice the red dome marking the oldest nunnery in the German-speaking world (established in 712) under the fortress and to the left. The real Maria from *The Sound of Music* taught in this nunnery's school. In 1927, she and Herr von Trapp were married in the church you see here (not the church filmed in the movie). He was 47. She was 22. Hmmmm.

At #19, find the carvings on the old door—notices from beggars to the begging community (more numerous after the economic dislocation caused by the wars over religion following the Reformation) indicating whether the residents would give or not. Notice the old-fashioned doorbells.

At #9, a plaque shows where Joseph Mohr, who wrote the words to "Silent Night," was born—poor and illegitimate—in 1792. Stairs lead from near here up to the monastery.

Across the street, on the corner you just passed, the wall is gouged out. This was left even after the building was restored so locals could remember the American GI who tried to get a tank down this road during a visit to #24.

By night, Steingasse is home to several trendy pubs (see "Steingasse Pub Crawl," page 540).

▲**St. Sebastian Cemetery**—Wander through this quiet place, so Baroque and so Italian (free, daily April–Oct 9:00–18:30, Nov–March 9:00–16:00, entry usually at Linzergasse 43). Mozart is buried in Vienna, his mom's in Paris, and his sister is in Salzburg's old town (St. Peter's)—but Wolfgang's father Leopold and his wife Constantia are buried here (from the Linzergasse entrance, take 17 paces and look left). When Prince-Archbishop Wolf Dietrich had the cemetery moved from around the cathedral and put here, across the river, people didn't like it. To help popularize it, he had his own mausoleum built as its centerpiece. Continue straight past the Mozart tomb to this circular building (English description at door).

Above the Old Town

These sights are atop the Mönchsberg, Salzburg's little mountain, hovering above the old town.

▲**Hohensalzburg Fortress**—Built on a rock 400 feet above the Salzach River, this fortress was never really used. That's the idea. It was a good investment—so foreboding, nobody attacked the town for a thousand years. One of Europe's mightiest, it dominates Salzburg's skyline and offers incredible views.

Running a racket for tourists, this place has an all-or-nothing proposal: you pay one price that includes the price of the funicular, as well as admission to the fortress grounds and all the museums—whether you want to see them or not (€9.60 round-trip). If you just went to see the view, consider going in the evening since the funicular serves the "castle concert," running 300 nights a year at 19:30, 20:00, and 20:30 (see "Concerts at the Fortress," page 527); even if you're not seeing the concert, you can ride up and down and see the fortress courtyard for €3.20 after 18:30.

The fortress visit has three parts: a relatively dull courtyard with some fine views, the Kuenburg Bastion (an overlook point accessed from the courtyard), and the palatial interior. The fortress is open daily year-round (June–Aug 9:00–19:30, May and Sept 9:00–19:00, Oct–April 9:00–17:30, last entry 30 min before closing, tel. 0662/8424-3011). On nights when there's a concert, the castle grounds are open until 21:30.

Courtyard: The courtyard is easy to tour on your own. Climb from the funicular to the inner courtyard. Immediately inside, circle left (counterclockwise, passing the audioguide booth with the only pricing scheme in Europe that charges you more to listen longer). The cannon were positioned to defend the city against the Turks. Skip the one-room marionette exhibit—you'll see more for free in its lobby than by paying €3 to go inside. The courtyard was the main square of a community of a thousand—which could be self-sufficient when necessary. The well dipped into a rain-fed cistern. The square was ringed by craftsmen, blacksmiths, bakers, and so on. The church is dedicated to St. George, the protector of horses (logical for an army church) and decorated by fine red marble reliefs (c. 1502). Behind the church is the top of the old lift that helped supply the church. (From here, steps lead back into the city, or to the "Mönchsberg Walk," described below.) Continue behind the church and turn left into the Kuenburg Bastion (once a garden) for fine city and castle views.

Kuenburg Bastion: Notice how the castle has three parts: the original castle inside the courtyard, the vast whitewashed walls (built when the castle was a residence), and the lower, beefed-up fortifications (built to defend against Turkish invasion). Survey Salzburg from here and think about fortifying an important city using nature. Mönchsberg natu-rally cradles the old town, with just a small gate between the mountain and the river needed to bottle up the place. The new town across the river needed a bit of a wall arcing from the river to its hill. Back then, only one bridge crossed the Salzach into town—with a fortified gate.

Back inside the castle courtyard, continue your circle. The Round Tower (1497) helps you visualize the inner original castle.

Fortress Palace Interior: Tourists are allowed inside the palace only with an escort. You'll go one room at a time, listening to a 45-minute audioguide. The decorations are from around 1500—fantastic animals and plants inspired by tales of New World discoveries. While the interior furnishings are mostly gone—taken by Napoleon—the rooms survived as well as they did because no one wanted to live there after 1500, so the building was never modernized. Your tour includes a room dedicated to the art of "intensive questioning" ("softening up" prisoners, in current American military jargon)—filled with tools of that gruesome trade. You'll get a sneak preview of the room used for the nightly fortress concerts. The last rooms show music, daily life in the castle, and an exhibit dedicated to the Salzburg regiment in the World Wars. The highlight is the commanding city view from the top of a tower.

▲**Mönchsberg Walk**—For a great 30-minute hike, exit the fortress by taking the steep lane down from the castle courtyard. At the first intersection, right leads into the old town, and left leads across the Mönchsberg. The lane leads 20 minutes through the woods high above the city (stick to the high lanes, or you'll end up back in town), taking you to the Gasthaus Stadtalm café (light meals, cheap beds—see page 533 of "Sleeping," and page 538 of "Eating"). From the Stadtalm, pass under the medieval wall and walk left along the wall to a tableau showing how it once looked. Take the switchback to the right and follow the lane downhill to the Museum of Modern Art (described below), where the elevator zips you back into town (€1.80 one-way, €2.90 round trip, daily Sept–June 8:00–19:00, July–Aug 8:00–24:00, closed off-season). If you stay on the lane past the elevator, you eventually pass the Augustine church that marks the rollicking Augustiner Bräustübl (see page 539).

In 1669, a huge Mönchsberg landslide killed more than 200 townspeople. Since then the cliffs have been carefully checked each spring and fall. Even today, you might see crews on the cliff, monitoring its stability.

Museum of Modern Art on Mönchsberg—The modern-art museum on top of Mönchsberg, built in 2004, houses Salzburg's Rupertinum Gallery, plus special exhibitions. While the collection is not worth climbing a mountain for, the restaurant has some of the best views in town (€8, Tue–Fri 10:00–18:00, Wed 10:00–21:00, closed Mon, at top of Mönchsberg elevator, tel. 0662/842-220, www.museumdermoderne.at).

More Salzburg Sights and Activities

▲▲**Riverside or Meadow Bike Ride**—The Salzach River has smooth, flat, and scenic bike paths along each side (thanks to medieval tow paths—cargo boats would float downstream and be dragged back up by horse). On a sunny day, I can think of no more shout-worthy escape from the city. The nearly four-mile path upstream to Hellbrunn Castle is easy, with a worthy destination (leave Salzburg on castle side). For a nine-mile ride, head out to Hallein (where you can tour a salt mine—see "Near Salzburg," below; the north, or new-town, side of river is most scenic). Perhaps the most pristine meadow farm-country route is the four-mile Hellbrunner Allee from Akademiestrasse. Even a quickie ride across town is a great Salzburg experience. In the evening, the riverbanks are a floodlit-spires world.

▲**Hellbrunn Castle**—The attractions here are a garden full of clever trick fountains and the sadistic joy the tour guide gets from soaking tourists. (Hint: When you see a wet place, cover your camera.) After buying your ticket, you wait for the English tour, laugh and scramble through the entertaining 40-minute trick-water toy tour, and are then free to tour the forgettable palace with an included audioguide (€8.50, July–Aug daily 9:00–18:00 with palace tour or until 22:00 with €8 fountain-only tour, May–June and Sept until 17:30, April and Oct until 16:30, closed Nov–March, tel. 0662/820-372, www.hellbrunn.at). Hellbrunn is nearly four miles south of Salzburg (bus #25 from station or from Staatsbrücke bridge in the center, 2/hr, 20 min). It's most fun on a sunny day or with kids, but, for many, it's a lot of trouble for a few water tricks. The Hellbrunn Baroque garden, one of the oldest in Europe, now features *S.O.M.*'s "Sixteen Going On Seventeen" gazebo.

Near Salzburg

▲**Bad Dürrnberg Salt Mine (Salzbergwerke)**—This salt mine tour above the town of Hallein (9 miles from Salzburg) is a fun experience. Wearing white overalls and sliding down the sleek wooden chutes, you'll cross underground from Austria into Germany while learning about the old-time salt-mining process. The visit also includes a "Celtic Village" open-air museum (€16, allow 2.5 hours for the visit, April–Oct daily from 9:00 with last tour at 17:00, Nov–March daily from 11:00 with last tour at 15:00, English-speaking guides—but let your linguistic needs be known loud and clear, easy bus and train connections from Salzburg, tel. 06245/852-8515, www.salzwelten.at). A convenient *Salz Erlebnis* ticket from Salzburg's train station covers admission, train, and shuttle bus tickets, all in one money-saving round-trip ticket (€19, buy ticket at train station).

Hallein Mountain Bobsled—The Zinkenlifte Bad Dürrnberg luge ride is the priciest, longest, and most exciting in Austria (7,200 feet, 1,600-foot drop, €8.50 per ride). It's just half a mile beyond the salt mines (accessible by same bus from Salzburg station, tel. 06245/85105).

▲**Berchtesgaden**—This alpine ski town in the region of the same name just across the German border (12 miles from Salzburg) flaunts its attractions very successfully. During peak season, you may find yourself in a traffic jam of desperate tourists trying to turn their money into fun. The **TI** is next to the train station (TI: German tel. 08652/967-150, from Austria tel. 00-49-8652/967-150, www.berchtesgadener-land.com).

At the Berchtesgaden **salt mines,** you put on traditional miners' outfits, get on funny little trains, and zip deep into the mountain. For one hour, you'll cruise subterranean lakes; slide speedily down two long, slick, wooden banisters; and learn how they mined salt so long ago. Call for crowd-avoidance advice. When the weather gets bad, this place is mobbed. You can buy a ticket early and browse through the town until your appointed tour

Greater Salzburg

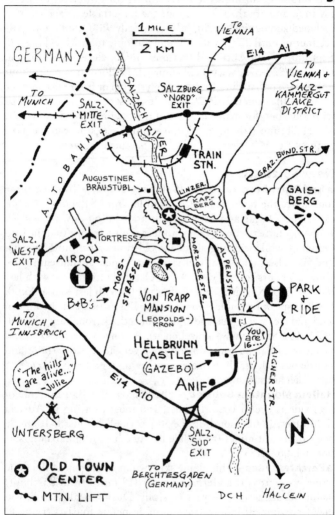

time. While tours are in German, English-speakers get audio-guides (€12.90; May–mid-Oct daily 9:00–17:00; mid-Oct–April Mon–Sat 11:30–15:00, closed Sun, German tel. 08652/60020, from Austria tel. 00-49-8652/60020).

Hitler's famous **Eagle's Nest**—where the Führer and his senior officers brainstormed the horrors they would release on the world—towers high above Obersalzberg near Berchtesgaden. The road and building were constructed in an impressive 13 months—just in time to be given to Hitler for his 50th birthday. The site is open to visitors (mid-May–Oct), but little remains of the alpine retreat Hitler visited only 10 times. Hitler's Berghof and most other Nazi buildings were blown up in 1952. The round-trip bus ride up the private road and the lift to the top (a 2,000-foot altitude gain) cost €16 from the station, €13 from the parking lot. Allow two hours for the visit.

The **Nazi Documentation Center,** next to the Eagle's Nest parking lot, includes a trip to the bunkers that burrow into the mountainside (€2.50, €2 for English audioguide, allow 90 min for visit, April–Oct daily 9:00–17:00, Nov–March Tue–Sun 10:00–15:00, closed Mon, last entry 1 hr before closing, German tel. 08652/947-960, from Austria tel. 00-49-8652/947-960, www .obersalzberg.de).

In 2005, the British hotel chain InterContinental Hotels and Resorts opened a luxury hotel very near the Eagle's Nest. Located on the precise spot where Nazi officers Bormann and Goering had their own villas, it's been nicknamed "Hotel Hitler" by the world press. Jewish groups such as the Simon Wiesenthal Center have called for a boycott. (At rooms that cost from $3000 a night, that shouldn't be too hard to do.)

Getting There: From Salzburg, the bus is more scenic and direct than the train (2/hr, 30 min, bus station across street from Salzburg's train station). Some travelers visit Berchtesgaden en route from Munich (hrly trains from Munich, 2.5 hrs, with 1 change). From the Berchtesgaden station, bus #9540 goes to the salt mines (a 20-min walk otherwise) and bus #9549 to the Nazi Documentation Center. Buses also go to the idyllic Königsee (popular €11, 1-hr scenic cruises, 2/hr, with the pilot demonstrating the lake's echo with a trumpet, stopovers anywhere, German tel. 08652/963-618, from Austria tel. 00-49-8652/963-618).

ENTERTAINMENT

Music Scene

▲▲**Salzburg Festival (Salzburger Festspiele)**—Each summer, from late July to the end of August, Salzburg hosts its famous Salzburg Festival, founded in 1920 to employ Vienna's musicians in the summer. This fun and festive time is crowded, but there are plenty of beds (except for a few August weekends). There are three big halls: the Opera and Orchestra venues in the Festival House, and the Landes Theater where German plays are performed. Tickets for the big festival events are generally expensive (€50–100) and sold out well in advance (bookable from Jan). Most tourists think they're "going to the Salzburg Festival" by seeing smaller non-festival events that go on during the festival weeks. For these lesser events, same-day tickets are normally available (the ticket

Sound of Music Debunked

Rather than visit the real-life sights from the life of Maria von Trapp and family, most tourists want to see the places where Hollywood chose to film this fanciful story. Local guides are happy not to burst any *S.O.M.* pilgrim's bubble, but keep these points in mind:

- "Edelweiss" is not a cherished Austrian folk tune or national anthem. Like all the "Austrian" music in the *S.O.M.*, it was composed for Broadway by Rodgers and Hammerstein. It was, however, the last composition that the famed team wrote together, as Hammerstein died in 1960—nine months after the musical opened.
- The *S.O.M.* implies that Maria was devoutly religious throughout her life, but Maria's foster parents raised her as a socialist and atheist. Maria discovered her religious calling while studying to be a teacher. After completing school, she joined the convent as a novitiate.
- Maria's position was not as governess to all the children, as portrayed in the musical, but specifically as governess and teacher for the Captain's second-oldest daughter, Maria, who was bedridden with rheumatic fever.
- The Captain didn't run a tight domestic ship. In fact, his seven children were as unruly as most. But he did use a whistle to call them—each kid was trained to respond to a certain pitch.
- Though the von Trapp family did have seven children, the show changed all their names and even their genders. Rupert, the eldest child, responded to the often-asked tourist question, "Which one are you?" with a simple, "I'm Leisl!"
- The family never escaped by hiking to Switzerland (which is a 5-hour drive away). Rather, they pretended to go on one of

office on Mozartplatz, in the TI, prints a daily list of concerts and charges a 30 percent fee to book them). For specifics on this year's festival schedule and tickets, visit www.salzburgfestival.at, or contact the Austrian National Tourist Office in the United States (P.O. Box 1142, New York, NY 10108-1142, tel. 212/944-6880, fax 212/730-4568, www.austria.info, travel@austria.info). While I've never planned in advance, I've enjoyed great concerts with every visit.

▲▲**Musical Events Year-Round**—Salzburg is busy throughout the year, with 2,000 classical performances in its palaces and churches annually. Pick up the events calendar at the TI (free, bimonthly). Whenever you visit, you'll have a number of concerts (generally small chamber groups) to choose from.

their frequent mountain hikes. With only the possessions in their backpacks, they "hiked" all the way to the train station (it was at the edge of their estate) and took a train to Italy. The movie scene showing them climbing into Switzerland was actually filmed near Berchtesgaden, Germany...home to Hitler's Eagle's Nest, and certainly not a smart place to flee to.

- The actual von Trapp family house exists...but it's not the one in the film. The mansion in the movie is actually two different buildings, one used for the front, the other for the back. The interiors were all filmed on Hollywood sets.

- For the film, Boris Levin designed a reproduction of the Nonnberg Abbey courtyard so faithful to the original (down to its cobblestones and stained-glass windows) that many still believe the cloister scenes were really shot at the abbey. And no matter what you hear in Salzburg, the graveyard scene (in which the von Trapps hide from the Nazis) was also filmed on the Fox lot.

- In 1956, a German film producer offered Maria $10,000 for the rights to her book. She asked for royalties, too, and a share of the profits. The agent explained that German law forbids film companies from paying royalties to foreigners (Maria had by then become a U.S. citizen). She agreed to the contract and unknowingly signed away all film rights to her story. Only a few weeks later, he offered to pay immediately if she would accept $9,000 in cash. Because it was more money than the family had seen in all of their years of singing, she accepted the deal. Later, she discovered the agent had swindled them—no such law existed.

Concerts at the Fortress (Festungskonzerte): There are nearly nightly concerts—Mozart's greatest hits for beginners—up at the fortress in the "prince's chamber," featuring small chamber groups (open seating after the first 5 more expensive rows, €31 and €38, at 19:30, 20:00, or 20:30, doesn't include funicular, doors open 30 min early, tel. 0662/825-858 to reserve, pick tickets up at the door). The medieval-feeling chamber has windows overlooking the city, and the concert gives you a chance to enjoy the grand city view and a stroll through the castle courtyard. (The €9.60 round-trip funicular is discounted to €3.20 within an hour of the show, ideal for people who just want to ascend for the view; see page 520.) Combine the concert with a four-course dinner (€47 and €51, includes concert and funicular, starts 2 hours before concert).

Concerts at the Mirabell Palace (Schlosskonzerte): The nearly nightly chamber music concerts at the Mirabell Palace are performed in a lavish Baroque setting. They come with more sophisticated programs and better musicians than the fortress concerts. Baroque music flying around a Baroque hall is a happy bird in the right cage (open seating after the first 5 more expensive rows, €30–36, at 19:30, 20:00, or 20:30, doors open 30 min early, tel. 0662/848-5860, www.salzburger-schlosskonzerte.at).

"Five O'Clock Concerts" (5-Uhr-Konzerte): These concerts—next to St. Peter's in the old town—are cheaper, since they feature young artists (€12, July–Sept at 17:00 daily except Wed, 45 min, tel. 0662/8445-7619, www.5-uhr-konzerte.com). While the series is formally named after the brother of Joseph Haydn, it offers music from various masters.

Marionette Theater: Salzburg's much-loved marionette theater offers operas with spellbinding marionettes and recorded music. Music-lovers are mesmerized by the little people on stage (€18–35, nearly nightly at 19:30 June–Sept except Sun, also some in May, some matinees, tel. 0662/872-406, www.marionetten.at).

Mozart Dinner Concert: For those who'd like some classical music but would rather not sit through a concert, Stiftskeller St. Peter offers a traditional candlelit meal with Mozart's greatest hits performed by a string quartet and singers in historic costumes gavotting among the tables. In this elegant Baroque setting, tourists clap between movements and get three courses of food (from Mozart-era recipes) mixed with three 20-minute courses of crowd-pleasing music (€45, Mozart-lovers with this guidebook receive a 20 percent discount if they book direct in 2006, almost nightly at 20:00, call to reserve at 0662/828-6950, www.mozartdinnerconcert.com). For more details, see page 537.

Sound of Salzburg Dinner Show: The show at the Sternbräu Inn (see page 537) is Broadway in a dirndl with tired food. But it's a good show, and *Sound of Music* fans leave with hands red from clapping. A piano player and a hardworking quartet of singers wearing historical costumes perform an entertaining mix of *S.O.M.* hits and traditional folk songs (€44 for dinner, €40 if you mention this book, dinner at 19:30). You can also come by at 20:30, pay €26 (if you mention this book, otherwise it's €29), skip the dinner, and get the show. Those who book direct (not through a hotel) and pay cash get a 10 percent discount with this book in 2006 (nightly mid-May–mid-Oct, Griesgasse 23, tel. 0662/826-617, www.soundofsalzburgshow.com).

SLEEPING

Finding a room in Salzburg, even during its music festival (mid-July–Aug), is usually easy. Rates rise significantly (20–30 percent) during the music festival, special Mozart events (celebrating his 250th birthday), and sometimes also around Easter and Christmas; these higher prices do not appear in the ranges I've listed. You'll often be charged 10 percent extra for a one-night stay.

Linzergasse and Rupertgasse

These listings are in a pleasant neighborhood (with easy parking) a 15-minute walk from the train station (for directions, see "Arrival in Salzburg," above) and a 10-minute walk to the old town. If you're coming from the old town, simply cross the main bridge (Staatsbrücke) to the mostly traffic-free Linzergasse. If driving, exit the highway at Salzburg-Nord, follow Vogelweiderstrasse straight to its end, and turn right.

$$$ Altstadthotel Wolf Dietrich, around the corner from Linzergasse on pedestrian-only Wolf-Dietrich Strasse, is well located (with half its rooms overlooking St. Sebastian Cemetery). With 27 rooms, it's a reasonable, big-hotel option, if that's what you want (Sb-€69–94, Db-€109–164, rates depend on room size, family deals, €40 more during festival time, complex pricing but readers of this book get a 10 percent discount on prevailing price in 2006, elevator, pool, sauna, garage-€12/day, Wolf-Dietrich Strasse 7, tel. 0662/871-275, fax 0662/882-320, www.salzburg-hotel.at, office@salzburg-hotel.at). Their annex across the street has 14 equally comfortable rooms (but no elevator, and therefore slightly cheaper prices).

Sleep Code

(€1 = about $1.20, country code: 43, area code: 0662)
S = Single, **D** = Double/Twin, **T** = Triple, **Q** = Quad, **b** = bathroom, **s** = shower only. Unless otherwise noted, credit cards are accepted and breakfast is included. All of these places speak English.

To help you sort easily through these listings, I've divided the rooms into three categories, based on the price for a standard double room with bath:

$$$ **Higher Priced**—Most rooms €90 or more.
$$ **Moderately Priced**—Most rooms between €60–90.
$ **Lower Priced**—Most rooms €60 or less.

Central Salzburg Hotels

1 Altstadthotel Wolf Dietrich
2 Hotel Trumer Stube
3 Hotel Goldene Krone
4 To Bergland Hotel &
   Hotel-Pension Jedermann
5 Institute St. Sebastian
6 Pension zum Jungen Fuchs
7 Blaue Gans Arthotel
8 Hotel Weisse Taube
9 Gasthaus zur Goldenen Ente
10 Hotel am Dom
11 Hotel/Rest. Weisses Kreuz
12 Christkönig Pension
13 Gasthaus Stadtalm
14 Hotel Amadeus
15 Launderette

$$$ Hotel Trumer Stube, three blocks from the river just off Linzergasse, has 20 clean, cozy rooms and a friendly, can-do owner (Sb-€60, Db-€100, Tb-€125, Qb-€140, top-floor rooms have lower ceilings and are €7 less expensive, 10 percent discount if you book direct with this book and pay cash in 2006, non-smoking, elevator, Internet access, Bergstrasse 6, tel. 0662/874-776, fax 0662/874-326, www.trumer-stube.at, info@trumer-stube.at, pleasant Silvia).

$$$ Hotel Amadeus is a 500-year-old building with 25 comfortable rooms, half of them on the very peaceful back side overlooking the Mozart family tomb (most of the year: Sb-€65, Db-€100, Tb-€135; late July–Aug and Dec: Sb-€88, Db-€170, Tb-€200; these special prices promised if you book direct with this book in 2006, 10 percent cash discount off-season, free Internet access, Linzergasse 43, tel. 0662/871-401, fax 0662/871-4017, www.hotelamadeus.at, salzburg@hotelamadeus.at, Margo).

$$ Hotel Goldene Krone, about five blocks from the river, is big, quiet, and creaky-traditional but modern, with comforts rare in this price range (25 rooms, Sb-€60, Db-€88, Tb-€128, claim your 10 percent discount off these prices with this book in 2006, elevator, relaxing backyard garden, Linzergasse 48, tel. 0662/872-300, fax 0662/8723-0066, office@hotel-goldenekrone .com, Claudia and Günther).

$ Institute St. Sebastian is in a somewhat sterile but very clean historic building next to St. Sebastian Cemetery. From October through June, the institute houses female students from various Salzburg colleges, and also rents 40 beds for travelers. From July through September, the students are gone and they rent all 100 beds (including 20 doubles) to travelers. The building has spacious public areas, a roof garden, a piano guests are welcome to play, and some of the best rooms and dorm beds in town for the money. The immaculate doubles come with modern baths and head-to-toe twin beds (S-€30, Sb-€37, D-€50, Db-€60, Tb-€74, Qb-€88, includes breakfast, elevator, self-service laundry-€4/load, reception open daily July–Sept 7:30–12:00 & 13:00–22:00, Oct–June 8:00–12:00 & 16:00–21:00, Linzergasse 41, enter through arch at #37, tel. 0662/871-386, fax 0662/8713-8685, www.st-sebastian -salzburg.at, office@st-sebastian-salzburg.at). Students like the €18 bunks in 4- to 10-bed dorms (€2 less if you have sheets, no lockout time, free lockers, free showers). You'll find self-service kitchens on each floor (fridge space is free; request a key).

$ Pension zum Jungen Fuchs terrifies claustrophobes and titillates troglodytes. It's plain and sometimes smelly, but sleepable and wonderfully located in a funky, dumpy old building (16 rooms, S-€28, D-€40-44, T-€50, no breakfast, cash only, Linzergasse 54, tel. 0662/875-496).

Pensions on Rupertgasse: These two hotels are about five blocks farther from the river up Paris-Lodron Strasse to Rupertgasse, a breeze for drivers but with more street noise than the places on Linzergasse. They're both modern and well-run—good values if you don't mind being a bit away from the old town. **$$$ Bergland Hotel** is charming and classy, with comfortable, neo-rustic rooms (Sb-€60, Db-€90, Tb-€107, Qb-€127, elevator, Internet access, English library, bike rental €6/day, Rupertgasse 15, tel. 0662/872-318, fax 0662/872-3188, www.berglandhotel.at, kuhn@berglandhotel.at, Kuhn family). The similar, boutique-like **$$ Hotel-Pension Jedermann,** a few doors down, is also tastefully done and comfortable, with artsy decor and a backyard garden (Sb-€55, Db-€85, Tb-€100, Qb-€120, much more during music festival, Internet access, Rupertgasse 25, tel. 0662/873-241, fax 0662/873-2419, www.hotel-jedermann.com, office@hotel-jedermann.com).

In or above the Old Town

$$$ Blaue Gans Arthotel is ultra-modern, giving you a break from charming old Salzburg with artsy public spaces and 40 sleek but nothing-special rooms beautifully located at the far end of Getreidegasse (Sb-€105–115, standard Db-€140, bigger superior Db-€170, fancier suites, elevator, Getreidegasse 41, tel. 0662/842-4910, fax 0662/842-4919, www.blauegans.at, office@blauegans.at).

$$$ Gasthaus zur Goldenen Ente is in a 600-year-old building with medieval stone arches and narrow stairs. Located above a good restaurant, it's as central as you can be on a pedestrian street in old Salzburg. The 17 rooms are modern yet worn, and the service is uneven (most of the year: Sb-€68, Db-€90; late July–Aug and Dec: Sb-€78, Db-€125; extra person-€29, elevator, parking-€14/day, Goldgasse 10, tel. 0662/845-622, fax 0662/845-6229, www.ente.at, hotel@ente.at). While this hotel's advertised rates are too high, these prices are substantially discounted for travelers with this book through 2006.

$$$ Hotel Weisse Taube is a big, quiet, old-feeling, 30-room place with more comfort than character, well-located about a block off Mozartplatz (Sb-€61, Db with shower-€93, bigger Db with bath-€106, 10 percent discount with this book and cash in 2006, elevator, Internet access, tel. 0662/842-404, fax 0662/841-783, Kaigasse 9, www.weissetaube.at, hotel@weissetaube.at).

$$$ Hotel am Dom, while pretty forgettable, is perfectly located—on Goldgasse a few steps from the cathedral. The 14 rooms are old and basic, but well-maintained (Sb-€76–79, Db-€79–117, extra bed-€33, prices slightly lower Nov–mid-June, non-smoking rooms, Goldgasse 17, tel. 0662/842-765, fax 0662/8427-6555, www.amdom.at, bach@salzburg.co.at).

$$ Hotel Restaurant Weisses Kreuz is a Tolkienesque little family-run place on a cobbled back street under the fortress. It's away from the crowds and offers a fine Balkan restaurant, four rooms, and a peaceful roof garden (small Db-€66, big Db-€90, Tb-€120, 10 percent more June–Aug, garage, Bierjodlgasse 6, tel. 0662/845-641, fax 0662/845-6419, weisses.kreuz@eunet.at).

$$ Christkönig Pension makes you feel like a guest of the bishop, with 25 rooms in a 14th-century church building just under the castle and behind the cathedral. You can even stay in the bishop's suite...if no one from the Vatican is visiting. This place offers a charming, quiet, and unique way to sleep well and cheaply in the old center (S-€36, Sb-€40, Db-€80, twin beds only, €6 extra for 1-night stays, cash only, Kapitelplatz 2a, tel. 0662/842627, www.christkoenig-kolleg.at, christkoenig-pension@salzburg.co.at, Frau Anna Huemer).

$ Gasthaus Stadtalm is a local version of a mountaineer's hut and a great budget alternative. Snuggled in a forest on the remains of a 15th-century castle wall atop the little mountain overlooking Salzburg, it has magnificent town and mountain views. While the accommodations are designed-for-backpackers rustic, the price and view are the best in town—it's a fine experience (26 beds, €15/person in 2-, 4-, and 6-bed dorms, includes breakfast and shower, cash only, no lockers, open mid-April–Oct, 2 min from top of €2.60 round-trip Mönchsberg elevator, Mönchsberg 19-C, tel. & fax 0662/841-729, Peter and Roland).

Near the Train Station

$$ Pension Adlerhof, a plain and decent old place, is two blocks in front of the train station (left off Kaiserschutzenstrasse), but a 15-minute walk from the sightseeing action. It has a quirky staff, a boring location, and 35 stodgy-but-spacious rooms (Sb-€55, D-€52, Db-€69–82, Tb-€87–105, Qb-€112–120, cash only, elevator, Elisabethstrasse 25, tel. 0662/875-236, fax 0662/873-663, www.pension-adlerhof.com, adlerhof@pension-adlerhof.at).

$ International Youth Hotel, a.k.a. the "Yo-Ho," is the most lively, handy, and American of Salzburg's hostels (€17 in 6- to 8-bed dorms, €20 in dorms with bathrooms, Q-€18/person, Qb-€21/person, sheets included, cheap breakfast, 6 blocks from station toward Linzergasse and 6 blocks from river at Paracelsusstrasse 9, tel. 0662/879-649, fax 0662/878-810, www.yoho.at, office@yoho.at). This easygoing place speaks English first; has cheap meals, 160 beds, lockers, Internet access, laundry, tour discounts, and no curfew; plays *The Sound of Music* free daily at 10:30; runs a lively bar; and welcomes anyone of any age. The noisy atmosphere and lack of a curfew can make it hard to sleep.

Zimmer (Private Rooms)

These are generally roomy and comfortable and come with a good breakfast, easy parking, and tourist information. Off-season, competition softens prices. These are a bus ride from town, but, with a €3.40 transit day pass *(Tageskarte)* and the frequent service, this shouldn't keep you away. In fact, most will happily pick you up at the train station if you simply telephone them and ask. Most will also do laundry for a small fee for those staying at least two nights. I've listed prices for two nights or more. If staying only one night, expect a 10 percent surcharge.

Beyond the Train Station

Both of these places have easy free parking, are a 30-minute walk or easy bus ride into the center, and are happy to pick up when you arrive. They're a 10-minute walk from station: Head for the river, cross the pedestrian Pioneer Bridge, turn right, and walk along the river a few minutes into a quiet suburban-feeling residential neighborhood.

$ Trude Poppenberger's three pleasant rooms share a long, mountain-view balcony (S-€25, D-€40, T-€57, Wachtelgasse 9, tel. & fax 0662/430-094, www.trudeshome.com, mail@trudeshome .com). From Pioneer Bridge, turn right, walk along the river 300 yards, cross the canal, go left on Linke Glanzeile for three minutes, and then turn right on Wachtelgasse to #9.

$ Brigitte Lenglachner rents six basic rooms with no public spaces (S-€24, D-€37, Db-€44, T-€50, Tb-€64, Qb-€88, bigger apartment, Scheibenweg 8, she pushes tours and charges a booking fee—save money and book your tours direct, tel. & fax 0662/438-044, bedandbreakfast4u@yahoo.de). From the Pioneer Bridge, walk along the river to the third street (Scheibenweg), turn left, and it's halfway down on the right.

On Moosstrasse

The busy street called Moosstrasse, southwest of Mönchsberg, is lined with *Zimmer*. (While it does come with lots of cows, *moos* means "moss.") Handy bus #16 connects Moosstrasse to the center frequently (Mon–Fri 4/hr until 17:00, then 2/hr; Sat 4/hr until 12:00, then 2/hr)—but service drops to a frustrating twice per hour on Sundays. To get to these from the train station, take bus #1, #5, #6, or #25 to Makartplatz, where you'll change to #16. If you're coming from the old town, catch bus #16 from Hanuschplatz, just downstream of the Staatsbrücke bridge near the *Tabak* kiosk. Buy a €1.80 *Einzelkarte-Kernzone* ticket (for 1 trip) or a €3.40 *Tageskarte* (day pass, good for 24 hours) from the streetside machine and punch it when you board the bus. The bus stop you use for each *Zimmer* is listed below. If you're driving from the center, go through the tunnel, continue straight on Neutorstrasse, and take the fourth left onto Moosstrasse. Drivers exit autobahn at *Süd* and then head in the direction of *Grodig*.

$ Frau Ballwein offers cozy, charming, and fresh rooms in two buildings, all with intoxicating view balconies (S-€23, D-€40, Db-€52, Tb-€65–70, family deals, cash only, farm-fresh breakfasts, non-smoking, small pool, Moosstrasse 69-A, bus stop: Gsengerweg, tel. & fax 0662/824-029, www.haus-ballwein.at, haus.ballwein@gmx.net).

$ Helga Bankhammer rents four nondescript rooms in a farmhouse, with a real dairy farm out back (D-€44, Db-€48, no surcharge for 1-night stays, family deals, non-smoking, laundry about €5 per load, Moosstrasse 77, bus stop: Marienbad, tel. & fax 0662/830-067, www.privatzimmer.at/helga.bankhammer, bankhammer@aon.at).

$ Haus Reichl, with three good rooms at the end of a long lane, feels the most remote (Db-€52, Tb-€66, Qb-€88, doubles and triples have balcony and view, non-smoking, between Ballwein and Bankhammer B&Bs, 200 yards down Reiterweg to #52, bus stop: Gsengerweg, tel. & fax 0662/826-248, www.privatzimmer .at/haus-reichl, haus.reichl@telering.at). Elizabeth offers free loaner bikes for guests (20 min to the center).

$ Pension Bloberger Hof, while more a hotel than a *Zimmer,* is comfortable and friendly, with a rural location and 20 farmer-plush, good-value rooms. It's the farthest out, but reached by the same bus #16 from the center (Sb-€41–51, Db-€60, big new Db with balcony-€85, extra bed-€15, Inge offers those booking direct with this book and paying cash a 10 percent discount in 2006, family apartment, non-smoking, restaurant for guests, free loaner bikes, free station pick-up if staying 3 nights, Hammerauerstrasse 4, bus stop: Hammerauerstrasse, tel. 0662/830-227, fax 0662/827-061, www.blobergerhof.at, office@blobergerhof.at).

EATING

In the Old Town

Salzburg boasts many inexpensive, fun, and atmospheric places to eat. I'm a sucker for big cellars with their smoky, Old World atmosphere, heavy medieval arches, time-darkened paintings, antlers, hearty meals, and plump patrons. Most of these eateries are centrally located in the old town, famous with visitors, but also enjoyed by the locals.

Gasthaus zum Wilden Mann is the place if the weather's bad and you're in the mood for *Hofbräu* atmosphere and a hearty, cheap meal at a shared table in one small, smoky, well-antlered room (€6–8 daily specials, Mon–Sat 11:00–21:00, closed Sun, 2 min from

Central Salzburg Restaurants

1. Gasthaus zum Wilden Mann
2. Stiftskeller St. Peter
3. St. Paul's Stub'n Beer Garden
4. Triangel Restaurant
5. Fisch Krieg Rest.
6. Sternbräu Inn
7. Café Tomaselli
8. To Augustiner Bräustübl
9. Restaurant Weisses Kreuz
10. Restaurant Yuen
11. To Bar Club Café Republic
12. Gasthaus Stadtalm
13. Toskana Cafeteria Mensa
14. Bosna Sausage Stand
15. Frauenberger Restaurant
16. Spicy Spices
17. Biergarten Weisse
18. Café Bazar
19. Steingasse Pubs & Restaurants

Mozart's birthplace, enter from Getreidegasse 22 or Griesgasse 20, tel. 0662/841-787). For a quick lunch, get the *Bauernschmaus,* a mountain of dumplings, kraut, and peasant's meats (€9.50). Manager Robert runs the place with Schwarzenegger-like energy.

Stiftskeller St. Peter has been in business for more than 1,000 years—it was mentioned in the biography of Charlemagne. It's classy and central as can be, serving uninspired traditional Austrian cuisine (€15–25 meals, daily 11:30–24:00, indoor/outdoor seating, next to St. Peter's Church at foot of Mönchsberg, restaurant tel. 0662/841-268). They host the Mozart Dinner Concert described in "Music Scene," on page 528 (€45, nearly nightly at 20:00, call 0662/828-6950 to reserve, book direct with this 2006 guidebook for 20 percent off). Over the centuries, they've learned to charge for each piece of bread and not serve free tap water.

St. Paul's Stub'n Beer Garden is a secret—tucked away under the castle with an ignore-the-tourists-attitude (menu in German only). The food is better than a beer hall, and the young, local clientele fills its troll-like interior and breezy tree-shaded garden (€10 daily specials, €10–15 plates, Mon–Sat 17:00–22:00, closed Sun, Herrengasse 16, tel. 0662/843-220).

Triangel Restaurant, just across from the festival concert hall, caters to local students and artists. They serve simple regional cuisine, including a €5 lunch special on weekdays (served Tue–Fri 12:00–13:30, 2 choices: meat or vegetarian; open Tue–Sat 11:00–24:00, closed Sun–Mon, good indoor and outdoor seating, Wiener Philharmonikergasse 7, tel. 0662/842-229).

Fisch Krieg Restaurant, on the river where the fishermen used to sell their catch, serves fast, fresh, and inexpensive fish with great riverside seating (€2 fishwiches to go, €7 meals, salad bar, Mon–Fri 8:30–18:30, Sat 8:30–13:00, closed Sun, Hanuschplatz 4, tel. 0662/843-732).

Sternbräu Inn is a sprawling complex of popular eateries (traditional, Italian, self-serve, and vegetarian) in a cheery garden setting—explore both courtyards before choosing a seat (most restaurants open daily 9:00–24:00). One fancy, air-conditioned room hosts the Sound of Salzburg dinner show (see description on page 528).

Café Tomaselli (with its Kiosk annex across the way) is the top place to see and be seen. While overpriced, it is good for lingering and people-watching. Tomaselli serves light meals and lots of drinks, keeps long hours daily, and has fine seating on the square, a view terrace upstairs, and indoor tables. Despite its fancy inlaid wood paneling, 19th-century portraits, and chandeliers, it is surprisingly low-key. Its greatest claim to fame is that Mozart's widow and her second husband lived upstairs in 1820 (€3–6 entrées, daily

7:00–21:00, until 24:00 during music festival, Alter Markt 9, tel. 0662/844-488).

Restaurant Weisses Kreuz, nestled quietly behind the cathedral and under the fortress, serves good Balkan cuisine in a pleasant dining room or under an ivy-roofed front porch (€11 3-course *menu*, daily 11:30–14:30 & 17:30–22:30, closed Tue Oct–mid-June, Bierjodlgasse 6, tel. 0662/845-641).

Restaurant Yuen affords a break from the wurst, with good Chinese food and friendly service (€7 buffet until 15:00, €8 buffet 18:00–21:00, open daily, indoors or on quiet courtyard at Getreidegasse 24, tel. 0662/843-770).

Bar Club Café Republic, a hip hangout for local young people near the end of Getreidegasse, serves good food with indoor and outdoor seating. It's ideal if you want something mod, untouristy, and un-wursty (trendy breakfasts 8:00–18:00, Asian and international menu, €5–9 plates, lots of hard drinks, daily until late, music with a DJ Fri and Sat from 23:00, Anton Neumayr Platz 2, tel. 0662/841-613).

Gasthaus Stadtalm, the local mountaineers' hut, sits high above the old town on the edge of the cliff with cheap prices, good food, and great views. If hiking across Mönchsberg, make this your goal (traditional food, salads, cliffside garden seating or cozy-mountain-hut indoor seating, an indoor view table booked for a decade of New Year's celebrations, 2 min from top of €2.60 round-trip Mönchsberg elevator, Mönchsberg 19-C, tel. & fax 0662/841-729, Peter and Roland).

Eating Cheaply in the Old Town

Toskana Cafeteria Mensa is the students' lunch place, fast and cheap—with indoor seating and a great courtyard for sitting outside with students and teachers instead of tourists. They serve a daily soup-and-main course special for €3.50 (Mon–Fri 9:00–15:30, hot meals served 11:00–13:30 only, closed Sat–Sun, behind the Residenz, in the courtyard opposite Sigmund-Haffnergasse 16).

Sausage stands serve the local fast food. The best places (like those on Universitätsplatz) use the same boiling water all day, which gives the weenies more flavor. Key words: *Weisswurst*—boiled white sausage, *Bosna*—with onions and curry, *Käsekrainer*—with melted cheese inside, *Debreziner*—spicy Hungarian, *Frankfurter*—our weenie, *frische*—fresh ("eat before the noon bells"), and *Senf*—mustard (ask for sweet—*süss* or sharp—*scharf*). Only a tourist puts the sausage in a bun like a hot dog. Munch alternately between the meat and the bread (that's why you have 2 hands), and you'll look like a local. Generally, the darker the weenie, the spicier it is. The locals' favorite spicy sausage is sold at the 55-year-old **Bosna Stand,** run by chatty Frau Ebner (€2.50, to go only, Mon–Fri 11:00–19:00, closed Sat–Sun, May–Dec also Sat 11:00–17:00, July–Dec also Sun 16:00–20:00, hiding down the tunnel marked #33 across from Getreidegasse 40).

Picnickers will appreciate the bustling morning **produce market** (daily except Sun) on Universitätsplatz, behind Mozart's house (see page 516).

Away from the Center

Augustiner Bräustübl, a monk-run brewery, is rustic and crude. It's closed for lunch, but on busy nights, it's like a Munich beer hall with no music but the volume turned up. When it's cool, you'll enjoy a historic setting with beer-sloshed and smoke-stained halls. On balmy evenings, it's a Monet painting with beer breath under chestnut trees in the garden. Local students mix with tourists eating hearty slabs of schnitzel with their fingers or cold meals from the self-serve picnic counter, while children frolic on the playground kegs. For your beer: Pick up a half-liter or full-liter mug (*schank* means self-serve price, *bedienung* is the price with waiter service), pay the lady, wash your mug, give Mr. Keg your receipt and empty mug, and you will be made happy. Waiters don't bring food—instead, go up the stairs, survey the hallway of deli counters, and assemble your own meal (or, as long as you buy a drink, you can bring in a picnic). For dessert—after a visit to the strudel kiosk—enjoy the incomparable floodlit view of old Salzburg from the nearby Müllnersteg pedestrian bridge and a riverside stroll home (open daily 15:00–23:00; about a 15-min walk along the river—with the river on your right—from the Staatsbrücke bridge, head up Müllner Hauptstrasse northwest along the river and ask for "Müllnerbräu," its local nickname; Augustinergasse 4, tel. 0662/431-246). Don't be fooled by second-rate gardens serving the same beer nearby. Augustiner Bräustübl is a huge, 1,000-seat place within the Augustiner brewery.

On or near Linzergasse

These cheaper places are near the recommended hotels on Linzergasse.

Frauenberger is a friendly, picnic-ready, and inexpensive deli, with indoor or outdoor seating. They'll make a sandwich to your specs, serve fancy breakfast until 18:00, and offer lots of delicious eat-in options (soups and wurst-€3–5, main course-€6–15, daily 8:00–24:00, across from Linzergasse 11, tel. 0662/874-413).

Spicy Spices is a trippy vegetarian-Indian restaurant where Suresh Syad serves tasty curry and rice take-out, samosas, organic salads, vegan soups, and fresh juices (€5 lunch specials, Mon–Sat 10:00–22:00, Sun 12:00–21:00, Wolf-Dietrich Strasse 1, tel. 0662/870-712).

Biergarten Weisse, close to the hotels on Rupertgasse and away from the tourists, is a long-time hit with locals (Mon–Sat 10:30–2:00, closed Sat–Sun, on Rupertgasse east of Bayerhamerstrasse, tel. 0662/872-246).

Café Bazar, overlooking the river between Mirabell Gardens and the Staatsbrücke bridge, is a great place for a classy drink with an old-town and castle view (Mon–Sat 7:30–23:00, closed Sun, Schwarzstrasse 3, tel. 0662/874-278).

Steingasse Pub Crawl

For a fun post-concert activity, crawl through medieval Steingasse's trendy pubs, open until the wee hours. This is a young and very hip scene: dark bars filled with well-dressed twentysomethings lazily smoking cigarettes and talking philosophy, with avant-garde Euro-pop throbbing on the soundtrack. Most of the pubs are in cellar-like caves...extremely atmospheric. (For more on Steingasse, see page 519.)

At the Linzergasse end of Steingasse are a couple of places that serve food and are lively earlier in the evening. **Pepe Gonzales,** with Mexican decor, serves tapas *con* cocktails (nightly 18:30–3:00 in the morning, Steingasse 3, tel. 0662/873-662). Next door, **Shrimps** is the least claustrophobic of these places, with international cuisine (spicy shrimp sandwiches and salads, nightly 17:00–1:00 in the morning, Steingasse 5, tel. 0662/874-484).

A block farther down Steingasse, the scene doesn't get rolling until later. **Saiten Sprung** wins the "Best Atmosphere" award (nightly 21:00–4:00 in the morning, Steingasse 13, tel. 0662/881-377). If the door's closed, ring the bell and enter its hellish interior—lots of stone and red decor, with mountains of melted wax beneath age-old candlesticks. Next door, the tiny **Fridrich,** with lots of mirrors and a silver ceiling fan, specializes in wine (€5–12 small entrées, nightly from 17:00, Steingasse 15, tel. 0662/876-218).

After you close down these four places, consider the next street down—the riverside Giselakai, also lined with trendy pubs.

TRANSPORTATION CONNECTIONS

By train, Salzburg is the first stop over the German–Austrian border. This means that if Salzburg is your only stop in Austria, and you're using a Eurail Selectpass that does not include Austria, you don't have to pay extra or add Austria to your pass to get here.

From Salzburg by Train to: Innsbruck (direct every 2 hrs, 2 hrs), **Vienna** (hrly, 3 hrs), **Hallstatt** (every 2 hrs, 50 min to Attnang Puchheim, 20-min wait, then 90 min to Hallstatt), **Reutte** (every 2 hrs, 4 hrs, transfer to a bus in Innsbruck), **Munich** (hrly, 2 hrs).

Train info: tel. 051-717 (to get an operator, dial 2, then 1).

By Car: To leave town driving west, go through the Mönchsberg tunnel and follow blue A1 signs to Munich. It's 90 minutes from Salzburg to Innsbruck.

Route Tips for Drivers

Into Salzburg from Munich (or the Autobahn): After crossing the border, stay on the autobahn, taking the Süd Salzburg exit in the direction of Anif. First, you'll pass Schloss Hellbrunn (and zoo), then the Salzburg Süd TI and a great park-and-ride service. Get sightseeing information and a €3.40 transit day pass *(Tageskarte)* from the TI (usually open Mon–Sat 10:00–18:00, opens at 9:00 July–Aug, closed Mon–Tue in May, closed Mon in June, and always closed Sun, Nov, and Jan–March, tel. 0662/8898-7360). Park your car (free) and catch the shuttle bus into town (€1.80, or included in day pass, every 5 min, bus #3, #7, or #8). Mozart never drove in the old town, and neither should you. If you don't believe in park-and-rides, the easiest, cheapest, most central parking lot is the 1,500-car Altstadt lot in the tunnel under the Mönchsberg (€14/day; note your slot number and which of the twin lots you're in, tel. 0662/846-434). Your hotel may provide discounted parking passes.

From Salzburg to Hallstatt (50 miles): Get on the Munich–Wien autobahn (blue signs), head for Vienna, exit at Thalgau, and follow signs to Hof, Fuschl, and St. Gilgen. The Salzburg-to-Hallstatt road passes two luge rides (see Hallstatt chapter), St. Gilgen (pleasant but touristy), and Bad Ischl (the center of the Salzkammergut with a spa, the emperor's villa if you need a Hapsburg history fix, and a good TI—Mon–Fri 8:00–18:00, Sat 9:00–15:00, Sun 9:00–12:00, tel. 06132/277-570).

Hallstatt is basically traffic-free. To park, try parking lot #1 in the tunnel above the town (free with guest card). Otherwise, try the lakeside lots (a pleasant 10- to 20-min walk from the town center) after the tunnel on the far side of town. If you're traveling off-season and staying downtown, you can drive in and park by the boat dock. (For more on parking in Hallstatt, see the next chapter.)

HALSTATT
and the SALZKAMMERGUT

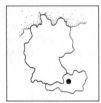

Commune with nature in Austria's lake district, the Salzkammergut. "The hills are alive," and you're surrounded by the loveliness that has turned on everyone from Emperor Franz Josef to Julie Andrews. This is *Sound of Music* country. Idyllic and majestic, but not rugged, it's a gentle land of lakes, forested mountains, and storybook villages, rich in hiking opportunities and inexpensive lodging. Settle down in the postcard-pretty, lake-cuddling town of Hallstatt.

Planning Your Time

While there are plenty of lakes and charming villages, Hallstatt is really the only one that matters. One night and a few hours to browse are all you'll need to fall in love. To relax or take a hike in the surroundings, give it two nights and a day. It's a relaxing break between Salzburg and Vienna. My best Austrian week: the two big cities (Salzburg and Vienna), a bike ride along the Danube, and a stay in Hallstatt.

ORIENTATION

(area code: 06134)
Lovable Hallstatt is a tiny town bullied onto a ledge between a selfish mountain and a swan-ruled lake, with a waterfall ripping furiously through its middle. It can be toured on foot in about 15 minutes. The town is one of Europe's oldest, going back centuries before Christ. The symbol of Hallstatt, which you'll see all over town, is two adjacent spirals—a design based on jewelry found in Bronze Age Celtic graves high in the nearby mountains.

Hallstatt

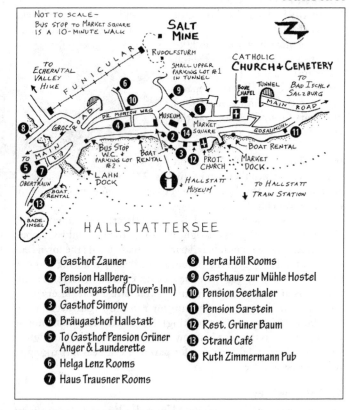

① Gasthof Zauner

② Pension Hallberg-Tauchergasthof (Diver's Inn)

③ Gasthof Simony

④ Bräugasthof Hallstatt

⑤ To Gasthof Pension Grüner Anger & Launderette

⑥ Helga Lenz Rooms

⑦ Haus Trausner Rooms

⑧ Herta Höll Rooms

⑨ Gasthaus zur Mühle Hostel

⑩ Pension Seethaler

⑪ Pension Sarstein

⑫ Rest. Grüner Baum

⑬ Strand Café

⑭ Ruth Zimmermann Pub

The charms of Hallstatt are the village and its lakeside setting. Go there to relax, nibble, wander, and paddle. While tourist crowds can trample much of Hallstatt's charm in August, the place is almost dead in the off-season. The lake is famous for its good fishing and pure water.

Tourist Information

The friendly and helpful TI, on the main drag, can explain hikes and excursions, arrange private tours of Hallstatt (€65), and find you a room (April–Oct Mon–Fri 9:00–17:00; in July–Aug also Sat 10:00–16:00, closed Sun; Nov–March Mon–Fri 9:00–13:00, closed Sat–Sun; a block from Marktplatz toward lakefront parking, above post office, Seestrasse 169, tel. 06134/8208, www.inneres-salzkammergut.at, hallstatt@inneres-salzkammergut.at).

The TI offers a €5 walking tour of the town in English at 10:00 on Wednesdays and Saturdays in July and August (confirm schedule at TI).

Arrival in Hallstatt

By Train: Hallstatt's train station is a wide spot on the tracks across the lake. *Stefanie* (a boat) meets you at the station and glides scenically across the lake

into town (€1.90, meets each train until about 18:30—don't arrive after that). The last depart-ing boat-train connection leaves Hallstatt around 18:00, and the first boat goes in the morning at 6:50 (9:20 on Sun). Walk left from the boat dock for the TI and most hotels. Since there's no train station in town, the TI can help you find schedule information, or check www.oebb.at.

By Car: The main road skirts Hallstatt via a long tunnel above the town. Parking is tight mid-June through mid-October. Hallstatt has several numbered parking areas outside the town cen-ter. Parking lot #1 is in the tunnel above the town (swing through to check for a spot, free with guest card). Otherwise, several num-bered lots are just after the tunnel. If you have a hotel reservation, the guard will let you drive into town to drop your bags (ask if your hotel has any in-town parking). It's a lovely 10- to 20-minute lakeside walk to the center of town from the lots. Without a guest card, you'll pay €4.20 per day for parking. Off-season parking in town is easy and free.

Helpful Hints

Internet Access: Try **Hallstatt Umbrella Bar** (€4/hr, summers only, weather permitting—since it's literally under a big umbrella, halfway between Lahn boat dock and Museum Square at Seestrasse 145).

Laundry: A small full-service **launderette** is at the campground up from the town's man-made island, Bade-Insel, just off the main road (about €8/load, mid-April–mid-Oct daily 7:00–12:00 & 15:00–22:00, closed off-season, tel. 06134/83224). In the center, **Hotel Grüner Baum** does laundry for non-guests (€11/load, facing Market Square).

Bike Rental: Hotel Grüner Baum rents bikes (€9/half-day, €16/day).

Parks and Swimming: Green and peaceful lakeside parks line the south end of Lake Hallstatt. If you walk 10 minutes south of town to Hallstatt-Lahn, you'll find a grassy public park, playground, and swimming area *(Badestrand)* with the fun Bade-Insel play-island.

Views: For a great view over Hallstatt, hike above Helga Lenz's *Zimmer* as far as you like (see page 553), or climb any path leading up the hill. The 40-minute steep hike down from the salt-mine tour gives the best views (see page 548).

SELF-GUIDED WALK

Welcome to Hallstatt

This short walk starts at the dock.

Boat Landing: There was a Hallstatt before there was a Rome. In fact, because of the importance of salt mining here, an entire epoch—the Hallstatt era, from 800 to 400 B.C.—is named for this important spot. Through the centuries, salt was traded and people came and went by boat. You'll still see the traditional *Fuhr* boats, designed to carry heavy loads in shallow water.

Towering above the town is the Catholic church. Its faded St. Christopher—patron saint of travelers with his cane and baby Jesus on his shoulder—watched over those sailing in and out. Until 1875, the only way into town was by boat. Then came the train and the road. The good ship *Stefanie* shuttles travelers back and forth from here to the Hallstatt train station immediately across the lake. The *Bootverleih* sign advertises boat rentals (see "Lake Trip," below).

Notice the one-lane road out of town (with the waiting time, width, and height posted). Until 1966, when a bigger tunnel was built above Hallstatt, all the traffic crept single file right through the town.

Look down the shore at the huge homes. Several families lived in each of these houses back when Hallstatt's population was about double its present 1,000; today, many of them rent rooms to visitors.

Parking is tight here in the tourist season. Locals and hotels have cards getting them into the prime town-center lot. From October through May, the barricade is lifted and anyone can park here. Hallstatt is snowbound for about three months each winter, but the lake hasn't frozen over since 1981.

See any swans? They've patrolled the lake like they own it since the 1860s, when Emperor Franz Josef and Empress Sissy—the Princess Diana of her day—made this region their annual holiday retreat. Sissy loved swans, so locals made sure she'd see them here. During this period, the Romantics discovered Hallstatt, many top painters worked here, and the town got its first hotel.

Tiny Hallstatt has two big churches—Protestant (with a grassy lakeside playground) and Catholic up above (described below, with its fascinating bone chapel). After the Reformation, most of Hallstatt was Protestant. Then, under Hapsburg rule, it was mostly Catholic. Today, 60 percent of the town is Catholic.

• *Walk over the town's stream, past the Protestant church, one block to the...*

Market Square: In 1750, a fire leveled this part of town. The buildings you see now are all late-18th-century and built of stone rather than flammable wood. Take a close look at the two-dimensional, up-against-the-wall pear tree (it likes the sun-warmed wall). The statue features the Holy Trinity.

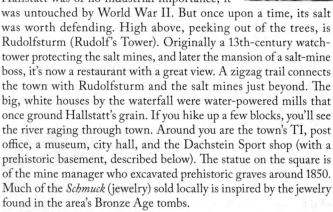

• *Continue a block past Gasthof Simony to the pair of phone booths and step into the...*

Museum Square: Because 20th-century Hallstatt was of no industrial importance, it was untouched by World War II. But once upon a time, its salt was worth defending. High above, peeking out of the trees, is Rudolfsturm (Rudolf's Tower). Originally a 13th-century watchtower protecting the salt mines, and later the mansion of a salt-mine boss, it's now a restaurant with a great view. A zigzag trail connects the town with Rudolfsturm and the salt mines just beyond. The big, white houses by the waterfall were water-powered mills that once ground Hallstatt's grain. If you hike up a few blocks, you'll see the river raging through town. Around you are the town's TI, post office, a museum, city hall, and the Dachstein Sport shop (with a prehistoric basement, described below). The statue on the square is of the mine manager who excavated prehistoric graves around 1850. Much of the *Schmuck* (jewelry) sold locally is inspired by the jewelry found in the area's Bronze Age tombs.

For thousands of years, people have been leaching salt out of this mountain. A brine spring sprung here, attracting Bronze Age people around 1500 B.C. Later, they dug tunnels to mine the rock, which was 70 percent salt, dissolved it into a brine, and distilled out salt—precious for preserving meat (and making french fries so tasty). For a look at early salt-mining implements, visit the museum.

SIGHTS AND ACTIVITIES

▲▲**Hallstatt's Catholic Church and Bone Chapel**—The Catholic church overlooks the town from above. From near the boat dock, hike up the covered wooden stairway and follow the *Kath. Kirche* signs. The lovely church has 500-year-old altars and frescoes dedicated to St. Barbara (patron of miners) and St. Catherine (patron of foresters—lots of wood was needed to fortify the many miles of tunnels and boil the brine to distill out the salt). The last priest modernized parts of the church, but since Hallstatt is a UNESCO World Heritage Site, now they're changing it all back to its original state.

Behind the church, in the well-tended graveyard, is the 12th-century **Chapel of St. Michael** (even older than the church). Its bone chapel—or charnel house *(Beinhaus)*—contains more than 600 painted skulls. Each skull has been lovingly named, dated,

and decorated (skulls with dark, thick garlands are oldest—18th century; those with flowers more recent—19th century). Space was so limited in this cemetery that bones had only 12 peaceful, buried years here before making way for the freshly dead. Many of the dug-up bones and skulls ended up in this chapel. They stopped this practice in the 1960s, about the same time the Catholic Church began permitting cremation (€1, daily July–Aug 10:00–18:00, Easter–mid-May 11:00–16:00, mid-May–June and Sept 10:00–16:00, Oct 10:00–17:00—weather permitting, closed Nov–Easter).

▲**World Heritage Hallstatt Museum**—This newly redone museum tells the story of Hallstatt—with a special focus on the Hallstatt period (800–400 B.C.), when this little village was the crucial salt-mining hub of a culture that spread from France to the Balkans. Back then, Celtic tribes dug for precious salt, and Hallstatt was, as its name means, the "place of salt."

First, you'll watch a video that takes you back in time 7,000 years. Then you'll walk through exhibits tracing the town's evolution to the present day. This fun museum—though pricey—is well organized into meaningful, bite-sized chunks. There are displays on everything from the region's flora and fauna to local artists and the surge in Hallstatt tourism during the Romantic age—and lots and lots of salt-mining artifacts. Everything's in German, but the €2 English guide explains most of it (€7, May–Sept 10:00–18:00, Oct–April Tue–Sun 11:00–15:00, always closed Mon, Seestrasse 56, adjacent to TI, tel. 06134/828-015). The **Dachstein Sport shop** across from the TI dug into a prehistoric site, and now its basement is another small museum (free).

▲**Lake Trip**—For a quick boat trip, you can ride the *Stefanie* across the lake and back for €3.80. It stops at the tiny Hallstatt train station for 30 minutes, giving you time to walk to a hanging bridge and enjoy the peaceful, deep part of the lake. Longer lake tours are also available (€7/50 min, €8.50/90 min, www.hallstatt.net /schiffahrt, sporadic schedules—especially off-season—so check chalkboards by boat docks for today's times). Those into relaxation can rent a sleepy electric motorboat to enjoy town views from the water. There are two rental places: **Riedler,** next to ferry dock or across from Bräugasthof (tel. 06134/8320), or **Hemetsberger,** near Gasthof Simony or past bridge before Bade-Insel (tel. 06134/8228). Both are open daily until 19:00 in-season and in good weather. Boats have two speeds: slow and stop (€11/hr, spend an extra €3/hr for faster 500-watt boats).

▲▲**Salt Mine Tour**—If you have yet to pay a visit to a salt mine, Hallstatt's—which claims to be the oldest in the world—is a good one. You'll ride a steep funicular high above the town (funicular-€8.50 round-trip, €5.10 one-way, daily May–mid-Sept 9:00–18:00, mid-Sept–Oct until 16:30, closed Nov–April), take a 10-minute hike, check your bag and put on old miners' clothes, hike 650 feet higher in your funny outfit to meet your guide, load onto the train, and ride into the mountain through a tunnel actually made by prehistoric miners. Inside, you'll watch a great video (English headsets), slide down two banisters, and follow your guide. While the tour is mostly in German, the guide is required to speak English if you ask—so ask (salt mine tour-€15.50, €21 combo-ticket includes entrance and round-trip funicular, you can buy mine tickets at cable-car station, daily May–mid-Sept 9:30–16:30, mid-Sept–Oct 9:30–15:00, closed Nov–April, the 16:00 funicular departure catches the last tour at 16:30, no children under age 4, rarely a long wait but arrive after 15:00 and you'll find no lines and a smaller group, tel. 06132/200-2400). The well-publicized ancient Celtic graveyard excavation sites nearby are really dead (precious little to see). If you skip the funicular, the scenic 40-minute hike back into town is (with strong knees) a joy.

At the base of the funicular, notice train tracks leading to the Erbstollen tunnel entrance. This lowest of the salt tunnels goes many miles into the mountain, where a shaft connects it to the tunnels you just explored. Today, the salty brine from these tunnels flows 25 miles through the world's oldest pipeline to the huge modern salt works (next to the highway) at Ebensee. You'll pass a stack of the original 120-year-old wooden pipes between the lift and the mine.

▲**Local Hikes**—Mountain-lovers, hikers, and spelunkers who use Hallstatt as their home base keep busy for days (ask the TI for ideas). Local hikes are well described in the TI's *Dachstein Hiking Guide* (€5.80, in English). A good, short, and easy walk is the two-hour round-trip up the Echerntal Valley to the Waldbachstrub waterfall and back. From the parking lot, follow signs to the salt mines, then follow the little wooden signs marked *Echerntalweg*. With a car, consider hiking around nearby Altaussee (flat, 3-hr hike) or along Grundlsee to Tolpitzsee. Regular buses connect Hallstatt with Gosausee for a pleasant hour-long walk around that lake. The TI can recommend a great two-day hike with an overnight in a nearby mountain hut.

Near Hallstatt

▲▲**Dachstein Mountain Cable Car and Caves**—For a refreshing activity, ride a scenic cable car up a mountain to visit huge, chilly caves.

Dachstein Cable Car: From Obertraun, three miles beyond Hallstatt on the main road (or right across the lake as the crow flies), a mighty gondola goes in three stages high up the Dachstein Plateau—crowned by Dachstein, the highest mountain in the Salzkammergut (over 9,000 feet). The first segment stops at Schönbergalm (4,500 feet, runs May–Oct), which has a mountain restaurant and two huge caves (described below). The second segment goes to the summit of Krippenstein (6,600 feet, runs mid-May–Oct). The third segment descends to Gjaidalm (5,800 feet, runs mid-June–Oct), where several hikes begin. For a quick high-country experience, Krippenstein is better than Gjaidalm. From Krippenstein, you'll survey a scrubby, limestone, karst landscape (which absorbs rainfall through its many cracks and ultimately carves all those caves) with 360-degree views of the surrounding mountains (round-trip cable-car ride to the caves-€14, to Krippenstein-€19.50, to Gjaidalm-€21, cheaper family rates available, last cable car back down usually around 17:00, tel. 06134/8400, www.dachstein.at).

Giant Ice Caves (Riesen-Eishöhle, 4,500 feet): These were discovered in 1910. Today, guides lead tours in German and English on an hour-long, half-mile hike through an eerie, icy, subterranean world, passing limestone canyons the size of subway stations. The limestone caverns, carved by rushing water, are named for scenes from Wagner operas—the favorite of the mountaineers who first came here. If you're nervous, note that the iron oxide covering the ceiling takes 5,000 years to form. Things are very stable.

At the lift station, report to the ticket window to get your cave appointment. While the temperature is just above freezing and the 600 steps help keep you warm, bring a sweater. Allow 90 minutes,

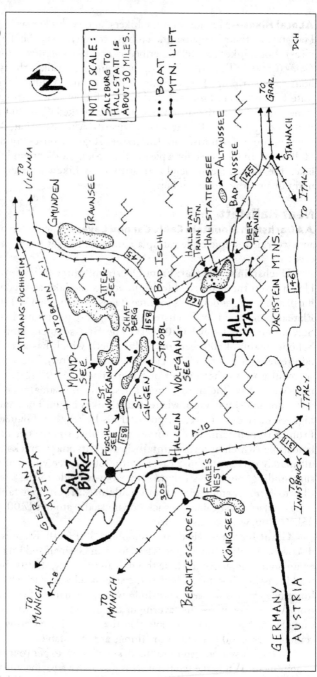

Salzkammergut

including the 10-minute hike from the station (€8.50, or €13.10 combo-ticket with Mammoth Caves—see below, open May–Oct, hour-long tours 9:00–16:00, stay in front and assert yourself for English information, tel. 06134/8400).

Drop by the little free museum near the lift station—in a local-style wood cabin designed to support 200 tons of snow—to see the cave-system model, exhibits about its exploration, and info about life in the caves.

Mammoth Caves (Mammuthöhle): While huge and well-promoted, these are much less interesting than the ice caves and—for most—not worth the time. Of the 30-mile limestone labyrinth excavated so far, you'll walk a half-mile with a German-speaking guide (€8.50, or €13.10 combo-ticket with ice caves, open mid-May–Oct, hour-long tours 10:00–15:00, call a few days before to check on the schedule for an English guide, entrance a 10-min hike from lift station).

Getting to Obertraun: The cable car to Dachstein leaves from Obertraun, right across the lake from Hallstatt. From Hallstatt, the handiest option is the bus (5/day June–Oct, 4/day off-season). Romantics can take the boat (€4, 5/day July–Aug, less off-season, 15 min)—but it's a longer hike to the lift station. The adventurous or impatient can consider hitching a ride—virtually all cars leaving Hallstatt to the south will pass through Obertraun in a few minutes.

Luge Rides on the Hallstatt–Salzburg Road—If you're driving between Salzburg and Hallstatt, you'll pass two luge rides. Each is a ski lift that drags you backward up the hill as you sit on your go-cart. At the top, you ride the cart down the winding metal course. It's easy: Push to go, pull to stop, take your hands off your stick and you get hurt. For more details, see "Luge Lesson" on page 115.

Each course is just off the road with easy parking. The ride up and down takes about 15 minutes. Look for *Riesen-Rutschbahn* or *Sommerrodelbahn* signs. The one near Fuschlsee (closest to Salzburg) is half as long and cheaper (€3.50/ride, 1,970 feet, tel. 06235/7297). The one near Wolfgangsee is a double course, more scenic with grand lake views (€5.50/ride, €36/10 rides, 4,265 feet, each track is the same speed, tel. 06137/7085). Courses are open Easter through October from 10:00 to 18:00 (July–Aug 9:30–19:00)—but will close in bad weather. These are fun, but the concrete courses near Reutte are better (see page 115).

SLEEPING

Hallstatt's TI can almost always find you a room (either in town or at B&Bs and small hotels outside of town—which are more likely to have rooms available and come with easy parking). Mid-July

Sleep Code

(€1 = about $1.20, country code: 43, area code: 06134)
S = Single, **D** = Double/Twin, **T** = Triple, **Q** = Quad, **b** = bathroom,
s = shower only. Unless otherwise noted, credit cards are accepted, English is spoken, and breakfast is included.

To help you sort easily through these listings, I've divided the rooms into three categories, based on the price for a standard double room with bath:

$$$ **Higher Priced**—Most rooms €80 or more.
$$ **Moderately Priced**—Most rooms between €50–80.
$ **Lower Priced**—Most rooms €50 or less.

and August can be tight. Early August is worst. Hallstatt is not the place to splurge—some of the best rooms are in *Zimmer,* just as nice and modern as the bigger hotels, at half the cost. A bed in a private home costs about €20 with breakfast. It's hard to get a one-night advance reservation. But if you drop in and they have a spot, one-nighters are welcome. Prices include breakfast, lots of stairs, and a silent night. *"Zimmer mit Aussicht?"* means "Room with view?"—worth asking for. Unlike many businesses in town, the cheaper places don't take credit cards.

$$$ Gasthof Zauner is run by a friendly mountaineer, Herr Zauner, whose family has owned it since 1914. The 12 pricey, pine-flavored rooms on the main square are decorated with sturdy alpine-inspired furniture. Lederhosen-clad Herr Zauner recounts tales of local mountaineering lore, including his own impressive ascents (Sb-€48–55, Db-€88–102, prices depend on season and view, closed mid-Nov–mid-Dec, Marktplatz 51, tel. 06134/8246, fax 06134/82468, www.zauner.hallstatt.net, zauner@hallstatt.at).

$$$ Pension Hallberg-Tauchergasthof (Diver's Inn), across from the TI, has five big rooms and a funky mini-museum of WWII artifacts found in the lake (Sb-€50–90, Db-€70–120, rooms for up to 5 also available, price depends on size, €20 less off season, cash preferred, tel. 06134/8709, fax 06134/20621, www.pension-hallberg.at.tf, hallberg@aon.at, Gerda the "Salt Witch" and Eckbert Winkelmann).

$$$ Gasthof Simony, my 500-year-old favorite, is on the square, with a lake view, balconies, creaky wood floors, slippery rag rugs, antique furniture, a lakefront garden for swimming, and a huge breakfast. Reserve in advance, ideally by phone or fax. For safety, reconfirm your room and price a day or two before you arrive and call again if arriving late (S-€38, D-€55, Ds-€65, Db-€80–85, third person-€30 extra, cash only, Markt 105, tel. & fax

06134/8231, www.hallstatt.net/gasthof/simony, Susanna Scheutz).

$$$ Bräugasthof Hallstatt is another creaky, friendly old place, a former brewery with eight clean, cozy, mostly lakeview rooms run by Susanna's sister and her family (Sb-€46, Db-€84, Tb-€120, just past TI on the main drag at Seestrasse 120, tel. 06134/8221, fax 06134/82214, www.brauhaus-lobisser.com, info@brauhaus-lobisser.com, Lobisser family).

$$ Gasthof Pension Grüner Anger is practical and modern, away from the medieval town center—the only hotel in town that doesn't squeak and creak. It's big and quiet, with 11 rooms, a few blocks from the base of the salt-mine lift, and a 15-minute walk from Market Square (Sb-€36, Db-€63, €3 more per room July–Aug, €3 more for 1-night stays July–Aug, third person-€15, non-smoking, Internet access, free parking, Lahn 10, tel. 06134/8397, fax 06134/83974, www.anger.hallstatt.net, anger@aon .at, Sulzbacher family).

$$ Pension Sarstein has 20 beds in basic, dusty, ancient-feeling rooms with flower-bedecked, lakeview balconies, in a charming building run by friendly Isabelle Fischer. You can swim from her lakeside garden (S-€18, D-€44, Ds-€50, Db-€56 with this book in 2006, Ds and Db have balconies, 1-night stays-€2 per person extra, cash only, non-smoking, leave the boat dock to the right and walk 200 yards to Gosaumühlstrasse 83, tel. 06134/8217, fax 06134/20635, www.pension-sarstein.at.tf, pension.sarstein @aon.at).

$ Helga Lenz's Zimmer is a steep five-minute climb above the Pension Seethaler (look for the green *Zimmer* sign). This large, sprawling, woodsy house has a nifty garden perch, wins the "Best View" award, and is ideal for those who sleep well in tree houses and don't mind the ascent from town (S-€18—only available April–June and Oct, D-€34, Db-€40, T-€45, Tb-€54, 1-night stays-€1 per person extra, family room, cash only, closed Nov–March, Hallberg 17, tel. & fax 06134/8508, www.hallstatt .net/privatzimmer/helga.lenz, haus-lenz@aon.at).

$ Two **Zimmer** are a few minutes' stroll south of the center, just past the bus stop/parking lot and over the bridge: **Haus Trausner** has four clean, bright, new-feeling rooms (Ds-€36, Db-€38, less for more than 1 night, cash only, Lahnstrasse 27, tel. 06134/8710, trausner1@utanet.at, Maria Trausner), while **Herta Höll** rents out three rooms in a riverside house crawling with kids (Db-€44, apartment-€60, cash only, Malerweg 45, tel. 06134/8531, fax 06134/825-533, frank.hoell@aon.at).

$ Gasthaus zur Mühle Jugendherberge, below the waterfall, has 46 of the cheapest good beds in town. It's popular for its great, inexpensive pizza (bed in 3- to 14-bed coed dorms-€11, D-€24, sheets-€3 extra, family quads, breakfast-€3, big lockers with a €15 deposit, closed Nov, reception closed Tue Sept–mid-May—so arrange in advance if arriving on Tue, below tunnel car park, Kirchenweg 36, tel. & fax 06134/8318, toeroe.f@magnet.at, Ferdinand Törö).

$ Pension Seethaler is a dark, homey old lodge with 45 beds and a breakfast room mossy with antlers, perched above the lake. The confusing floor plan is like an M. C. Escher house with fire hazards, and the staff won't win any awards for congeniality—*Zimmer* are friendlier and cheaper—but this place is a reasonable last resort (€20/person in S, D, T, or Q, €28/person in Db, Tb, or Qb, cash only, coin-op showers downstairs-€1/8 min, closed Nov, Dr. Morton Weg 22, find the stairs to the left of Seestrasse 116, at top of stairs turn left, tel. 06134/8421, pension-seethaler@aon.at).

EATING

You can enjoy good food inexpensively, with delightful lakeside settings. While everyone cooks the typical Austrian fare, your best bet here is trout. *Reinanke* trout is from Lake Hallstatt. Restaurants in Hallstatt tend to have unreliable hours and close early on slow nights, so don't wait too long to get dinner.

At **Restaurant Bräugasthof,** you can feed the swans while your trout is being cooked (fun menu and tasty food, May–Oct daily 10:00–21:00, closed Nov–April, cash only, tel. 06134/20012, also see listing on page 553). **Hotel Grüner Baum** is another lakefront option (daily May–Oct 11:30–22:00, closed Nov–April, at bottom of Market Square, tel. 06134/8263).

Gasthof Zauner's classy restaurant lacks a lakeside setting, but it's well-respected for its grilled meat and fish; the interior of its dining room is covered in real ivy that grows in through the windows (daily 11:30–14:30 & 17:30–22:00, closed Nov–mid Dec, reservations smart, also see page 552).

Gasthaus zur Mühle has the best pizza in town with a fun-loving local crowd. Chow down cheap and hearty here (daily 11:00–14:00 & 17:00–21:00, closed Tue and no lunch mid-Oct–mid-May, see "Sleeping" above).

Strand Café, a smoky local favorite, is a 10-minute lakeside hike away, near the town beach, or Bade-Insel (April–Oct Tue–Sun 10:00–21:00, closed Mon and Nov–March, great garden setting on the lake, Seelande 102, tel. 06134/8234).

For your late-night drink, savor Market Square from the trendy little pub called **Ruth Zimmermann** (daily June–Oct 9:00–2:00, Nov–May 12:00–2:00, tel. 06134/8306).

TRANSPORTATION CONNECTIONS

For tips for drivers coming here from Salzburg, see the end of the Salzburg chapter.

From Hallstatt by Train to: Salzburg (every 2 hrs, 90 min to Attnang Puchheim, short wait, 50 min to Salzburg), **Vienna** (hrly, 90 min to Attnang Puchheim, short wait, 2.5 hrs to Vienna). Day-trippers to Hallstatt can check bags at the Attnang Puchheim station. (Note: Connections there and back can be very fast—about 5 min; have coins ready for the lockers at track 1.) Train info: tel. 051-717 (to get an operator, dial 2, then 1).

INNSBRUCK AND HALL

Austria's Tirol region—in the country's pan-handle, south of Bavaria—is a winter sports mecca known for its mountainous panoramas. In the region's capital, Innsbruck, the Golden Roof glitters—but you'll strike it rich in neighboring Hall, which has twice the charm and none of the tourist crowds.

Innsbruck

Innsbruck is world-famous as a resort for skiers and a haven for hikers...but when compared to Salzburg and Vienna, it's stale strudel. Still, a quick look is easy and interesting. Innsbruck was the Hapsburgs' capital of the Tirol, and its medieval center—now a glitzy, tourist-filled pedestrian zone—still gives you the feel of a provincial medieval capital. The much-ogled Golden Roof (Goldenes Dach) is the centerpiece.

ORIENTATION

(area code: 0512)

Tourist Information

Innsbruck has two TIs: **downtown** (daily 9:00–18:00, Burggraben 3, 3 blocks in front of Golden Roof, tel. 0512/5356, www.innsbruck-tourismus.com) and at the **train station** (daily 9:00–19:00, tel. 0512/583-766). At either one, you can pick up a free city map (the €1 map, with more information on sights, isn't necessary) or book a room (€3 fee and 15 percent deposit).

Innsbruck and Hall

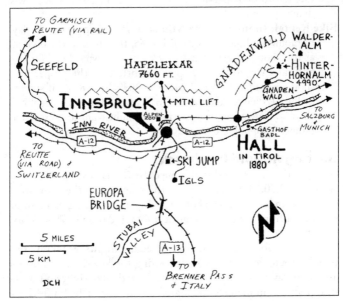

Innsbruck Card: The €23, 24-hour Innsbruck Card pays for itself only if you take the Mountain Lift (also covers Igls Lift, as well as the Sightseer mini-bus, buses, trams, museums, zoo, and palace).

Tours of Innsbruck: The TI offers a basic one-hour city walk of Innsbruck (€8, daily May–Oct at 11:00 and 14:00).

Arrival in Innsbruck

From the main train station (Hauptbahnhof), it's a 10-minute walk to the old-town center. Leave by veering right to Brixnerstrasse. Follow it past the fountain at Boznerplatz where it turns into Meranerstrasse and go straight until it dead-ends into Maria-Theresa Strasse. Turn right and head 300 yards into the old town (you'll pass the TI on Burggraben on your right), where you'll see the Golden Roof and Hotel Weisses Kreuz. The train station has lockers (€2–3.50), a post office (Mon–Sat 7:00–19:30, closed Sun), a supermarket (daily 6:00–21:00), and a *Reisezentrum*, where you can get rail information and tickets (daily 6:00–21:30).

Helpful Hints

Laundry and Internet Access: Bubble Point is a handy self-service launderette with Internet terminals (€6 per load, Mon–Fri 8:00–22:00, Sat–Sun 8:00–20:00, between train station and

Golden Roof at Brixnerstrasse 1, tel. 0512/5650-0750, www
.bubblepoint.com).

Bike Rental: Inntour has everything from city cruisers (€17/day)
to mountain bikes (€33/day). For €5, they'll drop the bike off
at your hotel or, even better, pick you up at your hotel for free
and take you to their shop to get fitted for the proper bike
(hours unreliable, so call Mike at 0699/1012-8730, if staying
at Hotel Weisses Kreuz they will phone for you). Also, call
them for any adventure sports you might want to do (such as
bungee jumping, etc.).

Getting Around Innsbruck

A single ticket for Innsbruck's buses or trams costs €1.60; a day
ticket is €3.50. Buy tickets from the machine at the tram stop,
at the TI, or at a tobacco shop (Tabak); single tickets can also be
purchased from the driver. Transit info: tel. 0512/530-7500, www
.ivb.at.

A made-for-tourists minibus called the **Sightseer** follows two
popular routes around town, connecting the key sights (€2.50 for
any one-way trip, €4 round-trip to a particular sight and back,
headphone commentary in English, May–Oct 2/hr 9:00–17:30,
Nov–April hourly 10:00–17:00). If visiting several outlying sights,
you can buy a day ticket (*Tagesticket*, €8, includes funicular) and
use the Sightseer as a hop-on, hop-off bus. It's pricey—more than
twice the cost of a day pass on public transit—but convenient (for
information and tickets, visit the TI).

SIGHTS AND ACTIVITIES

Innsbruck's Old Town

▲▲**The Golden Roof (Goldenes Dach) and Herzog-
Friedrichstrasse**—The three-block pedestrian street (Herzog-
Friedrichstrasse) in front of the Golden Roof is Innsbruck's
tourism central.

Stand in front of the Roof to get oriented. Emperor
Maximilian I loved Innsbruck, and built a palace here—including the balcony topped with 2,657 gilded copper tiles. The Golden
Roof (1494) offered Maximilian an impressive spot from which to
view his medieval spectacles.

Most buildings along this street are Gothic (notice the entry
arches), but across the street from the Golden Roof (to the left
as you face the Roof) is the frilly Baroque-style **Helblinghaus**
facade. Above you is the bulbous **city tower** *(Stadtturm)*, with
148 steps you can climb for a great view (€2.50, daily June–Sept
10:00–20:00, Oct–May 10:00–17:00, tel. 0512/561-500). This was
the old town watchtower (the prison was on the 2nd floor). Like

Innsbruck

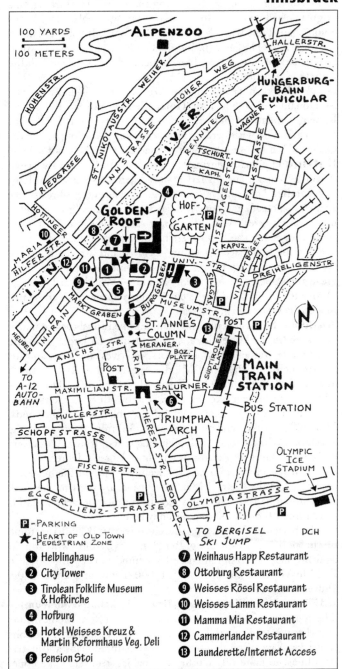

P - PARKING
★ - HEART OF OLD TOWN PEDESTRIAN ZONE

❶ Helblinghaus
❷ City Tower
❸ Tirolean Folklife Museum & Hofkirche
❹ Hofburg
❺ Hotel Weisses Kreuz & Martin Reformhaus Veg. Deli
❻ Pension Stoi

❼ Weinhaus Happ Restaurant
❽ Ottoburg Restaurant
❾ Weisses Rössl Restaurant
❿ Weisses Lamm Restaurant
⓫ Mamma Mia Restaurant
⓬ Cammerlander Restaurant
⓭ Launderette/Internet Access

many Austrian buildings (including the nearby Hofkirche), this originally had a pointy Gothic spire—but was replaced with this onion-shaped one when Baroque was in vogue. If you walk down the shop-lined Hofgasse (facing the Golden Roof, go right), you'll reach the Hofburg palace, Hofkirche, and the Tirolean Folklife Museum (see below).

A block in front of the Golden Roof—next to the McDonald's—is the historic **Hotel Weisses Kreuz**. It's built on Roman foundations, but has only been hosting guests for the last 500 years. The white cross *(weisses Kreuz)* is the symbol of the Order of Malta—knights who opened up guesthouses for Holy Land–bound pilgrims during the Crusades. In 1769, a 13-year-old Amadeus Mozart and his father stayed here on their way to Italy. A generation later, this hotel was one of the centers of resistance against Napoleon, and later still, against the Nazis (giving shelter to Jewish refugees). When the American soldiers moved in from Italy, they made the hotel their headquarters. Today, it's still a functioning hotel (see "Sleeping," below), and it recently hosted Otto von Hapsburg, the Man Who Would Be Emperor, if his great-great-uncle hadn't started—and lost—World War I. Though Otto could have stayed in the fanciest place in town, he chose this historic, comfortable inn instead.

▲▲**Hofkirche**—Emperor Maximilian I liked Innsbruck so much, he wanted to be buried here, surrounded by 28 larger-than-life cast-bronze statues of his ancestors, relatives, in-laws...and his favorite heroes of the dying Middle Ages (such as King Arthur). The good €1 English book tells you who everyone is. Don't miss King Arthur (as you face the altar, he's the 5th from the front on the right, next to the heavy-metal dude) and Mary of Burgundy, Maximilian's first—and favorite—wife (3rd from the front on the left). Some of these sculptures, including that of König Artur, were designed by German Renaissance painter Albrecht Dürer.

That's Maximilian himself, kneeling on top of the huge sarcophagus. Sadly, the real Max isn't inside. By the time he died, Maximilian had become notorious for running up debts, and his men weren't allowed to bring his body here.

Just inside the door to the church, you'll find the tomb of the popular Tirolean soldier Andreas Hofer, who fought against Napoleon (church entry-€3, combo-ticket with Tirolean Folklife Museum-€6.50, Mon–Sat 9:00–17:00, Sun 13:00–17:00, Universitätsstrasse 2).

▲▲**Tirolean Folklife Museum (Tiroler Volkskunst Museum)**— The museum, next door to the Hofkirche, offers the best look anywhere at traditional Tirolean lifestyles. Fascinating exhibits range from wedding dresses and gaily painted cribs and nativity scenes, to maternity clothes and babies' trousers. The upper

Emperor Maximilian I
(1459–1519)

The big name in Innsbruck is Emperor Maximilian I, who made this city a regional capital and built the Golden Roof. This Hapsburg emperor was a dynamic, larger-than-life Renaissance man—soldier, sculptor, and statesman (though not very good at any of these). At the same time, he clung to the last romantic fantasies of the Middle Ages; for example, he was the last Hapsburg who personally led his troops into battle.

Most people associate the Hapsburg Empire with Vienna—which was the capital of the empire's far-flung Eastern European holdings during its peak in the 17th and 18th centuries. But during Maximilian's time, two centuries earlier, the focus was on Italy—he took the "Roman" part of Holy Roman Emperor very seriously. This made Innsbruck very important, since it was the capital of Tirol (which then included much of today's northern Italy, and was on the Italian frontier).

This visionary emperor hoped that once all of Italy was his, Innsbruck would become the permanent capital of his empire. In reality, he was unlucky at war and ran up huge debts. But his strategic marriage to Mary of Burgundy set the stage for the large-scale expansion of the empire. Though he wanted to be a war hero, as with most Hapsburgs, his biggest victory came with a trip to the altar.

floors show Tirolean homes through the ages (€5, combo-ticket with Hofkirche-€6.50, daily Sept–June 10:00–17:00, July–Aug until 17:30, hard to appreciate without the €2 English guidebook, Universitätsstrasse 2, tel. 0512/584-302).

Hofburg—This 18th-century Baroque palace, built by Maria Theresa, is only worth a visit if you aren't going to the much bigger and better palaces in Vienna, Munich, or near Füssen (€5.45, daily 9:00–17:00, last entry 16:30, helpful €1.80 English booklet, €8 includes entry and 1-hr guided tour in English—May–Oct daily at 12:15, plus June–Sept at 15:15, tel. 0512/587-186, www.tirol.com/hofburg-ibk).

Maria-Theresa Strasse—The fine Baroque Maria-Theresa Strasse stretches south from the medieval center. **St. Anne's Column** (Annasäule) marks the middle of the old marketplace. This was erected in the 18th century by townspeople thankful that their army had defeated an invading Bavarian army and saved the town (it's the same idea as the plague columns you see throughout Europe).

At the far end of the street, the **Triumphal Arch** is a gate Maria Theresa built to commemorate a happy and a sad occasion. The happy: Her son Leopold II, archduke of Tuscany, met and married a Spanish princess here in Innsbruck—and Maria Theresa and her husband Franz came for the ceremony. But Franz partied a little too hard, and died the day after the wedding. (Maria Theresa wore black for the rest of her life.) The south-facing side of the arch—what you see as you approach the center—shows the interlocked rings of the happy couple. But the flipside, visible as you leave town, features mournful statuary.

▲**Slap Dancing**—For your Tirolean folk fun, Innsbruck hotels offer an entertaining evening of slap dancing and yodeling nearly nightly at 20:30 from April through October (€20 includes a drink with 2-hour show, tickets at TI). Every summer Thursday, the town puts on a free outdoor folk show under the Golden Roof (July–Sept, weather permitting).

Into the Mountains

▲**Ski Jump (Bergisel)**—A new, modern ski jump has been built in the same location as the original (demolished in 2000) that was used for the 1964 and 1976 Olympics. It's an inviting side-trip with a superb view, overlooking the city just off the Brenner Pass road on the south side of town (drivers follow signs to Bergisel, walkers take tram #1 from the center). For the best view, hike to the Olympic rings under the dishes that held the Olympic flame, where Dorothy Hamill and a host of others who brought home the gold are honored. Near the car park is a memorial to Andreas Hofer, the hero of the Tirolean battles against Napoleon. The lazy can zip up to the top in a funicular, then an elevator, for a great view and a panorama café (€8 for 2-min funicular, or 325 steps for free, daily 9:00–17:00, tel. 0512/589-259, www.bergisel.info).

Mountain Lifts and Hiking—A popular mountain-sports center and home of the 1964 and 1976 Winter Olympics, Innsbruck is surrounded by 150 mountain lifts, 1,250 miles of trails, and 250 hikers' huts. One lift goes right out of downtown. The first stage, a funicular (called Hungerburgbahn, €4.30), goes to the Alpenzoo. From there, cable cars lead up into the mountains (Nordkettenbahn Seegrube-Hafelekar, €19). If it's sunny, consider riding the lift right out of the city to the mountaintops above (€23 total).

Ask your hotel or hostel for a free Innsbruck Club card (different from the Innsbruck Card sold by TI), which offers overnight guests various discounts, bike tours, and free guided hikes in summer. Hikers meet in front of Congress Innsbruck daily at 8:45; each day, it's a different hike in the surrounding mountains and valleys (bring only lunch and water; boots, rucksack, and transport are provided; confirm with TI).

Alpenzoo—This zoo is one of Innsbruck's most popular attractions (understandable when the competition is the Golden Roof). You can ride the funicular up to the zoo (free if you buy your zoo ticket before boarding) and get a look at all the animals that hide out in the Alps: wildcats, owls, elk, vultures, and more (€7, daily May–Sept 9:00–18:00, Oct–April 9:00–17:00, Weiherburggasse 37, tel. 0512/292-323, www.alpenzoo.at).

Near Innsbruck
▲▲Alpine Side-Trip by Car to Hinterhornalm—In Gnadenwald, a village sandwiched between Hall and its Alps, pay a €5 toll, pick up a brochure, then corkscrew your way up the mountain. Marveling at the crazy amount of energy put into such a remote road project, you'll finally end up at the rustic Hinterhornalm Berg restaurant (often closed, mobile 0664/211-2745). Hinterhornalm is a hang-gliding springboard. On good days, it's a butterfly nest. From there, it's a level 20-minute walk to Walderalm, a cluster of three dairy farms with 70 cows that share their meadow with the clouds. The cows ramble along ridge-top lanes surrounded by cut-glass peaks. The ladies of the farms serve soup, sandwiches, and drinks (very fresh milk in the afternoon) on rough plank tables. Below you spreads the Inn River Valley and, in the distance, tourist-filled Innsbruck.

SLEEPING

$$ Hotel Weisses Kreuz, near the Golden Roof, has been housing visitors for 500 years (see page 558). While it still feels like an old inn, its 40 rooms are newly renovated and comfortable (S-€34–39, Sb-€58–62, D-€64–67, small Db-€90–97, the big Db at €98–112 is a better value, includes breakfast, non-smoking rooms, elevator, Internet access, 50 yards in front of Golden Roof, as central as can

---

Sleep Code

(€1 = about $1.20, country code: 43, area code: 0512)
S = Single, **D** = Double/Twin, **T** = Triple, **Q** = Quad, **b** = bathroom, **s** = shower only. Unless otherwise noted, credit cards are accepted, English is spoken, and breakfast is included.

To help you sort easily through these listings, I've divided the rooms into three categories, based on the price for a standard double room with bath:

$$ Higher Priced—Most rooms €70 or more.
 $ Lower Priced—Most rooms less than €70.

be in the old town at Herzog-Friedrichstrasse 31, tel. 0512/594-790, fax 0512/594-7990, www.weisseskreuz.at, hotel@weisseskreuz.at).

$ **Pension Stoi** rents 17 pleasant, basic rooms 200 yards from the train station (S-€30, Sb-€36, D-€49, Db-€59, T-€59, Tb-€69, Q-€70, Qb-€84, cash only, no breakfast, reception daily 8:00–21:00; on foot, head left as you leave the station to Salurnerstrasse, take first left on Adamgasse, then watch for signs in the courtyard on the right, Salurnerstrasse 7; tel. 0512/585-434, fax 05238/87282, pensionstoi@aon.at, Stoi family).

EATING

You'll find plenty of expensive places in the pedestrian zone around the Golden Roof; locals favor **Weinhaus Happ** (daily 11:00–23:00, on the left as you face the Roof at Herzog-Friedrichstrasse 14, tel. 0512/582-980) and **Ottoburg** (Tue–Sun 10:00–14:30 & 18:00–24:00, closed Mon, jog left down street in front of Roof to Herzog-Friedrichstrasse 1, tel. 0512/584-338).

Weisses Rössl is off the tourist track (Mon–Sat 7:00–15:00 & 17:00–24:00, closed Sun; facing the Roof, go one block left to Kiebachgasse 8, tel. 0512/583-057). Or stroll across the Innbrücke (bridge over the Inn River) and go left a half-block along the waterfront street to the smoky but very local **Weisses Lamm** (Fri–Wed 8:00–24:00, closed Thu, hiding upstairs at Mariahilfstrasse 12, tel. 0512/283-156).

Mamma Mia, an escape from traditional fare, dishes up hearty portions of pizza and pasta (€6, indoor/outdoor seating, daily 10:00–24:00, Kiebachgasse 2, tel. 0512/562-902), while **Cammerlander** is *the* place for a steak fix. Enjoy international cuisine in their sleek, candle-lit dining room, on the glassed-in veranda, or riverside with a mountain view (€8–22 entrées, daily 8:00–24:00, Innrain 2, tel. 0512/586-398).

Vegetarians can feast on tasty organic meals at **Martin Reformhaus,** a health-food store with an eat-in or take-out deli (€6 lunch specials, Mon–Fri 9:00–18:00, Sat 9:00–13:00, closed Sun, Herzog-Friedrichstrasse 29).

TRANSPORTATION CONNECTIONS

From Innsbruck by Train to: Hall (25 min; hrly trains, 15 min, Hall is the 2nd stop and is not always announced; 4 buses/hr, 25 min), **Salzburg** (every 2 hrs, 2 hrs), **Vienna** (every 2 hrs, 5.5 hrs), **Reutte** (every 2 hrs, 4 hrs with transfer in Garmisch; or by bus: 4/day, 2.5 hrs), **Bregenz** (every 2 hrs, some with transfer in Feldkirch, 2.5 hrs), **Zürich** (3/day, 4 hrs), **Munich** (every 2 hrs, 2 hrs), **Paris** (2/day, transfer in Munich or Salzburg, 11 hrs), **Milan**

(2/day, 5.5 hrs), **Venice** (1/day, 5 hrs). Night trains run to Vienna, Milan, Venice, and Rome. Train info: tel. 051-717 (to get an operator, dial 2, then 1).

Hall

Hall was a rich salt-mining center when Innsbruck was just a humble bridge *(Brücke)* town on the Inn River. Hall actually has

a larger old town than does its sprawling neighbor, Innsbruck. Hall hosts a colorful morning scene before the daily tour buses arrive, closes down tight for its daily siesta, and sleeps on Sunday. There's a brisk farmers' market on Saturday mornings. (For drivers, Hall is a convenient overnight stop on the long drive from Vienna to Switzerland.)

ORIENTATION

Tourist Information

Hall's helpful TI offers lots of town information and brochures on a wide range of topics. If it's not too busy, they can also help you find a room (Mon–Fri 8:30–18:00, Sat 9:00–12:00, closed Sun, just off main square at Wallpachgasse 5, tel. 05223/45544, regional info: www.regionhall.at, office@regionhall.at).

Arrival in Hall

By Bus: Coming from Innsbruck, get off at the Unterer Stadtplatz stop, just below downtown Hall. (If you stay on the bus, it makes a long loop beyond and then back into Hall, dropping you at the *Kurhaus* at the top of town, which is fine if you're staying at Gartenhotel Maria Theresia.) From the Unterer Stadtplatz bus stop, you're a five-minute uphill walk from the town square and TI.

By Train: Hall's train station is a 10-minute walk from the town center (exit straight ahead up Bahnhofstrasse, turn right at the busy road, and you'll soon reach the fountain that marks the bottom of town).

By Car: Drivers approaching on the Autobahn take the Hall-Mitte exit. You'll cross a big bridge, then you'll see two convenient parking lots (each one a 5-min walk to old center). Immediately after the bridge is P5 (€2/180 min, Mon–Fri 8:30–18:00, Sat until 13:00, free on Sun), and through the light and on the left is P2 (1 hr free, €1/each hr after that).

On Foot or Bike: Hall and Innsbruck are connected by a pleasant bike path along the Inn River and through some parks. From Innsbruck, simply follow the river downstream along the *Inntal Radweg*, minding signs to Hall. A comfortable 30-minute pedal will get you there.

SIGHTS AND ACTIVITIES

Main Square (Oberer Sadtplatz)—Hall's quaint main square at the top of town is worth a visit (TI just up the street). In the adjacent square (Pfarrplatz) is the Town Hall (Rathaus) and St. Nicholas Parish Church (Pfarrkirche St. Nikolaus). This much-appended Gothic church is decorated Baroque, with fine altars, a twisted apse, and a north wall lined with bony relics.

Hall Mint in Hasegg Castle (Münze Hall in Burg Hasegg)—Beginning in the 15th century, Hall began minting coins—most notably the *Taler* (which eventually became "dollar" in English). The former town mint, housed in Hasegg Castle, is between the river and the center at the south end of town. The Hall Mint Museum was renovated and expanded in 2003 to show off the town's proud minting heritage. The centerpiece is a huge, fully-functioning replica of a 16th-century minting press—powered by water and made entirely of wood. The newly renovated tower (Münzerturm), which contains a multimedia exhibit about the castle and the town, provides a medieval-style workout (202 steps) and a great view (€6, includes audioguide, €4 for tower, €8 combo-ticket for both, April–Oct Tue–Sun 10:00–17:00, closed Mon, Nov–March Tue–Sat 10:00–17:00, closed Sun–Mon, last entry 30 min before closing, tel. 05223/585-5165, www.muenze-hall.at). The bus from Innsbruck drops you off right by the castle (stop: Unterer Stadtplatz, go through door marked #17 and *Burg Hasegg*); from Gasthof Badl, it's the first big building you'll see after crossing the old pedestrian bridge.

Salt Museum (Bergbaumuseum)—Back when salt was money, Hall was loaded. Try catching a tour at this museum, where the town has reconstructed one of its original salt mines, complete with pits, shafts, drills, tools, and a slippery but tiny wooden slide (€3, €8 town walk price includes museum, call TI to confirm schedule and check on English-speaking guides, tel. 05223/45544). The museum is a block south of the main square at Eugenstrasse.

Walking Tours—The TI organizes one-hour town walks (€6, includes admissions, €8 also includes Salt Museum tour, above; May–Oct usually Mon–Sat 10:00 and 14:00, Sun 14:00, same English situation as Salt Museum, above). The TI can also put you in touch with an English-speaking private guide (around €80/1 hr).

Swimming—If you want to make a splash, check out Hall's magnificent *Freischwimmbad*, a huge outdoor pool complex with four diving boards, a giant lap pool, a big slide, and a kiddies' pool, all surrounded by a lush garden, sauna, mini-golf, and lounging locals (€3, mid-May–Aug daily 9:00–19:00, closed Sept–mid-May, at campground northwest of Hall, follow Schwimmbad signs from downtown to Scheidensteinstrasse 24, tel. 05223/454-6475, www.camping-hall.at).

Biking—You can rent bikes at the campground (about €14/day, see directions for "Swimming," above). The riverside bike path (7 miles from Hall to Volders) is a treat.

SLEEPING AND EATING

(€1 = about $1.20, country code: 43, area code: 05223)
Lovable towns that specialize in lowering the pulse of local vacationers line the Inn Valley. Hall, while the best town, has the shortest list of accommodations. Up the hill on either side of the river are towns strewn with fine farmhouse hotels and pensions. Most *Zimmer* charge about €20 per person but don't accept one-night stays.

$$ Gartenhotel Maria Theresia, just a 15-minute walk from the center of town, makes you feel a little bit like landed Tirolean gentry. This comfortable, family-run place is a fine splurge and makes a great hub from which to explore the Inn Valley (Sb-€44, standard Db-€88, deluxe Db-€104 and a better value, free parking, beautiful garden patio, restaurant, Reimmichlstrasse 25, tel. 05223/56313, fax 05223/44685, www.gartenhotel.at, info@gartenhotel.at). If you arrive by car from Innsbruck, take the Hall-Mitte exit, go over the bridge, and through the light. At the roundabout, veer left (you'll already see signs) onto Speckbacherstrasse. Go left on Scheidensteinstrasse, right on Badgasse and left on Reimmichelstrasse. If you are coming by bus, take it to the Kurhaus stop above town, then take Stadtgraben (with the town on your left) to Kathreinstrasse, which feeds into Scheidensteinstrasse.

$ Gasthof Badl is a big, comfortable, friendly place run by sunny Frau Steiner and her daughter, Sonja. I like its convenience, peace, big breakfast, easy telephone reservations, and warm welcome (25 rooms, Sb-€38, Db-€59–63, Tb-€85, Qb-€107–110, elevator, €6.50/day rental bikes for guests for fine riverside path, laundry-€7 per load, Innbrücke 4, tel. 05223/56784, fax 05223/567-843, www.badl.at, info@badl.at). Hall's kitchens close early, but Gasthof Badl's restaurant serves excellent dinners until 21:30 (€7–11 entrées, closed Tue). They stock the essential TI brochures and maps of Hall and Innsbruck in English. It's easy for drivers to find: From the east, it's immediately off the Hall-Mitte freeway exit; you'll see the orange-lit Bed sign. From Innsbruck, take the Hall-Mitte exit and, rather than turning left over the big bridge into town, go straight.

To reach Gasthof Badl from the bus station, go through the door next to the bus stop (marked #17 and *Burg Hasegg*), cut through a couple of courtyards until you're under the castle tower, exit left out of the courtyard, turn right on Münzergasse, and head toward the river. Go straight until you hit the train tracks, then go left to use the railroad underpass, which is about 10 yards away on your right. Coming out of the underpass, go right up the ramp and, from there, cross the old wooden bridge to the hotel.

From the train station, leave the station to the right, follow the tracks straight ahead, and as the street curves left, veer right on the footpath that follows the tracks to access the railroad underpass, then head straight across the old wooden bridge.

TRANSPORTATION CONNECTIONS

Innsbruck is the nearest major train station. Hall and Innsbruck are connected by train and bus. Trains do the trip faster but leave only hourly; bus #4 takes a bit longer (25 min, €2.40 each way) but leaves four times per hour and drops you closer to town (see "Arrival in Hall," page 565). Buses go to and from the Innsbruck train station, a 10-minute walk from the old-town center. Drivers staying in freeway-handy Hall can side-trip into Innsbruck on the bus.

Route Tips for Drivers
From Hall into Innsbruck and on to Switzerland: For old Innsbruck, take the autobahn from Hall to the Innsbruck Ost exit and follow the signs to *Zentrum*, then *Kongresshaus,* and park as close as you can to the old center on the river *(Hofgarden).*

Just south of Innsbruck is the new ski jump (from the autobahn take the Innsbruck Süd exit and follow signs to *Bergisel*). Park at the end of the road near the Andreas Hofer Memorial, and climb to the empty, grassy stands for a picnic.

Leaving Innsbruck for Switzerland, head west on the autobahn (direction: Bregenz). (If you're coming directly from Innsbruck's ski jump, go down into town along the huge cemetery—thoughtfully placed just beyond the jump landing—and follow blue *A12, Garmisch, Arlberg* signs). The eight-mile-long Arlberg tunnel saves you 30 minutes on your way to Switzerland, but costs you lots of scenery and €8.50 (Swiss francs and credit cards accepted). For a joyride and to save a few bucks, skip the tunnel, exit at St. Anton, and go via Stuben.

After the speedy Arlberg tunnel, you're 30 minutes from Switzerland. Bludenz, with its characteristic medieval quarter, makes a good rest stop. Pass Feldkirch (and another long tunnel) and exit the autobahn at Rankweil/Feldkirch Nord, following signs for *Altstätten* and *Meiningen (CH)*. Crossing the baby Rhine River, leave Austria.

Leaving Hall or Innsbruck for Reutte, go west (as above, direction: Switzerland) and leave the freeway at Telfs, where signs direct you to Reutte (a 90-min drive).

Side-Trip over Brenner Pass into Italy: A short swing into Italy is fast and easy from Innsbruck or Hall (45-min drive, easy border crossing). To get to Italy, take the great Europa Bridge over Brenner Pass. It costs about €8, but in 30 minutes you'll be at the border. (Note: Traffic can be heavy on summer weekends.)

In Italy, drive to the colorful market town of Vipiteno/ Sterzing. **Reifenstein Castle** is a unique and wonderfully preserved medieval castle, just south of town on the west side of the valley, down a small road next to the autobahn. The lady who lives at the castle leads tours nearly hourly in Italian and German, squeezing in whatever English she can (€5, open Easter–Oct; tours Sat–Thu at 10:30, 14:00, and 15:00; mid-July–mid-Sept also at 16:00, closed Fri; picnic spot at drawbridge; from Austria tel. 00-39-0472-765-879, from Italy tel. 0472/765-879).

GERMAN AND AUSTRIAN HISTORY

German History

There was no Germany before 1871, but the cultural heritage of the German-speaking people (of modern-day Germany and Austria) stretches back 2,000 years.

Romans (A.D. 1–500)

German history begins in A.D. 9, when Romans troops are ambushed and driven back by the German chief Arminius. For the next 250 years, the Rhine and Danube Rivers marked the border between civilized Roman Europe (to the southwest) and "barbarian" German lands (northeast). While the rest of Europe's future would be Roman, Christian, and Latin, Germany would follow its own pagan, *Deutsch*-speaking path.

Rome finally fell to the Germanic chief Theodoric the Great (a.k.a. Dietrich of Bern, A.D. 476). After that, Germanic Franks controlled northern Europe, ruling a mixed population of Romanized Christians and tree-worshipping pagans.

Charlemagne and the Franks (A.D. 500–1000)

For Christmas in A.D. 800, the pope gave Charlemagne the title of Holy Roman Emperor. Charlemagne, the king of the Franks, was the first of many German kings to be called *Kaiser* (Caesar) over the next thousand years. Allied with the pope, Charlemagne ruled an empire that included Germany, Austria, France, the Low Countries, and northern Italy.

Charlemagne (Karl der Grosse, or Charles the Great, ruled 768–814) stood a head taller than his subjects, and his foot became a standard measurement. The stuff of legend, Charles the Great had five wives and four concubines, producing descendants with names like Charles the Bald, Louis the Pious, and Henry the Quarrelsome. After Charlemagne died of pneumonia (814), his united empire did not pass directly to his oldest son but was divided into (what would become) Germany, France, and the lands in between (Treaty of Verdun, 843).

The Holy Roman Empire (1000–1500)

Chaotic medieval Germany was made of 350 small, quarreling dukedoms ruled by the Holy Roman Emperor. The title was pretty bogus, implying that the German king ruled the same huge European empire as the ancient Romans. In fact, he was "Holy" because he was blessed by the Church, "Roman" to recall ancient grandeur, and the figurehead "Emperor" of only a scattered kingdom.

Germany's emperors had less hands-on power than other kings around Europe. Because of the custom of electing emperors by nobles and archbishops, rather than bestowing the title through inheritance, they couldn't pass the crown father to son. This system gave nobles great power, and the peasants huddled close to their local noble's castle for protection from attack by the noble next door. There were no empire-wide taxes and no national capital.

When Emperor Henry IV (ruled 1056–1106) tried to assert his power by appointing bishops, he was slapped down by the nobles, and forced to repent to the pope by standing barefoot in the Alpine snow for three days at Canossa (north Italy, 1077).

Emperor Frederick I Barbarossa (1152–1190), blue-eyed and red-bearded (hence *barba rossa*), gained an international reputation as a valiant knight, gentleman, bon vivant, and lover of poetry and women. Still, his great victories were away in Italy and Asia (on the Third Crusade, where he drowned in a river), while back home nobles wielded real power.

This was the era of Germany's troubadours *(Meistersingers)*, who traveled from castle to castle singing love songs *(Minnesang)* and telling the epic tales of chivalrous knights (Tristan and Isolde, Parzival, and the Nibelungen) that would later inspire German nationalism and Wagnerian operas.

While France, England, and Spain were centralizing power around a single ruling family to create modern nation-states, Germany remained a decentralized, backward, feudal battleground.

Medieval Growth

Nevertheless, Germany was located at the center of Europe, and trading towns prospered. Several northern towns (especially Hamburg and Lübeck) banded together into the Hanseatic League, promoting open trade around the Baltic Sea. To curry favor at election time, emperors granted powers and privileges to

Why We Call Deutschland "Germany"

Our English name "Germany" comes from the Latin *Germania*, the name of one of the "barbarian" tribes. The French and Spanish call it *Allemagne* and *Alemania* after the Alemanni tribe. Italians call the country *Germania*, but the German language is known as *tedesco*, after another Germanic tribe.

To Germans, their country is *Deutschland*, a name used for at least 1,200 years. It probably derives from *deutsch*—which is what eighth-century folks called the common language that developed in the east half of the Frankish empire. *Alles klar?*

certain towns, designated Free Imperial Cities. Some towns, such as Köln, Mainz, Dresden, and Trier, held higher status than many nobles, as hosts of one of the seven Electors of the emperor.

Textiles, mining, and the colonizing of eastern lands made Germany an economic powerhouse with a thriving middle class. In towns, middle-class folks (burghers), not the local aristocrats, began running things. Around 1450, Johann Gutenberg of Mainz invented moveable type for printing, an invention that would allow the export of a new commodity: ideas.

Religious Struggles and the Thirty Years' War (1500–1700)

Martin Luther—German monk, fiery orator, and religious whistle-blower—sparked a century of European wars by speaking out against the Catholic Church (see sidebar).

Luther's protests ("Protestantism") threw Germany into a century of turmoil, as each local prince took sides between Catholics and Protestants. In the 1525 Peasant Revolt, peasants attacked their feudal masters with hoes and pitchforks, fighting for more food, political say-so, and respect. The revolt was brutally put down.

The German Emperor, Charles V (r. 1519–1556), sided with the pope. Charles was the most powerful man in Europe, having inherited an empire that included Germany and Austria, plus the Low Countries, much of Italy, Spain, and Spain's New World possessions. But many local German nobles took the opportunity to go Protestant—some for religious reasons, but also to seize Church assets and powers.

The 1555 Peace of Augsburg allowed each local noble to decide the religion of his realm. In general, the northern lands became Protestant, while the south (Bavaria, Austria) remained Catholic.

Unresolved religious and political differences eventually expanded into the Thirty Years' War (1618–1648). This Europe-wide

Germany before Unification

war fought mainly on German soil involved Denmark, Sweden, France, and Bohemia (in the modern-day Czech Republic), among others. It was one of history's bloodiest wars, fueled by religious extremism and political opportunism, and fought by armies of brutal mercenaries who worked on commission, and were paid in loot and pillage.

By war's end (Treaty of Westphalia, 1648), a third of all Germans had died, France was the rising European power, and the Holy Roman Empire was a medieval mess of scattered, feudal states. In 1689, France's Louis XIV swept down the Rhine, gutting and leveling its once-great castles, and Germany ceased to be a major player in European politics until the modern era.

Austria and Prussia (1700s)

The German-speaking lands now consisted of three "Germanies": Austria in the south, Prussia in the north, and the rest in between.

Prussia—originally colonized by celibate ex-Crusaders called Teutonic Knights—was forged into a unified state by two strong kings. Frederick I (the "King Sergeant," r. 1701–1713) built a modern state around a highly disciplined army, a centralized

Martin Luther
(1483–1546)

One of the most influential Germans of all time was Martin Luther, who defied the Catholic Church and forever divided its congregation. Luther was born on November 10, 1483, in Eisleben, south of Berlin. His dad owned a copper smelter, affording Luther a middle-class upbringing—a rarity in the medieval hierarchy of nobles, clergy, and peasants. At the University of Erfurt, Luther earned a liberal arts degree, entered law school, and earned himself two nicknames—"the philosopher" for his wide-ranging mind, and "the king of hops" for his life-long love affair with beer.

In 1505, while riding back to school after a trip home, a bolt of lightning knocked him to the ground. Terrified, he vowed to become a monk. By age 23 he was ordained a priest in Erfurt Cathedral and was on the fast track to become a professor of theology.

Martin soon got a teaching job at a brand new university in Wittenberg—the progressive city that would be his home for the rest of his life. Luther taught theology and mingled with the town's brightest thinkers and artists; he also spent hours alone in his cell (living quarters) in the Augustinian monastery. Consumed with the notion that he was a sinner, he devoured the Bible looking for an answer, finding it in Paul's letter to the Romans. Luther realized that God makes sinners righteous through their faith in Jesus Christ, not by earning it through good deeds. As this concept of grace took hold, Luther said, "I felt myself to have been born again."

Energized, he began a series of Bible lectures at Wittenberg's twin-towered St. Mary's City Church. The pews were packed as Luther quoted passages directly from the Bible. Speaker and audience alike began to see discrepancies between what the Bible said and what the Church was doing.

Coincidentally, a representative of the pope arrived in Wittenberg to raise money by selling letters of indulgence promising "full forgiveness for all sins." Luther was outraged at the idea that God's grace could be bought, and thought the subject should be debated openly. On October 31, 1517, Luther approached Wittenberg's Castle Church and nailed 95 "theses"—or topics for discussion—to the door, which was then used as a public bulletin board. The theses questioned indulgences and other Church practices and beliefs. Luther's propositions were printed and circulated from Wittenberg's new-fangled presses (some of Europe's first). It was the talk of Germany, and Luther became famous—or infamous—almost overnight.

The pope ordered Luther's writings to be burned and sent a letter excommunicating the rebellious monk. Luther was branded a heretic and ordered to Rome to face charges, but he refused to go. Finally, the most powerful man in Europe, Emperor Charles V, stepped in to arbitrate, calling an Imperial Diet (congress) at Worms (1521). Luther made a triumphal entry into Worms, greeted by cheering crowds.

The Diet convened, and Luther took his place in the center of the large hall, standing next to a stack of his books. Inquisitors grilled him while the ultra-Catholic Charles looked on from his throne. Luther refused to disavow his beliefs or books. "Here I stand," he told the assembly, "I can do no other. So help me God. Amen."

Given a few days to reconsider, Luther disappeared. Rumor was he was kidnapped, but in fact he'd escaped to safety in Wartburg Castle, overlooking his teenage home of Eisenach. Protected by a German prince opposed to Rome, he spent a year fighting depression and translating the New Testament from Greek into German. This "German King James Version" was revolutionary, bringing the Bible to the masses and shaping the modern German language. Finally, wearing a fake beard and disguised as a knight, Luther returned home to Wittenberg.

In 1525, 41-year-old Martin met 25-year-old Katherine von Bora, and within months, the ex-monk married the ex-nun in St. Mary's Church. He and "Katie" moved from the monastery to their own house. Martin and Katherine had six children and raised four orphans.

Though living in Wittenberg under the protection of German princes, Luther traveled, spreading the Protestant message. In 1529, at Marburg Castle just north of Frankfurt, he attended a summit of leading Protestants to try and forge an alliance against Catholicism (1529). They agreed on everything except a single theological point: whether Christ was present in the wine and bread of Communion in a physical sense (according to Luther) or symbolic sense (Ulrich Zwingli). The disagreement doomed the Protestant movement to splinter into dozens of sects.

In his 50s, Luther's health declined and he grew bitter, a fact made clear in such writings as "Against the Papacy at Rome Founded by the Devil" and "Of the Jews and their Lies." He died on February 18, 1546, and was buried in Wittenberg. To this day pilgrims bring flowers.

government, and national pride. His grandson, Frederick II "The Great" (r. 1740–1786), added French culture and worldliness, preparing militaristic Prussia to enter the world stage. A well-read, flute-playing lover of the arts and liberal ideals, Frederick also ruled with an iron fist—the very model of the "enlightened despot."

Meanwhile, Austria thrived under the laid-back rule of the Hapsburg family. Hapsburgs gained power in Europe by marrying it. They acquired the Netherlands, Spain, Bohemia, and Hungary that way—a strategy that didn't work so well for Marie-Antoinette, who married the king of France.

The Germanic lands in the 1700s became a cultural powerhouse, producing musicians (Bach, Haydn, Mozart, Beethoven), writers (Goethe, Schiller), and thinkers (Kant, Leibniz). But politically, feudal Germany was no match for the modern powers.

After the French Revolution (1789), Napoleon swept through Germany with his armies, deposing feudal lords, confiscating church lands, and forcing the emperor to hand over his crown (1806). After a thousand years, the Holy Roman Empire (or *Reich*) was dead.

German Unification (1800s)

Napoleon's invasion helped unify the German-speaking peoples by rallying them against a common foreign enemy. After Napoleon's defeat, the Congress of Vienna (1815), presided over by the Austrian Prince Metternich, realigned Europe's borders. "Germany" consisted of three Germanic nations—Prussia in the north, Austria in the south, and the German Confederation, a loose collection of small states in between. The idea of unifying these three into one began to grow, and by mid-century most German-speaking people favored forming a modern nation-state. The only question was whether the confederation would be under Prussian or Austrian dominance.

Economically, Germany was becoming increasingly modern, with railroads (1835), a unified trade organization (1834), mechanical engineering prowess, and factories booming on a surplus of labor.

Energetic Prussia took the lead in unifying the country. Otto von Bismarck (served 1862–1890), the strong minister of Prussia's weak king, used cunning politics to engineer a unified Germany under Prussian dominance. First he started a war with Austria, ensuring that any united Germany would be under Prussian control. (Austria-Hungary became a separate country.) Next, Bismarck provoked a war with France (Franco-Prussian War, 1870–1871). This united Prussia and the German Confederation against their common enemy, France.

Fueled by hysterical patriotism, German armies swept through France and, in the Hall of Mirrors at Versailles, crowned Prussia's Wilhelm I as Emperor *(Kaiser)* of a new German Empire uniting Prussia and the German Confederation (but excluding Austria). This Second Reich (1871–1918) featured elements of democracy (an elected *Reichstag,* or parliament) offset by a strong military and an emperor with veto powers.

A united and resurgent Germany was suddenly flexing its muscles in European politics. With strong industry, war spoils, overseas colonies, and a large and disciplined military, it sought its rightful place in the sun. *Volk* art flourished (Wagner's operas, Nietzsche's essays), fueled by nationalist fervor, reviving medieval German myths and Nordic gods. The rest of Europe saw Germany's rapid rise and began arming themselves to the teeth.

World War I and Hitler's Rise (1914–1939)

When Austria's heir to the throne was assassinated in 1914, all of Europe took sides as the political squabble quickly escalated into World War I. Germany and Austria-Hungary attacked British and French troops in France, but were stalled at the Battle of the Marne. Both sides dug defensive trenches, then settled in for four years of bloodshed, boredom, mud, machine-gun fire, disease, and mustard gas.

Finally, at 11:00 in the morning of November 11, 1918, fighting ceased. Germany surrendered, signing the Treaty of Versailles in the Hall of Mirrors at Versailles. The war cost the defeated German nation 1.7 million men, precious territory, colonies, their military rights, reparations money, and national pride.

A new democratic government called the Weimar Republic (1919) dutifully abided by the Treaty of Versailles and tried to maintain order among Germany's many divided political parties. But the country was in ruins, the economy a shambles, and the war's victors demanded heavy reparations. Communists rioted in the streets, fascists plotted coups, and a loaf of bread cost a billion inflated marks. War vets grumbled in their beer about how their leaders had sold them out. All Germans, regardless of their political affiliations, were fervently united in their apathy toward the new democracy. When the worldwide depression of 1929 hit Germany with brutal force, the nation was desperate for a strong leader with answers.

Adolf Hitler (1889–1945) was a disgruntled vet who had spent the post–World War I years homeless, wandering the streets of Vienna with sketchpad in hand, hoping to become an artist. In Munich, he joined other disaffected Germans to form the National Socialist (Nazi) party. In stirring speeches, Hitler promised to restore Germany to its rightful glory, blaming the country's

Germany During World War II
(1939–1945)

1939 Soldiers singing "Muss ich denn, Muss ich denn" ("I must leave my happy home") march off to war. On September 1, Germany invades Poland, sparking World War II. Germany, Italy, and Japan (the Axis) would eventually square off against the Allies—Britain, France, the United States, and the Soviet Union.

1940 The Nazi *Blitzkrieg* (lightning war) quickly sweeps through Denmark, Norway, the Low Countries, France, Yugoslavia, and Greece. With fellow fascists ruling Italy (Mussolini), Spain (Franco), and Portugal (Salazar), all of the Continent is now dominated by fascists, creating a "fortress Europe."

1941 Hitler invades his former ally, the U.S.S.R.. Bombastic victory parades in Berlin celebrate the triumph of the Aryan race over the lesser peoples of the world.

1942 Allied bombs begin falling on German cities. In the autumn and winter, German families receive death notices from the horrific Battle of Stalingrad. On the worst days, 50,000 men died. (America lost 58,000 total in Vietnam.) Back home, Nazi officials begin their plan for the "final solution to the Jewish problem"—systematic execution of Europe's Jews in specially built death camps.

current problems on Communists, foreigners, and Jews. After an unsuccessful coup attempt (the Beer Hall Putsch in Munich, 1923), Hitler was sent to jail, where he wrote an influential book of his political ideas, called *Mein Kampf (My Struggle)*.

By 1930, the Nazis—now wearing power suits and working within the system—had become a formidable political party in Germany's democracy. They won 38 percent of the seats in the *Reichstag* in 1932, and Hitler was appointed chancellor (1933). Two months later, the *Reichstag* building mysteriously burned to the ground—an apparent act of terrorism with a September 11–sized impact—and a terrified Germany gave Chancellor Hitler sweeping powers to preserve national security.

Hitler wasted no time in using this Enabling Act to jail opponents, terrorize the citizenry, and organize every aspect of German life under the watchful eye of the Nazi party. Plumbers' unions, choral societies, school teachers, church pastors, movie-makers, and artists all had to account to a Nazi party official about how their work furthered the Third Reich.

1943 Germany has to fight a two-front war: against tenacious Soviets on the chilly Eastern Front, and against Brits and Yanks advancing north through Italy on the Western Front. Germany's industrial output tries desperately to keep up with the Allies'. The average German suffers through shortages, rationing, and frequent trips to the bomb shelter.

1944 Hitler's no-surrender policy is increasingly unpopular, and he narrowly survives being assassinated by a bomb planted in an office. After the Allies reach France on D-Day, Germany counterattacks with a last-gasp offensive (the Battle of the Bulge) that slows but does not stop the Allies.

1945 Soviet soldiers approach Berlin from the east and Americans and Brits from the west. Adolf Hitler commits suicide, and families lock up their daughters to protect them from rapacious Soviet soldiers. When Germany finally surrenders on May 8, the country is in ruins, occupied by several foreign powers, divided into occupation zones, and viewed by the world as an immoral monster.

In the war's aftermath, many German citizens learn for the first time of the mass killings and atrocities committed by their leaders.

For the next decade, an all-powerful Hitler proceeded to revive Germany's economy, building the autobahns and rebuilding the military. Defying the Treaty of Versailles and world opinion, Hitler occupied the Saar region (1935) and the Rhineland (1936), annexed Austria and the Sudetenland (1938), and invaded Czechoslovakia (March 1939). The rest of Europe finally reached its appeasement limit.

Two Germanies (1945–1990)

After the war, the Allies divided occupied Germany into two halves, split down the middle by an 855-mile border that Winston Churchill called an "Iron Curtain." By 1949, Germany was officially two separate countries. West Germany (the Federal Republic of Germany) was democratic and capitalist, allied with the powerful United States. East Germany (the German Democratic Republic) was a socialist state under Soviet control. The former capital of Berlin, sitting in East German territory, was itself split into two parts, allowing a tiny pocket of Western life in the

Soviet-controlled East. Armed guards prevented Germans from crossing the border to see their cousins on the other side.

In 1948, Soviet troops blockaded West Berlin. The Allies responded by airlifting food and supplies into the stranded city, forcing the Soviets to back off. In 1961, the Soviets erected a 12-foot-high concrete wall through the heart of Berlin. The Berlin Wall—built at the height of the Cold War between the United States and the U.S.S.R.—was designed to prevent the westward flow of East German citizens. It came to symbolize divided Germany.

In West Germany, Chancellor Konrad Adenauer (who had suffered imprisonment under the Nazis), tried to restore Germany's good name, paying war reparations and joining international organizations of nations. Thanks to U.S. aid from the Marshall Plan, West Germany was rebuilt, democracy was established, and its "economic miracle" quickly exceeded pre-war levels. Adenauer was succeeded in 1969 by the U.S.-friendly Willy Brandt.

East Germany was ruled with an iron fist by Walter Ulbricht (who had been exiled by the Nazis). In 1953, demonstrations and protests against the government were brutally put down by Soviet—not German—troops. Erich Honecker (having endured a decade of Nazi imprisonment) succeeded Ulbrich as ruler of the East in 1971. Honecker was a kinder, gentler tyrant.

Throughout the 1970s and 1980s, both the United States and the Soviet Union used divided Germany as a military base. West Germans debated whether U.S. missiles aimed at the Soviets should be placed in their country. Economically, the West just got stronger while the East stagnated.

On November 9, 1989, East Germany unexpectedly opened the Berlin Wall. Astonished Germans from both sides climbed the Wall, hugged each other, shared bottles of beer, sang songs, and chiseled off souvenirs. Negotiations and elections immediately began to reunite the two Germanies. October 3, 1990, was proclaimed German Unification Day, with Berlin as the capital (1991).

Germany Today (1990–present)

Differences between *Ossis* (former East Germans) and *Wessis* remain, but they're diminishing as the two economies find equilibrium. Germany remains a major economic and political force in Europe. After a decade of a center-right government (under Chancellor Helmut Kohl), and a decade under the center-left Chancellor Gerhard Schroeder, Germany is at a crossroads. Elections in 2005 left no dominant political party, and the government is currently led by a loose coalition headed by a conservative Christian, Chancellor Angela Merkel. Germany is fully integrated into the international

Benedict XVI, the German Pope

When Josef Ratzinger became the 265th pope in 2005, he introduced himself as "a simple, humble worker in the vineyard of the Lord." But the man has a complex history, a reputation for intellectual brilliance, a flair for the piano, a penchant for controversy for his unbending devotion to traditional Catholic doctrine...and a Bavarian accent.

Born in 1927 in the small Bavarian town of Marktl am Inn (southeast of Munich), young Josef went to school in nearby Traunstein, studying in the seminary. When Hitler took power, he lived life under Nazi rule as many Germans did—outwardly obeying leaders while inwardly conflicted. Like many Germans, he joined the Hitler Youth, was drafted into the Army, sprayed flak from anti-aircraft guns (guarding a BMW plant), and saw Jews transported to death camps. Near the war's end, he deserted, and subsequently spent a brief time in an American P.O.W. camp near Ulm.

After the war, Ratzinger became a priest and a professor of theology, first at Munster then at the University of Tübingen. Originally a voice of liberal Catholicism, he became increasingly convinced that Church tradition was needed to offset the growing chaos of the world.

In 1977, he was made Archbishop of Munich. Ratzinger became Pope John Paul II's closest advisor and good friend. Every Friday afternoon for two decades, they met for lunch, intellectual sparring, and friendly conversation.

Under John Paul II, Ratzinger served as the Church's "enforcer" of doctrine, earning the nickname "God's Rottweiler." He spoke out against ordaining women, chastised Latin American priests for fomenting class warfare, reassigned bishops who were soft on homosexuality, reaffirmed opposition to birth control, and wrote thoughtful papers challenging the secular world's moral relativism.

The name of "Benedict" recalls both Pope Benedict XV (who healed World War I's divisions) and Europe's patron St. Benedict (c. 480–543), who symbolizes Europe's Christian roots. A true pan-European who speaks many languages, Benedict XVI is expected to continue John Paul's two priorities: defending Catholic doctrine in a changing world and building bridges with fellow Christians.

community as a member of the European Union—an organization whose chief aim was to avoid future wars with an aggressive Germany by embracing it in the economic web of Europe.

Austrian History

Austria's history marches in step with Germany's, but there are some differences that give Austria its distinct culture.

c. A.D. 1 The Romans occupy and defend the "crossroads of Europe," where the west–east Danube River crosses the north–south Brenner Pass through the Alps.

c. 800 Charlemagne designates Austria as one boundary of his European empire—the "Eastern Empire," or *Osterreich*.

1273 An Austrian noble from the Hapsburg family (Rudolf I) is elected Holy Roman Emperor, ruling Austria, Germany, and north Italy. From 1438 until 1806, every emperor but one is a Hapsburg. The Hapsburgs arrange strategic marriages for their children with other prominent royalty around Europe, gaining power through international connections.

1493 Maximilian I is crowned emperor. His marriage to Mary of Burgundy weds two kingdoms together, and their grandson, Charles V, will inherit a vast empire.

1519 Charles V (r. 1519–1556) is the most powerful man in Europe, ruling Austria, Germany, the Low Countries, parts of Italy, and Spain (with its New World possessions). Charles is responsible for trying to solve the problems of all those lands, including battling Turks in Vienna and Lutherans in Germany. While many lands north of the Danube would turn Protestant, Austria remains Catholic.

1522 Charles gives Austria (and the Turkish problem) to his little brother, Ferdinand, who four years later marries into the Bohemian and Hungarian crowns, as well.

1529 Muslim Turks besiege Vienna, beginning almost two centuries of battles between Austria and the Turks. In the course of the wars, Austria gains possession of Hungary.

1556 Charles V retires from the throne to enter a monastery, leaving his kingdom to his son (King Philip II of Spain), and to his brother, Ferdinand I of Austria, the crown of Holy Roman Emperor. From now on, Austria's rulers would concentrate on ruling their "Austro-Hungarian" empire, which includes part or all of present-day Austria, Hungary, the Czech Republic, Slovakia, Romania, Slovenia, Croatia, Bosnia, Serbia, north Italy (Venice), and, later, parts of Poland.

1648 The Thirty Years' War ends, leaving the "Holy Roman Empire" an empire only in name: a figurehead emperor of a scattered group of German-speaking people, mainly in Austria and Germany.

1683 Nearly 200,000 Muslims from Ottoman Turkey surround the city of Vienna. The Turks are driven off, leaving behind bags of coffee that help fuel a beverage craze around Europe. Vienna's first coffeehouse opens.

1672–1714 Three wars with Louis XIV of France (including War of the Spanish Succession) drain Austria.

1740 Maria Theresa (r. 1740–1780) has 16 children and still finds time to fight two wars in 25 years, defending her right to rule. Adored by her subjects for her down-to-earth personality, she brings Austria international prestige by marrying her daughters to Europe's royalty.

1781 Maria Theresa's son Joseph II, who frees the serfs and takes piano lessons from Mozart, rules as an "enlightened despot." Vienna becomes the world capital of symphonic music, home to Haydn (1732–1809), Mozart (1756–1791), and Beethoven (1770–1827).

1792 When his aunt, Marie-Antoinette, is imprisoned and (later) beheaded by revolutionaries in Paris, Austria's Emperor Franz II seeks revenge, beginning two decades of wars between revolutionary France and monarchist Austria.

1805 Napoleon defeats Austria at Austerlitz, his greatest triumph over the forces of monarchy. Napoleon forces Holy Roman Emperor Franz II to hand over the imperial crown (1806), ending a thousand years of empire, and he even marries Franz II's daughter, Marie-Louise.

1814–1815 An Austrian, Chancellor Metternich, heads the Congress of Vienna, reinstalling kings and nobles in lands now free of Napoleon.

1848 Emperor Franz Josef (Emperor of Austria, not of the Holy Roman Empire) rules for the next 68 years, maintaining white-gloved tradition while overseeing great change—Austria's decline as an empire and entrance into the modern industrial world.

1849 Nearly 100,000 Viennese attend the funeral of violinist Johann Strauss, responsible for the dance craze called the waltz. His son, Johann Strauss, Jr. (1825–1899), takes the baton of the Strauss Orchestra and waltzes on, writing "The Blue Danube."

1866 Prussia provokes war and defeats Austria, effectively freezing Austria out of any involvement in a modern German nation.

1914 Austria fires the opening shots of World War I to avenge the assassination of their heir to the throne.

1919 After its defeat in World War I, the Austro-Hungarian Empire is divided into separate democratic nations, with Austria assigned the borders it has today—small and landlocked.

1932 Mirroring events in Germany, a totalitarian government (of Engelbert Dollfuss) replaces a weak democracy floundering in economic depression.

1938 Nazi Germany—using the threat of force and riding a surge of Germanic nationalism—annexes Austria in the *Anschluss*, and leads it into World War II.

1945 Like Germany, a defeated Austria is divided by the victors into occupied zones, but Austria's are short lived.

1955 Modern Austria is born with the blessing of the international community.

1995 Austria joins the European Union.

2000 The European Union places sanctions on Austria (lifted a few months later) when the far-right Freedom Party—campaigning under the slogan "*Überfremdung:* Too many foreigners"—gains seats in Austria's parliament.

2002 The Freedom Party does badly in elections.

2004 Heinz Fischer, a center-left career politician, is elected president. Arnold Schwarzenegger, the Austrian-born "governator" of California, is criticized by Austrians for his historically-questionable comments calling Austria "socialist." Still, "Ah-nolt" remains popular in his native land, a symbol of the small-town boy who made good.

APPENDIX

Let's Talk Telephones

For specifics on Germany and Austria, see "Telephones" in this book's Introduction.

Making Calls Within a European Country: About half of all European countries use area codes (like we do in most of the U.S.); the other half use a direct-dial system without area codes.

To make calls within a country that uses a direct-dial system (Belgium, the Czech Republic, Denmark, France, Italy, Portugal, Norway, Spain, and Switzerland), dial the same number whether you're calling across the country or across the street.

In countries that use area codes (such as Germany, Austria, Britain, Croatia, Finland, Hungary, Ireland, the Netherlands, Poland, Slovakia, Slovenia, and Sweden), dial the local number when calling within a city, and add the area code if calling long-distance within the country.

Making International Calls: Always start with the international access code (011 if you're calling from the U.S. or Canada, 00 from anywhere in Europe), then dial the country code of the country you're calling (see chart below).

What you dial next depends on the phone system of the country you're calling. If the country uses area codes (like Germany and Austria), drop the initial 0 of the area code, then dial the rest of the number.

Countries that use direct-dial systems (no area codes) vary in how they're accessed internationally by phone. For instance, if you're making an international call to the Czech Republic, Denmark, Italy, Norway, Portugal, or Spain, simply dial the international access code, country code, and phone number. But if you're calling Belgium, France, or Switzerland, drop the initial 0 of the phone number.

European Calling Chart

Just smile and dial, using this key:
AC = Area Code, LN = Local Number.

European Country	Calling long distance within ...	Calling from the U.S.A./ Canada to ...	Calling from a European country to ...
Austria	AC + LN	011 + 43 + AC (without the initial zero) + LN	00 + 43 + AC (without the initial zero) + LN
Belgium	LN	011 + 32 + LN (without initial zero)	00 + 32 + LN (without initial zero)
Britain	AC + LN	011 + 44 + AC (without initial zero) + LN	00 + 44 + AC (without initial zero) + LN
Croatia	AC + LN	011 + 385 + AC (without initial zero) + LN	00 + 385 + AC (without initial zero) + LN
Czech Republic	LN	011 + 420 + LN	00 + 420 + LN
Denmark	LN	011 + 45 + LN	00 + 45 + LN
Finland	AC + LN	011 + 358 + AC (without initial zero) + LN	00 + 358 + AC (without initial zero) + LN
France	LN	011 + 33 + LN (without initial zero)	00 + 33 + LN (without initial zero)
Germany	AC + LN	011 + 49 + AC (without initial zero) + LN	00 + 49 + AC (without initial zero) + LN
Greece	LN	011 + 30 + LN	00 + 30 + LN
Hungary	06 + AC + LN	011 + 36 + AC + LN	00 + 36 + AC + LN
Ireland	AC + LN	011 + 353 + AC (without initial zero) + LN	00 + 353 + AC (without initial zero) + LN
Italy	LN	011 + 39 + LN	00 + 39 + LN

European Country	Calling long distance within ...	Calling from the U.S.A./ Canada to ...	Calling from a European country to ...
Netherlands	AC + LN	011 + 31 + AC (without initial zero) + LN	00 + 31 + AC (without initial zero) + LN
Norway	LN	011 + 47 + LN	00 + 47 + LN
Poland	AC + LN	011 + 48 + AC (without initial zero) + LN	00 + 48 + AC (without initial zero) + LN
Portugal	LN	011 + 351 + LN	00 + 351 + LN
Slovakia	AC + LN	011 + 421 + AC (without initial zero) + LN	00 + 421 + AC (without initial zero) + LN
Slovenia	AC + LN	011 + 386 + AC (without initial zero) + LN	00 + 386 + AC (without initial zero) + LN
Spain	LN	011 + 34 + LN	00 + 34 + LN
Sweden	AC + LN	011 + 46 + AC (without initial zero) + LN	00 + 46 + AC (without initial zero) + LN
Switzerland	LN	011 + 41 + LN (without initial zero)	00 + 41 + LN (without initial zero)
Turkey	AC (if no initial zero is included, add one) + LN	011 + 90 + AC (without initial zero) + LN	00 + 90 + AC (without initial zero) + LN

- The instructions above apply whether you're calling a fixed phone or mobile phone.
- The international access codes (the first numbers you dial when making an international call) are 011 if you're calling from the U.S.A./Canada, or 00 if you're calling from anywhere in Europe.
- To call the U.S.A. or Canada from Europe, dial 00, then 1 (the country code for the U.S.A. and Canada), then the area code and number. In short, 00 + 1 + AC + LN = Hi, Mom!

Country Codes

After you've dialed the international access code (00 if calling from Europe, 011 if calling from the U.S. or Canada), dial the code of the country you're calling.

Austria—43	Italy—39
Belgium—32	Morocco—212
Britain—44	Netherlands—31
Canada—1	Norway—47
Croatia—385	Poland—48
Czech Rep.—420	Portugal—351
Denmark—45	Slovakia—421
Estonia—372	Slovenia—386
Finland—358	Spain—34
France—33	Sweden—46
Germany—49	Switzerland—41
Gibraltar—350	Turkey—90
Greece—30	U.S.A.—1
Ireland—353	

Directory Assistance

Austria: National—tel. 16; international—tel. 08; train info—tel. 051717

Germany: National—tel. 11833; international—tel. 11834; train info—tel. 11861 (€0.50/min)

German Tourist Offices: Dial local code, then 19433.

U.S. Embassies

Austria (in Vienna): Boltzmanngasse 16, tel. 01/313-390, embassy@usembassy.at; consular services at Parkring 12, daily 8:00–11:30, tel. 01/313-397-535, www.usembassy.at, consulatevienna@state.gov

Germany (in Berlin): Neustädtische Kirchstrasse 4-5, tel. 030/83050; consular services at Clayallee 170, Mon–Fri 8:30–12:00, closed Sat–Sun, tel. 030/832-9233—Mon–Fri 14:00–16:00 only, www.usembassy.de, consberlin@state.gov

Festivals and Public Holidays

For specifics, contact Germany's and Austria's national tourist offices (see page 8) and check these Web sites: www.whatsonwhen .com and www.festivals.com. Vienna and Salzburg have music festivals nearly every month.

Jan	Perchtenlaufen (winter festival, parades), Tirol and Salzburg, Austria
Jan–Feb	Fasching (carnival season, balls, parades), throughout Austria and Germany

2006

JANUARY
S	M	T	W	T	F	S
1	2	3	4	5	6	7
8	9	10	11	12	13	14
15	16	17	18	19	20	21
22	23	24	25	26	27	28
29	30	31				

FEBRUARY
S	M	T	W	T	F	S
			1	2	3	4
5	6	7	8	9	10	11
12	13	14	15	16	17	18
19	20	21	22	23	24	25
26	27	28				

MARCH
S	M	T	W	T	F	S
			1	2	3	4
5	6	7	8	9	10	11
12	13	14	15	16	17	18
19	20	21	22	23	24	25
26	27	28	29	30	31	

APRIL
S	M	T	W	T	F	S
						1
2	3	4	5	6	7	8
9	10	11	12	13	14	15
23/30	24	25	26	27	28	29

MAY
S	M	T	W	T	F	S
	1	2	3	4	5	6
7	8	9	10	11	12	13
14	15	16	17	18	19	20
21	22	23	24	25	26	27
28	29	30	31			

JUNE
S	M	T	W	T	F	S
				1	2	3
4	5	6	7	8	9	10
11	12	13	14	15	16	17
18	19	20	21	22	23	24
25	26	27	28	29	30	

JULY
S	M	T	W	T	F	S
						1
2	3	4	5	6	7	8
9	10	11	12	13	14	15
16	17	18	19	20	21	22
23/30	24/31	25	26	27	28	29

AUGUST
S	M	T	W	T	F	S
		1	2	3	4	5
6	7	8	9	10	11	12
13	14	15	16	17	18	19
20	21	22	23	24	25	26
27	28	29	30	31		

SEPTEMBER
S	M	T	W	T	F	S
					1	2
3	4	5	6	7	8	9
10	11	12	13	14	15	16
17	18	19	20	21	22	23
24	25	26	27	28	29	30

OCTOBER
S	M	T	W	T	F	S
1	2	3	4	5	6	7
8	9	10	11	12	13	14
15	16	17	18	19	20	21
22	23	24	25	26	27	28
29	30	31				

NOVEMBER
S	M	T	W	T	F	S
			1	2	3	4
5	6	7	8	9	10	11
12	13	14	15	16	17	18
19	20	21	22	23	24	25
26	27	28	29	30		

DECEMBER
S	M	T	W	T	F	S
					1	2
3	4	5	6	7	8	9
10	11	12	13	14	15	16
17	18	19	20	21	22	23
24/31	25	26	27	28	29	30

Easter	Easter Festival, Salzburg
May 1	May Day with maypole dances, throughout Austria and Germany
May 20–28	Spring Horse Races (www.baden-galopp.de), Baden-Baden, Germany
May	Vienna Festival of Arts and Music
June 2–5	Meistertrunk Show (medieval costumes, parties in the beer gardens), Rothenburg, Germany
June	Frankfurt Summertime Festival (arts)
Late June	Midsummer Eve Celebrations, Austria
July 14–23	City Festival Week, Dresden, Germany
July 29	Lichter Festival (fireworks and music, www.koelnerlichter.de), Köln, Germany
Late July–Aug	Salzburg Festival (music)

Aug 25–Sept 3	Fall Horse Races (www.baden-galopp.de), Baden-Baden, Germany
Aug 27	Historical Parade, Dresden, Germany
Sept 1–3	Imperial City Festival (fireworks), Rothenburg, Germany
Sept 16–Oct 3	Oktoberfest (starts 3rd weekend, runs 16 days—18 in 2006, www.oktoberfest.de), Munich
Sept	Berlin Festwochen (arts festival); Imperial City Festival (costumes, parade, fireworks on 2nd weekend), Rothenburg, Germany
Nov	Berlin Jazz Festival; St. Martin's Day Celebrations (feasts), Austria and Bavaria
Dec	St. Nicholas Day parades, Austria; Christmas Fairs, Austria, Germany

World Cup 2006 Match Schedule

From June through early July of 2006, all (non-American) eyes will be on Germany's cities as the World Cup football (soccer) championship rolls into town. Be warned that host cities will be flooded by soccer fans around game time (book hotels well ahead or stay elsewhere). For more on the World Cup, see the sidebar on page 6 of the Introduction. Here's a complete list of host cities and match dates:

Berlin	June 8 (opening ceremony), 13, 15, 20, 23, 30 (QF); July 9 (F)
Dortmund	June 10, 14, 19, 22, 27; July 4 (SF)
Frankfurt	June 10, 13, 17, 21; July 1 (QF)
Gelsenkirchen	June 9, 12, 16, 21; July 1 (QF)
Hamburg	June 10, 15, 19, 22, 30 (QF)
Hannover	June 12, 16, 20, 23, 27
Kaiserslautern	June 12, 17, 20, 23, 26
Cologne	June 11, 17, 20, 23, 26
Leipzig	June 11, 14, 18, 21, 24
Munich	June 9, 14, 18, 21, 24; July 5 (SF)
Nürnberg	June 11, 15, 18, 22, 25
Stuttgart	June 13, 16, 19, 22, 25; July 8 (3P)

(QF = quarterfinal match; SF = semifinal match; 3P = 3rd-place match; F = final match.)

Climate

First line, average daily low; second line, average daily high; third line, days of no rain. For more detailed weather statistics for destinations throughout Germany and Austria (as well as the rest of the world), check www.worldclimate.com.

J	F	M	A	M	J	J	A	S	O	N	D
AUSTRIA • Vienna											
25°	28°	30°	42°	50°	56°	60°	59°	53°	44°	37°	30°
34°	38°	47°	58°	67°	73°	76°	75°	68°	56°	45°	37°
16	17	18	17	18	16	18	18	20	18	16	16
GERMANY • Berlin											
26°	26°	31°	39°	47°	53°	57°	56°	50°	42°	36°	29°
35°	37°	46°	56°	66°	72°	75°	74°	68°	56°	45°	38°
14	13	19	17	19	17	17	17	18	17	14	16
GERMANY • Munich											
23°	23°	30°	38°	45°	51°	55°	54°	48°	40°	33°	26°
35°	38°	48°	56°	64°	70°	74°	73°	67°	56°	44°	36°
15	12	18	15	16	13	15	15	17	18	15	16

Numbers and Stumblers

- Europeans write a few of their numbers differently than we do. 1 = 1, 4 = 4, 7 = 7. Learn the difference or miss your train.
- In Europe, dates appear as day/month/year, so Christmas is 25/12/06.
- Commas are decimal points and decimals, commas. A dollar and a half is $1,50, and there are 5.280 feet in a mile.
- When counting with fingers, start with your thumb. If you hold up your first finger to request one item, you'll probably get two.
- What Americans call the second floor of a building is the first floor in Europe.
- Europeans keep the left "lane" open for passing on escalators and moving sidewalks. Keep to the right.

Temperature Conversion: Fahrenheit and Celsius

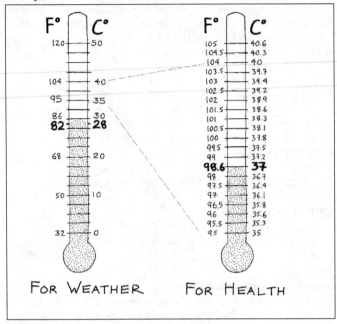

Europe takes its temperature using the Celsius scale, while we opt for Fahrenheit. For weather, remember that 28°C is 82°F—perfect. For health, 37°C is just right.

Metric Conversion (approximate)

1 inch = 25 millimeters	32°F = 0°C
1 foot = 0.3 meter	82°F = about 28°C
1 yard = 0.9 meter	1 ounce = 28 grams
1 mile = 1.6 kilometers	1 kilogram = 2.2 pounds
1 centimeter = 0.4 inch	1 quart = 0.95 liter
1 meter = 39.4 inches	1 square yard = 0.8 square meter
1 kilometer = 0.62 mile	1 acre = 0.4 hectare

German Survival Phrases

When using the phonetics, pronounce ī as the long I sound in "light."

Good day.	Guten Tag.	**goo**-tehn tahg
Do you speak English?	Sprechen Sie Englisch?	shprehkh-ehn zee **ehng**-lish
Yes. / No.	Ja. / Nein.	yah / nīn
I (don't) understand.	Ich verstehe (nicht).	ikh fehr-**shtay**-heh (nikht)
Please.	Bitte.	**bit**-teh
Thank you.	Danke.	**dahng**-keh
I'm sorry.	Es tut mir leid.	ehs toot meer līt
Excuse me.	Entschuldigung.	ehnt-**shool**-dig-oong
(No) problem.	(Kein) Problem.	(kīn) proh-**blaym**
(Very) good.	(Sehr) gut.	(zehr) goot
Goodbye.	Auf Wiedersehen.	owf **vee**-der-zayn
one / two	eins / zwei	īns / tsvī
three / four	drei / vier	drī / feer
five / six	fünf / sechs	fewnf / zehkhs
seven / eight	sieben / acht	**zee**-behn / ahkht
nine / ten	neun / zehn	noyn / tsayn
How much is it?	Wieviel kostet das?	**vee**-feel **kohs**-teht dahs
Write it?	Schreiben?	**shrī**-behn
Is it free?	Ist es umsonst?	ist ehs oom-**zohnst**
Included?	Inklusive?	in-kloo-**zee**-veh
Where can I buy / find...?	Wo kann ich kaufen / finden...?	voh kahn ikh **kow**-fehn / **fin**-dehn
I'd like / We'd like...	Ich hätte gern / Wir hätten gern...	ikh **heh**-teh gehrn / veer **heh**-tehn gehrn
...a room.	...ein Zimmer.	īn **tsim**-mer
...a ticket to ___.	...eine Fahrkarte nach ___.	ī-neh **far**-kar-teh nahkh
Is it possible?	Ist es möglich?	ist ehs **mur**-glikh
Where is...?	Wo ist...?	voh ist
...the train station	...der Bahnhof	dehr **bahn**-hohf
...the bus station	...der Busbahnhof	dehr **boos**-bahn-hohf
...tourist information	...das Touristen-informationsbüro	dahs too-**ris**-tehn-in-for-maht-see-**ohns**-bew-roh
...toilet	...die Toilette	dee toh-**leh**-teh
men	Herren	**hehr**-rehn
women	Damen	**dah**-mehn
left / right	links / rechts	links / rehkhts
straight	geradeaus	geh-**rah**-deh-**ows**
When is this open / closed?	Um wieviel Uhr ist hier geöffnet / geschlossen?	oom **vee**-feel oor ist heer geh-**urf**-neht / geh-**shloh**-sehn
At what time?	Um wieviel Uhr?	oom **vee**-feel oor
Just a moment.	Moment.	moh-**mehnt**
now / soon / later	jetzt / bald / später	yehtst / bahld / **shpay**-ter
today / tomorrow	heute / morgen	**hoy**-teh / **mor**-gehn

In the Restaurant

I'd like / We'd like...	Ich hätte gern / Wir hätten gern...	ikh **heh**-teh gehrn / veer **heh**-tehn gehrn
...a reservation for...	...eine Reservierung für...	ī-neh reh-zer-**feer**-oong fewr
...a table for one / two.	...einen Tisch für ein / zwei.	ī-nehn tish fewr īn / tsvī
Non-smoking.	Nichtraucher.	**nikht**-rowkh-er
Is this seat free?	Ist hier frei?	ist heer frī
Menu (in English), please.	Speisekarte (in Englisch), bitte.	**shpī**-zeh-kar-teh (in **ehng**-lish) **bit**-teh
service (not) included	Trinkgeld (nicht) inklusive	**trink**-gehlt (nikht) in-kloo-**zee**-veh
cover charge	Eintritt	**īn**-trit
to go	zum Mitnehmen	tsoom **mit**-nay-mehn
with / without	mit / ohne	mit / **oh**-neh
and / or	und / oder	oont / **oh**-der
menu (of the day)	(Tages-) Karte	(**tah**-gehs-) **kar**-teh
set meal for tourists	Touristenmenü	too-**ris**-tehn-meh-**new**
specialty of the house	Spezialität des Hauses	shpayt-see-ah-lee-**tayt** dehs **how**-zehs
appetizers	Vorspeise	**for**-shpī-zeh
bread	Brot	broht
cheese	Käse	**kay**-zeh
sandwich	Sandwich	**zahnd**-vich
soup	Suppe	**zup**-peh
salad	Salat	zah-**laht**
meat	Fleisch	flīsh
poultry	Geflügel	geh-**flew**-gehl
fish	Fisch	fish
seafood	Meeresfrüchte	**meh**-rehs-**frewkh**-teh
fruit	Obst	ohpst
vegetables	Gemüse	geh-**mew**-zeh
dessert	Nachspeise	**nahkh**-shpī-zeh
mineral water	Mineralwasser	min-eh-**rahl**-vah-ser
tap water	Leitungswasser	**lī**-toongs-vah-ser
milk	Milch	milkh
(orange) juice	(Orangen-) Saft	(oh-**rahn**-zhehn-) zahft
coffee	Kaffee	kah-**fay**
tea	Tee	tay
wine	Wein	vīn
red / white	rot / weiß	roht / vīs
glass / bottle	Glas / Flasche	glahs / **flah**-sheh
beer	Bier	beer
Cheers!	Prost!	prohst
More. / Another.	Mehr. / Noch ein.	mehr / nohkh īn
The same.	Das gleiche.	dahs **glīkh**-eh
Bill, please.	Rechnung, bitte.	**rehkh**-noong **bit**-teh
tip	Trinkgeld	**trink**-gehlt

Making Your Hotel Reservation

Most hotel managers know basic "hotel English." Faxing or e-mailing are the preferred methods for reserving a room. They're more accurate than telephoning and much faster than writing a letter. Use this handy form for your fax or find it online at www.ricksteves.com/reservation. Photocopy and fax away.

One-Page Fax

To: _____ @ _____
                   hotel   *fax*

From: _____@ _____
                     name   *fax*

Today's date: _____/_____ / _____
                  day   *month*   *year*

Dear Hotel _____ ,
Please make this reservation for me:

Name: _____

Total # of people: _____ # of rooms: _____ # of nights: _____

Arriving: _____ /_____ /_____   My time of arrival (24-hr clock): _____
         day *month* *year*   (I will telephone if I will be late)

Departing: ____ /____/____
        day *month* *year*

Room(s): Single _____ Double ___ Twin _____ Triple ___ Quad_____

With: Toilet _____ Shower _____ Bath _____ Sink only _____

Special needs: View___ Quiet ___ Cheapest ___ Ground Floor ___

Please fax, mail, or e-mail confirmation of my reservation, along with the type of room reserved and the price. Please also inform me of your cancellation policy. After I hear from you, I will quickly send my credit-card information as a deposit to hold the room. Thank you.

_____
Signature

_____
Name

_____
Address

_____
City   *State*   *Zip Code*   *Country*

_____
E-mail Address

INDEX

CREDITS

Contributor

Gene Openshaw

Gene is the co-author of eight Rick Steves books. For this book, he wrote material on art, history, and contemporary culture. When he's not traveling, Gene enjoys composing music, recovering from his 1973 trip to Europe with Rick, and living everyday life with his wife and daughter.

Researcher

Karoline Vass

Karoline Vass was born and raised in Munich, Germany. Passionate about anything alpine, she made her way to Seattle via the Swiss Alps and the Rocky Mountains. When not researching guidebooks and leading tours, she makes her living as a freelance violist.

Images

Front color matter:
Bavarian beer maid — Rick Steves

Front color matter:
Linderhof Castle, Bavaria — Andrew Wakeford/Getty Images/Photodisc Green

Front color matter:
Alphorn Music Celebration, Munich, Germany — Bachmann/Photophile

Front color matter: Burg Eltz — Dominic Bonucelli

Germany full-page:
Munich's Marienplatz — Dominic Bonucelli

Munich: Marienplatz — Rick Steves

Bavaria and Tirol:
Neuschwanstein Castle — Dominic Bonuccelli

Baden-Baden and the Black Forest: Baden-Baden — Cameron Hewitt

Rothenburg and the Romantic Road: Rothenburg — David C. Hoerlein

Würzburg: Würzburg Cityscape — Rick Steves

Frankfurt: Frankfurt Scene from Bridge — Rick Steves

Rhine Valley: Bacharach and the Rhine — Dominic Bonucelli

Mosel Valley: Beilstein — Cameron Hewitt

Trier: Market Square — Cameron Hewitt

Köln and the Unromantic Rhine:
Köln's Cathedral — Cameron Hewitt

Nürnberg: Market Square — Rick Steves

Dresden: Zwinger — Cameron Hewitt

Berlin: Gendarmenmarkt — Cameron Hewitt

Görlitz: Church of St. Peter — Lee Evans

Austria full-page: St. Peter's Church,
Vienna — Cameron Hewitt

Vienna: Schönbrunn Palace — Cameron Hewitt

Danube Valley: Danube River — Rick Steves

Salzburg: Salzburg Overview — Dominic Bonucelli

Hallstatt and the Salzkammergut:
Hallstatt — David C. Hoerlein

Innsbruck and Hall: Innsbruck — Rick Steves

Start your trip at
www.ricksteves.com

Rick Steves' website is packed with over 3,000 pages of timely travel information. It's also your gateway to getting FREE monthly travel news from Rick— and more!

Free Monthly European Travel News

Fresh articles on Europe's most interesting destinations and happenings. Rick will even send you an e-mail every month (often direct from Europe) with his latest discoveries!

Timely Travel Tips

Rick Steves' best money-and-stress-saving tips on trip planning, packing, transportation, hotels, health, safety, finances, hurdling the language barrier…and more.

Travelers' Graffiti Wall

Candid advice and opinions from thousands of travelers on everything listed above, plus whatever topics are hot at the moment (discount flights, packing tips, scams…you name it).

Rick's Annual Guide to European Railpasses

The clearest, most comprehensive guide to the confusing array of railpass options out there, and how to choo-choose the railpass that best fits your itinerary and budget. Then you can order your railpass (and get a bunch of great freebies) online from us!

Great Gear at the Rick Steves Travel Store

Enjoy bargains on Rick's guidebooks, planning maps and TV series DVDs— and on his custom-designed carry-on bags, wheeled bags, day bags and light-packing accessories.

Rick Steves Tours

Every year more than 6,000 lucky travelers explore Europe on a Rick Steves tour. Learn more about our 30 different one-to-three-week itineraries, read uncensored feedback from our tour alums, and sign up for your dream trip online!

Rick on Radio and TV

Read the scripts and run clips from public television's "Rick Steves' Europe" and public radio's "Travel with Rick Steves."

Respect for Your Privacy

Ordering online from us is secure. When you buy something from us, join a tour, or subscribe to Rick's free monthly travel news e-mails, we promise to never share your name, information, or e-mail address with anyone else. You won't be spammed!

Have fun raising your Travel I.Q. at
www.ricksteves.com

Travel smart...carry on!

The latest generation of Rick Steves' carry-on travel bags is easily the best—benefiting from two decades of on-the-road attention to what really matters: maximum quality and strength; practical, flexible features; and no unnecessary frills. You won't find a better value anywhere!

Convertible, expandable, and carry-on-size:

Rick Steves' Back Door Bag $99

This is the same bag that Rick Steves lives out of for three months every summer. It's made of rugged water-resistant 1000 denier Cordura nylon, and best of all, it converts easily from a smart-looking suitcase to a handy backpack with comfortably-curved shoulder straps and a padded waistbelt.

This roomy, versatile 9" x 21" x 14" bag has a large 2600 cubic-inch main compartment, plus three outside pockets (small, medium and huge) that are perfect for often-used items. And the cinch-tight compression straps will keep your load compact and close to your back—not sagging like a sack of potatoes.

Wishing you had even more room to bring home souvenirs? Pull open the full-perimeter expando-zipper and its capacity jumps from 2600 to 3000 cubic inches. When you want to use it as a suitcase or check it as luggage (required when "expanded"), the straps and belt hide away in a zippered compartment in the back.

Attention travelers under 5'4" tall: This bag also comes in an inch-shorter version, for a compact-friendlier fit between the waistbelt and shoulder straps.

Convenient, expandable, and carry-on-size:

Rick Steves' Wheeled Bag $129

At 9" x 21" x 14" our sturdy Rick Steves' Wheeled Bag is rucksack-soft in front, but the rest is lined with a hard ABS-lexan shell to give maximum protection to your belongings. We've spared no expense on moving parts, splurging on an extra-long button-release handle and big, tough inline skate wheels for easy rolling on rough surfaces.

Wishing you had even more room to bring home souvenirs? Pull open the full-perimeter expando-zipper and its capacity jumps from 2600 to 3000 cubic inches.

Rick Steves' Wheeled Bag has exactly the same three-outside-pocket configuration as our Back Door Bag, plus a handy "add-a-bag" strap and full lining.

Our Back Door Bags and Wheeled Bags come in black, navy, blue spruce, evergreen and merlot.

For great deals on a wide selection of travel goodies, begin your next trip at the Rick Steves Travel Store!

Visit the Rick Steves Travel Store at
www.ricksteves.com

Rick Steves

More *Savvy*. More *Surprising*. More *Fun*.

COUNTRY GUIDES 2006

England
France
Germany & Austria
Great Britain
Ireland
Italy
Portugal
Scandinavia
Spain
Switzerland

CITY GUIDES 2006

Amsterdam, Bruges & Brussels
Florence & Tuscany
London
Paris
Prague & The Czech Republic
Provence & The French Riviera
Rome
Venice

BEST OF GUIDES

Best of Eastern Europe
Best of Europe

As the #1 authority on European travel, Rick gives you inside information on what to visit, where to stay, and how to get there—economically and hassle-free.

www.ricksteves.com

PHRASE BOOKS & DICTIONARIES

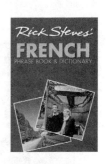

French
French, Italian & German
German
Italian
Portuguese
Spanish

MORE EUROPE FROM RICK STEVES

Easy Access Europe
Europe 101
Europe Through the Back Door
Postcards from Europe

RICK STEVES' EUROPE DVDs

All 43 Shows 2000-2005
Britain
Eastern Europe
France & Benelux
Germany, The Swiss Alps & Travel Skills
Ireland
Italy
Spain & Portugal

PLANNING MAPS

Britain & Ireland
Europe
France
Germany, Austria & Switzerland
Italy
Spain & Portugal

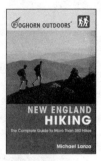
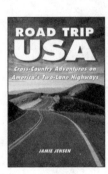